Connie Hanuck 2020

The Psychology of Negotiations in the 21st Century Workplace

New Challenges and New Solutions

The Organizational Frontier Series

SIOP Organizational Frontiers Series
Series Editor
Eduardo Salas
University of Central Florida

Goldman-Shapiro: (2012) *The Psychology of Negotiations in the 21ˢᵗ Century Workplace: New Challenges and New Solutions*

Ferris-Treadway: (2012) *Politics in Organizations: Theory and Research Considerations*

Jones (2011*) Nepotism in Organizations*

Hofmann-Frese (2011) *Error in Organizations*

Outtz: (2009) *Adverse Impact: Implications for Organizational Staffing and High Stakes Selection*

Kozlowski-Salas: (2009) *Learning, Training, and Development in Organizations*

Klein-Becker-Meyer (2009) *Commitment in Organizations: Accumulated Wisdom and New Directions*

Salas-Goodwin-Burke: (2009) *Team Effectiveness in Complex Organizations*

Kanfer-Chen-Pritchard: (2008) *Work Motivation: Past, Present and Future*

De Dreu/Gelfand: (2008) *The Psychology of Conflict and Conflict Management in Organizations*

Ostroff/Judge: (2007) *Perspectives on Organizational Fit*

Baum/Frese/Baron: (2007) *The Psychology of Entrepreneurship*

Weekley/Ployhart: (2006) *Situational Judgment Tests: Theory, Measurement and Application*

Dipboye/Colella: (2005) *Discrimination at Work: The Psychological and Organizational Bases*

Griffin/O'Leary-Kelly: (2004) *The Dark Side of Organizational Behavior*

Hofmann/Tetrick: (2003) *Health and Safety in Organizations*

Jackson/Hitt/DeNisi: (2003) *Managing Knowledge for Sustained Competitive Knowledge*

Barrick/Ryan: (2003) *Personality and Work*

Lord/Klimoski/Kanfer: (2002) *Emotions in the Workplace*

Drasgow/Schmitt: (2002) *Measuring and Analyzing Behavior in Organizations*

Feldman: (2002) *Work Careers*

Zaccaro/Klimoski: (2001) *The Nature of Organizational Leadership*

Rynes/Gerhart: (2000) *Compensation in Organizations*

Klein/Kozlowski: (2000) *Multilevel Theory, Research and Methods in Organizations*

Ilgen/Pulakos: (1999) *The Changing Nature of Performance*

Earley/Erez: (1997) *New Perspectives on International I-O Psychology*

Murphy: (1996) *Individual Differences and Behavior in Organizations*

Guzzo/Salas: (1995) *Team Effectiveness and Decision Making*

Howard: (1995) *The Changing Nature of Work*

Schmitt/Borman: (1993) *Personnel Selection in Organizations*

Zedeck: (1991) *Work, Families and Organizations*

Schneider: (1990) *Organizational Culture and Climate*

Goldstein: (1989) *Training and Development in Organizations*

Campbell/Campbell: (1988) *Productivity in Organizations*

Hall: (1987) *Career Development in Organizations*

The Psychology of Negotiations in the 21st Century Workplace

New Challenges and New Solutions

Edited by

Barry M. Goldman
University of Arizona

Debra L. Shapiro
University of Maryland

Routledge
Taylor & Francis Group
New York   London

Routledge
Taylor & Francis Group
711 Third Avenue
New York, NY 10017

Routledge
Taylor & Francis Group
27 Church Road
Hove, East Sussex BN3 2FA

© 2012 by Taylor & Francis Group, LLC
Routledge is an imprint of Taylor & Francis Group, an Informa business

Printed in the United States of America on acid-free paper
Version Date: 20111209

International Standard Book Number: 978-0-415-87115-0 (Hardback)

Library of Congress Cataloging-in-Publication Data

The psychology of negotiations in the 21st century workplace : new challenges
and new solutions / edited by Barry M. Goldman, Debra L. Shapiro.
  p. cm. -- (The organizational frontier series)
Includes bibliographical references and index.
ISBN 978-0-415-87115-0 (alk. paper)
  1. Negotiation in business. 2. Negotiation in business--Psychological aspects.
I. Goldman, Barry. II. Shapiro, Debra L.

HD58.6.P75 2012
658.4'052--dc23   2011043097

**Visit the Taylor & Francis Web site at
http://www.taylorandfrancis.com**

**and the Psychology Press Web site at
http://www.psypress.com**

Dedication

To my parents, Gilbert and Evelyn Goldman, with love

and appreciation for their sacrifices—actually, Mom

and Dad don't read academic books, so someone please

tell them about this or else they'll never know.

To my brother, Marty, a kind and loving soul.

B.M.G

To my Mom and, in loving memory, my Dad, and to my

nearest and dearest family and friends (who know who you

are), including Champagne and Tuxedo—all of whom have

taught me that the quality of all communications, including

negotiations, is greatest when everyone is genuine.

D.L.S

Contents

SECTION 3 Negotiators as Emotion Managers in the 21st Century

SECTION 4   Negotiators as Social Influence/ Group-Sensitive Managers in the 21st Century

Chapter 9 Social Networks and Negotiation 245

Daniel J. Brass and Giuseppe Labianca

Chapter 10 How Cultural Stereotyping Influences Intercultural
Negotiation 269

Catherine H. Tinsley, Nazli Turan, Laurie R. Weingart, and Robin L. Dillon-Merrill

Chapter 11 Gender and Negotiation 293

Michael P. Haselhuhn and Laura J. Kray

SECTION 5   Negotiators as Organizational Managers in the 21st Century

Series Foreword

We go through our lives by constantly negotiating. No one escapes it. We negotiate from the moment we are born. We negotiate with our parents, our kids, our teachers, our spouses, our friends, and our family and when we buy houses or cars. And, of course, we negotiate with our bosses, colleagues, customers, sponsors, and clients. Negotiation is prevalent at work and in many industries, agencies, and organizations (for profit as well as nonprofit). It is done by individuals, groups, or multiple organizations and entities. It takes many forms, and the stakes can be high if lives depend on it. So, the more we know about the process of negotiating, the better for all involved. The more we know about how, when, why, what, and if to negotiate, the better the outcomes. We, indeed, need to know much in this area.

We need to know what is fair and what matters in negotiations. We need to understand the emotions involved and how these influence outcomes. We need to get more insight regarding the cultural, sociopolitical, and personal attributes that help or hinder negotiations. The good news is that our science is well poised to begin to answer these questions and more. Our science is rich with theories, paradigms, methodologies, strategies, and interventions that matter in negotiations.

Barry M. Goldman and Debra L. Shapiro have put together a volume that is full of promising avenues of research that in due time will influence practice. There is a wealth of information, ideas, suggestions, and hypotheses on what matters and what the challenges in negotiations are—a volume that is both deep and broad on perspectives and approaches to think about when studying negotiation. This volume will motivate, we hope, the kind of research individuals, groups, and organizations need to negotiate well and avoid pitfalls. On behalf of the SIOP Frontier Series Editorial Board, Spring issue, thanks Barry and Debra! You and your contributors have done a tremendous service to our science and practice.

Eduardo Salas, PhD
University of Central Florida
Series Editor

Acknowledgment

The editors wish to thank David Welsh for his helpful comments to this volume.

About the Editors

Barry M. Goldman (PhD, JD, University of Maryland–College Park) is the McCoy–Rogers Faculty Fellow and an associate professor of management and organizations at the Eller College of Management at the University of Arizona. Prior to getting his PhD, he practiced corporate law for 10 years. At law school, he was managing editor of the law review. Before that, he studied politics and economics at Oxford University.

Dr. Goldman is presently the chair of the Conflict Management (CM) Division of the Academy of Management, after serving in all other elected executive board positions of the CM Division, starting with representative-at-large.

His primary area of research involves issues relating to negotiations and conflict management, particularly those involving legal issues relating to employees, including employment discrimination and organizational justice. His research has been published in journals such as *The Academy of Management Journal, Journal of Applied Psychology, Personnel Psychology, Journal of Management*, and the *Journal of Organizational Behavior*, among other outlets. His research has been featured in *The Wall Street Journal, Inc Magazine*, and by the Dalai Lama in his book, *The Art of Happiness at Work*.

His research has received the CM Division's Best Paper Award twice (2001 and 2007). He has also received the 2004 Best Paper Award from the *Journal of Management*. He is a member of the editorial boards of the *Journal of Applied Psychology (JAP)*, the *Journal of Management*, and the *Negotiations & Conflict Management Journal*. He was named an Ascendant Scholar by the Western Academy of Management (2005) and was the CM Division's nominee for the Newman Award (Best Dissertation, 1999). He teaches (or has taught) classes in negotiations, business law, human resources, and organizational behavior and has received Best Teacher awards from both MBA (2000, 2001, 2004, 2006, 2008) and undergraduate (1999, 2000, 2010) students. He has also been a visiting associate professor at the Tuck School of Business (Dartmouth), Wuhan University (China), and the Instituto de Empresa (Madrid, Spain).

Debra L. Shapiro (PhD, Northwestern University) is the Clarice Smith Professor of Management at the University of Maryland's Robert H. Smith School of Business. Prior to joining the Smith School, Dr. Shapiro was the Willard J. Graham Distinguished Professor of Management at University of North Carolina–Chapel Hill's Kenan-Flagler Business School (KFBS). While at KFBS (1986–2003), Dr. Shapiro was associate dean for doctoral programs 1998–2001, a role she served again July 2008–2011 after joining the Smith School.

Dr. Shapiro's service to the Academy of Management spans the Organizational Behavior (OB), Human Resource (HR), and CM Divisions, as well as All-Academy needs. Specifically, she served as an elected member of the AOM's Board of Governors (2002–2005), during which time she was chair of the Division and Interest Group Relations (DIGR) Committee; served as associate editor of *The Academy of Management Journal* (2005–2007); served as division chair of the CM Division (1994–1995) after serving in all other elected executive board positions of the CM Division, starting with representative-at-large; served as member of the AOM's All-Academy Social Events Task Force (1994–1995), Academy Council (2000), Best AMR Publication Award Committee (2001), Career Achievement Award Committee (2004–2005), and Terry Book Award Committee (2004–2005). For the AOM's HR Division, Dr. Shapiro served as a member of the Newman (Best Dissertation-based) Committee (2002) and Scholar Achievement Award Committee (2002); and for the OB Division, she served as a member of the L. L. Cummings Scholarly Achievement Award Committee (2010–2011) and Membership Outreach and Involvement (MOI) from 1996 to 2000.

An author of nearly 70 publications, her research generally regards managing conflict/perceived injustice in organizations, including resistance to managerial practices such as self-managing work team assignments and the various strategies (negotiation, third-party dispute resolution, mediation, arbitration, the provision of explanations or disclaimers and other impression management tactics) that can be used to defuse conflict or enhance perceived justice; in addition, Dr. Shapiro examines the cross-cultural challenges associated with these strategies. Her publications appear in *Administrative Science Quarterly* (ASQ), *Academy of Management Journal* (AMJ), *Academy of Management Review* (AMR), *Organizational Behavior & Human Decision Processes* (OBHDP), *Journal of Applied Psychology* (JAP), *Journal of Personality & Social Psychology* (JPSP), *Journal of Experimental Social Psychology* (*JESP*), and *Communication Research.* She is also the senior coeditor of the book *Managing Multinational Teams Global Perspectives* (with Mary Ann Von Glinow and Joe Cheng; Elsevier/JAI Press, 2005). She is a four-time recipient of the Best Paper Award in the CM Division (1991, 1992, 1996, and 2007); a recipient of the 1999 Best Empirical Paper Award from the International Association for Conflict Management; and a finalist for the 1998 Best Publication in Organizational Behavior Award offered by the AOM's OB Division; she has also received awards for teaching excellence, including the 1997 PhD Teaching Award at the University of North Carolina's Kenan-Flagler Business School and the Smith School's 2007 Krowe Teaching Award. Dr. Shapiro is a Fellow of the AOM, the Society of Organizational Behavior, and the Ethics Resource Center.

About the Contributors

Ritu Agarwal is professor and the Robert H. Smith Dean's Chair of Information Systems at the Robert H. Smith School of Business, University of Maryland, College Park. She has published over 80 papers on information technology (IT) management topics in journals such as *Information Systems Research, MIS Quarterly, Management Science, Communications of the ACM, Journal of Management Information Systems, Decision Sciences, IEEE Transactions,* and *Decision Support Systems* and has made presentations at a variety of national and international conferences. She is the editor in chief of *Information Systems Research.* Her current research is focused on the use of IT in health care settings, electronic markets, and consumer behavior in technology-mediated environments.

Animesh Animesh is an assistant professor in the information systems area at Desautels Faculty of Management, McGill University, Canada. Animesh has a PhD from the University of Maryland, a master's in information systems management from Carnegie Mellon University, and a bachelor's degree in business studies from Delhi University. His research focuses on the adoption, design, and impact of Internet technologies and electronic commerce. He has examined a wide variety of technology-enabled contexts such as paid search advertising, peer-to-peer electronic markets, and virtual world platform. His research has been published in top journals, such as *Information Systems Research, MIS Quarterly,* and *Marketing Science.* He has presented research papers at premier peer-reviewed academic conferences, including the International Conference on Information Systems (ICIS), Conference on Information Systems and Technology (CIST), Workshop on Information Technology and Systems (WITS), and Americas Conference on Information Systems (AMCIS).

Max H. Bazerman is the Jesse Isidor Straus Professor of Business Administration at the Harvard Business School. Dr. Bazerman's research focuses on decision making, negotiation, and ethics. He is the author, coauthor, or coeditor of 19 books (including *Blind Spots* (with Ann Tenbrunsel; Princeton University Press, 2011) and over 200 research articles and chapters. In 2006, he received an honorary doctorate from the University of London (London Business School), the Kulp-Wright Book Award from the American Risk and Insurance Association for Predictable Surprises. In 2008, Dr. Bazerman was named as one of Ethisphere's 100 Most Influential in Business Ethics, was named one of Daily Kos' Heroes from the Bush Era for going public about how the Bush Administration corrupted the RICO (Racketeer Influenced and Corrupt Organizations) Act tobacco trial, and received the Distinguished Educator Award from the Academy of Management. He has won numerous teaching awards, and his former doctoral students have accepted positions at leading business schools throughout the United States, including the Kellogg School at Northwestern, the Wharton School, the Fuqua School at Duke, Cornell, Carnegie-Mellon, Stanford, the University of Chicago, Notre Dame, Columbia, and the Harvard Business School.

William J. Becker is assistant professor of management, Neeley School of Business at Texas Christian University. He joined the management faculty after completing his PhD in management with a minor in cognitive neuroscience at the University of Arizona. He specializes in emotions in the workplace, and his research has appeared in the *Journal of Applied Psychology* and *Personnel Psychology*. He has also worked with firms to help employees be more confident and effective during negotiations.

Robert J. Bies is professor of management and founder of the Executive Master's in Leadership program at Georgetown University. He earned a PhD in organizational behavior from Stanford University, and a BA and MBA from the University of Washington. His research interests include leadership, the delivery of bad news, and organizational justice. Bies serves on the editorial boards of several academic journals, including *Journal of Organizational Behavior* and *Journal of Management*.

Daniel J. Brass received his PhD from the University of Illinois and is the J. Henning Hilliard Professor of Innovation Management and director of LINKS—The International Center for the Study of Social Networks in Business (http//www.linkscenter.org) at the Gatton College of Business and Economics at the University of Kentucky. He served as associate editor of *Administrative Science Quarterly* from 1995 to 2007. He has published articles in such journals as *Administrative Science Quarterly, Academy of*

Management Journal, Academy of Management Review, Journal of Applied Psychology, Organization Science, Organizational Behavior and Human Decision Processes, and *Science*. His research on the antecedents and consequences of social networks in organizations has been cited more than 5,000 times.

Joel Brockner is the Phillip Hettleman Professor of Business at Columbia Business School. He received a PhD in social/personality psychology from Tufts University. His research interests include the consequences of organizational change, organizational justice, self-processes in work organizations, regulatory focus theory, cross-national differences in employees' attitudes and behaviors, and the escalation of commitment to a failing course of action.

Donald E. Conlon is the Eli Broad Professor of Management in the Department of Management at Michigan State University. He received his PhD in organizational behavior from the University of Illinois at Urbana-Champaign. His research interests include justice issues in organizations, negotiation, third-party dispute intervention, and managerial decision making. He has written over 50 refereed journal articles and book chapters. He has served as division chair for the Conflict Management Division of the Academy of Management as well as president of the International Association for Conflict Management.

Russell Cropanzano is the Brian Lesk Professor of Organizational Behavior at the University of Arizona's Eller College of Management. Dr. Cropanzano's primary research areas include perceptions of organizational justice as well as on the experience and impact of workplace emotion. He has edited four books, presented over 100 papers, and published over 100 scholarly articles and chapters. In addition, he is a coauthor (with Robert Folger) of the book *Organizational Justice and Human Resources Management*, which won the 1998 Book Award from the International Association of Conflict Management. Dr. Cropanzano was also a winner of the 2000 Outstanding Paper Award from the *Consulting Psychology Journal*, as well as the 2007 Best Paper Award from the Academy of Management Perspectives. He is a past editor of the *Journal of Management* and a fellow in the Society for Industrial/Organizational Psychology and the Association for Psychological Science.

Jared R. Curhan is an associate professor of organizational behavior in the Sloan School of Management at the Massachusetts Institute of Technology. He received his PhD from Stanford University. His research focuses on subjective outcomes in negotiation as well as the influence of interpersonal relationship dynamics on negotiation performance.

Robin L. Dillon-Merrill is an associate professor in the McDonough School of Business at Georgetown University. Professor Dillon-Merrill seeks to understand and explain how and why people make the decisions that they do under conditions of uncertainty and risk. This research specifically examines critical decisions that people have made following near-miss events in situations with severe outcomes (i.e., hurricane evacuation, terrorism, NASA mission management, etc.). She has received research funding from the National Science Foundation, NASA, the Department of Defense, and the Department of Homeland Security through USC's National Center for Risk and Economic Analysis for Terrorism Events. She has served as a risk analysis and project management expert on several national academies committees, including the review of the New Orleans regional hurricane protection projects and the application of risk analysis techniques to securing the Department of Energy's special nuclear materials. She can be reached via e-mail at rld9@georgetown.edu.

Hillary Anger Elfenbein is a professor of organizational behavior in the Olin School of Business at Washington University in St. Louis. She holds a PhD in organizational behavior, a Master's degree in statistics, and undergraduate degrees in physics and Sanskrit, all from Harvard University. Her research interests focus on inherently relational phenomena, including the behaviors and outcomes of competitive and mixed-motive interactions and areas of social perception such as emotion recognition. Her work has appeared in the *Academy of Management Annals, Academy of Management Journal*, the *Journal of Applied Psychology*, the *Journal of Personality and Social Psychology, Organization Science, Psychological Bulletin*, and *Psychological Science*. Dr. Elfenbein recently testified before Congress as an expert witness on federally funded research in the social sciences.

Sara Parker Enlow is a principal with Vantage Partners LLC, where she helps to run the firm's outsourcing practice. Sara's consulting work is focused primarily on helping providers of outsourcing services and their customers more effectively manage their relationships. Recently, Sara coauthored a study titled "Managing Outsourcing Relationships: Essential Practices for Buyers and Providers," and she has written and published several other articles and white papers on the topics of outsourcing, negotiation, and relationship management for publications such as *Compensation and Benefits Review, Outsourcing Magazine, CIO Update, Computerworld. com, Cutter Consortium Sourcing and Vendor Relationships Executive Update,* and *SHRM Online.* She is a frequent speaker on the topics of negotiation, outsourcing, and relationship management. Prior to joining Vantage, Sara was a consultant with Accenture. She is a graduate of Bryant University, summa cum laude.

Joël Feldman is a graduate student at the Eller College of Management at the University of Arizona. His research interests include emotions, person–organization fit, organizational identification, and organizational justice.

Ya'akov (Kobi) Gal is a faculty member of the Department of Information Systems Engineering at the Ben-Gurion University of the Negev and an associate at the School of Engineering and Applied Sciences at Harvard University. His work investigates representations and algorithms for making decisions in heterogeneous groups comprising both people and computational agents. He has published over 30 papers in highly refereed venues on topics ranging from artificial intelligence to the learning and cognitive sciences. He is a recipient of the Marie Curie International Reintegration Grant for 2010, a two-time recipient of Harvard University's Derek Bok award for excellence in teaching, as well as the School of Engineering and Applied Science's outstanding teacher award.

Michele J. Gelfand is professor of psychology and Distinguished University Scholar Teacher at the University of Maryland, College Park. She received her PhD in social/organizational psychology from the University of Illinois. Gelfand's work explores cultural influences on conflict, negotiation, justice, revenge, and forgiveness; workplace diversity and discrimination; and theory and methods in cross-cultural psychology. Her work has been published in outlets such as *Science,* the *Journal of Applied Psychology,* the *Journal of Personality and Social Psychology, Organizational Behavior and Human Decision Processes, Academy of Management Review, Psychological Science Journal,* and the *Annual Review of Psychology.* She is coeditor of

The Handbook of Negotiation and Culture (with Jeanne Brett; Stanford University Press) and *The Psychology of Conflict and Conflict Management in Organizations* (with Carsten De Dreu; Erlbaum) and is the founding coeditor of the *Advances in Culture and Psychology* series (with C. Y. Chiu and Ying-Yi Hong, Oxford University Press).

Ralph Hanke is an assistant professor of entrepreneurship and strategy at the Missouri University of Science and Technology. He received his PhD in business administration from the Pennsylvania State University. His research interests include team creativity, organizational resources and their effects on firm performance, entrepreneurial pedagogy, and conflict and negotiation strategies in organizations.

Michael P. Haselhuhn is an assistant professor at the Sheldon B. Lubar School of Business, University of Wisconsin–Milwaukee. He received his PhD in organizational behavior from the University of California, Berkeley. His research interests include the role of motivation in information processing and decision making and the influence of implicit beliefs on ethics, trust, and negotiation.

Jonathan Hughes is a partner at Vantage Partners LLC and head of the firm's sourcing and supplier management practice. As an expert in supply chain management, strategic alliances, and change management, he has worked with leading companies across a range of industries in North and South America, Europe, Asia, Australia, and Africa. Jonathan is the lead author of a number of global research studies focused on negotiation, relationship management, and collaborative innovation and is also author of the chapter on negotiation systems and strategies in the 2008 *International Contracts Manual* (Thomson-West). He is a frequent keynote speaker on negotiation, alliances, and supply management and a regularly cited expert in the business and popular presses. Jonathan has published numerous articles in journals, including the *Harvard Business Review, Global Business and Organizational Excellence, The Journal of Strategic Alliances, CPO Agenda, Inside Supply Management, CIO Magazine, The Journal of Trading Partner Practices*, and *Asia Supply Chain Magazine*. He is a graduate of Harvard College.

Laura J. Kray is the Warren E. and Carol Spieker Professor of Leadership at the Walter A. Haas School of Business, University of California at

Berkeley. Kray earned her doctorate in social psychology, and she applies this lens to her work on gender and negotiations, counterfactual thinking, and decision making. In 2008, her work on gender and negotiations was recognized with the Most Influential Paper award from the Conflict Management Division of the Academy of Management.

Giuseppe (Joe) Labianca (PhD, business administration, Penn State) is a Gatton Endowed Associate Professor of Management at the University of Kentucky's Gatton College of Business and Economics. He was previously on the faculty at Emory's Goizueta Business School and Tulane's Freeman School of Business. His main research stream involves examining organizational behavior from a social network perspective, including recent work on network approaches to interpersonal conflict, groups, gossip, organizational justice, job satisfaction, and interpersonal control. His work has appeared in *Science*, the *Academy of Management Journal*, the *Academy of Management Review, Harvard Business Review, Organization Science, Strategic Organization*, and elsewhere. He is currently serving on the editorial board of *Organization Science* and as an executive committee member of the Academy of Management's Organization and Management Theory (OMT) Division. He recently won the OMT Division's Best Paper Award, Goizueta's Alumni Award for Excellence in Research, and the University of Kentucky Alumni Association's Great Teacher Award.

Roy J. Lewicki is the Irving Abramowitz Professor of Management and Human Resources at the Max M. Fisher College of Business, The Ohio State University. He received his PhD in social psychology from Columbia University. His research interests include negotiation and conflict management, trust development, organizational justice, and ethical decision making.

Brian Lucas is a doctoral student at Northwestern University's Kellogg School of Management. His program of study is management and organizations.

Deepak Malhotra is a professor at Harvard Business School. He received his PhD from the Kellogg School of Management at Northwestern University. His research interests include issues related to trust development, competitive escalation, negotiation, and international and ethnic conflict. He is the coauthor (with Max H. Bazerman) of *Negotiation Genius*, which was published by Bantam Books in 2007.

Robin L. Pinkley is a professor of management and organizations and director of the American Airlines Center for Labor Relations and Conflict Resolution at the Cox School of Business at Southern Methodist University, as well as the founder of the M2M Center for Profitable Negotiation. Sample clients include General Electric, Sony Ericsson, Southwest Airlines, and Yahoo!. Her research interests include the development of the gain–gain approach to negotiation, negotiator power, and the use of strategic anchors. She is coauthor (with Greg Northcraft) of *Get Paid What You're Worth: The Expert Negotiators Guide to Salary and Compensation*. Dr. Pinkley's awards include the runner-up for the Most Influential Article or Book Chapter Published in the Field of Conflict Management Between 1992 and 1996 Award and the 1990 Best Paper Award, both from the Conflict Management Division of the Academy of Management; the Cox Outstanding Researcher Award; Southern Methodist University's Golden Mustang Award for innovative teaching; and the Sewell Distinguished Service to the Community Award.

Erika Richardson is a third-year doctoral student in the management and organizations department at Northwestern University's Kellogg School of Management. Prior to entering her doctoral program, Erika spent 2 years as a research associate at Harvard Business School in the areas of entrepreneurship and accounting. Erika's primary research interests include gender, race, intersectionality, and negotiations. Erika has presented research on these topics, and others, throughout the United States and internationally.

Kathryn S. Roloff is a PhD candidate in the social-organizational psychology program at Columbia University. She received her BA in psychology and administrative science from Colby College and her MA in psychology from Boston University. Her research interests revolve around leading organizational change and learning, and perceptions of organizational justice.

William H. Ross is a professor of management at the University of Wisconsin–La Crosse. He received his PhD in industrial/organizational psychology from the University of Illinois at Urbana-Champaign. His research interests include negotiation, conflict management, alternative dispute resolution procedures, organizational justice, and the management of technological developments such as the use of social media and electronic monitoring at work. He has written over 50 refereed journal articles and book chapters.

Jessica Siegel is a doctoral candidate in the Department of Management and Organizations at the University of Arizona. Jessica's primary research areas include work team processes and shared cognition, conflict and negotiations, and the design of workplace selection systems. She has presented numerous research projects at the Academy of Management annual meeting and the annual conference of the Society for Industrial and Organizational Psychology. Jessica has an ongoing interest in conflict and negotiations and teaches a negotiations seminar at the Eller College of Management at the University of Arizona. She has also been invited for several guest lectures on various negotiation topics. In addition to her interest in negotiations at the organization level, Jessica is currently working on a program of research examining the effects of different emotions in negotiating dyads. Jessica received her bachelor's degree in psychology and sociology from the School of Science and Engineering at Tulane University and earned her master's degree at the University of Arizona, where she is currently working toward the completion of her PhD.

Leigh Thompson joined the Kellogg School of Management in 1995. She is the J. Jay Gerber Distinguished Professor of Dispute Resolution and Organizations. She directs the Leading High Impact Teams executive program and the Kellogg Team and Group Research Center, and codirects the Negotiation Strategies for Managers program. An active scholar and researcher, she has published over 100 research articles and chapters and has authored 9 books, including *The Mind and Heart of the Negotiator* (5th edition), Pearson Education, 2012; *Making the Team: A Guide for Managers* (4th edition), Pearson Education, 2011; *Creativity and Innovations in Organizational Teams* (with Hoon Seok Choi), Lawrence Erlbaum Associates, 2006; *Shared Cognition in Organizations: The Management of Knowledge* (with John M. Levine and David Messick), Lawrence Erlbaum Associates, 1999; *Negotiation Theory and Research*, Psychology Press, 2006; *The Social Psychology of Organization Behavior: Key Readings* (edited volume), Psychology Press, 2003; *Organizational Behavior Today*, Pearson Education, 2008; *The Truth About Negotiations*, Pearson Education, 2008; and *Conflict in Organizational Groups: New Directions in Theory and Practice*, Northwestern University Press, 2007. She is currently working on a new book, *The Creative Conspiracy*. Thompson has worked with private and public organizations in the United States, Latin America, Canada, Europe, and the Middle East. Her teaching style combines experiential learning with theory-driven best practices. For more information about Leigh Thompson's teaching and research, please visit http://www.LeighThompson.com.

Catherine H. Tinsley is a professor of management at the McDonough School of Business at Georgetown University and is the executive director of the Georgetown University Women's Leadership Initiative. She has received several grants from NASA, the National Science Foundation, and the Department of Homeland Security for her work on decision making and risk and from the Department of Defense and Army Research Office for her work on modeling culture's influence on negotiation and collaboration. Dr. Tinsley recently served on two committees for the National Academy of Sciences: Committee to Improve Intelligence Analysis for National Security and Committee on Unifying Social and Cultural Frameworks. She studies how factors such as culture, reputations, and gender influence negotiation and conflict resolution. She also studies how people make decisions under risk, applying decision analytic frameworks to understand organizational disasters, and individual and expert responses to natural disasters (such as hurricanes) and man-made disasters (terrorist attacks). She received her master's and doctoral degrees in organizational behavior from J. L. Kellogg Graduate School of Management at Northwestern University and her BA in anthropology from Bryn Mawr College.

Thomas M. Tripp is professor of management at Washington State University. He earned a PhD in organizational behavior from the Kellogg School of Management at Northwestern University and a BS in psychology from the University of Washington. Tripp serves on the editorial boards of several academic journals, including *Negotiations and Conflict Management Research* and the *International Journal of Conflict Management*.

Chia-Jung Tsay is a doctoral candidate in organizational behavior and social psychology at Harvard University. Her research has focused on rapid social judgment and evaluations of performance, with implications for human capital management and the quality of decision making in professional selection and advancement. Her work has been published in outlets such as *Organizational Behavior and Human Decision Processes, Journal of Experimental Social Psychology, Academy of Management Annals*, and *Emotion Review*. Prior to her doctoral studies, Tsay graduated Phi Beta Kappa from Harvard with an AB in psychology and an AM in history of science. She also graduated with an MM in piano performance and an MM in piano pedagogy from the Peabody Institute of Johns Hopkins University, where she later served as faculty.

Nazli Turan is a PhD candidate at the Organizational Behavior and Theory Department at Tepper School of Business at Carnegie Mellon University. Her research is mainly on negotiation, conflict resolution, and morality. Her current projects focus on intercultural negotiation schemas, concession making in negotiation, and morality at the workplace.

Siva Viswanathan is an associate professor at the Robert H. Smith School of Business, University of Maryland, College Park. Siva studies the economic and strategic impacts of emerging technologies in collaboration with leading firms in a variety of sectors, including consumer retailing, financial services, online advertising, and auto retailing. His current research focuses on the strategic impacts of online social networks and Web 2.0 technologies. Siva has a PhD from New York University, a master's in business administration from the Indian Institute of Management Bangalore, and a bachelor's degree in engineering. His publications have appeared in various international conference proceedings and top academic journals, including *Management Science, Information Systems Research, Journal of Marketing*, and *Decision Support Systems*.

Laurie R. Weingart is the Carnegie Bosch Professor of Organizational Behavior and Theory at the David A. Tepper School of Business, Carnegie Mellon University. She earned her PhD in organizational behavior from the Kellogg School of Management at Northwestern University in 1989. Dr. Weingart's research examines negotiation, conflict, and innovation in teams. Her early research focused on group processes and on social motives and tactical behavior in negotiation. Her more recent research examines cognition, conflict, and innovation in cross-functional teams. Professor Weingart has published over 50 articles and book chapters in the fields of management, social psychology, industrial psychology, and cognitive psychology. Dr. Weingart served as chair of the Conflict Management Division of the Academy of Management (2001) and president of the International Association for Conflict Management (2003–2004). She currently serves as the founding president of the Interdisciplinary Network for Group Research (2007–2012) (http://www.ingroup.net).

Jeff Weiss is a partner at Vantage Partners LLC and is an expert in negotiation, partnering, and change management. His consulting work is primarily focused on helping sales organizations and alliance groups of Fortune 500/Global 1,000 organizations. Prior to cofounding Vantage, Jeff helped to build Conflict Management Group, a nonprofit consulting firm focused on resolving international conflicts of public concern. He was also a member of the Harvard Negotiation Project. Jeff has published extensively as a contributing author to a number of books, research reports, and articles in the likes of *Harvard Business Review* and is a frequently cited expert in the popular press. He is a graduate of Dartmouth College and Harvard Law School and is a member of the Massachusetts Bar. In addition, he serves on the faculty of the Amos Tuck School of Business at Dartmouth College and the faculty of the United States Military Academy at West Point. Jeff is also a founder, and presently codirector, of the West Point Negotiation Project.

Batia Mishan Wiesenfeld, professor of management at New York University Leonard N. Stern School of Business, is the Robert and Dale Atkins Rosen Faculty Fellow and the Daniel P. Paduano Faculty Fellow. She received her PhD in management and organizational behavior from the Columbia University Graduate School of Business. Her research interests include esteem and identity threat in the context of organizational change and the intersection of justice, power, status, and social emotion.

Section 1

Introduction

1

Negotiation in the 21st Century Workplace: New Challenges and New Solutions

Barry M. Goldman and Debra L. Shapiro

INTRODUCTION

The 21st century workplace is a "new world" relative to the workplace that preceded it, and this new world (for reasons explained in this book) necessitates negotiating effectively in ways that have generally been understudied in prior negotiation or management studies. The "litigation explosion" (Groth, Goldman, Gilliland, & Bies, 2002; Olson, 1992) is among the ways distinguishing the 21st century workplace from work experiences in earlier days. The increasing cost and risk of lawsuits makes negotiation—rather than litigation—an attractive alternative. Additional attributes that distinguish the 21st century workplace from work experiences in earlier days include organizations': increasing willingness to restructure in ways that result in employee layoffs (unheard of in earlier times; cf. Levine, 2002); globalization of products and services (Friedman, 2005); greater employee diversity (van Knippenberg & Schippers, 2007); and greater reliance on technology-mediated communications among employees, including team members and suppliers (Bailey & Kurland, 2002; Valley, White, & Iacobucci, 1992) increasingly dispersed around the globe. Cumulatively, these changes in the nature of work necessitate negotiation skills for not only preventing or resolving disputes in ways less costly than litigation, but also conducting everyday as well as more complex business transactions. Not surprisingly, then, negotiation skills are increasingly viewed by organizations as strategically important for individual employees as well as managers and thus as a source of organizations' sustainable competitive advantage (Barney, 1991; Thompson, 2009).

The purpose of this book is to bridge the gap between management and negotiation research so that employees, managers, and their organizations can *all* become better negotiators and so that negotiators can be more effective within the organization. Collectively, the chapters in this book illuminate that 21st century employees (at all levels) can—via tactics that are informed by relevant negotiation or management research (often treated in isolation of each other)—become more effective (a) fairness managers, (b) emotion managers, (c) social or group-level managers, and (d) organizational managers. Each chapter specifies tactics likely to aid employees or managers in achieving their goal (such as effectively managing fairness, emotions, social influences, and organizational transaction costs), informed by relevant negotiation or management research. Each chapter concludes by noting the 21st century workplace challenges associated with using the advised tactics and thus the questions in need of future negotiation research. Taken together, the chapters in this book therefore promise to set the next generation's research agenda in negotiation. The research agenda emerging from this book's collection of chapters is likely to have strategic importance for both managers and negotiators since the future research needs named in each chapter's conclusion are guided, at least in part, by the 21st century workplace management challenges illuminated in each chapter.

A FUNDAMENTAL ASSUMPTION OF THIS BOOK: THE WORKPLACE OF THE 21st CENTURY NECESSITATES REVISITING EARLIER MANAGEMENT AND NEGOTIATION ADVICE

Before we describe the contents of this book, let us highlight its fundamental assumption: Previously prescribed advice pertaining to effectively managing employees in general or effectively managing negotiations in particular needs to be revisited in light of 21st century workplace characteristics. If this fundamental assumption is true, then one or both of the following statements must also be true: (a) the process of managing or negotiating differs in the 21st century workplace relative to earlier times; or (b) the management or negotiation context differs in the 21st century workplace relative to earlier times. To better understand these issues, let us step back a century.

In 1910, the Austrian economist Joseph Schumpeter was 27 years old and concerned with how an economy develops. He argued that change in the economy arose from "new combinations of productive means" (Arthur, 2009, p. 19; Kreps, 1990). Schumpeter identified innovation as the critical element of economic change (Pol & Carroll, 2006) and introduced new ways of viewing the field of economics at the time by stating that entrepreneurs disturbed the expected (at the time) equilibrium by introducing innovation (Schumpeter, 1961). In essence, Schumpeter glorified the end products produced by the entrepreneur. However, in emphasizing the contribution of the wild spirits ("*unternehmergeist*") of the entrepreneur to the "creative destruction" of the business cycle, Schumpeter put little emphasis on the process of negotiation as adding value to the economy or to leading to innovation in itself. This daring and innovative thinker was conspicuously silent regarding the potential for added value via the negotiation process. In essence, he treated it as a big black box in which a messy mystery occurs.

In recent decades, negotiation scholars have recognized that *integratively oriented* negotiations can lead to added value for each party in a negotiation (Raiffa, 2002) when, for example, parties value issues differently and make trade-offs that enable each side's highest-priority issue to be met. Modern negotiation researchers specifically discuss creativity, evidenced in part by negotiators sharing priorities to discover potential trade-offs that are mutually satisfying as one of the important elements of good negotiations. For example, Raiffa (2002, pp. 83–84) has said: "[Joint decision-making negotiation] widens the scope of its vision to include the invention of strategies, creation of new alternatives, and increases or decreases in the number of parties." As such, a century after Schumpeter's groundbreaking work on innovation that focused on means of production, negotiation researchers have added the potential for further innovation through a new vision of the *process of negotiation*. Is the process of negotiation in the 21st century different from the negotiation process identified in earlier times? "Yes" is the answer generally suggested by this book's chapters because so many contextual attributes of the workplace have changed over time (a point we turn to next). Since nearly all book contributors—including commentators Tsay and Bazerman (in Chapter 17), Gelfand and Gal (in Chapter 15), and Thompson, Richardson, and Lucas (in Chapter 16)—acknowledge that the management context has changed, it seems likely that there is need to rethink *how* (with these contextual changes in mind) managers in the 21st century workplace need to go about managing employees, including negotiating for support from employees for the types of outcomes managers seek—be these perceptions of fairness, feelings of trust, or behavioral cooperation that are among the variables examined by chapters in this book.

What are the contextual changes of the 21st century workplace to which we refer? As noted at the outset of our chapter, these include changes in organizational structure, the globalization of the marketplace, organizations' reliance on virtual technologies as a means of communicating with employees as well as customers, and the increased cultural diversity of the workplace. Such changes have dramatically affected the negotiation landscape. For example, these changes have created flatter organizations (i.e., with fewer layers of authorities and more temporary, contract-based employees), which in turn tend to value individual skills over organizational structure. As another example, these changes have created more complex negotiations involving organizational representatives spread across the globe and more technologically mediated (fewer face-to-face) negotiations. These contextual workplace changes over time reward negotiators (and the organizations they represent) who are effective at negotiating and persuading international partners, using cultural knowledge to incorporate diverse points of view, and mastering virtual (non-face-to-face) channels or technical skills that are not necessarily equally understood by all parties. Technology also provides a multitude of options that were not available to negotiators in previous, less technologically reliant times, such as greater potential for knowledge (a)symmetry as information can be discovered via Internet-based networking sites. In a larger sense, much of innovation today is a collective enterprise that relies on exchange and negotiations (see Arthur, 2009). How might employees and managers benefit *as negotiators* from the changes across time that have occurred in "the workplace" (which in the digital age increasingly lacks a unitary location)? Collectively, our book aims to answer this question.

KEY MESSAGES

More specifically, the chapters in Section 2 of this book illuminate the importance of employees (at all levels) enhancing perceptions of justice, or fairness, since these perceptions have consistently been linked to various forms of cooperation and other positive (relational and tangible) outcomes that help organizations and the units comprising them to function positively. The strategic importance of fairness in triggering cooperative types of behaviors is noted in Chapters 2–5; yet, each of these chapters differentially approaches this general tendency. More specifically, Chapter 2 by Donald Conlon and William Ross reviews the strategies that have theoretically and empirically been linked to higher levels of employees' perceived justice (of various types) and describes how these strategies can also help negotiators achieve higher levels of perceived fairness of their actions. Importantly, these authors also caution readers to question the applicability of the fairness-enhancing tactics they describe in light of the fact that nearly all of these tactics fail to consider one of the hallmark attributes of the 21st century workplace: that social media now exists (e.g., Facebook, MySpace, blogs, etc.) that make it more difficult for managers as well as (prospective and current) employees to control (alone) the information that they may wish others to know about, hence making it potentially more difficult for either of these parties to utilize information in their negotiations in ways they might like. The challenges noted in this chapter thus suggest that future research on negotiation needs to be sensitive to social media channels that have generally been neglected in prior negotiation- and justice-related research.

Chapter 3, by Kathryn Roloff, Joel Brockner, and Batia Wiesenfeld, extends Conlon and Ross's insights in Chapter 2 by alerting readers to the fact that fairness actions, even if taken, may *not* necessarily be perceived as authentic, and that perceived authenticity is essential if justice strategies (such as those reviewed in the prior chapter) are to have their typical cooperation-enhancing effects. These authors identify ways for negotiators to enhance their perceived authenticity, many of which require negotiators to have access to "rich" (face-to-face) cues involving nonverbal as well as verbal characteristics; yet, they note the difficulty of achieving perceived authenticity in the 21st century workplace, where employees (including managers) must increasingly: (a) interact *without* access to nonverbal cues that can aid perceptions of sincerity due to employees' increased reliance on virtual (relatively "leaner") communications and (b) interact with culturally diverse others whose "display rules" likely differ from their own, thereby complicating employees' ability to be perceived as authentically fair or to similarly perceive another's authenticity. As such, Roloff et al. identify the richness/leanness of communication media, the cultural diversity of negotiation participants, and negotiators' perceptions of others' authenticity as additional research needs.

The remaining two chapters in Section 2 reinforce and extend the insights of its initial chapters, first in the context of salary negotiation specifically (in Chapter 4 by Robin Pinkley) and next in a more general context in which outcomes of "subjective value" as well as "economic value" are sought (in Chapter 5 by Hillary Anger Elfenbein and Jared Curhan). More specifically, in Chapter 4, Robin Pinkley hones in on the salary negotiation context in particular and reviews the strategies that have traditionally been found to aid negotiators in obtaining the salary they seek. She notes that such strategies were identified in studies *not* characterized by some of the 21st century workplace characteristics today, such as increased cultural diversity of the workplace (in gender-based and nationally diverse ways) and increased use of online job applications (thus eliminating the richer information available in face-to-face negotiations) and access to salary data-related sites. In Chapter 5, Hillary Anger Elfenbein and Jared Curhan emphasize negotiators' desire to experience "subjective value" (such as enhanced perceptions of fairness and feelings of respect, among other things) in addition to economic value (such as an attractive salary agreement). They identify possible actions for enhancing subjective value, yet note the need to test these speculations empirically for two reasons. These are the near absence of data that speak to their recommended actions and the likely challenges of using the strategies they identify in the 21st century workplace, where face-to-face negotiations are increasingly rare (due to organizations' reliance on virtual work structures) and where flatter and more interdependent organizational structures are increasingly the norm, thereby potentially blurring the start and end of formal negotiations.

In contrast to Section 2, the chapters in Section 3 are devoted to issues associated with managing employees' affect, moods, or emotions. More specifically, Chapter 6 by Russell Cropanzano, William Becker, and Jöel

Feldman reviews how moods and emotions (which they are careful to distinguish) affect negotiation dynamics, Chapter 7 by Robert J. Bies and Thomas Tripp reviews literature regarding how negative affect and related behaviors such as anger and revenge affect cooperation, and Chapter 8 by Roy Lewicki and Ralph Hanke reviews literature regarding how deceptive strategies in negotiation affect feelings of distrust. Collectively, all three of these chapters illuminate the need for negotiators, hence also managers who must negotiate with their employees, to understand the role that affect of various kinds plays in determining how cooperative others will be and therefore how readily agreements can (or cannot) be negotiated. Given the tendency for more positive types of emotions to generally trigger more cooperative behaviors, the prescribed strategies in these chapters typically involve invoking positive (rather than negative) emotions. Importantly, these chapters each caution that achieving desired emotions may be more difficult in the 21st century workplace, where managers, as a result of increasingly remote work assignments, are increasingly less able to provide or read nonverbal cues that can aid in the building of mutual trust, and relatedly, they are less able to be the *sole* emotion manager due to social network-based information sources or other online, or "virtual," communication channels. In summary, the insights of the chapters comprising Section 3 reinforce the need for future negotiation research to examine how virtual communication channels affect negotiation dynamics and add to the need for such research to include measures, hence observations, associated with negotiation participants' affective states (of various kinds).

In Section 4 of this book, Chapters 9–11 explore the importance of employees (at all levels) managing social influences or group-sensitive phenomena. The need to do so is clearly identified by the social network perspective on negotiation provided in Chapter 9 (by Daniel J. Brass and Giuseppe Labianca). These authors note that few existing negotiation studies have investigated levels of analysis beyond the negotiating dyad, and that very little social network analysis examines negotiations. The need to do so, they explain, is because social network variables likely affect negotiators' degree of power or influence and because flatter and more decentralized organizations are more characteristic of the 21st century relative to earlier times, thereby necessitating employees' need to understand and utilize their networks as effectively as possible (a view that reinforces and extends insights found in Chapter 5 by Elfenbein and Curhan). In Chapter 10 (by Catherine H. Tinsley, Nazli Turan, Laurie Weingart, and Robin

L. Dillon-Merrill), the authors illuminate the increased tendency for the 21st century workplace to involve intercultural negotiations; hence, there is need for negotiators and managers to negotiate agreement among culturally diverse employees to avoid the tendency to engage in stereotyping during intercultural exchanges. Chapter 11 by Michael P. Haselhuhn and Laura J. Kray reinforces and extends insights found in Tinsley et al.'s Chapter 10 since they note that cultural stereotypes exist for males versus females, and that such stereotypes are part of the reason for the existence of a gender gap in negotiation. Their extension of insights found previously in the book is due to Haselhuhn and Kray's illumination of 21st century workplace characteristics that impede the resolution of this gender gap—namely, the tendency for organizations in the economically precarious 21st century to focus on observable, short-term outcomes that unwittingly cause these organizations to reward male (immediate financial performance) versus female (building client relationships) skill sets.

In the concluding Section 5 of this book, the chapters illuminate the fact that the nature of the 21st century workplace challenges facing negotiators makes it necessary for managers and employees to become more effective *organizational managers*—that is, to more effectively recognize and account for the fact that negotiations now occur within and between organizations, and not just between individuals. These chapters address the unique transaction costs involved in negotiating within and between organizations. The chapters in this section acknowledge that individuals are often embedded within organizational structures, something that has received relatively little attention by negotiation researchers to date.

Toward this goal, Chapter 12 (by Jonathan Hughes, Sara Enlow, Jessica Siegel, and Jeff Weiss) draws on concepts of organizational learning to identify strategies for aiding organizations in becoming better able to improve their negotiated results. On a more practical level, they emphasize how organizations can implement organizational systems to improve negotiated outcomes across the multitudinous negotiations that organizations conduct. In brief, they argue that managers can significantly improve organizational-level outcomes by implementing methods to capture knowledge from negotiations, translate that knowledge into organized systems, and disseminate this knowledge across the organization. Chapter 13 by Deepak Malhotra discusses the importance of managers not assuming, as they often do, that their role in negotiations ends when they hand an agreement to lawyers to finalize. He argues that managers—as negotiators—should continue to involve themselves in the "contracting phase," to better ensure that the interests and understandings they are concerned with are consistently applied to the final, negotiated agreement. Chapter 14 (by Ritu Agarwal, Siva Viswanathan, and Animesh Animesh) analyzes the recent and impending changes to negotiation related to new information technologies (ITs) and the effects of IT on negotiations. Moreover, they propose a framework that describes the manner in which IT during the pre-negotiation, negotiation, and post-negotiation phases may help to minimize transaction costs associated with negotiating business agreements.

Collectively, all of the chapters in this book illuminate the need for future research on negotiation to include variables associated with virtual communication channels (including, but not limited to, social media-based channels of communication) and the increasingly "blurry" boundary between who is versus who is *not* a "negotiation participant." In addition, this book's chapters illuminate the need for future research on negotiation to include variables associated with negotiation participants' emotions as well as perceptions, their degree of cultural (dis)similarity to each other, and the extent to which negotiation participants are negotiating in organizations whose structure is flatter versus taller, negotiating across organizational (and even national) boundaries, negotiating with others who are the same (or different) from those they negotiated with at earlier phases of the negotiation, and negotiating with the goal of achieving subjective or economic value.

This book also illuminates the need for future negotiation research to consider studying negotiation phenomena via new and different research methodologies. Related to this point, it is worth noting several important patterns in negotiation research identified in a recent review of methodology trends in negotiation research between 1965 and 2004, which indicated several important patterns (Buelens, Van De Woestyne, Mestdagh, & Bouckenooghe, 2008). Among these are the following: (a) negotiations research has grown exponentially during this period; (b) for the most recent decade reported, 59.7% of published negotiations research involved laboratory or experimental simulations, 26.7% were theoretical or conceptual articles, and only 2.1% of research involved field studies; (c) the focus of most research in the past decade was negotiator personality, emotions, and rationality and bias involving laboratory experiments and mathematical/game theory relating to theoretical/conceptual articles.

The commentary by Leigh Thompson, Erika Richardson, and Brian Lucas (in Chapter 16) elaborates on the view that future negotiation research should enable multilevel observations to occur, thus involving more team-level or organizational-level (even interorganizational) field studies than the approximate 2% of such studies that occurred between 1965 and 2004. Among their conclusions, for example, is their belief that "the organizational perspective in many ways holds the greatest promise for negotiation research," which leads them to forecast that "it is the field of sociology and macro organizational behavior that may very well represent the next frontier of research." Similarly, the commentary by Michele J. Gelfand and Ya'akov Gal (in Chapter 15) suggests that negotiation scholars' tool kit needs to expand to include tools that enable observations of negotiation phenomena whose complexity in the 21st century workplace *cannot* be adequately reflected in two-party simulated negotiation studies. Such tools, they suggest, will require negotiation scholars to adopt a more "open systems view of negotiation" and to study negotiation with a more interdisciplinary approach than has historically been the case, for example, via partnering with scholars who have expertise in cross-cultural phenomena, neuroscience, social psychology, economics, and decision-making biases. Similarly, in the commentary by Chia-Jung Tsay and Max Bazerman (in Chapter 17), they conclude, among other things, that "by more fully appreciating negotiations as a function not only of individual skill but also of relationships and organizational competence, negotiators stand to gain much in joint processes and outcomes."

Before assuming that these calls for new and different negotiation study approaches are worth heeding, it is important to consider the contrarian view that is also part of Tsay and Bazerman's commentary. Provocatively, this last commentary offers the following question: Is the process of negotiation in the 21st century *really* different from the negotiation process identified in earlier times? Contrary to the dominant affirmative view suggested by previous parts of the book, Tsay and Bazerman remind us of the features of negotiation that have remained unchanged over time. Indeed, Tsay and Bazerman suggest that the *contextual* changes to the nature of work over time illuminate merely *moderating* variables that need to be added to negotiation studies, thereby illuminating the *conditions in which* "the negotiation process" (unchanged in its fundamentals) will continue to be as previous publications have described it. In contrast, our own view (supported by the content of most of this book) is that these contextual changes alter directly the process of negotiation itself. The fact that there is debate on whether the process of negotiation has changed is part of the reason why this book promises to stir conversations about how (if at all) to change the scholarly and practical approaches used for understanding negotiations today. It is our hope that you will feel provoked by this controversy to revisit your own assumptions and methodological approach to testing these, relating to what effective negotiating or managing truly needs to be in the 21st century workplace of which we all are (whether we like it or not) a part.

In summary, this book points to a research agenda for future negotiation research that is highly sensitive to the 21st century workplace challenges identified in each chapter. Importantly, these challenges relate to the prescriptions that each chapter also identifies for enhancing process or outcome effectiveness in negotiations. As such, the research agenda that cumulatively results from this book illuminates numerous moderating variables (at varying levels of analysis) that may need to nuance the understanding currently held by managers or scholars about which actions most likely lead to positive relational and economic outcomes in negotiation exchanges. We hope this book will thus inspire the creation and dissemination of new knowledge about negotiation dynamics to occur so that, ultimately, future recipients of this knowledge will feel able to negotiate in the new world that the 21st century workplace has become.

REFERENCES

Arthur, W. B. (2009). *The nature of technology*. New York: Free Press.

Bailey, D. E., and Kurland, N. B. (2002). A review of telework research: Findings, new directions, and lessons for the study of modern work. *Journal of Organizational Behavior, 23*, 383–400.

Barney, J. (1991). Firm resources and sustained competitive advantage. *Journal of Management, 17*(1), 99–120.

Buelens, M., Van De Woestyne, M., Mestdagh, S., & Bouckenooghe, D. (2008). Methodological issues in negotiation research: A state-of-the-art-review. *Group Decision and Negotiation, 17*, 321–345.

Friedman, T. L. (2005). *The world is flat*. New York: Farrar, Straus, & Giroux.

Groth, M., Goldman, B., Gilliland, S., & Bies, R. (2002). Commitment to legal claiming: Influences of attributions, social guidance, and organizational tenure. *Journal of Applied Psychology, 87*, 781–788.

Kreps, D. M. (1990). *A course in microeconomic theory*. Princeton, NJ: Princeton University Press.

Levine, D. I. (2002). The new employment contract? *Employment Research, 9*(1), 4–6.

Olson, W. K. (1992). *The litigation explosion: What happened when America unleashed the lawsuit*. New York: Truman Talley Books.

Pol, E., & Carroll, P. (2006). *An introduction to economics with emphasis on innovation.* Philadelphia: Thomson.

Raiffa, H. (2002). *Negotiation analysis.* Cambridge, MA: Harvard University Press.

Schumpeter, J. A. (1961). *The theory of economic development: An inquiry into profits, capital, credit, interest, and the business cycle* (R. Opie, Trans.). New York: Oxford University Press.

Thompson, L. (2009). *The mind and heart of the negotiator* (4th ed.). Upper Saddle River, NJ: Prentice Hall.

Valley, K. L., White, S. B., & Iacobucci, D. (1992). The process of assisted negotiations: A network analysis. *Group Decision and Negotiation, 2,* 117–135.

van Knippenberg, D., & Schippers, M. C. (2007). Work group diversity. *Annual Review of Psychology, 58,* 515–541.

Section 2

Negotiators as Fairness Managers in the 21st Century

2

The Effect of Perceived/Felt (In)Justice on Cooperativeness: Implications for Negotiators as "Justice-Enhancing Communicators" in an Era of Social Networking

Donald E. Conlon and William H. Ross

INTRODUCTION

What makes a work situation fair? The present chapter addresses this question within the context of negotiation. After reviewing this question, we offer some justice-enhancing strategies for negotiators—particularly for managers seeking to manage conflicts in their organizations. Finally, the chapter looks at how the growth of Internet-based social networking websites (SNWs) changes both the context of negotiations and how managers might use justice-enhancing strategies. As we will make clear, social networking activities by job applicants and employees present challenges to managers who seek to balance their use of relevant information for decision making with their efforts to use justice-enhancing strategies.

While "fairness" may sometimes be considered from an objective perspective (e.g., if the facts in a dispute heavily weigh in favor of one side, then perhaps the settlement should also favor that side), usually fairness is considered from the perspective of the disputant. That is because people often act on their beliefs, and justice-related beliefs can be powerful (Lind, 2001). Generally, employees perceive higher levels of fairness under the following conditions: (a) the quantity and quality of outcomes received, such as a salary offer, pay raise, or working conditions, are greater (termed *distributive justice*; cf. Deutsch, 1975); (b) the quality of procedures employed to determine their outcomes, such as criteria and methods used for performance appraisals, seem appropriate (termed *procedural justice*; cf. Folger, 1987; Thibaut & Walker, 1975); (c) the quality of information they have received, such as explanations for organizational outcomes or procedures, is satisfactory (termed *informational justice*; cf. Greenberg, 1990); and (d) the quality of interpersonal treatment they have received during the enactment of procedures or explanations is respectful and considerate (termed both *interactional justice* [cf. Bies & Moag, 1986; Bies & Shapiro, 1987] and *interpersonal justice* [cf. Greenberg, 1993; Colquitt, 2001]).

When employees perceive greater fairness in any of these ways, they typically behave more "cooperatively." By this, we mean that the employees who perceive more fairness tend to comply more and to be more loyal and committed. Evidence of greater compliance from employees who perceive more fairness includes these employees filing fewer wrongful termination claims when terminated (Lind, Greenberg, Scott, & Welchans, 2000) and receiving fewer reprimands for noncompliance with organizational policies (Robbins, Summers, & Miller, 2000). Similarly, customers who feel more fairly treated have been found to comply more frequently with store requests for demographic and shopping habit information (Albrecht, 2002). Evidence of greater loyalty from those who perceive more fairness includes greater repeat business from customers who feel fairly treated (Conlon & Murray, 1996). Evidence of greater commitment from employees who perceive more fairness includes their tendency to go beyond mere compliance to assist organizations' goals—that is, to express organizational commitment (cf., Herscovitch & Meyer, 2002; Meyer, Srinivas, Lal, & Topolynytsky, 2007). Because organizations, managers, and even fellow employees benefit when they have more compliant, loyal, and committed employees and customers, it behooves organizational authorities, leaders, team leaders, and coworkers to understand how to enhance perceptions of fairness on the part of those who interact with them. This may explain why numerous studies have theorized and established a link between fairness and cooperation (e.g., Tyler, 1990; Tyler & Blader, 2003, 2005).

Curiously, few of the last studies and justice studies in general involve the context of negotiation—that is, in contexts in which (a) the parties have distinct, preferred solutions that are often incompatible and typically identified in advance of discussion; (b) the parties are interdependent, unable to obtain mutually acceptable outcomes without the cooperation of the other; and (c) discussion and persuasion are used to better understand each side's underlying interests and preferences or to influence the other party or parties to accept outcomes that they would not normally accept (Lewicki, Barry, & Saunders, 2010; Kipnis, Schmidt, & Wilkinson, 1980; Pruitt, 1981; Putnam & Roloff, 1992). As a result, a question that is unanswered by past justice research is: Do negotiators who perceive the other negotiator as treating them more (rather than less) fairly behave "more cooperatively"? For this question to be meaningful, we need to clarify what we mean by both "fairly" and "more cooperatively" in a negotiation context.

Negotiators who perceive "more fairness" perceive the other negotiators at the table treating them with interpersonal respect and sincerity (interactional justice), giving them adequate information such as factually supported explanations for requested concessions (informational justice); using unbiased, ethical criteria to guide requested concessions (procedural justice); and proposing outcomes, or concessions, that meet the proposal recipient's needs and hence do not impose hardship (distributive justice). Negotiators who act "more cooperatively" (a) comply more readily with the other negotiator's requested concessions; (b) ask questions about the other other parties' needs to genuinely learn how potentially to meet those needs in addition to their own; (c) make proposals that they believe can meet the needs of all parties at the table (helped by what they have learned during the negotiation about others' needs); or (d) decline requested concessions by others in interpersonally sensitive ways, such as by providing an explanation that helps focus the conversation on mutual needs and shared benefits associated with reaching a mutually satisfying agreement. All of the last behaviors, except for readily complying with concession-making requests, illustrate what has been called an "integrative" (mutual problem solving-oriented) approach to negotiating. The antithesis of this has been called a "distributive" approach and consists of a self-oriented approach often characterized by a contentious and dominating manner.

In summary, many past organizational justice studies have occurred outside a clear negotiation context (e.g., research has focused on reactions to layoffs, drug testing, selection, or performance appraisal decisions; cf. Cropanzano, 1993; Greenberg & Colquitt, 2005). Further, many negotiation studies have focused on factors other than issues of fairness. For example, many studies have investigated how personality variables (e.g., locus of control; cf. Rubin & Brown, 1975) or situational factors (e.g., time pressure; e.g., Yukl, 1974) affect negotiation; other studies have focused on cognitive (cf. Neale & Bazerman, 1991) and affective (e.g., Van Kleef, De Dreu, & Manstead, 2004) aspects of negotiation. Typically, when fairness is considered, it is only as a dependent variable that is measured post facto (e.g., Conlon & Ross, 1997). Yet, we know that in organizations, people have ongoing relationships and multiple opportunities for negotiation over time. These relationships and negotiation episodes are made more complex by the advent of new technologies. Because of a lack of research linking the topics of fairness and negotiation, we do not know whether negotiators who perceive more fairness (in all the ways described at the start of our chapter) will subsequently behave more cooperatively—either integratively or compliantly. We do not know exactly how unfairness interacts with other factors (such as information gathered via social networks) to affect subsequent negotiator behavior.

As a start toward answering these questions, we first review the relatively sparse literature linking perceptions of fairness to subsequent negotiation behaviors or outcomes and then identify strategies that negotiators may use to enhance others' perception of them as fair, as suggested by the negotiation studies we review and by the organizational justice literature. After doing this, we identify and discuss eight justice-enhancing strategies that can help those in conflict and negotiation settings experience fairness. We then consider the impact that Internet-based social networking and information search sites have on how our justice enhancement strategies can influence cooperation in negotiations. With these challenges in mind, we conclude by identifying questions in need of future research by negotiation scholars.

DO NEGOTIATORS WHO PERCEIVE FAIRNESS BEHAVE MORE COOPERATIVELY?

While there is surprisingly little work on justice and negotiation, some results clearly suggest that fairness will facilitate cooperation. Maxwell, Nye, & Maxwell (1999) show that priming "fairness" considerations among negotiators leads to somewhat larger initial concessions, significantly faster agreements, and significantly greater beliefs that the final settlement is equitable—even though the final settlement was not significantly different from when fairness concerns were not primed. Smith, Pruitt, and Carnevale (1982) suggested that negotiators consciously adjust their own concession rate based on the other party's bargaining positions and concession rate to arrive at fair outcomes via a process of equal concessions. This body of research implies that in organizational contexts, individuals are often willing to forgo highly favorable outcomes for themselves to establish fairness for themselves and others. Thus, while some justice arguments may coincide with a negotiator's self-interest, justice is distinguishable from favorable outcomes in negotiation situations (c.f., Maxwell et al., 1999; Messick & Sentis, 1983). Beliefs about justice within negotiation may carry over to subsequent interactions. Shapiro and Bies (1994) reported that negotiators who believe that the other party deliberately lied to them in a prior negotiation were subsequently more angry and less willing to cooperate with the other party.

It is hoped this brief review makes clear that injustice can lead to patterns of negotiating that are likely to be more competitive or distributive in nature. From the perspective of a negotiator, decrements in cooperation could manifest themselves as higher impasse rates, a lack of concessions, a refusal even to negotiate, or a refusal to live up to the terms of a negotiated or imposed (e.g., third-party or supervisor-determined) settlement. These reactions exemplify the behavioral consequences of moral outrage that Folger and Cropanzano (1998) noted often stem from feelings of exploitation and unfairness related to outcomes, procedures, information, or treatment. In addition to such behaviors, injustice leads to altered psychological states, including distrust, a desire for revenge/restoration of justice, and an analysis of power within the relationship (e.g., Aquino, Tripp, & Bies, 2006; Neves & Caetano, 2006).

WHICH STRATEGIES MAY ENHANCE NEGOTIATORS' PERCEIVED FAIRNESS?

What types of justice-enhancing strategies have a positive impact on justice perceptions and ultimately lead to more cooperation? Numerous books (e.g., Lewicki et al., 2010) and articles (e.g., Kipnis et al., 1980) offer managers advice on eliciting cooperation from others, even while seeking to negotiate satisfactory outcomes for themselves or those they represent. Space limitations do not permit us to recount all of the advice for successful influence and negotiation contained in those writings. Instead, we emphasize that negotiators may seek to use a variety of justice-enhancing strategies to elicit cooperation from those they negotiate with, be they superiors, peers, or subordinates. We discuss two strategies related to each of the four forms of justice previously noted.

Distributive Justice

Justice-Enhancing Strategy 1: Define the Standard

One strategy a negotiator might use on a target in an effort to enhance distributive justice is to get the target person to agree to use a comparison standard that will lead them to the conclusion that what is offered them is a fair outcome. Oldham, Kulik, Ambrose, Stepina, and Brand (1986) proposed a 3 ′ 3 framework of referent "possibilities" based on *type of referent* (self, other, or system, the last defined as comparisons to items contractually promised) and the *temporality of the referent* (located in the past, present, or future). Thinking about such possibilities might lead one to become aware of a large number of possibilities that one might try to invoke as the comparison standard that should be used. One of the authors remembered when he worked at a manufacturing center and the company posted the hourly wage increase information on a bulletin board. The author remembers seeing the new hourly wage and being pleased because it was an increase of 35 cents per hour over what he had been making (compared to self-present, it seemed fair) and a lot more than what he had made at his previous job (a self-past referent). Moments later, another employee walked up, read the same information and muttered about how unfair the raise was. When asked why, the other employee noted that a similar manufacturing center in the area just gave its employees an increase of 60 cents per hour (an other-present referent), and thus he believed his raise was unfair.

Justice-Enhancing Strategy 2:
Provide Generous Outcomes on Another Issue

Negotiators can also try to balance what might be seen as lower outcomes on one dimension by providing greater outcomes on other dimensions.

Martin and Harder (1994) differentiated organizational rewards based on whether they were financial versus socioemotional in nature and noted that people sometimes compensated for providing others with low outcomes on one dimension by providing higher outcomes on the other. Cropanzano, Bowen, and Gilliland (2007) suggest that employees often prefer that socioemotional rewards (e.g., parking spaces) be allocated on an equality basis and that financial rewards be allocated using a combination of equity and equality. Vermunt and Steensma (2001) also highlighted the idea of giving someone an additional—sometimes symbolic—positive reward (e.g., a nicer computer and printer) to compensate partially for an injustice on another reward (e.g., the loss of secretarial help). Of course, there are many issues regarding the appropriateness or inappropriateness of substituting some types of resources (e.g., money, social support) for others (e.g., goods, status). Wilson, Sin, and Conlon (2010) provided a comprehensive review of what types of rewards or resources might be viewed as appropriate or inappropriate exchanges.

Procedural Justice

Justice-Enhancing Strategy 3: Provide Opportunities for "Voice"

Regarding procedural justice, the classic justice-enhancing strategy is to provide targets with voice or, more typically, voice opportunity (the two are not the same). Having the opportunity to be "heard" enhances procedural justice (Lind & Tyler, 1988), and having the chance to express one's opinions is particularly important when people ultimately receive unfavorable outcomes (Brockner & Wiesenfeld, 2005; Folger, Rosenfield, Grove, & Corkran, 1979). Obviously, part of voice includes listening and showing appreciation for what the other party says (even if it suggests undesirable outcomes for oneself). In an experimental study on negotiation, Leung, Tong, and Ho (2004) found that dyads composed of negotiators trained to show understanding and a willingness to listen demanded less for themselves in negotiation, reached agreements more quickly, and endured no impasses in negotiation relative to dyads composed of negotiators trained to respond in ways that did not enhance voice (i.e., remarking that the other side was wrong, having impatience in listening, and providing frequent interruptions).

Justice-Enhancing Strategy 4: Incorporate the Recommendations of Leventhal

Other ways to enhance procedural justice with an eye toward gaining cooperation or compliance in negotiation can be culled from the work of Leventhal and his colleagues (Leventhal, 1980; Leventhal, Karuza, & Fry, 1980). These scholars argued that procedural justice was enhanced when procedures (a) were applied consistently in situations; (b) ensured that biases were suppressed; (c) relied on accurate information; (d) had a means to correct flawed decisions; (e) conformed to prevailing standards of ethics or morality; and (f) ensured that all affected subgroups had voice opportunity. These criteria suggest a variety of ways negotiators might work to procure agreement with another negotiator. For example, Vermunt and Steensma (2001) suggested that an earlier procedural injustice can be partially offset by subsequent procedural justice, which they called *mitigation*. Perhaps an unfair performance appraisal procedure may be partially offset by allowing the subordinate to add a note to his or her file disputing the way the procedure was designed or administered. This might enhance procedural justice because it makes the subordinate feel that the data are now more accurate and less biased and because it allowed the subordinate to engage in voice.

Interpersonal Justice

Justice-Enhancing Strategy 5: Treat Others With Politeness, Dignity, and Respect

It is not just what you say in negotiation, but how you say it that can often be the difference between reaching agreement or not. Regarding interpersonal justice, treating people with politeness, dignity, and respect—thereby preventing or calming hostile emotions—may enhance justice (Yang & Diefendorff, 2009). Surprisingly, there has been little work on interpersonal justice and negotiations, although with increasing attention being paid to subjective as well as objective outcomes from negotiation, we expect to see more work in the future on this topic. Leung et al. (2004, p. 407) argue that interpersonal justice signals trustworthiness to the other side; thus, fair interpersonal treatment should lead to "a smoother bargaining process characterized by fewer confrontations and disagreements." Looking at future intentions, a negotiation study by Kass (2008) suggested that interpersonal justice influenced negotiators' desire for future negotiations with the other party, suggesting a link between interpersonal justice and willingness to cooperate.

Justice-Enhancing Strategy 6: Behave in Trustworthy Ways

If a supervisor is trusted, then the supervisor may be seen as more interpersonally just by subordinates (Simons, Friedman, Liu, & McLean Parks, 2007). Malhotra and Murnighan (2002) related trust to cooperation using attribution theory: When another's cooperative behavior is seen as voluntary, the person is seen as trustworthy, eliciting cooperation; however, the same behavior does not elicit trust when it is attributable to external factors, such as if the behavior is required by a binding contract. Also, a "transformational leadership" style is related to trust and cooperation with the leader (Conchie & Donald, 2009). A transformational leadership style also leads to perceptions of interpersonal justice, which in turn lead to employees being more willing to cooperate with organizational change (Wu, Neubert, & Yi, 2007). Leaders who are trustworthy also tend to have subordinates who are more willing to cooperate by engaging in organizational citizenship behaviors—but this relationship is moderated by whether the leader has treated them with interpersonal justice (Chiaburu & Marinova, 2006).

Informational Justice

Justice-Enhancing Strategy 7: Offer Credible and Sincere Accounts

Finally, regarding informational justice, research suggests that if managers offer a credible explanation (an "account") for their position or actions, it will enhance justice effects compared to offering no explanation. Typically, organizational justice researchers, building on Scott and Lyman's (1968) taxonomy, compared three types of accounts: excuses, apologies, and justifications (Conlon & Murray, 1996; Shapiro, Buttner, & Barry, 1994). *Excuses* are explanations that remove one from responsibility for the outcome (e.g., a manager who has to give a work group an onerous new job responsibility may explain that it is necessary to comply with an order from a government regulatory agency). *Apologies* are explanations that include a strong element of admission of responsibility for an action as well as an expression of remorse (e.g., a manager must negotiate with a work group to downsize a percentage of the group, but makes it clear that he or she is sorry about having to do it and about the pain that it will cause). *Justifications* are explanations in which a party not only takes responsibility for the action but also attempts to minimize the negative impact or to reframe the action, perhaps by appealing to superordinate goals (e.g., a downsizing decision, while bad for the work group, is good for the organization as a whole). Bobocel and Zdaniuk (2005) noted that there are far fewer studies on apologies compared to the other two explanation types.

Shaw, Wild, and Colquitt's (2003) meta-analysis of explanations research concluded that explanations that allow for external attributions (excuses directing attention away from the supervisor and toward external factors) are frequently perceived as "just," but if there is no credible external explanation, then the subordinate is inclined to believe that the supervisor's position is simply attributable to the supervisor's own preference (internal attributions) unless the supervisor offers a compelling justification. This work highlights the importance of the explanation being seen as sincere and believable. Kass's (2008) work on informational justice and negotiation made a similar point, as informational justice perceptions (beliefs that explanations were reasonable and truthful) were positively related to outcome satisfaction and desire for future negotiations.

Justice-Enhancing Strategy 8: Offer Timely Accounts

In addition to the quality of an explanation, the timing of an explanation can also have an impact on its credibility and subsequent reaction to the explanation. Information received early on has greater impact on fairness judgments than later information (Van den Bos, Vermunt, & Wilke, 1997). Explanations received in advance of unfavorable outcomes provide a framework for the person to interpret the subsequent outcome, whereas explanations that are offered later do not have this effect (Weaver & Conlon, 2003). Together, conclusions from these studies fit anecdotal suggestions that negotiators eschew their natural tendency to submit a proposal and then offer explanations if requested. Rather, it may be beneficial for negotiators to explain their logic prior to offering a proposal so that the other party understands how the proposal was formulated and what facts were considered (Graham & Sanyo, 1984). This also means that in a negotiation situation, a delay in receiving an explanation for why something is occurring may lead parties to perceive the explanation more negatively once it is received (Shapiro et al., 1994). Justice delayed can be justice denied.

Some Caveats Regarding the Use of These Eight Strategies

This discussion assumes that managers will use these strategies in ways that enhance fairness. Fortin and Fellenz (2008), building on a framework offered by Lukes (2005), cautioned that the subjective beliefs of employees about what is fair may not match either objective standards of fairness (e.g., equality) or standards rooted in philosophy (e.g., Solomon's 1992 "virtue ethics" or Rawls's 1971 theory of justice). They note that managers may manipulate employee impressions of fairness in three ways. First, managers may seek to manipulate such impressions by how they respond to complaints about unfairness of either outcomes or procedures. Second, managers may seek to use their power to prevent conflict by limiting which topics are discussed or negotiated or preventing certain groups from forming and raising issues (e.g., General Motors faced a lawsuit because the company allowed certain "affinity groups" to form and meet on company facilities while forbidding other groups from forming; Clark, 2004). Third, managers use long-term methods such as socialization and organizational culture manipulation (e.g., using carefully selected language and symbols) to shape employee expectations so that employees may not even recognize that they have grievances. For example, without aggregate data, individual women often do not realize that they have been victims of sex discrimination in salary negotiations with their employers (Tomasson, Crosby, & Herzberger, 1996). The consequence may be that employees believe a manager's actions and positions on issues are reasonable and fair when they actually are not. Thus, managers are admonished to use "fairness" research in ways that not only appear fair but actually are fair, at least according to commonly used objectives or philosophical standards.

21ST CENTURY CHALLENGES TO USING JUSTICE-ENHANCING STRATEGIES

Until now, our review of the justice-enhancing strategies to facilitate cooperation in negotiation has focused exclusively on the parties actively engaged in the negotiation, be it two employees, a manager and an employee or employee group, and so on. Moreover, we have implicitly assumed that the negotiating parties have considerable control over what information is presented to and considered by the other side. However, the 21st century workplace makes this assumption highly suspect. In fact, technological changes in the workplace have strong implications for justice judgments and the connections that can be drawn between our justice-enhancing strategies outlined in the previous section and the achievement of cooperation. So, let us consider how our review of justice-enhancing strategies might be impacted by new information technologies present in the workplace. We do this by focusing on SNWs and related information technologies (e.g., weblogs or "blogs," sometimes grouped under the broad heading of "social media").

Social Networking, the Internet, and Organizational Justice

From relatively simple beginnings in the mid-1990s, SNWs have grown in technological sophistication (e.g., allowing users to post photographs) and popularity (e.g., in 2010 the SNWS Facebook exceeded 500 million users; Starr, 2010). Consider how easily people can now find information on, opinions of, and feedback from friends, professional colleagues, and even strangers by searching SNWs such as LinkedIn, Facebook, and MySpace. Such websites also often allow other individuals (e.g., "friends") the opportunity to post their opinions as well.

SNWs relate to conflict at work in several ways. First, using SNWs can be a source of conflict. It creates conflict if employees are spending their time visiting these popular websites instead of working. One survey reported that 27% of employees aged 18–29 spend 3 or more hours of work time per week visiting SNWs (Thomas, 2007). This type of conflict can be managed in many ways, including technologically prohibiting employees from accessing such websites while at work. Twentyman (2008) reported that nearly two-thirds of human resource (HR) managers in the United Kingdom block their employees from accessing SNWs while at work. Second, the content of SNWs may be a source of conflict. If employees are posting information that compromises company trade secrets, promotes hatred toward coworkers who are minority group members, or sexually harasses coworkers, then the content of the SNW posting may be a source of conflict, perhaps warranting managerial intervention or employee discipline (Wessel, 2004).

Third, SNWs may relate to conflict and negotiation in that they may allow each side to have access to an unprecedented amount of information about the other, which may affect subsequent negotiations. When one combines the relational computing power of SNWs and other social media (such as Twitter or personal weblogs) with the rise of powerful search engines such as Google, the amount of information potentially available becomes massive relative to what individuals had access to only a few years ago. We wish to focus on this third relationship between SNWs and conflict. Rather than the relatively straightforward implementation of technological barriers or development of policies regulating SNW use and content, the implications of information availability via SNWs and related websites are complex and may affect negotiation. For example, when considering a job offer, the applicant may be able to look up information about the prospective manager that he or she may be able to incorporate into impression management attempts to be seen as deserving a higher starting salary. Similarly, the manager may discover information about the applicant that may lead to a lower salary offer and cause the manager to resist adjusting the amount upward in negotiation. In the past, such information (including information that may provide a direct assessment of the other person's preferred outcomes; see Walton & McKersie, 1965) was not available without exhaustive research—and perhaps hiring private detectives.

Information has traditionally been considered a source of power in negotiation, as negotiators gather facts to support their positions or develop their expertise in particular issues and carefully present their arguments in a controlled fashion designed to secure a favorable agreement (e.g., Brodt, 1994). Also, if information flows through persons who are considered central in an information network, it may give such persons power (Brass, 1984). In other contexts such as automobile sales, the development of the ability to research price information (and even bargain) via the Internet has shifted the balance of power between car dealers and consumers; it has empowered consumers and resulted in lower car prices (Blumenstein, 1997). We expect altered negotiations in the workplace also as both managers and employees (or applicants) gather information via SNWs.

As noted, information acquisition and control provide a source of power in negotiations. The fundamental change in information acquisition and control that SNWs engender may have an impact on the ability of negotiators to use many of the justice-enhancing strategies just described. We now consider these linkages.

SNWs and Distributive Justice

Certainly, Justice-Enhancing Strategy 1 (defining the comparison standard to be used) becomes much more challenging when information is available through SNWs. In the past the organization might have provided a set of potential referents; the advent of SNWs and concomitant search tools like Google means that a negotiator can have a much wider set of referents to consider. This can make it much more difficult to agree on what referent should be used as the standard by which fairness is determined. Consider a professor engaged in a salary adjustment negotiation who is told by his or her department chair he or she is well paid—and produces selected salary survey data to support that position. In the past, the professor might be limited to accepting such information or talking to a few friends who are academics to determine what a fair salary is. Now, the professor can access the opinions of hundreds of colleagues through SNWs or can search electronic databases, where such information can be verified across many universities, allowing the professor to have more information to use in making a case (e.g., the Collegiate Times Higher Education Salary Database, http://www.collegiatetimes.com/databases/salaries). Of course, the ability to accumulate more information does not guarantee that better decisions are made (O'Connor, 1997). The ability of both parties to gather more information may reduce the information asymmetry that might have previously existed. However, it can also lead one or both to "anchor" on an improper reference point (Neale & Bazerman, 1991), which might complicate negotiations and make subsequent justice judgments less favorable, leading to less cooperation in the future.

People often discuss their personal lives on their SNWs, including sometimes work-related interests or preferred work outcomes. From a strictly distributive justice perspective, the ability of a manager to discover an employee's or applicant's preferred work outcomes through the Internet may allow the manager to use Justice-Enhancing Strategy 2: Providing generous outcomes on another issue if it is not possible to do so on a focal issue. For example, a manager may be unable to provide a pay raise to an employee but may be able to provide more time off because the manager discovered that the employee wanted to help his grown son move. However, using SNWs to uncover these other possibly preferred outcomes could be challenging because some employees do not use SNWs, while others who do may not always write about what their other preferred outcomes are—leading to the possibility that a manager might provide an employee an outcome that the employee does not want or one that has little value. It is also the case that monitoring employee SNWs even for the purpose of improving or personalizing employee outcomes raises numerous procedural and interpersonal justice issues. These are considered next.

SNWs and Procedural Justice

To the degree that negotiators engage in electronic self-expression by posting their statements (e.g., weblogs) and behaviors (e.g., YouTube videos or photos), they are creating instances of voice expression; thus, our Strategy 3 comes into play. Prior studies have shown that exercising voice has a "value-expressive" quality (meaning that the sheer expression of voice enhances one's sense of justice, even if such voice cannot influence the ultimate outcome received; cf. Lind & Tyler, 1988). The irony is that by encouraging the other in a negotiation to express his or her opinions (privately or publicly) about the negotiation process or the outcomes under discussion in negotiation, these voice expressers should ultimately be more accepting of the outcome they receive. However, exercising voice via SNWs may not have the same salutary outcomes as is the case when we think about voice as part of a formal dispute resolution process or system: One might discover that this "unsanctioned" or unregulated system for expressing voice runs counter to organizationally preferred systems for voice opportunity. The voice a negotiator engages in "off-line" via SNWs or websites that are critical of the employer may be amplified by others who share the same concern or feel they have shared a similar injustice. This might lead to the focal negotiator becoming even more angry, making the likelihood of reaching an acceptable agreement more difficult.

A second consequence of voice or self-expression on the Internet is that it provides information that the other negotiator may be able to use in negotiation if the other side can access the information. Such information may be used against the voice expresser if the other negotiator feels he or she now has an information advantage over the voice expresser. It has been shown that mutual trust leads people to share information via social media (Chai & Kim, 2010), and the long-term consequence is that people (e.g., employees) may trust others (e.g., their managers) less if they become aware that their information had been accessed. One of the authors encountered a situation in which a job candidate had done such extensive research about each member of the department that some faculty members grew uncomfortable, and the department decided not to bring the candidate on campus for an interview. In sum, the proliferation of SNWs means that negotiators have the potential to learn a lot more about each other as they prepare for negotiations.

The awareness that employees use SNWs to voice their opinions or publicize their behaviors can lead to numerous temptations that can compromise a manager's ability to act in justice-enhancing ways. The material presented on SNWs could be used against the voice expresser. For example, employees who criticize their employers or managers online are sometimes disciplined, even if the employees make these criticisms when off duty and on non-work-related websites (Ross, 2005). This would seem to violate the "ethicality" dimension of fair procedures noted by Leventhal (mentioned in our Strategy 4). Consider some possibilities from the hiring arena: One survey reported that approximately 41% of job candidates admitted to having posted information to SNWs about their own excessive drinking or drug use (Copeland, 2009). Bohnert and Ross (2010) examined how qualifications and SNW information affected people's willingness to interview and hire an applicant. They found that respondents were less likely to interview (hypothetical) applicants with alcohol-oriented information on websites, and they would offer such applicants significantly less money for a starting salary than applicants with family-oriented or professional information on SNWs. What one posts may even affect whether one receives an offer: Approximately one-third of employers have declined to offer at least one job candidate a position based on finding unflattering material in an Internet search (Parker, 2007). Clearly, what one decides to "voice" on SNWs has consequences.

SNWs and Interpersonal Justice

The discussion of how postings on SNWs might be used by others in negotiation situations is apparently something that those who post feel is inappropriate. Thus, treating people with politeness, dignity, and respect (Justice-Enhancing Strategy 5) and behaving in trustworthy ways (Justice-Enhancing Strategy 6) would also seem to be "in play" depending on what a manager did with SNW-generated voice. One poll found that 56% of those with SNWs consider it unethical for prospective employers to investigate them using SNWs, and 43% said that they would "feel outraged" if they knew that a prospective employer looked at their web page when deciding whether to hire them ("Workers Naïve," 2007). Such outrage is central to interpersonal justice judgments of status, dignity, and respect (Justice-Enhancing Strategy 5). Those who post on SNWs can argue that since most social networking host sites state that the content is not to be used for commercial purposes, its use in a hiring context is unethical or even illegal. In 2010, Germany first considered a proposed law to make such queries illegal (Jolly, 2010). If an interviewer or prospective coworker asks about aspects of an applicant's life reported only on the applicant's social network page, the applicant may feel that his or her privacy is violated and that he or she is not being treated with respect. It might also cause the employee to question the trustworthiness of the interviewer and, by extension, the company (thereby compromising Justice-Enhancing Strategy 6).

SNWs and Informational Justice

Managers may try to justify their use of information found on SNWs. For instance, Fernando (2008) suggests that managers who do not use such information neglect their "due diligence" obligations to the organization and to customers. Thus, continuing with our "new hire" scenario, the manager could try to explain his or her behavior or company policy of examining this information to the focal party. The success or failure of this explanation may depend on the last two justice-enhancing strategies: Was the explanation provided to the focal person sincere and believable (Justice-Enhancing Strategy 7)? Was it delivered in a timely fashion (Justice-Enhancing Strategy 8)? In the case of information gleaned from SNWs, it might be best to tell a potential applicant *before* investigating SNWs that the company will be looking at such information and why. This gives the applicant the opportunity to edit or delete information.

FUTURE RESEARCH NEEDS

To this point, we have described eight justice-enhancing strategies parties might use in negotiation and subsequently identified how social networks (and Internet search technologies) may create challenges for the use of those strategies. We now turn our attention to questions that remain unanswered and warrant future investigation.

Research Questions Related to Distributive Justice-Enhancing Strategies

Powerful parties frequently use information to obtain advantageous outcomes. For example, research suggests that those with power are more likely to engage in deceptive conflict management and negotiating strategies (Crott, Kayser, & Lamm, 1980; Boles, Croson, & Murnighan, 2000), are generally less concerned about the social consequences of their actions (Keltner, Gruenfeld, & Anderson, 2003), and are specifically less attentive to the less-powerful party's interests (Mannix & Neale, 1993). If "information is power" in negotiation and employees use the Internet to identify standards and "referent others," then the Internet affords opportunities for the weaker party to "level the playing field" by engaging in substantial research. Does this actually occur? If so, how does the more powerful party react? For example, in a hiring scenario, if a job candidate has done extensive research on comparable salary levels, does the manager simply raise the salary offer, respond with additional research of his or her own, or assert that his or her own information is more authoritative than the information gathered informally, perhaps through SNWs, by the candidate? What approach is seen as most fair by each party in such a scenario?

One justice-enhancing strategy is to provide generous outcomes on a second issue when favorable outcomes on a first issue are not forthcoming. A manager (or employee) may learn more about the other person via SNWs. Thus, the manager may better tailor desirable outcomes to the specific worker or job applicant by using SNWs. Under what conditions are managers actually likely to do this? And, how will employees react if they suspect that a manager visited their SNWS? Clearly, distributive justice may interact with other forms of justice when managers visit employee or applicant SNWs—even if the proposed outcome is highly favorable.

Significant cultural differences may also exist with regard to justice evaluations of cooperative behavior in organizations (Leung, 2005). For example, many Americans believe that it is perfectly fair for the person with more bargaining power to seek more favorable outcomes. By contrast, in Japan most respondents believe that it is the more powerful party's responsibility to take care of the weaker party by offering the weaker party more favorable outcomes (Buchan, Croson, & Johnson, 2004). Future research should investigate how cultural variables affect negotiation and conflict management strategies when SNWs offer the possibility of changing the balance of power in a relationship—and whether such change produces fairer outcomes.

Research Questions Related to Procedural Justice-Enhancing Strategies

One justice-enhancing managerial strategy is to provide opportunities for voice. However, as noted, employees or job applicants may resent that employers accessed the voice that they exercise via SNWs. This raises the obvious question: Under which conditions does it enhance justice for managers to access employee "off-duty voice," and under which conditions does it seem procedurally unjust for managers to access such voice information? For example, suppose a firm provides a website where each employee can host a weblog ("blog"). Further suppose that an employee posts a desire for a specific transfer on his or her weblog. Is it fairer for a manager to access such information (and then negotiate over what the employee must do to earn such a transfer) from such a company-provided website than from a similar nonwork website?

Of Leventhal's many recommendations, we wish to relate the "ethicality" dimension to future research questions. Is it appropriate for managers and employees to "friend" each other when they must later negotiate with each other? Is it unethical for recruiters to use aliases to gain access to job applicant SNWs? Do the job duties (e.g., working with children) justify certain information-gathering procedures that would otherwise be seen as unethical?

Leventhal noted that using accurate information is also an important aspect of procedural justice. Job candidates may feel that certain types of information on personal SNWs does not present an accurate picture of them *as employees*. Therefore, will candidates see it as fairer if a recruiter gives a job candidate advance notice that he or she plans to look at the candidate's SNW (so that the candidate has the opportunity to alter or remove information)? Will recruiters view it as fairer if they do not give candidates such advance notice? One of the chapter authors knows of a recruiter who, in the middle of job interviews, hands interviewees a laptop computer and asks them to pull up their SNW so that they can both see it simultaneously. Will candidates view this procedure as fairer than not being told until after they were hired that such information was accessed?

How much will it matter if such information affected the opening offer managers made in salary negotiations?

Research Questions Related to Interpersonal Justice-Enhancing Strategies

The growth of "temporary" (short-term or contract workers) and geographically disparate organizational relationships means that employees will have fewer instances of personal history with the parties with which they negotiate. Thus, they may rely even more heavily on SNW resources and technology to determine the strategies and medium through which they will negotiate. One problem here is of course that electronic negotiations are not as "media rich" as face-to-face negotiations, and the lack of ability to make eye contact and to hear one's tone of voice may neutralize the effectiveness of some of the justice-enhancing strategies and make it harder to establish trust (Ross, Chen, & Huang, 2007). How does the reliance on SNWs and technology, applied to organizational relationships with more distance and less history, influence the process and outcomes of negotiation? Goals of treating others with politeness (Justice-Enhancing Strategy 5) and behaving in trustworthy ways (Justice-Enhancing Strategy 6) would both seem to be more challenging to attain if negotiations are conducted via technology and if such negotiations involve parties with limited knowledge of each other. At least one study suggested that people are often less cooperative when negotiating via e-mail and feel justified in being less cooperative when using this medium compared to bargaining face to face; the feeling that competitiveness is justified mediated the relationship between the communication medium used and competitive behavior (Naquin, Kurtzberg, & Belkin, 2008).

Research Questions Related to Informational Justice-Enhancing Strategies

Negotiator reputations for behaving competitively can limit their ability to claim value if opponents are aware of this reputation (cf. Tinsley, O'Connor, & Sullivan, 2002). The presence and permanence of information on many SNWs and websites more generally could make it difficult to change one's reputation. How does SNW information about a negotiator's interpersonal style influence how others respond to this negotiator? SNWs can result in people having reputations (positive or negative) that can "stick" far longer than they should, depending on the permanence of the information on the site (Fernando, 2008). For instance, perhaps a focal negotiator engaged in an underhanded negotiation tactic 10 years ago. Someone can write about that action and post a description of it at any time. The focal negotiator may no longer negotiate in this fashion, but if the negotiator's opponent in an upcoming negotiation discovers the Web posting and reads it, the opponent is likely to infer that this is the current approach the focal negotiator may take in negotiation. This could make negotiations far more difficult than they should be because the opponent will perceive that (a) the focal negotiator cannot be trusted and (b) that the focal negotiator will behave in a contentious fashion. Research suggested that a competitive orientation leads to competitive behavior in negotiation, but expectations of mutual success can lead to both a higher likelihood of settlement and a greater belief that such a settlement is fair (Deutsch, 1960; Liberman, Anderson, & Ross, 2010). Posted incidents of a focal negotiator behaving unfairly in the past would have similar impact. It would be interesting to examine how newly discovered evidence of "injustice from the past" affects current negotiations. Would behaving in trustworthy ways in a current negotiation be sufficient to overcome such reputational effects?

Finally, we note that one of the benefits of electronic communication can be the speed with which people receive responses. This could be a two-edged sword in negotiations. SNWs may be in the process of altering what people perceive is an acceptable amount of time to wait for a reply. How fast is too fast? If one responds immediately to a question in a negotiation, it is possible that the other will perceive the response as less thoughtful and perhaps less valuable than it should be. On the other hand, if one does not respond quickly via technology, is this "delay" taken as an affront? Perhaps negotiators view a slow-to-respond opponent as less trustworthy. Issues of timing can lead to new problems erupting in negotiations.

FINAL THOUGHTS

Issues of power, technology, and employee relationships are just a few of the many potential moderating factors that can influence the relationship between applying the justice-enhancing strategies we have discussed and engendering cooperation in negotiation situations. But, the impact of fairness can go far beyond cooperation. In fact, justice perceptions have recently been characterized as a central variable in social exchange models that link workplace characteristics to a variety of organizational outcomes beyond cooperation (see Cropanzano & Mitchell, 2005, for a recent review). From this perspective, justice serves as a benefit to employees that is reciprocated through the expression of beneficial attitudes (e.g., job satisfaction, organizational commitment, trust in supervisor) and behaviors (task performance, organizational citizenship behavior, and counterproductive work behavior). Thus, while we focus on how the application of eight justice-enhancing strategies can have a positive impact on cooperation, there are many other potential benefits if or when such strategies can be applied successfully. It is hoped that this chapter will alert negotiation and justice researchers to their need, ideally together rather than separately, to examine the "if" and "when" justice-enhancing strategies can be applied successfully in light of the 21st century workplace realities we identified in this chapter.

REFERENCES

Albrecht, K. 2002. Supermarket cards: The tip of the retail surveillance iceberg. *Denver University Law Review, 79*, 534–539, 558–565, 587–592.

Aquino, K., Tripp, T., & Bies, R. (2006). Getting even or moving on? Power, procedural justice, and types of offense as predictors of revenge, forgiveness, reconciliation, and avoidance in organizations. *Journal of Applied Psychology, 91*, 653–668.

Bies, R. J., & Moag, J. F. (1986). Interactional justice: Communication criteria of fairness. In R. J. Lewicki, B. H. Sheppard, & M. H. Bazerman (Eds.), *Research on negotiations in organizations* (Vol. 1, pp. 43–55). Greenwich, CT: JAI Press.

Bies, R. J., & Shapiro, D. L. (1987). Interactional fairness judgments: The influence of causal accounts. *Social Justice Research, 1*, 199–218.

Blumenstein, R. (1997, December 30). Haggling in cyberspace transforms car sales. *The Wall Street Journal*, pp. B1, B6.

Bobocel, D. R., & Zdaniuk, A. (2005). How can explanations be used to foster organizational justice? In J. Greenberg & J. A. Colquitt (Eds.), *Handbook of organizational justice* (pp. 469–498). Mahwah, NJ: Erlbaum.

Bohnert, D., & Ross, W. H. (2010). The influence of social networking Websites on the evaluation of job candidates. *CyberPsychology, Behavior, and Social Networking, 13*, 341–347.

Boles, T., Croson, R., & Murnighan, J. (2000). Deception and retribution in repeated ultimatum bargaining. *Organizational Behavior and Human Decision Processes, 83*, 235–259.

Brass, D. J. (1984). Being in the right place: A structural analysis of individual influence in an organization. *Administrative Science Quarterly, 29,* 518–539.

Brockner, J., & Wiesenfeld, B. (2005). How, when, and why does outcome favorability interact with procedural fairness? In J. Greenberg & J. A. Colquitt (Eds.), *Handbook of organizational justice* (pp. 525–554). Mahwah, NJ: Erlbaum.

Brodt, S. E. (1994). "Inside information" and negotiator decision behavior. *Organizational Behavior and Human Decision Processes, 58,* 172–202.

Buchan, N. R., Croson, R. T. A., & Johnson, E. J. (2004). When do fair beliefs influence bargaining behavior? Experimental bargaining in Japan and the United States. *Journal of Consumer Research, 31,* 181–190.

Chai, S., & Kim, M. (2010). What makes bloggers share knowledge? An investigation on the role of trust. *International Journal of Information Management, 30,* 408–415.

Chiaburu, D., & Marinova, S. (2006). Employee role enlargement: Interactions of trust and organizational fairness. *Leadership and Organization Development Journal, 27*(3), 168–182.

Clark, M. M. (2004, August). Religion versus sexual orientation. *HR Magazine, 49*(8), 54–59.

Colquitt, J. A. (2001). On the dimensionality of organizational justice: A construct validation of a measure. *Journal of Applied Psychology, 86,* 386–400.

Conchie, S., & Donald, I. (2009). The moderating role of safety-specific trust on the relation between safety-specific leadership and safety citizenship behaviors. *Journal of Occupational Health Psychology, 14*(2), 137–147. doi:10.1037/a0014247.

Conlon, D. E., & Murray N. M. (1996), Customer perceptions of corporate responses to product complaints: The role of expectations. *Academy of Management Journal, 39,* 1040–1056.

Conlon, D. E., & Ross, W. H. (1997). Appearances do count: The effects of outcomes and explanations on disputant fairness judgments and supervisory evaluations. *International Journal of Conflict Management, 8*(1), 5–31.

Copeland, D. (2009, January 19). Keep it clean, kid, software's watching. *Boston Globe,* B-5.

Cropanzano, R. (Ed.). (1993). *Justice in the workplace: Approaching fairness in human resource management.* Hillsdale, NJ: Erlbaum.

Cropanzano, R., Bowen, D. E., & Gilliland, S. W. (2007). The management of organizational justice. *Academy of Management Perspectives, 21,* 34–48.

Cropanzano, R., & Mitchell, M. S. (2005). Social exchange theory: An interdisciplinary review. *Journal of Management, 31,* 874–900.

Crott, H., Kayser, E., & Lamm, H. (1980). The effects of information exchange and communication in an asymmetrical negotiation situation. *European Journal of Social Psychology, 10,* 149–163.

Deutsch, M. (1960). The effect of motivational orientation upon threat and suspicion. *Human Relations, 13,* 122–139.

Deutsch, M. (1975). Equity, equality, and need: What determines which value will be used as the basis of distributive justice? *Journal of Social Issues, 31*(3), 137–149.

Fernando, A. (2008). Communiqué: The social media resume. *Communication World, 25,* 8–9.

Folger, R. (1987). Distributive and procedural justice in the workplace. *Social Justice Research, 1,* 143–159.

Folger, R., & Cropanzano, R. (1998). *Organizational justice and human resource management.* Thousand Oaks, CA: Sage.

Folger, R., Rosenfield, D., Grove, J., & Corkran, L. (1979). Effects of "voice" and peer opinions on responses to inequity. *Journal of Personality and Social Psychology, 37,* 2253–2261.

Fortin, M., & Fellenz, M.. (2008). Hypocrisies of fairness: Towards a more reflexive ethical base in organizational justice research and practice. *Journal of Business Ethics, 78,* 415–433.

Graham, J. L., & Sanyo, Y. (1984). *Smart bargaining: Doing business with the Japanese.* Cambridge, MA: Ballinger.

Greenberg, J. (1990). Looking fair versus being fair: Managing impressions of organizational justice. In B. M. Staw & L. L. Cummings (Eds.), *Research in organizational behavior* (Vol. 12, pp. 111–157). Greenwich, CT: JAI Press.

Greenberg, J. (1993). The social side of fairness: Interpersonal and informational classes of organizational justice. In R. Cropanzano (Ed.), *Justice in the workplace: Approaching fairness in human resource management* (pp. 79–103). Hillsdale, NJ: Erlbaum.

Greenberg, J., & Colquitt, J. A. (Eds.). (2005). *Handbook of organizational justice.* Mahwah, NJ: Erlbaum.

Herscovitch, L., & Meyer, J. P. (2002). Communication, procedural justice, and employee attitudes: Relationships under conditions of divestiture. *Journal of Management, 26,* 63–83.

Jolly, D. (2010, August 26). German law would limit the use of Facebook in hiring. *New York Times,* p. 8.

Kass, E. (2008). Interactional justice, negotiator outcome satisfaction, and desire for future negotiations: R-E-S-P-E-C-T at the bargaining table. *International Journal of Conflict Management, 19,* 319–338.

Keltner, D., Gruenfeld, D., & Anderson, C. (2003). Power, approach, and inhibition. *Psychological Review, 110,* 265–284.

Kipnis, D., Schmidt, S., & Wilkinson, I. (1980). Intraorganizational influence tactics: Explorations in getting one's way. *Journal of Applied Psychology, 65,* 440–452.

Leung, K. (2005). How generalizable are justice effects across cultures? In J. Greenberg & J. A. Colquitt (2005). *Handbook of organizational justice* (pp. 555–586). Mahwah, NJ: Erlbaum.

Leung, K., Tong, K., & Ho, S. S. (2004). Effects of interactional justice on egocentric bias in resource allocation. *Journal of Applied Psychology, 89,* 405–415.

Leventhal, G. S. (1980). What should be done with equity theory? New approaches to the study of fairness in social relationships. In K. Gergern, M. Greenberg, & R. Willis (Eds.), *Social exchange: Advances in theory and research* (pp. 27–55). New York: Plenum Press.

Leventhal, G. S., Karuza, J., & Fry, W. R. (1980). Beyond fairness: A theory of allocation preferences. In G. Mikula (Ed.), *Justice and social interaction* (pp. 167–218). New York: Springer-Verlag.

Lewicki, R. J., Barry, B., & Saunders, D. M. (2010). *Negotiation* (6th ed.). Boston: McGraw-Hill/Irwin.

Liberman, V., Anderson, N. R., & Ross, L. (2010). Achieving difficult agreements: Effects of positive expectations on negotiation processes and outcomes. *Journal of Experimental Social Psychology, 46,* 494–504.

Lind, E. (2001). Fairness heuristic theory: Justice judgments as pivotal cognitions in organizational relations. In J. Greenberg & R. Cropanzano (Eds.), *Advances in organizational justice* (pp. 56–88). Stanford, CA: Stanford University Press.

Lind, E., Greenberg, J., Scott, K., & Welchans, T. (2000). The winding road from employee to complainant: Situational and psychological determinants of wrongful-termination claims. *Administrative Science Quarterly, 45,* 557–590.

Lind, E. A., & Tyler, T. (1988). *The social psychology of procedural justice.* New York: Plenum.

Lukes, S. (2005). *Power–A radical view* (2nd ed.). Hampshire, UK: Palgrave.

Malhotra, D., & Murnighan, J. K. (2002). The effects of contracts on interpersonal trust. *Administrative Science Quarterly, 47,* 534–559.

Mannix, E. A., & Neale, M. A. (1993). Power imbalance and the pattern of exchange in dyadic negotiation. *Group Decision and Negotiation, 2,* 119–133.

Martin, J., & Harder, J. W. (1994). Bread and roses: Justice and the distribution of financial and socioemotional rewards in organizations. *Social Justice Research, 7,* 241–264.

Maxwell, S., Nye, P., & Maxwell, N. (1999). Less pain, same gain: The effects of priming fairness in price negotiations. *Psychology and Marketing, 16,* 545–562.

Messick, D. M., & Sentis, K. (1983). Fairness, preference, and fairness biases. In D. Messick & K. Cook (Eds.), *Equity theory* (pp. 61–94). New York: Praeger.

Meyer, J. P., Srinivas, E. R., Lal, J. B., & Topolnytsky, L. (2007). Employee commitment and support for an organizational change: Test of the three-component model in two cultures. *Journal of Occupational and Organizational Psychology, 80,* 185–211.

Naquin, C., Kurtzberg, T., & Belkin, L. (2008). E-mail communication and group cooperation in mixed motive contexts. *Social Justice Research, 21,* 470–489.

Neale, M. A., & Bazerman, M. H. (1991). *Cognition and rationality in negotiation.* New York: Free Press.

Neves, P., & Caetano, A. (2006). Social exchange processes in organizational change: The roles of trust and control. *Journal of Change Management, 6,* 351–364.

O'Connor, K. M. (1997). Motives and cognitions in negotiation: A theoretical integration and an empirical test. *International Journal of Conflict Management, 8,* 114–131.

Oldham, G. R., Kulik, C. T., Ambrose, M. L., Stepina, L. P., & Brand, J. F. (1986). Relations between job facet comparisons and employee reactions. *Organizational Behavior and Human Decision Processes, 38,* 28–47.

Parker, K. (2007, March 13). There are no secret indiscretions anymore. *Tampa* [FL] *Tribune,* p. 13.

Pruitt, D. G. (1981). *Negotiation behavior.* New York: Academic Press.

Putnam, L. L., & Roloff, M. E. (1992). Communication perspectives on negotiation. In L. L. Putnam & M. E. Roloff (Eds.) *Communication and negotiation* (pp. 1–20). Newbury Park, CA: Sage.

Rawls, J. (1971). *A theory of justice.* Cambridge, MA: Harvard University Press.

Robbins, T., Summers, T., & Miller, J. (2000). Intra- and inter-justice relationships: Assessing the direction. *Human Relations, 53,* 1329–1355.

Ross, W. H. (2005). What every human resource manager should know about web logs. *Society for the Advancement of Management Advanced Management Journal, 70,* 4–14.

Ross, W. H., Chen, J. V., & Huang, S. F. (2007). Adapting different media types to trust development in the supply chain. *International Journal of Management and Enterprise Development, 4,* 373–386.

Rubin, J. Z., & Brown, B. (1975). *The social psychology of bargaining and negotiation.* New York: Academic Press.

Scott, M. B., & Lyman, S. M. (1968). Accounts. *American Sociological Review, 33,* 46–62.

Shapiro, D., & Bies, R. (1994). Threats, bluffs, and disclaimers in negotiations. *Organizational Behavior and Human Decision Processes, 60,* 14–35.

Shapiro, D. L., Buttner, E. H., & Barry, B. (1994). Explanations: What factors enhance their perceived adequacy? *Organizational Behavior and Human Decision Processes, 58,* 346–368.

Shaw, J. C., Wild, E., & Colquitt, J. A. (2003). To justify or excuse? A meta-analytic review of the effects of explanations. *Journal of Applied Psychology, 88,* 444–458.

Simons, T., Friedman, R., Liu, L., & McLean Parks, J. (2007). Racial differences in sensitivity to behavioral integrity: Attitudinal consequences, in-group effects, and "trickle down" among Black and non-Black employees. *Journal of Applied Psychology, 92,* 650–665. doi:10.1037/0021-9010.92.3.650.

Smith, D. L., Pruitt, D. G., & Carnevale, P. J. D. (1982). Matching and mismatching: The effect of own limit, other's toughness, and time pressure on concession rate in negotiation. *Journal of Personality and Social Psychology, 42,* 876–883.

Solomon, R. (1992). Corporate roles, personal values: An Aristotelian approach to business ethics. *Business Ethics Quarterly, 2,* 317–340.

Starr, T., (2010, September). Face the facts about Facebook. *Quick Printing, 33*(12), 29, 31.

Thibaut, J., & Walker, L. (1975). *Procedural justice: A psychological analysis.* Hillsdale, NJ: Erlbaum.

Thomas, K. (2007, March 28). A generation waiting to play havoc with company security. [London, UK] *Financial Times,* p. 1.

Tinsley, C. H., O'Connor, K. M., & Sullivan, B.A. (2002). Tough guys finish last: The perils of a distributive reputation. *Organizational Behavior and Human Decision Processes, 88,* 621–642.

Tomasson, R. F., Crosby, F. J., & Herzberger, S. D. (1996). *Affirmative action: The pros and cons of policy and practice.* Washington, DC: American University Press.

Twentyman, J. (2008, January 8). Talking about my second generation. *Personnel Today,* pp. 20–23.

Tyler, T. R. (1990). *Why people obey the law.* New Haven, CT: Yale University Press.

Tyler, T. R., & Blader, S. L. (2003). The group engagement model: Procedural justice, social identity, and cooperative behavior. *Personality and Social Psychology Review, 7,* 349–361.

Tyler, T. R., & Blader, S. L. (2005). Can businesses effectively regulate employee conduct? The antecedents of rule following in work settings. *Academy of Management Journal, 48,* 1143–1158.

Van den Bos, K., Vermunt, R., & Wilke, H. A. (1997). Procedural and distributive justice: What is fair depends more on what comes first than on what comes next. *Journal of Personality and Social Psychology, 72,* 95–104.

Van Kleef, G., De Dreu, C., & Manstead, A. (2004). The interpersonal effects of emotions in negotiations: A motivated information processing approach. *Journal of Personality and Social Psychology, 87,* 510–528. doi:10.1037/0022-3514.87.4.510.

Vermunt, R., & Steensma, H. (2001). Stress and justice in organizations: An exploration into justice processes with the aim to find mechanisms to reduce stress. In R. Cropanzano (Ed.), *Justice in the workplace, Vol. 2: From theory to practice.* Mahwah, NJ: Erlbaum.

Walton, R. E., & McKersie, R. B. (1965). *A behavioral theory of labor negotiations: An analysis of a social interaction system.* New York: McGraw-Hill.

Weaver, G., & Conlon, D. (2003). Explaining façades of choice: Timing, justice effects, and behavioral outcomes. *Journal of Applied Social Psychology, 33,* 2217–2243. doi:10.1111/j.1559-1816.2003.tb01882.x.

Wessel, H. (2004, July 20). Blogs find their way into the workplace. *Orlando* [FL] *Sentinel.* Retrieved October 22, 2004 from http://libweb.uwlax.edu:2055/hottopics/inacademic/?

Wilson, K. S., Sin, H. P., & Conlon, D. E. (2010). What about the leader in leader-member exchange? The impact of resource exchanges and substitutability on the leader. *Academy of Management Review, 35,* 358–372.

Workers naïve over online presence. (2007). *Strategic Communication Management, 12,* 9.

Wu, C., Neubert, M., & Yi, X. (2007). Transformational leadership, cohesion perceptions, and employee cynicism about organizational change: The mediating role of justice perceptions. *Journal of Applied Behavioral Science, 43,* 327–351.

Yang, J., & Diefendorff, J. (2009). The relations of daily counterproductive workplace behavior with emotions, situational antecedents, and personality moderators: A diary study in Hong Kong. *Personnel Psychology, 62,* 259–295.

Yukl, G. (1974). Effects of situational variables and opponent concessions on a bargainer's perception, aspirations, and concessions. *Journal of Personality and Social Psychology, 29,* 227–236. doi:10.1037/h0036013.

3

The Role of Process Fairness Authenticity in 21st Century Negotiations

Kathryn S. Roloff, Joel Brockner, and Batia Mishan Wiesenfeld

INTRODUCTION

One of the cardinal principles of organizational justice theory and research is that people react more positively when they are treated with greater fairness (e.g., Greenberg & Colquitt, 2005). For example, employees who perceive more fairness generally have been found to support organizational decisions, trust their supervisors, and feel committed to organizations (Brockner et al., 1994; Masterson, Lewis, Goldman, & Taylor, 2000; Tyler & Smith, 1997; Van den Bos, Wilke, & Lind, 1998) relative to their counterparts who perceive less fairness. Even negative work-related outcomes, such as layoff decisions, have generally been found to be more acceptable when recipients of these outcomes (e.g., layoff victims or survivors who witness colleagues being laid off) perceive them to be accompanied by a fairer process (Brockner & Wiesenfeld, 1996; Chen, Choi, & Chi, 2002).

Most studies of organizational justice have occurred *outside* the negotiation setting (although see Chapter 2, this volume, and Brockner, Chen, Mannix, Leung, & Skarlicki, 2000, for some exceptions). Thus, further research is needed to evaluate whether fellow negotiators who are perceived to be more procedurally fair will elicit more positive reactions (e.g., support for their requested concessions). Pending further research, we believe that negotiators who treat the other party fairly will gain greater support for their proposed outcomes, given people's tendency to judge outcome fairness or "distributive justice" (cf. Deutsch, 1985) as higher when they believe that they have been treated with higher levels of "procedural justice" (cf., Thibaut & Walker, 1975).

The tendency for people to react more positively when they have been treated with greater procedural fairness has been called the "fair process effect" (Folger, Rosenfield, Grove, & Corkran, 1979; Van den Bos, Lind, & Wilke, 2001; Van den Bos, Vermunt, & Wilke, 1997). The fair process effect suggests that negotiators are likely to gain support for offers or outcomes they request if they provide the other party with adequate reasons, with opportunities for input, and with considerate treatment (see Chapter 2, this volume, for additional strategies negotiators may use to appear fair). Under such circumstances, the negotiation is more likely to be a positive experience for all parties and thus likely to help negotiation parties arrive at viable agreements, to promote successful interpersonal interactions, and to set the stage for positive future relations (e.g., Chen, Brockner, & Greenberg, 2003).

Importantly, the predicted positive effects of process fairness on negotiators' reactions are based on the assumption that the other party's fairness-related behaviors are viewed as genuine. For example, if a negotiator expresses a desire to help satisfy a need expressed by another party, this expressed desire to be helpful would be inauthentic if the negotiator does not truly want to help. If the negotiator is perceived to be inauthentic, then the negotiator's expressed desire to help (which could be coded as "cooperative" by observers analyzing the interaction, e.g., Brett, Shapiro, & Lytle, 1998) would probably backfire if the party on the receiving end believes that the negotiator has no true intention of helping. The recipient's skepticism may be due to his or her history with the negotiator *prior to* the current negotiation or due to incongruence *during* the current negotiation between the negotiator's helpful expressions and proposals that he or she offers that seem to ignore the recipient's concerns.

A negotiator's authenticity is ultimately determined by the perceived congruence between what the negotiator says are his or her (cooperative) intentions and the negotiator's actual behavior. Much of the prior theory and research on authenticity has examined the *intra*personal consequences of acting (or not acting) in accordance with one's internal states (e.g., Harter, 2002). In contrast, we consider authenticity from an *inter*personal perspective (see also Kernis & Goldman, 2006). More specifically, our focus on authenticity is as it is seen through the eyes of one's fellow negotiator. For present purposes, authenticity pertains to the extent to which negotiators perceive the other party to be acting congruently with their internal states, in particular their values and intentions.

CHAPTER PURPOSES AND OVERVIEW

The present chapter examines the role of authenticity on the fair process effect in the context of negotiations. It consists of five parts. First, we outline the process of *forming* perceptions of authentic fairness in negotiations. Second, we describe the likely *consequences* of perceived fairness inauthenticity for both negotiation processes (e.g., the extent to which negotiators openly share information about their real needs and priorities) and negotiation outcomes (e.g., the likelihood of negotiators reaching mutually satisfactory agreements). Third, because negative consequences are likely for negotiators who are perceived to be inauthentically fair, we identify strategies that may help negotiators enhance their perceived fairness authenticity. Fourth, we consider two prominent characteristics of the 21st century workplace (i.e., increased cultural diversity and increased physical distance/virtuality among employees) that may make it challenging for negotiators to be seen as authentic in their expressions of process fairness; we also suggest in the fourth section ways that negotiators may overcome the challenges engendered by these two characteristics. Fifth, in light of these 21st century workplace characteristics, we conclude with questions in need of future research.

Cumulatively, the chapter is designed to raise awareness about (a) the theoretical and practical importance of the construct of process fairness authenticity, (b) the challenge of inducing culturally diverse or virtually communicating negotiators to be seen as authentic in their expression of process fairness (Gibson & Grubb, 2005; Shapiro, Furst, Spreitzer, & Von Glinow, 2002), and (c) strategies for enhancing fairness-authenticity in negotiations in the context of the realities of contemporary organizations.

PERCEPTIONS OF (IN)AUTHENTICITY IN NEGOTIATIONS: WHAT ARE THEIR LIKELY ANTECEDENTS AND CONSEQUENCES?

Process fairness subsumes a variety of types of fairness, such as procedural, interactional, and informational justice (Colquitt, 2001). Whereas outcome fairness is a primary concern in negotiations, the perceived authenticity of process fairness may be more variable than the perceived authenticity of outcome fairness. Put differently, it may be easier for people to judge outcome fairness objectively. After all, outcome fairness refers to "the bottom line." Thus, negotiators are likely to know whether the other party has given them an outcome that is truly fair. In contrast, high process fairness may be more "fake-able" than is high outcome fairness. It is for this reason that we restrict our analysis to authenticity as it relates to process fairness rather than outcome fairness; it is not to suggest that process fairness is necessarily more important than outcome fairness in negotiations or to say that the authenticity of process fairness is more consequential than is the authenticity of outcome fairness.

Fairness in negotiations is important for many reasons. In particular, fairness sends an important message to parties about their expectations of the negotiation process. By definition, negotiations are highly uncertain social interactions; neither party is entirely sure how the process will unfold, what their tangible outcomes will be, or what their intangible outcomes (such as how they are viewed by the other party) will be. Presumably, both sides of the negotiation seek to reduce or manage their uncertainty. In so doing, they look for clues about whether their partner is trustworthy or will treat them well. Indeed, research has shown that individuals are particularly likely to engage in sense-making processes in uncertain situations, which makes them susceptible to influence by the other party's process fairness (Van den Bos & Lind, 2002). Fairness heuristic theory purports that people use process fairness information to form expectations about their outcomes when such information is not explicit or available (Van den Bos, Lind, Vermunt, & Wilke, 1997). In short, process fairness informs negotiators about a number of matters of importance to them.

Fairness considerations are relevant at various points in the negotiation process, such as (a) at the time of the initial offer, (b) in response to the demands of the opposing party, (c) when the decision to settle or to counteroffer is made, and (d) at the time an impasse is reached. Indeed, as Welsh (2004) has noted, understanding the importance of fairness in negotiations in legal settings "undermines the iconic image of two rational negotiators locked in a battle of logic, economics, and will" (p. 766). Although such symbolic images of negotiators are ubiquitous, more recent conceptualizations of negotiations take into account the importance of forging personal relationships and connections, building positive rapport, and finding cooperative processes and agreements. Perceptions of fairness have an important influence on these relational components of the negotiation process.

In discussing fair processes in negotiations, we do not consider behaviors that are clearly unfair; rather, we are interested in understanding how perceived authenticity can undermine or enhance the positive effects of process fairness in negotiations. Therefore, our analysis is limited to those actions that are consistent with conventional conceptualizations of fair process behaviors, such as providing advanced notice, involving people in decisions, treating others with dignity and respect, and providing clear and transparent information. But first, we need to consider how perceptions of authentic process fairness are formed in negotiations.

Forming Perceptions of Authentic Process Fairness in Negotiations: How?

The notion of authenticity has deep historical roots. The age-old adage coined by Greek scholars, "Know thyself," is a well-known tenet of Western philosophy. Developmental psychologists define authenticity as "the extent to which one acts in accord with the true self," and it "involves owning one's personal experiences, thoughts, emotions, needs, wants, preferences, or beliefs" (Harter, 2002, p. 382). Definitions of authenticity in organizational behavior follow history's adages; they typically refer to the extent to which people's actions are in alignment with their inner worlds. For example, in the context of constructing professional images, authenticity has been defined as "the degree of congruence between internal values and external expressions" (Roberts, 2005, p. 699). In research on leadership, authenticity has been defined as "being transparent in linking inner desires, expectations, and values in interactions" (May, Chan, Hodges, & Avolio, 2003, p. 248). Harvey, Martinko, and Gardner (2006) describe authentic leaders as those "who possess self-awareness of, and act in accordance with, their values, thoughts, emotions, and beliefs…and understand the moral implications of their actions" (p. 1). Other leadership scholars claim that "being true to oneself" is among the most essential leadership characteristics (May et al., 2003). Indeed, the idea of being true to oneself, that is, acting in accordance with one's internal workings, is considered to be a highly valued personality trait, particularly in individualistic cultures (Peterson & Seligman, 2004; Seligman, 2002).

Whereas the various definitions of authenticity refer to the congruence between people's behavior and their inner sense of self, much of the existing research on authenticity ignores, or at least underemphasizes, the role played by others' perceptions of authenticity. The focus in the present chapter is on authenticity *as perceived by the other party*. In other words, we propose that the construct of authenticity can and should be expanded to reflect the perspective of the party toward whom one's (negotiation) behaviors are directed. Therefore, as mentioned at the outset, our focus is on *perceived authenticity* as seen through the eyes of the fellow negotiator; that is, the extent to which Party B in a negotiation believes that Party A's behavior is congruent with Party A's inner workings, such as values and intentions. Furthermore, the dimension along which judgments of authenticity will be evaluated is fairness, in particular, process fairness.

Two related but conceptually distinct attributions are likely to influence the extent to which process fairness behaviors are seen as authentic. The first type of attribution refers to people's judgments of causality for the enactment or origination of behavior. In some instances, the impetus for a certain behavior is seen as residing *within* the focal person. For example, negotiators may take it on themselves to provide an explanation or to invite input from the other party. No one is telling them to do this, and they are not seen as coerced or tempted by external forces to exhibit the behavior. On other occasions, however, negotiators may be seen as acting with high process fairness *because of* external factors. In such instances, they are responding to their environments, which may be forcing or constraining them to act in certain ways. For example, one element of fair process is to provide people with advanced notification of an upcoming change in circumstances. The Worker Adjustment and Retraining Notification Act (WARN) requires employers to give employees a 60-day notice of an impending plant closing or large-scale layoffs. It was enacted partly to ensure procedural justice, on the grounds that it is only fair for employees to be informed about such a significant disruption in their lives well in advance.

Whereas employers technically are required to comply with WARN, not all of them do. Moreover, among those that do, they are likely to vary in the extent to which they are seen as providing advanced notice to be "in compliance" versus doing so out of their own accord. Extending this example to the negotiation setting, we posit that the more that negotiators judge their partner's fair process behaviors as internally originated, the more likely they are to perceive those behaviors as authentic. In the language of DeCharms (1968), behaviors for which people are seen as "origins" are likely to be judged as more authentic than behaviors for which they are seen as "pawns." In fact, DeCharms (1968) further suggested that people are more influenced by others' behavior that is self-originating. For example, apologies are more effective when they are seen as sincere (Bies, 1987; De Cremer & Schouten, 2008; Tomlinson, Dineen, & Lewicki, 2004). We suggest that to be perceived as authentically fair, and to subsequently reap the positive benefits therein, negotiators' acts of process fairness must be seen as self-determined.

A second type of attribution that people make to judge authenticity pertains less to the perceived cause of the behavior and more to its perceived consequences, in particular, whether the process fairness-related behavior is *intended* to help their partner (or to be constructive for the negotiations) or is motivated by other reasons, such as to benefit the self ("ulterior motives"). Often inextricably linked in people's minds to their judgments of the other's behaviors are the consequences associated with those behaviors, in particular whether the other party meant to bring those consequences about. For example, giving the other party voice may be undertaken with the intent to find an integrative solution, or it may be motivated by the desire to unearth information that will be used against that individual. Process fairness behaviors enacted with good intentions are likely to be seen as more authentic than are those same behaviors that are not so benignly motivated. Indeed, the expressions negotiating "in good faith" or "in bad faith" essentially amount to a referendum on the other party's intentions, which is akin to a judgment of whether the other party "really meant it."

In summary, for negotiators to elicit positive reactions in their counterparts we suggest that they need to be seen not only as fair, which already has been noted by justice theorists (e.g., Greenberg, 1988), but also as authentically fair. Two bases of perceived authenticity are for negotiators' process fairness behaviors to be seen as (a) self-originating and (b) intended to produce positive consequences for the other party or for the negotiation process more generally.

Unpacking Authentic Fairness

Whereas the previous two bases of perceived authenticity judgments are conceptually distinct, they are likely to covary in actual negotiation settings. That is, given that negotiators are simultaneously making judgments about both the source of a fair process behavior and the intention behind it, it is likely that these two judgments will influence or at least be positively related to each other. To form a judgment about the source of a behavior, people will generally categorize events as either within a person's control or outside their control (Weiner, 1982). The former is referred to as an internal attribution or a determination that the cause of an event is due to personality, values, beliefs, moods, attitudes, abilities, or effort (Heider, 1958). The latter is referred to as an external attribution or a determination that the cause of an event is due to situational factors, such as the actions of others or luck.

This reasoning may be applied to how negotiators judge the authenticity of the other party's process fairness behavior during the course of the negotiation. Kelley (1967) outlined three types of information that people use to evaluate whether the cause of behavior resides within the actor or within the actor's environment. Information about *consensus* refers to the extent to which others act similarly to the target individual in the same situation. Information about *consistency* refers to the extent to which the target individual acts the same way in that situation over time. Information about *distinctiveness* refers to the extent to which a target individual's behavior varies across situations (e.g., treating different people differently) rather than acting the same way across situations. Kelley's attribution process suggests that people are more likely to see another's behavior as coming from within (and hence view the behavior as more authentic) when each of consensus and distinctiveness is low and when consistency is high. In the context of negotiations, people are more likely to see the other party's process fairness behaviors as internally caused and hence authentic if (a) most others did not act fairly in negotiations similar to the one at hand (low consensus), (b) the other party acted fairly toward the focal

TABLE 3.1

Application of the Kelley Covariation Principle to Judgments of Fairness Authenticity

Why Did This Negotiator Treat Me With High Process Fairness?		
Consensus	*Low*—Others have not treated me fairly in negotiations.	*High*—Others have treated me fairly in negotiations.
Consistency	*High*—This person has treated me fairly before (in other negotiations).	*Low*—This person has not treated me fairly in other negotiations.
Distinctiveness	*Low*—This person always treats others fairly in negotiations.	*High*—This person never treats others fairly in negotiations.
Most common attribution	*Internal attribution*: This person is responsible for acting fairly toward me. Hence, this person's process fairness behavior is high in authenticity.	*External attribution*: The situation caused the person to act fairly toward me. Hence, this person's process fairness behavior is low in authenticity.

negotiator in prior interactions (high consistency), and (c) the other party acted fairly toward other negotiation partners (low distinctiveness). (See Table 3.1 for an application of Kelley's Covariation Principle.)

To form a judgment about the intention behind a fair process behavior, negotiators may use various sources of information. For example, negotiators may use information about their impression of their fellow negotiator's personality, information received from colleagues who have had prior interactions with the negotiator, or expectations about the negotiation process. In general, negotiators are more likely to be seen as authentically fair if they can effectively convey that they are behaving fairly due to a desire to achieve mutually satisfying outcomes or because of a strong belief in the moral principles of fairness. Evidence from economics suggests that it is important to account for a person's intention to act fairly in addition to whether the outcomes they achieve are fair (e.g., Falk, Fehr, & Fischbacher, 2008; Falk & Fischbacher, 2006). Negotiators bring scripts and schemas into the negotiation that may bias their perceptions of their partner's fairness intentions. If, for example, a fairness recipient holds an expectation that the negotiation will be highly competitive or "win-lose" in nature, he or she may consider an offer of fairness to be a subversive tactic leveraged to obtain a greater concession later in the process. Although it is not always entirely clear how negotiators form perceptions about the other party's intentions, it is clear that apparent acts of fairness do not always convey an intention *to be* fair.

In summary, when making judgments about the source or intent of process fairness behavior, negotiators may see such behavior as more versus less authentic. All else being equal, process fairness behaviors are likely to lead to better negotiation outcomes (broadly defined) when the behaviors are seen as more authentic. In the ensuing section, we discuss the penalties negotiators may experience when their process fairness behaviors are not perceived to be authentic.

PERCEPTUAL CONSEQUENCES OF INAUTHENTIC FAIRNESS IN NEGOTIATIONS

"Inauthentic process fairness" may be an oxymoron of sorts; it may be difficult, if not impossible, for negotiators to be seen as high in process fairness and inauthentic at the same time. For example, research has shown that voice (a cardinal element of procedural fairness) is perceived to be considerably fairer when people believe that their views were *truly* considered by the decision maker (Shapiro & Brett, 1993). When people's views are not truly considered, they may infer that their negotiation partner has an ulterior motive. Indeed, in some cases, inauthentic "fairness" in negotiations may engender more negative reactions than procedures that are clearly unfair. Whereas clearly unfair behaviors are predictable, albeit in a negative way, inauthentic fairness sends confusing interpersonal messages. Negotiators may respond less negatively to behaviors that are clearly unfair than to process fairness-related behaviors that are seen as inauthentic. At the very least, people can better understand the motives driving process behaviors that are clearly unfair than those driving acts of inauthentic process fairness; the devil you know may be better than the devil you do not know.

In an extreme case, inauthentic process fairness can become an unethical business practice, especially when it stems from self-interest. For example, the fact that negotiators can increase others' acceptance of unfavorable outcomes by acting with high process fairness may lead to exploitation of the other party. Chen et al. (2002) found that local employees accepted a lower wage than their expatriate colleagues if the advantaged expats treated the locals with high process fairness. Surely, the spirit of theory and research on justice does not endorse the exploitation of fairness principles for personal gain at others' expense. However, certain negotiators may infer that if they can *appear* to be authentic in their expressions of process fairness (even though they are not), they will be able to claim greater value from the negotiations. Somewhat reassuringly, there is some research to suggest that devious (read: inauthentic) offers of fairness are thwarted when those on the receiving end "smell a rat" (as they often do). Most negotiators are wary of and can detect instances of disingenuous or "sham" process fairness. In research conducted outside the negotiation venue, Lind (1998) noted that "false (or inauthentic) representations of fair treatment" may engender "extremely negative reactions" (p. 187). For example, consider a negotiation between a homebuyer and seller. If the seller is seen as inauthentic in his or her expressions of "high" process fairness, the buyer may believe that he or she is not being treated with dignity and respect (e.g., "Does the seller think I am some sort of dimwit who will not be able to see right through him [her]?"—hardly the essence of seeing oneself as being treated with dignity and respect).

Moreover, the authenticity of fair process behavior may influence a variety of important dimensions. That is, negotiation outcomes may be assessed not only with respect to traditional objective measures such as individual or joint economic gains but also with respect to more subjective measures. According to Curhan, Elfenbein, and Xu (2006), "subjective value" may be captured by four types of measures: perceptions about the *instrumental outcomes*, perceptions about *the self*, perceptions about the *negotiation process*, and perceptions about *the relationship*. In what follows, we discuss the benefits of exhibiting high process fairness in negotiations and suggest that it is not sufficient to be seen as fair, but rather it is necessary to be seen as *authentically* fair to achieve these benefits.

Curhan and colleagues (2006) stated that the attainment of high subjective value in negotiations is important for three reasons: (a) It is useful in its own right, (b) it acts as a heuristic for negotiators to evaluate their economic outcomes, and (c) it fosters positive future relations and outcomes. Indeed, process fairness in negotiations is important for the same reasons. Inferences about process fairness are inherently linked to evaluations of subjective value as both are primarily focused on the interpersonal nature of social exchanges in negotiations. Traditionally, subjective outcomes have received somewhat less attention in negotiations in favor of a focus on economic outcomes. However, we suggest that the two types of outcomes may be linked: Improving processes that heighten subjective outcomes also can promote more favorable economic outcomes.

Perceptions About Instrumental Outcomes

It is well known that people use fairness information to form expectations about the outcomes they are likely to receive. Specifically, individuals who perceive process fairness as relatively high are more optimistic about the favorability or fairness of their future outcomes (Van den Bos, Lind, et al., 1997; Van den Bos et al., 1998). However, process fairness information will only have this positive effect on expectations of future outcomes when it is perceived as a reliable indicator of how the other party will behave over time. If process fairness is perceived as inauthentic, it is less likely to be viewed as a reliable basis for future expectations.

The authenticity of process fairness not only is an important predictor of negotiators' expectations about future outcomes but also shapes their perception of the fairness of, and hence their satisfaction with, current outcomes. It may be difficult for negotiators to determine the fairness of their agreement because objective standards often are absent. However, when treated with higher process fairness, recipients are more likely to be satisfied with lower outcomes (Brockner & Wiesenfeld, 1996; Van den Bos, Lind, et al., 1997; Van den Bos et al., 2001). Moreover, given that negotiators' interests usually are opposed to one another (thus creating potential suspicion of the other side's true motives), people may be more likely to use process fairness information to evaluate their negotiation agreement when they perceive that the negotiation process was authentically fair. In addition, recipients weight unfavorable outcomes less strongly, and are more willing to accept them, if they are treated with higher process fairness because process fairness offers psychological benefits (such as pride and respect; Tyler, Degoey, & Smith, 1996) that people may be willing to trade for economic outcomes. Once again, however, these benefits are likely to depend on whether the process fairness is perceived as authentic. For example, while being treated with authentic process fairness leads negotiators to feel respected, inauthentic expressions of the same behavior are likely to be perceived as disrespectful.

Perceptions About the Negotiation Process

Justice theorists suggested that individuals may attain a sense of control by having input into the process (Tyler, 1987). A sense of control enhances perceptions of predictability and reduces the anxiety that may arise from an undefined future. Indeed, negotiations may activate a need for predictability and hence control because they are inherently uncertain, leading negotiators to initiate strategies to gain control and establish predictability in their interactions with their partner. Thus, when a negotiator invites the other party to engage actively in determining the nature of the negotiation process (e.g., by giving the other party voice), the other party may feel a greater sense of control, but only if the other party perceives that the invitation is authentic. The sense of control created by an authentically fair process creates a feeling of trust in the other party and the perception that events are more predictable. Both parties are likely to be confident about the success of their actions and strategies.

In fact, enacting authentically fair processes in negotiations can determine the path of the negotiation process itself. Fair processes may give rise to "integrative" negotiations, in which parties attempt to reconcile opposing or diverging points of view by openly sharing their interests as opposed to becoming entrenched in positions (Johnson & Johnson, 2003). However, integrative negotiation strategies are likely to arise when the parties treat each other with authentically high process fairness, such as by providing accurate information, by representing the interests of all parties, and by not entirely acting with self-interest (Leventhal, Karuza, & Fry, 1980). Indeed, many integrative negotiation strategies mirror common conceptions of process fairness behaviors. In sum, authentic process fairness is likely to enhance perceptions of the negotiation process.

Perceptions About the Self

Research on process fairness has shown that individuals feel better about themselves when they are treated with higher process fairness (Folger, 1986, 1993; Tyler et al., 1996; Vermunt, Wit, Van den Bos & Lind, 1996). Fair treatment is interpreted as a sign of respect toward the recipient, whereas unfair treatment is interpreted as disrespect (Tyler et al., 1996; Tyler & Lind, 1992). Fair treatment signals to people that others consider them worthy of such conduct. Once again, however, this effect is likely to depend on the perceived authenticity of the fair treatment. That is, when fair treatment is seen as authentic, it is more likely to be interpreted as a signal that the other party holds one in high regard.

Being treated with authentically high process fairness also enhances the recipient's sense of inclusion, acceptance, and recognition (De Cremer,

2002; Wayne, Shore, Bommer, & Tetrick, 2002). Moreover, these positive feelings about the self are likely to lead to other beneficial outcomes, such as more cooperative behavior, more support for authorities and organizations, and an increase in organizational citizenship behaviors. When negotiators are made to feel good about themselves by their partners, they are more likely to want to maintain the relationship, to accept terms of agreements otherwise denied, and to put in extra effort to come to cooperative, mutually beneficial solutions.

Perceptions About the Relationship

An authentically fair process also enhances the relationships between negotiators by helping to build trust. In contrast, inauthentic process fairness may undermine trust by leading negotiators to feel deceived. Particularly when information about trust is not available, individuals may use the authenticity of process fairness information to determine the trustworthiness of their partners. When negotiators build trusting bonds, both parties are likely to evaluate the relationship positively, thereby increasing the likelihood that they will invest time and effort into maintaining a good rapport. Mutual trust makes it more likely that negotiators will provide veridical information to one another by reducing their fear that their partner will use this information to take advantage of them (De Dreu, Giebels, & Van de Vliert, 1998; Pruitt & Kimmel, 1977; Rubin & Brown, 1975). Information exchange helps negotiating partners identify mutually favorable agreements (De Dreu, Beersma, Stroebe, & Euwema, 2006; Pruitt, 1981; Thompson & Hastie, 1990), which simultaneously enhances value creation and strengthens the relationship between the parties.

It is important to note that both parties to a negotiation are at once the agents and the recipients of process fairness behaviors. As such, the interactions described in this section are likely to be dynamic and self-reinforcing. That is, without intervention, perceived inauthenticity can lead to a reciprocation of insincere fairness, thereby continuing the cycle. Alternatively, perceived authenticity is likely to be met with an enthusiastic return of genuine fairness. In either case, these mutually reinforcing patterns of interaction can serve to significantly enhance or undermine positive reactions to process fairness behaviors during negotiations. Given the important consequences of the authenticity of process fairness for both objective and subjective outcomes, it is important to consider how negotiators may improve their chances of coming across as authentically fair. In what follows, we explore three strategies for increasing the likelihood of being perceived as authentically fair.

STRATEGIES TO BOOST PERCEPTIONS OF FAIRNESS AUTHENTICITY IN NEGOTIATIONS

To date, much of the practical advice on enhancing authenticity in organizations comes from the leadership literature. In particular, authentic leaders are exhorted to be "true to themselves," that is, to act on personal values through increased self-awareness and self-regulation (Avolio & Gardner, 2005; Shamir & Eilam, 2005). However, there are several important differences between the work on authentic leadership and our conceptualization of authentic fairness in negotiations. First, authentic leadership is focused on encouraging leaders to become more aware of their guiding values to align their behavior with their beliefs (Avolio & Gardner, 2005; Erickson, 1995). In contrast, we assume that negotiators already are in touch with their inner workings (values, intentions). The key challenge in the present analysis is for them *to be seen by their negotiation partner as authentic* in their expressions of process fairness.

Second, whereas prior theorizing has posited that authentic leader behavior fosters positive relationships with followers, it has not addressed how people come to see their leaders (that is, their interaction partners) as authentic or explored the consequences for people when the other party perceives their process fairness behaviors to be inauthentic. In contrast, the present analysis has focused on how individuals form perceptions of authenticity about their interaction partners, rather than simply assuming that self-perceptions of authenticity will be socially validated. Given our focus on process fairness authenticity as perceived by one's negotiation partner, it may be useful to identify strategies to enhance such authenticity. Three approaches that are likely to enhance perceived authenticity are (a) soliciting feedback, (b) enhancing emotional intelligence (EQ), and (c) building trust and rapport.

To enhance process fairness authenticity in negotiations, people need to be able to see themselves from their partners' perspective; doing so may help them to bridge the gap between their true intentions and others' interpretations. This skill can be developed by soliciting feedback from others, such as through formal mechanisms (e.g., 360 performance appraisals, executive coaching) as well as through informal mechanisms (e.g., eliciting feedback in nondefensive ways and then demonstrating that the feedback has been taken seriously). In addition to providing insight into how people are seen by others, multirater feedback provides the opportunity to promote authentic fairness through self-reflection about the relationship between one's behaviors and others' perceptions. For example, consider multiparty negotiations in which negotiators not only may be directly involved in negotiating on their own behalf but also may serve as a witness or third party to exchanges between other parties. While negotiators may perceive themselves as behaving in accordance with fairness principles by treating different negotiation partners differently, parties witnessing these exchanges may interpret this inconsistency as a *lack* of authentic process fairness (e.g., Leventhal et al., 1980). Multirater feedback allows negotiators to recognize the ways that their behavior is interpreted not only by people with whom they have regular interaction but also by people with whom they interact less frequently, whose perceptions of process fairness authenticity are important nonetheless.

Expanding negotiators' EQ is another way for them to take greater advantage of the implicit cues about how one is perceived. EQ includes the abilities to perceive emotions in the self and in others, use emotions to facilitate performance, understand emotions and emotional knowledge, and regulate emotions in the self and in others (Mayer & Salovey, 1997). Higher levels of EQ expand negotiators' social bandwidth, allowing them to better bridge distances and make sense of a wider range of cues, including those that come from people who are not similar to or near them. Enhancing EQ requires increased self-awareness, such as can be achieved through soliciting feedback. However, EQ goes beyond simply boosting self-knowledge; EQ aids negotiators in choosing words and demeanors that reflect their true intentions. For example, even if a negotiator intends to act authentically fairly, inviting voice in a rude or impetuous manner will diminish the likelihood that recipients will see the offer of fairness as authentic. That is, if a negotiator "invites" voice by yelling in a harsh tone, "What would you do?" the recipient may not perceive the extension of fairness to be authentic. Thus, a higher EQ would allow negotiators to know (a) that they are transmitting a negative emotion, and (b) that being seen by others as frustrated may reduce the extent to which others perceive them as authentically fair. Furthermore, the emotional self-regulation associated with EQ suggests that once negotiators are aware of their emotional impact on the other party, and its effect on undermining perceptions of fairness, they then are able to reflect on their actions to change their behavior to convey their intentions more successfully. This process of "connecting the dots" from intention to impact can greatly enhance a negotiator's ability to come across as authentically fair. It is not enough simply to develop self-awareness; negotiators must know how to *enact* EQ with others, which includes but is not limited to regulating negative emotions they may experience during the negotiations.

Negotiations are commonly characterized as competitive, thereby inducing low levels of trust in the other party. Therefore, building trust may enhance the perceived authenticity of fair process behaviors. A study by Robinson, Lewicki, and Donahue (2000) showed that most students studying for a master's in business administration endorsed "traditional competitive bargaining" tactics in negotiations. Such tactics include asserting false time pressure, starting with a demand higher than needed, and undermining their opponent's confidence. As such, on entering a negotiation, individuals may be suspicious about their partner's expression of even high process fairness, instead perceiving it to be a tactic for an ulterior motive as opposed to seeing it as authentic. For example, they may believe that the partner is misrepresenting the resources available, the policies and procedures, the constraints on their behavior, or the treatment others have received. As a result, even processes that may be authentically fair from the negotiator's perspective may be perceived as inauthentic. The suspicion or lack of trust that negotiators feel toward one another already has been shown to influence their perceptions of the substance or content of the other party's behavior. Ross and Stillinger (1991) have shown that negotiators exhibit "reactive devaluation," a tendency to see the other party's offers or concessions as less valuable, simply because they came from or were initiated by the opposing side. In a related vein, we are suggesting that the suspicion or lack of trust between negotiators may cause them to see the other party's process fairness behaviors as inauthentic; for example, an outside observer who is not directly involved in the negotiations (and therefore has less reason to suspect the negotiator's motives) may perceive the exact same behavior as relatively authentic. Therefore, it is important for negotiators to build trust and rapport with one another before entering into the negotiation process. During this initial "getting-to-know-you" phase, negotiators have the opportunity to establish their integrity by demonstrating consistency in their actions and fostering a sense of predictability.

Multirater feedback, developing EQ, and building trust and rapport early in the negotiation are just a few strategies that may serve to enhance the perceived authenticity of process fairness in negotiations. We view these strategies as complements to strategies such as self-discovery that have been suggested by previous writings on authentic leadership (e.g., George, 2007). That is, negotiators may be more likely to be perceived as authentic in their process fairness behaviors (which is the focus of the present chapter) if they are acting in ways that are "true to themselves" (which has been the focus of previous work on authenticity in the workplace and which may be enhanced through strategies such as self-discovery). Therefore, we build on authentic leadership work by exploring how individuals can increase their chances of being perceived as authentic, assuming that their self-perceptions of authenticity have been established. While considerable anecdotal and practical insight supports the suggestions made here, future research is needed to determine the relationships between these general strategies—soliciting feedback, enhancing EQ, and building trust and rapport—and process fairness authenticity in negotiations in particular.

21st CENTURY BARRIERS TO AUTHENTICITY

The motives of corporate executives frequently have been called into question in light of the ethical transgressions in Enron, Worldcom, and Tyco and more recently, with the scandal involving Bernard Madoff, the civil lawsuit filed against Goldman Sachs, and many other events. As such, the current business climate is operating with a set of norms that encourage observers to interpret "moral" behavior, such as fair processes, with suspicion. Individuals frequently question the "true" motives behind the actions of organizational authorities. For example, consider the case of the cigarette manufacturing company Phillip Morris, which funds many advertisements inviting people to participate in smoking cessation and healthy living programs. It is obviously difficult for a cigarette manufacturing company to convince the public that it is truly invested in the health and well-being of Americans. Instead, people are likely to question the motives behind these advertisements. Is it a marketing ploy? Is it a public relations campaign? Is it mandated by a legal settlement? Regardless of the intention, the effectiveness of such a message is significantly undermined by its perceived inauthenticity. Likewise, the disclaimers Goldman Sachs has made to clients that they may hold trading positions contrary to those they promote to their clients call into question the extent to which their efforts at transparency (and thus fairness) in such disclosures are in fact authentic.

We suggest that in today's business environment concerns about perceived authenticity in negotiations are high. Relatedly, modern-day work settings also pose significant barriers to conveying authenticity in negotiations. Some of these barriers to authentic process fairness are based on physical distance, whereas others are based on psychological distance. *Physical distance* refers to negotiations that take place across geographical space and time through technologically mediated negotiations. *Psychological distance* refers to negotiations that take place across cultures and customs in an increasingly global economy.

Physical distance may reduce negotiators' chances of coming across as authentically fair because the other party is unlikely to have access to the full array of social information negotiators use to communicate, such as body language or vocal inflections. Relatedly, whereas virtual forms of communication, such as e-mail, can reduce some types of bias and stereotyping (Straus, Miles, & Levesque, 2001) and can improve the efficiency of communication (DeSanctis & Monge, 1999), these types of positive outcomes are most apt to occur when the relationship between parties is highly transactional or takes place in a setting in which favorable impressions already have been formed. Negotiations, in contrast, involve a high degree of shared meaning making in which social cues found in face-to-face interactions can be of high importance (Zack & McKenney, 1995). This can be particularly critical in forming perceptions of authenticity as the parties may not have a strong foundation of shared meaning prior to the negotiation. Therefore, it may be more difficult to see the other negotiator's process fairness as authentic (if indeed it is) when communicating across virtual realms.

Psychological distance also may undermine negotiators' perceived authenticity because people often approach out-group members with suspicion. For instance, behaviors by an out-group that appear to be fair to third parties may be viewed skeptically by those directly involved in the negotiation with the out-group because people tend to see things consistently with their prior beliefs. By virtue of being opposing parties in a negotiation, the two sides are automatically divided into ingroup/out-group membership. When such intergroup fault lines occur, people have a tendency to assign positive features to their ingroup and negative features to their out-group (Alderfer, 1987; Brockner et al., 2000). As such, when psychological distance is introduced in a negotiation, whether due to cultural differences, religious differences, or simply by being on opposing sides of the "table" (Ross & Stillinger, 1991), negotiators may be less likely to see expressions of process fairness as authentic. Ironically, fair process behaviors may be seen as inauthentic even if they are offered sincerely. In today's global economy, both physical distance and psychological distance are likely to occur simultaneously in negotiations. In addition, both of these 21st century features pose barriers to achieving the aforementioned authenticity-boosting strategies of seeking feedback, enhancing EQ, and building trust and rapport, as we explain in the following discussion; see Table 3.2 for a summary.

Twenty-first century negotiators need to be aware of the particular challenges of coming across as authentically fair. Even the strategies we suggested to enhance authenticity (seeking feedback, enhancing or at least conveying EQ, and building trust and rapport) may be made more difficult by physical or psychological distance. For example, it may be hard for negotiators to solicit feedback on how they are being perceived by their partners when negotiating across virtual media. In face-to-face interactions with similar others, feedback may be volunteered without prompting, whereas when physical and psychological distance are high,

TABLE 3.2

Workplace Features That Challenge Perceived Fairness Authenticity

	Physical Distance	**Psychological Distance**
Feedback	Less opportunity for informal feedback	Different norms for providing feedback
Emotional intelligence	Leaner media, cannot effectively convey emotions	Discrepancies in emotion "display rules"
Trust and rapport	Fewer interpersonal cues to convey integrity	Out-group suspicion and mistrust

negotiators may need to request feedback explicitly and proactively. When face-to-face, feedback may occur frequently, immediately, and informally, either during the course of conversation or through other nonverbal cues. When negotiating across e-mail, over the phone, or through another virtual setting, feedback may need to be formalized, leading to a less-candid interaction, less-frequent feedback, gaps in time between events and when feedback is given, and sometimes less-detailed and less-specific feedback. Physical distance can further introduce complications by increasing the chances for miscommunication among negotiation partners because virtual communication tends to be less effective as a means of conveying nuance and meaning (Daft, Lengel, & Trevino, 1987). Also, if negotiators have different cultural backgrounds, and thus have different norms that guide interpersonal interactions, feedback may be misunderstood. For example, in some cultures it is important to be polite and agreeable in interpersonal settings. A negotiator who intends to be fair but who communicates in a way that is frank or blunt may be perceived as disrespectful. Consequently, the authenticity of their process fairness behavior may be questioned.

Virtual negotiation settings also pose challenges for conveying EQ. That is, physical distance may disrupt a negotiator's ability to *enact* EQ as well as the negotiator's ability to *develop* EQ. For example, an e-mail that is written with the intention of conveying time urgency may be interpreted as voicing frustration with the recipient. According to Daft et al. (1987), different communication methods vary in degree of "media richness" or the volume of direct and indirect cues about the message being conveyed. Therefore, different communication methods provide more or less ease in transmitting messages about a person's emotions. Furthermore, psychological distance, which may result from cultural differences, also may hinder a negotiator's ability to convey EQ due to differences in emotional "display rules" across cultures (Ekman & Friesen, 1969). Thus, it can be difficult for negotiators to decide whether and when to amplify, suppress, modify, or qualify their emotions during interactions with a partner from a different culture (Matsumoto, LeRoux, & Yoo, 2005). They also may misinterpret emotional cues from their partners, such as interpreting a smile as agreement when it was merely intended to convey affiliation.

In addition, physical distance may make it difficult to build trust and rapport. Thompson, Nadler, and Lount (2006) proposed "the schmooze effect" as a strategy to address the challenges of technologically mediated negotiations. They suggested that forming a strong rapport at the beginning of a negotiation can replace the behavioral synchrony that is formed in face-to-face negotiations. Negotiators can implement getting-to-know-you exchanges that allow them to learn more about each other while forming a foundation of trust. Researchers have shown that simple steps such as sending biographical information and photographs (Moore, Kurtzberg, Thompson, & Morris, 1999) or initiating a brief phone conversation prior to negotiations (Morris, Nadler, Kurtzberg, & Thompson, 2002) have positive effects on negotiations. Schmoozers elicited greater trust and less frustration and achieved agreements more frequently than nonschmoozers in negotiations entailing physical distance. By extension, it is likely that efforts to get to know the other side on a personal basis also may serve to overcome challenges related to psychological distance between negotiators, perhaps enabling negotiators to be perceived as authentically enacting process fairness despite the challenges of physical and psychological distance.

In summary, physical distance can cause communication problems for negotiators because they are less able to develop a shared understanding of each other's context. Psychological distance can arouse distrust and suspicion, which diminishes negotiators' motivation to interpret process fairness as authentic. To complicate matters further, it is likely that both of these forms of distance exist concurrently in a negotiation; negotiations that take place across geographies are likely to transpire across cultural boundaries as well. Considering the increasingly global business market, these concerns are likely to become more important as organizations continue to expand their reach across countries. In the next section, we consider the implications of our analysis for theory and how future research may explore these barriers to process fairness authenticity in modern-day negotiation contexts.

THEORETICAL IMPLICATIONS AND FUTURE RESEARCH QUESTIONS

The present chapter advanced existing research on authenticity in two ways. First, we focused on how authenticity is perceived by one's negotiation partner, rather than on whether negotiators are being "true to themselves." Second, we suggested that it is the perceived authenticity of fair process behaviors, and not simply the fair process behaviors themselves, that influences a host of negotiation outcomes. Our focus on the relatively underemphasized perspective of interaction partners suggests the need to understand how attribution processes influence perceptions of authenticity. We expect that when process fairness behaviors are attributed to the volition of the individual, perceived authenticity will be higher than when an external attribution is made for those same behaviors. Future research also should consider how perceptions of intentionality influence judgments of authenticity. Moreover, our discussion of the twin 21st century challenges of physical and psychological distance helped us understand why it may be difficult for negotiators' process fairness behaviors to be seen as authentic.

We highlighted the value of feedback and the development of EQ as strategies that may enable negotiators to enhance the authenticity of their expressions of process fairness. Tools that may facilitate these strategies include the use of 360 performance evaluations, which provide extensive feedback and inform negotiators about how their and others' emotional expressions are perceived. However, our discussion of the physical and psychological distance prevalent in 21st century work organizations raises some practical issues that warrant further investigation. For example, multirater evaluations generally aggregate feedback by the status rank of the evaluator (i.e., supervisor, peer, subordinate). Given the physical and psychological distance among negotiators in organizations, it may be important to create feedback reports that are differentiated by evaluator characteristics, such as cultural background or whether interactions are virtual, so that negotiators can identify the challenges to perceived fairness authenticity derived from these types of distance. Thus, the growing psychological and physical distance in 21st century work organizations may require revision of management tools such as 360 performance appraisals.

Whereas the various sources of physical and psychological distance in contemporary organizations generally reduce perceived authenticity, this may not always be the case. For example, research has found that computer-mediated communication such as e-mail reduces social context cues and therefore leads people to be less likely to edit themselves or actively manage others' social impressions of them (Kiesler & Sproull, 1992). These reduced social context cues in computer-mediated communication have been associated with greater identification and trust (Wiesenfeld,

Raghuram, & Garud, 1999), perhaps setting the stage for greater perceived authenticity. Research evaluating the effect of computer-mediated communication on perceived authenticity may be best pursued in field studies in which the influence of contextual variables is highly realistic and reflective of the actual experience of negotiators across physical and psychological distance.

In general, our analysis has focused on authenticity in fairness behaviors for negotiators themselves; however, the challenges of psychological and physical distance associated with 21st century business may be even more acute for third-party observers. In many multiparty negotiations and in organizational settings more generally, negotiations are witnessed by third parties who subsequently interact with the negotiators and whose attitudes and behaviors also may be shaped by their perceptions of the authenticity of negotiators' fairness behaviors. Consider line employees of an organization that has been acquired: Although they may not have been party to the acquisition negotiations, they have become organization members as a result of the acquisition. Their perception of the authenticity of the fairness behaviors of the acquiring firm's leaders is likely to influence their level of engagement in the organization after the acquisition. To the extent that they perceive that leaders of the acquiring firm were only "going through the motions" rather than being authentically fair, they may refuse to contribute fully once the acquisition has been finalized. Importantly, their role as third parties to the initial exchange often may be replete with psychological and physical distance (e.g., they may be immersed in different national and organizational cultures, and as third parties, the information they receive may often be secondhand). Such distance will further complicate the efforts of leaders who wish to be perceived as authentically fair and thereby elicit high employee engagement. In sum, in organizational settings the effects of the authenticity of negotiators' process fairness behaviors may reverberate beyond the parties to the negotiation, to include third parties whose greater distance may lead to even lower perceptions of authentic fairness.

In conclusion, whereas years of research on process fairness have established the numerous linkages between fair treatment and favorable reactions, more recent work has revealed that process fairness does not yield universally positive outcomes (e.g., Brockner, Wiesenfeld, & Diekmann, 2009). We propose that one possible explanation for the wide range of recipient reactions is related to perceptions of fairness authenticity. It may not be sufficient for negotiators to be seen as fair; rather, they may have to been seen as *authentically fair* to elicit high levels of objective and subjective value. The consideration of process fairness authenticity in negotiations may be especially important in that many contemporary negotiations take place in contexts that pose barriers to authenticity. We hope that our analysis can stimulate future research and practical knowledge on this important topic for 21st century negotiators.

REFERENCES

Alderfer, C. P. (1987). An intergroup perspective on group dynamics. In J. W. Lorsch (Ed.), *Handbook of organizational behavior* (pp. 190–222). Englewood Cliffs, NJ: Prentice-Hall.

Avolio, B. J., & Gardner, W. L. (2005). Authentic leadership development: Getting to the root of positive forms of leadership. *Leadership Quarterly, 16*, 315–338.

Bies, R. J. (1987). Beyond "voice": The influence of decision-maker justification and sincerity on procedural justice judgments. *Representative Research in Social Psychology, 17*, 3–14.

Brett, J. M., Shapiro, D. L., & Lytle, A. I. (1998). Breaking the bonds of reciprocity in negotiations. *Academy of Management Journal, 43*, 410–424.

Brockner, J., Chen, Y., Mannix, E., Leung, K., & Skarlicki, D. (2000). Culture and procedural fairness: When the effects of what you do depend upon how you do it. *Administrative Science Quarterly, 45*, 138–159.

Brockner, J., Konovsky, M., Cooper-Schneider, R., Folger, R., Martin, C., & Bies, R. J. (1994). The interactive effects of procedural justice and outcome negativity on the victims and survivors of job loss. *Academy of Management Journal, 37*, 397–409.

Brockner, J., & Wiesenfeld, B. M. (1996). An integrative framework for explaining reactions to decisions: The interactive effects of outcomes and procedures. *Psychological Bulletin, 120*, 189–208.

Brockner, J., Wiesenfeld, B., & Diekmann, K. (2009). Towards a "fairer" conception of process fairness: How, when and why more may not be better than less. In J. Walsh & A. Brief (Eds.), *The Academy of Management annals* (Vol. 3, pp. 183–216). New York: Routledge.

Chen, C. C., Choi, J., & Chi, S. C. (2002). Making sense of local-expatriate compensation disparity. *Academy of Management Journal, 45*, 807–817.

Chen, Y., Brockner, J., & Greenberg, J. (2003). When is it "a pleasure to do business with you"? The effects of status, outcome favorability, and procedural fairness. *Organizational Behavior and Human Decision Processes, 91*, 1–21.

Colquitt, J. A. (2001). On the dimensionality of organizational justice: A construct validation measure. *Journal of Applied Psychology, 86*, 386–400.

Curhan, J. R., Elfenbein, H. A., & Xu, H. (2006). What do people value when they negotiate? Mapping the domain of subjective value in negotiations. *Journal of Personality and Social Psychology, 91*, 493–512.

Daft, R. L., Lengel, R. H., & Trevino, L. K. (1987). Message equivocality, media selection, and manager performance: Implications for information systems. *MIS Quarterly, 11*, 355–366.

DeCharms, R. (1968). *Personal causation: The internal affective determinants of behavior.* New York: Academic Press.

De Cremer, D. (2002). Respect and cooperation in social dilemmas: The importance of feeling included. *Personality and Social Psychology Bulletin, 28*, 1335–1341.

De Cremer, D., & Schouten, B. (2008). When apologies for injustice matter: The role of respect. *European Psychologist, 13*, 239–247.

De Dreu, C. K. W., Beersma, B., Stroebe, K., & Euwema, M. (2006). The interaction between social motives and epistemic motives in negotiation. *Journal of Personality and Social Psychology, 90*, 927–943.

De Dreu, C. K. W., Giebels, E., & Van de Vliert, E. (1998). Social motives and trust in integrative negotiation: The disruptive effects of punitive capability. *Journal of Applied Psychology, 83*, 408–422.

DeSanctis, C., & Monge, P. (1999). Introduction to the special issue: Communication processes for virtual organizations. *Organization Science, 10*, 693–703.

Deutsch, M. (1985). *Distributive justice: A social psychological perspective.* New Haven, CT: Yale University Press.

Ekman, P., & Friesen, W. V. (1969). The repertoire of nonverbal behavior: Categories, origins, usage, and coding. *Semiotica, 1*, 49–98.

Erickson, R. J. (1995). The importance of authenticity for self and society. *Symbolic Interaction, 18*, 121–144.

Falk, A., Fehr, E., & Fischbacher, U. (2008). Testing theories of fairness—Intentions matter. *Games and Economic Behavior, 62*, 287–303.

Falk, A., & Fischbacher, U. (2006). A theory of reciprocity. *Games and Economic Behavior, 54*, 293–315.

Folger, R. (1986). A referent cognitions theory of relative deprivation. In J. M. Olson, C. P. Herman, & M. P. Zanna (Eds.), *Social comparison and relative deprivation: The Ontario symposium* (Vol. 4, pp. 33–55). Hillside, NJ: Erlbaum.

Folger, R. (1993). Reactions to mistreatment at work. In J. K. Murnighan (Ed.), *Social psychology in organizations: Advances in theory and research* (pp. 161–183). Englewood Cliffs, NJ: Prentice Hall.

Folger, R., Rosenfield, D., Grove, J., & Corkran, L. (1979). Effects of "voice" and peer opinions on responses to inequity. *Journal of Personality and Social Psychology, 37*, 2243–2261.

George, W. W. (2007). *True north: Discovering your authentic leadership.* San Francisco: Jossey-Bass.

Gibson, C. B., & Grubb, A. R. (2005). Turning the tide in multinational teams. In D. L. Shapiro, M. A. Von Glinow, and J. L. Cheng (Eds.), *Managing multinational teams: Global perspectives* (pp. 69–96). Oxford, UK: Elsevier/JAI Press.

Greenberg, J. (1988). Cultivating an image of justice: Looking fair on the job. *Academy of Management Executive, 2*, 155–158.

Greenberg, J., & Colquitt, J. A. (2005). *Handbook of organizational justice.* Mahwah, NJ: Erlbaum.

Harter, S. (2002). Authenticity. In C. R. Snyder & S. Lopez (Eds.), *Handbook of positive psychology* (pp. 385–394). London: Oxford University Press.

Harvey, P., Martinko, M. J., & Gardner, W. (2006). Promoting authenticity in organizations: An attributional perspective. *Journal of Leadership and Organizational Studies, 12*, 1–11.

Heider, F. (1958). *The psychology of interpersonal relations.* New York: Wiley.

Johnson, D. W., & Johnson, R. T. (2003). Field testing integrative negotiations. *Peace and Conflict: Journal of Peace Psychology, 9*, 39–68.

Kiesler, S., & Sproull, L. (1992). Group decision-making and communication technology. *Organizational Behavior and Human Decision Processes, 52,* 96–123.

Kelley, H. H. (1967). Attribution theory in social psychology. In D. Levine (Ed.), *Nebraska symposium on motivation* (pp. 192–238). Lincoln: University of Nebraska Press.

Kernis, M. H., & Goldman, B. M. (2006). A multi-component conceptualization of authenticity: Research and theory. In M. P. Zanna (Ed.), *Advances in experimental social psychology* (pp. 284–357). San Diego, CA: Academic Press.

Leventhal, G. G., Karuza, J., & Fry, W. R. (1980). Beyond fairness: A theory of allocation preferences. In G. Mikula (Ed.), *Justice and social interaction: Experimental and theoretical contributions from psychological research* (pp. 167–218). New York: Springer-Verlag.

Lind, E. A. (1998). Procedural justice, disputing, and reactions to legal authorities. In A. Sarate, M. Constable, D. Engel, V. Hans, & S. Lawrence (Eds.), *Everyday practices and problem cases* (pp. 177–198). Evanston, IL: Northwestern University Press.

Matsumoto, D., LeRoux, J. A., & Yoo, S. H. (2005). Emotion and intercultural communication. *Kwansei University Journal, 99,* 15–38.

Masterson, S. S., Lewis, K., Goldman, B. M., & Taylor, M. S. (2000). Integrating justice and social exchange: The differing effects of fair procedures and treatment on work relationships. *Academy of Management Journal, 43,* 738–748.

May, D. R., Chan, A. Y. L., Hodges, T. D., Avolio, B. J. (2003). Developing the moral component of authentic leadership. *Organizational Dynamics, 32,* 247–260.

Mayer, J. D., & Salovey, P. (1997). What is emotional intelligence? In P. Salovey & D. Sluyter (Eds.), *Emotional development and emotional intelligence: Implications for educators* (pp. 3–31). New York: Basic Books.

Moore, D. A., Kurtzberg, T. R., Thompson, L. L., & Morris, M. W. (1999). Long and short routes to success in electronically mediated negotiations: Group affiliations and good vibrations. *Organizational Behavior and Human Decision Processes, 77,* 22–43.

Morris, M., Nadler, J., Kurtzberg, T., & Thompson, L. L. (2002). Schmooze or lose: Social friction and lubrication in email negotiations. *Group Dynamics Theory, Research, and Practice, 6,* 89–100.

Peterson, C., & Seligman, M. (2004). *Character strengths and virtues: A classification and handbook.* New York: Oxford University Press.

Pruitt, D. G. (1981). *Negotiation behavior.* New York: Academic Press.

Pruitt, D. G., & Kimmel, M. J. (1977). Twenty years of experimental gaming: Critique, synthesis, and suggestions for the future. *Annual Review of Psychology, 28,* 363–392.

Roberts, L. M. (2005). Changing faces: Professional image construction in diverse organizational settings. *Academy of Management Review, 30,* 685–711.

Robinson, R., Lewicki, R., & Donahue, E. (2000). Extending and testing a five factor model of ethical and unethical bargaining tactics. *Journal of Organizational Behavior, 21,* 649–664.

Ross, L., & Stillinger, C., (1991). Barriers to conflict resolution, *Negotiation Journal, 7,* 389–404.

Rubin, J. Z., & Brown, B. R. (1975). *The social psychology of bargaining and negotiation.* New York: Academic Press.

Seligman, M. (2002). *Authentic happiness.* New York: Free Press.

Shamir, B., & Eilam, G. (2005). What's your story?—Toward a life-story approach to authentic leadership. *Leadership Quarterly, 16,* 395–417.

Shapiro, D. L., & Brett, J. M. (1993). Comparing three processes underlying judgments of procedural justice: A field study of mediation and arbitration. *Journal of Personality and Social Psychology, 65,* 1167–1177.

Shapiro, D. L., Furst, S., Spreitzer, G., & Von Glinow, M. A. (2002). Teams in the electronic age: Is team identity and high-performance a risk? *Journal of Organizational Behavior, 23*, 455–468.

Straus, S. G., & Miles, J. A., & Levesque, L. (2001). The effects of videoconference, telephone, and face-to-face media on judgments in employment interviews. *Journal of Management, 27*, 363–381.

Thibaut, J. W., & Walker, L. (1975). *Procedural justice: A psychological analysis.* Hillsdale, NJ: Erlbaum.

Thompson, L. L., & Hastie, R. (1990). Social perception in negotiation. *Organizational Behavior and Human Decision Processes, 47*, 98–123.

Thompson, L., Nadler, J., & Lount, R. B. (2006). Judgmental biases in conflict resolution and how to overcome them. In M. Deutsch, P. T. Coleman & E. C. Marcus (Eds.), *The handbook of conflict resolution* (pp. 243–267). San Francisco: Jossey-Bass.

Tomlinson, E. C., Dineen, B. R., & Lewicki, R. J. (2004). The road to reconciliation: Antecedents of victim willingness to reconcile following a broken promise. *Journal of Management, 30*, 165–188.

Tyler, T. R. (1987). Conditions leading to value expressive effects in judgments of procedural justice: A test of four models. *Journal of Personality and Social Psychology, 52*, 333–344.

Tyler, T. R., Degoey, P., & Smith, H. (1996). Understanding why the justice of groups matters: A test of the psychological dynamics of the group-value model. *Journal of Personality and Social Psychology, 70*, 913–930.

Tyler, T. R., & Lind, E. A. (1992). A relational model of authority in groups. *Advances in Experimental Social Psychology, 25*, 115–191.

Tyler, T. R., & Smith, H. J. (1997). Social justice and social movements. In D. Gilbert, S. Fiske, & G. Lindsey (Eds.), *Handbook of social psychology* (4th edition, Vol. 2, pp. 595–629). New York: McGraw-Hill.

Van den Bos, K., & Lind, E. A. (2002). Uncertainty management by means of fairness judgments. In M. P. Zanna (Ed.), *Advances in experimental social psychology* (Vol. 34, pp. 1–60). San Diego, CA: Academic Press.

Van den Bos, K., Lind, E. A., Vermunt, R., & Wilke, H. A. M. (1997). How do I judge my outcome when I do not know the outcome of others? The psychology of the fair process effect. *Journal of Personality and Social Psychology, 72*, 1034–1046.

Van den Bos, K., Lind, E. A., & Wilke, H. A. M. (2001). The psychology of procedural and distributive justice viewed from the perspective of fairness heuristic theory. In R. Cropanzano (Ed.), *Justice in the workplace, from theory to practice* (Vol. 2, pp. 49–66). Mahwah, NJ: Lawrence Erlbaum Associates.

Van den Bos, K., Vermunt, R., & Wilke, H. A. M. (1997). Procedural and distributive justice: What is fair depends more on what comes first than on what comes next. *Journal of Personality and Social Psychology, 72*, 95–104.

Van den Bos, K., Wilke, H. A. M., & Lind, E. A. (1998). When do we need procedural fairness? The role of trust in authority. *Journal of Personality and Social Psychology, 75*, 1449–1458.

Vermunt, R., Wit, A., Van den Bos, K., & Lind, E. A. (1996). The effects of unfair procedures on negative affect and protest. *Social Justice Research, 9*, 109–119.

Wayne, S. J., Shore, L. M., Bommer, W. H., & Tetrick, L. E. (2002). The role of fair treatment and rewards in perceptions of organizational support and leader-member exchange. *Journal of Applied Psychology, 87*, 590–598.

Weiner, B. (1982). The emotional consequences of causal attributions. In M. S. Clark & S. T. Fiske (Eds.), *Affect and cognition: The 17th annual Carnegie symposium on cognition* (pp. 185–210). Hillsdale, NJ: Erlbaum.

Welsh, N. (2004). Making deals in court-connected mediation: What's justice got to do with it? *Washington University Law Quarterly, 79,* 786–861.

Wiesenfeld, B. M., Raghuram, S., & Garud, R. (1999). Communication patterns as determinants of organizational identification in a virtual organization. *Organization Science, 10,* 777–790.

Zack, M. H., & McKenney, J. L. (1995). Social context and interaction in ongoing computer-supported management groups. *Organization Science, 6,* 394–422.

4

The Effect of Perception on Judgments About "Fair" Compensation: Implications for Negotiators as Price Justifiers

Robin L. Pinkley

> All the world's a stage,
> And all the men and women merely players;
> They have their exits and their entrances,
> And one man in his time plays many parts,
> His acts being seven ages.

William Shakespeare, *As You Like It*, 1599

One of the most important stages on which one plays is one's work life. Since most people on average switch jobs 12 times during their careers (U.S. Bureau of Labor Statistics, 2004), the ability to manage the exits and entrances onto that stage and to make decisions concerning if and how to negotiate the compensation package is crucial. By "compensation," I refer to any issue of relevance and value to the employer or to the employee (whether potential or existing) that can be included in an employment package. Such issues might include those shown in Table 4.1. The variability of the issues included in this list reinforces Milovich and Newman's (2004) view that compensation typically incorporates issues tied to organizational profitability, employee quality of life, and the viability of the long-term relationship due to employee performance, motivation, satisfaction, and recidivism—and as such involves issues other than mere salary levels. Despite this, Malhotra and Bazerman (2007) have suggested that negotiators' vulnerability to the "vividness bias," or the tendency to

TABLE 4.1

Potential Compensation Issues

Basic pay-related issues	**Vacation and time issues**
Salary	Vacation time
Overtime pay	Sick days
Commissions	Flextime
Signing bonus	Paternity/maternity/family leave
Incentive bonus	
Profit sharing	**Relocation benefits**
401(k) plan (matched or unmatched)	Moving expenses
Pension plan	Brokers' fees
Stock plan	Legal fees
Stock purchase plan	Job search assistance for spouse
Stock options	Severance packages (golden parachutes)
Ownership equity	Temporary housing
Guaranteed age of retirement	
	Job description and evaluation
Health benefits	Title
General coverage	Location
Medical insurance	Performance review date
Dental insurance	Promotion schedule
Vision insurance	
Business travel insurance	**Perks**
Life insurance	Home office expenses
Accidental death and dismemberment insurance	Mobile phone or expenses
	Car allowance
Disability insurance (short or long term)	Company car or repair
Prescription card	Garage or parking
	Tolls
Professional development	Mileage
Club memberships	Expense accounts
Fraternal memberships	Travel expenses
Professional associations	Company jet usage
Conference fees and expenses	Child care/eldercare facilities
Training programs	Valet services
Sabbaticals	

overweight the importance of the most vivid or prestigious aspects of an employment package lead them to focus most on salary, especially when such aspects are easier to quantify, evaluate, and compare across offers or employee options than issues. The issues listed in Table 4.1 serve as a visual reminder that salary is only one of many potential compensation issues open for negotiation.

Compensation-related negotiation, which is the focus of this chapter, occurs when (a) a compensation-related offer by an employer or a compensation-related request by a job seeker or existing employee falls short of "yes" from the receiver and (b) the parties in this exchange keep talking to find ways to accommodate each other's concerns ultimately to reach agreement on the employment package. The antithesis of compensation negotiation, which is outside the scope of this chapter, is what Krannich and Krannich (2005) called a "negotiation transaction," illustrated when either party (the employer or the employee, either existing or potential) responds to the other's compensation-related communication with either an immediate, unqualified acceptance or a move to terminate discussion by walking away to rejoin the employment line (if one is on the employee side) or to seek to fill the position with an alternative applicant (if one is the employer). The reason this chapter focuses, instead, on compensation-related negotiation is twofold. First, most job offers and many compensation review discussions leave room for negotiation, in which case the ultimate form of the compensation agreement is more an interpersonal decision-making process informed by both the employer and potential (in the case of a job offer) or existing (in the case of a compensation review) employee than it is a single-solution transaction informed by only one of the interdependent parties (Thompson, 2005). Second, this chapter aims to highlight that, despite the availability of more than one solution to compensation-related requests or offers, people often fail to recognize this and thereby underutilize opportunities to negotiate compensation (Pinkley & Northcraft, 2000).

Now that what the focus of this chapter and what is meant by compensation negotiation are clarified, the remainder of this chapter proceeds as follows: First, I review those prenegotiation preparation strategies and proactive and reactive exchange strategies touted in the popular press and scholarly literature to assist negotiators engaged in compensation negotiations in terms of (a) "claiming value," or getting their own needs met (Lax & Sebenius, 1986; see also Lewicki, Barry, & Saunders, 2010, for a review); (b) "creating value," or getting the needs of *both*, themselves and their counterpart, met (Lax & Sebenius, 1986; cf. Lewicki et al., 2010); and (c) avoiding "suboptimal agreements," that is, agreements that leave value on the negotiation table that is undiscovered and unclaimed by either party or agreements that leave at least one party feeling unfairly treated, thereby leading to future costs. An example of unclaimed value in compensation negotiation is failing to recognize that an earlier start date of employment could potentially have resolved differences of opinion regarding salary base level. Examples of future costs associated with agreements that left at least one party feeling unfairly treated are quick turnover, depressed performance, and even organizational sabotage or mutiny (Gomez-Mejia, Berrone, & Franco-Santos, 2010; Merryman, 2010).

Second, I discuss how the negotiator actions named might be specifically used for compensation negotiations by employers, as well as by potential and existing employees.

Third, I highlight that the conventionally prescribed negotiation strategies described in this chapter were generally identified in research utilizing face-to-face simulation-based negotiations comprised of participants who shared the same characteristics, such as gender and nationality; as such, it is questionable how applicable some or all of the conventionally prescribed negotiation strategies are for helping negotiators effectively negotiate compensation when negotiators do not see the face of their counterpart (as is the case when job applications are solely online; My Career, 2007) and when negotiators' counterparts are diversified (as is increasingly the case due to labor pool changes caused by changing demographics, enhanced gender diversity, and globalization; Benko & Weisberg, 2007). To illustrate the latter point, I select one of the conventionally prescribed exchange strategies described and note how applying that strategy may differ when the negotiators are *not* face to face and *not* demographically homogeneous.

Fourth, and last, I identify questions in need of future negotiation research whose derivation is guided by the compensation negotiation strategy alterations I speculated may be necessary when the negotiators are (a) in situations involving electronic (e.g., online) rather than face-to-face communications; (b) in situations involving demographcally heterogeneous (rather than nationally similar) counterparts; and (c) in situations involving *both* (rather than just one) of these characteristics. As will become clear in this chapter, the available negotiation literature does not answer these questions, and the 21st century workplace trends involving these two characteristics are unlikely to cease any time soon. Cumulatively, I hope this chapter enables readers to learn what the conventionally prescribed negotiation strategies are, how these strategies may be applied to compensation negotiations in particular, and why the time has come to revisit the applicability of these strategies in light of the fact that the 21st century workplace involves negotiations that are electronically based in a context of diversity that has generally (with rare but important exceptions) been missing from the contexts studied by negotiation scholars. Ultimately, ideally readers will feel inspired to consider to what extent current research applies to those negotiating compensation within the context of the 21st century workplace so that future negotiators and negotiation scholars can better understand how (if at all) conventionally prescribed negotiation strategies may need to change.

CONVENTIONALLY PRESCRIBED PREPARATION AND EXCHANGE STRATEGIES THAT ENABLE NEGOTIATORS TO CLAIM VALUE, CREATE VALUE, OR AVOID SUBOPTIMAL AGREEMENTS

Table 4.2 provides a list of the strategic actions most frequently named in the conventional negotiation literature to enable negotiators to claim value, create value, or avoid suboptimal agreements during the preparation and exchange process stages of negotiation. While the objective of

TABLE 4.2

Conventionally Prescribed Compensation Negotiation Strategies

---

Act I: Preparation and Planning Strategies

1. Do your homework to obtain objective data concerning both internal (within an organization) and external (across organizations) market norms.
2. Develop attractive real and phantom alternatives (i.e., BATNA—*b*est *a*lternative to *t*he *n*egotiated *a*greement) to increase negotiator power.
3. Create a MAP to guide you during the negotiation that reflects what you want, why you want it, and how much you want it.

Act II: Exchange Process Strategies

1. Avoid the use of unprincipled strategies such as using lies, bluffs, and threats.
2. Attempt to anchor (and enhance the other party's perception of value) by making the highest first offer one can defend.
3. Avoid being overly influenced by the other side's anchor attempts.
4. Manage the concession process and the message that it sends to the other party.
5. Look for mechanisms to create and claim value.
6. Strategically share information about time deadlines, but not about time costs.
7. Compare the final offer to your MAP and know whether, when, and how to walk away.

---

negotiation is to claim value, claiming strategies must be coupled with those that create value and avoid suboptimal agreements according to Raiffa (1982) if agreement is to be reached in most cases. This is because few if any negotiators will agree to deals that lack value or satisfaction for them, providing value only to the other. Thus, savvy negotiators will look for strategies that combine mechanisms for *getting value* (i.e., value-claiming strategies) with mechanisms for *giving value* in return for what one gets (i.e., value-creating strategies), in the most *optimal* way possible (i.e., avoid suboptimal agreement strategies).

In this section, each strategic action component is described in turn.

Preparation and Planning

Arguably the most important part of any negotiation is what occurs before the parties actually meet. The failure to prepare for negotiation is the first mistake that many people make and one that likely results in less-optimal outcomes (Thompson, 2005). The preparation process lays the ground-work and sets the stage for what is to come. To be fully prepared, both parties need to (a) obtain objective comparison information that might inform outcome expectations and perceptions of fairness (i.e., research internal and external market information); (b) work to assess and create sources of power (i.e., create real and phantom alternatives, such as BATNA, best alternative to a negotiated agreement); (c) clearly determine details concerning what one wants, must have, and will be willing to give in return (i.e., make a MAP [my actual preferences] as a guide); and (d) begin to formulate a plan for the information one wants to share, with-hold, and find out (i.e., create an information exchange strategy) (Pinkley & Northcraft, 2000).

The first preparation and planning strategy shown in Table 4.2 refers to the need for negotiators to collect data from objective sources, such as comparative market information, that will likely enable them to make requests or offers that both sides will view as fair (i.e., how the compensation package in question compares to the internal and external market). Research suggests that in situations of great ambiguity, people are more persuaded regarding what is appropriate, desirable, and correct when they have *social proof* about the choices made by similar others (Cialdini, 2001). Doing this has been called "using objective standards" by Fisher, Ury, and Patton (1991), which also coincides with what justice scholars have referred to as "procedural justice" (cf. Colquitt, Conlon, Wesson, Porter, & Ng, 2001). In essence, this means being able to justify one's proposal with criteria that any objective party would choose as unbiased in nature, hence favoring no negotiator's stance more than that of another. Reliance on objective criteria is illustrated, for example, when car buyers and car sellers each consult Web sites or other information pertaining to a car's market value, as influenced by the car's age, mileage, current condition, and so on.

In addition to enhancing fairness judgments, acquiring objective standards to support compensation requests or offers is important because it increases negotiator realism and decreases overconfidence or the tendency for negotiators to overestimate their ability, correctness, accuracy, or value to the other party (Bottom & Paese, 1999). Although Bottom and Paese (1999) suggested that overconfidence can help negotiators resist being too conciliatory and thereby improve their ability to claim value, Bazerman and Neale (1982) cautioned negotiators against being overconfident since negotiators who overestimate their own worth and the probability that the other will acquiesce are less successful and obtain fewer agreements. To avoid overconfidence, negotiators should base their claims on information that is as objective as possible, enhancing also the legitimacy of their requests.

The second strategy referenced in Table 4.2 concerns a mechanism for enhancing negotiator power, which Barada (2008) has argued is one of the most overlooked but important dynamics affecting compensation negotiations today. Kim, Pinkley, and Fragale (2005) have defined negotiator power as the "underlying capacity of negotiators to obtain benefits from their agreements." While negotiator power has been operationalized in many ways, including resource contribution or status (Komorita, Sheposh, & Braver, 1968); reward structures (Rubin & Brown, 1975); influence tactics (Kipnis & Schmidt, 1983); and inequities in negotiator alternatives, typically referred to as negotiator BATNAs (Pinkley, Neale, & Bennett, 1994), the value of a negotiator's BATNA has been found to have the most profound impact on behavior and outcome. Negotiators with high-quality BATNAs pick higher reservation points due to a decreased dependence on the other party and increased feelings of leverage in negotiation (Lewicki et al., 2010; Pinkley et al., 1994). This greater leverage may explain why these negotiators are more likely to make the first offer (Magee, Galinsky, & Gruenfeld, 2007), make more extreme first offers (Buelens & Van Poucke, 2004; Pinkley et al., 1994), and achieve more "individual gains"—that is, obtain more value than their opponents from the negotiated agreement (cf. Shapiro & Bies, 1994). In addition, negotiators who communicate the existence of their high-quality BATNAs enhance the perceived fairness of the request (cf. Buelens & Van Poucke, 2004), possibly because it provides social proof regarding the value that the high-BATNA negotiator brings to the table and a sense of scarcity given that the high-BATNA negotiator may walk away to accept the alternative (i.e., job opportunity or potential employee) (Cialdini, 2001). Consistent with this notion, Pinkley and Vandewalle (2010) found that recruiters informed of a job candidate's high-quality BATNA changed their perceptions of both the candidate's market value (i.e., how much it would take to hire the candidate) and actual value (i.e., the value of the candidate to the organization). Some of the yielding behavior of negotiators faced with a high-BATNA opponent may also be due to their desire to prevent the counterpart from terminating negotiations to pursue their BATNA (e.g., go to work for a competitor). Thus, coercive power is also enhanced on the part of negotiators who provide information about a favorable BATNA (cf. Shapiro & Bies, 1994).

Pinkley and Vandewalle (2010) discovered that negotiators who have phantom (potential, but unavailable) alternatives obtain as much benefit to outcome as those who have real BATNAs. For example, a candidate who has had a positive second interview with an alternative company but has not received an offer from the alternative company and has no idea whether or not he or she can expect an offer in the future can be said to have a phantom BATNA (i.e., an impasse in the current negotiation will result in zero value to both the candidate and the recruiter should they fail to reach agreement). Although the BATNA literature would suggest that the phantom BATNA that is not available at the time of the current negotiation should give the person who holds it no additional power, their findings suggest otherwise, in that candidates with phantom BATNAs obtained as much value from the negotiation as those with real, high-valued alternatives. In fact, even when both parties were given probability information regarding the likelihood that the candidate would obtain the phantom alternative in the future (increasing the value of the phantom above zero points of value, to some expected value between 0% [which is equivalent to no BATNA] and 100% [which is equivalent to an acquired BATNA]), they failed to calibrate the expected value of the future opportunity in a manner that justified the power boost obtained by the candidates in all of the phantom conditions. It is unclear whether the recruiters failed to *recognize* that the candidate's phantom alternative had an expected value that was of significantly less than a distributive, compromise solution; failed to *explain* this to the candidates; or failed to *convince* the candidate of this reality. Regardless of which pattern is correct, taken together, the BATNA-related research suggested that negotiators are well advised to obtain real and phantom alternatives, share information concerning real BATNAs of high value, and share information about phantom BATNAs, while being candid about their phantom (i.e., probable vs. real) nature.

A third strategy relates to the creation of a MAP, which is a document that helps negotiators organize their thoughts; clarify their objectives and requirements; identify the information that they will need to obtain from the other party; plan their bidding, counterbidding, value-claiming, and value-creating strategies; track the process of negotiation; and compare and contrast the value of your alternatives (Pinkley, 2009). In essence, the MAP does exactly what the name implies: It provides a guide to keep negotiators on track. Table 4.3 provides a detailed example of a candidate's MAP.

The MAP can be created as a simple paper-and-pencil exercise but is most efficiently created as an Excel spreadsheet that includes information pertaining to: (a) *who* the decision makers are in the negotiation (this is simplest and possibly more effective when a third party such as a head-hunter is not involved given that research has shown that the intervention of third parties can decrease the quality of joint agreements; Valley, White, & Iacobucci, 1992); (b) *what* issues are of importance to either party and all of the options that are acceptable for each issue; (c) *how much*, that is, what the relative value of each issue option to all others is; (d) *why* this particular configuration of issues and options fulfills the overall interests of the negotiator (Lewicki et al., 2010); (e) *BATNA*, the value that will be obtained should the parties reach an impasse in the current compensation negotiation (Fisher et al., 1991); (f) *bottom line*, the least amount of value that a negotiator can accept before walking away from the deal (i.e., for both sides, this means calculating both the cost and the benefits associated with the agreement); (g) *target*, the highest value they can hope to achieve from the negotiation; and (h) *offers and counteroffers*, with negotiators preplanning their bidding/counterbidding strategies and tracking them in the course of the negotiation (Lewicki et al., 2010). Failure to select a bottom line leads negotiators to exhibit what Pinkley et al. (1994) have called a *bias toward settlement,* and Cohen, Leonardelli, and Thompson (2010) have coined an *agreement bias,* or the tendency to view any deal as preferable to an impasse. Research suggested that the most advantageous

TABLE 4.3

Sample of a Candidate MAP with a BATNA and Market Substantiated First Offer

Issues	My Options	My Utility	My BATNA	Their Utility	Other's BATNA	1st Offer	2nd Offer	3rd Offer
Explicit Value Why:								
Salary	$85,000	40				40		
40%	$80,000	26.33	26.33					
[15,000/40]=375	$75,000	13					13	
	$70,000	0						
Bonus	15%	3				3	3	
3%	10%	2	2					
[15/3]=5	5%	1						
	0%	0						
Vacation	18 Days	5				5		
5%	14 Days	3.18						
[11/5]=2.2	11 Days	1.81						
	7 Days	0	0				0	

		Target	Bottom Line		
Health benefits 15% [75/15]=5					
	75%	15		15	
	50%	10	10		
	25%	5			5
	No Coverage	0			0
Car allowance 2% [400/2]=200					
	$400	2	2	2	
	$300	1.5			
	$200	1			
	$0	0			0
Implicit Value Why:					
Content 10%	Contingent	0–10	5	6	6
Culture fit 5%	Contingent	0–5	2	3	3
Challenge 20%	Contingent	0–20	10	18	18
Total		100	56.99	92	48

manner for negotiators to manage to avoid this tendency and motivate themselves to acquire high-quality outcomes is to couple a bottom line based on the value of one's BATNA (Bazerman, Moore, & Gillespie, 1999) with a higher aspiration or target that one can work to try to achieve, thus resulting in significantly superior outcomes (Locke & Latham, 1984; Simon, 1955).

Beyond committing to a bottom line and focusing on a target point for the overall value of the compensation agreement, Fisher et al. (1991) recommend that negotiators attempt to be *firm regarding the value* they wish to obtain from the agreement but *flexible* in terms of the *form of that agreement.* To do this, one needs to understand *why* it is that one desires a specific issue or issue option and *how much* one wants it relative to other issues so that one can (a) obtain his or her underlying interests even if unable to obtain the original issue or stated position (e.g., the employer provides a stock value guarantee in return for a smaller stock offering such that the final stock value is equivalent to the stock value requested by the job seeker) and (b) trade issues of less importance in return for issues of greater importance if such a trade increases benefit (e.g., the employer gives the employee a new title that the employee has long coveted instead of a salary increase that the organization can ill afford) (Lewicki et al., 2010).

Building on the system long used by scholars and practitioners, Pinkley (2009) has created a simple system for determining issue values that allow negotiators to compare the relative value of every issue option to every other issue option across issues. This system increases negotiator flexibility and allows the negotiator to calculate the value of any offer quickly. This system allows the negotiator to translate all issues into the same metric, preventing the candidate from having to determine in the heat of negotiation how many days of vacation would make a good trade for extra dollars of salary.

Table 4.4 provides an example of how two of the issues (salary and health benefits) included in Table 4.3 were calculated, although all of the utilities calculated for every option listed in Table 4.3 were calculated this way. Although the example provided here might be made by a job seeker preparing for an upcoming negotiation with a human resource (HR) representative, any member of an organization can create a similar MAP that translates all of the issues into the same metric, enhancing efficiency and effectiveness and preventing the negotiator from having to determine in

TABLE 4.4

Guidelines for Making a MAP to Guide You Through the Process of Negotiation

Step 1 = Two issues – Salary and Health Benefits

Step 2 = For each issue pick a target, bottom line, and multiple options

Step 3 = Divide 100 pts across the issues in terms of relative value

Step 4 = For each issue determine the issue distance from bottom line to target

Step 5 = Divide assigned issue points by issue distance

- **Issue 1 is worth 40% so (15,000/40) = $375 of salary = 1 point of value**

  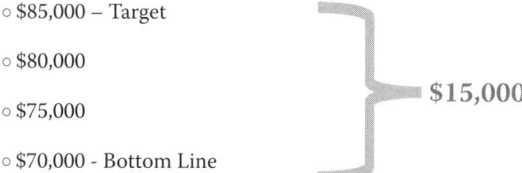

  ○ $85,000 – Target

  ○ $80,000

  ○ $75,000 — $15,000

  ○ $70,000 - Bottom Line

- **Issue 2 is worth 15% so (75/15) = 5% of benefits = 1 point of value**

  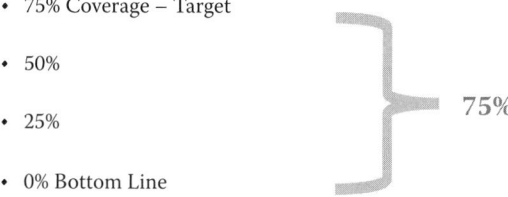

  • 75% Coverage – Target

  • 50%

  • 25% — 75%

  • 0% Bottom Line

the heat of negotiation how many days of vacation might make a good trade for a thousand extra dollars of salary.

Exchange Process

Regardless of how carefully one prepares for a negotiation and MAPs out a strategy, one must inevitably implement that strategy in the dynamic social context of the compensation exchange (Lax & Sebenius, 2006). As seen in Table 4.2, the exchange process strategies heretofore identified as the most profoundly important for enhancing negotiator ability to claim value, create value, or avoid suboptimal outcomes in the context of compensation negotiations are (a) avoiding the use of unprincipled strategies such as using lies, bluffs, and threats; (b) anchoring the negotiation (and enhancing the other party's perception of value) by making the most extreme first offer one can defend; (c) avoiding the influence of the other side's anchor attempts; (d) managing the concession process and the message that it sends to the other party: (e) strategically sharing information about time deadlines, but not information about time costs; (f) looking for mechanisms to create and claim value; and (g) comparing the final offer to one's MAP and knowing whether, when, and how to walk away. Each strategy is reviewed in turn.

The negotiation exchange process has been informed by numerous literatures, including psychology, economics, anthropology, biology, political science, communication, labor relations, law, and sociology (Pruitt, 1981) Much of this work suggests that given the social context of negotiation, most negotiators are concerned with both the economic (e.g., money, salary, and other resources of value to the negotiator) and interpersonal (e.g., developing and building the relationship and establishing trust) outcomes that may be achieved. As a consequence, Shapiro and Bies (1994) encouraged negotiators to be as transparent and straightforward as possible and cautioned against the use of "bluffs" and threats that one cannot or will not in actuality take since credibility once lost is difficult to regain. The first exchange strategy listed in Table 4.2 is thus to avoid the use of unprincipled strategies such as lies, bluffs, or threats. Of course, this does not imply that all questions should be answered or that the timing of information sharing is not important (Bazerman & Malhotra, 2007), just that that it is far better to say "No" or decline to answer a question than it is to lie. More than any other strategy in negotiation, lying is judged to be unethical (Lewicki et al., 2010). Because reputations are as informed by secondhand (i.e., what we hear from someone else) as firsthand experience, lying or even the perception of lying can cost negotiators far more than it can benefit them (Goates, 2008). Therefore, negotiators need to think as carefully about what they will say, will not say, and will not do in the course of a negotiation as what they need to find out. For example, a negotiator should not share his or her bottom line until the negotiator is ready to change the negotiation into a transaction in which the other party either accepts the offers as made or no agreement is reached.

Of the strategies evaluated in the conventional literature, the strategy found to account for the greatest variance in outcome (85% to be exact) is the bidding strategy used in negotiation (see Table 4.2, Exchange Process

Strategy 2). According to the findings of Galinsky and Mussweiler (2001), it is advantageous to make the first offer because the first offer serves as a powerful anchor against which all other offers will be compared. While the true playing field lies between the bottom lines of the two parties, negotiators who lack this information come to perceive the distance between the first bid and the first counterbid as the true playing field when in fact, negotiator bids tend to be strategic. People normatively track and compare the concessions made by each party (consciously or unconsciously), so agreements generally fall near the statistical average of the first two offers that the parties perceive to be fair, although it may fall far off the statistical average of the bottom lines of the two parties (Raiffa, 1982).

Research by Galinsky and Mussweiler (2001) further refined our understanding of the relationship between offers and outcomes to find that agreements fall significantly closer to the first offer than the counteroffer. This means that negotiators should attempt to make the first offer—when armed with market information. First offers made in the absence of market information may be disadvantageous in that they may be made incorrectly at a level that is costly rather than beneficial or may lead to a decrease in credibility in the negotiation and possibly harm to one's reputation (Tinsley, Cambria, & Kupfer-Schneider, 2006). Thus, to accrue the benefits associated with the first mover advantage (Exchange Strategy 2) and avoid the costs associated with bluffing (Exchange Strategy 1), a rule of thumb concerning how extreme to make one's first bid (or one's counterbid should the other make the first bid) is to make it as *extreme as one can defend*. This suggests that a negotiator should present the first bid as a specific figure or point rather than as a range that implies (correctly or incorrectly) the negotiator's bottom line and target (Pinkley & Northcraft, 2000).

Given that first bids are often strategic, Exchange Process Strategy 3 suggests that it is important to avoid being anchored and biased by the other party's first bid (Galinsky & Mussweiler, 2001). Effective negotiators keep their eye on the prize by measuring their own success in terms of how far above their bottom line and how close to their target they are able to move in the course of the negotiation, as well as how much value they are able to achieve over the lifetime of the relationship (Krannich & Krannich, 2005). This means that should the other party make the first bid, the negotiator should: (a) ask questions designed to test the validity of the bid (should it be manipulative or strategic rather than substantive in nature) and explore the underlying interests that motivate the bid, and

(b) make a counteroffer that reflects one's target and is substantiated by objective market information. That is, a counteroffer should be no more or less extreme than a first offer or be influenced or anchored by the first offer that it follows (Pinkley, 2009). Thus, bids (whether first bids or counter-bids) made in the first round should include no compromise of any kind. Instead, ideas regarding strategic concessions and trade-offs should be reserved for second-round moves (Stillenger, Epelbaum, Keltner, & Ross, 1990).

The fourth exchange strategy mentioned in the conventional literature concerns the process used for making concessions. While counterintuitive, rather than being satisfied, a negotiator is likely to be dissatisfied when his or her first offer is met with acceptance since immediate acceptance of an offer implies that the negotiator *could* have done better (Galinsky, Seiden, Kim, & Medvec, 2002). Why is this? The answer lies in the fact that negotiator outcomes are evaluated in context, and that part of the context is *how* the outcome is obtained. This means that effective negotiators manage the *actual value* of what they give and the *perceived value* of what they give through the process of concession making. Research suggested that negotiators fare better when the cost of the concession to the negotiator is made salient and traded for something else to combat *reactive devaluation* or the tendency for negotiators to devalue the other party's concessions just because they were made (Stillenger, Epelbaum, Keltner, & Ross, 1990). One wants to avoid the signal that one's initial offer is strategically inflated and thus that one can and will move significantly. Concession patterns have been found to communicate the ability to move during the course of the negotiation, with people expecting smaller and smaller concessions as one gets closer to one's bottom line (Malholtra & Bazerman, 2007). In the same vein, delayed concessions are perceived to be more valuable than immediate concessions (Kwon & Weingart, 2004).

While a negotiator's MAP provides an efficient mechanism for organizing the negotiator's own issues and interests, *how that negotiator's interests compare to those of the other party* is what determines how much value is available for division, the degree of flexibility regarding the form that value can take, and the strategies that will be most effective for mining that value (see Table 4.2, Exchange Strategy 5) (Raiffa, 1982). In multiissue negotiations, different issues provide different opportunities for creating and claiming value and thus require a different set of strategies. If we compare the preferences and priorities of negotiators, we can determine the kinds of issues embedded in the negotiation and which strategies might be the most effective for uncovering, creating, and claiming value (Lax & Sebenius, 1986). In fact, Pinkley, Griffith, and Northcraft (1995) found that the more negotiators were able to recognize the relationship between their preferences and priorities, the higher the value of their joint and individual outcomes was. Issue types vary along two dimensions: (a) do the parties have the same or opposite *within-issue preferences* (e.g., during a salary review negotiation, an employer and employee have opposite within-issue preferences when the employee prefers a high salary increase and the employer a low salary increase and the same preferences when they both want the employer to transfer to the Seattle office) and (b) do the parties have the same or different *across-issue priorities* (e.g., the employer and employee have the same priorities when salary is more important to both of them than office location, and they have different priorities when the employer cares more about office location and the employee about salary increase). The four issue types most commonly found in compensation negotiations that vary along these dimensions are: (a) distributive issues, (b) logrolling issues, (c) congruent issues, and (d) add-on issues. Each issue type is discussed in turn.

For a *distributive issue*, each party expresses opposite preferences but shares equal priority, so that one party's gain translates into the other's loss. If a negotiator's strategy is self-focused, then there is the tendency to treat the entire negotiation as if the benefit to one party costs an equal amount of value to the other. This approach is also called a distributive negotiation orientation (cf. Lewicki et al., 2010; Malhotra & Bazerman, 2007). In addition to focusing on threats or thinking about or communicating concerns and desired solutions that meet only one's own needs, distributively oriented negotiators tend to have a *single-issue focus* (Weingart, Bennett, & Brett, 1993), which means planning strategies to ensure that one's self-interests are met, including that one has met, at a minimum, his or her reservation point and ideally obtained his or her highest-priority issues. By focusing on single issues, negotiators who succeed in extracting concessions on their highest-priority interests do so unilaterally, that is, without having to concede anything in return. In compensation negotiations, it is unlikely that the overall deal will be distributive (i.e., there is usually some overlap in the parties' interests or the potential for trade-offs), although there will likely be an issue or two that is distributive. Although not always distributive, the issues most likely to be distributive are those concerning salary; for example, an employer and employee engaged in a performance review negotiation may care equally about salary, with the employer pushing for a small increase and the employee a large increase (Lewicki et al., 2010; Malhotra & Bazerman, 2007).

Negotiators have a tendency to assume that both parties in compensation negotiations have opposite preferences (e.g., the employer wants to pay the job seeker a small signing bonus, and the job seeker wants the highest bonus achievable) and equal priorities (i.e., the issues of greatest importance to the employer are also those of greatest importance to the job seeker). This biased assumption, called the *fixed-pie bias,* is costly because it stems from and perpetuates the tendency for negotiators to refuse to share information about their needs and priorities (Thompson & Hastie, 1990). In multiissue compensation negotiations, it is more likely that the two share the same preferences on some issues (i.e., the parties' interests are congruent) and different priorities on others, so that what is of greatest importance to one is of less importance to the other, providing opportunities for making trade-offs (Thompson & Hrebec, 1996). Going back to our Table 4.3 example, we see that the recruiter and job seeker have been through one offer–counteroffer exchange. If each were merely to state *what* they want from the agreement (*positional bargaining*), they would know only that the job seeker wants a high salary and high percentage of health coverage, while the recruiter wants to offer a low level of each. Should they add information concerning *how much* they value each issue relative to the other (priority information consistent with *interest-based bargaining*), they would discover that salary is crucial to the job seeker, while skyrocketing health care costs have enhanced the importance of this issue for the organization, providing an efficient and fortuitous trade-off opportunity. Coupling information about priorities with that of preferences promotes integrative solutions, which can enhance mutual value and individual benefit (Kemp & Smith, 1994; Thompson, 1991). Thus, an *integrative negotiation strategy*, as opposed to a distributive strategy, that recognizes opportunities for aligning the interest of both parties is most effective when dealing with the remaining issue types: logrolling, congruent, and add-on issues.

Logrolling is possible when the issue or issues of greatest importance to the organization are not the same as those that are of greatest importance to the employee. When this is the case, a negotiator can often gain more value from exchanging those issues of less value personally (but more value to the other party) for those of more value personally (but less value to the counterpart) than the negotiator would have if he or she had compromised on these issues (Tajima & Fraser, 2001). Logrolling or negotiated trade-offs result in an increase of the overall value for both parties (Thompson, 2005).

A *congruent* issue exists when both parties share the same preference, as in the example provided when both parties preferred that the employee transfer to the Seattle office rather than remain in New York. Although one might expect that such issues would be easy to detect and resolve, Thompson and Hastie (1990) found that about 50% of people failed to recognize that the other party had interests completely congruent or compatible with their own, resulting in agreements of less value for both parties or what they called the "lose-lose effect." Why does this occur? The lose-lose effect results when one or both parties lie about their preferences or make a first bid or counterbid that reflects a unilateral compromise rather than a target preference or a negotiator mishears or misinterprets the opponent's stated preference due to the fixed-pie bias (Thompson & Hastie, 1990). These are all errors that the Table 4.2 strategies are designed to alleviate.

Add-on issues are those that are not originally included in the compensation negotiation but are added during the course of the negotiation when one party discovers that they are valued by the other party and they are able to add it to the mix. For example, a recruiter may be able to add an extra week of paid vacation to the candidate's first year *only* (after learning of the candidate's wedding plans) but then combine that issue in the discussion of a signing bonus. One common mistake, however, is to treat add-on issues as pure benefit to the opponent without calculating the cost to oneself. Any changes to the MAP should be reflected in your calculations. An add-on issue should only be added to the mix if (a) it is of more benefit to the other party than it costs the focal negotiator and (b) the focal negotiator is able to get more value in return (i.e., get value for giving value) for the add-on than it costs them to provide to the other party (Malholtra & Bazerman, 2007; Pinkley, 2009).

As anyone whose severance payments have run out will tell you, time pressure has implications in negotiation and is the focus of Exchange Strategy 6. While most negotiators believe that *time cost* (e.g., legal fees, strike costs) and *time deadline* (e.g., nonrefundable airline tickets) information should be withheld, the wisdom of this strategy is contingent on the type of time pressure involved (Moore, 2004). Negotiators with climbing time costs should withhold this information since opponent delay tactics will lead to disadvantageous concessions, while those with time deadlines should share this information so that both parties are equally motivated to find a solution before time runs out. Otherwise, only the negotiator with the time deadline feels the rush to find a solution and makes unilateral concessions (Lim & Murnighan, 1994; Moore, 2004). So, how might negotiators combat the problem of time costs? Moore suggested the strategic use of final deadlines to spread responsibility for agreement among the parties, increase the sense of urgency, and aid in reaching agreement.

Scholars and practitioners have long used payoff matrices similar to Pinkley's (2009) MAP to teach executives, those with MBAs, undergraduate students, and others to track the value of their outcomes to avoid the documented tendency to accept agreements below the value of one's BATNA and the costly *agreement bias* (Cohen et al., 2010). The last exchange process strategy listed in Table 4.2 (see Exchange Strategy 7) is thus to compare the final offer of the negotiation to one's best alternative and to walk away should the agreement provide value that falls below the value of one's BATNA (Pinkley & Northcraft, 2000). Just as important as whether one walks away, however, is *how* one walks away since all the world is a stage and that stage has gotten smaller and smaller with the advancement of all forms of technology (e.g., global travel, telecommunications). This means that compensation negotiations should never be viewed as discrete, independent events with no past or future ramifications. The negotiation does not end with an agreement or impasse but is an ongoing process with ongoing benefits or costs. One should never underestimate the value and potential carryover effects of a good reputation and costs of a poor reputation (Tinsley et al., 2006). Social utility in negotiation involves not only the value of liking (which some value more than others) but also the value (and potential cost) of human capital— sustainable value in the form of networking, job referrals, and even online recommendations through commonly used Web outlets such as LinkedIn, Xing, and even Facebook. These Web-based outlets mean that negotiators can have an impact on one's reputation like never before, enhancing the importance of the fairness perceptions in negotiation. Thus, at the end of the exchange, both parties should be particularly respectful and pleasant. Thank you notes and signs of appreciation are always welcome and perhaps even more important in the case of impasse. In fact, research showed that negotiators are liked most when they are initially negative and resistive and become positive and personable over time (Aronson & Linder, 1965). Responding with a "thank you" is an *appreciative move* (Kolb & Williams, 2001) that can help to alleviate or prevent contentiousness in negotiations and thus is a simple mechanism for reestablishing rapport. When things do not work out, it never hurts to give the other face and mention how difficult it was to reach the decision to walk away (Brown & Robbennolt, 2006).

How can negotiators use the conventionally prescribed preparation and exchange process strategies shown in Table 4.2 specifically to negotiate compensation agreements, and does this advice change contingent on whether one sits on the employer or employee side of the table? Additional advice more specifically tailored to employer and employee roles are provided in the next section.

SPECIFIC ADVICE FOR EMPLOYERS AND EMPLOYEES REGARDING THE APPLICATION OF CONVENTIONALLY PRESCRIBED COMPENSATION NEGOTIATION STRATEGIES

If the two sets of conventionally prescribed negotiation strategies (summarized in Table 4.2 and described in the previous sections of this chapter) are to be used to negotiate *compensation* specifically, what might negotiators do? Employers *and* employees should complete the preparation process well before they engage in the first interview or compensation-related meeting to avoid missteps such as sharing information that is strategically costly or the tendency to bluff, exaggerate, or deceive when faced with an unexpected question. Such reactions rarely help one's case, decrease the hope of finding mutually advantageous solutions, elicit perceptions of distrust, and endanger one's reputation. Before the interview process begins, negotiators should investigate industry standards to determine the market rate companies pay for the job in question and how much the existing and potential employees *might be paid* given that salary is often the issue of highest concern to both parties (Malhotra & Bazerman, 2007). This means tapping into career centers, professional associations, and Internet salary sites to determine industry starting salaries in general and specific geographic areas that apply to the skill level, education, and experience needed for the job in question. It is also beneficial to network and contact professional organizations to obtain annual salary surveys, read professional publications, and have open dialogues with friends, family, and coworkers about what people might expect to be compensated, given a specific role. If possible, it is helpful to learn if employers are bounded by salary limits and internal equity issues, knowledge that is more easily obtained if the job seeker is seeking a new position within his or her current organization or if the job seeker knows employees at the organization he or she is hoping to join as a new employee.

Table 4.5 shows Web site sources that provide various types of comparative market information. Relying on these sources can help negotiators (on both sides of the table) avoid overconfidence. With regard to the salary ranges, it is important to treat, for example, the generalized averages as just that—*averages*—and to recognize the potential flaws in the data, including data sources (i.e., employee self-report or HR professionals), recency (i.e., the data should not be more than a year or so old), and fit (i.e., select on location, company size, and detailed job description instead of mere job title). Negotiators should also remember that salary data are easier to come by than information concerning other forms of compensation (such as those listed in Table 4.1), and that it is the value of the overall deal (in terms of both cost and benefit) that should determine whether an agreement is reached. It is important, therefore, *not* to become too fixated on market salary data or to use it to base one's reservation point (or bottom lines) solely on this issue since doing so risks becoming single-issue focused, thereby forgetting to focus on multiple issues and to look for opportunities to *exchange* concessions and logroll to enhance mutual satisfaction and personal benefit (as described in the section pertaining to value-creating actions).

Specific Advice for the Employer

The possession of an alternative signals not just what the job seeker *might* get but what the job seeker *can get* (i.e., market value). Although BATNA information should only convey the job seeker's *market value* (i.e., how much it will take to get the job seeker) as opposed to the job seeker's *actual value* (i.e., the value that the job seeker is expected to bring to the

TABLE 4.5

Web-Based Salary Information Resources

http://www.acinet.org
- A government site that is part of the Department of Labor's CareerOneStop portal. The data can be dated, so be sure to check the age of any search that you do on this site.

http://online.wsj.com/public/page/news-career-jobs.html
- A Dow Jones & Company site that features salary information as well as job-hunting tips and features from *The Wall Street Journal* concerning industry trends.

http://www.homefair.com
- Provides cost of living comparison information for various U.S. cities.

http://www.jobstar.org
- A link to over 300 salary surveys, many of which are industry specific. The data can be dated, so be sure to check the age of any search that you do on this site.

http://www.payscale.com
- Salary reports, wage calculators, and compensation reports for candidates, employees, and human resources professionals based on job title, location, education, skills, and experience.

http://www.salary.com
- Includes salary data, employee benefits, and customized salary range for nearly 2,000 job descriptions with various levels of experience, education, and so on in specified locations. Also market analysis, pricing software, and competitive pay data are available.

http://www.salaryexpert.com
- Salary surveys, wage calculators, compensation reports, and salary advice.

http://www.vault.com
- Salary data categorized by company, industry, and profession.

organization based on predetermined objective criteria such as the job seeker's performance history and the interview process), recent work by Pinkley and Vandewalle (2010) found that recruiters change their perceptions of job seeker quality, as well as market value, on hearing of the job seeker's high-valued alternative. BATNA-related research cautions existing and potential employees to take care when reacting to information about existing and potential employee real and potential alternatives, particularly the tendency to shift perceptions of their actual value (i.e., as opposed to market value) irrationally and, as a consequence, one's own bottom line. A negotiator's bottom line should be based on the value of one's own alternatives and what it will take to make the deal profitable for oneself and one's constituency rather than on the value of the other party's bottom line (Pinkley & Vandewalle, 2010).

Employers should also listen for employee attempts to segment their BATNA (Pinkley & Vandewalle, 2010), such as when an employee wishing to renegotiate a compensation agreement tells the employer about the increased salary and additional vacation time procured from a competing organization. In such cases, the natural tendency is to counter the BATNA by upping the employee's compensation on both issues, although it is prudent to remember that it is the relative total value of the compensation packages that matter, not the relative value of a subset of issues contained in the compensation contracts (i.e., salary and vacation time), and negotiators often segment their BATNAs (i.e., mention only those pieces of the alternative that are less attractive than the current negotiation even if the overall value of the current negotiation exceeds the overall value of the BATNA) in a way that benefits them strategically. Thus, rather than responding with an immediate concession, the employer might congratulate the employee, assure the employee of his or her interest in finding a solution that works (if this is sincere and true), remind the employee that his or her compensation agreement includes many issues, only a very few of which he or she has mentioned, and then explore the alternative offer in much more detail. Having done so, the two parties can revisit the current compensation package and work together to find possible trade-offs should the BATNA changes in salary and vacation time be more important to the employer than some of the other issues included in the current employee contract. Should trade-offs not be possible and a unilateral concession be the employer's only recourse, the two parties may be able to determine additional performance criteria that the employee can offer in return for enhanced compensation. This is consistent with the recommendation that negotiators attempt to get value in exchange for what they give (i.e., make bilateral compromises rather than unilateral concessions) whenever possible.

Specific Advice for the Existing and Potential Employee

Given the power of real and phantom BATNAs and the impact that they have on employee and employer perceptions of value, job seekers are advised to create alternatives whenever possible (Pinkley et al., 1994). In terms of *strategic action*, this means that job seekers with high-valued

BATNAs should inform the other party that they have an alternative offer but share the value of that alternative in a manner that is strategically viable. This means, for example, that they share information about those pieces of the alternative that are more attractive than the offer made by the potential employer, when strategically beneficial (i.e., they understand the power of strategically segmenting the BATNA). This also means that when an employee has a potential, but not yet obtained, job offer, the employee should inform the employer of this phantom possibility (Pinkley & Vandewalle, 2010). Such behavior will only serve to legitimize the power of the job seeker's position and increase the ability to claim value. Job seekers are cautioned to be *candid* about whether the alternative they hold is available or phantom given that credibility and reputation are irreplaceable commodities (Anderson & Shirako, 2008), and phantom BATNAs provide as much power as those obtained.

In terms of *strategic thinking*, this research makes salient the importance of recognizing the difference between available (i.e., what a job seeker *has* obtained), phantom (i.e., what a job seeker *has some chance* of obtaining), and ghost alternatives (i.e., what a job seeker *might* obtain given what others have obtained, such as market value). Pinkley and Vandewalle (2010) gave preliminary evidence that suggests that negotiators are also influenced by ghost information, even when that information is about similar others as opposed to the negotiator in question. Thus, we caution job seekers to remember that they are likely to exaggerate the expected value of their phantom alternatives due to overconfidence, and that exaggerated estimations of certainty will lead them to make inaccurate forecasts and poor decision choices (Hensher & Johnson, 1981; Sivanathan & Galinsky, 2007). While it is important to recognize the strategic power of real, phantom, and even ghost alternatives in compensation negotiation, it is equally important to accurately (a) recognize the true value of one's BATNA, (b) select a bottom line based on one's true BATNA (rather than illusions), and (c) assess one's value relative to the employer's BATNA. In terms of substantiating employee value, Vogt (2009) suggested that the more prospective and existing employees emphasize issues related to money, time, and amounts, the more employers are likely to recognize employee worth and future potential. This means being specific about how employees have saved, earned, or managed money; saved, made, or managed time; and how much or how many of these things the employee has done.

In tough economic times, job seekers and employees requesting salary increases are often reminded that there are others waiting in the wings to take their place or that others have been satisfied with similar offers. Such entreaties of *social proof* regarding an employer's potential BATNA can increase one's sense of *scarcity*, particularly when presented by an *authority* figure to whom one does or may report, which leads to an enhanced sense of urgency and greater compliance (Cialdini & Goldstein, 2004). While these feelings are natural, the employer's BATNA should not shift one's own bottom line, perception of alternatives, or bidding strategy, given that the first two should be based on one's own BATNA rather than on the employer's, and the third should be based on objective criteria that one can support and verify, such as market comparisons. In fact, one should proceed exactly as one would have before hearing about the employer's alternative. The point here is that while the employer's BATNA (if real as opposed to strategic or phantom) will likely influence what the employer is willing to accept (the employer's bottom line) and the final outcome of the negotiation (the compensation agreement), it should not alter the job seeker's or employee's first bid (which will only serve to decrease the value of the final compensation agreement to him or her in the end) or walkaway point (one's own bottom line).

Employees preparing to ask for an increase in compensation are encouraged to consider the employer's likely reaction to attempts to invoke a BATNA. Some employers are sadly unable to recognize an employee's true value without social proof in the form of an alternative job offer and so require this information before increasing one's compensation. Others view the acquisition of an alternative as disloyal and so respond to news of alternatives with the recommendation that the employee take the offer (Pinkley & Vandewalle, 2010). These differences highlight the importance of incorporating the historic reactions of the other party into one's strategy; particularly when power strategies are part of one's approach.

Job seekers must carefully consider when and how to share information about salary history and expectations. When asked to state salary expectations preoffer, job seekers tend to ask for too little, fearing that they will be dropped from consideration, anchoring the negotiation in a manner that is disadvantageous to them (Pinkley & Northcraft, 2000). As a consequence, conventional advice has been to advise job seekers to decline salary expectation discussions until they have an offer in hand. Although this may sound inconsistent with Exchange Strategy 2 (see Table 4.2), which advises negotiators to anchor the negotiation by making the first offer, it is not. This advice simply refines Exchange Strategy 2 by suggesting that the timing of the first offer is an important feature of compensation negotiation. Although salary history may be required, job seekers can delay discussion about salary and strategic anchoring until an offer is made by saying something like: "While I understand the importance of salary and other forms of compensation and will be more than willing to discuss my expectations once you have decided that I am the preferred candidate for this position and an offer is forthcoming, it is my hope that decisions regarding my potential employment can be based on the quality of my credentials, what you think I can bring to this organization, and how well this opportunity fits with my own goals and objectives. If you can agree, I would like to table that important conversation until then." Such a statement prevents the job seeker from the tendency to lowball oneself and sets up the compensation negotiation nicely by suggesting that the job seeker will specify salary expectations when an offer is forthcoming.

APPLYING PREVIOUSLY PRESCRIBED COMPENSATION NEGOTIATION STRATEGIES TO THE 21st CENTURY WORKPLACE

To this point, this chapter has reviewed conventionally prescribed negotiation preparation and exchange strategies for claiming value, creating value and avoiding suboptimal agreements (summarized in Table 4.2) and noted how each of these strategies might be used to negotiate compensation in particular—from the perspective of the employer as well as the existing employee or job seeker. All of these strategies have theoretical merit and practical appeal, but it is important to remember that the identification of these strategies occurred largely from simulated negotiation studies that comprise the bulk of the negotiation literature (Friedman, 1994) and that these characteristics include some that do *not* characterize the way compensation negotiations occur in the 21st century workplace, although the results of these studies have been found to be generalizable in most cases. Specifically, past simulation-based negotiation studies involved: (a) negotiators interacting with others who knew all the issues that could be raised during the negotiation, as well as each side's BATNAs, since simulation materials typically provided this information to the participants (Lewicki et al., 2010); (b) negotiators communicating face to face (Galin, Gross, & Gosalker, 2007; Moore, Kurtzberg, Thompson, & Morris, 1999); and (c) negotiators interacting with others who shared their own nationality or gender, with most negotiating dyads consisting of male, U.S. Americans, or the issue of gender of little consideration. In contrast to these characteristics, increasingly more job seekers communicate with job recruiters, at least during the application process, via online channels of communication, hence *not* face to face (e.g., Galin et al., 2007); increasingly, there is diversity among job seekers and job hirers due to the increase of women in the workforce and globalization of the labor pool (Towers Watson, 2010), due at least in part to organizations' increased reliance on multinational teams (cf. Von Glinow, Shapiro, & Brett, 2004) and global virtual teams (e.g., Amichaei-Hamburger & McKenna, 2006). Online communications prevent participants from obtaining nonverbal cues that may enable them to see or hear, hence potentially interpret, which issues are of primary concern to the other side; individual difference issues such as gender and national diversity between negotiators increase the chance that negotiators may *not* feel equally comfortable about explicitly raising issues of concern that need to be negotiated or may *not* mutually understand whatever communications or nonverbal cues may be sent (cf. Von Glinow, et al., 2004).

Hereafter, I focus on two of the contextual conditions characterizing the 21st century workplace—its increasing diversity and increasing use of electronic forms of communication—to answer the questions: Do the compensation-related negotiation strategies identified in Table 4.2 need to be altered when negotiators are *not* negotiating with a counterpart who shares their gender or are *not* face to face? If so, how? For illustrative purposes, I explore this possibility by revisiting the applicability of only one of the compensation negotiation strategies described previously; the strategy that I have selected pertains to the second exchange strategy discussed in Table 4.2—anchoring the negotiation (and enhancing the other party's perception of value) by making the most extreme first offer one can defend. Specifically, I examine how conventional advice about strategic anchoring in compensation negotiation may need to be updated or altered for (a) female rather than male negotiators given what we know about gender differences and (b) online rather than face-to-face negotiation exchanges due to what we know about the impact of technology in the context of negotiation.

21st Century Gender Diversity and Implications Regarding Strategic Anchoring

Given the mix of generations, genders, ethnic groups, and cultural origins found in most organizations, diversification is more the rule than the exception in the 21st century workplace. Because each of us is an amalgamation of these characteristics (and many more, including but not limited to religious affiliation, economic status, and political perspective), it is important to explore the individual across the table rather than assume that the individual will negotiate in a manner consistent with the norms associated with one demographic feature. Still, the plethora of recent findings concerning gender differences in the propensity to negotiate compensation suggests that this individual difference feature deserves our attention (Babcock, Gelfand, Small, & Stayn, 2007; Kray, Reb, Galinsky, & Thompson, 2004), most particularly since women are expected to account for 52.2% of the total labor force growth between 2008 and 2018 (U.S. Department of Labor, Bureau of Labor Statistics, 2009), and the majority of management and professional jobs are projected to be held by women in 2030 (Benko & Weisberg, 2007).

Research consistently finds that women are less likely to negotiate compensation then are men (Babcock & Laschever, 2003), and that when they do, they are likely to obtain agreements of less value (Gerhart & Rynes, 1991), due at least in part to lower expectations, target points, and bottom lines (Kaman & Hartel, 1994). Research concerning gender differences in negotiation suggested that in terms of anchoring strategies, when compared to men, women will be less likely to (a) anchor the negotiation by making the first offer and (b) make extreme first offers and counteroffers. Given this tendency and the fact that Bowles, Babcock, and McGinn (2005) found that when women negotiate, they are less comfortable with ambiguous information, but as information becomes more available, it is essential that women seek to obtain concrete information about *all aspects* of the compensation package (not just about salary) from every available source to enhance the sense of comfort and willingness to anchor the negotiation. It is also recommended that women (as well as men) on both sides of the table openly share the statistics they obtain (even a computer printout from the Internet) with the other party. Transparency is a good thing and can only help to consolidate the objectivity of one's position.

Because research found that gender differences disappear or women outperform their male counterparts under certain conditions, women are advised to (a) treat salary expectation requests as just that, a *request* or *ask* rather than a negotiation (Small, Gelfand, Babcock, & Gettman, 2007); (b) recognize the exponential cost to one's family, as well as oneself, when one fails to negotiate compensation because a job seeker who is offered an $80,000 starting salary and who fails to negotiate the 1% increase negotiated by her male counterpart will have to work an additional 9 years to earn the same amount of money obtained over the male's lifetime (Babcock & Laschever, 2003); and (c) remember that one is indeed powerful having been made an offer in that she has been invited to the dance but has not yet accepted (Small et al., 2007).

21st Century Information Technology and Implications Regarding Strategic Anchoring

While most would agree that the *communication age* is a perfect description of the 21st century, much of that communication takes place through an ever-expanding array of information technology (IT) devices such as laptops, mobile phones, and personal digital assistants (PDAs). Collectively, these ITs have changed the way that organizational citizens think about work processes, not only providing new options for negotiation but also changing the very fabric of how these relationships are negotiated (Lewicki & Dineen, 2002). One consequence of the *world as market effect* (i.e., access to worldwide job postings) is that the entire process from job posting to new hire compensation negotiation to year-end compensation review can transpire *virtually* with limited or even no face-to-face contact among the involved parties. This means that the strategies available to each party will be influenced and limited by the format used. For example, the online job posting process used by many organizations requires job seekers to post their salary expectations *before they receive an interview,* much less a job offer. As a consequence, job seekers are unable to postpone the discussion of their salary expectations and manage the timing of the strategic anchoring as previously advised.

Although it is nice to have an offer before talking numbers, if handled carefully, one's salary expectations (i.e., based on future value relative to the market) can be leveraged against information concerning one's current or past salary history (i.e., which is the figure that employers like to base future salary on instead), which is beneficial strategically since what one *hopes to earn* is a better anchor than what one *currently or used to earn*. The problem is that job seekers asked for this information preoffer tend to ask for too little for the sake of ensuring inclusion in the interview pool (given the tight market during tough economic times). This costly strategy can be avoided by using a *sequential anchoring process* by which the job seeker states online that "salary expectations are commensurate with the market and negotiable, contingent on the job scope and overall compensation package" (some semblance of that message contingent on the space provided) and then on receiving an offer provides a specific anchor in the form of a salary and compensation request. Should one be required to provide a specific figure online, the figure should be based on substantiated market information given the job description, one's experience, education level, and past performance rather than in terms of one's current or past salary. If room permits, the job seeker should add that "salary is negotiable and contingent on the job scope and overall compensation package." Of course, it is important that you obtain as much information as possible about the job's scope, description, location, and so on and related market information before providing any figures (Pinkley, 2010).

Job seekers whose salary histories reflect pay cuts need to raise this issue directly so that employers make the correct attribution rather than assuming that it reflects employee performance or is an appropriate part of the compensation calculation. Furloughs and across-the-board pay cuts are a fact of life during tough economic times. The goal is to minimize the cost of past events as one moves forward.

Negotiations that take place over the computer tend to alleviate cues regarding status and individual differences (Chakravarti, Loewenstein, Morris, Thompson, & Kopelman, 2004). As a result, those who have less status or are more comfortable with less-direct forms of communication (i.e., like women or individuals from some cultures) may prefer to negotiate over the Internet or at least submit their initial compensation requests through this format. In contrast, those with high status or who prefer direct forms of communication should prefer to conduct all compensation negotiations face to face. This means that women may actually benefit from posting information regarding salary requests and anchors over the Internet as long as they have done their homework and use the other strategies suggested for managing the natural tendencies that lead negotiators to underbid themselves. Of course, research suggests that non-task related *schmoozing* that focuses on building rapport, and relationship-focused conversations are grossly lacking in negotiations that occur through e-mail (Morris, Nadler, Kurtzberg, & Thompson, 2002); thus, conversations of this type decrease the impasse rate, improve outcomes, and increase optimism regarding the future relationship. Fortunately, researchers have found that these benefits can be obtained in person or over the phone before the negotiation begins, so those involved in compensation decisions are advised to conduct the interview process through these formats instead whenever possible. When this is not possible, negotiators may still want to attempt to have a brief discussion when the offer is made before they begin the negotiation to establish rapport and obtain the benefits of schmoozing (Morris et al., 2002).

FUTURE RESEARCH NEEDS AS GUIDED BY 21st CENTURY CHALLENGES

The issues raised in the previous section make clear that there is need for future negotiation research to study compensation negotiation strategy dynamics in (a) situations involving electronic (e.g., online) rather than face-to-face communications and (b) situations involving negotiators interacting with counterparts who do not share their own gender or nationality. Such situations characterize the 21st century workplace, and as such, negotiators need to understand how to apply conventionally prescribed negotiation strategies in these situations.

Given the very important role that anchors play in the negotiation of compensation and the increased access that people now have to relevant information of all kinds in the communication age, additional research should be done to determine the various potential anchors that organizations and employers attend to and use in the context of compensation negotiations (Galinsky & Mussweiler, 2001). Numerous variables might predict the selection of anchors, such as the (a) specific type, category, or content of the anchor; (b) presentation or persuasive account associated with the anchor; (c) the strategic viability of the anchor for one's position; (d) the order in which the anchors are accessed; or (e) expected value or model that incorporates all of the anchors. In the context of compensation negotiations, dueling anchors are likely to be the rule, rather than the exception, but there may be individual differences or contextual features that influence the pattern of anchors, including negotiator role, the economic market, technology or form of presentation, and individual differences.

It would be interesting to consider dimensions in addition to that of a "gain-loss" comparison that might account for the impact of strategic anchors in negotiation and underline the meaning that people associate with the outcomes that they obtain. It is quite possible that the meaning that people derive from outcome comparisons are far more complex and that numerous dimensions underlie the sense-making process and the manner in which anchors inform subsequent decisions like the acceptance and rejection of offers, satisfaction with outcome, fairness perceptions, and retention. According to Curhan and his colleagues (Curhan, Elfenbein, & Kilduff, 2009; Curhan, Elfenbein, & Xu, 2006), negotiator perceptions of value are subjective as well as objective and fall into four factors: (a) feelings about *instrumental* outcomes (e.g., outcome satisfaction and perceptions of fairness regarding how the outcomes are divided among the negotiators); (b) feelings about the self or one's *principles* (e.g., saving face and living up to one's own standards); (c) feelings about the negotiation *process* (e.g., perceptions about whether the negotiation process was fair and whether they had voice or the ability to have an impact on the process; and (d) feelings about the *relationship* (e.g., trust and a good foundation for the future). In fact, Curhan, Elfenbein, and Kilduff (2009) found that one year following the negotiation of a job offer, subjective evaluations of the offer rather than economic outcomes predicted compensation satisfaction, job satisfaction, and turnover intention, proving the importance of understanding and managing subjective evaluations such as fairness in the course of compensation negotiations. These dimensions correspond nicely with the four types of interests that Lax and Sebenius (1986) hypothesized might have both intrinsic (negotiators value it in and of itself) and instrumental (negotiators value it because of the implications it may have for other outcomes in the future) to negotiators and may also inform outcome-anchor comparison judgments.

Rather than assuming that the other party will interpret the meaning of their outcomes as intended through a comparison of their outcome to a strategic anchor, it may be more powerful to combine the anchor with an account that communicates, explains, substantiates, or provides the account with the strategic meaning of that account. Given the tendency of negotiators to suspect the motives of others, it would likely be more effective to provide the other party with the desired meaning behind the anchor than it would be to wait and hope that they draw the conclusion intended. If so, a fruitful direction for future research would be to investigate the components of an account needed to have the most effective impact on meaning in negotiation and the variables that influence that effectiveness. For example, it may be that the most effective accounts directly address both of the dimensions (i.e., objective value and subjective value) that the work by Curhan et al. (2006, 2009) and Lax and Sebenius (1986) suggest influence people's perceptions of what they get in return for what we give them. Alternatively, it may be better to provide an anchor as a request without an account. Work conducted by Ert and Bazerman (2010) found that buyers were more likely to accept offers made by computers devoid of communication than from human sellers with whom they communicated since communication increased buyer concerns about seller truthfulness, but that the difference between computer and human sales rates disappeared when the human sellers did not communicate with the buyers. Clearly, further research should be conducted to determine (a) if an account regarding *why* an offer is appropriate enhances counterpart acceptance, (b) the types of accounts that may beneficial or costly, (c) under what conditions an account is beneficial or costly, and (d) whether an account that explains the *why* behind a negotiator's own offer is a distinct construct and perceived to be different from a persuasive argument used to move a counterpart away from his or her own offer.

Neale and Bazerman (1991) have found that people overestimate their value in negotiation when they have limited information. Although Neale and Bazerman (1991) did not look at gender differences, the findings of Bowles et al. (2005) would predict the opposite pattern for women in that they found that when women lack information, they tended to undervalue themselves, but that this pattern dissipated as they obtained objective information. This suggests that the overconfidence bias reported by Neale and Bazerman (1991) may be more normative for men, but that women are more likely to exhibit an *underconfidence bias* when information is lacking, with the accuracy of both genders improving with the availability of objective information. Along with investigating this pattern, we might find that gender differences dissipate with the Internet generation given their Internet search capabilities (i.e., comfort with searching for and obtaining information) and MySpace, Skype, and YouTube networking acumen.

As mentioned, Neale and Bazerman (1991) suggested that negotiators overestimated their value in negotiation when they had limited information. This means that they would predict that negotiators who researched the market to obtain comparative salary data should exhibit *less* of an over-confidence bias and be more concessionary than those not privy to these data. Pinkley and Vandewalle's (2010) work on phantom BATNAs (i.e., potential but as yet unavailable alternatives) suggests that these negotiators should be *more* likely to exhibit an overconfidence bias. They would make this prediction because rather than being presented as specific data points, salary data are presented in the form of ranges and vary significantly across Web sources. While bounded, data in this form are open to self-serving interpretation, and as Messick and Sentis (1979) reminded us, even when motivated by fairness, people have difficulty interpreting information in an unbiased manner. Clearly, additional research is needed to determine how the form in which the information is presented may increase or decrease overestimations and perceptions of value (e.g., means, ranges, and single, person-specific data points). In addition, it would be interesting to see whether reactions to the data change in terms of the medium of interaction (i.e., face to face, over the phone, or electronic forums) (Thompson & Nadler, 2002), and whether the role (i.e., employer or employee/job seeker) and characteristics (e.g., gender, nationality) of the negotiator leads to differential, self-serving interpretations (Messick & Sentis, 1979). Also, it would be interesting to see if the findings of Neale and Bazerman (1991) and Pinkley and Vandewalle (2010) are actually consistent in that negotiators (or at least some of them given gender differences) are so susceptible to ego-enhancing, phantoms that their illusions are unbounded, and thus they are more overconfident in the absence of market information ranges than in the presence of market information ranges.

In summary, this chapter reviewed the negotiation preparation and exchange process strategies touted in the popular press and scholarly literature to be most likely to assist negotiators in their efforts to claim value, create value, and avoid suboptimum agreements. It then examined how these strategies might be used for compensation negotiations by employers, as well as by potential and existing employees. While most of these strategies have been found to have a high degree of generalizability and practical appeal, they have on the whole been identified in research utilizing face-to-face, simulation-based negotiations, comprised of participants who share the same characteristics, such as gender and nationality. It is argued, therefore, that some of these strategies could benefit from further refinement as they are applied in the 21st century workplace environment. Recommendations were made regarding how one exchange process strategy—anchoring the negotiation—might be further refined and developed (a) for female rather than male negotiators given what we know about gender differences and (b) for online rather than face-to-face negotiation exchanges due to what we know about the impact of technology in the context of negotiation. Finally, a number of ideas worthy of future investigation were considered with the hope that readers might be inspired to test these or related relationships in a matter more consistent with 21st century workplace trends so that future negotiators and negotiation scholars can better understand how (if at all) conventionally prescribed negotiation strategies may need to change.

REFERENCES

Amichaei-Hamburger, Y., & McKenna, K. Y. A. (2006). The contract hypothesis reconsidered: Interacting via the internet. *Journal of Computer-Mediated Communication, 11*, 825–843.

Anderson, C., & Shirako, A. (2008). Are individuals' reputations related to their history of behavior? *Journal of Personality and Social Psychology, 94*, 320–333.

Aronson, E., & Linder, D. (1965). Gain and loss of esteem as determinants of interpersonal attractiveness. *Journal of Experimental Social Psychology, 1*, 156–171.

Babcock, L., Gelfand, M., Small, D., & Stayn, H. (2007). Propensity to negotiate: A new look at gender variation in negotiation behavior. In D. De Cremer, M. Zeelenberg, & J. K. Murnighan (Eds.), *Social psychology and economics* (pp. 239–262). Mahwah, NJ: Erlbaum.

Babcock, L., & Laschever, S. (2003). *Women don't ask*. Princeton, NJ: Princeton University Press.

Barada, P. (2008). *Power relationships and negotiation*. Retrieved from http://www.career-advise.Monster.com/salary-negotiation/Power-Relationship-and-Negotiation/home.asp

Bazerman, M. H., Moore, D. A., & Gillespie, J. J. (1999). The human mind as a barrier to wiser environmental agreements. *American Behavioral Scientist, 42*, 1277–1300.

Bazerman, M. H., & Neale, M. A. (1982). Improving negotiator effectiveness under final offer arbitration: Role of selection and training. *Journal of Applied Psychology, 67,* 543–548.

Benko, C., & Weisberg, A. (2007). *Mass career customization: Aligning the workplace with today's nontraditional workforce.* Boston: Harvard Business School Press.

Bottom, W. P., & Paese, P. W. (1999). Judgment accuracy and the asymmetric cost of errors in distributive bargaining. *Group Decision and Negotiation, 8,* 349–364.

Bowles, H. R., Babcock, L., & McGinn, K. L. (2005). Constraints and triggers: Situational mechanics of gender in negotiation. *Journal of Personality and Social Psychology, 89,* 951–965.

Brown, J. G., & Robbennolt, J. K. (2006). Apology in negotiation. In A. Kupfer Schneider & C. Honeyman (Eds.), *The negotiator's field book: The desk reference for the experienced negotiator* (pp. 425–434). Chicago: American Bar Association.

Buelens, M., & Van Poucke, D. (2004). Determinants of a negotiator's initial opening offer. *Journal of Business and Psychology, 19,* 23–35.

Chakravarti, A., Loewenstein, J., Morris, M., Thompson, L., & Kopelman, S. (2004). At a loss for words: Negotiators disadvantaged in technical knowledge are vulnerable to verbal domination and economic losses as a function of communication. *Organizational Behavior and Human Decision Processes, 98,* 28–38.

Cialdini, R. B. (2001) *Influence: Science & practice* (4th ed.). Boston: Allyn & Bacon.

Cialdini, R. B., & Goldstein, N. J. (2004). Social influence: Compliance and conformity. *Annual Review of Psychology, 55,* 591–621.

Cohen, T., Leonardelli, G., J., & Thompson, L. (2010). T*he agreement bias in negotiation: Teams facilitate impasse.* Paper presented at the International Association of Conflict Management, Annual Meeting, June, Boston.

Colquitt, J. A., Conlon, D. E., Wesson, M. J., Porter, C. O. L. H., & Ng, K. Y. (2001). Justice at the millennium: A meta-analytic review of 25 years of organizational justice research. *Journal of Applied Psychology, 86,* 425–445.

Curhan, J. R., Elfenbein, H. A., & Kilduff, G. J. (2009). Getting off on the right foot: Subjective value versus economic value in predicting longitudinal job outcomes from job offer negotiations. *Journal of Applied Psychology, 94,* 524–534.

Curhan, J. R., Elfenbein, H. A., & Xu, H. (2006). What people value when they negotiate? Mapping the domain of subjective value in negotiation. *Journal of Personality and Social Psychology, 91,* 493–512.

Dawson, R. (2006). *Secrets of power salary negotiating: Inside secrets from master negotiator.* New Jersey: Career Press.

Ert, E., & Bazerman, M. H. (2010). If you want to sell, sell. Don't talk: When talking to buyers increases skepticism. Paper presented at the International Association of Conflict Management Annual Meeting, June, Boston.

Fisher, R., Ury, W., & Patton, B. (1991). *Getting to yes: Negotiating agreement without giving in* (2nd ed.). New York: Penguin.

Friedman, R. (1994). *Front stage, backstage: The dramatic structure of labor negotiations.* Cambridge, MA: MIT Press.

Galin, A., Gross, M., & Gosalker, G. (2007). E-negotiation versus face-to-face negotiation what has changed—if anything? *Computers in Human Behavior, 23,* 787–797.

Galinsky, A., & Mussweiler, T. (2001). First offers as anchors: The role of perspective taking and negotiator focus. *Journal of Personality and Social Psychology, 81,* 657–669.

Galinsky, A., Seiden, V. L., Kim, P. H., & Medvec, V. H. (2002). The dissatisfaction of having your first offer accepted: The role of counterfactual thinking in negotiations. *Personality and Social Psychology Bulletin, 28,* 271–283.

Gerhart, B., & Rynes, S. (1991). Determinants and consequences of salary negotiations by male and female MBA graduates. *Journal of Applied Psychology, 76,* 256–262.

Goates, N. (2008). *Reputation as a basis for trust: Social information, emotional state, and trusting behavior.* Paper presented at the Academy of Management annual meetings.

Gomez-Mejia, L. R., Berrone P., & Franco-Santos, M. (2010). *Compensation and organizational performance: Theory, research, and practice.* New York: Sharp.

Hensher, D. A., & Johnson, L. W. 1981. *Applied discrete-choice modeling.* London: Croom Helm.

Jost, J. (2010). *Finding job satisfaction: Myths and tips for employees.* http://www.salary.com/articles/ArticleDetail.asp?part=par599

Kaman, V. S., & Hartel, C. E. (1994). Gender differences in anticipated pay negotiation strategies and outcomes. *Journal of Business and Psychology, 9,* 183–197.

Kemp, K. E., & Smith, W. P. (1994). Information exchange, toughness, and integrative bargaining: The roles of explicit cues and perspective-taking. *International Journal of Conflict Management, 5,* 5–21.

Kim, P. H., Pinkley, R. L., & Fragale, A. (2005). Power dynamics in negotiation. *Academy of Management Review, 30,* 799–822.

Kipnis, D., & Schmidt, S. M. (1983). An influence perspective on bargaining within organizations. In M. Bazerman & R. Lewicki (Eds.), *Negotiating in organizations* (pp. 303–319). Beverly Hills, CA: Sage.

Kolb, D. M., & Williams, J. (2001). Breakthrough bargaining. *Harvard Business Review, 79,* 89–97.

Komorita, S. S., Sheposh, J. P., & Braver, S. L. 1968. Power, the use of power, and cooperative choices in a two person game. *Journal of Personality and Social Psychology, 8,* 134–142.

Krannich, R., & Krannich C. (2005). *Salary negotiation tips for professionals.* Manasses Park, VA: Impact.

Kray, L., Reb, J., Galinsky, A., & Thompson, L. (2004). Stereotype reactance at the bargaining table: The effect of stereotype activation and power on claiming and creating value. *Personality and Social Psychology Bulletin, 30,* 399–411.

Kwon, S., & Weingart, L. R. (2004). Unilateral concessions from the other party: Concession behavior, attributions, and negotiation judgments. *Journal of Applied Psychology, 89,* 263–278.

Lax, D., & Sebenius, J. (1986). *The manager as negotiator: Bargaining for cooperation and competitive gain.* New York: Free Press.

Lax, D., & Sebenius, J. (2006). *3-D negotiation.* Boston: Harvard Business School.

Lewicki, R. J., Barry, B., & Saunders, D. M. (2010). *Negotiation* (6th ed.). Boston: McGraw-Hill/Irwin.

Lewicki, R. J., & Dineen, B. R. (2002). Negotiating in virtual organizations. In R. Heneman & D. Greenberger (Eds.), *Human resource management in virtual organizations* (pp. 263–294). New York: Wiley.

Lim, S. G., & Murnighan, J. K. (1994). Phases, deadlines, and the bargaining process. *Organizational Behavior and Human Decision Processes, 58,* 153–1171.

Locke, E., & Latham, G. (1984). *Goal setting: A motivational technique that works!* Englewood Cliffs, NJ: Prentice Hall.

Magee, J. C., Galinsky, A. D., & Gruenfeld, D. (2007). Power, propensity to negotiate, and moving first in competitive interactions. *Personality and Social Psychology Bulletin, 33,* 200–212.

Malhotra, D., & Bazerman, M. H. (2007). *Negotiation genius.* New York: Bantam Books.

Merryman, A. (2010). *Organizational mutiny: Employee experiences in leader oustings.* Paper presented at International Association of Conflict Management Conference, June, Boston.

Messick, D. M., & Sentis, K. P. (1979). Fairness and preference. *Journal of Experimental Social Psychology, 15,* 418–434.

Milovich, G., & Newman. J. (2004). *Compensation* (8th ed.). Boston: McGraw-Hill/Irwin.

Moore, D. A. (2004). The unexpected benefits of final deadlines in negotiation. *Journal of Experimental Social Psychology, 40,* 121–127.

Moore, D. A., Kurtzberg, T., Thompson, L., & Morris, M. W. (1999). Long and short routes to success in electronically mediated negotiations: Group affiliations and good vibrations. *Organizational Behavior and Human Decision Processes, 77,* 22–43.

Morris, M. W., Nadler, J., Kurtzberg, T., & Thompson, L. (2002). Schmooze or lose: Social friction and lubrication in email negotiations. *Group Dynamics: Theory, Research, and Practice, 6,* 89–100.

My Career. (2007). *Mastering the art of online job applications.* Retrieved from http://content.mycareer.com.au/advice-research/search/mastering-the-art-of-online-job-applications.aspx

Neale, M. A., & Bazerman, M. H. 1991. *Cognition and rationality in negotiation.* New York: Free Press.

Pinkley, R. L. (2009). *Building trust and successful negotiation handbook: A gain-gain approach to profitable negotiation.* Dallas, Texas: Collins Center Press, Southern Methodist University.

Pinkley, R. L. (2010). Managing negotiations: Pay attention to the process and the issues. *Leadership Excellence Magazine: The Magazine of Leadership Development, Managerial Effectiveness, and Organizational Productivity, 27*(9), 17–20.

Pinkley, R. L., Griffith, T., & Northcraft, G. B. (1995). Fixed pie-a la mode: Information availability, information processing, and the negotiation of sub-optimal agreements. *Organizational Behavior and Human Decision Processes, 62*(1), 101–112.

Pinkley, R. L., Neale, M. A., & Bennett, R. J. (1994). The impact of alternatives to settlement in dyadic negotiation. *Organizational Behavior and Human Decision Processes, 57,* 97–116.

Pinkley, R. L., & Northcraft, G. B. (2000). *Get paid what you're worth: The expert negotiators' guide to salary and compensation.* New York: St. Martin's Press.

Pinkley, R. L., & Vandewalle, D. (2010). *Reconciling the way things ought to be, with the way things are: The role of real and phantom BATNAs in dyadic negotiation.* Cox Working Papers Collection, Southern Methodist University, Dallas, TX.

Pruitt, D. G. (1981). *Negotiation behavior.* New York: Academic Press.

Raiffa, H. (1982). *The art and science of negotiation.* Cambridge, MA: Belknap.

Rubin, J. Z., & Brown, B. R. (1975). *The social psychology of bargaining and negotiation.* New York: Academic Press.

Shakespeare, W. (1599). *As you like it.* Act 2, scene 7, 139–143.

Shapiro, D. L., & Bies, R. J. (1994). Threats, bluffs, and disclaimers in negotiation. *Organizational Behavior and Human Decision Processes, 60,* 14–35.

Simon, H. (1955). A behavioral model of rational choice. *Quarterly Journal of Economics, 69*, 99–118.

Sivanathan, N., & Galinsky, A. (2007). *Power and overconfidence.* Paper presented at the International Association of Conflict Management Meeting, July, Budapest, Hungary.

Small, D. A., Gelfand, M., Babcock, L., & Gettman, H. (2007). Who goes to the bargaining table? The influence of gender and framing on the initiation of negotiation. *Journal of Personality and Social Psychology, 93*, 600–613.

Stillenger, C., Epelbaum, M., Keltner, D., and Ross, L. (1990). *The "reactive devaluation" barrier to conflict resolution.* Working paper, Stanford University, Palo Alto, CA.

Tajima, M., & Fraser, N. M. (2001). Logrolling procedure for multi-issue negotiation. *Group Decision and Negotiation, 10*, 217–235.

Thompson, L. (1991). Information exchange in negotiation. *Journal of Experimental Social Psychology, 27*, 161–179.

Thompson, L. (2005). *The heart and mind of the negotiator.* Englewood Cliffs, NJ: Prentice Hall.

Thompson, L., & Hastie, R. (1990). Social perception in negotiation. *Organizational Behavior and Human Decision Processes, 47*, 98–123.

Thompson, L., & Hrebec, D. (1996). Lose-lose agreements in interdependent decision making. *Psychological Bulletin, 120*, 396–409.

Thompson, L., & Lowenstein, G. (1992). Egocentric interpretations of fairness and interpersonal conflict. *Organizational Behavior and Human Decision Processes, 51*, 176–197.

Thompson, L., & Nadler, J. (2002). Negotiating via information technology: Theory and application. *Journal of Social Issues, 58*, 109–124.

Tinsley, C. H., Cambria, J. J., & Kupfer-Schneider, A. (2006). Reputations in negotiation. In A. Kupfer Schneider & C. Honeyman (Eds.), *The negotiator's field book: The desk reference for the experienced negotiator* (pp. 203–214). Chicago: American Bar Association.

Towers Watson (2010). *From recession to recovery: How far, how fast, how well prepared?* New York: Towers Watson.

U.S. Bureau of Labor Statistics (2004). *Number of jobs held, labor market activity, and earnings growth among younger baby boomers: Recent results from a longitudinal survey.* Retrieved from http://www.bls.gov/nls/nlsy79r20.pdf

U.S. Department of Labor, Bureau of Labor Statistics. (2009). *Employment and earning. 2009 annual averages and the monthly labor review.* http://www.bls.gov/cew/cewbultn09.htm

Valley, K. L., White, S. B., & Iacobucci, D. (1992). The process of assisted negotiations: A network analysis. *Group Decision ad Negotiation, 2*, 117–135.

Vogt, P. (2005). 6 answers interviewers need to hire you. http://artbistro.monster.com/careers/articles/8868-6-answers-interviewers-need-to-hire-you?print=true

VonGlinow, M. A., Shapiro, D. L., & Brett, J. M. (2004). Can we talk, and should we? Managing emotional conflict in multicultural teams. *The Academy of Management Review, 29*, 578–592.

Weingart, L. R., Bennett, R. J., & Brett, J. M. (1993). The impact of consideration of issues and motivational orientation on group negotiation process and outcome. *Journal of Personality and Social Psychology, 78*, 504–517.

5

The Effects of Subjective Value on Future Consequences: Implications for Negotiation Strategies

Hillary Anger Elfenbein and Jared R. Curhan

INTRODUCTION

Conventional wisdom holds that the objective value (OV) of a deal—that is, the explicit set of terms regarding the agreement—is the barometer of successful negotiation performance, bar none. By contrast, how one feels afterward is considered a fleeting emotion, subject to heuristics and biases. Offering a counterpoint to this rationalist assumption, in this chapter and elsewhere we maintain descriptively that negotiators care about how they feel and about how their counterparts feel. Going a step further, we maintain prescriptively that negotiators *should* care. Simply put, these subjective feelings during and after negotiations have objective consequences. The formal term we use for these feelings is *subjective value* (SV)—defined by Curhan, Elfenbein, and Xu (2006, p. 494) as the "social, perceptual, and emotional consequences of a negotiation."

The present chapter's purpose is fourfold. First, we review theory and recent evidence documenting that SV not only matters to negotiators but also can matter in some cases more than OV. Second, we describe some specific negotiator actions, or tactics, that existing research suggests are associated with promoting or depleting a negotiation counterpart's SV. Third, we identify two trends in the 21st century workplace that seem likely to strengthen the need for negotiators to pay attention to SV. These trends are: (a) the so-called flattening of hierarchical organizations and (b) the increased frequency of communication via "lean" channels such as e-mail and other text-only formats. We refer to these formats as lean because text-based communication limits participants from accessing the range of nonverbal cues, which carry additional affective meaning to enhance the appropriate regulation of social interaction (for a review, see Elfenbein, 2007). While describing each of these trends, we attempt to explain why they are likely to strengthen the need for the negotiation process to enhance counterparts' SV. Fourth, and last, we identify research questions about SV that would be valuable to examine in future work, as guided by the dynamics of the 21st century workplace.

WHAT IS SUBJECTIVE VALUE?

In contrast to *objective economic outcomes*, which are the explicit terms or products of a negotiation (also called *objective value*, or OV), *social psychological outcomes* refer to the attitudes and perceptions of those involved (Oliver, Balakrishnan, & Barry, 1994; Thompson, 1990). Within these social psychological outcomes, SV refers to those ends that a negotiator actually desires to achieve. In trying to map out the terrain of SV, we and our colleagues conducted a series of studies that identified inductively and validated the importance of a broad range of negotiators' psychologically valued outcomes.

Negotiators Care About SV

In conducting this empirical research, we started with the most basic question: "What do people value when they negotiate?" (Curhan et al., 2006). Participants included graduate students enrolled in negotiations courses, professional negotiation practitioners, and even community members we recruited outside grocery stores in the Boston area. Rather than limiting respondents to preconceived categories, we provided a broad definition of negotiation ("any situation in which people are trying to accomplish a goal and have to communicate with at least one other person in order to achieve that goal") alongside an open-ended opportunity for participants to generate examples of their own valued outcomes in recent negotiations in both business and personal contexts. To encourage a comprehensive listing, 16 blank spaces were provided, and participants were invited to continue on the back side of the page if desired. After listing each item, respondents also rated how important that particular item was to them. Taken together, our goal in the study was to access the lay theories negotiators hold regarding what it means to "succeed" in a negotiation.

What we found was surprising. Participants reported an extremely diverse range of negotiation goals, with 20 different distinct categories that emerged. Interestingly, although participants more frequently mentioned factors associated with their objective negotiation outcomes—that is, terms of the agreement that were either quantifiable (e.g., money or delivery time) or not readily quantifiable (e.g., high quality)—the importance ratings of these objective outcome terms were in fact no higher than the stated importance the subjective factors they named, such as relationship quality, fairness, listening, apology for wrongdoing, maintaining one's morality, and having positive feelings. Further, although tangible terms of agreements appeared more frequently than any other single factor, in their open-ended responses, 20% of participants did not mention any tangible outcomes at all. These findings suggest that subjective negotiation outcomes may be dramatically underrated in their real-world importance.

We continued this work by asking professional negotiators to sort into factors the 20 categories that emerged from these open-ended responses. Applying multidimensional scaling to these negotiators' responses led to a four-factor model of SV—for which we wrote and validated questionnaire items to establish the psychometric properties of convergent, discriminant, and criterion validity for the resulting 16-item scale.[1] The four factors in the model of SV encompass distinct yet related constructs: *Instrumental SV* is the subjective perception that the economic outcome is beneficial, balanced, and consistent with principles of legitimacy and precedent. *Self SV* comprises losing face versus feeling competent and satisfied that one has behaved appropriately. *Process SV* includes the perception that one has been heard and treated justly, and that the process was efficient. *Relationship SV* involves positive impressions, trust, and a solid foundation for working together in the future. The third and fourth factors together form a broader construct of *rapport*. As such, the umbrella construct of SV represents an integrative framework that connects existing lines of negotiation research on related topics, such as trust, justice, relationships, and outcome satisfaction.

WHY DOES SUBJECTIVE VALUE MATTER?

Theoretical Arguments

There are at least three reasons why SV can be important to negotiators (Curhan et al., 2006). First, SV is a good in itself. Feelings of satisfaction, confidence, pride, and connection with others are intrinsically rewarding (Lax & Sebenius, 1986; Miller, 1999; Mills, 1940), beyond any extrinsic value that may result. We seek these feelings for ourselves, and if we care about the person with whom we are negotiating, we seek these feelings for others as well.

Second, one's SV is often the best-available intuition that negotiators have about their own OV. It can be difficult, if not impossible, in real-world settings to obtain enough direct information to create a detailed analysis of one's performance. It is critical how to know whether you succeeded in a negotiation, and one's subjective sense of performance is often the best-available proxy. As such, SV can influence learning and future behaviors. However, we note that these performance intuitions are often inaccurate and flawed, given that information about our performance tends to be noisy, challenging to access, and potentially biased when provided by counterparts. Our own empirical findings suggest the imperfect nature of SV as a performance predictor—for example, we typically find only modest-size partial correlations between instrumental SV and objective outcomes themselves ($r = .26$; Curhan et al., 2006). On a descriptive level, real-world negotiators tend to use SV as a diagnosis of their performance—even if, on a prescriptive level given this modest association, there is a risk that experience can be a lousy teacher if one's conclusions about that experience are flawed.

Third, the SV resulting from one negotiation may feed back, typically in a positive direction, into future economic outcomes. On theoretical grounds, we propose that SV is an asset that can be "cashed in" at a future time to extract OV. This is true both for the SV that one experiences as well as the SV that one provides to others. For oneself, those who feel that they have succeeded instrumentally in past negotiations may experience greater confidence and self-efficacy (Sullivan, O'Connor, & Burris, 2006)—rather than feeling complacent. Many negotiators would benefit from the corresponding increase in their motivation, perseverance, and aspirations going forward—although confidence can be a drawback when taken to the extreme of overconfidence (e.g., Hayward, Shepherd, & Griffin, 2006). The SV that one elicits in negotiation counterparts is also a valuable asset. Negotiators are more willing to compromise with counterparts they know and like (Druckman & Broome, 1991). By contrast, being seen as focusing only on one's own needs can invoke defensive behaviors from counterparts (Tinsley, O'Connor, & Sullivan, 2002). Thus, high SV can lead a counterpart to provide more slack to a negotiator and to interpret more charitably the negotiator's ambiguous behavior. A climate of positive relationship satisfaction can be flattering and even disarming to a counterpart, who may underestimate the negotiator and reveal valuable information. Finally, those who develop the smooth interpersonal functioning associated with relationship and process SV are more likely over time to learn their counterpart's preferred negotiation style, for example, the type of arguments the counterpart will find convincing and which strategies and techniques tend to be successful at eliciting concessions with minimal conflict (Valley, Neale, & Mannix, 1995). At the dyadic level, SV may improve the climate for integrative bargaining. It can serve as a shared resource to be leveraged at a future time to create value for the pair—by enhancing genuine concern for one's counterpart, which is important according to the dual-concern model (Pruitt & Rubin, 1986); by increasing negotiators' commitment and sheer endurance to meet the challenge of reaching an effective integrative settlement; and by preventing disruptive tactics and encouraging information sharing, reciprocity, creative problem-solving mindsets, charitable interpretations of ambiguous behaviors, familiarity with counterparts' preferred influence styles, and efficient time management, which are factors crucial for reaching efficient negotiation settlements (Barry & Oliver, 1996; Bazerman, Curhan, & Moore, 2001; Lind & Tyler, 1988; Pruitt & Rubin, 1986; Tinsley et al., 2002; Valley et al., 1995). Developing closer, more trusting relationships can create a comfortable environment within which to share information and smooth over the rough edges of bargaining.

Empirical Data

Several of our empirical studies have validated this third assertion—that is, high SV from a negotiation is associated subsequently with more favorable objective outcomes. To state this differently, SV matters not only privately to negotiators but also has tangible positive future consequences.

Our studies suggested, intriguingly, the understated value of SV. Two studies examined master's level students taking place in simulated negotiation exercises, and a third examined the long-term consequences of negotiations regarding participants' actual full-term employment contracts.

We examined (Curhan et al., 2006) the consequences of SV following a mixed-motive negotiation simulation conducted among students in an introductory negotiations course at the master's in business administration (MBA) level. In this class—in which bargaining outcomes were the sole determinant of students' grades—there was a final exercise for which their recorded preferences determined the assignment of a teammate in a team-against-team negotiation. Students who experienced higher SV, as reported immediately after their earlier mixed-motive exercise, subsequently reported a greater preference for working together in a future cooperative task in which part of their actual course grade was at stake. By contrast, participants' actual objective outcome of the negotiation had no such impact on teammate preference ratings. In the second test conducted among the same participants, at the end of the semester they recorded semibehavioral intentions in the form of their opinions about their counterpart's worthiness for future professional contact. To enhance realism, we used questions designed to sample from the type of networking activities common to the alumni of highly rated MBA programs (e.g., Would you want to have this person as your business partner? How likely is it that you will seek to remain in contact with this person? If you were considering whether or not to join a firm, and you found out that this person works there, would that make you more or less likely to join?). For these ratings of behavioral intentions, participants who had reported greater SV earlier in the semester subsequently expressed greater intentions to maintain a positive professional connection with their counterpart. We found it particularly noteworthy that objective outcomes did not show an association in any of these analyses. However, there was a clear influence from subjective outcomes that endured over time.

We followed up this research by examining the consequences of SV when the same negotiators worked together on multiple occasions (Curhan, Elfenbein, & Eisenkraft, 2010). In this study, negotiators took part in a two-round mixed-motive simulation and maintained the same roles and partners for both. Supporting the value of SV, we found that positive feelings resulting from one negotiation can be economically rewarding in a second negotiation. Negotiators claimed more OV in their second negotiation if they had reported greater SV following the first negotiation. Further, negotiation dyads created more joint value in their second negotiation if partners had reported greater average SV in the first negotiation. In both cases, the effects were significant for the Instrumental and Relationship factors of SV, as well as for global SV as a whole, even after controlling for OV. In this respect, our study demonstrates the economic value of relational capital, which theorists have argued is a resource for negotiators (Gelfand, Major, Raver, Nishii, & O'Brien, 2006). This first study provided suggestive evidence that subjective impressions may pay off economically in subsequent negotiations—and can serve as more than a figurative pat on the back or a mere consolation prize for a meager settlement. In addition to achieving better subsequent economic outcomes, negotiators who experienced greater SV in the first round reported a greater desire to negotiate again with their counterparts. By contrast, objective performance had no such predictive power, which is striking because, rationally, one should prefer to negotiate with counterparts against whom one has performed objectively well. This differed from the result reported previously, in that SV predicted not only future cooperative interactions with their counterpart (Curhan et al., 2006) (i.e., to sit on the same side of the table, so to speak) but also negotiators' willingness to enter into further mixed-motive interactions (Curhan et al., 2010) (i.e., to sit on the opposite side of the table).

Finally, we tested the theory that SV can have important long-term consequences in a real-world setting (Curhan, Elfenbein, & Kilduff, 2009) by examining the OV and SV achieved by MBA students while negotiating the terms of their full-time employment job offers and using these measures to predict their subsequent job attitudes and turnover intentions as employees one year later.

This field study was unique for attempting to craft a controlled measurement of OV in a high-stakes real-world negotiation. Respondents accepted jobs across a wide range of industries and positions, yet the study retained a relatively high degree of control in that respondents were all graduating at the same time from the same elite degree program. As the first measure, graduating students provided their initial compensation in terms of their *base salary* (i.e., paid continuously over 12 months) plus their *other guaranteed compensation* (e.g., bonuses, relocation allowances, tuition reimbursement, and other commitments). Total salary was a worthwhile control variable in light of a number of studies that indicated a link between pay and job attitudes (e.g., Williams, McDaniel, & Nguyen, 2006). Second, students listed in free response all of the concessions that they received during their job offer negotiation, to serve as a measure of their OV. We (this chapter's two authors) coded these into 15 different categories and found, consistent with the original inductive study described, that these desired outcomes represented a diverse range from salary and signing bonus to less financially tangible concessions on starting dates, vacation time, additional job training, and even the ability to delay making a decision about the job offer. Participants were then asked to monetize their concessions with the following question: "In order to assess the approximate dollar value of what you negotiated, please estimate the *minimum* amount of money you would be willing to accept (in dollars) in exchange for forfeiting all concessions you received in your negotiation." Given that it is challenging to quantify objectively the value of a negotiation settlement outside a laboratory setting, this measure provided a metric for the *economic value* of concessions. Importantly, this measure also ensured that participants were aware of their own economic value. Third, students reported their SV resulting from the job negotiation. One year later, these respondents were now alumni of the MBA program, and we surveyed again those who were working full time at the same jobs for which they negotiated these settlements. They repeated all of the original measures of OV and SV to describe the negotiation that had taken place a year earlier. As suggestive evidence of the validity of these measures, test–retest reliability was fairly robust at .72 for OV and .74 for SV.

As the key outcome measures of our study, alumni also reported three different types of job attitudes: compensation satisfaction, job satisfaction, and turnover intentions. These factors have potentially far-reaching implications for both employees and the organizations that hire them (Bateman & Organ, 1983; Currall, Towler, Judge, & Kohn, 2005; Osterman, 1987; Williams et al., 2006) and make the results of this study relevant beyond the field of negotiations research. The results showed that SV from job offer negotiations predicted greater subsequent compensation satisfaction and job satisfaction and lower subsequent turnover intention. Analyses controlled for potentially extraneous factors such as sex, predegree base salary, positive and negative trait affect, job industries and job functions, as well as expectations of future interaction with the particular counterpart involved with the job negotiation. Surprisingly, negotiators' objective outcomes had no apparent effects on these long-term measures of job attitudes—a particularly provocative finding given the high economic stakes involved with these job negotiations. It seemed striking to us that the SV that incoming employees achieved during their job offer negotiations significantly predicted compensation satisfaction, job satisfaction, and turnover intention measured over one full year after the negotiations had taken place. During this time, participants presumably were exposed to a wide range of other intervening factors that could have affected their job attitudes, such as the characteristics of their jobs, their interactions with supervisors and coworkers, and the success of the company. Thus, our results demonstrated not only the robustness of SV but also the halo that it casts over future consequences in a real-world setting with high stakes.

Taking together the evidence presented, we argue that SV is highly valued by negotiators, surprisingly robust over time, and in our initial studies seem to be predictive of important long-term consequences—in some cases, even more predictive than OV. In spite of the considerable enthusiasm that has developed around social psychological outcomes in negotiation, empirical work has been relatively sparse in comparison to that on economic outcomes—indeed, according to a relatively recent review article, subjective factors appear in less than one quarter of published articles on negotiation (Mestdagh & Buelens, 2003). We hope that this description of the field becomes merely historical as researchers increasingly incorporate SV into their studies of negotiations.

HOW CAN NEGOTIATORS ENHANCE THEIR COUNTERPART'S SUBJECTIVE VALUE?

Given the substantial benefits of SV, how does one create it? And how does one do so without undermining one's OV? Our next studies attempted to unpack these challenging questions. Given the early stage within the research program, some of the following advice is grounded in empirical data but some is necessarily speculative.

In the first of these studies (Elfenbein, Curhan, Eisenkraft, Shirako, & Baccaro, 2008), we found evidence that certain individuals consistently felt greater SV after their negotiations, and that certain individuals consistently brought out greater SV in their counterparts. We used Kenny's

(1994) social relations model (SRM), which is a theoretical model designed for understanding how individuals influence the unfolding of inherently dyadic interactions. After all, in a negotiation, "it takes two to tango." The SRM requires that participants participate in a series of interactions while continually switching partners, and it uses specialized statistical algorithms to examine the cross-negotiation consistency of each individual. Using the "round-robin" design of the SRM, students in an introductory MBA-level negotiations class were assigned to groups of five, in which each person took part in a one-on-one mixed-motive exercise separately with each other person in the group. The SRM analyses provided coefficients that can be interpreted akin to an R-squared statistic. The results showed that a significant 6.4% of the variance in SV resulted from individual-level consistency in negotiators' experiences, and 12.5% of the variance resulted from individual-level consistency in the experience that negotiators tended to elicit in others. This is consistent with other evidence that there is individual-level consistency in the emotional states that people tend to elicit in others—known as *affective presence*—in addition to individual differences in the trait affect that people tend to experience themselves (Eisenkraft & Elfenbein, 2010).

Armed with these findings showing that some individuals systematically feel and evoke more SV than others, we conducted a follow-up study in which we videotaped negotiators taking part in similar round-robin designs in an attempt to identify the specific actions and tactics associated with systematically increasing and depleting the SV of others (Elfenbein, Curhan, Eisenkraft, Shirako, & Brown, 2010). We coded these videotapes and the resulting verbal transcripts by examining the specific negotiation tactics that individuals used to move the process forward, while also examining more generally the negotiators' use of language and even their nonverbal behavior. We discuss findings from this study further in the chapter.

In this chapter, we have made the point that there is value to both the degree of SV that a negotiator experiences as well as the degree of SV that the negotiator instills in others. From this point forward, in which we discuss prescriptive steps for increasing SV, our focus is on the latter of these two sides of the coin—that is, how much SV each of us can bring out in our negotiation counterparts. The reasons for this are both theoretical and empirical. First, theoretically, the feelings that one tends to have on a chronic basis are central to the psychological notion of *personality*. Accordingly, on an empirical basis, we find that negotiators' own SV tends to be at least moderately associated with enduring personality traits such as positive affect, extraversion, agreeableness, and self-esteem (Elfenbein et al., 2008). Further, outwardly observable tactics and behaviors in our research do not seem to be strongly predictive of negotiators' own SV (Elfenbein et al., 2010)—which further suggests that the root cause of the SV a negotiator tends to experience is at least in part dispositional, rather than strictly a matter of situational factors and controllable behavior that unfold over the course of the negotiation. The popularity of lengthy psychotherapeutic treatments suggests that changes to one's fundamental personality traits are not as simple as quick prescriptive recommendations that would be possible in a book chapter. However, for a discussion about influences on negotiators' own SV—including some inwardly controllable processes as well as factors associated with the negotiation setting—we direct readers to Curhan and Brown's (in press) recent comprehensive review.

There is relatively little firm empirical evidence for prescriptive actions to enhance a negotiation counterpart's SV. For this reason, the advice provided is necessarily speculative. We consider several specific actions and tactics that hold promise for enhancing negotiators' ability to bring out the greatest SV in others (for additional discussion of others, see Curhan & Brown, in press). After all, a counterpart's high SV predicts a greater willingness to work together again, to cooperate and forgo competitive tactics, greater value creation in subsequent negotiations, and greater commitment to the long-term professional relationship. For a detailed review of existing research with implications for increasing SV, see the work of Curhan and Brown (in press).

Identifying Subjectively Valued Outcomes

Although it may seem obvious, we suggest that the first step to increasing a counterpart's SV is to attempt to identify the particular outcomes that he or she subjectively values, however imperfect such an attempt may be. This is a matter of expanding the typical preparation—for which we counsel negotiators to identify the issues valued by their counterpart—by emphasizing the need to include subjectively valued issues in this process. One way to be systematic in doing so is to use the questionnaire items of the Subjective Value Inventory (SVI; Curhan et al., 2006) as a guide that can prompt a negotiator to think about whether each element of SV is a priority to the counterpart in any particular setting. Ultimately, this task involves communication and brainstorming to try to understand what the other party wants. Why are they at the negotiating table? What are the particular life goals or problems that they seek to enhance through reaching a negotiated settlement? Who are the constituents observing the negotiation whose opinions are important to the counterpart? A rich example of this kind of analysis can be seen in histories of the real-world negotiation setting for the final contract renewal of the television show *Frasier* (e.g., Subramanian, 2001). Whereas the company Paramount producing the show was interested in earning as much money as possible with the contract, the show's star, Kelsey Grammer, was more interested in the duration of the contact to ensure that *Frasier* tied the record for the longest-running character in television history. Grammer was also interested in repairing the pride that was damaged by his perception that the NBC network had not sufficiently appreciated the show's many achievements. The second step is trying to increase these subjectively valued outcomes once you know what they are—which is easier said than done.

Assess Whether There Is a Trade-off of SV Versus OV

We distinguish between two types of advice based on whether there is a particular kind of trade-off involved: In this negotiation, does a person's SV need to come at the expense of that person's OV? The fact that we pose this trade-off as a question rather than a certainty is intentional. Conventional wisdom might presume that the only way to make another person satisfied with a negotiated settlement is to increase that person's claimed value. However, in every single research study that we have conducted on the topic of SV—including all of the articles reviewed—we found that the association between individuals' OV and instrumental SV is small and often nonsignificant. That is, negotiators often have only relatively modest accuracy regarding the OV that they achieve. Thus, even if their satisfaction were based purely on their outcome, they know their outcome only imperfectly. This convergence is likely to be particularly weak when information about typical deal terms is difficult to come by, and therefore intuition about one's OV tends to be modest at best. Thus, we argue that, more often than negotiators may realize, the expected trade-off of SV versus OV can be unnecessary and strictly perceptual—that is, their imperfect convergence makes it perfectly possible to increase one for the counterpart without giving away the other for oneself. Of course, in any given negotiation context, the four distinct factors of SV can correspond with OV to a different extent—or even in different directions—so that the advice that follows is necessarily general.

Manage Perceptions When There Is No Trade-off

For accomplishing this, the most important action that a negotiator can take is to frame the favorable nature of settlement to the other party. That is, it is important to explain why the other party should see this particular deal as appropriate and, indeed, as beneficial. This tactic involves being as explicit as possible with a counterpart regarding the norms and explanations for the proposed settlement. For example, in selling a car or home, an analysis of book values or comparable transactions could be presented to show the favorable nature of the current offer. Of course, this tactic can be used in a manipulative way—for example, by the car salesperson who keeps repeating that you are getting a great deal—but it can also be used authentically. Ideally, negotiators can probe in conversation with their counterparts to reveal which norms or standards they find most relevant and can make a calm yet convincing case for the norms that would suggest that the outcome achieved is a fair one. Put simply, if you provide your reasoning, then the other party cannot see you as unreasonable. As a consequence, if you can present yourself as reasonable, then your counterpart is likely to see the resulting deal as balanced and legitimate. Going one step further, it is valuable to help the other party to see the deal not only as balanced but also as highly favorable to their side. We find empirically that negotiators' instrumental SV tends to be more sensitive to a partner's loss than it is to the negotiator's own gain (Elfenbein et al., 2008). Note that this is possible mathematically due to the imperfect negative correlation of outcomes in a mixed-motive scenario—and suggests, intriguingly, that we are better at tracking the value of concessions from the other party's perspective than from our own. This may be an extension of the fixed-pie bias, in that we assume that losses to the other party come at our gain and thus focus on the former when evaluating the favorability of a deal. This means, prescriptively, that it might be worthwhile to let your counterpart see clearly when you are bending. Of course, this tactic can also be used in an authentic versus manipulative way—for example, by the car salesperson who pretends no longer to be able to feed his or her family. Unless your counterpart knows the true efforts you have made to accommodate his or her concessions, then it is hard for those concessions to be fully appreciated. The act of conceding may itself have a limited effect on evoking goodwill from others. As a guiding principle to this prescriptive advice, realizing that negotiators achieve only imperfect accuracy regarding their settlements opens the possibility for advocating that these settlements are attractive and appropriate. In sum, when the SV-versus-OV trade-off is a false one, there is no downside for anyone in enhancing the other party's SV.

Acknowledge When the SV-Versus-OV Trade-off Is Real

Sometimes, however, there is a real and unavoidable trade-off between SV and OV. This is particularly the case when information about the nature of the deal is readily available to the parties. After all, it is imperfect information about deals that enhances the divergence between SV and OV—and therefore limits the trade-off between them. However, the trade-off can also be real when certain tactics are needed to reach a favorable deal, and these tactics deplete the SV of others. In our study mentioned that examined videotaped negotiations in detail (Elfenbein et al., 2010), perhaps not surprisingly we found that many of the competitive tactics that help negotiators to claim value were also the same actions that tended to irritate their counterparts in the form of lower reported SV. Listed in Table 5.1, these competitive tactics included—in order of just how irritating partners found them—referring to one's outside alternatives (i.e., best alternative to a negotiated agreement, or BATNA), providing arguments to support one's position, providing reactions to a counterpart's offer, providing misleading information, making numerous offers, referring to oneself as high in status, being highly talkative, saying negative words such as "no" or "never."[2] To the extent that these tactics may be necessary to reach a favorable settlement—which is admittedly impossible to know with certainty in advance—then low SV for a counterpart may be an unfortunate but unavoidable consequence. In these cases, for which there may exist a real trade-off between OV and SV, one must prioritize them. If you judge competitive tactics as necessary to reach a favorable settlement, then that should mean acknowledging this to yourself and being comfortable with the likelihood that it comes at a subjective cost to the other party.

Often, a negotiator will feel that the trade-off of OV over SV will be worthwhile, but sometimes he or she will not. Negotiators might choose

TABLE 5.1

Competitive Tactics That Claim Objective Value Yet Decrease Partner's Subjective Value

Tactic
Providing misleading information
Referring to one's outside alternatives
Making numerous offers
Appealing to fairness
Saying negative words such as "no" or "never"
Making arguments
Referring to oneself as high in status
Providing reactions to a counterpart's offer
Being highly talkative
Referring to competitors

Note: Items appear in order from greatest to least association with claimed value.
Source: From Elfenbein, H. A., Curhan, J. R., Eisenkraft, N., Shirako, A., & Brown, A. (2010). *Why are some negotiators better than others? Opening the black box of bargaining behaviors.* Paper presented at the 23rd Annual Meeting of the International Association for Conflict Management. Cambridge, Massachusetts. Retrieved from http://ssrn.com/abstract=1336257

SV as the more important outcome particularly in the context of ongoing relationships in which the relationship is itself more valuable than the settlement at hand (Curhan, Neale, Ross, & Rosencranz-Engelmann, 2008). In keeping with the advice regarding framing, similarly in such cases we would advocate that a negotiator make sure the counterpart is at least partly aware of the value of the concessions. At the risk of providing one's relationship partners with a long list of every sacrifice one has ever made, the risk of not doing so even a little is to have these sacrifices overlooked entirely. The last thing that a negotiator should want, when making a relational accommodation to a valued counterpart, is to be seen merely as having been a poor negotiator.

We offer another distinct piece of prescriptive advice for increasing SV: Treat your counterpart with clear respect. As an example of specific tactics that negotiators can take, Curhan and Brown (in press) discussed the particular behavior of asking questions. Asking questions has a wide range of benefits—it can signal an interest in the other party, create a flow of conversation in both directions, and increase the exchange of deal-relevant information. We found in our study examining detailed negotiator behaviors that people tend to be relatively consistent in the extent to which they ask questions from one negotiation to the next (Elfenbein et al., 2010). However, in spite of these apparent individual differences in the use of this tactic, it is feasible for all negotiators to incorporate more questions into their behavioral repertoire. In addition to asking questions, being explicit about the logic and standards behind offers is a way to communicate to a counterpart that he or she is respected. A different form of respect also involves the interpersonal dynamics that unfold over the course of the negotiation, such as listening to your counterpart, showing yourself to be trustworthy through your words and actions, helping the process to be efficient, and trying to save face for the other party—in other words, treating your counterpart like a valued relationship partner. One can use the SVI itself as a kind of checklist to suggest behaviors that enhance a counterpart's SV. For example, the question, "Do you feel your counterpart(s) listened to your concerns?" can remind a negotiator to listen to the concerns voiced by the other party. Likewise, the question, "Did you 'lose face' (i.e., damage your sense of pride) in the negotiation?" can remind negotiators to save face for their counterparts.

WHY ENHANCING SUBJECTIVE VALUE IN NEGOTIATIONS MAY BE PARTICULARLY IMPORTANT IN THE 21st CENTURY WORKPLACE

We believe that the settings particular to the 21st century workplace are likely to demonstrate an even greater potential value to SV. Among the innumerable changes under way to the modern workplace, we highlight two in particular for their potential influence on SV: the so-called flattening of hierarchical organizations and the increased frequency of communication via lean channels such as e-mail and other text-only formats.

Flatter organizations are likely to mean that more negotiations over time are woven into day-to-day relationships among colleagues. Formal organization has merged into informal organization, which means that much of daily organizational life takes place outside hierarchical levels that guide the work-related decisions that need to be made. Thus, on a regular basis more of these decisions will require agreements to be reached jointly among individuals whose underlying interests are largely but incompletely aligned—which is the operational definition of a *negotiation*. This increase in negotiations taking place on a daily basis on the job is likely to increase greatly the importance of SV in organizations.

Having greater relational consequences to the outcomes of negotiations means that more of "success" in a work-related negotiation stretches beyond the confines of the tangible terms for any particular deal—because it includes the ability to work together effectively and feel positively about their interactions. Thus, SV should matter more for counterparts who are enmeshed within an ongoing relationship—for which the trade-off between OV and SV, when true, would lean at least partly in the direction of SV. For this reason, of the tactics described, negotiators may particularly need to improve their skills at identifying counterparts' subjectively valued outcomes and analyzing the extent to which these outcomes can be provided without coming at the expense of the negotiator's objective settlement.

Interestingly, these negotiations within flatter organizations may take many of the parties by surprise. If, as in Kolb and Williams's (2000) concept of the *shadow negotiation*, these negotiations are so interwoven into daily interaction that parties do not even realize they are happening, then it is more difficult to follow the steps we outlined and to prepare for high SV as one might normally do for a formal negotiation. In particular, the surprise nature of many negotiations in the 21st century organization may prevent parties from following the prescriptive advice regarding their thorough assessment of counterparts' subjectively valued outcomes, as well as their assessment of the trade-off. Colleagues are in continual contact with each other and can initiate a negotiation at any time, so that negotiators will not have the same advanced notice to prepare, even if they realize that preparation is necessary.

A second change particular to the 21st century organization is the increased use of lean channels of communication media. Electronic mail, text messages, and instant messaging have become commonplace for conveying information among colleagues. However, this poses a communication challenge that is exacerbated by the other change described, namely, the interwoven nature of negotiations in day-to-day colleague interactions. Our prescriptive advice focused on learning the other party's subjectively valued outcomes, making the counterpart aware of the choice to forgo some OV for the sake of the relationship and showing respect. All of these communication goals are challenging enough under normal circumstances, but all the more so when using leaner channels that limit the flow of affective information (Curhan & Brown, in press; Drolet & Morris, 2000; McGinn & Croson, 2004). Further, the asynchronous nature of these communication channels makes it more difficult to adjust the flow of conversation out of responsiveness to the signals that are typically conveyed in real time by a counterpart.

Highlighting the particular example of a tactic that can increase SV—that is, asking questions, we suggest that both of the changes to the 21st century organization outlined can make this tactic more difficult to use effectively. First, the proliferation of negotiations that take place within flatter organizations means that many counterparts are enmeshed within a single organization, and negotiators may take for granted their shared context to avoid asking questions. For example, two colleagues in the same department might assume that they share the same priorities when working out details for an upcoming project and not ask each other about their preferred outcomes on specific issues—even though they would typically ask such questions when negotiating with someone at arm's length. They might also experience awkwardness if they feel that they should already know the answers, such as if calculating the value of a potential deal involves inputs that one party does not recall or to which that party does not have access. Parties might not even have the meta-awareness to know what to ask, particularly when the negotiation takes them by surprise. Second, the use of leaner communications media may impede the natural rhythm of questions. That is, the use of asynchronous communications media makes it cumbersome to create a true back-and-forth interaction, which is needed for multiple iterations of question asking and answering. It can be easier to leave alone a confusing topic when each round of e-mail exchange adds long hours to the interaction rather than the mere minutes it would take for a minor interruption from live interaction. Indeed, one of the benefits of asking questions is the flow of conversation that it generates due to its iterative nature, and this is decreased for the virtual negotiator. Further, the lean nature of text-based communications makes it difficult to provide context—in the case of asking questions, context can be valuable for interpreting what information is truly being requested. Face to face, a negotiator can ask a question simply and without the need to articulate it clearly, for example, "I don't understand," whereas this would be too vague to elicit a helpful response in an e-mail dialogue. In these ways, using leaner means of communication creates a barrier for negotiators to ask questions, as just one example of how changes in the 21st century organization may change negotiators' ability to increase SV.

FUTURE RESEARCH NEEDS GUIDED BY CHALLENGES IN ENHANCING SUBJECTIVE VALUE IN THE 21st CENTURY WORKPLACE

Given the nature of our prescriptive advice, there are particular challenges that negotiators face in attempting to increase the SV of their counterparts in the 21st century organization. Notably, we suggest that the negotiator needs to learn the other party's subjectively valued outcomes to make the counterpart aware of the choice to forgo some OV for the sake of the relationship and to show respect. However, these are precisely the most difficult types of activities when using communication media that limit the flow of affective information (Byron, 2008). As a result, one area for future negotiation research is to examine the extent to which negotiators can effectively enhance SV when they use leaner rather than richer channels of communication. On a related note, future research is needed to study how negotiators can attempt to enrich the leaner channels of communication that they are using and how doing so can potentially help them to enhance their SV. As one example, e-mail was still in its relative infancy when the need to convey emotional expression led to the development of "emoticons" to assist with the flow of affective details. Future research may be able to help us to understand further how negotiators can convey positive affect and respect across lean media and the extent to which various strategies for doing so effectively enhance SV. Our best prescriptive advice in the interim is for negotiators to make active choices about their communication media.

We also noted that enhancing SV may be especially important in the flatter hierarchical structures characterizing the 21st century workplace, yet potentially more difficult because flatter structures can also give rise to negotiations among colleagues that are impromptu enough to limit preparation. As a result, a second need for negotiation research is to study the effectiveness with which negotiators enhance SV in flatter versus more hierarchical organizational structures. Such studies would require examining negotiation phenomena: (a) at multiple levels of analysis, such as the organization level, rather than at solely the dyadic level that has dominated negotiation research; and (b) over longer periods of time than typically observed in studies with simulated negotiation exercises. The absence of these qualities from conventional negotiation research has led some to describe this literature as isolated from its social, relational, historical, and future contexts (e.g., Barley, 1990; Oliver et al., 1994). Studying negotiation phenomena in these ways—which include longer periods of time and multiple levels of potential influence—promises to enhance our understanding about negotiation in a way that more closely reflects the real-world negotiations context. Such understanding will also better reflect 21st century workplace challenges. We advocate for research designs that capture as much as possible the conditions faced by real negotiators in the 21st century organization. Simulation studies can incorporate greater realism along these lines ideally by including multiple rounds of negotiations so that the results achieved in one round feed directly into what takes place in further rounds (e.g., Shapiro & Bies, 1994). This enables such studies to capture how earlier objective and subjective negotiation experiences affect those parties' later subjective and economic outcomes together.

To focus on longer-term outcomes, future research designs will also ideally focus on compliance as an outcome—that is, the extent to which parties follow through with promises of future actions that they make during a negotiation. After all, it is rare for a bargaining agreement to cover issues that are immediately and irrevocably implemented, without room for alternative interpretations, broken promises, or delays. Such compliance requires ample goodwill following the negotiation (Fortgang, Lax, & Sebenius, 2003; Walton, Cutcher-Gershenfeld, & McKersie, 1994), which can be enhanced by negotiators' satisfaction with their settlements (Barry & Oliver, 1996). This makes issues of opportunism and trustworthiness very important and thus also raises in importance the need to examine the potential role of SV with postsettlement compliance.

This research agenda is intended to help complement existing work in the negotiations field. Theorists working in a rationalist behavioral framework have long focused on the potential pitfalls of social psychological factors, such as subjective feelings and close interpersonal relationships in negotiation (for a review, see Bazerman et al., 2001). By contrast, our own and related research consistently suggest that such factors can also be tangible assets within the context of an ongoing working relationship. We argue that negotiators can enhance their long-term financial outcomes by paying attention to the "softer side" and maximizing the subjective experience for themselves and for counterparts. The challenge that this poses in the best of cases is augmented by new challenges while the role of negotiation in organizational life evolves. It is our hope that the areas for future research outlined will help to provide guidance for the negotiator facing life in the 21st century organization.

ACKNOWLEDGMENTS

We are deeply grateful to our co-authors who have taken part in the research reviewed in this chapter: Lucio Bacarro, Ashley Brown, Noah Eisenkraft, Gavin Kilduff, Aiwa Shirako, and Alice Xu. We also thank Debra Shapiro and Barry Goldman for their guidance and support.

NOTES

1. This 16-item Subjective Value Inventory (SVI) is freely available for research use and printed in full with scoring information in the work of Curhan et al. (2006).
2. Interestingly, the tactic of trying to appeal to the other party's sense of sympathy was greatly irritating to counterparts and reduced joint gains, without demonstrating any benefit to the individual negotiator.

REFERENCES

Barley, S. R. (1990). Contextualizing conflict: Notes on the anthropology of disputes and negotiations. In M. H. Bazerman, R. J. Lewicki, & B. H. Sheppard (Eds.), *Research on negotiation in organizations* (Vol. 3, pp. 165–199). Greenwich, CT: JAI Press.

Barry, B., & Oliver, R. L. (1996). Affect in dyadic negotiation: A model and propositions. *Organizational Behavior and Human Decision Processes, 67*, 127–143.

Bateman, T. S., & Organ, D. W. (1983). Job satisfaction and the good soldier: The relationship between affect and employee "citizenship." *Academy of Management Journal, 26*, 587–595.

Bazerman, M. H., Curhan, J. R., & Moore, D. A. (2001). The death and rebirth of the social psychology of negotiation. In G. J. O. Fletcher and M. S. Clark (Eds.), *Blackwell handbook of social psychology: Interpersonal processes* (pp. 196–228). Oxford, UK: Blackwell.

Byron, K. (2008). Carrying too heavy a load? The communication and miscommunication of emotion by email. *Academy of Management Review, 33*, 309–327.

Curhan, J. R., Elfenbein, H. A., & Eisenkraft, N. (2010). The objective value of subjective value: A multi-round negotiation study. *Journal of Applied Social Psychology, 40*, 690–709.

Curhan, J. R., Elfenbein, H. A., & Kilduff, G. J. (2009). Getting off on the right foot: Subjective value versus economic value in predicting longitudinal job outcomes from job offer negotiations. *Journal of Applied Psychology, 94*, 524–534.

Curhan, J. R., Elfenbein, H. A., & Xu, H. (2006). What do people value when they negotiate? Mapping the domain of subjective value in negotiation. *Journal of Personality and Social Psychology, 91,* 493–512.

Curhan, J. R., Neale, M. A., Ross, L., & Rosencranz-Engelmann, J. (2008). Relational accommodation in negotiation: Effects of egalitarianism and gender on economic efficiency and relational capital. *Organizational Behavior and Human Decision Processes, 107,* 192–205.

Currall, S. C., Towler, A. J., Judge, T. A., & Kohn, L. (2005). Pay satisfaction and organizational outcomes. *Personnel Psychology, 58,* 613–640.

Drolet, A. L., & Morris, M. W. (2000). Rapport in conflict resolution: Accounting for how face-to-face contact fosters mutual cooperation in mixed-motive conflicts. *Journal of Experimental Social Psychology, 36,* 25–50.

Druckman, D., & Broome, B. J. (1991). Value differences and conflict resolution: Familiarity or liking? *Journal of Conflict Resolution, 35,* 571–593.

Eisenkraft, N., & Elfenbein, H. A. (2010). The way you make me feel: Evidence for individual differences in affective presence. *Psychological Science, 21,* 505–510.

Elfenbein, H. A. (2007). Emotion in organizations: A review and theoretical integration. *Academy of Management Annals, 1,* 371–457.

Elfenbein, H. A., Curhan, J. R., Eisenkraft, N., Shirako, A., & Baccaro, L. (2008). Are some negotiators better than others? Individual differences in bargaining outcomes. *Journal of Research in Personality, 42,* 1463–1475.

Elfenbein, H. A., Curhan, J. R., Eisenkraft, N., Shirako, A., & Brown, A. (2010). *Why are some negotiators better than others? Opening the black box of bargaining behaviors.* Paper presented at the 23rd Annual Meeting of the International Association for Conflict Management, June. Cambridge, MA. Retrieved fromhttp://ssrn.com/abstract=1336257

Fortgang, R. S., Lax, D. A., & Sebenius, J. K. (2003). Negotiating the spirit of the deal. *Harvard Business Review, 81*(2), 66–76.

Gelfand, M. J., Major, V. S., Raver, J. L., Nishii, L. H., & O'Brien, K. (2006). Negotiating relationally: The dynamics of the relational self in negotiations. *Academy of Management Review, 31,* 427–451.

Hayward, M. L. A., Shepherd, D. A., & Griffin, D. (2006). A hubris theory of entrepreneurship. *Management Science, 52,* 160–172.

Kenny, D. A. (1994). *Interpersonal perception: A social relations analysis.* New York: Guilford Press.

Kolb, D. M., & Williams, J. (2000). *The shadow negotiation: How women can master the hidden agendas that determine bargaining success.* New York: Simon and Schuster.

Lax, D. A., & Sebenius, J. K. (1986). Interests: The measure of negotiation. *Negotiation Journal, 2,* 73–92.

Lind, E. A., & Tyler, T. R. (1988). *The social psychology of procedural justice.* New York: Plenum.

McGinn, K. L., & Croson, R. (2004). What do communication media mean for negotiators? A question of social awareness. In M. J. Gelfand & J. Brett (Eds.), *The handbook of negotiation and culture* (pp. 334–349). Palo Alto, CA: Stanford University Press.

Mestdagh, S., & Buelens, M. (2003). *Thinking back on where we're going: A methodological assessment of five decades of research in negotiation behavior.* Paper presented at the 16th Annual IACM Conference, June. Melbourne, Australia.

Miller, D. T. (1999). The norm of self-interest. *American Psychologist, 54,* 1053–1060.

Mills, C. W. (1940). Situated actions and vocabularies of motive. *American Sociological Review, 5,* 904–913.

Oliver, R. L., Balakrishnan, P. V., & Barry, B. (1994). Outcome satisfaction in negotiation: A test of expectancy disconfirmation. *Organizational Behavior and Human Decision Processes, 60,* 252–275.

Osterman, P. (1987). Turnover, employment security, and the performance of the firm. In M. M. Kleiner, R. N. Block, M. Roomkin, & S. W. Salsburg (Eds.), *Human resources and the performance of the firm* (pp. 275–317). Washington, DC: BNA Press.

Pruitt, D. G., & Rubin, J. Z. (1986). *Social conflict: Escalation, stalemate, and settlement.* New York: McGraw-Hill.

Shapiro, D. L., & Bies, R. J. (1994). Threats, bluffs, and disclaimers in negotiations. *Organizational Behavior and Human Decision Processes, 60,* 14-35.

Subramanian, G. (2001). *Frasier series.* Cambridge, MA: Harvard Business School Publishing, Teaching cases 9-801-447 and 9-801-448.

Sullivan, B. A., O'Connor, K. M., & Burris E. R. (2006). Negotiator confidence: The impact of self-efficacy on tactics and outcomes. *Journal of Experimental Social Psychology, 42,* 567–581.

Thompson, L. (1990). Negotiation behavior and outcomes: Empirical evidence and theoretical issues. *Psychological Bulletin, 108,* 515–532.

Tinsley, C. H., O'Connor, K. M., & Sullivan, B. A. (2002). Tough guys finish last: The perils of a distributive reputation. *Organizational Behavior and Human Decision Processes, 88,* 621–645.

Valley, K. L., Neale, M. A., & Mannix, E. A. (1995). Friends, lovers, colleagues, strangers: The effects of relationships on the process and outcome of dyadic negotiations. *Research on Negotiation in Organizations, 5,* 65–93.

Walton, R. E., Cutcher-Gershenfeld, J. E., & McKersie, R. B. (1994). *Strategic negotiations: Theory of change in labor–management relations.* Cambridge, MA: Harvard Business School Press.

Williams, M. L., McDaniel, M. A., & Nguyen, N. T. (2006). A meta-analysis of the antecedents and consequences of pay level satisfaction. *Journal of Applied Psychology, 91,* 392–413.

Section 3

Negotiators as Emotion Managers in the 21st Century

6

The Effect of Moods and Discrete Emotions on Negotiator Behavior

Russell Cropanzano, William J. Becker, and Jöel Feldman

INTRODUCTION

Over the years, scholars have had frequent occasion to observe that moods and emotions are vital for understanding the negotiation process, simultaneously lamenting on the paucity of empirical evidence (see reviews by Barry, 1999; Barry, Fulmer, & Goates, 2006; Barry, Fulmer, & van Kleef, 2004; Barry & Oliver, 1996; Fisher & Shapiro, 2005; Kumar, 1997; Thompson, Neale, & Sinaceur, 2004). Trying to account for negotiator behavior while neglecting a role for affect was always problematic. However, changes in 21st century business have created an environment in which it is no longer possible to emphasize rational decision making at the expense of the emotional negotiator (Thompson, Nadler, & Kim, 1999). Many attributes of this new landscape will be apparent to all, although their implications for affect may not be widely understood. Let us consider just three of these.

One obvious change is the use of new communication technology, such as electronic mail and virtual conferencing (Friedman et al., 2004). Such technologies can lack richness, leading to impasses (Stuhlmacher & Citera, 2005). This problem can be attenuated if the two negotiators express their feelings to one another. As an example of this, consider the work of Moore, Kurtzberg, Thompson, and Morris (1999). Moore et al. found that even during electronically mediated negotiations with an out-group member, mutual self-disclosure caused bargainers to express more positive affect toward their counterparts. In addition, the expression of these good feelings produced greater rapport and more agreements. Consequently, attention to affect helped to overcome the impoverished electronic communication environment.

A second change lies in the increasing globalization of national economies. In 1947, the total world trade was about US$57 billion. By the late 1990s, this figure had climbed to $6 trillion (Steger, 2003). Figures such as this illustrate that modern organizations are encountering a different and more diverse environment than they were a generation ago. With the rise of the global economy and international business, research on cross-cultural negotiations is becoming increasingly important. There are cultural differences in the manner in which affect is expressed and interpreted during bargaining sessions (Kumar, 2004). Such research is becoming critical, although to date empirical evidence remains limited (George, Jones, & Gonzales, 1998).

Third, individuals in organizations often find themselves working in horizontal teams and networks (Pettigrew, Massini, & Numagami, 2000), many of which are transnational (Subramaniam & Venkatramen, 2001). In these types of teams, effective negotiation is likely to be an important factor in business success, although there is relatively little research to guide team-oriented interventions (Schweiger, Atamer, & Calori, 2003). Given that many of these teams function outside the formal authority hierarchy, issues of informal power and status are likely to become important. Such issues are closely tied to affect during negotiations (Van Kleef, De Dreu, Pietroni, & Manstead, 2006).

This chapter proposes that we must look back before we can look forward to solve the challenges facing us in the 21st century. That is, we must take stock of what we have, what we lack, and what we will need for the next generation of research on affect and negotiations. Specifically, the goals of this chapter are: (a) to review the literature to emphasize the distinction between moods and emotions and (b) to discuss how these affect various negotiator behaviors. As we will see, scholars have provided more tools than are generally realized, although these are scattered throughout a number of different literatures, such as psychology, economics, and management. When we pull this body of knowledge together, we find that while it is sizable, it is fragmented and incomplete. It is for that reason that we make a number of practical suggestions throughout.

DEFINING AFFECT: MOODS AND EMOTIONS

Generally speaking, affect refers to how people feel. A number of psychologically relevant constructs are said to contain affect, such as physical symptoms and perhaps attitudes (Fredrickson, 2001). For our present purposes, the two most important affectively relevant concepts are moods and emotions (Barry et al., 2004, 2006). While they are often confused, a careful comparison of emotions and moods reveals that they differ in several important respects (Daly, 1991; Kumar, 1997; Morris & Keltner, 2000).

First, emotions are tied to a specific target. For example, I may be *angry* (an emotion) at my *negotiation counterpart* (the target), for *making an unfair offer* (this generates anger; see Daly, 1991). On the contrary, mood states are not associated with a particular event or object (Morris & Keltner, 2000). This is not to say that moods lack a cause, of course, but only that the target is not specifically part of the mood's phenomenology. The target of emotions is important. For example, we will review the work of Steinel, van Kleef, and Harinck (2008), who found that the expression of anger and happiness has differential effects, depending on whether these emotions are targeted at people or at behaviors.

Second, emotions are generally felt more strongly, often so overwhelmingly that rational thought becomes difficult (Pham, 2007; Shapiro, 2002, 2005). Moods are usually less intense. They tend not to disrupt our thinking as much, although they can positively or negatively bias our thoughts (e.g., Carnevale, 2008; Carnevale & Isen, 1986; Conlon & Hunt, 2002). In their bargaining research, Lawler and Yoon (1997) viewed this distinction as the most critical. They saw "mood" as a less-intense form of "emotion."

Third, some emotion researchers have argued that there are differences in duration. According to these scholars, emotions are often understood to last a shorter time than moods. Emotions are like a flash flood. They tend to strike quickly and intensely but dissipate rapidly (Kumar, 1997; Morris & Keltner, 2000). Moods are less intense but usually linger. We caution the reader that we have presented these durational differences to reflect current conceptual thinking accurately. However, this particular distinction between moods and emotions is less certain than others, and we are personally skeptical. While it is often the case that moods are longer, there is noteworthy evidence contrary to this supposition, as some research shows long-duration emotions (for a review, see Frijda, Mesquita,

Sonnemans, & van Goozen, 1991). For negotiation scholars with an interest in integrating affect into their thinking, the possibility that emotions could last as long as moods is more than a casual question. If emotion generated at one point in time can be maintained for a long duration, then it might continue to influence bargaining well into the future. This phenomenon has been empirically observed. In a study we discuss further, Ketelaar and Au (2003, Study 2) found that individuals who felt guilty about the way they treated a bargaining partner were more generous when they renegotiated 1 week later. For similar week-long effects, see the work of Thompson, Valley, and Kramer (1995, Study 2).

Fourth, emotions and moods have been organized into different taxonomies. Emotions tend to be classified into a set of discrete or specific emotions (Butt, Choi, & Jaeger, 2005; Morris & Keltner, 2000). As we will see, negotiation scholars have studied guilt (Ketelaar & Au, 2003), disappointment (Thompson et al., 1995), anger (van Kleef & Côté, 2007; van Kleef, De Dreu, & Manstead, 2004a), and fear (van Kleef, De Dreu, & Manstead, 2004b; Kugler, Ordóñez, & Connolly, 2009, among others). Moods, on the other hand, are usually organized into a small number of (usually two) broad dimensions, such as negative affectivity (NA) and positive affectivity (PA) (e.g., by Curhan, Elfenbein, & Kilduff, 2009; Anderson & Thompson, 2004).

Fifth, emotions have a number of component processes, whereas moods tend to be relatively "pure" affect. Emotions consist of feelings, characteristic cognitions, and behavior predisposition (Daly, 1991; Frank, 1988). In this section, we pay special attention to the action tendencies that are linked to emotions, as these are especially important for negotiation researchers (Shapiro, 2005). When we feel an emotion, we automatically experience an unbidden desire to behave in a certain way. For example, in two experiments, Kugler, Ordóñez et al. (2009) examined the impact of fear and anger on decision making. In both of their studies, these two emotions pushed individuals in opposite directions. After finding support for their theory, Kugler, Ordóñez et al. (2009) then averaged fear and anger together to construct an index of overall negative affect. As one might expect, this index was not predictive. The opposing tendencies of fear and anger canceled one another out, and the strong effects for the two specific emotions were wiped away (for additional findings, see Lerner, Gonzalez, Small, & Fischhoff, 2003).

Within the negotiation literature, research efforts on mood and affect have proceeded separately. For this reason, our review has separate sections for each. We show that both types of affect provide keys for understanding the bargaining process.

MOOD AND NEGOTIATION

The pervasive influence of moods is well documented. A number of affect scholars judged moods to be as, or even more, important than emotions. For example, Forgas and George (2001, p. 5) argue that "moods often have a more subtle and insidious influence on organizational behavior precisely because they lack elaborate cognitive content and those often escape conscious scrutiny." In a similar fashion, Barsade (2002, p. 656) suggests that moods have "more broad-ranging effects as compared to other types of affect." Thompson, Medvec, Seiden, and Kopelman (2002) add that emotions may be less important than moods, to the extent that emotions are found to have shorter durations. In this chapter, we stop short of making a relative statement. We take the position that moods and emotions are both important to the bargaining process, and that neither should be ignored.

The Dual-Process Model of Positive Moods: Sociability and Innovation

Early research on affect posited that favorable moods produce more effective bargaining outcomes than do neutral (and certainly negative) feeling states (e.g., Barry et al., 2006; Barry & Oliver, 1996; Lawler & Yoon, 1997). One explanation of these benefits was offered by scholars such as Carnevale and Isen (1986) and Baron (1990). For convenience, we term this perspective the *dual-process model* because it argues that pleasant feelings have two beneficial effects. *Inter*personally, the dual-process model suggests that people who are in a good mood often become more sociable. That is, positive affect makes us less contentious, more generous, and more helpful toward others. *Intra*personally, the model suggests that pleasurable moods lead to more innovative problem solving. While some evidence has supported the dual-process model, other studies provided more mixed results. This prompted later extensions to this model, as we now discuss.

Evidence Favoring the Dual-Process Model

An early experiment by O'Quinn and Aronoff (1981) was primarily concerned with humor. The researchers argued that joking could put one's counterpart into a better mood, thereby making them more cooperative. In O'Quinn and Aronoff's experiment, undergraduate research participants bargained with a confederate. A simple joke about a pet frog caused participants to laugh and smile (although women expressed more positive affect than men). As predicted, O'Quinn and Aronoff found that humor induced subjects to make more concessions. In a later experiment, Carnevale and Isen (1986) studied bargainers' ability to reach integrative or collaborative solutions that met the needs of both parties. These researchers suggested that more sociability and additional integrative problem solving should produce "win-win" solutions. When pleasant feelings were induced in both parties, individuals used fewer contentious tactics, made more trade-offs, and achieved higher joint outcomes. Finally, a study by Baron (1990) was primarily concerned with the impact of pleasant (vs. neutral) scent. He suspected that enjoyable smells induce positive affect. This affect, in turn, creates sociability and innovativeness. In this experiment, participants who were exposed to pleasurable scents reported more pleasant moods than did those exposed to neutral scents. The former subjects also set higher monetary goals for their bargaining but were willing to make more concessions to attain them.

Caveat and Concerns

While the three experiments cited offered support for the dual-process model, other experimental studies have produced more mixed findings (e.g., Baron, Fortin, Frei, Hauver, & Shack, 1990). Conlon and Hunt's (2002) even backfired, with happy faces creating *less* trust and cooperation. Of course, it is difficult to interpret such unexpected findings. Still, some evidence suggests that the dual-process model may be too simplistic. Positive moods do not always produce greater cooperation and superior thinking than neutral moods (e.g., Forgas, 1995, 1998, 2000).

This possibility is underscored by Hertel, Neuhof, Theuer, and Kerr (2000). Hertel and his colleagues pointed out that, under certain conditions, people in positive moods utilize more heuristic decision-making strategies, employing quick and efficient "rules of thumb." Those in negative moods tend to be more systematic and deliberate in their decision making (Forgas & George, 2001). Based on this, Hertel et al. suggested that heuristic thinking could at least partially explain the seeming cooperation that had been observed in previous studies. According to these scholars, heuristic thinking causes us to mimic the behavior of our counterpart. Alternatively, when we consider an event in an effortful and systematic manner, we are more likely to form our own opinion. This makes it less likely that we will blindly copy our negotiation partner. For that reason, we may imitate more when we feel good and less when we are in a neutral or negative mood. In two experiments, Hertel et al. found support for these propositions. Happy (Experiment 1) and secure (Experiment 2) individuals tended to model their counterpart's behavior. These findings suggested that the dual-process model is incomplete. With these observations in mind, we now turn to a number of alternative conceptual frameworks that could address the limitations of the dual-processing model.

Forgas's Affect Infusion Model

Forgas's (1995, 1998, 2000) *affect infusion model* (AIM) was not formulated specifically to study mood and negotiation. Rather, it is a comprehensive framework for explicating the role of affect in decision making. Since bargaining involves decisions, of course, then the AIM makes predictions relevant to negotiation. However, to understand this effect, we need to step back and examine the AIM more closely. We open with a brief summary of the model.

Overview of the Affect Infusion Model

In defining his principal idea, Forgas (2000, p. 255) claimed that "*affect infusion* refers to the process whereby affectively loaded information exerts an influence on, and becomes incorporated into cognitive and judgment processes, entering into a person's deliberations and eventually coloring the outcome" (italics in original). In other words, according to AIM our feelings permeate our judgments (Forgas, 1995; Forgas & George, 2001). An interesting feature of the AIM is that affect can be more or less infused into thinking. This depends on the strategy being used to render a decision. To illustrate this, we need to examine the four processing strategies described by Forgas (1995):

- *Direct access* is simply retrieving a judgment from long-term memory. When a stored evaluation is recalled, the influence of affect is likely to be relatively small.
- *Motivated processing* refers to thinking or judging in the service of a specific objective. Motivated processing tends to be focused narrowly on a particular goal. As such, there tends to be limited affective influence.
- *Heuristic processing* occurs when one uses rules of thumb or efficient aids to quick decision making. Affect should have some influence when we process information heuristically.
- *Substantive or systemic processing* takes place when one is using a generative strategy to formulate a judgment. This is an open and constructive type of thinking whereby new ideas and concepts are created. Although substantive processing is effortful and deliberate, there is likely to be a good deal of affect infusion.

As can be seen, Forgas's (2000) AIM describes four processing strategies, each with its own characteristic amount of affect infusion. What remains to be seen is how this framework describes negotiator behavior.

Forgas's Affect Infusion During Negotiations

Forgas (1998, Experiment 1) argued that, in general, negotiation is "complex and indeterminate" (p. 575). As a consequence, it will often engender substantive or generative processing. Given our previous comments about the substantive processing strategy, affect infusion should be high during many bargaining sessions. To test this, Forgas (1998, Study 1) gave research participants bogus feedback on a mock test of verbal abilities. In so doing, he placed these students into a positive or negative mood. Following this mood manipulation, Forgas then had the students bargain with one another.

Since negotiation was seen as encouraging generative processing, Forgas (1998) expected strong infusion effects. Findings were supportive. Consistent with the AIM, people in a good mood expected more cooperation and planned to use more integrative bargaining strategies than did those placed in a less-pleasant frame of mind. During the bargaining sessions, these plans were implemented, with the result that subjects placed in a positive mood were more cooperative and earned superior outcomes than did those placed in negative moods.

Forgas's Motivated Processing During Negotiations

Experiment 2 (Forgas, 1998) extended these findings by examining another aspect of the theory. As we have already seen, Forgas (1995, 2000) argued that individuals with a motivated processing strategy targeted on a particular goal will not demonstrate the strong infusion effects characteristic of those with more open processing strategies. Forgas (1998) went further, asserting that certain personality traits predispose people to use motivated processing when bargaining. Those who are high in machiavellianism have a desire to be successful manipulators, while those high in need for approval want to look good to others. Consistent with these ideas, Forgas (Study 2) found that bargainers who were high in either machiavellianism or in need for approval showed weaker infusion effect, presumably due to their motivated processing strategy.

Forgas's Integral Affect and Bargaining

According to Pham (2007) affect can be studied in two ways. *Incidental* feelings are unrelated to the object or event being judged or evaluated. *Integral* feelings are directly tied to the person or thing under consideration. Forgas's (1998) first experiment studied incidental mood since the affect induction was from a test of verbal ability that had nothing to do with negotiation. In his third experiment, Forgas explored integral mood. He argued that feelings expressed by a counterpart could in turn influence the mood of a negotiator. Since bargaining often involves generative processing (see Forgas's first experiment), then counterpart mood creates affect infusion. In his third study, Forgas again found support for the AIM.

The Affect Infusion Model: Some Closing Thoughts

We have devoted some attention to the AIM because it offers the promise of being a comprehensive conceptual framework for understanding the relationship between mood and negotiator behavior. Given the aforementioned problems with the dual-process model, the success of the AIM should be seen as encouraging. Mood effects may be complex at times, but they are intelligible and important.

Affectivity as an Individual Difference

As we have seen, negotiation researchers have generally emphasized affective *states,* or one's current mood. A few scholars have also considered affective *traits,* which refer to dispositional tendencies that generalize to a lesser degree across situations and times. Unfortunately, investigations of affective states are limited, although they would seem to hold considerable promise. In two experimental studies, Anderson and Thompson (2004) found that trait positive affectivity (PA) predicted the ability of dyads to reach effective integrative solutions. However, this effect was due to the PA of the more powerful party. The trait PA of the less-powerful party did not facilitate joint gains. Anderson and Thompson (2004) further learned that when the most powerful negotiator possessed a high level of trait PA, this engendered trust within the bargaining dyad. This shared trust in turn partially mediated the relationship between PA and integrative agreements. Interestingly, trait PA had no effect on distributive agreements in either of Anderson and Thompson's experiments.

Mixed results were obtained in a longitudinal study by Curhan et al. (2009). Curhan and his colleagues were studying two types of value: economic value (what negotiators actually earned) and subjective value (their individual appraisal of worth). (For a review of this important topic, see Elfenbein and Curhan's Chapter 5 in this book.) Trait PA and trait NA were used as predictors of each type of value. Interestingly, Curhan et al. (2009) found that PA and NA did not predict economic value. The results of the negotiation did not seem to be impacted by dispositional affectivity. However, these NA and PA did predict subjective value. Even so, the significant correlation between NA and subjective value disappeared when other variables were included. The predictability of PA fared somewhat better, although the findings were not entirely consistent.

The disappointing findings for trait NA and trait PA, reported by Curhan and his colleagues, make sense in light of Anderson and Thompson's (2004) results. Curhan et al. surveyed individuals who were negotiating job offers. Such individuals would be unlikely to have greater power consistently than would the organizations with whom they were bargaining. To the extent that trait affect exerts greater influence when it comes from the more powerful party, as found by Anderson and Thompson, then one would anticipate weaker effects for job candidates.

Behavioral Decision-Making Approaches to Mood in Negotiation

In the past few decades, the behavioral decision paradigm has been the most successful and influential approach for studying bargaining behavior (Malhotra & Bazerman, 2008). This research has generally used models from decision-making research to better understand negotiation (Bazerman & Neale, 1992). Some of this work is relevant to our investigation of affect. We next review this eclectic body of research.

Mood and Self-Enhancement

Consistent with the dual-process model, Kramer, Newton, and Pommerenke (1993) agreed that positive mood could boost negotiator performance. However, Kramer and his colleagues posed a somewhat different theoretical account. These authors suggested that positive mood works by causing self-enhancement biases. To induce positive moods in the appropriate conditions, they showed participants a humorous video. Before they began bargaining, subjects who saw the amusing video were placed in a more positive mood. In turn, they became more self-confident and rated themselves as more likable and trustworthy. Subsequent to the bargaining session, those exposed to a positive mood induction showed higher performance when negotiating.

Mood and Decision Framing

Negotiation researchers who take a decision-making approach have studied an interesting phenomenon called *framing* (Bazerman & Neale, 1992). When bargainers frame their positions in terms of potential losses, they tend to accept more risk. One manifestation of this phenomenon is that they make fewer concessions even though doing so could lead to an impasse. Conversely, when bargainers frame their positions in terms of potential gains, they are inclined to accept less risk. That is, they make more concessions and reach agreements more quickly.

Carnevale (2008) further argued that an agreeable mood causes people to see things in a more positive light (similar to Forgas, 1998). This optimistic outlook alters the negotiators' reference points. The result of this altered orientation is that positive affect reverses the traditional framing effect. Specifically, those with optimistic gain frames become *more* willing to make concessions, while those with negative gain frames become *less* willing to make concessions. Carnevale (2008) examined these possibilities in an experimental study of bargaining dyads. Positive affect was induced by gift giving. People who were placed in good moods tended to be tougher bargainers, giving less to their counterpart. Conversely, when those with loss frames were placed in good moods, they became more generous and cooperative. Significantly, among participants who did not receive gifts, and therefore experienced lower levels of positive affect, the traditional framing effect was obtained.

Trust in Feelings

A very different approach to affect and negotiation has been taken by Stephens and Pham (2008; see also Pham, 2007). These authors accepted the widely recognized premise that individuals use their feelings as information, which they then incorporate into their decisions. This phenomenon has been termed *affect-as-information* (by Ketelaar, 2006; Mullen, 2007), the *affect heuristic* (by Slovic, Finucane, Peters, & MacGregor, 2002), and the *somatic-marker hypothesis* (by Damasio, 1994). As Stephens and Pham (p. 1052) put it: "It [affect] triggers a qualitatively distinct form of decision-making." These authors presented two specific changes.

- Feelings lead individuals to think in terms of cognitive images or mental pictures. As such, they tend to prefer unambiguous categories, placing less emphasis on qualifying or nuanced information, such as probability judgments.
- People who rely on affect tend to extract and employ simplified summaries or essences, focusing on the "gist" of the situation. As opposed to their more cognitively oriented counterparts, people who trust their feelings tend to avoid complex or intricate representations of the situation.

As a consequence of these two processes, trusting one's feelings tends to have an impact on how people negotiate. This was tested in three studies by

Stephens and Pham (2008). In each of these experiments, trust in feelings was increased by a memory task. Specifically, research participants were told to recall two past real-life episodes in which they relied on their feelings to make a decision and the outcome was successful. Following this manipulation, subjects played a variant of the ultimatum bargaining game (Güth, Schmittberger, & Schwarze, 1982).

In the standard ultimatum bargaining game, two participants are told to divide a pool of money. One individual, usually the subject, serves as the "proposer." He or she suggests a division that allocates a certain proportion of the funds to each participant. The second subject serves as the "responder." He or she can accept or reject the offer. If the responder accepts the offer, then each individual receives the division offered by the proposer. If the responder rejects the offer, then neither individual receives anything. Generally speaking, research suggested that proposers prefer to take a larger share of the money (Prasnikar & Roth, 1992; Straub & Murnighan, 1995; for exceptions, see Van Dijk & Tenbrunsel, 2002). Unfortunately for them, if the suggested division is unequal, the recipient may reject the offer and leave them with nothing. To avoid penury, proposers tend to behave strategically, keeping the division at a level that will provide them a maximal payoff while still maintaining a deal (Pillutla & Murnighan, 1995, 1996). This ultimatum bargaining task has been used to examine trust in feelings.

In their first experiment, Stephens and Pham (2008) had individuals play the standard ultimatum bargaining game. The authors reasoned that those who trusted their feelings would tend to take a more literal approach to the interchange. Since these individuals tend to prefer concrete and unambiguous representations, they were predicted to seek the most desirably payout, attending less to the likelihood that the responder will reject their offer. Findings confirmed this prediction. Those who trusted their feelings were less generous than those who did not. That is, when relying on their feelings to decide how to allocate money, individuals tended to claim a larger share for themselves. They claimed less when not relying on their feelings.

In the second experiment, Stephens and Pham (2008) allowed the responder to make a counteroffer. In so doing, the researchers transformed the ultimatum bargaining game into something akin to distributive bargaining. Stephens and Pham found that those high on trust in feelings were relatively unresponsive to this manipulation. That is, they tended to make offers similar to the ones that were made in the first experiment. On the other hand, those who had not received the trust-in-feeling manipulation, and who presumably gave more credence to cognitive analysis, behaved differently when they knew that the responder could make a counteroffer. Specifically, their original proposal became *less* generous. (This was probably because they wanted to begin the bargaining with a low offer, which is a widely used tactic in distributive negotiation.) The result was that those who trusted their feelings became *more* generous than those who did not trust their feelings. Notice that trusting one's feelings can cause an individual to become more generous (Experiment 2) or less (Experiment 1), depending on the parameters of the situation. In a subsequent experiment, Stephens and Pham would turn these findings around one more time.

In their third experiment, Stephens and Pham (2008) switched to a dictator game. This paradigm mirrors the ultimatum bargaining game, except that the responder cannot respond: He or she is powerless and must accept whatever offer the proposer elects to make. Stephens and Pham reasoned that participants who had received the trust-in-feelings manipulation would consider only the simple gist of the situation, construing it as a straightforward allocation task. As a consequence, relying on feelings would make one less concerned with "extraneous" issues, such as justice. Those who had not received the trust-in-feelings manipulation would represent the task in a more complicated fashion, with attention to issues of fair play and social justice. Results were again supportive. Those who trusted their feelings offered very little to the responder. Those who did not were much more generous.

The trust-in-feelings literature, though small, is potentially important. Knowing that people have feelings is only part of the puzzle. This is the case for two reasons. First, individuals do not always rely on their feelings to make decisions. Trusting our affect qualitatively alters our decision processes (Pham, 2007). Second, the effect of our feelings on our behavior is not always constant. It can change depending on the particulars of the negotiation. Affect can make us either more (Experiment 1 and Experiment 3) or less (Experiment 2) generous. As Forgas (1995, 2000) argued, affect has an impact on how we understand or construe a situation. Behavior is a more distal outcome that results from these processing effects.

Contrasting Positive and Negative Moods: Practical Advice for Using Mood

As we have seen, negotiation researchers generally treat mood as either positive or negative. For practitioners, though, this is a limited point of view. A single individual can switch mood during the course of a bargaining session, switching from agreeable to hostile. These shifts from one mood valence to the other can dramatically alter the direction being taken by the two counterparts. Two traditions of study have examined this possibility.

Incompatible Response Model

Some years ago, Baron (1976) argued that positive feelings were incompatible with negative ones. Hence, one response can cancel out the other. In a later experiment, Baron (1984) applied this idea to bargaining. To test his theory, Baron had laboratory subjects discuss a business case with an experimental confederate. The confederate always disagreed with the subject. In the incompatible response condition, this confederate then gave the participant a gift, explained that tests had made him "uptight" (sympathy), or showed the subject funny cartoons (humor). These simple manipulations caused the subject to rate the disagreeable confederate more favorably and indicated a desire to resolve future conflicts in a more constructive fashion. The positive events were able to "break" the impact of negative feelings.

Emotional Punctuation

A somewhat different approach to affective shifts has been taken by McGinn and Keros (2002). McGinn and Keros were interested in the approaches that dyads naturally take when negotiating an issue. To examine these ideas, they coded the dialogue between undergraduates while they bargained with one another. Some of these bargainers were friends, and others were strangers. Consistent with their theory, McGinn and Keros found that most pairs quickly fell into one of three improvisations:

- *Opening up:* This was driven by a logic of complete honesty with one another.

- *Working together:* This was driven by a logic of shared problem solving.
- *Haggling:* This was driven by a logic of competition and self-gain.

Most pairs fell into one of these improvisations quickly and remained there throughout the session. Each of these logics seems to have been somewhat stable over time. However, there were occasions when at least one of the participants wished to alter the initial improvisation. This required that one bargainer "break set" and push the counterpart to think about the bargaining session in a different way. Such changes were brought about by one of three transitions:

- *Trust testing:* Asking whether the counterpart was honest.
- *Process clarification:* An explicit questioning of the underlying logic.
- *Emotional punctuation:* Displaying emotion to break set. This is obviously of most interest in our present chapter.

Thus, the display of one's emotions was a tactic for abruptly changing the logic of an improvisation. Emotional punctuation could be either positive or negative, but in either case, it served to convey dissatisfaction. It was most likely to be used when the two negotiators were strangers and did not know each other in advance. Also, it was frequently used during a haggling or competitive improvisation. Unfortunately, emotional punctuation often did not achieve its desired aim. Usually, the result was a bargaining session in which the final improvisation was asymmetric or more competitive.

Concluding Thoughts Before Moving to Emotion

In this section, we reviewed a number of different approaches that have proven useful to understand the impact of mood on the negotiation process: the dual-process model, the AIM, affect as an individual difference, behavioral decision making, and contrasting positive and negative moods. As we have seen, there has been a steady evolution in thinking. The early dual-process model was inclined to view positive affect's impact on negotiation outcomes as superior to that of negative affect (e.g., Baron, 1990; Baron et al., 1990; Carnevale & Isen, 1986; O'Quinn & Aronoff, 1981). This early thinking was not entirely successful, and some of the findings associated with it were mixed. Later work began to pay closer attention to cognitive processing (e.g., Forgas & George, 2001; Stephens & Pham, 2008) and cognitive heuristics (e.g., Carnevale, 2008; Kramer et al., 1993). What emerged from this work was an interesting nuance, with greater consideration of the costs and benefits of good and bad feelings (e.g., Hertel et al., 2000). Consequently, the literature on mood and bargaining exhibits a promising cumulativeness, becoming not only steadily more complex but also steadily more realistic. As this literature has evolved, scholars interested in mood have taught us much about the negotiation process.

SPECIFIC EMOTIONS AND NEGOTIATION

It is well established that negotiating can cause one to experience emotions. For example, Hegtvedt and Killian (1999) found that procedural fairness during bargaining reduced depressive feelings regarding one's earnings. Treating others fairly reduced one's guilt, while being treated fairly sometimes made negotiators feel guilty. These are interesting findings but not directly relevant to the issue we are considering here. Our focus is less on the feelings that result from bargaining and more on how emotions have an impact on the bargaining process. We illustrate this possibility by organizing our review around a number of discrete emotional states.

Anger

Anger is probably the most widely discussed emotion by negotiation researchers (e.g., Allred, 1999; Daly, 1991). There is evidence that "irrational" anger prevents us from being exploited while bargaining. This has generally been studied by scholars interested in the "commitment problem" (Ketelaar, 2006, p. 432). The commitment problem emerges when short- and long-term interests collide. Let us first consider the short term. If an individual falls into an infuriated rage, then he or she may spitefully and irrationally act to harm the other party (Davidson & Greenhalgh, 1999). When this occurs, the angry individual usually ends up paying a financial cost for the satisfaction of getting revenge (Allred, 1999; Daly, 1991). This is a potential short-term danger of anger: Our emotions may overpower our rational judgment at the expense of our economic interests.

However, when this is viewed over the long term, there is a silver lining. Negotiators need to behave strategically (Thompson et al., 1999). That is, the best option could depend on the choices made by their counterpart now and in the future. If you believe that your contentious offer will cause your opponent to become furious, then you are less likely to make that offer in the first place. In this way, strong emotions can bring long-term benefits, but only as long as they are perceived to be sincere (Frank, 1988, 1990, 2004). In other words, strong emotions signal a person's "commitment" to a potentially risky course of action. Anger can have long-term benefits even if it comes with short-term costs.

Anger With Power

Anger can bring benefits as irritation may signal a cessation of concessions, which may bring a counterpart to agree to settle (cf., for a theoretical account, see van Kleef, 2009). However, this must be done carefully. Power relationships between negotiating dyads are argued to moderate emotional responses to hostility. When the expresser of anger is in a position of power, the emotion may lead to greater gains for him or her. When one is not in a position of relative power, however, it is more dangerous to vent one's frustration.

A number of studies have examined this possibility empirically; see especially the work of van Kleef and his colleagues (van Kleef & Côté, 2007; van Kleef et al., 2004a, 2004b, 2006). Similarly, Sinaceur and Tiedens (2006) posited that when a negotiating partner has few alternatives other than to negotiate (i.e., low bargaining power), expressions of anger by the high-power partner allow for greater claiming of value by him or her. They argued that this would occur because anger communicates toughness, and when faced with a negotiating partner in a position of weakness caused by a lack of alternatives, toughness leads to greater gains. Their proposition was supported in two experiments.

Relevant findings were also reported in a study of online dispute resolution by Friedman et al. (2004). Friedman and his colleagues were examining mediation. As such, there was a claimant who raised a concern regarding a respondent. Friedman et al. found that expressions of anger did not affect resolution rates when claim respondents had little power (in this case, where large amounts of money were at stake), but anger did produce settlements along with greater power. Anger can be useful, at least in the short term, when one has the power to back it up.

The work of van Kleef and Côté (2007), van Kleef et al. (2004a, 2004b, 2006), and Sinaceur and Tiedens (2006) suggests that showing one's ire during a bargaining session can increase individual gains and settlement rates (Friedman et al., 2004), but that this occurs primarily among those who are high in power. One recent experiment provided less-supportive results. A study by Campagna, Bottom, Kong, and Mislin (2010) was unable to replicate these findings. In their study, anger did not enable powerful negotiators to claim more value. As we shall discuss, there may be other moderators of this relationship, such as whether the expression of anger is appropriate (Gibson, Schweitzer, Callister, & Gray, 2009).

Rather than individual value claiming, other researchers have examined joint gains. Joint value may also be impacted by the expression of anger, although the evidence is not completely consistent. An experiment by Butt and his colleagues (2005) found that angry negotiators not only used more dominating bargaining tactics but also reduced joint gains. Conversely, a more recent experiment by Overbeck, Neale, and Govan (2010) found that having an angry person in the negotiation dyad tended to produce more integrative agreements. Overbeck and her colleagues found that this effect was strongest when the more powerful party was angry, but that it existed (albeit to a lesser degree) even for the low-power bargainer. Anger sometimes works, in the sense of improving joint gains, and sometimes does not. We explore this in more detail in the following.

The Appropriate Expression of Anger

Anger is more effective when it is expressed appropriately (Gibson et al., 2009). An interesting example of this can be found in three cross-cultural studies by Adam, Shirako, and Maddux (2010). These scholars agreed that negotiators who express anger often receive superior payouts (e.g., van Kleef et al., 2004a, 2004b). However, they argued that annoyance may be viewed as more appropriate among Westerners, such as Dutch negotiators (e.g. van Kleef et al., 2006), and less appropriate in an Asian cultural context. Adam and his colleagues found this to be the case. In their first two studies, Asian and Asian American negotiators conceded less to an angry counterpart than did European Americans. In their third experiment, Adam et al. found that telling subjects that anger was appropriate eliminated these cultural differences; Asians and Asian Americans showed patterns of concessions that were similar to European Americans. Likewise, indicating that anger was *in*appropriate caused European Americans to make concessions in a fashion that was similar to Asians and Asian Americans. The authors concluded that expressing anger could increase one's payoffs, but only when it was done in an appropriate fashion. When the anger is counternormative, such as when it is strongly expressed in an Asian cultural context, then it could well reduce one's outcomes.

The appropriateness of one's anger interacts with relationship power. As we have seen, expressing anger tends to benefit powerful negotiators more than it benefits less-powerful ones (Overbeck et al., 2010). This difference may be weaker when the anger of the low-power party is legitimate. Research by van Kleef and Côté (2007) found that the extent to which the expresser's anger is perceived as justified has a greater impact, even when one is bargaining with a more powerful counterpart. Specifically, they showed that respondents in a powerful position often demanded more value when faced with an angry negotiator, but mostly when the anger was seen as unjustified. When the anger of the low-power individual was seen as justified, then even powerful negotiators were apt to moderate their demands.

Anger With Happiness

Van Kleef (2009) argued that emotional expression serves as a nonverbal signal of negotiation intentions. The observing of these signals is referred to as *tracking*. While anger signals that a negotiation partner is no longer willing to make concessions, happiness signals ongoing cooperation. Van Kleef and his colleagues (2004a) found support for their model in two experiments: The first showed that negotiators conceded more to an angry participant than to a happy one; the second showed that these differing concessions were predicted by tracking, or the monitoring of the other negotiators' emotions. Van Kleef and colleagues (2006) replicated these effects in a series of five experiments using three different methods (experiment, field study, and scenario) and different sample populations (managers, students, and general population).

Steinel et al. (2008) extended these findings by examining whether the target or orientation of the happiness and anger were people or behaviors. That is, one could become angry at a counterpart as a person or could simply become angry over a particular offer. Specifically, participants received one of the following types of communication: angry and behavior oriented, happy and person oriented, angry and person oriented, or happy and behavior oriented. When the emotions were aimed at behaviors, previous findings were replicated, with greater concessions being made to angry negotiators than to happy ones. However, the findings were reversed when the emotions were person oriented, with greater concessions made to happy, person-oriented negotiators than to angry, person-oriented negotiators. When attacked in a personal way, people are less likely to yield ground.

Emotional Regard: Compassion Minus Anger

Allred, Mallozzi, Matsui, and Raia (1997) defined emotional regard as each negotiator's level of compassion minus his or her level of anger. In a laboratory experiment, they found that negotiating dyads with lower aggregate levels of compassion had a lower desire to work together in the future and realized fewer joint gains. However, they did not find that negotiators with lower levels of compassion claimed higher levels of individual values for themselves.

Fear

Fear has usually been studied alongside anger. This goes back at least to the work of Adler, Rosen, and Silverstein (1998), who argued that the two most pervasive and nefarious emotions with an impact on negotiations were anger and fear. Although they treated each emotion independently, their discussion suggests that anger and fear are often tied and mutually reinforcing. For example, they described how the fear of "losing face" leads negotiators to express anger, which escalates the fear to an even greater extent. Substantiating this idea, van Kleef and his colleagues (2004a) posited and found support for the idea that anger may cause a negotiator to pay less attention to his or her negotiation partner's emotions. Anger has these effects because it engenders greater levels of fear. According to this view, anger thus causes fear, which in turn has an impact on internegotiator emotional communication. Consistent with Adler and his colleagues' thinking, anger and fear are discrete emotions, but they may co-occur in real life. This is not to say, of course, that anger and fear have an impact on behavior in the same way. Evidence suggests otherwise.

In an interesting experiment, Young, Jung, and Bauman (2010) induced either fear or anger in male and female research participants. Contrary to earlier work, neither anger nor fear had consistent effect. When angry men and angry women were given the opportunity to negotiate payment, angry men earned more than did angry women. Fear had a somewhat different effect. When fearful men and fearful women were given the opportunity to negotiate payment, fearful men were less likely to bargain and, as one might expect, earned less. Fearful women, on the other hand, were more likely to bargain and claimed more value. In other words, men earned more than women when they both experienced neutral or angry emotions, but women earned more than men when both experienced fear.

Kugler, Ordóñez, et al. (2009) presented two studies that compared three emotions: anger, fear, and happiness. They argued that each emotion is accompanied by a distinct cognitive appraisal. Fear tends to be associated with a lack of individual control and attributions of environmental uncertainty. Thus, one who is fearful will be especially cautious when confronting ambiguity from a nonhuman agent, such as a lottery. Anger is associated with feelings of individual control and with attributions of certainty. As a result, one who is angry will be less concerned with environmental uncertainty but more circumspect toward human decision makers. Happiness, like anger, is associated with both control and certainty. However, since happiness is a positive emotion, people are motivated to maintain their good moods. This prompts individuals to reduce their risks when stakes are high. Hence, happy people should make choices that are intermediate between those of fearful and those of angry individuals. In support of these contentions, Kugler, Ordóñez et al. found that fearful individuals were *less* risk averse than happy or angry ones when the risk was based on the decision of another person (Study 2), but fearful people became *more* risk averse than angry persons when the risk was based on a randomizing device (Study 1).

Guilt

Work on the effect of guilt in negotiations is rather limited. Although the results are not in complete agreement, the few findings hint at the fact that feelings of guilt lead to more concessions. In one experiment, Butt and his colleagues (2005) measured the guilt/shame of both negotiators and their counterparts. Neither party's guilt/shame had the predicted effects on compromise behavior. Likewise, neither negotiator nor counterpart guilt/shame had an impact on the outcomes of the bargaining session.

Two other pertinent experiments were also reported by Thompson et al. (1995). These scholars were interested in the "bittersweet" feelings of success and their effect on later negotiations. To test this, they had participants negotiate with either an ingroup or an out-group member. They found that when participants found out that when an ingroup member was disappointed in the negotiation outcomes, the participants made more concessions in a negotiation held 1 week later. This effect was weaker when the negotiating partner was an out-group member.

Using an affect-as-information theoretical paradigm, Ketelaar and Au (2003) investigated the effects of guilt experienced following a social bargaining game on a subsequent negotiation. They predicted that guilt experienced following a negotiation task would be considered as a cost by participants and would have an impact on cost-benefit analyses of gains the next time they negotiated with the same partner. In support of their hypotheses, the authors found that negotiators who experienced guilt due to their actions in a negotiation were more likely to make concessions when negotiating with the same partner a week later.

Sadness

There is little research on sadness during negotiations. Lerner, Small, and Loewenstein (2004) argued that sadness invokes feelings of helplessness and motivates people to strive to change their current circumstances. Hence, they predicted opposing effects on buyers and sellers. For a seller, a change results from disposing of current possessions; therefore, sadness *lowers* the seller's asking price. Buyers, on the other hand, change their situation by acquiring new items. Hence, sadness *raises* the amount that a seller is willing to pay. These effects run contrary to typical endowment effects. In an experiment in which incidental sadness was evoked prior to individuals participating in a buy–sell decision task, these propositions were supported. Sad participants were willing to sell for less and buy for more than neutral participants.

Anxiety

Anxiety represents another discrete negative emotion that is likely to accompany negotiations and influence their outcomes. We found only one, relatively old, experiment by Tedeschi, Burrill, and Gahagan

(1969). Tedeschi and his colleagues had research participants complete the Manifest Anxiety Scale (MAS). Then, they had pairs of subjects play a version of the prisoner's dilemma game; one individual had a weaker position, and one had a stronger one. No communication was allowed between participants, but the scenario was repeated many times. They found that anxiety did not predict the behavior of those in the strong position. However, among weaker participants, those who were more anxious were more likely to defect (i.e., were less cooperative than they could have been). This suggests that anxious individuals with high MAS scores behaved more conservatively and exhibited more defensive (less-submissive) behavior to prevent exploitation in an interactive decision task. This finding suggests that anxious negotiators are more defensive but not necessarily more submissive.

Envy

Moran and Schweitzer (2008) investigated the envy that arises before and during a negotiation. The authors argued that envy leads one to devalue relationships with the target of one's jealousy. As a result, envy can increase one's willingness to use deception to maximize profits. In their first study, envious individuals reported being more willing to use deception in upcoming negotiations with the object of their envy. Their second study investigated actual negotiation behaviors in an ultimatum bargaining game. In this experiment, the participant of interest (the proposer) knew the size of the pie to be divided, but the other player did not. In the envy condition, proposers used deception more often than in the nonenvy condition. Further, envious proposers used deception to make lower offers. These initial findings suggest that envy can arise before and during negotiations, and these emotions have important consequences for the conduct and outcome of the negotiations.

Embarrassment

Embarrassment is another emotion that has been examined infrequently. In the first study conducted by Brown (1968), individuals participated in a bargaining exercise against a competitive confederate with controlled observer feedback. Players frequently retaliated when taken advantage of by the other party. However, this behavior was not driven only by anger.

Players were more likely to retaliate despite the significant cost of doing so when they received feedback that they had lost face and when they believed observers were unaware of the cost of retaliation. In short, vindictiveness was likely to occur when one could restore lost "face" but do so in a way that did not cause one to look economically inefficient.

In two other experiments, Brown (1970) had college-age males perform an embarrassing task (put pacifiers in their mouths) or a nonembarrassing task (describe a rubber soldier). Later, they chose between explaining their observations in front of a group of people (higher payoff) or anonymously (lower payoff). Subjects in the embarrassing task were much more likely to give up potential earnings to avoid public exposure and save face. As the reader will observe, Brown's (1968, 1970) research on embarrassment is decades old. We think it is time for negotiation scholars to take a new look at this research. While the evidence is limited, Brown's research suggests that embarrassment could prove to have an important influence on negotiator behavior.

Positive Emotions

As one can see, much of the emotion research has emphasized negative states, such as regret, anger, and guilt. However, some work exists on positive emotions. In their experimental study, Butt et al. (2005) assessed two discrete emotions: pride-achievement (which they viewed as a single emotional state) and gratitude. They found that when a counterpart expressed pride-achievement, the negotiator was likely to reciprocate by displaying integrative behavior. However, when a negotiator was feeling pride-achievement, he or she was less apt to acquiesce to the demands of a counterpart. Gratitude produced somewhat different effects. When a negotiator felt gratitude, he or she was more likely to yield to another person's requests. Hence, these two emotions did not have the same behavioral outcomes, even though they were both positive. Lawler and Yoon (1993) explored interest/excitement and pleasure/commitment and found positive effects for repeated negotiations. We return to their experiment when we discuss interpersonal relationships.

Anticipated Emotions: Regret and Happiness

Thus far, we have considered emotions that are directly experienced or expressed during a bargaining session. Working from a different theoretical standpoint, other scholars have emphasized the emotions that one might *anticipate* feeling. A good example of this line of inquiry can be found in two studies by Brown and Curhan (2010), who explored the misattribution of arousal. In their first experiment, the authors found that incidental physical arousal (i.e., due to walking briskly on a treadmill) led to more extreme ratings of subjective value during a bargaining session. Those who looked forward to bargaining were especially favorable when their heart rates were high, whereas those who dreaded bargaining were especially negative when in the same state. More pertinent to our present discussion was Brown and Curhan's second study. The authors found that people with *high* arousal who also looked forward to negotiating rated an imagined bargaining session as having *higher* subjective value because they believed that they would experience *positive* emotions. Conversely, people with *high* arousal who did not look forward to negotiating rated the imagined bargaining session as having *lower* subjective value because they believed that they would experience *negative* emotions.

To summarize, Brown and Curhan (2010) found that physical arousal interacts with individuals' feelings about negotiating. In so doing, it causes them to anticipate either positive emotions (when they are favorably predisposed to bargaining) or negative emotions (when they are unfavorably predisposed). These anticipated emotions—both positive and negative—have an impact on subjective value. This is an important possibility, and it has also been explored by researchers interested in regret (Reb & Connolly, 2009) and, more recently, happiness (Kong, Tuncel, & Parks, 2010).

Anticipated Regret

Anticipated regret pertains to the remorse that one expects to feel subsequent to a given choice or decision. In general, anticipated regret has been found to cause decision makers to become more vigilant and careful in their thinking (Reb, 2008; Connolly & Zeelenberg, 2002; Reb & Connolly, 2010). As one might imagine, this should be an important phenomenon in bargaining situations. Unfortunately, anticipated regret has not received sufficient attention in negotiation settings. One important experiment was conducted by Kugler, Connolly, and Kausel (2009, Study 2). Consistent with this earlier work, Kugler et al. determined that the anticipation of regret led to lower levels of trust for the partner. Anticipated regret also caused subjects to take fewer interpersonal risks. Transposing this to a negotiation context, these results suggest that negotiators who anticipate regret will be less trusting and less willing to make concessions while bargaining.

Anticipated Happiness

While anticipated regret pertains to the expectation of a negative emotion, anticipated happiness holds forth the promise of good feelings. Kong et al. (2010) argued that anticipated happiness activates a "promotion focus," whereby the individual is oriented toward personal growth, accomplishment, and potential gains. As a result of this promotion focus, people are more likely to pursue worthwhile opportunities when they anticipate being happy. Kong et al. tested these ideas in two studies. When participants anticipated being happy, they were likely to initiate negotiatons (Study 1). They also made higher opening offers (Study 2). As expected, these effects were mediated by a promotion focus. As these two experiments used a scenario design, Kong and his colleagues were unable to examine whether the happiness-promotion focus produced greater value for bargainers. Nevertheless, these are promising findings and worthy of additional research attention.

Practical Advice: Three Strategies for Using Emotion While Negotiating

With only a few exceptions (such as Barry, 1999), much of the research advising working people has not always been driven by a strong empirical foundation (e.g., Adler et al., 1998; Daly, 1991; Fisher & Shapiro, 2005; Shapiro, 2002, 2005). An exception is the work of Thompson et al. (2002), who reviewed three possible tactics that could be inferred from the available literature. We briefly discuss each, supplementing our comments with other work.

The Rational Negotiator ("Poker Face")

The perspective of the rational negotiator argues that one should be as logical and rational as possible during negotiations. Negotiators should therefore endeavor to keep emotion out of the process to avoid irrational consequences, such as conflict spirals. Thompson and her colleagues (2002) suggested that the "poker face" could be most useful in cases involving "competitive independence." This pertains to distributive bargaining, when the two parties need each other but have opposing interests and the likelihood of repeated interaction is low. Since competition is necessary, it is probably best to remain logical and nonemotional to obtain the Pareto-optimal solution for both parties.

The "Rant-'n'-Rave" Approach

The "rant-'n'-rave" approach involves using hostile emotions, such as anger, to demand one's own way. We have already discussed circumstances when fury, feigned or actual, may be useful. These include situations when the irate person has greater power (Friedman et al., 2004; Overbeck et al., 2010; Sinaceur & Tiedens, 2006; van Kleef et al., 2004a, 2004b, 2006), when the anger is justified (van Kleef & Côté, 2007), and when the expression of rage is normatively appropriate (Adam et al., 2010). Shapiro (2005) further suggested that there are three conditions under which expressing ire might be functional: (a) You do not care about your relationship with the other person, (b) the negotiation is zero sum (people often overestimate the likelihood of this, however), and (c) your counterpart has a weak BATNA (e.g., the work of van Kleef et al., 2004a, 2004b, 2006). Despite the empirical support for negative emotion, real-world negotiations are seldom likely to meet these conditions, and negative emotion should be expressed with great care and restraint.

The Positive Emotion Approach

Three experiments by Kopelman, Rosette, and Thompson (2006) found that expressing positive emotions can generate more beneficial bargaining outcomes than does expressing negative emotions (see also Anderson & Thompson, 2004). Thompson and her colleagues (2002) maintained that the positive approach is superior in mixed-motive games and integrative negotiations, for which each individual must balance cooperation and competition. Shapiro (2005) recommended that one should display positive emotions when (a) the relationship is important and (b) there is an opportunity to create and distribute value. Notice that Shapiro's latter recommendation is consistent with Thompson et al.'s advice that positive emotion is best for mixed-motive situations. Unfortunately, there is relatively little evidence pertaining to the use of positive discrete emotions (see Butt et al., 2005, for an important exception). This is an important topic for future inquiry.

In summary, it is clear that the expression of emotion has important consequences for negotiations. Emotions not only influence the behavior of individual negotiators but also convey information to the other party. The findings suggest that negotiators need to be aware of their emotional feelings and expressions. No one strategy for expressing emotions will always be appropriate. Rather, the adept negotiator must know when to suppress or express positive and negative emotions. The more complex the negotiation, the more likely that multiple approaches will be required to varying degrees.

EMOTION IN RELATIONSHIPS

In this section, we consider a series of articles that purport to examine emotions in general as they relate to relationships between parties in negotiation. While these studies do not fit neatly into either the "mood" or "emotion" sections that we have already discussed, they are interesting because they focus on the development of interpersonal relationships between dyadic negotiators. The general idea is that stronger and more committed attachments have an impact on bargaining outcomes. This is especially important in light of the emphasis on building relationships found in the practical advice of Thompson et al. (2002) and Shapiro (2005).

Lawler and Yoon's Social Exchange Theory

In an interesting theoretical chapter, Lawler and Yoon (1997) applied social exchange theory to the study of affect during negotiations. They argued that negotiators in a work context are likely to negotiate more than once. If they are able to reach a number of repetitive agreements, then these successes will engender reciprocated positive emotion. This positive emotion in turn will lead the individuals to "objectify" their dyadic relationship. That is, they will see their friendship as having an existence beyond each of them as individuals. When this is done, the two counterparts will show higher commitment and become more generous with one another. Two studies supported these theoretical propositions, although their applicability may depend somewhat on the type of positive affect considered (Lawler & Yoon, 1993; Lawler, Yoon, Baker, & Large, 1999).

In their first experiment, Lawler and Yoon (1993) had research participants negotiate a number of times, rather than reaching a single agreement. When the bargaining was between parties of equal power, the frequency of interaction was beneficial. It increased the number of mutual concessions and the number of agreements. As expected by the theory, repeated bargaining tended to increase pleasure/satisfaction. However, interest/excitement decreased over time. This suggests that the establishment of stable relationships increased pleasure but reduced excitement. In the later study, Lawler and colleagues (1999) found that dyads of equal power and higher mutual dependency increased the frequency of agreement in early interactions. More important, early-round agreement was positively related to later-round agreement even when more lucrative options became available. This supports the notion that habitualized exchange relationships developed over time, and that these were characterized by mutual trust. Further, these relationships had a strong emotional component that was tied to feelings of pleasure/happiness.

It is unfortunate that Lawler and Yoon's (1993, 1997) findings have not received more attention. Their work is generally comparable with the aforementioned experiment by Anderson and Thompson (2004, Study 2), who found that trait PA boosted dyadic trust, which in turn produced integrative agreements. Lawler and Yoon's work is also consistent with the McGinn and Keros (2002) study, in which negotiators who were friends were less likely to try to benefit at the other party's expense. Clearly, emotions arising from social exchange play an important role in the development of relationships during repeated negotiations.

Additional Effects: From Positive Affect to Future Interactions and Rapport

Similar findings were also obtained in three experiments reported by Kopelman et al. (2006). These experimenters did not use the term *mood*, but spoke of "positive, neutral, and negative emotions" (p. 81). Kopelman et al. found that positive emotions led bargainers to be more successful than did either neutral or negative emotions. So far, these findings share much in common with earlier work that we have already discussed (e.g., Anderson & Thompson, 2004; Baron, 1990; Carnevale & Isen, 1986).

Most relevant here were the findings regarding future interactions. In their first experiment, Kopelman and her colleagues found that when bargainers expressed positive feelings the two counterparts were more desirous of future collaboration. Indeed, they were likely to incorporate a longer-term business relationship into their contract. These findings are consistent with other research (e.g., Allred et al., 1997). Even third-party observers can be influenced by the relationship between opponents. Thompson and Kim (2000) had simulated mediators watch a videotape of two individuals negotiating a dispute. The third parties proposed better solutions when the two bargainers expressed a positive relationship than when they expressed a negative relationship.

Relationship effects are also important during electronic negotiations, in which the two counterparts may not have an opportunity to see each other face to face. In an e-mail negotiation experiment conducted by Moore et al. (1999), participants bargained with either an ingroup member from the same university or an out-group member from a rival university. Subjects who established a positive affective rapport tended to have fewer impasses. Affective rapport could be built through either being an ingroup member (i.e., both were from the same university) or practicing self-disclosure. Either of these two manipulations boosted the expression of positive affect. This affect, in turn, increased rapport, which lowered the incidence of impasses. We note that the Moore et al. study is quite similar to the findings reviewed by Lawler and Yoon (1997).

DIRECTIONS FOR FUTURE RESEARCH

In this section, we discuss four directions for future research. This section deals with a number of theoretical issues that remain, including the need for more research integrating moods and emotions, investigating the benefits of negative mood states, exploring positive emotions, and assessing complementarity.

Integrating Moods and Emotions

As we have seen, scholars interested in the study of affect during bargaining have emphasized either moods or emotions. Very little work has tried to emphasize both (for an exception, see Mullen, 2007). When preparing this chapter, this demarcation was quite evident to us. At times, it felt as if we were writing two "subchapters," one on mood and a second on emotion. Since moods and emotions are both viable affective processes, and since both appear to influence negotiation processes, at times concurrently, we would encourage future scholars to design conceptual frameworks that include both, as well as discussing the interaction between them.

Negative Mood States

Researchers investigating mood and emotion have often viewed positive affect as beneficial and negative affect as hazardous to one's outcomes (for an exception, see Carnevale, 2008). As we have seen, this is often a reasonable starting assumption. But, there are times when negative moods might actually help one to become a better bargainer. For example, Forgas's (1995, 1998, 2000; Forgas & George, 2001) AIM suggests that, in some circumstances, people in positive moods consider their alternatives less systematically. Depending on the context, negative mood might be useful to the extent that it leads one to more effortful thinking. These sorts of effects, where positive moods are not necessarily advantageous, are worthy of additional inquiry.

Positive Discrete Emotions

There has been considerable work on negative emotions, such as anger (van Kleef et al., 2004a, 2004b), guilt (Ketelaar & Au, 2003), fear (Young et al., 2010), and so on. Relatively little research has compared one discrete positive emotion to another discrete positive emotion. In this regard, we discussed the work of Butt et al. (2005), who investigated pride-achievement and gratitude, and Lawler and Yoon (1993), who examined interest/excitement and pleasure/commitment. Given these promising findings, it could be that negotiation researchers might be missing an opportunity. According to Fredrickson's (1998) *broaden-and-build* model there are a number of specific positive emotions. These include joy, interest, contentment, pride, and love. Fredrickson (2001) listed specific action tendencies that come with each. Much as anger and fear impel us in different ways (Kugler, Ordóñez, et al., 2009), each of these positive emotions may have unique effects on the negotiation process (for evidence, see Butt et al., 2005; Lawler & Yoon, 1993).

Complementary Emotions

It is important to take a closer look at the interpersonal effects of emotions. Generally speaking, when negotiation scholars think of emotions in a dyad, they assume that one person "catches" the feelings of the other (for a good review, see Thompson et al., 1999). However, as Thompson and her colleagues observed, this is not always the case. Emotions evolved to help human beings communicate with one another. Sometimes, they will provoke similar responses, as when an angry person makes you angry, but other times they will not. Keltner and Haidt (1999) and Folger and Cropanzano (2010) maintained that certain emotions come in complementary pairs. For example, we have seen that anger can provoke fear in people when it is targeted at an individual with low power (van Kleef et al., 2004a). Likewise, when one is engaged in distributive bargaining with an out-group member, a counterpart's disappointment can cause a negotiator to be pleased with his or her performance (Thompson et al., 1995). This complementarity seems to be relatively automatic and might even occur in response to expectations. In one interesting study, Lanzetta and Englis (1989) found that the expectation of cooperation led to physiological changes (e.g., activation of facial muscles) consistent with an empathic reaction. On the other hand, Lanzetta and Englis also found that the expectation of competition led to physiological changes consistent with a counterempathic reaction. These are important effects that deserve greater attention.

CONCLUSIONS

In closing, we emphasize our general conclusions. Ultimately, one cannot remove feelings from the negotiation process. As Shapiro (2002, p. 68) put it, human beings are almost always in a state of "perpetual emotion." We cannot ignore our feelings but must try to understand and manage them. Given this observation, it is important for scholars to better understand the relationship between affect and the negotiation process. We hope that our chapter has contributed to this understanding.

REFERENCES

Adam, H., Shirako, A., & Maddux, W. W. (2010). Cultural variance in the interpersonal effects of anger in negotiations. *Psychological Science, 21,* 882–889.

Adler, R. S., Rosen, B., & Silverstein, E. M. (1998, April). Emotions in negotiation: How to manage fear and anger. *Negotiation Journal,* pp. 161–179.

Allred, K. G. (1999). Anger and retaliation: Toward an understanding of impassioned conflict in organizations. In R. J. Bies, R. J. Lewicke, & B. H. Sheppard (Eds.), *Research on negotiation in organizations* (pp. 27–58). Stamford, CT: JAI Press.

Allred, K. G., Mallozzi, J. S., Matsui, F., & Raia, C. P. (1997). The influence of anger and compassion on negotiation performance. *Organizational Behavior and Human Decision Processes, 70,* 175–187.

Anderson, C., & Thompson, L. L. (2004). Affect from the top down: How powerful individuals' positive affect shapes negotiations. *Organizational Behavior and Human Decision Processes, 95,* 125–139.

Baron, R. A. (1976). The reduction of human aggression: A field study of the influence of incompatible responses. *Journal of Applied Social Psychology, 6,* 260–274.

Baron, R. A. (1984). Reducing organizational conflict: An incompatible response approach. *Journal of Applied Psychology, 69,* 272–279.

Baron, R. A. (1990). Environmentally induced positive affect: Its impact on self-efficacy, task performance, negotiation, and conflict. *Journal of Applied Social Psychology, 20,* 368–384.

Baron, R. A., Fortin, S. P., Frei, R. L. Hauver, L. A., & Shack, M. L. (1990). Reducing organizational conflict: The role of socially-induced positive affect. *The International Journal of Conflict Management, 1,* 133–152.

Barry, B. (1999). The tactical use of emotion in negotiation. In R. J. Bies, R. J. Lewicki, & B. H. Sheppard (Eds.), *Research on negotiation in organizations* (Vol. 7, pp. 93–121). Stamford, CT: JAI Press.

Barry, B., Fulmer, I. S., & Goates, N. (2006). Bargaining with feeling: Emotionality in and around negotiation. In L. L. Thompson (Ed.), *Negotiation theory and research* (pp. 99–127). New York: Psychology Press/Hove.

Barry, B., Fulmer, I. S., & van Kleef, G. A. (2004). I laughed, I cried, I settled: The role of emotion in negotiation. In M. J. Gelfand & J. M. Brett (Eds.), *The handbook of negotiation and culture* (pp. 71–94). Stanford, CA: Stanford Business Books.

Barry, B., & Oliver, R. L. (1996). Affect in dyadic negotiation: A model and propositions. *Organizational Behavior and Human Decision Processes, 67,* 127–143.

Barsade, S. G. (2002). The ripple effect: Emotional contagion and its influence on group behavior. *Administrative Science Quarterly, 47,* 644–675.

Bazerman, M. H., & Neale, M. A. (1992). *Negotiating rationally.* New York: Free Press.

Brown, A. D., & Curhan, J. R. (2010, August). *Misattribution of arousal in negotiation: How physiological arousal and construal of negotiation interact to predict subjective outcomes.* Paper presented at the annual meeting of the Academy of Management. Montréal, Québec.

Brown, B. R. (1968). The effects of need to maintain face on interpersonal bargaining. *Journal of Experimental Social Psychology, 4,* 107–122.

Brown, B. R. (1970). Face-saving following experimentally induced embarrassment. *Journal of Experimental Social Psychology, 6,* 255–271.

Butt, A. N., Choi, J. N., & Jaeger, A. M. (2005). The effects of self-emotion, counterpart emotion, and counterpart behavior on negotiator behavior: A comparison of individual-level and dyad-level dynamics. *Journal of Organizational Behavior, 26,* 681–704.

Campagna, R., Bottom, W., Kong, K., & Mislin, A. (June, 2010). *Flying bagels and social graces: The impact of strategic expressions of emotion on distrust and post settlement behavior.* Boston: International Association for Conflict Management.

Carnevale, P. J. (2008). Positive affect and decision frame in negotiation. *Group Decision and Negotiation, 17,* 51–63.

Carnevale, P. J., & Isen, A. M. (1986). The influence of positive affect and visual access on the discovery of integrative solutions in bilateral negotiation. *Organizational Behavior and Human Decision Processes, 37,* 1–13.

Conlon, D. E., & Hunt, C. S. (2002). Dealing with feelings: The influence of outcome representation on negotiation. *International Journal of Conflict Management, 13,* 38–58.

Connolly, T., & Zeelenberg, M. (2002). Regret in decision making. *Current Directions in Psychological Science, 11,* 212–220.

Curhan, J. R., Elfenbein, H. A., & Kilduff, G. J. (2009). Getting off on the right foot: Subjective value versus economic value in predicting longitudinal job outcomes from job offer negotiations. *Journal of Applied Psychology, 94,* 524–534.

Daly, J. P. (1991, January). The effects of anger on negotiations over mergers and acquisitions. *Negotiation Journal,* pp. 31–39.

Damasio, A. R. (1994). *Descartes' error: Emotion, reason, and the human brain.* New York: Putnam.

Davidson, M. N., & Greenhalgh, L. (1999). The role of emotion in negotiation: The impact of anger and race. In R. J. Bies, R. J. Lewicki, & B. H. Sheppard (Eds.), *Research on negotiation in organizations* (Vol. 7, pp. 3–26). Greenwich, CT: JAI Press.

Fisher, R., & Shapiro, D. (2005). *Beyond reason: Using emotions as you negotiate.* New York: Viking.

Folger, R., & Cropanzano, R. (2010). Social hierarchies and the evolution of moral emotions. In M. Schminke (Ed.) *Managerial ethics: Managing the psychology of morality* (pp. 207–234). New York: Routledge/Psychology Press.

Forgas, J. P. (1995). Mood and judgment: The affect infusion model (AIM). *Psychological Bulletin, 117,* 39–66.

Forgas, J. P. (1998). On feeling good and getting your way: Mood effects on negotiator cognition and bargaining strategies. *Journal of Personality and Social Psychology, 74,* 565–577.

Forgas, J. P. (2000). Affect and information processing strategies: An interactive relationship. In J. P. Forgas (Ed.), *Feeling and thinking: The role of affect in social cognition* (pp. 253–282). Cambridge, UK: Cambridge University Press.

Forgas, J. P., & George, J. M. (2001). Affective influences on judgments and behavior in organizations: An information processing perspective. *Organizational Behavior and Human Decision Processes, 86,* 3–34.

Frank, R. H. (1988). *Passions within reason: The strategic role of emotions.* New York: Norton.

Frank, R. H. (1990). A theory of moral sentiments. In J. J. Mansbridge (Ed.), *Beyond self-interest* (pp. 71–96). Chicago: University of Chicago Press.

Frank, R. H. (2004). Introducing moral emotions into models of rational choice. In A. S. R. Manstead, N. H. Frijda, & A. H. Fischer (Eds.), *Feelings and emotions: The Amsterdam symposium* (pp. 422–440). New York: Cambridge University Press.

Fredrickson, B. L. (1998). What good are positive emotions? *Review of General Psychology, 2,* 300–319.

Fredrickson, B. L. (2001). The role of positive emotions in positive psychology: The broaden-and-build theory of positive emotions. *American Psychologist, 56,* 218–226.

Fredrickson, B. L. (2009). *Positivity: Groundbreaking research reveals how to embrace the hidden strength of positive emotions, overcome negativity, and thrive.* New York: Random House.

Friedman, R., Anderson, C., Brett, J., Olekalns, M., Goates, N., & Lisco, C. C. (2004). The positive and negative effects of anger on dispute resolution: Evidence from electronically mediated disputes. *Journal of Applied Psychology, 89,* 369–376.

Frijda, N. H. Mesquita, B., Sonnemans, J., & van Goozen, S. (1991). The duration of effective phenomena or emotions, sentiments, and passions. In K. T. Strongman (Ed.), *International review of studies on emotion* (Vol. 1, pp. 187–225). New York: Wiley.

George, J. M., Jones, G. R., & Gonzales, J. A. (1998). The role of affect in cross-cultural negotiations. *Journal of International Business Studies, 29,* 749–783.

Gibson, D. E., Schweitzer, M. E., Callister, R. R., & Gray, B. (2009). The influence of anger expression on outcomes in organizations. *Negotiation and Conflict Management Research, 2,* 236–262.

Güth, W., Schmittberger, R., & Schwarze, B. (1982). An experimental analysis of ultimatum bargaining. *Journal of Economic Behavior and Organization, 3,* 411–429.

Hegtvedt, K. A., & Killian, C. (1999). Fairness and emotions: Reactions to the process and outcomes of negotiations. *Social Forces, 78,* 269–303.

Hertel, G., Neuhof, J., Theuer, T., & Kerr, N. L. (2000). Mood effects on cooperation in small groups: Does positive mood simply lead to more cooperation? *Cognition and Emotion, 14,* 441–472.

Keltner, D., & Haidt, J. (1999). Social functions of emotions at four levels of analysis. *Cognition and Emotion, 13,* 505–521.

Ketelaar, T. (2006). The role of moral sentiments in economic decision making. In D. De Cremer, M. Zeelenberg, & J. K. Murnighan (Eds.), *Social psychology and economics* (pp. 97–116). Mahwah, NJ: Erlbaum.

Ketelaar, T., & Au, W. T. (2003). The effects of guilt feelings on the behavior of uncooperative individuals in repeated social bargaining games: An affect-as-information interpretation of the role of emotion in social interaction. In C. Crawford & C. Salmon (Eds.), *Evolutionary psychology, public policy and personal decisions* (pp. 145–168). Mahwah, NJ: Erlbaum.

Kong, D. T., Tuncel, E., & Parks, J. M. (2010, June). *Anticipated happiness and negotiation decisions.* Boston: International Association for Conflict Management.

Kopelman, S., Rosette, A. S., & Thompson, L. (2006). The three faces of Eve: Strategic displays of positive, negative, and neutral emotions in negotiations. *Organizational Behavior and Human Decision Processes, 99,* 81–101.

Kramer, R. M., Newton, E., & Pommerenke, P. L. (1993). Self-enhancement biases and negotiator judgment: Effects of self-esteem and mood. *Organizational Behavior and Human Decision Processes, 56,* 110–133.

Kugler, T., Connolly, T., & Kausel, E. E. (2009). The effect of consequential thinking on trust game behavior. *Journal of Behavioral Decision Making, 22,* 101–119.

Kugler, T., Ordóñez, L., & Connolly, T. (2009). *Emotion, decisions, and risk: Betting on gambles vs. betting on people.* Unpublished manuscript.

Kumar, R. (1997). The role of affect in negotiations: An integrative overview. *Journal of Applied Behavioral Science, 33,* 84–100.

Kumar, R. (2004). Culture and emotions in intercultural negotiations: An overview. In M. J. Gelfand & J. M. Brett (Eds.), *The handbook of negotiation and culture* (pp. 95–113). Stanford, CA: Stanford Business Books.

Lanzetta, J. T., & Englis, B. G. (1989). Expectations of cooperation and competition and their effects on observers' vicarious emotional responses. *Journal of Personality and Social Psychology, 56,* 543–554.

Lawler, E. J., & Yoon, J. (1993). Power and the emergence of commitment behavior in negotiated exchange. *American Sociological Review, 58,* 465–481.

Lawler, E. J., & Yoon, J. (1997). Structural power and emotional processes in negotiation: A social exchange approach. In R. M. Kramer & D. M. Messick (Eds.), *Negotiation as a social process* (pp. 143–165). Thousand Oaks, CA: Sage.

Lawler, E. J., Yoon, J., Baker, M. R., & Large, M. D. (1999). Mutual dependence and gift giving in exchange relations. In B. Markovsky, J. O'Brien, & K. Heimer (Eds.), *Advances in group processes* (Vol. 12, pp. 271–298). Greenwich, CT: JAI Press.

Lerner, J. S., Gonzalez, R. M., Small, D. A., & Fischhoff, B. (2003). Effects of fear and anger on perceived risk of terrorism: A national field experiment. *Psychological Science, 14,* 144–150.

Lerner, J. S., Small, D. A., & Loewenstein, G. (2004). Heart strings and purse strings: Carryover effects of emotions on economic decisions. *Psychological Science, 15,* 337–341.

Malhotra, D., & Bazerman, M. H. (2008). Psychological influence in negotiation: An introduction long overdue. *Journal of Management, 34,* 509–532.

McGinn, K. L., & Keros, A. T. (2002). Improvisation and the logic of exchange in socially embedded transactions. *Administrative Science Quarterly, 47,* 442–473.

Moore, D. A., Kurtzberg, T. R., Thompson, L. L., & Morris, M. W. (1999). Long and short routes to success in electronically mediated negotiations: Group affiliations and good vibrations. *Organizational Behavior and Human Decision Processes, 77,* 22–43.

Moran, S., & Schweitzer, M. E. (2008). When better is worse: Envy and the use of deception. *Negotiation and Conflict Management Research, 1,* 3–29.

Morris, M. W., & Keltner, D. (2000). How emotions work: The social functions of emotional expression in negotiations. In B. M. Staw & R. I. Sutton (Eds.), *Research in organizational behavior* (Vol. II, pp. 1–50). Amsterdam: JAI.

Mullen, E. (2007). The reciprocal relationship between affect and perceptions of fairness. In K. Tornblom & R. Vermunt (Eds.), *Distributive and procedural justice: Research and social applications* (pp. 15–37). Burlington, VT: Ashgate.

O'Quinn, K., & Aronoff, J. (1981). Humor as a technique of social influence. *Social Psychology Quarterly, 44,* 349–357.

Overbeck, J. R., Neale, M. A., & Govan, C. L. (2010). I feel, therefore you act: Intrapersonal and interpersonal effects of emotion on negotiation as a function of social power. *Organizational Behavior and Human Decision Processes, 112,* 126–139.

Pettigrew, A., Massini, S., & Numagani, T. (2000). Innovative forms of organizing in Europe and Japan. *European Management Journal, 18,* 259–273.

Pham, M. T. (2007). Emotion and rationality: A critical review and interpretation of empirical evidence. *Review of General Psychology, 11,* 155–176.

Pillutla, M. M., & Murnighan, J. K. (1995). Being fair or appearing fair: Strategic behavior in ultimatum bargaining. *Academy of Management Journal, 38,* 1408–1426.

Pillutla, M. M., & Murnighan, J. K. (1996). Unfairness, anger, and spite: Emotional rejections of ultimatum offers. *Organizational Behavior and Human Decision Processes, 68,* 208–224.

Prasnikar, V., & Roth, A. E. (1992). Considerations of fairness and strategy: Experimental data from sequential games. *Quarterly Journal of Economics, 55,* 865–888.

Reb, J. (2008). Regret aversion and decision process quality: Effects of regret salience on decision process carefulness. *Organizational Behavior and Human Decision Processes, 105,* 169–182.

Reb, J., & Connolly, T. (2009). Myopic regret avoidance: Feedback avoidance and learning in repeated decision making. *Organizational Behavior and Human Decision Processes, 109,* 182–189.

Reb, J., & Connolly, T. (2010). The effects of action, normality, and decision carefulness on anticipated regret: Evidence for a broad mediating role of decision justifiability. *Cognition and Emotion, 24,* 1405–1420.

Schweiger, D. M., Atamer, T., & Calori, R. (2003). Transnational project teams and networks: Making the multinational organization more effective. *Journal of World Business, 38,* 127–140.

Shapiro, D. L. (2002). Negotiating emotions. *Conflict Resolution Quarterly, 20,* 67–82.

Shapiro, D. L. (2005). Enemies, allies, and emotions the power of positive emotions in negotiation. In M. L. Moffitt & R. C. Bordone (Eds.), *The handbook of dispute resolution* (pp. 66–82). San Francisco, CA: Jossey-Bass.

Sinaceur, M., & Tiedens, L. Z. (2006). Get made and get more than even: When and why anger expression is effective in negotiation. *Journal of Experimental Social Psychology, 42,* 314–322.

Slovic, P., Finucane, M., Peters, E., & MacGregor, D. G. (2002). The affect heuristic. In T. Gilovich, D. Griffin, & D. Kahneman (Eds.), *Heuristics and biases: The psychology of intuitive judgments* (pp. 397–420). New York: Cambridge University Press.

Steger, M. B. (2003). *Globalization: A very short introduction.* Oxford, UK: Oxford University Press.

Steinel, W., van Kleef, G. A., & Harinck, F. (2008). Are you talking to *me?!* Separating the people from the problem when expressing emotion in negotiation. *Journal of Experimental Social Psychology, 44,* 362–369.

Stephens, A. T., & Pham, M. T. (2008). On feelings as a heuristic for making offers in ultimatum negotiations. *Psychological Science, 19,* 1051–1058.

Straub, P., & Murnighan, J. L. (1995). An experimental investigation of ultimatums: Information, fairness, expectations, and lowest acceptable offers. *Journal of Economic Behavior and Organization, 27,* 345–365.

Stuhlmacher, A. F., & Citera, M. (2005). Hostile behavior and profit in virtual negotiation: A meta-analysis. *Journal of Business and Psychology, 20,* 69–93.

Subramaniam, M., & Venkatramen, N. (2001). Determinants of transnational new products development capability: Testing the influence of transferring and deploying tacit overseas knowledge. *Strategic Management Journal, 22,* 359–378.

Tedeschi, J., Burrill, D., & Gahagan, J. (1969). Social desirability, manifest anxiety, and social power. *Journal of Social Psychology, 77,* 231–239.

Thompson, L. L., & Kim, P. H. (2000). How the quality of third parties' settlement solutions is affected by the relationship between negotiators. *Journal of Experimental Psychology: Applied, 6,* 3–14.

Thompson, L. L., Medvec, V. H., Seiden, V., & Kopelman, S. (2002). Poker face, smiley face, and rant 'n' rave: Myths and realities about emotion in negotiation. In M. A. Hogg & R. S. Tindale (Eds.), *Blackwell handbook of social psychology: Group processes* (pp. 139–163). Malden, MA: Blackwell.

Thompson, L. L., Nadler, J., & Kim, P. H. (1999). Some like it hot: The case for the emotional negotiator. In L. L. Thompson, J. M. Levine, & D. M. Messick (Eds.), *Share cognition in organizations: The management of knowledge* (pp. 139–161). Mahwah, NJ: Erlbaum.

Thompson, L. L., Neale, M., & Sinaceur, M. (2004). The evolution of cognition and biases in negotiation research: An examination of cognition, social perspective, motivation, and emotion. In M. J. Gelfand & J. M. Brett (Eds.), *The handbook of negotiation and culture* (pp. 7–44). Stanford, CA: Stanford Business Books.

Thompson, L. L., Valley, K. L., & Kramer, R. M. (1995). The bittersweet feeling of success: An examination of social perception in negotiation. *Journal of Experimental Social Psychology, 31,* 467–492.

Van Dijk, E., & Tenbrunsel, A. (2002). The battle between self-interest and fairness. In S. W. Gilliland, D. D. Steiner, D. P. Skarlicki, & K. van den Bos (Eds.), *What motivates fairness in organizations?* (pp. 31–48). Greenwich, CT: Information Age.

Van Kleef, G. A. (2009). The emotions as social information (EASI) model. *Psychological Science, 18,* 184–188.

Van Kleef, G. A., & Côté, S. (2007). Expressing anger in conflict: When it helps and when it hurts. *Journal of Applied Psychology, 92,* 1557–1569.

Van Kleef, G. A., De Dreu, C. K. W., & Manstead, A. S. R. (2004a). The interpersonal effects of anger and happiness in negotiation. *Journal of Personality and Social Psychology, 86,* 57–76.

Van Kleef, G. A., De Dreu, C. K. W., & Manstead, A. S. R. (2004b). The interpersonal effects of emotions in negotiations: A motivated information processing approach. *Journal of Personality and Social Psychology, 87,* 510–528.

Van Kleef, G. A., De Dreu, C. K. W., Pietroni, D., & Manstead, A. S. R. (2006). Power and emotion in negotiation: Power moderates the interpersonal effects of anger and happiness on concession making. *European Journal of Social Psychology, 36,* 557–581.

Young, M. J., Jung, H., & Bauman, C. W. (2010, June). *What helps women ask for more? The role of incidental fear in the initiation of negotiation.* Boston: International Association for Conflict Management.

7

Negotiating the Peace in the Face of Modern Distrust: Dealing With Anger and Revenge in the 21st Century Workplace

Robert J. Bies and Thomas M. Tripp

INTRODUCTION

As we enter the second decade of the 21st century, while looking back at the first decade, we are reminded of the introductory sentences of *A Tale of Two Cities* by Charles Dickens (1859/1997, p. 13):

> It was the best of times, it was the worst of times, it was the age of wisdom, it was the age of foolishness, it was the epoch of belief, it was the epoch of incredulity, it was the season of Light, it was the season of Darkness, it was the spring of hope, it was the winter of despair.

We began the new millennium filled with great possibilities only to be met with 9/11. The first decade began with great prosperity driven by globalization only to end with global recession and growing distrust of organizations and those who lead and manage them. The decade that began with hope and optimism had given way to fear and pessimism.

A Puzzle for the 21st Century

One would hope that, in this "age of instability" and constant, even chaotic change, that leaders and managers would take advantage of the new techniques and technologies available to them to mitigate the effects of this "brave new world" and negotiate an effective peace to create superior deals. However, we worry that a 21st century danger is that employees will increasingly retaliate instead of negotiate or retaliate as a form of negotiation. As such, in this chapter we focus on how leaders and managers can create a workplace environment that promotes candor and transparency, which are essential ingredients for building trust and negotiating the peace between individuals and between organizational units in the 21st century workplace. While 21st century technology can help create transparency and candor (e.g., instant Internet searches for information about a product or service being negotiated), other aspects of technology may undermine the peace and blow up profitable deals. In particular, we investigate the growing problem of far-flung employees relying on distance-bridging technologies, including e-mail and social media, to interact and negotiate.

We say "problem" because, as revenge scholars, we worry about whether enough trust exists in many such virtual relationships to buffer against misunderstandings; without such buffers, employees often retaliate rather than cooperatively negotiate. For instance, as the ultimatum bargaining literature has made quite clear, people will "cut off one's own nose to spite one's face" by rejecting profitable deals when they believe the other side is exploiting them. We further worry that not only might social media and other tele-presence technologies not overcome deficits in trust, but also they may, in fact, create those deficits, resulting in the greater likelihood of revenge in the 21st century workplace.

The damage that such revenge can cause is incalculable. For example, working employee relationships are interrupted, if not broken beyond repair. They can even escalate into tit-for-tat feuds, dragging whole departments and branch locations into the feud. Other times, employees get even with customers when they do not like how the customers negotiate. As one coffee barista confessed, "I give decaf to people who are rude to me" (Tripp & Bies, 2009). In return, such customers increasingly go online and complain about bad service on a review site or complaint site, or construct their own anticorporate Web site (e.g., http://www.starbucked.com), or make a music video and post it on YouTube (Gregoire, Tripp, & Legoux, 2009).

Chapter Overview

Given such potential costs, what can managers do to prevent employees retaliating and instead get them to negotiate more cooperatively? To answer that, one must first understand why employees seek revenge. Thus, in this chapter, we explore the ways that employees and negotiators seek revenge, what triggers such revenge, and what other factors can attenuate such revenge. We define revenge as an action in response to some perceived harm or wrongdoing by another party that is intended to inflict damage, injury, discomfort, or punishment on the party judged responsible (Aquino, Tripp, & Bies, 2001). We then examine how new technologies may amplify this tendency, leading to harmed relationships and bad negotiation deals. Next, we suggest research directions to see whether the technologies do, in fact, amplify. Finally, we explore ways that negotiators and leaders can create trust to make negotiations less vengeful and more cooperative.

WHY EMPLOYEES ENGAGE IN REVENGE: EVIDENCE AND INSIGHTS FROM THE EMPIRICAL STUDIES

Much research, especially in the past 15 years, has examined why employees seek revenge and otherwise deliberately misbehave (for reviews, see Fox & Spector, 2005; McCullough, 2008; Miller, 2001; Tripp & Bies, 2009). This research has uncovered how to get employees to behave more productively and cooperatively. Negotiation and game theory research has also long been interested in the problem of cooperation (e.g., Axelrod, 1984, 1997; Pruitt & Rubin, 1986), although not of revenge per se. In this chapter, we draw from both streams of research to explain how and why revenge occurs, both within and outside negotiations.

To begin, we examine how revenge (in general, not just within negotiations) occurs. In our book (Tripp & Bies, 2009), we reviewed the empirical research and summarized five conclusions about revenge in the workplace: (a) revenge is triggered; (b) righteous anger sustains the desire for revenge; (c) inferences of the offenders' motives drive anger; (d) revenge can be expressed in many forms; and (e) strategies exist to weaken the desire for revenge. We briefly elaborate on these key conclusions.

Triggers of Revenge

Our research (e.g., Bies & Tripp, 1996) and that of others (e.g., Allred, 1999; Skarlicki & Folger, 1997) made it clear that revenge is a provoked, or "triggered," behavior. Triggers include (a) goal obstruction; (b) violation of rules, norms, and promises; and (c) status and power derogation. The last two sources of provocation are rooted in the sense of injustice, while goal obstruction is not necessarily a justice event.

Goal Obstruction

When one frustrates the attainment of goals in organizations, it can lead to acts of revenge in response (Morrill, 1992). Goal obstruction can lead to frustration (Buss, 1962), and that frustration can lead to an aggressive response like revenge (Neuman & Baron, 1997).

Violation of Rules, Norms, or Promises

Employees are motivated to seek revenge when the formal rules of the organization are violated (Bies & Tripp, 1996). One such example is organizational decision makers who change the rules or criteria of decision making after the fact to justify a self-serving judgment (Bies & Tripp, 1996). Another example of rule violation involves a formal breach of a contract between an employee and employer, which can lead to litigation (Bies & Tyler, 1993).

Violations are not limited to formal rules, but also include breaches of social norms and etiquette. For example, when bosses or coworkers make promises but then break them, or even lie outright, the victims may be motivated to avenge such wrongs (Bies & Tripp, 1996). More broadly, any perceived inequities on the job or violations of fairness norms can motivate revenge (cf. Skarlicki & Folger, 1997). Examples of such inequities and violations include bosses or coworkers who shirk their job responsibilities, take undue credit for a team's performance, or outright "steal" ideas (Bies & Tripp, 1996). The revenge motive may also be salient when private confidences or secrets are disclosed to others inside or outside the organization—that is, when people feel "betrayed" by someone they trusted (Bies, 1993).

Status and Power Derogation

Several studies suggest that attempts to derogate a person's status or power can motivate revenge (Bies & Tripp, 1996). For example, bosses who are hypercritical, overdemanding, and overly harsh—even cruel—in their dealings with subordinates over time can spark revenge cognitions and emotions (Bies & Tripp, 1996, 1998). Other revenge-provoking incidents include destructive criticism (Baron, 1988), public ridicule intended to embarrass a subordinate or coworker (Morrill, 1992), or a boss or peer wrongly accusing the employee (Bies & Tripp, 1996).

Righteous Anger Sustains the Desire for Revenge

Revenge may be a dish best served cold, but it usually is cooked in a very hot oven. Vengeance-minded employees are very angry employees (Allred, 1999). In our earlier research in which we content analyzed nearly 600 stories of workplace revenge, as well as in others' research (Hornstein, 1996; Mikula, 1986; Mikula, Petri, & Tanzer, 1990), the nature of the anger became clear. That is, anger has many facets, including: *moral righteousness, intensity,* and *rumination.*

Moral Righteousness

Victims are more than mad; they moralize. That is, they focus on the harm as a violation of norms of fair treatment. They were not just hurt; they were *wronged.* Given the types of injustice that provoke revenge, especially status derogation and rule violations, it is not surprising that victims' anger often reflects a sense of violation that was more than mere "unmet expectations." For example, in the work of Bies and Tripp (1996), one individual described a betrayed confidence as causing her world to be "shattered," as what she assumed to be "sacred and true—the trust of a friend" was violated, if not destroyed forever. It is the sense of injustice that commands their attention. And, it is this sense of injustice that they feel must be balanced and quenched with an act of justice, even vigilante justice.

Intensity

Victims often focus on the intensity of the emotions they experience in injustice. The intensity reveals a strong visceral response of physiological and psychological pain. In fact, the initial emotions of injustice are often described as "white hot," "furious," "bitter," and "volatile," characterized by expressions of pain, anger, and rage (Bies & Tripp, 1996). One person described herself as "inflamed," "enraged," and "consumed" by thoughts of revenge, while another person needed to satisfy the "burning desire of revenge." Others have reported a variety of physiological symptoms, including uncontrollable crying, "knots in the stomach," and physical exhaustion.

Rumination

Further, the emotions of injustice can create a psychological and physiological stranglehold over the individual. The emotions of revenge can endure over time, sometimes for days, even weeks and months, if not longer. Indeed, the emotions of revenge can be like a "social toxin" (Hornstein, 1996), "poisoning" their professional and personal lives over time. For an extreme example, Matthews (1988) recounted an example of an individual who let a harmdoer "live inside his head rent free" for over 10 years after the initial injustice. And, as Bies and Tripp (1996) found, often the emotions endure due to the social support of coworkers who continually "vent" about the injustice, or what Morrill (1992) referred to as "bitch sessions."

Inferences of the Harmdoer's Motives Drive Anger

What really makes victims angry enough to become avengers is not simply that some "harmdoer" obstructed their goals, broke the rules, or derogated their status, but the *reason why* the harmdoer did it. The more intentional the reason, then the greater the anger and subsequent desire for revenge is (Bies & Tripp, 1996; Crossley, 2009; Gregoire, Laufer, & Tripp, 2010). Crossley (2009) showed that the more the victim inferred that the harmdoer was motivated to harm that particular victim (i.e., "malice" motive)—as opposed to being willing to harm any person who would advance the harmdoer's agenda (i.e., "greed" motive)—the angrier the victim became, and the more revenge and avoidance, and less reconciliation, the victim sought. Gregoire et al. (2010) found a similar relationship with customers who had received bad service from a firm: Customers who perceived that firms caused bad service for greed-based reasons (e.g., to save money) rather than unintentionally (e.g., an honest mistake) became angrier, desired revenge more strongly, and actually sought revenge.

If the victim can blame the harmdoer, then the victim will likely construe the harmdoer's action as a personal attack (Bies, 2001), an act of aggression that will trigger anger (Cahn, 1949; Frank, 1987). As such, revenge often is viewed as a "legitimate" and rational response of self-defense in response to an aggressive action by another. Indeed, revenge is, in many cases, a response to a perceived injustice (Skarlicki & Folger, 1997). Thus, revenge is most often intended to restore justice. For instance, while engaging in revenge, people reported their strong belief that they were "doing the right thing" and that they were "doing justice." (Tripp & Bies, 1997). Therefore, revenge has its own moral imperative (Bies & Tripp, 1996; McLean & Parks, 1997). The justice rationality can be a powerful motivation and justification for revenge.

Because blame and inferences of a harmdoer's motive are such key elements of revenge episodes, it is worth considering how this inference process can go awry. In other words, what aspects of the justice-centered sense-making process can amplify the emotions of revenge? Our research on revenge has identified several such cognitive processes that can bias the blame assignment process (Bies, Tripp, & Kramer, 1997). First, there is the *overly personalistic attribution* (Bies & Tripp, 1996) by which victims believe the motive for harm was more intentional than it really was. A second important cognitive process contributing to individuals' perceptions that they are being intentionally harmed or singled out unfairly is the *biased punctuation of conflict* (Bies et al., 1997). Biased punctuation of conflict refers to a tendency for individuals to construe the history of conflict with others in a self-serving way. That is, individuals remember the conflict such that the other person started the conflict originally and started each new round of conflict. For example, in a tit-for-tat feud, each party perceives itself as the avenging victim and perceives its opponent as the aggressor against whom one must defend. A third cognitive process that may intensify blame is an *ego defensiveness,* by which one perceives that one did no wrong. We discuss these cognitive dynamics in the context of negotiation.

The Many Expressions of Revenge

The enactment of revenge can take many forms, depending on the situation and the objective (Bies & Tripp, 1996, 1998; Skarlicki & Folger, 1997; Tripp & Bies, 1997). For example, some forms of revenge resembled inequity reduction responses. For instance, people might *avoid the harmdoers* for a short period of time, refusing to greet them or even acknowledge their presence. Or, people might *withhold effort or work* (Bies & Tripp, 1996; Tripp & Bies, 1997), such as deliberately not supporting the harmdoer when support is needed or intentionally turning in poor work performance. Other people sometimes *transfer out of the job or department* as the ultimate act of withholding support and friendship. In all these acts, the benefit the harmdoer receives from the avenger is reduced or eliminated, thus restoring equity in the relationship.

In other cases, the act of revenge not only may focus on avoiding or not helping the harmdoer but also may focus on going out of one's way to harm the harmdoer. We found (Bies and Tripp, 1996; Tripp and Bies, 1997) such aggressive elements in the following types of revenge: public complaints designed to humiliate another person, public demands for apologies that are intended to embarrass the perpetrator, "bad-mouthing" the perpetrator, whistle-blowing, and litigation.

Some avengers prefer a more direct approach, such as private confrontations with the harmdoers to problem-solve and negotiate "fair" resolutions to their situations. Thus, justice can also be served when the harmdoers receive feedback that particular behaviors or attitudes hurt others or are inappropriate (Bies & Tripp, 1996). Often, the harmdoers are unaware of the harms they commit against coworkers, and being made aware is sufficient for them to correct their behaviors. In these situations, the avengers seek to restore justice by eliminating the source of the injustice, but they do not necessarily seek recompense beyond the discomfort such private confrontations inflict on the perpetrators.

Revenge-Weakening Strategies and Contexts

Even when victims are angry and strongly desire revenge, they do not always seek it. They may cope instead by forgiving or reconciling. Which coping response victims choose depends on several factors, including the victim's power relative to the harmdoer (Kim, Smith, & Brigham, 1998), the victim's hierarchical status in the organization (Aquino et al., 2001; Aquino, Tripp, & Bies, 2006), and the procedural justice climate in the organization (Aquino et al., 2006).

Victim's Power and Hierarchical Status

One situational factor that has been researched is the victim's power. In a laboratory study, Kim et al. (1998) found that the relative power of the victim to the harmdoer influences whether victims will seek revenge. In short, when the victims have more power than their harmdoers, they are much more likely to get even than when the victims have less power than their harmdoers. This effect occurs because those with more status have more means for revenge and thus also have less fear of counterretaliation from the harmdoer/target because the harmdoer/target has fewer means available. Aquino et al. (2001, 2006) twice confirmed Kim et al.'s findings in field settings showing that victims who have higher relative hierarchical status are more likely to seek revenge (albeit when the procedural justice climate is low; this is discussed next). Aquino et al. (2001, 2006) further showed that the victim's absolute hierarchical status in the organization also influences the choice of coping response, independently of the offender's organizational status. Specifically, Aquino et al. (2001) found that the higher in the organization the victim is, the less likely the victim will seek revenge. This effect occurs perhaps because those lower in status possess fewer symbolic, self-affirming resources (e.g., prestigious titles, important assignments, high salaries, positions of authority) and therefore may be more sensitive to interpersonal slights and insults than those who possess a surplus of such resources (Aquino et al., 2006; Baumeister, Smart, & Boden, 1996; Wicklund & Gollwitzer, 1982).

Procedural Justice Climate

Aquino et al. (2006) also found that the procedural justice climate of the organization influences the choice of coping response. When victims perceive an organization has fair grievance procedures, victims more likely pursue justice through official, organizational channels; however, when victims perceive that organizations have unfair grievance procedures, then victims will consider pursuing justice on their own, much as vigilantes "take the law into their own hands." Moreover, the effect of power depends on the perceived procedural justice climate. The pattern of this interaction is such that revenge is more likely (and forgiveness and reconciliation less likely) when relative status is highly in the victim's favor, but when both relative status is low and procedural justice climate is high, revenge is less likely (and forgiveness and reconciliation more likely).

VENGEANCE IN NEGOTIATIONS: IS IT REALLY SUCH A GOOD IDEA?

In the previous section, we examined the triggers, processes, and expressions of revenge in the generic workplace. Next, we turn to revenge that is specific to negotiations. Common experience and folklore suggest many ways that vengeance may play out in negotiation. Such vengeance can fit into one of two categories: tactical or emotional. That is, sometimes vengeance is a cold act committed by calculating negotiators who have not lost sight of their goal, which is to get the best outcome possible. Other times, vengeance is a hot response, committed by angry negotiators who may have lost sight of their original goal. Unfortunately, both kinds of vengeance often do not turn out as intended because both kinds can escalate the conflict. We consider each kind of vengeance in turn.

Tactical Vengeance

Tactical vengeance comprises those actions that are designed to shape the behavior of the other party. If the other party behaves too aggressively or competitively, the first party may wish to "teach a lesson" to the other party. For instance, if one party withholds information, the second party may in return withhold information. Also, if another party uses a dirty trick, like the snow job, then the second party may also use a dirty trick. Such tit-for-tat exchanges may be intended to turn a competitive negotiation into a more cooperative negotiation. Indeed, many negotiation courses teach tit for tat as a strategy to get the other party to cooperate when it is not cooperating. Given this common advice, it is worthwhile to analyze the pros and cons of tit-for-tat vengeance as a negotiation strategy, which we do next.

The Case for Tit for Tat

The best-known case for tit for tat came from Robert Axelrod (1984). Axelrod designed a computer simulation to determine the best strategy for playing an iterated prisoner's dilemma (PD) game. In this game, tit for tat was the best strategy because it did the best job of *encouraging* other strategies to cooperate. To understand this counterintuitive result, a little more explanation is provided.

A PD game is perhaps the best-known game in all of game theory and is used to model conflict between two parties when there is some incentive to cooperate and some incentive to compete (just like in a negotiation). In short, the game has two players who must decide either to cooperate or to compete with each other. However, the parties make this choice simultaneously, each party not knowing what the other party is choosing and unable to communicate about the choice. Both parties receive higher rewards if they both choose to cooperate than if they both choose to compete; however, if one party chooses to compete while the other party chooses to cooperate, the party who competes get a very large reward (the largest possible in the game), while the party who cooperates gets a very small reward (the smallest reward possible in the game). Thus, here is the dilemma: Both parties are better off if both cooperate than if both compete, but from an individual party's perspective, no matter what the other party chooses to do, one is always better off choosing to compete.

In an *iterated* PD game, two players make this choice not once, but many times over many rounds. Moreover, each player learns what the other player decided for a round after that round is completed, but before the next round is played. This provides players opportunities to respond to what the other player is choosing.

In Axelrod's famous iterated PD tournament, he had participants submit strategies (as algorithms) for playing a 200-round game; furthermore, it was a round-robin tournament, meaning that every strategy played every other strategy once. The strategy that accumulated the most points over the course of the tournament, but not necessarily the strategy that won the most matches, was declared the winner. Anatol Rappoport submitted the winning strategy: tit for tat. Tit for tat makes the cooperative choice on Round 1, and then on each subsequent round, it repeats the choice its opponent made in the previous round: If the opponent cooperated in Round r, tit for tat cooperates in Round $r + 1$; if the opponent competed in Round r, then tit for tat defects in Round $r + 1$.

Tit for tat won the tournament because it was the most successful of all strategies at getting its opponent to make cooperative choices. That is, tit for tat did the best job of avoiding costly escalations of conflict in which each player punishes the other with frequent defections. Axelrod published the results of this tournament in *Science* and then held a second, identical tournament (Axelrod & Hamilton, 1981). Tit for tat also won the second tournament.

Axelrod (1984) identified four properties that make tit for tat so successful. First, it is "nice" in that it never defects first. Second, it "responds" in that it retaliates to a defection with a defection. Third, it "forgives" in that as soon as its opponent makes a cooperative choice, tit for tat cooperates the very next round; tit for tat does not "hold grudges." Fourth, tit for tat is a very "simple" strategy in that it is easy to predict: in particular, the opponent can predict that any cooperative choice will be rewarded by tit for tat with cooperation, and any defection choice will be punished by tit for tat with a defection.

Tit for tat is, at its core, a revenge strategy (Gibson, Bottom, & Murnighan, 1999). Tit for tat takes an "eye for an eye." Tit for tat communicates, "If you don't cooperate with me, I will get even with you next time." In fact, in an iterated prisoner's dilemma game such as Axelrod's, all tit for tat can do is literally even the score: Every round, tit for tat either ties or is tied with its opponent in terms of points accumulated during the match; tit for tat can never pull ahead. It is these properties and messages that can make tit for tat very useful in negotiations to get the other party to cooperate. Thus, it suggests that revenge can be a good idea in negotiations.

The Case Against Tit for Tat

While tit for tat is a rational, utility-maximizing strategy within the strict and tamed confines of a well-specified PD game, what is it in the untamed, unspecified, unconfined, and generally messy realm of real human negotiations? Real human negotiation is "messy" because it is contextually embedded, full of misperceptions, and driven by emotionally clouded judgments. Yet, the classic tit-for-tat game is anything but messy: Full information regarding the payoffs, penalties, and sequence of moves radically minimizes misperceptions; in short, both parties are keeping the same scorecard. Fisher and Brown (1988, p. 201) stated, "Since relationships do not fit the Prisoners' Dilemma model, the analysis suggesting tit-for-tat does not apply. Furthermore, trying to pursue tit-for-tat on relationship issues may be dangerous." So, just because tit for tat performs well in PD games does not mean that it would be effective in many negotiation settings. When it would or would not largely depends on how accurate the scorecard is—how much both parties' scorecards show the same score.

The scorecard can be inaccurate in several ways. First, in the PD games, which literally have a scorecard that all players can see, the magnitude of payoffs and penalties are objective, known, and agreed on by both players; each party knows how many points or dollars are contained in the reward payoff. Also, each party knows not only what he or she gets but also what the other party gets. It is all spelled out. However, it is not all spelled out in real workplace negotiations: Outcomes are neither objective nor perceived similarly by all parties. We explain how this is so next.

Rewards and punishments come in varying shapes and sizes that cannot always be quantified. That is, negotiated rewards include not only the easily quantified outcomes like money but also the unquantifiable outcomes like certainty, praise, and respect. Negotiated punishments include not only the easily quantified monetary penalties but also the unquantifiable insults, disrespects, being ignored, being yelled at, and so on. Also, whatever the intrinsic value of such outcomes, parties to a negotiation may misjudge the value that each other places on these items.

Not only may parties make errors when judging the impact of rewards and punishments on others, but also these errors may not occur only randomly. In fact, conflicting perceptions of the value of outcomes may be egocentrically biased. That is, to protect one's ego, one may inflate or shrink one's own perception of various outcomes. For example, suppose a person wants to "play the victim," perhaps to claim the moral high ground or even to use the rhetoric of injustice for personal gain. This person may inflate all his or her sacrifices and the punishments that the other party inflicted on him or her and deemphasize the rewards received and the punishments inflicted on the other party. If, instead, one wants to feel superior, like he or she has "won" the conflict by getting a "good deal," the person may deemphasize personal sacrifices and the punishment the other party has inflicted (e.g., "Oh *that*? *That* didn't hurt") and inflate the rewards received and the severity of the punishments inflicted on the other party.

So far, we have discussed misperceptions that may occur in any one round. But, misperceptions may occur or accumulate across rounds over time. If the problem of objectively evaluating a single exchange of favors or punishments is severe enough, then the difficulty of objectively evaluating a history of exchanges multiplies the errors. For not only may perceptions be faulty, but also memory may be. Thus, as each exchange recedes into the ongoing history of the extended negotiation, the evaluation of each round, and of the aggregation of rounds, can become even more egocentrically distorted.

The biased punctuation of the conflict history can explain the aggregate impact of selectively remembered events on the final scorecard. Biased punctuation of conflict history refers to a tendency for individuals to construe the history of conflict with others in a self-serving and provocative fashion. In particular, in a two-party conflict, each party believes the other party "started it." In an iterated PD game, such as Axelrod's, it is clear to both parties when Round 1 is, and the scorecard reveals who defected first, thus "starting" exchanges of defections. But without such a scorecard, and with imperfect memory, what happens if the parties no longer remember who defected first? Indeed, what if each party believes the other party defected first? Then, each party views the other party as having started the dirty play, which also means that for every subsequent pair of defections, each party views the other's defections as escalations, whereas one's own defections are retaliations. As such, each party is convinced it is the innocent victim, and the other party is the hostile aggressor. Each party is also convinced one's own aggressive actions merely tie the score, while the other's aggressive actions put the other "in the lead."

To summarize, we have argued that parties in a feud cannot keep the same scorecard. They are unlikely to agree on who did what to whom, how bad or good it was, and who started it. As such, cold, calculated vengeance in negotiations is likely to escalate conflict rather than encourage cooperation. Consequently, tit for tat should be avoided.

Emotional Vengeance

Negotiators do not always, if usually, respond to others' offenses coolly; sometimes, negotiators get very angry (Lewicki, Barry, & Saunders, 2010). When angered, they may lose sight of their goals or change their goals. For example, negotiators may deliberately sabotage good deals to deny the other party any satisfaction, as when a consumer, after feeling poorly treated by the salesperson, walks away from what the consumer knows is a good deal. Alternatively, negotiators who feel unfairly treated, instead of walking away, may negotiate more competitively and less cooperatively. This is what Allred, Mallozzi, Matsui, and Raia (1997) found: Angry negotiators often fail to cooperate and then achieve suboptimal gains.

Tripp, Sondak, and Bies (1995) interpreted the ultimatum bargaining game literature as examples of negotiators willfully forgoing cash to punish stingy parties. In the typical ultimatum bargaining game experiment, a pair of subjects has a fixed sum of money to divide; one subject, the proposer, proposes a division, and the other subject, the decider, chooses to accept or reject the division offered by the proposer. If the decider rejects the suggested division, neither subject receives any money. A "rational" proposer should maximize one's own outcome by offering the decider only slightly more than zero and demanding everything else for him- or herself. Because even a very small amount of money is still more desirable than nothing, a rational decider should accept such an offer. However, the typical results substantially differ from this rational solution: The median division suggested by the proposers is 60%/40%; this offer is usually accepted. Those subjects who offer less than 40% to the deciders usually find their offers rejected. In short, deciders are willing to reject a profitable offer if it is too stingy.

Why would the deciders be so willing to cut off their noses to spite their faces? Rabin (1993) suggested that rather than being either entirely selfish or altruistic, individuals prefer to (a) help those who are kind to them and (b) harm those who are unkind. In other words, they want to get even.

Is wanting to get even a rational goal? On the one hand, if the goal of getting even is a goal that exists only in the heat of the moment—and later negotiators cool down and regret their sabotaging a deal that would have better met the goals they begin with *and that they still hold* (e.g., a profitable deal)—then getting even is a mistake. On the other hand, if getting even satisfies other, stable goals or values that dwarf the original goal (e.g., a profitable deal), then getting even may be worth it. Elfenbein and Curhan (Chapter 5, this volume) provide evidence that negotiators do seek to satisfy values other than instrumental ones, such as "self-values" (e.g., feeling competent), "process values" (e.g., being treated fairly), and "relationship values" (e.g., building a trusting relationship). Nonetheless, even if these other values are satisfied, getting even still may not be worth it if getting even escalates the negotiation into resource- and time-consuming conflict.

Rational or not, negotiators want not only good deals but also fair deals and fair treatment, and not only in terms of equitable outcomes but also in terms of process, respect, and trustworthy behaviors. Moreover, if they do not get it, they may retaliate, as the research on generic workplace revenge would suggest.

THE 21st CENTURY CHALLENGES

We suspect that 21st century technologies too often will make negotiators retaliate more, not less. As the 21st century opens, one trend is clear: Interactions, including negotiations, are increasingly negotiated at a distance, and often the distance is bridged by communication technology, such as e-mail, text messaging, and VOIP (Voice Over Internet Protocol) phone calls. However, such communication technology in many ways makes a dangerous substitute for face-to-face negotiations. Not only do communication technologies provide new means for revenge, such as badmouthing offenders online via social networking sites (e.g., Facebook) and business-related complaint sites (e.g., http://www.rippedoffreport.com), but also during computer-mediated negotiating, misperceptions occur easily, thus trust is harder to manage, making revenge more likely to occur and forgiveness harder to achieve.

Much research in the information systems literature has documented the problems inherent in computer-mediated communications (e.g., see Baltes, Dickson, Sherman, Bauer, & LaGanke, 2002). One such problem is the "flame war," in which online misunderstandings escalate tit for tat into increasingly hostile or insulting exchanges. Media richness theory (Daft & Lengel, 1986) offers insights into how misunderstandings and escalations occur. Media richness theory argues that face-to-face communication is the richest communication medium and leads to better performance on "equivocal" tasks (those tasks for which information can lead to many, possibly conflicting, interpretations), in part because immediate feedback and redundant communication channels make misunderstanding less likely (Dennis & Kinney, 1998).

In an experiment testing media richness theory in negotiations, Kahai and Cooper (2003) found that deleterious features of computer-mediated communication led to worse negotiations. Specifically, the deleterious features were (a) relative lack of immediate feedback, feedback that is helpful for "rapid bidirectional communication and, hence, rapid reinterpretation and clarification of messages" (p. 266); (b) fewer cues, such as vocal inflections and body gestures; and (c) reduced socioemotional communication (i.e., showing friendliness and support or hostility and rejection). In their experiment, they showed that these features in turn caused less-accurate social perceptions and less perceived ability to detect others' deception, thus resulting in lower-quality outcomes in mixed-motive negotiations.

Beyond media richness theory, the biases we have analyzed in our revenge research can explain further the problems inherent in media-lean communications and thus in negotiating at a distance. In short, sense making of an offense, which is difficult enough in face-to-face encounters, is likely even more error prone in computer-mediated encounters. Put another way, computer mediation of communications strips information and thus adds ambiguities—ambiguities that provide a breeding ground for the paranoid biases that lead to overly sinister attributions about the other negotiator's intent. To elaborate, in face-to-face encounters, tone of speech (e.g., the inflections in one's voice) communicates beyond the text of a person's words the person's intention.

For example, if one negotiator asks the other, "What do you need?" the negotiator can communicate different intentions by vocally emphasizing different words: "What do you *need*?" versus "*What* do you need?!" or even, "What do *you* need?" In the first question, the negotiator communicates that he or she wants to understand the other's needs that underlay the other's requests. Clearly, the intention is positive. In the second question, the negotiator communicates exasperation and annoyance with the other's withholding of information. This may suggest an intention to accuse or blame and thus not care about hurting the other's feelings. In the third question, the negotiator communicates a concern for helping the other negotiator meet his or her needs. Clearly, the intention is positive and other-centered. If the negotiators are speaking face to face, the inflection and emphasis (and perhaps body language) make clear which of the three messages the correct message is and how much the negotiator intends to help the other. But, suppose instead this question is asked in abbreviated text via e-mail, or even instant messaging (IM) texting, as, "what u need?" Then, neither tone nor intention is communicated.

So, with a lack of information about intention, what could go wrong? Wouldn't the negotiator just infer the most favorable intention of concern for helping—or at least be equally likely to infer each of the three inferences? We suspect not. While *rational* negotiators should construe a lack of information about intentions as neutral, negotiators are not rational. In particular, let us revisit the irrationalities discussed previously in this chapter.

The sinister attribution error (Kramer, 1994) suggests that when information is ambiguous about intentions, the tendency is to err on the side of inferring sinister intentions more than inferring benign intentions, particularly when negotiation processes or outcomes do not go as wished. Similar evidence exists in the justice literature of people making judgments in the absence of direct information (Lind, 2001). For instance, when outcomes are unfair but no information about processes exists, recipients of bad outcomes infer anyway that the processes must also be unfair (Daly & Tripp, 1996). The problem in electronically mediated negotiations is that much more of the information is ambiguous.

Rumination may also be more prevalent in electronically mediated negotiations than in some face-to-face negotiations. At least, for simple negotiations, in the face-to-face setting the negotiations occur relatively quickly, with fewer pauses for negotiators to ruminate about what may have just occurred. By contrast, in e-mail negotiations, the negotiation often is broken up into discrete rounds; minutes, if not days, can pass between rounds. These breaks offer negotiators opportunities to ruminate. Even worse, during these rumination breaks, negotiators have time to use social information to confirm their worst suspicions. When ambiguous information about intentions arises, the negotiator may ask one's friends if they also see the sinister intent that the negotiator sees. Taken together, these electronically mediated, media-lean negotiations are ripe for distrust.

All this begs the question of whether these types of negotiations will dominate the 21st century. Ten years into the century, these negotiations are becoming more prevalent. Even worse, the media may be getting leaner and leaner as more and more people switch from face-to-face interaction or phone calls to e-mail and even from e-mail to texting. This is a dangerous trend for negotiators. Many more negotiations may stop before they get started; alternatively, many more negotiations will resemble (if not turn into) flame wars through tit-for-tat escalation.

CONFLICT-MITIGATING STRATEGIES: PRACTICAL ADVICE FOR LEADERS AND MANAGERS

Given what the research has uncovered so far, we can recommend a number of conflict mitigation strategies. We divide our advice into strategies for (a) managing new communication technologies and (b) building the organizational foundations of trust that will facilitate negotiation in these difficult economic times of the 21st century.

Managing New Technologies

There are other technologies increasingly available to close the distance between geographically separated negotiators. One such technology is high-definition videoconferencing. Such technology is nearly face to face, offering all the aural cues and many of the visual cues that provide context to messages. This technology is becoming increasingly cheap and reliable; indeed, most personal computers and laptops manufactured now include built-in cameras just for this purpose. As of this writing, cell phones also now are beginning to include user-facing cameras strictly for the purpose of videoconferencing.

On the other hand, just because the technology exists does not mean that employees will prefer to use it. Indeed, the telephone has long offered a much richer communication medium than e-mail, but increasingly employees prefer to write e-mail messages than to use the telephone. In general, witness the now-common workplace practice of sending e-mails to colleagues whose offices are two doors down the hallway.

Thus, we advise managers to encourage their employees to use media-rich technologies rather than media-lean methods. When employees would text, tell them to send a detailed e-mail. When employees would e-mail, tell them to pick up the phone. And, when they schedule a meeting for the phone, tell them to set up a videoconference. Wherever possible and affordable, employees should meet in person, especially for sensitive negotiations.

We also recommend that negotiations begin with a media-rich format before using a media-lean one. For instance, before negotiating via e-mail (if one must), at least begin with a face-to-face meeting so the negotiators can get a read on each other and see each other as real humans. This will help build a base level of trust that may buffer any future misunderstandings (e.g., reduce the sinister attribution error), about which we have more to say in the next section. Also, meeting people in person makes them less anonymous, which may reduce the "bombardier effect" (Milgram, 1974); that is, it is easier to hurt anonymous, invisible people at a distance than to hurt visible people one knows, much as it is easier to kill people as a bombardier bombing them from an altitude of 30,000 feet than it is for a foot soldier shooting them at point-blank range.

These recommendations should work because richer communication and closer contact should help reduce the various cognitive biases that encourage negotiators to believe that the other negotiators are out to harm or exploit them intentionally. Without this sinister belief, negotiators will be less motivated to retaliate. Without retaliation, conflicts will not escalate, and more cooperative and peaceful negotiations should ensue.

The difficulty, however, is getting younger generations of employees to use media-rich technologies. Younger generations are very comfortable with high-tech, media-lean technologies, and many shun using low-tech, media-rich media. Indeed, many people have given up the richer landline, corded telephones (richer in that they have significantly higher audio quality) for leaner cell phones. And even then, instead of talking, many people often text. Managers will have to overcome this by insisting to their employees that negotiations occur in the richest format available.

Building the Foundation of Organizational Trust in Difficult Economic Times

One of the primary roles for leaders is to infuse their institutions with values that will guide its members in cooperation to achieve organizational effectiveness and mission success (Selznick, 1957). These values become the background and context for relationships and interaction in the workplace. In a world of new technologies, economic uncertainty, and bad news, one of the key leadership challenges is to infuse the organization with the values of trust to promote cooperation and peace (Bies, 2010). In our view, trust acts as a "lubricant" to facilitate the possibility of negotiation when distrust is prevalent; trust also acts as a "social glue" to keep organizational members focused on a common goal, which will facilitate negotiation and the possibility of peace.

What leaders in the 21st century will be increasingly called to do is build—and, in many cases, rebuild—the foundations of organizational trust to facilitate successful negotiation in the face of anger, distrust, and revenge. Over the past two decades, most of the negotiation theory and research has focused on dyadic exchange and the social cognitive dynamics of negotiators to the relative neglect of the organizational and relational context that is the foundation of any negotiation (Tripp et al., 1995). One major exception is research on cross-cultural negotiations. Some research showed that collectivist cultures, and in particular Japan, reach more cooperative integrative outcomes than individualist cultures (Lituchy, 1997). It is likely that differences in such outcomes are due to the processes used (Lewicki et al., 2010). Lewicki et al. (2010) summarized numerous processes and social cognitions that explained the superior outcomes collectivists achieve, but one process we focus on here is the relational focus. For instance, the Japanese first build trustworthy relationships within their own organizations and then with others and *then* negotiate. In all their relationships, they strive to make negotiation partners feel like family (March, 1989). By establishing solid, trustworthy relationships first, the Japanese believe that any potential conflicts that arise can then be better resolved.

Presuming the Japanese are correct, we advise organizational leaders first to build trustworthy relationships by making employees trust the leader so that they can trust the organization and thus trust each other more. We draw on the work of Bies (2010) to provide practical advice for building trust for leaders in the 21st century.

Bies (2010) argued that there are four basic principles that should guide leaders in building the organizational foundation of trust. These leadership principles are to tell the truth, listen (and listen even more), share information on a regular basis, and overcommunicate to employees. Each of these principles focuses on leadership communication as a key strategy to "signal" the importance of trust and facilitate the building of trust, which follows from the "mundane tools" of change as suggested by Peters (1978). But, these leadership principles are consistent with the negotiation principles that guide the integrative approach to effective negotiation (Lewicki et al., 2010), which emphasizes the importance of building trust in relationships (Tripp et al., 1995). And, given the expected economic instability and uncertainty that will be part of the social fabric of the 21st century workplace, the signaling and building of trust will become an even more critical leadership function to keep employees focused, engaged—and trusting each other.

Principle 1: Tell the Truth

With all due respect to Jack Nicholson in the movie *A Few Good Men*, people *can* handle the truth. What they find difficult is handling the lies. So, tell the truth.

If leaders' actions played a role in creating a bad situation, then they must explain their actions. What employees are looking for first in the offering of truth is a sincere and honest explanation. The explanation must acknowledge responsibility, not only privately but also publicly.

Employees want an explanation for controversial management decisions and for leaders' behaviors, particularly when these result in bad news (Bies, 2010). In the face of bad news, secrecy seems to be the default response of many leaders (Browning & Folger, 1994). Too often, leaders say it is "on a need to know basis and *you* don't need to know." To rebuild trust, tell the truth and take responsibility for your actions. Do not shift the blame or pass the buck. This will "signal" the right behavior that will build trust. One challenge to potentially using this strategy in the 21st century workplace will be how leaders can communicate the truth in ways that enable their recipients to be only those they wish to hear it. If the truth is sensitive information, such as the organization's potentially precarious competitive position at the moment, leaders will need to balance how to be not only truthful yet also organizationally protective (Bies, 2011). This balancing act generally suggests that the communication channel that is used needs to be in the speaker's (not receiver's) control; as such, verbally communicating this information face to face is ideal for sensitive communications (Bies, 1993, 2001). However, as we noted in this chapter, one of the challenges of the 21st century workplace is the increased need for employees and their managers to be separated geographically from each other, with face-to-face communications more difficult and sometimes *not* possible. As a result, one of the research needs for future negotiation researchers is how leaders can (re)build trust by "telling the truth" when communication channel options may be leaner than ideal.

Principle 2: Listen, Listen, and Then Listen

In the era of bad news, people are looking to their leaders. Employees are asking themselves, Do leaders care? Leaders are signal senders. One of the most important signals that leaders can send to convey that they care is this: Listen!

Listening is the most important leadership skill. Why? Because when leaders listen, employees will tell them *lots* of stuff (Bies, 2010). And, when leaders listen, and we mean *really* listen, employees feel valued and important (Bies, 2001). Listening is absolutely critical for (re)building trust (Lewicki, McAllister, & Bies, 1998). And as leaders listen, they should do the following: listen for the *content* (what are people concerned about?);

listen for the *emotions* (what are people afraid of?); also listen to *act* (are people suggesting solutions or new ideas to act on, to help the organization?) (Bies, 2010).

These listening principles are helpful not only for building trust but also as a key to successful negotiation when parties are geographically separated (Lewicki et al., 2010). One challenge to potentially using this strategy in the 21st century workplace will be how to demonstrate to employees that leaders are indeed listening when the employees and leaders are geographically separated, hence in situations for which nonverbal cues associated with listening are unavailable. As a result, studying how leaders can demonstrate listening in situations for which their employees are (vs. are not) physically distant is another need for future research.

Principle 3: Share Information on a Regular Basis

Another important way that leaders (re)build trust is to share information with their people—early and often. Keep employees informed regarding how things are going, whether it is good news or bad news. Sharing information is one of the sure ways to (re)build trust.

But, often leaders want to withhold information out of the need for control or power. Leaders operate under the mistaken belief that by sharing the information, it will only make matters worse. But, by withholding information, it will only make matters worse for them in terms of (re) building trust—and impede effective negotiation.

Why? The reason is that in the absence of information, people will create rumors, which contributes to everyday paranoia in the workplace (Kramer, 1998). What are the situational conditions that encourage rumors? There are two conditions: lack of information and the existence of an important issue (Bies, 2010). What are the situational conditions that encourage paranoia in the workplace? There are also two conditions: lack of information and the existence of employee status uncertainty (Kramer, 1998). What do rumors and paranoia have in common? Both are fueled by a lack of information. While rumors and paranoia are created by the landscape of bad news, leaders can lessen their negative impact on the workplace by sharing information on a regular basis. As we noted, however, how leaders share sensitive information (especially when their communication channels are leaner than ideal) yet protect the organization from unintended receivers hearing this is one of the needs for future research.

Principle 4: Practice C³ and Overcommunicate

In these times of turbulent change, leaders need to first practice C³: *crystal clear communication*. Second, leaders must overcommunicate their vision, their strategy, their plans, and their message. Repetition is absolutely critical. Why? First, not everybody hears you as they are distracted, if not fearful. Second, not everybody hears the message accurately if it is only said once, and not everybody hears the message at the same time. Third, repetition breeds familiarity, which can lead to understanding, which can lead to trusting you and supporting your initiatives. As a rule of thumb, communicate more than feels normal. By the way, because overcommunication will involve all the senior leadership team—make sure everyone stays on message.

In addition to the 21st century workplace challenges already noted, another major difficulty in heeding the advice has become clear in the early 21st century: An increasingly litigious environment has made many managers afraid to communicate fully. They fear that always telling the truth may promote lawsuits. For instance, telling the truth about why one coworker was fired, but others were not, may encourage the fired worker to file a defamation lawsuit or a wrongful termination lawsuit. Also, many managers fear that apologizing may be taken as an admission of guilt in a court of law. It is not that such fears have no basis in reality; they do. However, if managers listen to their legal counsel more than to their employees, they may find themselves building a culture of distrust that lowers motivation and increases conflict. And, ironically, they may actually invite *more* lawsuits.

More lawsuits were precisely what lawsuit-fearing medical doctors discovered. Historically, many medical doctors feared apologizing to patients when malpractice occurred because patients might take this as an admission of guilt, thus motivating them to sue. In actuality, doctors who give apologies for medical errors are sued for malpractice *less* often than doctors who refuse to give apologies (Kraman & Hamm, 1999). As Richard C. Boothman, chief risk officer for the University of Michigan, explained to the U.S. Senate, "People go to lawyers not because they want a million-dollar payout. People go to lawyers because they want answers and they don't trust their caregivers to give them answers. People go to lawyers because they don't get any information at all" (Barsella, 2007). This is why many states have considered bills for "I'm sorry" laws that would give doctors legal immunity for admitting mistakes ("Doctor's Apology," 2006). The purpose of such bills is to help improve communication between doctors and their patients and avoid conflict escalation.

NEW NEGOTIATION RESEARCH QUESTIONS FOR 21ST CENTURY CHALLENGES

To better judge the soundness of the strategies we suggest, there are many questions that research must address, some of which we noted. To begin such research, however, it would be wise to study revenge in negotiations in general, not just revenge that is negotiated at a distance. We know of little systematic research, outside of game theory, that measures the causes and varieties of revenge within negotiation. So, in what ways might negotiators retaliate? How common is a tit-for-tat style escalation? When does tit for tat produce cooperation and superior outcomes, and when does it increase hostility and inferior outcomes? When is it cold and calculated versus a hot, angry impulse?

In particular, qualitative research is needed to inventory the ways in which negotiators get even in the negotiating-at-a-distance context. For instance, how often do negotiators: withhold more information? Make accusations? Withdraw offers? Ask for even larger concessions? Walk away from the table? Never come back? Next, *when* do negotiators respond in these ways? What kind of actions by the other negotiator would trigger these responses? How much do various media-lean technologies amplify these responses? What other circumstances (e.g., length of relationships, power) would attenuate these responses? For instance, when one negotiator has a worse alternative to a negotiated agreement and thus needs a deal more than the other negotiator, the first negotiator likely will not walk away or engage in other avoidance tactics. As Baltasar Gracián observed over 350 years ago, "We tolerate those the most on whom we most depend" (1647/2009, p. 159). But, which of these alternatives they choose, and when, is unknown.

Once we understand the basics, then we can examine the 21st century context. Perhaps the first question here is: Which technology in fact does amplify revenge in negotiation, and how? For instance, does texting lead to inferior outcomes more than does negotiating via e-mail? To the extent that media-lean technologies amplify escalation, is that because stripped-down communication breeds suspicions and other sinister attributions, thus hampering sense making? More practically, how high-definition must be video (or audio for that matter, considering the drastic drop in average audio quality in cell phones compared to landlines) to attenuate sinister attributions and reduce the bombardier effect? Finally, whatever the difference in negotiation behavior and outcomes between media-rich and media-lean technologies, is there less of a difference in organizations that promote a culture of trust and open communication?

CONCLUSION

In this chapter, we investigated the dynamics of revenge in the 21st century workplace. In particular, we focused on when and why people are more or less likely to seek revenge and how managers can use that knowledge to negotiate the peace and avoid the destructive consequences of revenge. We also focused on how the rational approach of negotiation theory and interest-based bargaining can help cooler heads prevail, while also missing the mark to escalate conflict. In addition, we noted strategies that are likely to help managers or leaders (re)build trust in their organizations, thereby lessening the likelihood that employees will respond to their occasional bad news with revenge or negotiate in vengeful ways. Last, we identified 21st century workplace challenges that are likely to complicate effective use of the prescribed strategies, which thereby lead to future research needs associated with how *21st century managers and leaders* can lessen the likelihood of revenge and lead to successful negotiation of peace.

In exploring these 21st century challenges, we focused particularly on managing new technologies and how they shape revenge and negotiation dynamics. Geographic separation and the "speed" of communication and social media have created a brave new world for leaders, managers, and their organizations—and a fertile ground for new research for negotiation scholars. Acting on our proposed research agenda is a matter of practical as well as theoretical importance since the 21st century workplace, characterized by economic uncertainty and employee fears (hence the age of instability), is likely to have anger, distrust, and revenge as a constant presence (Bies, 2010).

REFERENCES

Allred, K. G. (1999). Anger driven retaliation: Toward an understanding of impassioned conflict in organizations. In R. J. Bies, R. J. Lewicki, & B. H. Sheppard (Eds.), *Research on negotiations in organizations* (Vol. 7, pp. 27–51). Greenwich, CT: JAI Press.

Allred, K. G., Mallozzi, J. S., Matsui, F,, and Raia, C. P. (1997). The influence of anger and compassion on negotiation performance. *Organizational Behavior and Human Decision Processes, 70*, 175–187.

Aquino, K., Tripp, T. M., & Bies, R. J. (2001). How employees respond to personal offense: The effects of blame attribution, victim status, and offender stat us on revenge and reconciliation in the workplace. *Journal of Applied Psychology, 86*, 52–59.

Aquino, K., Tripp, T. M., & Bies, R. J. (2006). Getting even or moving on? Power, procedural justice, and types of offense as predictors of revenge, forgiveness, reconciliation, and avoidance in organizations. *Journal of Applied Psychology, 91*, 653–658.

Axelrod, R. (1984). *The evolution of cooperation.* New York: Basic Books.

Axelrod, R. (1997). *The complexity of cooperation: Agent-based models of competition and collaboration.* Princeton, NJ: Princeton University Press.

Axelrod, R., & Hamilton, W. D. (1981). The evolution of cooperation. *Science, 211*, 1390–1396.

Baltes, B. B., Dickson, M. W., Sherman, M. P., Bauer, C. C., & LaGanke, J. S. (2002). Computer-mediated communication and group decision making: A meta-analysis. *Organizational Behavior and Human Decision Processes, 87*, 156–179.

Baron, R. A. (1988). Negative effects of destructive criticism: Impact on conflict, self-efficacy, and task performance. *Journal of Applied Psychology, 73*, 199–207.

Barsella, R. M. (2007). *Sincere apologies are priceless.* Retrieved August 1, 2008 from http://www.sorryworks.net/article50.phtml

Baumeister R. F., Smart L., & Boden, J. M. (1996). Relation of threatened egotism to violence and aggression: The dark side of high self-esteem. *Psychological Review, 103*, 5–33.

Bies, R. J. (1993). Privacy and procedural justice in organizations. *Social Justice Research, 6*, 69–86.

Bies, R. J. (2001). Interactional (in)justice: The sacred and the profane. In J. Greenberg & R. Cropanzano (Eds.), *Advances in organizational behavior* (pp. 89–118). Palo Alto, CA: Stanford University Press.

Bies, R. J. (2010, April). *Leading change in the era of bad news: Dealing with anger, distrust, and revenge in the workplace.* Paper presented at the ProSci Global Conference, Las Vegas, NV.

Bies, R. J. (2011). *Truth and justice: Reexamining the foundations of fairness.* Unpublished manuscript.

Bies, R. J., & Tripp, T. M. (1996). Beyond distrust: "Getting even" and the need for revenge. In R. M. Kramer & T. Tyler (Eds.), *Trust and organizations* (pp. 246–260). Thousand Oaks, CA: Sage.

Bies, R. J., & Tripp, T. M. (1998). Two faces of the powerless: Coping with tyranny. In R. M. Kramer & M. A. Neale (Eds.), *Power and influence in organizations* (pp. 203–220). Newbury Park, CA: Sage.

Bies, R. J., Tripp, T. M., & Kramer, R. M. (1997). At the breaking point: Cognitive and social dynamics of revenge in organizations. In R. A. Giacalone & J. Greenberg (Eds.), *Antisocial behavior in organizations* (pp. 18–36). Thousand Oaks, CA: Sage.

Bies, R. J., & Tyler, T. (1993). The "litigation mentality" in organizations: A test of alternative psychological explanations. *Organization Science, 4*, 352–366.

Browning, L. D., & Folger, R. (1994). Communication under conditions of litigation risk: A grounded theory of plausible deniability in the Iran Contra affair. In S. B. Sitkin & R. J. Bies (Eds.), *The legalistic organization* (pp. 251–280). Newbury Park, CA: Sage.

Buss, A. H. (1962). *The psychology of aggression.* New York: Wiley.

Cahn, E. (1949). *The sense of injustice.* New York: New York University Press.

Crossley, C. D. (2009). Emotional and behavioral reactions to social undermining: A closer look at perceived offender motives. *Organizational Behavior and Human Decision Processes, 108*, 14–24.

Curhan, J. R., & Elfenbein, H. A. (2012). Chapter 5 in this volume.

Daft, R. L., & Lengel, R. H. (1986). Organizational information requirements, media richness and structural design. *Management Science, 32*, 554–571.

Daly, J. P., & Tripp, T. M. (1996). Is outcome fairness used to make procedural fairness judgments when procedural information is inaccessible? *Social Justice Research, 9*, 327–349.

Dennis, A. R., & Kinney, S. T. (1998). Testing media richness theory in the new media: The effects of cures, feedback and task equivocality. *Information Systems Research, 9*, 256–274.

Dickens, C. (1859/1997). *A tale of two cities.* New York: Signet Classics.

Doctor's apology: Evidence or not? (2006, February 2). *The Daily Herald*, p. A5.

Fisher, R., & Brown, S. (1988). *Getting together: Building a relationship that gets to yes.* Boston: Houghton Mifflin.

Fox, S., & Spector, P. (2005). *Counterproductive work behavior: Investigations of actors and targets.* Washington, DC: American Psychological Association.

Frank, J. D. (1987). The drive for power and the nuclear arms race. *American Psychologist, 42*, 337–344.

Gibson, K., Bottom, W., & Murnighan, K. (1999). Once bitten: Defection and reconciliation in a cooperative enterprise. *Business Ethics Quarterly, 9*, 69–85.

Gracián, B. (2009). *The art of worldly wisdom.* (J. Jacobs, Trans.). Charleston, SC: BiblioLife. (Original work published 1647)

Gregoire, Y., Laufer, D., & Tripp T. M. (2010). A comprehensive model of customer direct and indirect revenge: Understanding the effects of perceived greed and customer power. *Journal of the Academy of Marketing Sciences, 28*, 738–758.

Gregoire, Y., Tripp, T. M., & Legoux, R. (2009). Customer revenge and avoidance overtime: Insights about a longitudinal "love becomes hate" effect. *Journal of Marketing, 73*, 18–32.

Hornstein, H. A. (1996). *Brutal bosses and their prey.* New York: Riverhead Books.

Kahai, S. S., & Cooper, R. B. (2003). Exploring the core concepts of media richness theory: The impact of cue multiplicity and feedback immediacy on decision quality. *Journal of Management Information Systems, 20*, 263–299.

Kim, S. H., Smith, R. H., & Brigham, N. L. 1998. Effects of power imbalance and the presence of third parties on reactions to harm: Upward and downward revenge. *Personality and Social Psychology Bulletin, 24*, 353–361.

Kraman, S. S., & Hamm, G. (1999). Risk management: Extreme honesty may be the best policy. *Annals of Internal Medicine, 131*, 963–967.

Kramer, R. M. (1994). The sinister attribution error. *Motivation and Emotion, 18*, 199–231.

Kramer, R. M. (1998). Paranoid cognitions in social systems: Thinking and acting in the shadow of doubt. *Personality and Social Psychology Review, 2*, 251–275.

Lewicki, R. J., McAllister, D. J., & Bies, R. J. (1998). Trust and distrust: New relationships and realities. *Academy of Management Review, 23,* 438–458.

Lewicki, R. J., Barry, B., & Saunders, D. M. (2010). *Negotiation* (6th ed.). New York: McGraw-Hill/Irwin.

Lind, E. A. (2001, August). When and how are heuristics used in making judgments? In J. Greenberg (Chair), *Controversial issues in organizational justice.* Paper presented as part of a symposium at the annual meeting of the Academy of Management, Washington, DC.

Lituchy, T. R. (1997). Negotiations between Japanese and Americans: The effects of collectivism on integrative outcomes. *Canadian Journal of Administrative Sciences, 14,* 386–395.

March, R. M. (1989). *The Japanese negotiator: Subtlety and strategy beyond western logic.* Tokyo: Kodansha.

Matthews, C. (1988). *Hardball: How politics is played—Told by one who knows the game.* New York: Summit Books.

McCullough, M. L. (2008). *Beyond revenge: The evolution of the forgiveness instinct.* San Francisco: Jossey-Bass.

McLean Parks, J. M. (1997). The fourth arm of justice: The art and science of revenge. In R. J. Lewicki, R. J. Bies, & B. H. Sheppard (Eds.), *Research on negotiation in organizations* (Vol. 6, pp. 113–144). Greenwich, CT: JAI Press.

Mikula, G. (1986). The experience of injustice: Toward a better understanding of its phenomenology. In H. W. Bierhoff, R. L. Cohen, & J. Greenberg (Eds.), *Justice in interpersonal relations* (pp. 103–123). New York: Plenum Press.

Mikula, G., Petri, B., & Tanzer, N. (1990). What people regard as just and unjust: Types and structures of everyday experiences of injustice. *European Journal of Social Psychology, 20,* 133–149.

Milgram, S. (1974). *Obedience to authority.* New York: Harper & Row.

Miller, D. T. (2001). Disrespect and the experience of injustice. *Annual Review of Psychology, 52,* 527–553.

Morrill, C. (1992). Vengeance among executives. *Virginia Review of Sociology, 1,* 51–76.

Neuman, J. H., & Baron, R. A. (1997). Aggression in the workplace. In R. A. Giacalone & J. Greenberg (Eds.), *Antisocial behavior in organizations* (pp. 37–67). Thousand Oaks, CA: Sage.

Peters, T. (1978). Symbols, patterns, and settings: An optimistic case for getting things done. *Organizational Dynamics, 7,* 3–23.

Pruitt, D. G., & Rubin, J. Z. (1986). *Social conflict.* New York: Random House.

Rabin, M. (1993). Incorporating fairness into game theory and economics. *American Economic Review, 83,* 1281–1302.

Selznick, P. (1957). *Leadership in administration: A sociological interpretation.* New York: Harper and Row.

Skarlicki, D. P., & Folger, R. (1997). Retaliation in the workplace: The roles of distributive, procedural, and interactional justice. *Journal of Applied Psychology, 82,* 434–443.

Tripp, T. M., & Bies, R. J. (1997). What's good about revenge? The avenger's perspective. In R. J. Lewicki, R. J. Bies, & B. H. Sheppard (Eds.), *Research on negotiation in organizations* (Vol. 6, pp. 145–160). Greenwich, CT: JAI Press.

Tripp, T. M., & Bies, R. J. (2009). *Getting even: The truth about workplace revenge—and how to stop it.* San Francisco: Jossey-Bass.

Tripp, T. M., Sondak, H., & Bies, R. J. (1995). Justice as rationality: A relational perspective of fairness in negotiations. In R. J. Bies, B. H. Sheppard, & R. J. Lewicki (Eds.), *Research on negotiations in organizations* (Vol. 5, pp. 45–64). Greenwich, CT: JAI Press.

Wicklund, R. A., & Gollwitzer, P. M. (1982). *Symbolic self-completion.* Hillsdale, NJ: Erlbaum.

8

Once Fooled, Shame on You! Twice Fooled, Shame on Me! What Deception Does to Deceivers and Victims: Implications for Negotiators When Ethicality Is Unclear

Roy J. Lewicki and Ralph Hanke

Oh, what a tangled web we weave
When first we practise to deceive!

Sr. Walter Scott, *Marmion*, Canto vi. Stanza 17

INTRODUCTION

Negotiation is a central and ubiquitous process in the workplace, although it has only been in recent years that its commonality has been recognized. In the early literature of negotiation, the dominant focus was in two areas: the purchasing function in corporations (Leenders & Fearon 2008) and the formalized dynamics of labor relations (e.g., Kochan & Katz, 1980; Walton & McKersie, 1965). In the last half century, both descriptive and prescriptive negotiation theory has evolved to encompass the great scope of everyday negotiating activity in organizations. Managers negotiate with subordinates; team members negotiate with each other to coordinate their work; agents of the organization negotiate outside organization boundaries to purchase raw materials, sell products and services, and manage relationships with other organizations and regulatory agencies. Finally, senior managers negotiate to structure mergers and acquisitions, leverage financial resources, and manage critical relationships with a variety of stakeholders: other corporations, governmental organizations, advocacy groups, and their various communities.

Negotiation theorists David Lax and Jim Sebenius (1986) defined negotiation as "a process of potentially opportunistic interaction by which two or more parties, with some apparent conflict, seek to do better through jointly decided action than they could otherwise." (p. 11). The central *tangible* currency of negotiation is information, and the essence of negotiation is the management of that information. Parties in a negotiation assemble and use information to persuade the other party to accept a particular perspective, point of view, or line of argument. They engage each other in a conversation in which the objective is to have the other side say "yes" to that perspective or line of argument. And because receiving that yes is so important to many negotiators, information is often exaggerated, embellished, distorted, or even outright "invented" to construct the most persuasive case—that is, they lie and deceive. And, the consequences of this exaggeration, embellishment, or distortion are a breakdown in trust and credibility, the central *psychological* currencies of the negotiation process.

PURPOSE OF THE CHAPTER

Because the accuracy of information and the process of its exchange are central to effective negotiation, researchers for years have been interested in all aspects of the ways that information is positioned and exchanged and how this exchange leads to concession making in reaching an agreement. But, given that Lax and Sebenius (1986) defined negotiation as "potentially *opportunistic* [italics added] interaction," incidents of opportunistic interaction can frequently occur. Further, in the 21st century workplace a variety of new online information exchange media have become ubiquitous, and this opportunistic interaction takes on a new dimension.

In this chapter, we hope to accomplish four major things. First, we argue that trust is the critical psychological currency in negotiation, and that trust is essential to effective negotiations. Moreover, increased deception in negotiation increases distrust, which significantly impedes negotiation. Second, as we point out from past research, acts of deception during negotiation cause negotiations to deteriorate, decreasing trust and increasing distrust, hence also increasing the probability that negotiations will either terminate prematurely or lead to highly suboptimal outcomes. Third, if negotiators understand these dynamics, then it seems paradoxical that negotiators would continue to use deceptive tactics. While a naïve negotiator might attempt deceptive tactics, it is puzzling that experienced negotiators would continue to attempt deceptive tactics and presume that they could "get away with it." So, we identify the strategies that negotiators typically use when attempting to deceive others without invoking harm to themselves, and we also identify the strategies that "victims" (i.e., targets of deceit) can use to prevent themselves from being deceived. Finally, we consider the various implications that new online media have on trust/distrust, deception during negotiation, and the ability and motivation to deceive.

TRUST, DISTRUST, AND THE MANAGEMENT OF INFORMATION IN NEGOTIATION

In an early treatise on the social psychology of negotiation, Harold Kelley (1966) focused on the central essence of opportunism in the information exchange process. Kelley described two dilemmas in negotiation exchanges: the *dilemma of honesty* and the *dilemma of trust*. The dilemma of honesty concerns how much of the truth about one's bargaining position one should divulge to the other party. On the one hand, telling the other party everything about your needs, preferences, or position may give that person the opportunity to take advantage of you. So, for example, if you divulge your walkaway point (least-acceptable deal) to the manager in a salary negotiation, the manager will certainly pay you no more than your walkaway point and may try to get you to take less. On the other hand, if you do not divulge enough information about your needs, preferences, or desired salary to the manager, it will not be possible for the manager to know what you want and help you achieve it. Conversely, the dilemma of trust concerns how much a negotiator should believe what the other party is telling him or her. If our negotiator in the salary negotiation believes everything the manager tells him or her about what the company can "afford," then the negotiator may be easily manipulated by the other's deception and may settle for a less-than-optimal compensation package; in contrast, if the negotiator believes nothing of what the other party is telling him or her, then once again agreement may be difficult to achieve (the parties may have to resort to a more formal exchange of written documents rather than be able to achieve a deal on a handshake). Trust and honesty are thus at the central core of negotiation; each negotiator must decide how honest to be, and how much to trust the other, in the process of shaping and disclosing information to achieve a viable, acceptable agreement. In general, we can view honesty as the "sender's responsibility" in the information exchange and trust as the "receiver's responsibility," but each person's actions and reactions are intimately tied to the other. We focus first on trust.

THE NATURE OF TRUST: DIFFERENT KINDS OF TRUST

We define *trust* as "confident positive expectations regarding another's conduct" (Lewicki, McAllister, & Bies, 1998, p. 439). Three major factors contribute to an individual's trust level: the individual's general disposition to trusting others (i.e., personality and past experience); the expectations that this individual has for the other party, often shaped by reputation or the history of their relationship; and situational factors such as power, communication dynamics, and so on. Trust can be expressed through one's intentions, expectations, emotions, and dispositions toward the other party and by making trusting choices in a situation in which one has to communicate and coordinate with the other party (cf. Lewicki, Tomlinson, & Gillespie, 2006, for one review).

Early studies of trust (e.g., Deutsch, 1958; Mayer, Davis, & Schoorman, 1995) talked about trust as a single unidimensional construct. However, more recent research indicated that trust and distrust are separate and distinct constructs (Lewicki et al., 1998). If *trust* is considered to be confident positive expectations of another's conduct, *distrust* is defined as confident negative expectations of another's conduct—that is, an actor can confidently predict that some other people will act to take advantage of us, exploit our good faith and goodwill, or manipulate the relationship to their own personal ends.

In the research literature, understanding the important role of trust in negotiation has a long and established tradition. Experiments began in the 1960s and repeated since then have shown, not unsurprisingly, that higher levels of trust and lower levels of distrust make negotiation easier, while lower levels of trust (and higher levels of distrust) make negotiation more difficult. Similarly, more cooperative (integrative) negotiation processes tend to increase trust, while more competitive (distributive) negotiation processes are likely to decrease trust (cf. Lewicki, Barry, & Saunders, 2010, for a complete review). A few of the more interesting wrinkles in this literature have also shown the following:

- Contrary to the expectation that trust in another party begins at "zero trust," or even with distrust, many people approach a new relationship with an unknown other party with remarkably high levels of trust, even with very little information or knowledge about the other (Kramer, 1994; Meyerson, Weick, & Kramer, 1996).
- Trustors, and those trusted, may focus on different things as trust is built (Malhotra, 2004). Trustors focus primarily on the risks of being trusted (e.g., how vulnerable they are), while those being trusted focus on the benefits to be received from the trust. These different foci may reveal a *framing bias* (Lewicki & Brinsfield, 2011) or a biased judgmental perspective that shapes how the other's actions are viewed and interpreted. Trustors are more likely to trust when the perceived risk of trusting is low. However, the receiver (trustee) is more likely to trust when the benefits to be received from trust are high. In a sense, then, whether one is the trustor or the trustee heavily shapes what the individual pays attention to in a trust-building or trust-related conversation.
- Finally, face-to-face negotiation encourages greater trust development than negotiation online. Parties anticipating an online negotiation expect less trust before the negotiations begin, are less satisfied with their negotiation outcomes, are less confident in the quality of their performance during the negotiation, trust the other less after the negotiation, and have less desire for a future interaction with the other party (Naquin & Paulson, 2003).

If trust is so critical to effective negotiations, then what leads negotiators to use deception, which undermines honesty and the potential for more effective negotiation? The answer lies in the "negotiator's dilemma" identified at the beginning of the chapter: the temptation to gain a temporary competitive advantage by using deceptive tactics and the biases in judgment that lead negotiators to believe they can be successful at executing this deceit without being detected (or suffering the possible negative consequences), which enhances the tendencies to use deceit. We now turn to a discussion of deception in negotiation and its consequences for trust and distrust.

DO NEGOTIATORS ENGAGE IN DECEPTIVE TACTICS?

The answer to the question of whether negotiators engage in trust is, "Yes—but not always!"

Ethically ambiguous tactics are common in negotiation; these are "tactics which are open to more than one interpretation of what is right or appropriate" (Lewicki et al., 2010, p. 265). Tactics can be judged based on what is ethical (appropriate based on some standard of moral conduct) versus what is legal (what the law allows or how certain tactics might be viewed in legal contracting) versus what is prudent (wise or smart based on the impact that their use may have on the negotiation outcomes and on the relationship between the parties) versus what is practical (what a negotiator can actually execute in a given conversation) (Missner, 1980).

Most of the ethics issues in negotiation are concerned with ambiguity about standards of truth telling—that is, how much of the truth, the whole truth, and (something less than) the truth should be told or should be believed in the other's communication. Researchers have identified the following six types of marginally ethical negotiation tactics (Barry, Fulmer, & Long, 2000; Robinson, Lewicki, & Donahue, 2000):

- traditionally competitive bargaining (not disclosing your walkaway, making an inflated opening offer);
- emotional manipulation (faking anger, fear, disappointment, elation, satisfaction);
- misrepresentation (distorting information or negotiation events in describing them to others);
- misrepresentation to others' networks (corrupting your opponent's reputation);

- inappropriate information gathering (bribery, infiltration, spying, etc.); and
- bluffing (insincere threats or promises).

These researchers examined the perceived appropriateness of these tactics and willingness of negotiators to use the tactics. Most interestingly, because most negotiators do *not* expect the other party to tell the whole truth and do *not* expect to be fully disclosing themselves (back to the core dilemmas of honesty and trust), the first two categories of tactics—traditional competitive bargaining and emotional manipulation—are *generally* seen as *appropriate* and *ethical* in successful competitive (distributive) bargaining. The other four groups of tactics are *generally* seen as *inappropriate* and *unethical*, even though they are frequently used. We have emphasized the word *generally* because perceptions of appropriateness and inappropriateness will vary significantly depending on the parties involved and the norms or informal rules that govern their interaction. Other researchers have aggregated tactics into lies of omission (omitting important or critical facts) versus lies of commission (intentionally misrepresenting information) (Carson, Wokutch, & Murrmann, 1982). Overall, O'Connor and Carnevale (1997) indicated that 28% of dyads in a negotiation simulation misrepresented the common value.

Like the use of deception in general, the use of deception in negotiation is driven by a variety of individual differences and situational factors. As we have noted, deception in negotiation is primarily driven by the negotiator's need to increase his or her power. Information is the dominant source of power in negotiation because people understand negotiation to be an exchange of information in an effort to "persuade" the other to accept one's point of view. If power can be enhanced by manipulating information in a self-serving manner to gain temporary advantage, it is more likely to occur (Shapiro & Bies, 1994). Negotiators who are more competitively oriented, or think the other is likely to be competitive and use marginal tactics, will also be more likely to use deception (Lewicki & Spencer, 1991; O'Connor & Carnevale, 1997). Larger incentives available to a negotiator increased the frequency of misrepresentation (Tenbrunsel, 1998). In addition, older negotiators and women were more honest; negotiators from some cultures were more likely to be honest, and a variety of situational factors, such as the operational norms of the negotiating environment, characteristics of the other party, past experience with using deceptive tactics, and how the parties communicate with each other, including the availability of communication channels, can all affect tactic use (see Lewicki et al., 2010, for one review).

In sum, research indicated that we know a lot about the factors that might increase the use of deception in negotiation: opportunities for opportunism, availability of tactics that are only marginally ethical, a competitive orientation to the negotiation, and a variety of situational influences that would make it easier for negotiators to act deceptively and without easy detection. No single factor can predict whether any given negotiator is more likely to use deception in a given situation, although we can state that the tactics from the first two groups identified—traditional competitive bargaining and emotional manipulation—frequently occur in many negotiation encounters (Fulmer, Barry, & Long, 2008; Lewicki & Robinson, 1998).

DO DECEPTIVE NEGOTIATORS EXPERIENCE INEFFECTIVE NEGOTIATIONS?

What do we mean by effective or ineffective? The answer has two aspects: Does the negotiator achieve his or her objectives, and are there long-term consequences that result from the deception? The answers to these questions, based on this research, are, generally, yes to the first, and no to the second. Deceptive negotiators clearly experience short-term success, but the long-term consequences are far more serious.

Short-Term Success

A number of studies have examined the consequences of negotiators using deceptive tactics. These studies showed that if the deception is performed carefully and not detected by the other, negotiators are more successful in the short term. Shapiro and Bies (1994) demonstrated that negotiators who used deception increased their perceived power, while Carney (2010) has shown that powerful people are better liars because power shields the liar from the stress of lying and hence increases their ability to deceive others. Moreover, a collection of studies (e.g., Aquino, 1993; Chertkoff &

Baird, 1971; Shapiro & Bies, 1994) have clearly demonstrated that negotiators who used deceptive tactics clearly achieved better outcomes over their opponent than those who did not use these tactics, while negotiators who did not use deceptive tactics achieved more equitable or "midrange" negotiating solutions. Moreover, negotiators who lied by omission secured better outcomes than negotiators who did not lie, and negotiators who lied by commission achieved better outcomes than by using lies of omission (Schweitzer & Croson, 1999). Liars who used emotional manipulation tactics (e.g., faking anger, happiness, etc.) performed more effectively than those who were emotionally honest (Fulmer et al., 2008). Finally, in a complex negotiating simulation, Boles, Croson, and Murnighan (2000) reported that "proposers" of first offers lied to the other (the responder) more when the stakes were large and the other party did not know how much money was at stake and when they knew that the other side had a weak BATNA (best alternative to a negotiated agreement; Fisher & Ury, 1981). Both proposers and responders who lied performed better in the negotiation than those who did not lie.

Long-Term Consequences

While deceptive negotiators may benefit in the short term, it is clear that using deception has consequences for both the deceiver and the deceived. These consequences are twofold: direct consequences to the deceiver if the deception is discovered and subsequent negotiations occur and more indirect consequences to the deceiver's reputation. Evidence on the first set of consequences is relatively clear-cut. Shapiro and Bies (1994) studied negotiations after one party had deceived (bluffed) the other. If the bluff was exposed to the responder, both negotiator parties negotiated less effectively in subsequent negotiations. If the bluff was labeled "unethical," it was even more difficult for the deceiver to recover. Boles et al. (2000) found that revealed deception lead to significantly more retribution on the part of the deceived but also significantly lower joint outcomes—that is, the act of retribution often led the responder to suffer as well.

Deception can also lead to significant consequences for a deceiver's reputation. Boles et al. (2000) and Tinsley, O'Connor, and Sullivan (2002), showed that the respondent rated opponents as less trustful and less trustworthy, and that the respondent had a significantly lower desire to work with those opponents in the future. (However, Barry et al. [2000] have shown that misrepresentation of positive emotions can actually lead to an increase in reputation, suggesting that the content of the deception may be more important than whether the communication is honest or dishonest.) McCornack and Levine (1990) found that victims had strong emotional reactions to deception, particularly when they already had a strong trusting relationship with the other, when the stakes of the negotiation were high, and when deception was judged by the deceived as an unacceptable form of behavior in the negotiation. The more deception was serious, personal, and highly consequential, the more destructive it was to the relationship.

So, in summary, as we see in many other examples of problematic and unethical conduct, short-term thinking can lead negotiators to take advantage of the opportunity to use deception to maximize the short-term results. But, the advantages of using deception can be significantly outweighed by the long-term consequences (unless, of course, the deception goes undetected).

HOW DO DECEPTIVE NEGOTIATORS ESCAPE PUNITIVE CONSEQUENCES?

There are two ways that deceptive negotiators escape punishment. First, they are clever enough to avoid getting caught. Second, if they do get caught, they use a variety of strategies—mostly verbal—to "manage" their relationship with the opponent and it is hoped minimize revenge, retribution, and negative consequences to reputation.

First, *avoid getting caught.* There can be several avenues to achieving this objective. A first approach may be to *minimize the amount of information* that is shared with the victim. If the victim does not know that a deception has occurred, "ignorance may be bliss." In the Boles et al. (2000) study discussed, when the receiver of the offer did not disclose the size of the financial pool to be shared, the victim was more satisfied. Similarly, in the Shapiro and Bies (1994) study, if the bluff was not exposed, the victim was more satisfied than if the bluff was later disclosed. Second, and more broadly, *minimize communication channels and access.* If a negotiator can eliminate face-to-face interaction with the other and control what kind of communication the victim receives, he or she may not arouse the victim's suspicions or the ability of the victim to detect any signals that deception has occurred.

Such monitoring affects the deceiver as well; Schweitzer, Brodt, and Croson (2002) demonstrated that deceivers who could monitor their target's reaction to the lie (through visual access) lied more and were more effective at maintaining trust with the deceived in spite of the deception. Finally, if a negotiator is also able to second guess the victim's potential suspicion, then he or she may discover ways not to arouse the victim's suspicions.

Third, *if caught, be able to use a variety of verbal strategies* (i.e., accounts, explanations, and justifications) to "mitigate" the consequences of the deception. Explanations and justifications by the actor can have an impact on how the victim interprets and reacts to the deception. "It was an accident," "I didn't think [the deception] was that big a thing," "I thought you would probably try to deceive me so I was just protecting myself," "All's fair in love and war," or (most likely) "I'm really sorry; I got carried away, and I will never do this again" are common explanations and deceptions. The more a subject feels that the partner's explanation is adequate to account for a deception, the less he or she expresses feelings of injustice, disapproval, and punitiveness toward the partner (Shapiro, 1991). Further, Shapiro found that if victims were mildly upset, the explanations had more impact than if the victims were strongly upset. Moreover, explanations had the most impact when the deceiver stated that the deception was unintentional, less impact when the deception was altruistic, and the least impact when the deception was selfishly motivated. At times, denying the deception may also be effective, particularly when the veracity of the deceptive message cannot be monitored. For example, Kim, Ferrin, Cooper, and Dirks (2004) have shown that denying actions may be more effective in repairing trust when the violator's trustworthiness was based in his or her integrity. Since the use of deceptive tactics is largely seen by victims as indicators of a deceiver's integrity (i.e., their honesty and credibility), under some conditions denial may be more effective.

Researchers have also examined the impact of deception at the organization level. Researchers Etty Jehn and Elizabeth Scott (2007) examined what has become a "classic" situation of skepticism and distrust—airline passenger reactions to information and announcements provided by the airline company (gate agents, pilots, and flight attendants). Not unsurprisingly, passengers frequently recognized that they are being lied to about staff intentions ("The flight attendant always says she will bring a pillow, but never does"), beliefs (whether it is really too foggy for the plane to take off), and intentional misrepresentation of emotions ("The attendants always smile and say they are happy to serve you on the flight, but we know they really are bored silly!"). Not unsurprisingly, the widespread belief that these representatives of the airline are frequently lying affects how passengers respond when they are telling the truth, customer perceptions of the airline company, and customer satisfaction.

HOW DO DECEPTIVE NEGOTIATORS REPAIR/REGAIN TRUST?

Since 2008, there has been an extensive research literature on a variety of trust repair activities (cf. Kramer & Lewicki, 2010, for one review). It is important to note that these studies have emphasized activities designed to rebuild trust and not necessarily to manage distrust as we have noted in our previous discussion. It is also important to note that the findings across many of these studies indicated that "simple" trust repair actions, such as an apology or provision of reparations (repayment for the victim's loss), are not consistently effective. Thus, while much has been done, more refined research is necessary. We selectively present several studies here.

First, one seminal study evaluated a number of the tactics that actors (violators) often use to repair calculus-based trust following a deception (a broken promise) and how these actions were viewed by victims (Tomlinson, Dineen, & Lewicki, 2004). The authors manipulated several repair tactics used by the deceiver (nature of the apology, timeliness of the reparative act, and sincerity of the apology) and characteristics of the relationship between offender and victim (quality of their past relationship and probability of a future relationship) on the victim's willingness to reconcile a professional relationship. The findings indicated that apologies in general, explicit and specific apologies that take responsibility for the offense, timely apologies, and sincere apologies were all more effective than an offender's efforts simply to "placate" the victim. The sincerity of an apology demonstrated the strongest positive effect. Second, the magnitude of the trust violation played a major role, and the effectiveness was related to the strength of the past relationship. When a serious violation occurs, victims look to the quality of the past relationship between the parties to determine whether to reconcile and are likely to terminate all future interactions; when the violation is small, parties instead try to estimate whether future violations are likely to occur, and what the costs might be, as a determinant for reconciliation.

Relatively comparable results were obtained in a later study by Schweitzer, Hershey, and Bradlow (2006). Using a laboratory simulation game called "the trust game," the researchers investigated how subjects (victims) responded to untrustworthy behavior by an actor and whether that untrustworthy behavior was also coupled with a deceptive message (a broken promise). The results indicated that when the actor changed from untrustworthy to a series of trustworthy decision choices over time, trust improved. However, when the untrustworthy actions were also accompanied by a deceptive message, trust never fully recovered—even when the victim received a promise to improve, an apology for past behavior, and a series of trustworthy moves in future rounds of the game. Thus, when deception is involved, previous trust levels may never fully recover to predeception levels. In terms of the trust–distrust distinctions made, we would interpret this result as indicating that deception specifically increases distrust, and that actions designed to rebuild trust (sincere or timely apologies) may not adequately address the distrust and suspicion that deception has created.

After a trust violation, some people are quick to forgive, while others never trust again. Researchers Haselhuhn, Schweitzer, and Wood (2010) determined that the victim's perception of the moral character of the actor was an important intervening factor. When victims believed that an actor's moral character can change over time, they were more willing to trust after the actor apologized and exhibited some trustworthy behavior than when the victim believed that moral character cannot change.

HOW DO NEGOTIATORS AVOID BEING VICTIMS OF DECEPTION? STRATEGIES FOR RECOGNIZING, CONFRONTING, AND MINIMIZING DECEPTION IN NEGOTIATIONS

A number of authors have provided excellent advice for detecting and responding to deceptive communications. Much of the early work focused on helping the deceived recognize various deceptive verbal and written statements. For example, Kalbfleisch (1994) proposed 38 different approaches for detecting deception, organized into 15 different categories.

We do not review all 38 but review a few of the key approaches that are most salient to negotiation.

One factor in minimizing the level of deception in negotiations is the level of personal interaction present in a negotiation. Schweitzer and Croson (1999) argued that developing a relationship with the other helps both to build and to understand trust better, and this increase in trust minimizes the frequency and severity of deception. Olekalns and Smith (2005) pointed out that how you portray trustworthiness also influences the amount and efficacy of deception. For example, if one portrays benevolence, integrity, and competence to the other (the three components of trustworthiness; Mayer et al., 1995), the other negotiator is more likely to use sins of omission tactics (withholding information) rather than sins of commission tactics (outright lying). Certainly, this is not a panacea, but at least a step in the right direction.

Second, asking questions is a powerful way to respond to deception. Lewicki et al. (2010) provided the following advice for counteracting deception: (a) ask probing questions, (b) phrase questions in a variety of different ways to see if one is receiving a consistent answer, (c) force the other party's deceptive communications into either a direct answer or a retreat, and (d) test the other party with questions to which you already know the answer. Schweitzer and Croson (1999) also argued for the use of direct questions. Their research showed that friends involved in negotiations who asked for information got more accurate information than friends who did not; strangers who asked for specific information got more accurate information than strangers who did not (but not as much as friends). Further, focusing questions by asking about a specific problem increased the frequency of disclosure of information about that problem. Finally, Thompson (1998) argued that negotiations can be more effective and less fraught with deception when the consistency of information is tested by asking many questions, such as asking for proof and documentation of the answers whenever possible.

Another important factor for fighting deception is to establish the "rules of the game" clearly. Aquino (1993) argued that making ethical standards more salient leads to more ethical behavior. Thus, the negotiator can make it explicit at the outset that the negotiator both intends to negotiate ethically and expects ethical behavior in return; this communication can go a long way to alleviating the potential for deception. Aquino's research showed that specifically coaching students on the ethical climate of the negotiation positively affected the ethicality of negotiating behavior that led to lower levels of deception. Similarly, Shapiro, Lewicki, and Devine (1995) argued that making policies that explicitly rule out deception or making clear what constitutes accepted practice in the context of an industry where negotiation is common (e.g. purchasing, real estate) is important for fostering a negotiation process that can have lower levels of deception. Tripp (1993) and colleagues (Trip, Sondak, & Bies, 1995) also suggested that negotiators (or those who oversee the process) can create rules and standards for what is "fair" in a negotiation process or outcome; these standards can provide a clear path for negotiators to follow that not only will minimize the occurrence of deception but also will facilitate a smoother interaction and flow to negotiations. However, setting those rules must be specific to the narrow negotiation context. Schweitzer and Croson (1999) showed that if negotiators had taken a course in business ethics, simply taking the course had no impact on use of deception. All in all, these findings clearly underscore the importance of negotiating not only with honesty and integrity but also with a healthy dose of skepticism and vigilance.

A final tool for protecting against deception is to have a strong BATNA or an alternative way to have one's needs met (Aquino, 1993). While having a BATNA did not directly affect negotiation behavior one way or the other, it did give a negotiator the power to walk away from deception and protect one's self-interest without creating (or experiencing) harm with a fellow negotiator. Sharing that BATNA with the other may be an instrumental part of that defense. Boles et al. (2000) showed that when respondents did not share private information (i.e., their BATNA), they were less likely to be exploited than when they did share this information, suggesting that a negotiator needs to be careful about deciding with whom to reveal one's BATNA.

As shown, there are a number of strategies that can be used to detect deception. Two comprehensive works (Kalbfleisch, 1994; Lewicki et al., 2010) summarized a variety of additional tactics for countering deception. Table 8.1 provides a convenient summary list of these tactics and how and when they can be used to counter deception.

21st CENTURY WORKPLACE CHARACTERISTICS THAT MAY AFFECT NEGOTIATORS' ABILITY TO USE DECEPTIVE MANAGEMENT STRATEGIES

Probably the single most important change in the 21st century workforce is the increased "virtualness" of organizational work. A number

TABLE 8.1

Responding to Deception

Type	Strategy
Direct pressure	A. *Intimidation.* Confront the deceiver to admit that he or she used deception by actively identifying and "calling" the deception.
	B. *Futility.* Signal the deceiver that further deception efforts will not work.
	C. *Inducing guilt or fear of public disclosure.* Threaten to let others know about the deceiver's behavior or actually disclose it to invoke public humiliation.
Reverse psychology	A. *Gentle prods.* Encourage pursuit of truthful and honest communication. Minimize direct accusations. Praise honest communication.
	B. *Minimizing consequences.* Allow the deceiver to offer excuses or apologies, minimize the impact, or shift the blame to others.
	C. *Self-disclosure.* Build trust through reciprocal honesty and empathy: "If I tell you the truth, will you tell me the truth?"
Listening	*Find inconsistencies.* Let the deceiver reveal information about themselves, their intentions, and explanations for their past behavior to catch them in factual distortions or contradictory statements.
Reputation effects	*Appeal to pride, "face," and honor.* Invoke the deceiver's sense of personal integrity: "Just tell me the truth." "What will people think if they knew you lied so blatantly?" "You don't want to be known as a liar in this community, do you?"
Silence	*Do not respond.* Force a deceiver to spontaneously respond with additional information, a corrected response, or an acknowledgment that earlier statements may not have been true.

of authors have noted the dramatic organizational changes that have required an increase in virtual work: flatter and more geographically dispersed organizations, increased globalization of trade and the workforce that conducts it, a workforce that is more culturally diverse, increased requirements for parties to work across organizational boundaries in joint ventures and partnerships, and a shift from an economy driven primarily by manufacturing and production (located in one or two facilities) to an economy highly driven by information and services (which are more broadly distributed geographically) (Heneman & Greenberger, 2002).

As these authors (and others; see Lewicki & Dineen, 2002) have noted, the primary consequences of increased virtuality is that it decreases the amount of face-to-face communication possible in a negotiation.

Decreased face-to-face communication has been shown to have a variety of impacts on negotiation. It can keep the negotiation more focused on the substantive issues because much of the informal, conversational interaction is omitted, conversation that is often encouraged and reinforced by face-to-face connectivity. It can minimize or enhance the effects of stereotypic judgments of the other party; "level the playing field" by minimizing status and power differences; and minimize the impact of informal norms that can govern what kind of behavior is appropriate in a negotiation (i.e., honest or deceptive communication). These consequences have been shown to have an impact on negotiation behavior. While most of these studies have focused specifically on counteracting deception in virtual negotiation, we enrich these results somewhat from the broader understanding of deception in virtual or low-context situations.

The total amount of verbal and nonverbal information cues sent or received in communication with the other is a key factor in signaling and detecting deception. "High-context" situations are ones in which negotiators have access to the other's facial expressions, eye contact, body language, voice tone, emotionality, and the words themselves, while "low-context" situations may contain only words (e.g., e-mail, fax, or even a short "chat"). Another term for this impact of context is the degree of *media richness* (Daft, Lengel, & Trevino, 1987; Trevino, Lengel, & Daft, 1987); the richer the media, the greater the number of verbal, visual, and emotional cues that are available to sender and receiver. The richness of a medium can be based on the following four criteria (Daft et al., 1987): timeliness, richness, accuracy, and adaptability. Following this breakdown, it can be argued that e-mail, for example, has the same media richness as paper-and-pencil letters. Nevertheless, it is argued that e-mail is generally viewed as less permanent, less restrained, more negative, and less personal than are other forms of communication, including those with pen and paper (Naquin, Kurtzberg, & Belkin, 2010). Therefore, an e-mail communication may trigger different psychological responses than does an identical content paper-and-pencil communication in signaling what constitutes appropriate behavior, in large part because an e-mail communication is usually viewed as creating more "psychological distance" between the actor and the victim of the deception. As a result, users of e-mail may feel subconsciously less accountable for their harmful actions, such as being deceptive (Naquin et al., 2010). Hence, evidence suggests that levels of media richness in computer-mediated communication matter. For example, the characteristics that define technology-mediated interaction, such as depersonalized communication, may also increase uncooperative behavior in mixed-motive situations (e.g., O'Sullivan & Flanagin, 2003). Moreover, in groups using a leaner (less-rich) communication medium, depersonalization lessens proper communication behavior and increases the difficulty of detecting deception (Wilson, Straus, & McEvily, 2006). Therefore, contexts that are media rich (i.e., in which the deceived has full visual and voice access to the deceiver) will provide more cues to the deceived that can be used to detect deception. We briefly review the consequences of this decreased media richness on negotiation dynamics.

First, Rockmann and Northcraft (2008) found that media richness affected behavior in mixed-motive situations by influencing individuals' *perceptions of trust*; this relationship played out in terms of both the bonds they created with other group members (affective trust) and knowledge of what other group members were going to do (cognitive trust). Rockmann and Northcraft found that cognitive-based trust influenced whether participants decided to cooperate but was not related to deception. Affective-based trust, on the other hand, seemed to play a role in determining both cooperative and deceptive behavior. As a consequence, they argued, when compared to other communication media, interacting in real time via computer seemed to be problematic for effective cooperation (compared to other communication media), yielding high defection and deception rates, receivers being less confident they knew what others were going to do, and receivers being less willing to rely on others (Rockmann & Northcraft, 2008).

Second, less-rich media (e-mail) may inspire more negative language ("flaming"; Kiesler & Sproull, 1986), more uninhibited behavior, and conformance to fewer social norms (e.g., the disinhibition effect; Beer, Knight, & D'Esposito, 2006; Goleman, 1995; Kiesler & Sproull, 1986; Suler, 2004) than do face-to-face interactions. It seems people have come to see and use e-mail as (a) less permanent, (b) less restrained and hence more negative, and (c) less personal; one consequence of this impact may be that individuals will perceive deception on e-mail to be a more justifiable behavior than is lying on paper, although they might be less conscious of the reasons contributing to that perception (Naquin et al., 2010). As we noted, researchers have shown that the use of emotionally manipulative tactics is one form of acting deceptively (Barry et al., 2000).

Third, a study of the effect of distance on deception found that geographical distance between collaborating partners influences one's willingness to initiate deception on the partner using e-mail. In particular, people were more likely to give deceptive (positive) portrayals about themselves to a partner that they believed to be in a remote city (Bradner & Mark, 2002). One reason for this is that deceptive parties may actually assume a different "identity" or "persona" in a remote communication. Galanxhi and Nah (2007) tried to determine if the intention to deceive others influenced one's choice of an avatar (persona) in an online chat environment. They also investigated if communication medium (text only vs. avatar-supported chat) influenced one's perception of trustworthiness of the communication partner. They found that in the text-only chat environment, subjects who were deceiving their partner experienced higher anxiety levels than those who were truthful to their partner; however, the same phenomenon was not observed in an avatar-supported chat environment. This suggests that "wearing a mask" in cyberspace may reduce the anxiety people experience in deceiving others. In addition, they found deceivers were more likely to choose avatars different from their real selves (Galanxhi & Nah, 2007), thereby perhaps making it easier to practice deception. What remains unknown, however, is if someone more inclined to deception is also more inclined to choose an avatar different from his or her real self.

The level and efficacy of deception are also influenced by the kind of interaction—synchronous or asynchronous—regardless of the richness of the media. *Synchronicity* refers to the timing of message exchange within a given time frame: In face-to-face communication, message exchange occurs in real time and is referred to as synchronous communication, while asynchronous communication occurs when time lapses separate conversational turns. Instant messaging, text chat, and text-based online virtual reality systems are different forms of synchronous communication, while e-mail and electronic bulletin or message boards are forms of asynchronous communication.

However, the power of deception in synchronous and asynchronous environments seems to operate in a counterintuitive fashion. One might expect that, based on the findings we have been summarizing, in an asynchronous environment deceivers would be better able to "spin their yarns" than in synchronous communication. However, the results showed that highly motivated deceivers can effectively promote a credible image, and can parlay their credibility into persuading others to make faulty decisions, *regardless* of whether the communication mode is synchronous or asynchronous (Hancock, Woodworth, & Goorha, 2010). Further, in a study of the effects of deception on group decision making, Burgoon, Burgoon, Broneck, Alvaro, and Nunamaker (2002) found that although synchronous interaction produced greater interactivity (e.g., involvement and mutuality)—an important aid to deception—than asynchronous interaction, synchronicity of communication neither impaired nor aided deceivers. It turned out that asynchronous forms of communication weakened the sense of engagement among participants. Apparently, asynchronous communication resulted in users having less trust for one another and viewing one another in a less-favorable light. This may be the case because asynchronous communication creates a level of detachment that may be an excellent shield against misinformation, manipulation, and misrepresentation. It enables users to resist bad arguments and to engage in more thoughtful analysis (Burgoon, Chen, & Twitchell, 2010). The combination of deception and synchronous communication may, however, be the most dangerous because deceivers can create a pseudorelationship when interactivity is high and can then capitalize on the truth bias that is more pronounced under real-time conditions (Burgoon et al., 2010). This finding is especially intriguing given that Rockmann and Northcraft (2008) found that there is no discernible difference between face-to-face communication and video-based computer-mediated communication when it came to deception. It seems people are equally bad at spotting deceptive tactics in both contexts.

HOW THE DECEIVER PRESENTS DECEPTIONS

Given people's poor capacity for spotting deceptive tactics in computer-mediated communication, it would be important to consider how deceivers go about online deception. To begin, deceivers in computer-mediated communication portray themselves as somewhat more credible than truth tellers, especially in terms of being sociable, composed, and dominant, all of which favor successful deception. However, they are not perceived as more persuasive than truth tellers (Burgoon et al., 2010). In addition, deceivers start by employing various strategies to withhold truthful information, followed by opting for vagueness and uncertainty if withholding does not work, and finally resorting to nonimmediacy if the first two fail (Burgoon, Buller, Guerrero, Afifi, & Feldman, 1996). Further, deceivers are more likely to employ mixed pauses in their speech, make fewer spontaneous corrections of their own speech, employ less talking time, and take longer to respond to the other (DePaulo et al., 2003). Moreover, deceivers have fewer ordinary imperfections in their speech and are less forthcoming than truth tellers. In addition, because they are dominantly preoccupied with fabricating deceptive information in their presentation, deceivers tend to fail to make spontaneous changes and participate more actively in discussions than truth tellers by taking shorter pauses between messages and initiating discussions (Zhou, 2005). Finally, deceivers may capitalize on the involvement and mutuality present in interactive computer-mediated communication modes to foster trust and impressions of truthfulness (Burgoon, Stoner, Bonito, & Dunbar, 2003).

Deceptive messages also differ from truthful messages along several linguistic dimensions. For example, deceptive messages tend to be longer, more informal and uncertain, more expressive and nonimmediate, less complex, and less diverse than truthful messages. Uncertainty and nonimmediacy are also consistent with deceivers' general strategies of obfuscation and equivocation. By using indirect and vague language, deceivers may seem submissive, thus dampening receivers' suspicion about a message (Carlson, George, Burgoon, Adkins, & White, 2004).

DETECTING DECEPTION IN THE 21st CENTURY VIRTUAL NEGOTIATION ENVIRONMENT

As we have noted, detecting online deception is particularly challenging for three reasons. First, online communication restricts nonverbal behavior of communication partners. Second, in an online environment, participants often lack visual and emotional cues, which depersonalizes the situation and may prevent the deceived from engaging in active dialogue with the other, questioning and checking comments and statements that could verify the truth of a message. Third, online communication provides deceivers with more time and opportunities to plan and rehearse their messages than in traditional face-to-face communication, thereby lowering even further the "leakage" of deceptive behavior (Zhou, Burgoon, Nunamaker, & Twitchell, 2004). For example, in computer-mediated communication, a communicator has the flexibility of deleting and updating a message as many times as he or she wants before sending, leaving no trace for the victim's use (Zhou, 2005).

A variety of tools is available to the 21st century negotiator that embellish on the broader strategies we discussed previously in this chapter (maximizing personal interaction, asking questions, enforcing normative ground rules, having a strong BATNA, and the broader strategies elaborated in Table 8.1). Here are several specific suggestions:

Learn to recognize the clues to deception that are unique to the virtual environment. For example, deceivers are more likely to have mixed pauses, fewer spontaneous corrections, shorter talking time, and longer response length (DePaulo et al., 2003). Compared with truth, deception contains fewer unique words and self-references, fewer superfluous repetitions of words or phrases, and fewer incomplete sentences. Deception also shows more negative emotion and sounds more evasive, unclear, uncertain, and impersonal (Zhou & Zhang, 2008). Further, those attempting to deceive may give briefer responses (fewer words, sentences) than truth tellers. By disclosing less information, they think they decrease the chances of being detected (Zhou, Burgoon, Twitchell, Qin, & Nunamaker, 2004). In addition, deceivers' messages may lack vivid and specific details because they do not have corresponding experiences to generate such details (DePaulo et al., 2003). Grazioli (2004) proposed that certain cues, including exaggerated claims, implausible scenarios, poor grammar, misspelled words, and other message indicators that do not meet the level of communication normally expected from the message source, are therefore critical cues for detecting deception on the Internet. Further, the language style used to tell the deceptive story may contain clues about the deceiver's state of mind. These "slips" in language can reveal underlying anxiety, guilt, or arousal, so deceptive intention is likely to be reflected in linguistic features. These include message erasing, response delays, cognitive complexity, and spontaneous correction (Zhou & Zhang, 2008).

While people involved in computer-mediated communication reveal an overall "truth bias," which may make them less alert to the possibility that they are being deceived, there does appear to be some increasing sensitivity (Hancock et al., 2010). Two contributing factors seem to influence success in detecting deception: past experience with fraud and deception, whether online or not, and a degree of awareness and conscientiousness about the informal rules and expectations in the computer-mediated communication environment (Wright, Chakraborty, Basoglu, & Marett, 2010). Recognizing these cues may prompt the deceived to ask a number of questions to clarify and elaborate on messages or insist on a face-to-face meeting at which suspicions can be verified. For example, with visual access, the deceived can learn to read the other's nonverbal signals; Thompson et al. (Thompson, Kray, & Lind, 1998) suggested people insist on negotiating in person so that one can have access to as many visual and verbal cues as possible. But, it turns out that people are not as sophisticated as one might think in either being deceptive or accurately reading deception in the other's verbal or visual cues. Psychologist Paul Ekman (2009), an expert on reading nonverbal behavior, has shown that even when people deliberately try to conceal their emotions (and truthful statements), they still exhibit a very brief facial expression (less than a second) that reveals their true emotional state. Thus, even "trained liars" emit these cues, and "trained victims" can learn to read these cues—but it does take training. Learning to read and detect these "microexpressions" is key to being able to detect deception when visual facial cues are available.

But, even in contexts that are less media rich (i.e., telephone, e-mail, or exchange of faxes), there are a number of other strategies that can be used to detect and respond to deception, as we have noted. If suspicions about deception are confirmed (either through visual detection of possible deception or through evasive responses to questions), the deceived may then move to a second step, in which the deceiver confronts the deceived, attempts to set ground rules for more honest communication, institutes mechanisms for monitoring and verifying agreements, or cultivates a BATNA (i.e., alternative ways to meet one's objectives without having to deal with the deceived).

Another mechanism for detecting deception is to turn to technology. While the technology that drives online negotiation can sometimes inhibit people's ability to detect deception, that same technology may also be used as an aid to spot deception in computer-mediated communication. For example, Jensen, Meservy, Burgoon, and Nunamaker (2010) developed a computer-assisted approach for automatically extracting behavioral indicators of deception from video, audio, and text-based interactions and used those indicators to predict human-interpretable judgments of a deceiver's involvement, dominance, tension, and arousal—all markers of the behavior of deceivers. They found that the accuracy of detection of deceptive behaviors by their computer-based system was substantially higher than typical human deception detection performance. Their research provided the prospect of improving people's negotiating ability through the development of automated systems for flagging hostile, deceptive, or suspicious communication by negotiators involved in online interactions. (Similar results were obtained through various computer modeling procedures of verbal and emotional linguistic cues, developed by Zhou, Burgoon, Twitchell, et al., 2004, and Zhou & Zhang, 2008.) Finally, results of studies detecting deception outside the negotiation arena showed that it is possible to classify cognitive and physical stress conditions (compared to non-stress conditions) accurately based on changes in computer keystroke use and speech patterns (Vizer, Zhou, & Sears, 2009). This research has confirmed that an individual's typing patterns are not stable, and changes have been attributed to stress, the environment, or gradual changes in cognitive or physical function (Monrose & Rubin, 2000). Given that most deceivers experience increased cognitive and physical stress while deceiving, it seems realistic to consider these methods as feedback mechanisms to help discover deceptions.

Imagine that such computer programs were available to a negotiator who is negotiating live, over a computer-mediated teleconference, or even by telephone or e-mail. So, for example, while negotiating in a chat environment, a negotiator might be able to use software on his or her own machine to analyze the keystrokes and linguistic turns being generated by the negotiation partner. The negotiator can load these programs on a laptop, computer notebook, or in the future, cell phone application. While the negotiator is using these devices to negotiate, the technology can also be monitoring that conversation and be attuned to detect various text, verbal, and even visual deception cues and can alert the negotiator to any indicators in the opponent's behavior—or even his or her *own* behavior—suggesting deceptive communications. While such programs clearly will not provide definitive indicators of deceptive behavior during negotiations, they can be used as indicators for increasing one's wariness of a fellow negotiator.

Such approaches, of course, are probably fraught with ethical dilemmas and carry the specter of a machiavellian big brother who is constantly watching us. Although we certainly do not support the idea of clandestine spying in computer-mediated communication, we certainly celebrate the possibility that open and honest communication in computer-mediated communication can be supported—and even enhanced—using the very technology that is also used to communicate directly. Would parties be willing to use this technology? What is their obligation to inform their opponent that such technology is in use? What is their obligation to have the technology used on themselves if they use it on others? Presumably, this will not be an issue for those willing to be forthright and open in their negotiations, but even for those who intend to behave in a forthright manner, the ethical issues are real and significant.

The final word on this may rest with a comment made by Wright et al. (2010). Their research showed that people should not ignore their feelings of apprehension when engaging in computer-mediated communication. Evidence suggested that individuals who are suspicious (as determined through personality-based traits, their knowledge-based awareness, or past Web experience) tend to be successful detectors of online deception. Thus, even with significantly enhanced computer-based monitoring, the best "detector" of deception may be a negotiator's capability to trust, while at the same time having a carefully honed capacity to distrust and to smell—and confront—deceit when it is in the air.

FUTURE RESEARCH NEEDS

In spite of the extensive research already completed on deception in negotiation, some research studies have been contradictory in their findings (e.g., whether deception is more or less likely to occur in face-to-face interaction), while other topics deserve more intense examination.

Most important, we believe that the opportunity to monitor communication technologically to detect deception deserves research on both the practical and ethical dimensions. From the practical perspective, there are a variety of tools (keystrokes, semantic structure of messages, spoken voice analysis, nonverbal cues) that can be monitored and detected electronically; research should examine whether these tools can actually be used by a negotiator and what the impact is of having these tools available—or in use—on negotiation processes and outcomes. What is the impact of being monitored on deception use and on negotiation effectiveness? Does a negotiator have lower initial trust in a partner when the partner knowingly uses electronic monitoring as part of the negotiation? Does the existence of electronic monitoring influence the effectiveness of parties, all other factors held constant? Is someone who has had to rebuild trust less likely to practice deception when being monitored than someone who has not been caught out in previous deceptions? In other words, does electronic monitoring itself undermine the negotiation process and so should not be used?

In addition, there are a host of questions that arise from an ethics perspective, examining how negotiators view the appropriateness and use of such technology, how the use of technology relates to trust and distrust dynamics, and how the use of this technology would relate to the perceived appropriateness of using various deceptive tactics themselves (Robinson et al., 2000).

In addition, our review has surfaced a number of other important questions for future investigation:

1. Do people actually believe they can get away with more deception online than in face-to-face negotiations? If so, do they plan accordingly?
2. Are certain deception tactics used in different amounts in face-to-face negotiations versus online negotiations? For example, do people use bluffs more in online negotiations? Relatedly, which are more prevalent in online negotiation: lies of commission or lies of omission?
3. Do trust and distrust play out differently in virtual space than in real space? Rockmann and Northcraft (2008) argued that affective and cognitive-based trust mediate the relationships between media richness and defection and deception. Therefore, is distrust higher in online environments than in real space? Also, is initial trust higher online or off-line? Is initial distrust higher?
4. Given that online communication helps us to negotiate around the world and hence a variety of cultures engage in online negotiation, what mechanisms would allow the establishment of ethical norms for online negotiation? While there has been no significant indication that certain cultures are more prone to using deception in negotiation, deception may be harder to detect because of other ways that culture affects interpersonal communication processes.
5. Finally, what factors influence trust repair online? What effects do original levels of trust have on trust repair? Is trust repair harder

online or in face-to-face negotiations? Is trust repair easier after deception in a "one-shot" negotiation than in a negotiation that has multiple iterations? Are people less inclined to try trust repair online? Do they think they are unable to make the kinds of connections (particularly visual cues and the transmission of emotion) required to help repair trust when the communication medium and relationship are primarily technology mediated?

SUMMARY

In this chapter, we have discussed the impact of deception on negotiation processes. Managers, including human resource (HR) professionals, negotiate all the time—with employees, with their own managers, with vendors, and with regulatory agencies, to name a few. In these negotiations, the opportunity for deception is always available—that is, one or both parties will see the opportunity to misrepresent information in the negotiation to gain advantage. While research has shown that this misrepresentation (bluffing, withholding critical facts, overdrawn emotional hysterics, or even outright lying) can create short-term negotiating advantage for the deceiver, the deception may produce significant negative long-term consequences, as well as destroy trust, the relationship "glue" that is central to creating productive negotiating agreements. We have also attempted to advise HR professionals about ways to detect, protect against, and respond to others' deceptive communications. Finally, we have shown how the dramatic changes in the technology of communication—e-mail, voice-only communication, videoconferencing, and so on—have increased not only the variety of ways people can use deceptive tactics but also the number of possible ways to detect and defuse it. Much has been done to enhance our understanding of deception in negotiation, but there is still work to be done.

ACKNOWLEDGMENT

Our thanks to Mathew Shaner for his assistance in assembling the literature for this chapter.

REFERENCES

Aquino, K. (1993). The effects of ethical climate and the availability of alternatives on the use of deception during negotiation. *International Journal of Conflict Management, 9,* 195–217.

Barry, B., Fulmer, I. S., & Long, A. (2000). *Ethically marginal bargaining tactics: Sanction, efficacy, and performance.* Paper presented at a meeting of the Academy of Management, Toronto, August.

Beer, J. S., Knight, R. T., & D'Esposito, M. (2006). Integrating emotion and cognition: The role of frontal lobes in distinguishing between helpful and hurtful emotion. *Psychological Science, 17,* 448–453.

Boles, T. L., Croson, R. T. A., & Murnighan, J. K. (2000). Deception and retribution in repeated ultimatum bargaining. *Organizational Behavior and Human Decision Processes, 83,* 235–259.

Bradner, E., & Mark, G. (2002). Why distance matters: Effects on cooperation, persuasion and deception. In *Proceedings of the 2002 ACM conference on computer supported cooperative work.* New Orleans, LA, November.

Burgoon, J. K., Buller, D. B., Guerrero, L. K., Afifi, W. A., & Feldman, C. M. (1996). Interpersonal deception XII: Information management dimensions underlying deceptive and truthful messages. *Communication Monographs, 63*(1), 50–69.

Burgoon, J., Burgoon, M., Broneck, K., Alvaro, E., & Nunamaker, J. J. (2002). *Effects of synchronicity and proximity on group communication.* Paper presented at the annual meeting of the National Communication Association, New Orleans, LA, November.

Burgoon, J., Chen, F., & Twitchell, D. P. (2010). Deception and its detection under synchronous and asynchronous computer-mediated communication. *Group Decision and Negotiation, 19,* 345–366.

Burgoon, J. K., Stoner, G., Bonito, J., & Dunbar, N. (2003). *Trust and deception in mediated communication.* Paper presented at the Proceedings of the 36th Annual Hawaii International Conference on Systems Sciences, Big Island, HI, January.

Carlson, J. R., George, J. F., Burgoon, J. K., Adkins, M., & White, C. H. (2004). Deception in computer-mediated communication. *Group Decision and Negotiation, 13*(1), 5–28.

Carney, D. (2010, May). Powerful people are better liars. *Harvard Business Review,* pp. 32–33.

Carson, T. L., Wokutch, R. E., & Murrmann, K. F. (1982). Bluffing in labor negotiations: Legal and ethical issues. *Journal of Business Ethics, 1*(1): 13–22.

Chertkoff, J. M., & Baird, S. L. (1971). Applicability of the big lie technique and the last clear chance doctrine to bargaining. *Journal of Personality and Social Psychology, 20,* 298–303.

Daft, R. L., Lengel, R. H., & Trevino, L. K. (1987). Message equivocality, media selection, and manager performance: Implications for information systems. *MIS Quarterly: Management Information Systems, 11,* 355–366.

DePaulo, B. M., Lindsay, J. J., Malone, B. E., Muhlenbruck, L., Charlton, K., & Cooper, H. (2003). Cues to deception. *Psychological Bulletin, 129*(1), 74–118.

Deutsch, M. (1958). Trust and suspicion. *Journal of Conflict Resolution, 2,* 265–279.

Ekman, P. (2009). *Telling lies: Clues to deceit in the marketplace, politics, and marriage* (3rd ed.). New York: Norton.

Fisher, R., & Ury, W. (1981). *Getting to yes.* Boston: Houghton Mifflin.

Fulmer, I. S., Barry, B., & Long, D. A. (2008). Lying and smiling: Informational and emotional deception in negotiation. *Journal of Business Ethics, 88*, 691–709.

Galanxhi, H., & Nah, F. F. H. (2007). Deception in cyberspace: A comparison of text-only vs. avatar-supported medium. *International Journal of Human Computer Studies, 65*, 770–783.

Goleman, D. (1995). *Emotional intelligence.* New York: Bantam Books.

Grazioli, S. (2004). Where did they go wrong? An analysis of the failure of knowledgeable Internet consumers to detect deception over the Internet. *Group Decision and Negotiation, 13*, 149–172.

Hancock, J., Woodworth, M., & Goorha, S. (2010). See no evil: The effect of communication medium and motivation on deception detection. *Group Decision and Negotiation, 19*, 327.

Haselhuhn, M., Schweitzer, M.E., & Wood, A. (2010). How implicit beliefs influence trust recovery. *Psychological Science, 21*, 645–648.

Heneman, R., & Greenberger, D. (2002). *Human resource management in virtual organizations.* New York: Wiley.

Jehn, K. A., & Scott, E. D. (2007). Perceptions of deception: Making sense of responses to employee deceit. *Journal of Business Ethics, 80,* 327–347.

Jensen, W., Meservy, T. O., Burgoon, J., & Nunamaker, J. F. (2010). Automatic, multimodal evaluation of human interaction. *Group Decision and Negotiation, 19*, 367.

Kalbfleisch, P. J. (1994). The language of detecting deceit. *Journal of Language and Social Psychology*, *13*, 469–496.

Kelley, H. H. (1966). A classroom study of the dilemmas in interpersonal negotiation. In K. Archibald (Ed.), *Strategic interaction and conflict: Original papers and discussion* (pp. 49–73). Berkeley, CA: Institute of International Studies.

Kiesler, S., & Sproull, L. (1986). Response effects in the electronic survey. *Public Opinion Quarterly, 50*, 402–413.

Kim, P., Ferrin, D., Cooper, C., & Dirks, K. (2004). Removing the shadow of suspicion: The effects of apology vs. denial for repairing competence- versus integrity-based trust violations. *Journal of Applied Psychology*, *83*, 104–118.

Kochan, T., & Katz, H. C. (1980). *Collective bargaining and industrial relations: From theory to policy and practice.* Homewood, IL: Irwin.

Kramer, R. (1994). The sinister attribution error: Paranoid cognition and collective distrust in organizations. *Motivation and Emotion*, *18,* 199–203.

Kramer, R., & Lewicki, R.J. (2010). Repairing and enhancing trust: Approaches to reducing organizational trust deficits. *Academy of Management Annals, 4*, 245–277.

Lax, D., & Sebenius, J. (1986). *The manager as negotiator: Bargaining for cooperation and competitive gain.* New York: Free Press.

Leenders, M. R., & Fearon, H. E. (2008). Developing purchasing's foundation. *Journal of Supply Chain Management, 44*, 17–27.

Lewicki, R. J., Barry, B., & Saunders, D. (2010). *Negotiation* (6th ed.). New York: McGraw-Hill.

Lewicki, R., & Brinsfield, C. (2012) Trust as a heuristic. In W. A. Donohue, R. R. Rogan, & S. Kaufman (Eds.). *Framing in negotiation: State of the art.* New York: Peter Lang.

Lewicki, R. J., & Dineen, B. R. (2002). Negotiating in virtual organizations. In R. Heneman & D. Greenberger (Eds.), *Human resource management in virtual organizations* (pp. 263–294). New York: Wiley.

Lewicki, R. J., McAllister, D., & Bies, R. H. (1998). Trust and distrust: New relationships and realities. *Academy of Management Review*, *23*, 438–458.

Lewicki, R. J., & Robinson, R. (1998). A factor-analytic study of negotiator ethics. *Journal of Business Ethics*, *18,* 211–228.

Lewicki, R. J., & Spencer, G. (1991, August). *Ethical relativism and negotiating tactics: Factors affecting their perceived ethicality.* Paper presented at a meeting of the Academy of Management, Miami, FL.

Lewicki, R. J., Tomlinson, E., & Gillespie, N. (2006). Models of interpersonal trust development: Theoretical approaches, empirical evidence and future directions. *Journal of Management, 32*(6), 991–1022.

Malhotra, D. K. (2004). Trust and reciprocity decisions: The differing perspectives of trustors and trusted parties. *Organizational Behavior and Human Decision Processes, 94,* 61–73.

Mayer, R. C., Davis, J. H., & Schoorman, D. F. (1995). An integrative model of organizational trust. *Academy of Management Review, 20,* 709–734.

McCornack, S. A., & Levine, T. R. (1990). When lies are uncovered: Emotional and relational outcomes of discovered deception. *Communication Monographs, 57,* 119–138.

Meyerson, D., Weick, K. E., & Kramer, R. M. (1996). Swift trust and temporary groups. In R. M. Kramer & T. R. Tyler (Eds.), *Trust in organizations: Frontiers of theory and research* (pp. 165–190). Thousand Oaks, CA: Sage.

Missner, M. (1980). *Ethics of the business system.* Sherman Oaks, CA: Alfred.

Monrose, F., & Rubin, A. D. (2000). Keystroke dynamics as a biometric for authentication. *Future Generation Computer Systems, 16,* 351–359.

Naquin, C. E., Kurtzberg, T. R., & Belkin, L. Y. (2010). The finer points of lying online: E-mail versus pen and paper. *Journal of Applied Psychology, 95,* 387–394.

Naquin, C. E., & Paulson, G. D (2003). Online bargaining and interpersonal trust. *Journal of Applied Psychology, 88,* 113–120.

O'Connor, K. M., & Carnevale, P. J. (1997). A nasty but effective negotiation strategy: Misrepresentation of a common-value issue. *Personality and Social Psychology Bulletin, 23,* 504–515.

Olekalns, M., & Smith , P. (2005). Metacognition, trust and outcomes in dyadic negotiations. *Personality and Social Psychology Bulletin, 31,* 1696–1707.

O'Sullivan, P. B., & Flanagin, A. J. (2003). Reconceptualizing "flaming" and other problematic messages. *New Media and Society, 5,* 69–94.

Robinson, R., Lewicki, R. J., & Donahue, E. (2000). Extending and testing a five factor model of ethical and unethical bargaining tactics: The SINS scale. *Journal of Organizational Behavior, 21,* 649–664.

Rockmann, K. W., & Northcraft, G. B. (2008). To be or not to be trusted: The influence of media richness on defection and deception. *Organizational Behavior and Human Decision Processes, 107,* 106–122.

Schweitzer, M. E., Brodt, S., & Croson, R. T. A. (2002). Seeing and believing: Visual access and the strategic use of deception. *International Journal of Conflict Management, 13,* 258–275.

Schweitzer, M. E., & Croson, R. (1999). Curtailing deception: The impact of direct questions on lies and omissions. *International Journal of Conflict Management, 10,* 225–248.

Schweitzer, M., Hershey, J., & Bradlow, E. (2006). Promises and lies: Restoring violated trust. *Organizational Behavior and Human Decision Processes, 101,* 1–19.

Shapiro, D. L. (1991). The effects of explanations on negative reactions to deceit. *Administrative Science Quarterly, 36,* 614–630.

Shapiro, D. L., & Bies, R. (1994). Threats, bluffs and disclaimers in negotiations. *Organizational Behavior and Human Decision Processes, 60,* 14–35.

Shapiro, D., Lewicki, R. J. and Devine, P. (1995). When do employees choose deceptive tactics to stop unwanted organizational change: A negotiation theory perspective. In R. H. Bies, B. H. Sheppard, & R. J. Lewicki (Eds.), *Research on negotiation in organizations* (Vol. 5, pp. 155–184). Greenwich, CT: JAI.

Suler, J. R. (2004). The psychology of text relationships. In R. Kraus, J. Zack, & G. Striker (Eds.), *Online counseling: A manual for mental health professionals* (pp. 20–50). London: Elsevier Academic.

Tenbrunsel, A. E. (1998). Misrepresentation and expectations of misrepresentation in an ethical dilemma: The role of incentives and temptation. *Academy of Management Journal, 41*, 330–339.

Thompson, L. (1998). *The mind and heart of the negotiator.* Upper Saddle River, NJ: Prentice Hall.

Thompson, L., Kray, L. J., & Lind, E. A. (1998). Cohesion and respect: An examination of group decision making in social and escalation dilemmas. *Journal of Experimental Social Psychology, 34*, 289–311.

Tinsley, C. H., O'Connor, K. M., & Sullivan, B. A. (2002). Tough guys finish last: The perils of a distributive reputation. *Organizational Behavior and Human Decision Processes, 88*, 621–642.

Tomlinson, E., Dineen, B., & Lewicki, R. (2004). The road to reconciliation: Antecedents of victim willingness to reconcile following a broken promise. *Journal of Management, 30*, 165–188.

Trevino, L., Lengel, R., & Daft, R. (1987). Media symbolism, media richness, and media choice in organizations: A symbolic interactionist perspective. *Communication Research, 14*, 553–574.

Tripp, T. (1993). Power and fairness in negotiations. *Social Justice Research, 6*, 19–38.

Tripp, T., Sondak, H., & Bies, R. (1995). Justice as rationality: A relational perspective on fairness in negotiations. In R. J. Bies, R. J. Lewicki, & B. H. Sheppard (Eds.), *Research on negotiations in organizations* (Vol. 5, pp. 45–64). Greenwich, CT: JAI.

Vizer, L. M., Zhou, L., & Sears, A. (2009). Automated stress detection using keystroke and linguistic features: An exploratory study. *International Journal of Human Computer Studies, 67*, 870–886.

Walton, R., & McKersie, R. (1965). *A behavioral theory of labor relations.* New York: McGraw-Hill.

Wilson, J. M., Straus, S. G., & McEvily, B. (2006). All in due time: The development of trust in computer-mediated and face-to-face teams. *Organizational Behavior and Human Decision Processes, 99*, 16–33.

Wright, R., Chakraborty, S., Basoglu, A., & Marett, K. (2010). Where did they go right? Understanding the deception in phishing communications. *Group Decision and Negotiation, 19*, 391.

Zhou, L. (2005). An empirical investigation of deception behavior in instant messaging. *IEEE Transactions on Professional Communication, 48*, 147–160.

Zhou, L., Burgoon, J. K., Nunamaker, J. F., Jr., & Twitchell, D. (2004). Automating linguistics-based cues for detecting deception in text-based asynchronous computer-mediated communication. *Group Decision and Negotiation, 13*, 81–106.

Zhou, L., Burgoon, J. K., Twitchell, D. P., Qin, T., & Nunamaker, J. F., Jr. (2004). A comparison of classification methods for predicting deception in computer-mediated communication. *Journal of Management Information Systems, 20*, 139–165.

Zhou, L., & Zhang, D. (2008). Following linguistic footprints: Automatic deception detection in online communication. *Communications of the ACM, 51*, 119–122.

Section 4

Negotiators as Social Influence/Group-Sensitive Managers in the 21st Century

9

Social Networks and Negotiation

Daniel J. Brass and Giuseppe Labianca

Man's economy, as a rule, is submerged in his social relationships.

Polanyi, 1944, p. 46

While Polanyi's comment may have come as a surprise to economists (as pointed out in Granovetter's 1985 critique), the effects of social relationships on economic outcomes are well understood by people working for tips (e.g., hairdressers and waiters) and parents of Girl Scouts trying to sell cookies. Behavior, even buying and selling behavior, is embedded in networks of interpersonal relationships. People rely on and are affected by social relationships of many types, including friendships, advice ties, and kinship ties, even in what appear to be perfectly open commodity markets (cf. Abolafia & Kilduff, 1988). Introductions between buyers and sellers are often facilitated through networks of these ties; referrals on who is trustworthy and who is to be avoided based on prior negotiations, who has useful knowledge and whose views are dated, and who is to be respected and who is to be feared are also transferred through these social networks (cf. Kilduff & Krackhardt, 1994).

This all makes it surprising that we find relatively few examples of the effects of these networks of social relationships on negotiation outcomes. Like power and conflict, negotiations inherently involve more than one party, and Bazerman and colleagues (Bazerman, Curhan, Moore, & Valley, 2000) have noted a history and recent resurgence in interest in the role of social relationships on negotiations. Yet, the focus of most negotiation research remains on the "behavioral decision" perspective (cf. Malhotra & Bazerman, 2008) and its emphasis on cognitive heuristics and predictable biases that affect negotiator behaviors. Social relationships have been relatively neglected (Valley, Neale, & Mannix, 1995), and few studies have gone beyond the negotiating dyad (Valley, White, & Iacobucci, 1992) to consider the role of third parties or the wider network of social relationships on negotiations. Yet, the negotiators' social networks, and the networks of individuals observing the outcome of the negotiations, will affect both the process and the outcomes of negotiations. To the extent that negotiations involve the exercise of an inherently relational phenomenon—power—the structural perspective of social network analysis may add to the predictive ability of negotiation research. In return, the more cognitive and behavioral insights from the behavioral decision perspective on negotiations may provide the understanding of the process mechanisms often missing from network analysis.

To that end, both the negotiations literature and the social network literature may benefit by informing each other. As a start toward this goal, our chapter's aims include: (a) to provide a brief general primer on social networks (for more depth, see Borgatti & Foster, 2003; Brass, 2011; Brass, Galaskiewicz, Greve, & Tsai, 2004; Kilduff & Brass, 2010); (b) to identify social network relationships that are likely to affect the extent to which negotiators have "power," or the ability to influence others to accommodate their requests; (c) to identify characteristics of the 21st century workplace that may affect social networks and negotiations; and (d) to identify questions in need of future research by both negotiation scholars and social network scholars. Cumulatively, this chapter's goal is to provide readers enough information to consider how they might increase their power/influence in negotiation situations with social network variables in mind and to encourage more research on the social network structure of negotiations.

A PRIMER ON SOCIAL NETWORKS

Much contemporary research on negotiations focuses on cognitive heuristics and biases that undermine the illusion that negotiators are perfectly rational and is conducted in the context of two-party (dyadic) negotiations. Another major stream of negotiations research focuses on how the structure of the game (e.g., how many times the two parties will negotiate, whether there is common knowledge of the potential outcomes) affects negotiations. We do not mean to suggest that these are not important aspects of negotiation processes and outcomes. Rather, we suggest an alternative, complementary perspective—that of social networks—that does not focus on the minds of negotiators or the structure of the game but rather on the structure of social relationships in and around the negotiations. This perspective assumes that social actors (whether individuals, groups, or organizations) are embedded within a web (or network) of interrelationships with other actors. The focus is on the structure or arrangement of relationships rather than the attributes or cognitions of the actors. It is this intersection of relationships that defines an actor's position in the social structure. It is these networks of relationships that provide opportunities and constraints that are as much the causal forces of negotiation outcomes as the strategies or cognitions of the actors and have an impact on how the structure of the negotiation itself might be viewed.

We define a social network as a set of actors (e.g., individuals, groups, organizations) and the set of ties representing some relationship or absence of relationship between the actors. Actors can be connected on the basis of (a) similarities (e.g., physical proximity, membership in the same group, or similar attributes such as gender); (b) social relations (e.g., kinship, roles, affective relations such as friendship); (c) interactions (e.g., talks with, gives advice to); or (d) flows (e.g., information, money) (Borgatti, Mehra, Brass, & Labianca, 2009). In organizational research, the links typically involve some form of interaction, such as communication or advice, and the flow of information or represent expressions of affect, such as interpersonal trust or friendship. Ties may be binary (present or absent) or valued (e.g., by frequency, intensity, or strength of ties), and some ties may be asymmetric (Dan likes Joe, but Joe does not like Dan) or directional (Joe goes to Dan for advice).

A major tenet of this perspective is that having the "right" network can determine whether someone is able to achieve better outcomes than someone with equal skills and abilities; it is both what you know and who you know. As differentiated from human capital (an individual's skills, ability, intelligence, personality, etc.) or financial capital (money), the popularized concept of social capital refers to benefits derived from relationships with others (see Adler & Kwon, 2002, for a cogent discussion of the history of usage of the term). Most organizational researchers explain these improved outcomes for individuals by reference to flows of resources through the individual's personal network. For example, a central actor in the network may benefit because he or she has greater access to information flows than a more peripheral actor. Podolny (2001) coined the term *pipes* to refer to the "flow" aspect of networks. He also noted, however, that networks can serve as "prisms," conveying mental images of the actor's status to those observing the network interactions.

The idea of a network implies more than one link, and the added value of the network perspective is that it goes beyond individual actors or dyads of actors to providing a way of considering the structural arrangement of many actors. The focal actor in a network is referred to as *ego*; the other actors with whom ego has direct relationships in his or her personal network are called *alters*. As Wellman (1988, p. 20) noted, "It is not assumed that network members engage only in multiple duets with separate alters." The focus is on the relationships among all the dyadic relationships within all the actors' personal networks that form the overall network in which all the actors are embedded. Typically, a minimum of two links connecting three actors is implicitly assumed in order to have a network and establish such notions as indirect links and paths (e.g., "six degrees of separation" and the common expression, "It's a small world"; see Watts, 2003).

SOCIAL NETWORKS AND IMPLICATIONS FOR NEGOTIATIONS

The Effect of Network Centrality

Consider the diagrams in Figure 9.1. One does not need to be an expert on social networks or negotiations to suggest that the central actor (Position A) in Figure 9.1a is the most powerful position and will almost certainly acquire better negotiation outcomes than any of the other positions. Outcomes can include both ego's ability to influence others to accommodate ego's needs (win–lose outcomes) or ego's ability to influence negotiations to satisfy both ego's and alter's needs (win–win outcomes), but the important point is that A is in the best position to attempt to dictate the terms of the negotiation.

We make these judgments based simply on the pattern or structure of the nodes (actors) and ties, without reference to the cognitions, strategies, or skills of the actors. From a purely structural perspective, a tie is a tie is a tie, and a node is a node is a node, only differentiated on the basis of

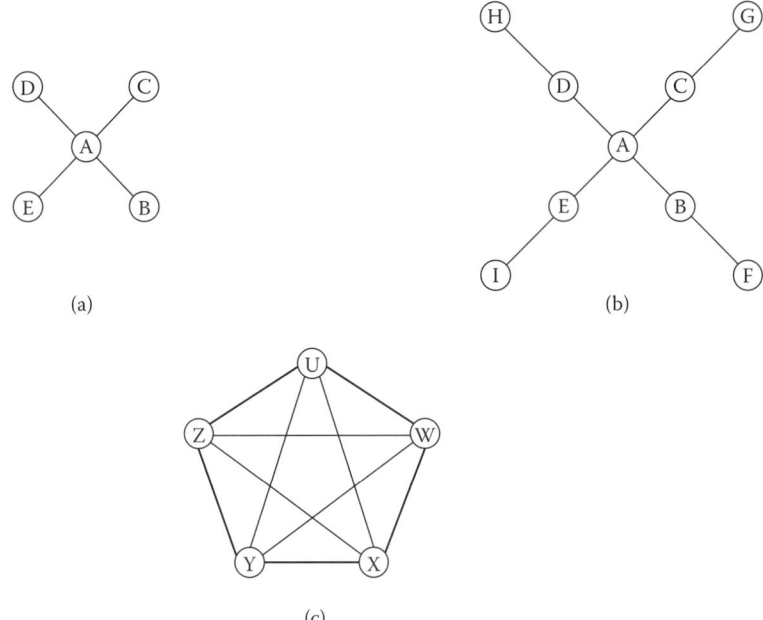

FIGURE 9.1
How control and access affect the power of nodes in a bargaining network.

structural position in the network. It is the *pattern* of relationships that provides the opportunities and constraints that affect outcomes.

We can now imagine that Figure 9.1a refers to a potential negotiation setting, where Actor A is negotiating with Actors B, C, D, and E. In explaining the power of a central position, we might note that Actor A is not dependent on any one other node because A has four potential negotiating partners, while all the other nodes are dependent on A as their sole negotiating partner (Brass, 1984). Negotiation researchers might recognize that this exchange theory explanation is consistent with the well-known notion of relative BATNA (best alternative to a negotiated agreement) determining negotiation power. The ability of the central actor to play one party off against the other to seek the best deal is not only because Actor A has multiple alternatives but also because those alternatives are not negotiating among themselves either to provide each other alternatives or potentially to work together to force a better deal on A. Network measures of centrality are not attributes of isolated individual actors; rather, they represent the actor's relationship within the network. If any aspect of the network changes, the actor's relationship within the network also changes. For example, simply adding an additional relationship to each of the alters (see Actors B, C, D, and E in Figure 9.1b) will substantially reduce Actor A's power. These additional actors provide bargaining alternatives for Actors B, C, D, and E, thereby increasing their BATNAs in relation to Actor A. In experimental settings, these actors have been found to have more power than Actor A, who is now surrounded and somewhat contained by individuals with other alternatives (Cook, Emerson, Gilmore, & Yamagishi, 1983).

In contrast to viewing the network as a potential source of exchange partners that can be played off one another, we can also view it as a potential source of cooperative information flows critical to negotiations. In these types of cooperative exchanges, Position A in Figure 9.1a acquires relatively more information than the other positions by virtue of its central position in the network. But now adding additional alters for Positions B, C, D, and E (Figure 9.1b) does not decrease Position A's power but rather adds increased access to information flows via indirect links in the network. Indeed, negotiators may attempt to increase their information access more dramatically by connecting to alters who have many connections rather than alters who have few connections. While negotiating with powerful others (actors with many connections) would be disadvantageous in competitive situations that require control and power-oriented negotiating approaches, being tied to well-connected alters would benefit ego in a cooperative situation. Thus, it is important to consider the nature of the ties as well as the structure of relationships.

Central actors, compared to peripheral actors, may also benefit from having better knowledge of what the overall network looks like outside their own particular connections, as well as a better idea of "who knows what." These accurate perceptions of the entire network are associated with power (Krackhardt, 1990) and might prove particularly beneficial for those engaged in coalition building (Murnighan & Brass, 1991).

While the networks depicted in Figures 9.1(a) and 9.1(b) provide various control, access, and perceptual advantages to different actors depending on their relative positions, the network in Figure 9.1(c) depicts a very different situation. These actors (U, W, X, Y, and Z) are "structurally equivalent"; each has the same number of ties to other actors similarly situated in the network. In that sense, the role that each actor plays in this network is equivalent and interchangeable with each other actor, and we would not expect that the network would affect the relative power of any of the individuals in a negotiation. Here, any differences in outcomes are more likely to be based on individual differences in negotiation skills.

Building a Network

The implications for negotiators in both competitive and cooperative negotiation situations are to build extensive networks of alternative transaction partners or information sources. Yet, it is important to note that relationships are not solely controlled by any single actor. Not every invitation for a date in high school is accepted. Little research has investigated strategies for "winning friends and influencing people." Yet, research focusing on antecedent correlates of network connections provides some clues on how to build networks. Several prescriptions follow: (a) be in temporal and physical proximity by intentionally placing yourself in the same place at the same time as others; (b) recognize the power of homophily (a strong human preference for interacting with similar others) and seek out the ways in which you are similar to someone you meet to create a connection; (c) increase your human capital (people with skills and expertise are sought out by others) as a way of increasing your status because people prefer to be attached to people of higher status ("preferential attachment"); (d) leverage existing relationships to create new relationships using balance theory tenets (e.g., a friend of a friend is a friend); and (e) recognize that certain personality traits are more attractive (positive, outgoing individuals) and that personality can be somewhat malleable over time (for elaboration, see Brass, 2011). Remember that relationships also hinge on the cognitive interpretations of actions by the parties involved. For example, we are not likely to form relationships with people whom we perceive as trying to use us. Perceptions of calculated self-interest inhibit relationship building.

The Effects of Structural Holes

Other things being equal, building larger networks is advantageous but is, of course, time intensive. Burt (1992) has argued that a person can increase the efficiency with which his or her network delivers valuable resources by focusing on developing a network with a specific pattern of relationships: maintaining relationships with those who are not themselves connected. When ego is connected to alters who are not themselves connected, there are many "structural holes" in ego's personal network (Actor A in Figure 9.1a). This creates many open triads (e.g., Triad A, B, C), which are focused around ego (Simmel, 1950). Burt noted the advantages to ego of being the "tertius gaudens" (i.e., "the third who benefits"). The tertius is in a position to control the information flow between the disconnected alters (i.e., broker the relationship) or play them off against each other. The advantages in negotiation from this control are obvious. An additional, less-obvious advantage is the access of the tertius to nonredundant information. Alters who are connected share the same information and are often part of the same social circles and knowledge pools. Alters who are not connected often represent different social circles and are sources of different, nonredundant information—information that may prove useful in providing different perspectives that lead to creative problem solving in negotiations. However, the two advantages of control and unique information access appear to be a trade-off: To play one off against the other, the two alters need to be sufficiently similar to be credible alternatives (e.g., it is difficult for most people to use a boat dealer as leverage against a car dealer in a negotiation). In addition, the irony of the structural hole strategy is that connecting to any previously disconnected alter creates structural hole opportunities for the alter as well as for ego (Brass, 2009). However, the research evidence indicated advantages to actors who occupy structural holes (Brass, 2011), and we would expect the same in negotiations.

The Effects of "Closed" Networks

An alternative to Burt's focus on the structural holes of individual actors is Coleman's (1990) focus on the collective and the often-cited reference to social capital as norms of reciprocity, trust, and mutual obligations, as well as monitoring and sanctioning of inappropriate behavior, which result from "closed" networks. Closed networks result from a high number of interconnections between members of a group; ego's alters are connected to each other as in Figure 9.1(c), as compared to the open networks depicted in Figures 9.1(a) and 9.1(b). Closed networks allow for the development of shared norms, social support, and a sense of identity. Information circulates easily within closed networks, and the potential damage to one's reputation discourages unethical behavior and, consequently, fosters generalized trust among members of the network (Brass,

Butterfield, & Skaggs, 1998). Third parties in closed networks have incentives to mediate conflicts and preserve the trust and social support of a tightly knit group, rather than "divide and conquer" as they would from a tertius gaudens perspective (Burt, 1992). They also serve as an audience for all negotiations that occur within the collectivity, which creates potential reputational liabilities for parties that negotiate too competitively with fellow group members. This creates a strong incentive for negotiations conducted within closed networks to be more cooperative, more likely to focus on mutual interests, more likely to focus on the shadow of the future, and less likely to exhibit unethical or opportunistic behavior and hence produce more lasting agreements.

The two perspectives seem to offer contradictory predictions concerning negotiations. At the individual level, connecting to disconnected others results in a negotiation advantage for the ego occupying the tertius position; at the collective level, connecting to others who are themselves connected results in closure in the network and the growth of the negotiation advantages of trust, norms, and group sanctions. However, not everything about closed networks is positive; an individual can become "trapped in your own net" as closed networks can constrain action (Gargiulo & Benassi, 2000). Indeed, both approaches are based on the underlying network proposition that densely connected networks constrain attitudes and behavior. In one case (Coleman, 1990), this constraint promotes good outcomes (trust, norms of reciprocity, monitoring and sanctioning of inappropriate behavior); in the other case (Burt, 1992), constraint produces bad outcomes (redundant information, a lack of novel ideas, an inability to outcompete the other actors). Negotiators may attempt to balance their networks by maintaining a core group of densely tied close friends while extending their external networks to include alters who are not connected (Burt, 2005; Reagans, Zuckerman, & McEvily, 2004).

The Effects of Tie Strength

In addition to focusing on the structure or overall pattern of relationships, social network researchers attempt to differentiate ties according to their content. The main focus from this perspective has been on the strength of the relationships in social networks and has been dominated by Granovetter's (1973) theory of the "strength of weak ties." Tie strength is a function of its interaction frequency, intimacy, emotional intensity (mutual confiding), and degree of reciprocity (Granovetter, 1973, p. 348). Strong ties often characterize friend and family relationships; weak ties tend to be acquaintances. Granovetter noted that our friends are likely to be connected, while our acquaintances are not. Thus, his structural explanation for the strength of weak ties is that weak ties are not likely to be connected and represent bridges to disconnected social circles that may provide useful, nonredundant information, similar to, but preceding, Burt's structural hole argument.

Strong ties, on the other hand, are thought to be more influential on ego, more motivated to provide information, and with easier access than weak ties. For example, Krackhardt (1992) showed that strong ties were influential in determining the outcome of a union election. Hansen (1999) found that while weak ties were more useful in searching out information, strong ties were useful for the effective transfer of information. Uzzi (1997) found that "embedded ties" were characterized by higher levels of trust, richer transfers of information, and greater problem-solving capabilities when compared to "arms-length" ties. On the downside, strong ties require more time and energy to maintain and come with stronger obligations to reciprocate.

The expected effects of tie strength have been confirmed in research on dyadic-level negotiating (Valley & Neale, 1993): Friends achieve higher joint utility than strangers. However, some research suggests that there might be a curvilinear relationship between tie strength and joint utility (e.g., lovers may be overly concerned about avoiding damage to the relationship and be unwilling to press for an adequate resolution to their issues). As Valley et al. (1995) noted, relationship strength affects not only the outcome but also the process of dyadic negotiation—the quantity of moves available, as well as the quality of the interaction.

Moving beyond the negotiating dyad, we expect that third-party friends (or enemies) may facilitate the negotiation toward cooperative solutions, while third-party acquaintances may provide diverse information that facilitates creative solutions. Extending the network outward, balance theory (Heider, 1958) predicts that clusters of friends will form closed networks that can engender trust but may also be constraining. As ingroup/out-group biases develop, negotiation across clusters may be particularly difficult. In addition, research on negative ties (i.e., ongoing ties between individuals who dislike one another) suggests that negative relationships may be more powerful predictors of behaviors, outcomes, and attitudes in organizations than positive relationships (Labianca & Brass, 2006). For example, Labianca, Brass, and Gray (1998) found that while having positive relationships with out-group members (such as friends in another department) did not reduce perceptions of intergroup conflict as one might expect, having a negative relationship with a member of the out-group (such as disliking someone in another department) did increase perceptions that one's entire group was in conflict with the other group.

Another focus of this school of research is on whether a tie transmits only one type of content, or whether it can be appropriated for a different type of use, thus making the tie stronger. As in the case of Girl Scout cookies, one type of tie (friend, neighbor) might be appropriated for a different use (cookie sales). However, there is some evidence that appropriating one type of tie for a different use is not totally acceptable for some. For example, Ingram and Zou (2008) found that people prefer affective friendship relations and instrumental business relations to remain separated. While friendship should lubricate negotiations, taking advantage of friends for commercial purposes may sever the strong tie, as is often the case when individuals engaged in multilevel marketing schemes attempt to involve their friends.

Effects of Ties to Powerful Alters

Rather than assume that all alters are the same, some social network researchers have argued that we need to weight the value of ties by the amount of resources that alters possess. Lin (1999) has argued that tie strength and the disconnection among alters is of little importance if the alters do not possess resources useful to ego. In response to Granovetter's (1973) findings on the importance of weak ties in finding jobs, Lin, Ensel, and Vaughn (1981) found that weak ties reached higher-status alters, and that alters' occupational prestige was the key to ego obtaining a high-status job. For example, Brass (1984) found that links to the dominant coalition of executives in a company were related to power and promotions for nonmanagerial employees. Extrapolating these results, we would predict that negotiation outcomes would be contingent on the resources possessed by the negotiators' alters. In cooperative situations, connecting to powerful others will help ego; in a competitive situation, negotiating with a powerful other will be disadvantageous to ego.

In addition to the resource advantage of connecting to powerful others, the *perception* of being connected to powerful others may be an additional source of power for ego. For example, when approached for a loan, the wealthy Baron de Rothschild replied, "I won't give you a loan myself, but I will walk arm-in-arm with you across the floor of the Stock Exchange, and you will soon have willing lenders to spare" (Cialdini, 1989, p. 45). Kilduff and Krackhardt (1994) found that being perceived to have a prominent friend had more effect on one's reputation for high performance than actually having a prominent friend in the organization. Likewise, Podolny (2001) noted how the market relations between firms are not only affected by the transfer of resources but also by how third parties perceive the quality of the relationship. You are known by the company you keep. Networks are not only pipes through which resources flow but are also prisms viewed by others. Perceptions of the network, whether accurate or inaccurate, may affect negotiation outcomes. Negotiators who are perceived as connected to powerful alters may reap the rewards of such perceptions, and subtly allowing the other party to learn about those connections can often be useful.

Effects of Knowledge of the Network

Bazerman and colleagues (2000) observed that there has been a transition in negotiation research from focusing on the structure of the game (the objective features of negotiations) to focusing on behavioral decision making, in part because the structure of the game is often beyond the control of individual negotiators. This implies that researchers and practitioners might more practically spend their efforts on factors that negotiators can control, such as strategies based on cognitive biases. The same question might be raised about the study of network structures on negotiations. To what extent do individual negotiators have control over social relationships? Even one's direct relationships are in part outside the individual's control because there is always another party to the relationship who may or may not be motivated to reciprocate the relationship. If important outcomes are affected by indirect links (over which ego has even less control), the effects of agency become inversely related to the path distance of alters whose relationships may affect ego. Structural determinism increases to the extent that relationships many path lengths away affect ego. For example, a study, popularized in the press, showed that a person's happiness was associated with the happiness of friends or family members up to a distance of three path lengths in the network (Fowler & Christakis, 2008).

While negotiators may not be able to change relationships easily, especially those far removed, knowledge of the existing network may prove particularly helpful. For example, Figure 9.2 illustrates the friendship network of a group of ministers. These ministers were all located in one geographical district in the Deep South of the United States that had a history of both slavery and segregation based on race. As a consequence, despite being in the same denomination, the predominantly black and white churches remained segregated and had largely developed their own traditions and methods of worship separately. This separation had led to tension within the broader community, and the ministers were interested in leading a racial reconciliation effort—a broad, community-based negotiation attempting to break down intergroup biases and generate momentum to tackle the community's problems together.

After administering a survey to all of the ministers asking about who they were friends with among the other ministers, who they spoke with

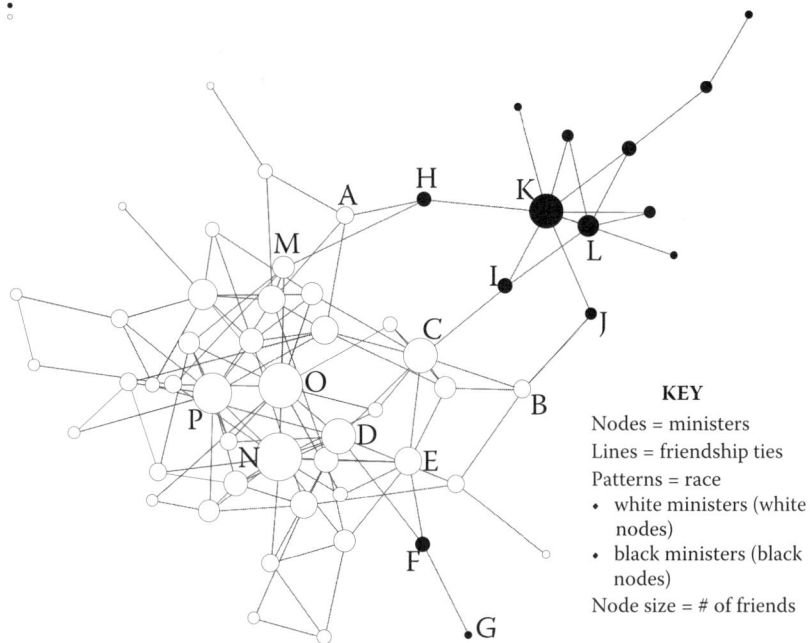

FIGURE 9.2
Friendship ties in a network of ministers.

on a regular basis, who they shared advice with, and who they gave material support to, we plotted the various networks, as shown in Figure 9.2. The checkered dots are the white ministers, the dashed dots are the black ministers, the lines indicate friendships among the ministers, and the size of the dots indicates the number of people who have nominated that minister as a friend, which is an indication of how well liked that minister is. Although expecting some separation, it stunned the ministers to see just how separate they were; visually, they could see that there were few connections between black and white ministers.

At this point, the ministers realized that prior to beginning a racial reconciliation in the broader community, they needed to begin within their own group. They decided to form a task force to lead the way in terms of negotiating underlying issues and proposing solutions that would help bring them together. The question of how to staff the task force then became critical. A network perspective was useful in thinking through these selection issues and ensuring the right mix of individuals formed the task force.

The ministers recognized that it would be useful to have individuals who were already bridging the racial divide. Figure 9.2 shows that among the white ministers, Ministers A, B, C, D, E, and M already had friendships with black ministers. Having one or two of these individuals on the task force would be useful because they were already acting as bridges between the two racial communities. Thus, the extent to which an individual sat between the white and black ministerial communities was the first criterion evaluated. Not wanting to make the task force unwieldy in terms of size, they had to decide on only one or two of these five "bridging" ministers. The network map provided further guidance. While Ministers D and E were friends with a black minister (Minister F), F only had one friend (Minister G), who in turn had no friends. D and E's contacts into the black ministerial committee were not as potentially useful as A, B, C, and M's contacts, which reached into the heart of the black church. This notion that it is not only your direct contacts that make you valuable but also the access provided by your contact's contacts was the reason why D and E would not be strong candidates for the task force.

When thinking about both direct and indirect contacts, Minister C stands out. Not only does Minister C have a lot of friends within the white church, but also his friends have a lot of well-connected friends there. In addition, Minister C's friend in the black church (Minister I) is friends with the most well-connected black ministers. Minister C has the type of network connections that would be useful in attempting a collaborative negotiation in which the main goal is to access the whole network and attempt to increase interconnections in the whole network. Similarly, Minister I has the same type of network profile among the black ministers and would likely be a good pick, all else being equal.

The task force also ultimately had to influence and change behavior. In that respect, it is useful to have people on the committee who are powerful in terms of interpersonal influence. From a network perspective, ministers who are nominated as friends by many people (or have "high in-degree centrality") would likely be good choices. Among the white ministers, N, O, and P were frequently nominated and likely choices, while K and L would be likely choices among the black ministers. Thus, ultimately a combination of individuals who are influential within their group, as well as individuals who can bridge the gap between groups, would be the optimal mix of negotiators to include on this task force. They have both the potential to negotiate on the task force itself, as well as later to influence successfully the broader network in which they are embedded, extending the collective social capital across the racial divide that exist currently.

The Effects of Adversaries

While the network perspective has much to inform the study of negotiations, we believe that negotiations research is equally likely to contribute to important elaborations of network studies. Most network research currently focuses on positive or neutral ties between individuals (e.g., friendship, advice, required workflow) while ignoring ties that convey any type of negative content (cf. Labianca & Brass, 2006). In contrast, negotiations researchers are often quite interested in politically charged situations in which individuals are actively vying for preeminence by both enhancing their own position and potentially harming another's position (e.g., Siegel, 2007). A real-world example of this phenomenon is occurring in international political networks: As Iran attempts to build its domestic nuclear industry, the United States, its current adversary, is intentionally introducing faulty equipment into the supplier network in an attempt to stall Iran's ambitions. This in turn motivates Iran to find many like-minded allies to oppose the United States (e.g., Venezuela) so it is not too dependent on any one ally. Many networks have these types of negative, threatening ties

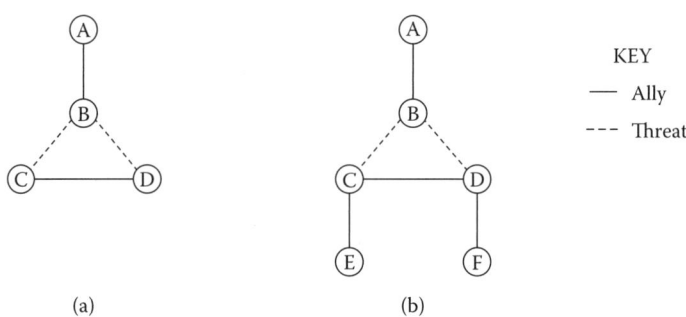

KEY

—— Ally

--- Threat

(a)　　　　　　　　　　(b)

FIGURE 9.3
Politically charged bargaining networks.

that seek to undermine the flows or interactions within the network and in which individuals might be trying to build coalitions to counter other individuals' actions (Murnighan & Brass, 1991). Most network analysis assesses the favorability of a node's position without regard to these types of negative threat ties.

We can examine this type of situation in the following network (see Figure 9.3(a)): Nodes A and B are political allies, as are Nodes C and D (allies are denoted by solid lines), but Node B is a political adversary of both Nodes C and D (adversaries are denoted by dashed lines). Who has the most favorable position in this network heading into a negotiation? One method of attempting to decide this would be simply to count the number of allies an individual has and then subtract the number of adversaries that same individual has. Using this simple method based on degree centrality, Actor A is in the best position (1 ally minus 0 adversaries = +1 score), while Actor B is in the worst position (1 ally minus 2 adversaries = -1), with C and D having identical scores in the middle range (1 - 1 = 0). Imagine A and B heading into a negotiation. B is under threat from both C and D and has only one alternative to turn to, Actor A. This creates a huge amount of dependence for B on A, placing B in an extremely vulnerable position.

We would argue that this position is even worse qualitatively than the one we showed in Figure 9.1(a), in which B was entirely dependent on A, who had many alternatives. When an actor is being threatened by another actor, that negative tie creates greater anxiety and motivates stronger reaction to attempt to resolve the situation as compared to being in a situation that does not involve threat, a phenomenon referred to as "negative asymmetry" (e.g., Labianca et al., 1998; Taylor, 1991). People assign more importance to negative information, and it outweighs positive information in decision making and judgments (see Labianca & Brass, 2006, for a summary of this research). We would expect this to carry over into this realm of negotiation as well.

Simply using these ally and adversary counts to determine the favorability of a node's position in the network does not adequately take into account the different levels of threat that can be created through coalition building. For example, compare Figure 9.3(a) to Figure 9.3(b). If we focus on Actors A, B, C, and D, their counts of allies and adversaries are identical in both networks. What has changed in Figure 9.3(b) is that C and D are no longer direct allies. C and D would thus have a more difficult time coordinating a response to Actor B, and thus we might expect that B's position would be more favorable in Figure 9.3(b) than in Figure 9.3(a). Unfortunately, no existing network measure is able to capture this type of logic at the moment, including Bonacich power centrality (Bonacich, 2007; Bonacich & Lloyd, 2004). While research is ongoing in an attempt to resolve this (e.g., Agneessens, 2010; Smith, Kidwell-Lopez, Borgatti, & Labianca, 2010), greater integration with the work that is already ongoing in conflict and negotiations might be fruitful.

21st CENTURY CHALLENGES AND OPPORTUNITIES

Organizations in the 21st century have become flatter, with more decentralized decision making and less reliance on formal authority. This suggests greater decision making involving negotiations among all employees. As the reliance on formal authority decreases and reliance on knowledge-intensive work increases, the informal network of contacts will continue increasing in importance. Employees are increasingly engaged in negotiations that cross departmental boundaries and organizational boundaries. As an example, firms are now migrating a great deal of their new product development outside the firm. Where negotiations were previously held only between research and development scientists and some other departments internally, these negotiations now increasingly draw in academic scientists, government employees, and representatives of nongovernmental organizations. This necessitates greater negotiating skill at maintaining a broader negotiating network while also maintaining a greater degree of flexibility in negotiating. This has also driven negotiations increasingly out of the realm of face-to-face negotiations and into negotiations through various other digital media, including e-mail, videoconferencing, and online marketplaces. This not only opens many questions about the strength of the ties between the negotiators, which are undoubtedly weaker in these digital settings, but also creates interesting research questions about how the ties might migrate from a digital to face-to-face setting and back again and how this affects the underlying negotiations.

The increasingly turbulent global business environment also ushered in another fundamental change to organizations in the 21st century: the demise of the vertically integrated organization. Very few industries continue to have organizations that manage the entire production process from generating the inputs, processing them into outputs, and managing the final customer relationship. Instead, we have seen a dramatic shift toward organizations being focused on a core set of competencies and then relying on other members of their supply chain to execute their own core competencies, with the resulting product or service created by a network of organizations. This change to a network form of organizing, coupled with pushing decision making lower into the organization, has driven dramatic increases in the need for negotiation skills among organizational members. Organizational members are now expected to negotiate across departmental and organizational boundaries with other parties, needing to determine to what extent the future relationship with the party is important, as well as whether there are audiences that will create potential positive or negative reputational effects from the negotiation. They have to decide what their bargaining networks look like. For example, should a focal firm bring two suppliers of the same component together to increase standardization, share development costs, and lower everyone's cost of doing business, while making their firm vulnerable to the two suppliers working in concert to affect their next round of negotiation? Or, should the firm keep them in as competitive a situation as possible and intentionally create "Bake-Offs" to maintain their position as the tertius gaudens? Many of those answers will increasingly need to be considered in the broader light of their entire supply chain network. Firms might choose to increase their vulnerability in certain areas of their network to increase access to certain resources while maintaining control over other parties in other areas of their network to arrive at the best portfolio of bargaining ties for their organization.

On the other hand, "maintaining control over other parties" may be more challenging in the 21st century workplace because employees now must increasingly conduct business transactions with people who are located across the globe, without a common context in which to develop densely shared networks or to see a face or shake a hand—traditional sources for tie strengthening. Virtual negotiations also may hinder knowledge of the network. The likely change of negotiators between the negotiation's start and its completion in global transactions further weakens any single negotiator's ability to control their own centrality or structural holes in the course of the negotiation. As such, the strategies for increasing power in social networks may likely be more challenging to use in general and for negotiation in particular in the 21st century workplace.

CONCLUSIONS

Overall, we have demonstrated how a social network perspective might contribute to understanding negotiations. In the process, we noted challenges and opportunities for future research. While the network provides a map of the highways, seldom is the traffic measured (Brass, 1984; Stevenson & Gilly, 1991). Future network research will need to measure the processes and mechanisms involved in negotiations to get a fuller understanding of the value of particular structural patterns. For example, does a structural hole provide the advantage of alternative bargaining partners, or is ego attempting to mediate a conflict? Should ego play one alter off another or connect the alters in hopes of synergistic solutions or the benefits of future reciprocation?

The next logical growth in network research is the evolution of networks, how they change over time. Although there are few longitudinal studies of network change at the individual level (e.g., Barley, 1990; Burkhardt & Brass, 1990), access to archival, longitudinal alliance data (e.g., Gulati, 2007) is fueling such studies at the interorganizational level. In addition, network scholars have actively devised computer simulations of network change (e.g., Buskens & van de Rijt, 2008; Gilbert & Abbott, 2005).

Several opportunities exist for both researcher and practitioner. How are negotiation ties maintained, and what causes them to decay or be severed? Can strong ties and dense networks be developed and maintained via electronic media? What strategies help negotiators become central in social networks associated with negotiated transactions, and do these differ when the transactions involve technology-mediated versus face-to-face exchanges? Can technology-enhanced communication provide a more accurate knowledge of the network? Are strategies such as building structural holes effective when negotiation participants change during the course of the negotiation? What are the effects of past ties on negotiations? Can dormant, inactive ties from past negotiations be reactivated? As in the case of the ministers, can external agents (i.e., managers) affect the network formation and change of others? Traditional research methods used in negotiation studies (simulations, laboratory-based experiments) may prove useful when information about social networks is included/manipulated. In addition, the Internet may prove to be both a convenient and a useful setting for studying technology-mediated/virtual negotiations. For example, Centola (2010) demonstrated how experimental studies can be conducted in online social networks. Many opportunities exist for research on the dynamics of networks in negotiations, and online social networks may be particularly useful in documenting change over time. It is hoped this chapter will foster collaborative research efforts on negotiations and social networks.

ACKNOWLEDGMENT

We are indebted to Steve Borgatti, Ajay Mehra, Dan Halgin, and the other faculty and doctoral students at the LINKS Center (http://www.linkscenter.org), as well as Filip Agneessens, for the many interesting and insightful discussions that formed the basis for chapters such as this.

REFERENCES

Abolafia, M. Y., & Kilduff, M. (1988). Enacting market crisis: The social construction of a speculative bubble. *Administrative Science Quarterly, 33*, 177–193.

Adler, P. S., & Kwon, S. (2002). Social capital: Prospects for a new concept. *Academy of Management Review, 27,* 17–40.

Agneessens, F. (2010). *Utilizing balance theory triads to determine political independence.* Unpublished manuscript, University of Groningen, the Netherlands.

Barley, S. R. (1990). The alignment of technology and structure through roles and networks. *Administrative Science Quarterly, 35,* 61–103.

Bazerman, M. H., Curhan, J. R., Moore, D. A., & Valley, K. L. (2000). Negotiations. *Annual Review of Psychology, 51,* 279–314.

Bonacich, P. (2007). Some unique properties of eigenvector centrality. *Social Networks, 29,* 555–564.

Bonacich, P., & Lloyd, P. (2004). Calculating status with negative relations. *Social Networks, 26,* 331–338.

Borgatti, S. P., & Foster, P. C. (2003). The network paradigm in organizational research: A review and typology. *Journal of Management, 29,* 991–1013.

Borgatti, S. P., Mehra, A., Brass, D. J., & Labianca, G. (2009). Network analysis in the social sciences. *Science, 323,* 892–895.

Brass, D. J. (1984). Being in the right place: A structural analysis of individual influence in an organization. *Administrative Science Quarterly, 29,* 518–539.

Brass, D. J. (2009). Connecting to brokers: Strategies for acquiring social capital. In V. O. Bartkus & J. H. Davis (Eds.), *Social capital: Reaching out, reaching in* (pp. 260–274). Northhampton, MA: Elgar.

Brass, D. J. (2011). A social network perspective on industrial/organizational psychology. In S. W. J. Kozlowski (Ed.), *The Oxford handbook of organizational psychology.* New York: Oxford University Press.

Brass, D. J., Butterfield, K. D., & Skaggs, B. C. (1998). Relationships and unethical behavior: A social network perspective. *Academy of Management Review, 23,* 14–31.

Brass, D. J., Galaskiewicz, J., Greve, H. R., & Tsai, W. (2004). Taking stock of networks and organizations: A multilevel perspective. *Academy of Management Journal, 47,* 795–819.

Burkhardt, M. E., & Brass, D. J. (1990). Changing patterns or patterns of change: The effect of a change in technology on social network structure and power. *Administrative Science Quarterly. 35,* 104–127.

Burt, R. S. (1992). *Structural holes: The social structure of competition.* Cambridge, MA: Harvard University Press.

Burt, R. S. (2005). *Brokerage and closure: An introduction to social capital.* Oxford, UK: Oxford University Press.

Buskens, V., & van de Rijt, A. (2008). Dynamics of networks if everyone strives for structural holes. *American Journal of Sociology, 114,* 371–407.

Centola, D. (2010). The spread of behavior in an online social network experiment. *Science, 329,* 1194–1197.

Cialdini, R. B. (1989). Indirect tactics of impression management: Beyond basking. In R. A. Giacalone & P. Rosenfield (Eds.), *Impression management in the organization* (pp. 45–56). Hillsdale, NJ: Erlbaum.

Coleman, J. S. (1990). *Foundations of social theory.* Cambridge, MA: Harvard University Press.

Cook, K. S., Emerson, R. M., Gilmore, M. R., & Yamagishi, T. (1983). The distribution of power in exchange networks: Theory and experimental results. *American Journal of Sociology, 89,* 275–305.

Fowler, J. H., & Christakis, N. A. (2008). The dynamic spread of happiness in a large social network. *British Journal of Medicine, 337*(a2338), 1–9.

Gargiulo, M., & Benassi, M. (2000). Trapped in your own net: Cohesion, structural holes and the adaptation of social capital. *Organization Science, 11*, 183–196.

Gilbert, N., & Abbott, A. (2005). Introduction. *American Journal of Sociology, 110*, 859–863.

Granovetter, M. S. (1973). The strength of weak ties. *American Journal of Sociology, 6*, 1360–1380.

Granovetter, M. (1985). Economic action and social structure: The problem of embeddedness. *American Journal of Sociology, 91*, 481–510.

Gulati, R. (2007). *Managing network resources: Alliances, affiliations and other relational assets*. Oxford, UK: Oxford University Press.

Hansen, M. T. (1999). The search–transfer problem: The role of weak ties in sharing knowledge across organization subunits. *Administrative Science Quarterly, 44*, 82–111.

Heider, R. (1958). *The psychology of interpersonal relations*. New York: Wiley.

Ingram, P., & Zou, X. (2008). Business friendships. In A. P. Brief & B. M. Staw (Eds.), *Research in organizational behavior* (Vol. 28, pp. 167–184). London: Elsevier.

Kilduff, M., & Brass, D. J. (2010). Organizational social network research: Core ideas and key debates. In J. P. Walsh & A. P. Brief (Eds.), *Academy of Management annuals* (Vol. 4, pp. 317–357). London: Routledge.

Kilduff, M., & Krackhardt, D. (1994). Bringing the individual back in: A structural analysis of the internal market for reputation in organizations. *Academy of Management Journal, 37*, 87–108.

Krackhardt, D. (1990). Assessing the political landscape: Structure, cognition, and power in organizations. *Administrative Science Quarterly, 35*, 342–369.

Krackhardt. D. (1992). The strength of strong ties: The importance of Philos. In N. Nohria & R. Eccles (Eds.), *Networks and organizations: Structure, form, and action* (pp. 216–239). Boston: Harvard Business School Press.

Labianca, G., & Brass, D. J. (2006). Exploring the social ledger: Negative relationships and negative asymmetry in social networks in organizations. *Academy of Management Review, 31*, 596–614.

Labianca, G., Brass, D. J., & Gray, B. (1998). Social networks and perceptions of intergroup conflict: The role of negative relationships and third parties. *Academy of Management Journal, 41*, 55–67.

Lin, N. (1999). Social networks and status attainment. *Annual Review of Sociology, 25*, 467–487.

Lin, N., Ensel, W. M., & Vaughn, J. C. (1981). Social resources and strength of ties: Structural factors in occupational status attainment. *American Sociological Review, 46*, 393–405.

Malhotra, D., & Bazerman, M. H. (2008). Psychological influences in negotiation: An introduction long overdue. *Journal of Management, 34*, 509–531.

Murnighan, J. K., & Brass, D. J. (1991). Intraorganizational coalitions. In M. Bazerman, B. Sheppard, & R. Lewicki (Eds.), *Research on negotiations in organizations* (Vol. 3, pp. 283–307). Greenwich, CT: JAI Press.

Podolny, J. M. (2001). Networks as the pipes and prisms of the market. *American Journal of Sociology, 107*, 33–60.

Polanyi, K. (1944). *The great transformation: The political and economic origins of revolution*. Boston: Beacon Press.

Reagans, R., Zuckerman, E., and McEvily, B. (2004). How to make the team: Social networks vs. demography as criteria for designing effective teams. *Administrative Science Quarterly, 49*, 101–133.

Siegel, J. (2007). Contingent political capital and international alliances: Evidence from South Korea. *Administrative Science Quarterly, 52*, 621–666.

Simmel, G. (1950). *The sociology of Georg Simmel.* (K. H. Wolff, Ed.). New York: Free Press.

Smith, J., Kidwell-Lopez, V., Borgatti, S. P., & Labianca, G. (2010). T*he political independence index.* Unpublished manuscript, University of Kentucky.

Stevenson, W. B., & Gilly, M. C. (1991). Information processing and problem solving: The migration of problems through formal positions and networks of ties. *Academy of Management Journal, 34,* 918-929.

Taylor, S. (1991). Asymmetrical effects of positive and negative events: The mobilization-minimization hypothesis. *Psychological Bulletin, 110*(1), 67–85.

Uzzi, B. (1997). Social structure and competition in interfirm networks: The paradox of embeddedness. *Administrative Science Quarterly, 42*, 35–67.

Valley, K. L., & Neale, M. A. (1993). *Intimacy and integrativeness: The role of relationships in negotiations.* Working paper, Cornell University, Ithaca, NY.

Valley, K. L., Neale, M. A., & Mannix, E. A. (1995). Friends, lovers, colleagues, strangers: The effects of relationships on the process and outcome of dyadic negotiations. *Research on Negotiation in Organizations, 5*, 65–93.

Valley, K. L., White, S. B., & Iacobucci, D. (1992). The process of assisted negotiations: A network analysis. *Group Decision and Negotiation, 2*, 117–135.

Watts, D. J. (2003). *Six degrees: The science of a connected age.* New York: Norton.

Wellman, B. (1988). Structural analysis: From method and metaphor to theory and substance. In B. Wellman & S. D. Berkowitz (Eds.), *Social structures: A network approach* (pp. 19–61). New York: Cambridge University Press.

10

How Cultural Stereotyping Influences Intercultural Negotiation

Catherine H. Tinsley, Nazli Turan,
Laurie R. Weingart, and Robin L. Dillon-Merrill

INTRODUCTION

In 2005, Thomas Friedman declared, *The World Is Flat* (Friedman, 2005), delineating how most commerce now consists of complex global supply chains spanning multiple countries and cultures involving different parties from around the world. Moreover, many organizations are themselves multinational, comprised of employees from many different cultures, some of whom may be in teams that are colocated, others working in teams that are geographically dispersed. Thus, intercultural negotiations are now commonplace, sometimes occurring over electronic media, and abilities to navigate these exchanges are critical.

Although there is an important corpus of literature devoted to culture and negotiation, one underexamined focus is how culture is used by negotiators for the social category information (i.e., the stereotypes) it contains and how this cultural membership-cued stereotyping will affect negotiations.

Introduced to social psychology as "pictures in our heads" (Lippman, 1922), stereotypes are cognitive structures that contain our knowledge, beliefs, and expectations about a social group (Hamilton & Sherman, 1994). The national cultural group membership of the counterpart is a notable characteristic that is commonly used as a basis for stereotyping.[1] As in any stereotyping process, a negotiator first assigns the other party to a cultural category based on knowledge of the other party's background (what one might call "cultural group categorizing"), then uses his or her knowledge of that cultural group to infer characteristics to the other party ("a key element of 'stereotyping'"). These inferred characteristics are then present in the negotiation and can influence both the process and the outcomes.

In this chapter, we use knowledge of the stereotyping process to improve our understanding of intercultural negotiation and to extend our understanding of stereotyping in intercultural negotiation by exploring *how* cultural membership-cued stereotyping influences a negotiation. We argue that it will depend on: (a) the accuracy of parties' stereotypic information about the other cultural group, (b) the level of ethnocentrism (or negative bias) that is triggered, and (c) the consistency with which each party conforms to their cultural group stereotype.

Although stereotypes are technically a cognitive phenomenon, they usually carry an emotional concomitant (Fiske, Cuddy, Glick, & Xu, 2002); by this, we mean that stereotypes carry an emotional "valence" (positive or negative) depending on how the negotiator thinks about the social group from which the stereotype is derived. More specifically, thoughts or feelings about a particular social group generally lead to positive versus negative stereotypes when these thoughts or feelings are positive versus negative, respectively. So, for example, stereotypes that are more negative will likely be held among interacting negotiators who are representing countries with hostile rather than friendly relations. Consider negotiations over the restructuring of two companies following the merger of a U.S. American firm and a Pakistani firm in which the U.S. firm is keen on sending a considerable number of managers to the Pakistani headquarters to assist with this transition. The problematic state of U.S.-Pakistani relations during the Iraqi and Afghan wars makes it quite possible during that time that the Pakistani negotiator will hold a *negative* stereotype of the U.S. negotiator as someone who is overbearing and controlling. Now, instead imagine that the other side of the merger is an Indian company; under these circumstances, since nonhostile relations are present between the United States and India, it is quite possible that the Indian negotiator will react to the same actions exhibited by the U.S. negotiator with a *positive* stereotype of the American as someone who is meticulous in his or her job. Assuming that the intent of the U.S. company is a mix of getting the most efficient restructuring from the merger and establishing some form of power, the negative and positive stereotypes are each inaccurate or incomplete; as such, the stereotype activations during this negotiation risk preventing the negotiators from achieving integrative, or win-win, outcomes (i.e., deals that satisfy the mutual interests of both parties).

Although the influence of such valenced stereotypes has been studied in the negotiation literature, it has been through the lens of gender. In a series of studies, Kray, Thompson, and Galinsky (2001) examined the effects of stereotype activation on female negotiators' performance across positive, negative, and neutral stereotype conditions. Results support the idea that the valence of a stereotype, when made salient, influences behavior of members of the stereotyped category. Kray et al. (2001) found that females set higher goals, felt more prepared, and outperformed males when a positive female stereotype was activated. In contrast, the differences were reversed in favor of males when the stereotype for women was affect neutral or negative. The Kray et al. study showed that stereotypes can influence the negotiation process and outcome via their effects on the target of the stereotype. In addition, there may be spillover effects when stereotype activation influences the negotiation counterpart. Kray and Thompson (2005) discussed how males performed better and were more confident against females after *female* negative stereotypes were activated.

We believe that such stereotyping effects will apply to cross-cultural negotiations as well. However, it is interesting to note that research on culture in negotiation has not examined such effects. This may be because research to date has focused on first developing a systematic understanding of how people from different cultures negotiate both within their own culture and with those that are outside it. Now that there has been considerable research that has provided us with a more descriptive account of cross-cultural negotiations, it is time to unravel the more intricate relationship between emotional and cognitive mechanisms that cross-border negotiators may engage in when they bring their stereotypes of each other to the table.

STEREOTYPING AND SOCIAL CATEGORIZATION

To understand how cultural stereotypes function, one must first understand the higher-level cognitive mechanism on which they are based, which is social categorization (Tajfel, 1982). Individuals, as social creatures, tend to carve their social landscape into groups in part to construct their own identities (Tajfel & Turner, 1986). People come to understand who they are by the groups to which they do and do not belong (Smith & Berg, 1987). Similarly, others tend to be seen, first and foremost, as members of a social category (Brewer & Feinstein, 1999; Fiske, Lin, & Neuberg, 1999), and these social categorization processes happen relatively effortlessly (Fiske, 1998), often based on visually prominent and culturally relevant features, such as race (Brewer & Feinstein, 1999; Fiske, 1998).

While people often form their group categorizations of others and fit new individuals into these categories, it is also true that group categorization occurs in the opposite direction as well. That is, people extend the individual characteristics of the people they know to others who have a common group membership. In particular, they tend to extrapolate category-level information from first encounters with individuals of that category (Kahneman & Miller, 1986). In the former case, if you think of lawyers as a group to be hardworking, it is likely that you will assume that the next lawyer you meet is hardworking, especially in the absence of any other professional information about him. This also suggests that if your neighbor Bob, who is a lawyer, is a very hardworking individual, you may conclude that lawyers as a group are hardworking people.

As can be inferred from the functioning of group categorization, these processes often lead to stereotyping, which consists of mental models based on the target's social category membership (Fiske & Taylor, 1991). An individual can be a member of many social categories, some of which are more salient than others. We argue that culture is a very salient and visible category. Culture has been defined as a shared social blueprint for life—the constellation of values, assumptions, beliefs, and behavioral norms that define a group of people (Kroeber & Kluckhohn, 1952). Culture has also been defined to include more macrolevel laws, organizations, and structures of a society (Brett, Tinsley, Janssens, Barsness, & Lytle, 1998; Lytle, Brett, Barsness, Tinsley, & Janssens, 1995). The nature or character of a culture can be defined by some pattern of dimensions. These dimensions are adjectives that describe the nature of a cultural group's character in relative terms. For example, a culture might be more collective and hierarchical than other cultures or more progressive and risk tolerant. How the culture (as a whole) is characterized might then (through stereotype transference) be attributed to any negotiator who happens to be a member of that culture.

STEREOTYPING, CULTURE, AND NEGOTIATION

Once a negotiator acknowledges the cultural group membership of the opponent, this recognition can have an effect on the negotiation process. This influence happens whether the two parties come from the same culture or from a different culture and whether the information that each has about the other's culture is shared and accurate or whether it is disparate and wildly inaccurate. All that matters is that one negotiator characterizes the other as a member of a social group. Once the cultural group membership has been established, how it will influence the negotiation depends on (a) the accuracy of the stereotype that characterizes the group as a whole, (b) the positive versus negative emotions associated with that stereotype, and (c) whether the culturally different negotiation counterpart will actually behave in ways consistent with the group stereotype. We consider each of these in turn.

Accuracy of Cultural Stereotypes

The first factor we consider with regard to how cultural group membership influences intercultural negotiations pertains to cultural stereotype accuracy, or the extent to which an observer negotiator correctly identifies characteristics of the counterpart's cultural group. For instance, consider a negotiation between a U.S. American and Japanese businesspeople. The U.S. American's cultural stereotype accuracy is the extent to which he or she can correctly describe characteristics of Japanese people, as a whole, and vice versa. Stereotype information can be learned through personal experience (living, visiting, or working in another culture) or through formal training programs and even stories of others' experience. The level of direct personal experience in the other culture should positively correlate to the accuracy someone has of another cultural group's stereotypic behavior. The further one gets from direct personal experience in learning about another cultural group, the more that information is subject to distortions and inaccuracies.

Perhaps the largest threat to cultural stereotype accuracy is the marked inability of negotiators to understand the difference between intracultural and intercultural settings. That is, most people, when characterizing the cultural stereotype of the other side, tend to focus on how people from that "other" culture behave with each other (intraculturally)—rather than how people from that other culture behave with members of different cultures (interculturally). For example, Adair, Taylor, and Tinsley (2008) found that both U.S. American and Japanese businesspeople, who had experience negotiating with people from the other culture, tended to characterize the culturally different other in stereotypic terms that were consistent with each culture's intracultural interactions, ignoring any intercultural adjustments. The U.S. Americans anticipated a Japanese counterpart who was very traditionally "Japanese"; the Japanese anticipated a U.S. American counterpart who was very traditionally "American," and neither set of negotiators realized that the counterparts might behave differently in an intercultural (Japanese American) setting. Such fallacy of assuming intracultural negotiation styles will play out in the same manner in an intercultural setting has indeed been one of the consistent empirical findings in this area (Adler & Graham, 1989). Thus, in summary, the accuracy of intercultural stereotypes tends to be lower than the accuracy of intracultural stereotypes.

Emotions Associated With Stereotypes

The second factor we consider regarding how cultural group membership influences intercultural negotiations pertains to ethnocentrism, or the extent to which people put their own group at the center of the universe. Anthropologists find that people learn to be ethnocentric through socialization in a particular social system, which rewards appropriate thought and behavior while sanctioning inappropriate thought and behavior (Segall, Dasen, Berry, & Poortinga, 1990). Hence, members come to believe that their own group's values, beliefs, behaviors, and organizing principles are superior to those of any other group. Evolutionary psychology considers ethnocentrism to be an innate outgrowth of nepotism (Van de Berghe, 1981), meaning ethnocentrism has a natural survival value for the group.

There are two reasons why ethnocentrism increases the probability that intercultural negotiators (relative to intracultural negotiators) hold images of each other that are more negative. The first relates to a psychological manifestation of ethnocentrism—namely, ingroup bias, or the tendency to see members of one's own group in a more positive light relative to members of other groups. Across a variety of studies, people have judged members of their ingroups to be smarter, more attractive, more coopera-tive, fairer, more trustworthy and more hardworking than members of out-groups (Brewer, 1979; Tajfel, 1970, 1982). Moreover, ingroup bias can occur with or without direct interaction (such as attitudinal biases that arise simply through observation or awareness of an out-group member), and without any prior personal history between the parties involved. Hence, simply acknowledging that a negotiation counterpart is from a "different" culture can elicit emotions that are more negative than when one is negotiating with a same culture counterpart.

A second reason leading to the likelihood of negative stereotypes amongst intercultural negotiators relates to "homophily," or the tendency to be attracted to those who are similar to oneself (Berscheid & Reis, 1998; Blau, 1977); this in turn suggests that the simple recognition that a coun-terpart is from a different culture can produce a negative bias and decrease cooperation (at least relative to a counterpart who is seen as more similar to oneself). As Kramer (2005, p. 20) noted:

> The problem of securing cooperation between interdependent groups has been a central and recurring theme in the study of intergroup relations from its inception (Sherif, 1966; Sumner, 1906). Whether they are minimal groups created in laboratory settings (Tajfel, 1970), groups of boys at sum-mer camp (Sherif, Harvey, White, Hood, and Sherif, 1961), groups within organizations (Blake & Mouton, 1986), or even nation-states (Kahn and Zald, 1990), reciprocal antipathy between groups seems to develop with surprising frequency and alacrity.

Assume that an ethnocentric negotiator actually holds a stereotype of the other party that evokes negative affect. Perhaps because of the his-tory of interaction between the two negotiators' cultures, each could hold a set of negative assumptions about the other party. One could imagine that an Iraqi and a U.S. businessperson might each think that the other is self-interested, competitive, and not particularly trustworthy. Here, it will be very hard for negotiators to share any sensitive information with each other, which might be necessary to create an integrative outcome. Tinsley, O'Connor, and Sullivan (2002) found that when just one negotiator (of a negotiating dyad) assumes his or her counterpart is competitive, that neg-ative view of the counterpart shuts down information exchange, so that these dyads fail to reach outcomes as integrative (or mutually satisfying) as dyads in which both parties held neutral expectations of their counterpart. Thus, in summary, there tend to be emotions with higher negativity associated with intercultural negotiations than intracultural negotiations (a negativity bias).

Counterpart Consistency With Cultural Group Stereotypes

The third factor we consider with regard to how cultural group membership influences intercultural negotiations relates to how well the stereotype describes the actual individual counterpart in any particular negotiation. Counterparts do not always behave in stereotype-consistent ways. Consider when an American manager is to negotiate with a Saudi counterpart who arrives at the meeting wearing a *thawb* and *ghutra an iqal* (traditional Saudi clothing). The American negotiator might assume his or her counterpart is stereotypically Saudi. Yet, it might as well be the case that the Saudi negotiator has had his or her entire education in the West, and that his or her perspective toward business relationships is more Western than Middle Eastern. Similarly, the Saudi negotiator could be dressed in a suit but may have never stepped out of his or her country and may simply be dressed in a Western way because he or she thought that was expected by the U.S. counterpart. Clearly, individual negotiators are *not* always consistent with their cultural group stereotype, and physical cues such as clothing do *not* always offer robust guidance regarding an individual's consistency. The question of when negotiation counterparts will behave in ways that are consistent with their cultural group stereotype and when they will not is a critical one.

Unfortunately, the answer is not simple. It will depend, to some extent, on whether the individual negotiator has had exposure to or socialization within other cultures and his or her personal preferences for one set of cultural values and behaviors over another. That is, knowledge of the individual negotiator's background and personality will certainly be invaluable. However, other factors may influence whether a negotiator behaves in ways consistent with the stereotype of his or her cultural group.

First, contextual cues have been found to influence a person's consistency with his or her cultural group stereotype. For example, research on biculturals (people who affiliate with two cultural groups) has found that biculturals react to the part of their double identity that is subconsciously primed. More specifically, Benet-Martinez, Leu, Lee, and Morris (2002) showed that Chinese Americans responded in ways congruent with the Chinese culture after being exposed to Chinese primes and with the U.S. American culture after being exposed to U.S. American primes. Although this effect has been supported in experimental situations, it can be expected to occur in real-life negotiations as well, with the prime being the *context* of the negotiation. For instance, Chinese Americans might tap into their Chinese identity when negotiating intra- or interculturally in China and into their American identity when negotiating in the United States. It is possible that cultural contextual cues might influence monocultural negotiators as well, particularly those who have been trained to be sensitive to cultural differences.

On the other hand, researchers have found that when women are consciously reminded of the gender-based stereotypes of how women negotiate (with instructions, for example, that remind them that women are nice to the other party but not very effective in meeting their own interests), they react against this stereotype and strive to behave in stereotype-inconsistent ways (Kray, Thompson, & Galinsky, 2001). So, what explains these discrepancies? Why do bicultural negotiators react to stereotypic primes by behaving consistent with the primed stereotype, whereas women negotiators react against the stereotypic prime? We believe the answer lies in (a) the consciousness of the prime and the (b) negativity of the stereotype evoked.

When a negative stereotype is primed through an explicit process, we believe the target will reject the stereotype as applicable to him- or herself. The target should engage in ego-defending mechanisms that ensure that the negative stereotype does not apply to the self, producing stereotype-inconsistent behavior. For instance, a Japanese negotiator may purposefully deny any hierarchical behaviors to escape a perceived negative stereotype, thus acting in ways that are unexpected by his or her counterpart. On the other hand, when positive or affect-neutral stereotypes are implicitly primed, the negotiator may embrace these subtle messages as part of his or her identity. For example, a Japanese negotiator may embrace a subtle cue indicating Japanese seek harmony, as that characteristic likely has a positive valence, and it may lead the Japanese negotiator toward softer negotiation tactics. This is an area that is ripe for systematic research.

ADVICE FOR INTERCULTURAL NEGOTIATORS

Given the current state of research on culture, stereotypes, and negotiations, what is the best advice for intercultural negotiators? One tempting piece of advice is simply to ignore culture in the first place since, as our literature review suggested, (a) negotiators' cultural-level stereotypes are likely to be inaccurate, (b) negotiators' focus on cultural differences is likely to lead to ethnocentrism and negatively valenced stereotypes, and (c) negotiators in intercultural exchanges may *not* necessarily behave in ways that are consistent with their cultural group's stereotype. As tempting as it sounds to forget about culture, we believe that this approach has proved neither fruitful nor practical (as evidenced by many failed intercultural negotiations for which the negotiators themselves admitted that they ignored cultural differences to their peril). It is also impractical to ignore culture because people *do* attend to social category information. In fact, some research showed that intentional suppression of stereotypic thought can produce the very thoughts one is trying to suppress (Macrae, Bodenhausen, Milne, & Jetten, 1994; Wegner, 1994). Moreover, suppression can function as a repetitive prime that actually increases a stereotype's accessibility (Higgins, 1989; Macrae et al., 1994). Thus, intentionally trying to ignore that someone is from a different culture is *not* likely to produce favorable results.

It would be more helpful to understand what cultural group information does for negotiators. Cultural information and stereotypes serve a function in a negotiation situation to reduce uncertainty. Automatic characterization processes such as cultural information or stereotype formation not only help individuals' self-identify but also allow people to form a basic understanding of the culturally different other (Bodenhausen, Macrae, & Sherman, 1999). That is, cultural information about one's negotiation opponent functions like any cognitive heuristic in reducing information complexity about the situation. Reducing this complexity is critical because negotiations are mixed-motive interactions.

Negotiations are characterized as mixed-motive because at any point during a negotiation a negotiator may cooperate with his or her partner to create gains that benefit both sides or may compete with the other side to claim the bigger share of the gains (Lax & Sebenius, 1986; McGrath, 1966). In their post hoc analyses of negotiation exchanges, scholars routinely distinguish tactics that create value (i.e., integrative tactics, such as asking the other side about his or her priorities and making trade-offs among issues) from those that claim value (i.e., distributive tactics, such as making demands and threats) (Lax & Sebenius, 1986; Olekalns & Smith, 2003; Weingart, Thompson, Bazerman, & Carroll, 1990). To negotiators bargaining in real time, however, the intentions lurking behind these tactics may be far less clear. Imagine that an opponent asks, "What is more important to you—the start of the lease or the monthly payment?" Is this opponent trying to identify your priorities in an effort to find ways to make a mutually beneficial trade-off between the two issues? Or, is the opponent trying to figure out the relative priority of the two issues to you to extract a sizable concession on your lower-priority issue? Shifting and opaque motives of any opponent make the job of interpreting tactics difficult. Facing this uncertainty (about the opponent's motives), negotiators will look for information that helps them to characterize their opponent. Information about the opponent's cultural group may seem relevant and thus receives attention. So, how can a negotiator best work with this information? Next, we suggest four strategies.

Intercultural Negotiation Strategy 1: Increase the Accuracy of Cultural Stereotype Information

One possible strategy for effectively negotiating in intercultural exchanges is to learn how members of your opponent's cultural group think, behave, evaluate, and negotiate, which can be critical to negotiation success; doing so enhances the accuracy of cultural stereotype information. There have been decades of research detailing cultural differences in various mixed-motive interactions, including problem solving, negotiation, and dispute resolution. For example, Tinsley (1998, 2001) documented that U.S. Americans tend to use an "interest-based" approach (appealing to the unique needs of both parties) to resolving workplace disputes, whereas Germans tend to use a "rights-based" approach (appealing to standard rules, operating procedures, and laws), and Japanese tend to use a "status power-based" approach (turning it over to a high-status third party). Similarly, Tinsley and Pillutla (1998) found that U.S. Americans tend to view a buyer–seller negotiation as a task for which the goal of the negotiation is to maximize joint gain, whereas Hong Kong Chinese, engaging in the same negotiation, tend to assume the goal is to minimize the difference between each party's outcomes. This goal discrepancy corresponded with the groups' actual outcomes and with parties' satisfaction with those outcomes.

In general, scholars and practitioners who specialize in cross-cultural comparative research have focused on how socialization in different cultures produces different thoughts, decisions, or behavioral interactions. What they have achieved is a large body of knowledge about how, all else being equal, people from different cultures react to the same stimuli with different choices of behavior or different strategies for solution. Although this research is helpful, it is important to remember that most of these results are in an intracultural context; thus, negotiators are well advised to spend time thinking about how their counterparts might be adjusting to the intercultural context (specifically, how these counterparts are reacting to the prospect of negotiating with the negotiators themselves). For example, negotiators might ask themselves how they plan on adjusting to the *intercultural* context and make logical inferences about their counterpart doing this same adjustment.

Intercultural Negotiation Strategy 2:
Pay Attention to the Situation

A second possible strategy for effectively negotiating in intercultural exchanges is to pay attention to the specifics of the intercultural situation. As we noted, more recent cross-cultural research conceptualizes culture as a more dynamic force with variable influence on individual behavior, *depending on context* (e.g., Benet-Martinez et al., 2002). This research focused on detailing that any particular culture can have both dominant characteristics (such as promoting collective values and beliefs) and recessive characteristics (such as also promoting individualistic values and beliefs). Whereas the more traditional approach to culture focused on direct cultural difference effects (culture as a "main effect" variable) and on pulling apart the various social groups, dynamic culture research focused on more indirect cultural difference effects (culture as a variable that interacts with specific situations) and on noting the wide variety of possible behavior within any culture. For example, Brett, Tinsley, Shapiro, and Okumura (2007) found that when resolving disputes between employees, Chinese managers tended to behave as egalitarian as U.S. American managers did (and significantly more egalitarian than did Japanese managers) when they were intervening as a third party *peer*, yet when the Chinese managers were intervening as a supervisor, they instead tended to behave as authoritarian as their Japanese colleagues did (and significantly more authoritarian than did the U.S. American managers). The *situational cue* of whether the manager was intervening as a supervisor versus as a peer thus determined the extent to which Chinese managers behaved autocratically, consistent with their cultural group's traditional cultural value of hierarchy, or with high power distance (cf. Hofstede, 1980), as compared to a lower power distance, or an egalitarian way, which is more characteristic of U.S. Americans (cf. Hofstede, 1980).

In other situations, the norms may be so strong they attenuate or even wipe out the effect of any other cultural variance. In such a strong situation, it would likely be the case that negotiators would be able to look beyond culture in their interactions. For example, when British investment bank Barclays negotiated with the U.S. American investment bank Lehman Brothers regarding which of Lehman's assets it might purchase and at what price, the general negotiation norms governing the banking industry as well as the particular (crisis) situation (of Lehman's impending failure) were likely to exert a much stronger influence on the tenor of these negotiations than any U.S.-British cultural differences. In summary, we are suggesting here that negotiators may more effectively handle intercultural transactions if they pay special attention to the social cues in the specific situation in which they are negotiating in addition to the strength of the cultural norms associated with their counterpart's cultural group.

Intercultural Negotiation Strategy 3: Recognize the Individual Negotiator

A third strategy for effectively negotiating in intercultural transactions, specifically to lessen the likelihood of negatively stereotyping cultural groups, is to advocate a "culture-blind" approach. Doing this entails increasing the personalization of the opponent and decreasing any cultural group distinctiveness. There are a number of ways through which one may achieve a culture-blind approach, one of which is individuation of the culturally different other (called here a target). The more personalized someone's contact is with the target, the less he or she stereotypes that target (Brewer, 1996). Unfortunately, this individuation process takes mental energy (Neuberg & Fiske, 1987). And as noted, ironically, intentional suppression of stereotypic thought can produce the very thoughts one is trying to suppress (Macrae et al., 1994; Wegner, 1994).

On the other hand, perspective taking, which merges the self with the other (Davis, Conklin, Smith, & Luce, 1996), may be one mechanism to induce the culture-blind approach. During perspective taking, the self-concept becomes activated, and because mental categories compete with each other (Bruner, 1957) and one category seems to dominate at a time (Macrae, Bodenhausen, & Milne, 1995), the self-concept is applied to the target. Perspective taking is a conscious process but entails a subconscious social categorization of the target. Thus, perspective taking increases an actor's empathy for and assistance to a target (Batson, 1991) and decreases people's tendency to attribute target behaviors to target dispositions (Regan & Totten, 1975). Galinsky and Moskowitz (2000) found that asking people to imagine a day in the life of a target from another social group decreased stereotype activation and ethnocentrism. Moreover, Galinsky and colleagues have also found that perspective taking increases negotiators' ability to discover hidden agreements and both claim and create value in the negotiation (Galinsky, Maddux, Gilin, & White, 2008).

Creating a superordinate goal across groups also decreases intergroup bias (Sherif, 1966). This likely occurs because the superordinate goal, like perspective taking, collapses the social categorical distinctions between people from different groups. Similarly, decreasing group distinctiveness by having members of other groups disclose personal information or by removing cues of social dissimilarity decreases intergroup bias (Gollwitzer, 1999). All these interventions are likely effective for reducing the negative bias because they function subconsciously on people. Negotiators are not aware of the social categorization processes or, more specifically, that the target's categorical distinction from them has evaporated. In sum, this research tends to suggest that processes that make culturally different counterparts seem less like members of other groups should attenuate the negative stereotyping associated with differences. Two of these processes are taking on the perspective of the counterpart and increasing the salience of any superordinate (shared) goals.

Intercultural Strategy 4: Recognize the Benefits of a Multicultural World

A fourth strategy for effectively negotiating in intercultural transactions is to take a "multicultural approach," which tries to change the discriminatory focus of the intergroup differences to see the other group (or target) more favorably. There is some evidence that people can update their stereotypes with more positive beliefs about the target (Kawakami, Dion, & Dovidio, 1998). This evidence includes observations by Goff, Steele, and Davies (2008) that people who were primed with a learning goal orientation tended to feel less threatened and to view the target group more benevolently, and observations by Cronin, Bezrukova, Weingart, and Tinsley (2011) that "cognitive integration" (i.e., the degree to which people understand each others' interpretive frameworks or ways of thinking about a problem) can improve the performance of teams composed of salient subgroups. These findings are consistent with the theorizing of Cramton and Hinds (2005) that culturally distinct groups can show a mutual positive distinctiveness, meaning that each group can be taught to recognize and value differences. Apparently, it is the ability to understand the target's way of doing things, and to value the differences between oneself and the target, that increases intercultural performance.

In intercultural negotiations, this multicultural approach may play out as reminding negotiators of the good attributes of their opponent's culture, which might be easy to overlook in a potentially competitive situation such as negotiation. Such an approach should remind negotiators that all cultures have positive and negative traits, and that being different does *not* necessarily mean being in opposition. A multicultural approach is particularly relevant for a 21st century workforce with increasing levels of cultural diversity.

Looking at the empirical research that compared the culture-blind and multicultural approaches, one study (Wolsko, Park, Judd, & Wittenbrink, 2000) actually tested the efficacy of these two approaches on two facets of ethnocentrism (both ingroup favoritism and the out-group homogeneity effect). They found that both approaches actually decreased ingroup favoritism, but that the multicultural approach did nothing to attenuate out-group homogeneity effects. In fact, participants in this multicultural condition were more likely to overattribute both positive and negative stereotypical traits to the out-group ("overattribute" relative to actual data for the group). Thus, in their study the multicultural approach tended to heighten stereotypes or the tendency to assume the culturally different other matches the prototypic categorization for the group. However, it should also be noted that participants in the culture-blind condition tended to overestimate the prevalence of *counter*stereotypical features of the out-group (again relative to actual data for the out-group). That is, the culture-blind participants tended to go a bit overboard in judging out-group targets as individuals distinct from their actual group categorization. They seemed intent on characterizing the target as different from any group prototype. Hence, neither prime led to any more accuracy about the out-group, but both primes attenuated ingroup favoritism.

Based on these findings, if multicultural and culture-blind approaches attenuate ingroup favoritism, then these two approaches can complement our previous suggestion that negotiators try to let go of cultural stereotypes that may move the negotiation away from a cooperative frame. Negotiators' cultural stereotypes of their counterparts are likely to be most pernicious when they are negative and the negotiation itself has integrative potential. Thus, increasing knowledge (particularly direct knowledge) of the counterpart's cultural group to increase one's own stereotype accuracy, noting the positive characteristics of the counterpart's culture, and paying attention to situational cues and the counterpart's individual behavior may be the best negotiation advice currently available.

21st CENTURY WORKPLACE CHALLENGES AND THEIR RESEARCH IMPLICATIONS FOR CROSS-CULTURAL NEGOTIATIONS

As noted at the beginning of the chapter, 21st century commerce is global. Companies interact in a complex web of global supply chains, and employees work in an increasingly multicultural environment. As such, both *inter-* and *intra*organizational interactions will increasingly be affected by cultural membership-cued stereotyping. In intraorganizational multicultural settings, people share a common organizational identity, although they may not be colocated and may come from different cultures (e.g., when employees work in transnational teams whose members represent different nationalities). In intraorganizational negotiations, shared organizational identities might serve as a strong situational cue that swamps negative stereotype biases and thereby may help to mitigate the propensity of culturally different members to rely on stereotypes or to form negative stereotypes (Espinosa, Cummings, Wilson, & Pearce, 2003, Li & Hambrick, 2005). In interorganizational multicultural settings, the lack of shared identity and clear organizational distinctions and norms may reinforce the reliance on stereotypes and differentiation between "us" and "them." To test these possibilities, future negotiation research is needed that compares dynamics associated with intercultural versus intracultural negotiations in settings that are within versus across organizational boundaries.

The types of interventions one might use to increase the accuracy of cultural stereotypes might differ across inter- and intraorganizational settings. In interorganizational settings, people might rely more on third-party sources, whereas in intraorganizational settings, direct contact across cultures/locations (e.g., site visits, exchanges) may be more feasible as a means to improve stereotype accuracy. When trying to predict the behavior of others from different cultures, a negotiator in an interorganizational (rather than intraorganizational) negotiation must pay attention to a broader set of situational cues. More specifically, the interorganizational negotiator must consider not only the implications of national cultural norms on his or her counterpart's actions but also the implications of his or her counterpart's organizational norms. As such, this reinforces the need for future research to consider how culture-cued stereotyping differentially influences negotiator cognition and behavior in intra- versus interorganizational negotiations.

In the 21st century workplace, inter- and intraorganizational negotiations also increasingly involve participants who are globally dispersed (cf., Shapiro, Von Glinow, & Cheng, 2005); this means that negotiations may also require negotiators to interact remotely and to rely on virtual technology to mediate their communication. Negotiating via teleconference, telephone, instant messaging, or e-mail is a double-edged sword that on the one hand brings great ease by eliminating distances and on the other introduces challenges by limiting the proximal interpersonal contact. We know that the communication medium that negotiators use influences the information being shared, how it is communicated, and how it will be interpreted (Carnevale & Probst, 1997; McGinn & Croson, 2004; Valley, Moag, & Bazerman, 1998). An interaction that may be clear and concise when speaking face to face may be very different over e-mail, just as certain types of exchanges may be easier electronically due to the common e-communication language that has evolved. In this way, e-communication for cross-border negotiators may bring both a challenge and an advantage. The challenge obviously is the fact that most of the communication richness that is present in face-to-face exchange, such as body language, gestures, or even tone of voice, is absent with electronic media (Daft & Lengel, 1986). As a result of such absence of communication richness, social presence of the individuals is reduced (Weisband & Atwater,1999), social distance between them is increased (Sproull & Kiesler, 1986), and negotiators' social awareness of each other is limited (McGinn & Croson, 2004).

This restricted social interaction can have two contrasting effects on the negotiation process. First, negotiators may focus more on the content of the electronic exchange since it is the main source of information in the absence of social cues (Ocker & Yaverbaum, 1999). This may be an advantage in cross-border negotiations because it will substantially decrease possible negative stereotyping of the opponent. Research has shown that group differences and social status are less salient in e-mail exchanges (Kiesler & Sproull, 1992). On the other hand, negotiators may rely too heavily on surface features of the message since there are no contextual cues in the exchange beyond the content. At the most simple level, negotiators may make attributions based on the cultural prototypicality of the other party's name. Relying on a foreign name to access a stereotype in an e-mail exchange is very similar to relying on clothing in a face-to-face exchange. However, updating of the stereotype might be much more difficult when relying on e-communication because of the limited contextual cues as compared to face-to-face interactions. If so, then negotiators will need to expend even greater effort implementing the approaches described in this chapter to reduce negative stereotyping.

How likely is it, however, that *virtual intercultural* negotiators can expend enough effort actually to reduce negative stereotyping or to gather additional cues to test the appropriateness of stereotypes? We see both of these outcomes as unlikely, despite intercultural negotiators' effort level, since the absence of communication richness associated with e-communication should exacerbate the tendency for negotiators to rely on stereotypes in cross-cultural negotiations. Yet, these are questions to be empirically examined, thus offering additional opportunities for future negotiation research.

SUMMARY

In this chapter, we reviewed literature suggesting that culture will affect a negotiation by eliciting stereotypes each party holds of their counterpart's cultural group. In addition, we noted that how this cultural group-cued stereotyping influences any particular negotiation likely depends on (a) the accuracy of both parties' stereotypic information about the other cultural group, (b) the level of ethnocentrism (or negative bias) that is triggered by the stereotypic information, and (c) the consistency with which each party conforms to the cultural group stereotype. Although cultural group stereotypes will generally make intercultural negotiations more difficult than intracultural negotiations, we are hopeful that increased understanding about why stereotypes are activated helps offer some advice for how to approach these increasingly prevalent intercultural exchanges effectively. Such advice may be more difficult to utilize in light of 21st century workplace challenges, also noted in this chapter, and these challenges illuminate future research needs for negotiation scholars, who themselves are increasingly likely to encounter intercultural negotiations in the work that they as scholars do. As the world becomes "more global" and "more wired," it is increasingly vital that managers as well as management scholars learn the conditions in which intercultural negotiations, especially but not only across borders, are more versus less effective. This chapter ideally will inspire future studies to examine intercultural negotiation phenomena in the many ways we have identified as needed and, ultimately in so doing, help negotiators understand how to build connections with others with whom they are culturally different or geographically apart.

ACKNOWLEDGMENT

Many thanks to the support provided by the de la Cruz Family Faculty Fellowship program at the McDonough School of Business as well as the Army Research Institute (ARO grant W911NF-08-1-0301).

NOTE

1. Other counterpart characteristics (age, gender, career) can also be used as a basis for stereotyping of that counterpart and can also influence the negotiation. Our emphasis here, though, is in delineating cultural influences.

REFERENCES

Adair, W. L., Taylor, M. S., & Tinsley, C. H. (2008). Starting out on the right foot: Negotiation schemas when cultures collide. *Negotiation and Conflict Management Research, 2,* 138–163.

Adler, N., & Graham, J. (1989). Cross-cultural interaction: The international comparison fallacy. *Journal of International Business Studies, 20,* 37–49.

Batson, D. (1991). *The altruism question: Toward a social psychological answer.* New York: Erlbaum.

Benet-Martinez, V., Leu, L., Lee, F., & Morris, M. (2002). Negotiating biculturalism: Cultural frame switching in biculturals with oppositional versus compatible cultural identities. *Journal of Cross-Cultural Psychology, 33,* 492–515.

Berscheid, E., & Reis, H. (1998). Attraction and close relationships. In D. Gilbert, S. Fiske, & G. Lindzey (Eds.), *The handbook of social psychology* (2nd ed., pp. 193–274). New York: Oxford University Press.

Blake, R., & Mouton, J. (1986). From theory to practice in interface problem solving. *Psychology of Intergroup Relations,* 118–134.

Blau, P. (1977). *Inequality and heterogeneity: A primitive theory of social structure.* New York: Free Press.

Bodenhausen, G., Macrae, C., & Sherman, J. (1999). On the dialectics of discrimination: Dual processes in social stereotyping. In S. Chaiken & Y. Trope (Eds.), *Dual process theories in social psychology* (pp. 271–290). New York: Guilford Press.

Brett, J. M., Tinsley, C. H., Janssens, M., Barsness, Z. I., & Lytle, A. L. (1997). New approaches to the study of culture in I/O psychology. In P. C. Earley & M. Erez (Eds.), *New perspectives on international/organizational psychology* (pp. 75–129). San Francisco: Jossey-Bass.

Brett, J., Tinsley, C., Shapiro, D., & Okumura, T. (2007). Intervening in employee disputes: How and when will managers from China, Japan and the USA act differently? *Management and Organization Review, 3,* 183–204.

Brewer, M. (1979). In-group bias in the minimal group situation: A cognitive-motivational analysis. *Psychological Bulletin, 86,* 307–324.

Brewer, M. B. (1996). When stereotypes lead to stereotyping: The use of stereotype in person perception. In C. N. Macrae, C. Stangor, & M. Hewstone (Eds.), *Stereotypes and stereotyping* (pp. 254–275). New York: Guilford Press.

Brewer, M., & Feinstein, A. (1999). Dual processes in the cognitive representation of persons and social categories. In S. Chaiken & Y. Trope (Eds.), *Dual processes in social psychology* (pp. 255–270). New York: Guilford Press.

Bruner, J. S. (1957). On perceptual readiness. *Psychological Review, 64,* 123–152.

Carnevale, P., & Probst, T. (1997). Conflict on the Internet. In S. Kiesler (Ed.), *Culture of the Internet* (pp. 233–255). New York: Routledge.

Cramton, C., & Hinds, P. (2005). Subgroup dynamics in internationally distributed teams: Ethnocentrism or cross-national learning? *Research in Organizational Behavior, 26,* 233–265.

Cronin, M. A., Bezrukova, K., Weingart, L. R., & Tinsley, C. H. (2011). Subgroups within a team: The role of cognitive and affective states. *Journal of Organizational Behavior, 32,* 831–849.

Daft, R., & Lengel, R. (1986). Organizational information requirements, media richness and structural design. *Management Science, 32,* 554–571.

Davis, M., Conklin, L., Smith, A., & Luce, C. (1996). Effect of perspective taking on the cognitive representation of persons: A merging of self and other. *Journal of Personality and Social Psychology, 70,* 713–744.

Espinosa, J. A., Cummings, J. N., Wilson, J. M., & Pearce, B. M. (2003). Team boundary issues across multiple global firms. *Journal of Management Information Systems, 19*(4), 157–190.

Fiske, S. (1998). Stereotyping, prejudice and discrimination. In D. Gilbert, S. Fiske, & G. Lindzey (Eds.), *The handbook of social psychology* (pp. 357–411). New York: McGraw-Hill.

Fiske, S. T., Cuddy, A., Glick, P., & Xu, J. (2002). A model of (often mixed) stereotype content: Competence and warmth respectively follow from status and power. *Journal of Personality and Social Psychology, 82,* 878–902.

Fiske, S., & Taylor, S. (1991). *Social cognition.* New York: McGraw-Hill.

Fiske, S., Lin, M., & Neuberg, S. (1999). The continuum model: Ten years later. In S. Chaiken & Y. Trope (Eds.), *Dual process theories in social psychology* (pp. 231–254). New York: Guilford Press.

Friedman, T. L. (2005). *The world is flat: A brief history of twenty-first century.* New York: Farrar, Straus and Giroux.

Galinsky, A., & Moskowitz, G. (2000). Perspective taking: Decreasing stereotype expression, stereotype accessibility and in-group favoritism. *Journal of Personality and Social Psychology, 78,* 708–724.

Galinsky, A., Maddux, W., Gilin, D., & White, J. (2008). Why it pays to get inside the head of your opponent: The differential effects of perspective-taking and empathy in negotiations. *Psychological Science, 19,* 375–382.

Goff, P. A., Steele, C. M, & Davies, P. G. (2008). The space between us: Stereotype threat and distance in interracial contexts. *Journal of Personality and Social Psychology, 94*(1), 91–107.

Gollwitzer, P. M., (1999). Implementation intentions: Strong effects of simple plans. *American Psychologist, 54,* 493–503.

Hamilton, D., & Sherman, J. (1994). Stereotypes. In J. Wyer & T. Srull (Eds.), *Handbook of social cognition* (pp. 1–68). Hillsdale, NJ: Erlbaum.

Higgins, E. (1989). Self-discrepancy theory: What patterns of self-beliefs cause people to suffer? In L. Berkowitz (Ed.), *Advances in experimental social psychology* (pp. 133–168). New York: Guilford Press.

Hofstede, G. (1980). *Cultures consequences.* Newbury Park, CA: Sage.

Kahn, R., & Zald, M. (1990). *Organizations and nation-states: New perspectives on conflict and cooperation.* New York: Jossey-Bass.

Kawakami, K., Dion, K. L., & Dovidio, J. F. (1998). Racial prejudice and stereotype activation. *Personality and Social Psychology Bulletin, 24,* 407–416.

Kahneman, D., & Miller, D. T. (1986). Norm theory: Comparing reality to its alternatives. *Journal of Personality and Social Psychology, 93,* 136–153.

Kiesler, S., & Sproull, L. (1992). Group decision making and communication technology. *Organizational Behavior and Human Decision Processes, 52,* 96–123.

Kramer, R. (2005). A failure to communicate: 9/11 and the tragedy of the informational commons. *International Public Management Journal, 8,* 23–34.

Kray, L. J., & Thompson, L. (2005). Gender stereotypes and negotiation performance: A review of theory and research. *Research in Organizational Behavior Series, 26,* 103–182.

Kray, L. J., Thompson, L., & Galinsky, A. (2001). Battle of the sexes: Gender stereotype confirmation and reactance in negotiations. *Journal of Personality and Social Psychology, 80,* 942–958.

Kroeber, A. L., & Kluckhohn, F. R. (1952). *Culture: A critical review of concepts and definitions* (Peabody Museum Papers, 47(1)). Cambridge, MA: Harvard University.

Lax, D., & Sebenius, J. (1986). *The manager as negotiator: Bargaining for cooperation and competitive gain*. New York: Free Press.

Li, J. T., & Hambrick, D. C. (2005). Factional groups: A new vantage on demographic faultlines, conflict, and disintegration in work teams. *Academy of Management Journal, 48*(5): 794–813.

Lippman, W. (1922). *Public opinion*. New York: Harcourt Brace.

Lytle, A., Brett, J., Barsness, Z., Tinsley, C., & Janssens, M. (1995). A paradigm for confirmatory cross-cultural research in organizational behavior. In E. Cummings & B. Staw (Eds.), *Research in organizational behavior* (pp. 167–214). Greenwich, CT: JAI Press.

Macrae, C., Bodenhausen, G., & Milne, A. (1995). The dissection of selection in person perception: Inhibitionary processes in social stereotyping. *Journal of Personality and Social Psychology, 69*, 397–407.

Macrae, C., Bodenhausen, G., Milne, A., & Jetten, J. (1994). Out of mind but back in sight: Stereotypes on the rebound. *Journal of Personality and Social Psychology, 67*, 808–817.

McGinn, K., & Croson, R. (2004). What do communication media mean for negotiators? A question of social awareness. In M. Gelfand & J. Brett (Eds.), *The handbook of negotiation and culture* (pp. 334–350). Stanford, CA: Stanford University Press.

McGrath, J. E. (1966). A social psychological approach to the study of negotiation. In R. V. Bowers (Ed.), *Studies in behavior in organizations* (pp. 101-134). Athens: University of Georgia Press.

Neuberg, S., & Fiske, S. (1987). Motivational influences on impression formation: Outcome dependency, accuracy-driven attention, and individuating processes. *Journal of Personality and Social Psychology, 53*, 431–444.

Ocker, R., & Yaverbaum, G. (1999). Synchronous computer-mediated communication versus face-to-face collaboration: Results on student learning, quality and satisfaction. *Group Decision and Negotiation, 8*, 427–440.

Olekalns, M., & Smith, P. (2003). Social motives in negotiation: The relationships between dyad composition, negotiation processes and outcomes. *International Journal of Conflict Management, 14*, 233–254.

Regan, D., & Totten, J. (1975). Empathy and attribution: Turning observers into actors. *Journal of Personality and Social Psychology, 32*, 850–856.

Segall, M. H., Dasen, P. R., Berry, J. W., & Poortinga, Y. H. (1990). *Human behavior in global perspective*. New York: Pergamon.

Shapiro, D. L., Von Glino, M. A., & Cheng, J. 2005. *Managing multinational teams: Global perspectives*. San Diego, CA: Elsevier.

Sherif, M. (1966). *In common predicament: Social psychology of intergroup conflict and cooperation*. Boston: Houghton Mifflin.

Sherif, M., Harvey, O., White, B. H., Hood, W. R., & Sherif, C. (1961). *Intergroup conflict and cooperation: The robbers cave experiment*. Norman: University of Oklahoma Press.

Smith, K., & Berg, D. (1987). *Paradoxes of group life: Understanding conflict, paralysis and movement in group life*. New York: Jossey-Bass.

Sproull, L., & Kiesler, S. (1986). Reducing social context cues: Electronic mail in organizational communications. *Management Science, 32*, 1492–1512.

Sumner, W. (1906). *Folkways*. Boston: Ginn.

Tajfel, H. (1970). Experiments in intergroup discrimination. *Scientific American, 223*, 96–102.

Tajfel, H. (1982). *Social identity and intergroup relations.* Cambridge, UK: Cambridge University Press.

Tajfel, H., & Turner, J. (1986). The social identity theory of intergroup behavior. In S. Worchel & W. Austin (Eds.), *Psychology of intergroup relations* (pp. 7–24). Chicago: Nelson.

Tinsley, C. (1998). Models of conflict resolution in Japanese, German and American cultures. *Journal of Applied Psychology, 83,* 316–323.

Tinsley, C. (2001). How negotiators get to yes: Predicting the constellation of strategies used across cultures to negotiate conflict. *Journal of Applied Psychology, 86,* 583–593.

Tinsley, C., O'Connor, K. S., & Sullivan, B. A. (2002). Tough guys finish last: The perils of a distributive reputation. *Organizational Behavior and Human Decision Processes, 88,* 621–642.

Tinsley, C., & Pillutla, M. (1998). Negotiating in the United States and Hong Kong. *Journal of International Business Studies, 29,* 711–728.

Valley, K., Moag, J., & Bazerman, M. (1998). A matter of trust: Effects of communication on the efficiency and distribution of outcomes. *Journal of Economic Behavior and Organization, 34,* 211–238.

Van de Berghe, P. (1981). *The ethnic phenomenon.* New York: Elsevier.

Wegner, D. M. (1994). Ironic processes of mental control. *Psychological Review, 101,* 961–977.

Weingart, L., Thompson, L., Bazerman, M., & Carroll, J. (1990). Tactical behavior and negotiation outcomes. *International Journal of Conflict Management, 1*(1), 7–31.

Weisband, S., & Atwater, L. (1999). Evaluating self and others in electronic and face-to-face groups. *Journal of Applied Psychology, 84,* 632–639.

Wolsko, C., Park, B., Judd, C. M., & Wittenbrink, B. (2000). Framing interethnic ideology: Effects of multicultural and color-blind perspectives on judgments of groups and individuals. *Journal of Personality and Social Psychology, 78,* 635–654.

11

Gender and Negotiation

Michael P. Haselhuhn and Laura J. Kray

INTRODUCTION

Despite the substantial progress women have made in the workplace over the last century, striking gender gaps in pay and advancement persist in the 21st century. In this chapter, we examine gender differences in business contexts by exploring how men and women approach and experience the negotiation process. With women comprising approximately 30% of current enrollment for a master's in business administration (MBA) at top business schools, the gender disparity in business is alarming. Although professional degree programs such as law and medicine have achieved gender parity in enrollment, women's absence in the MBA classroom persists. Not surprisingly, women are also relatively scarce in the upper echelons of business. Although women make up 46% of the U.S. labor force, they comprise just 3% of Fortune 500 chief executive officers (CEOs) and only 15.2% of Fortune 500 board seats ("U.S. Women in Business," 2009). This gender disparity extends to differences in earnings as well: In 2009, the median annual income for women working full time was 23% lower than that of similarly employed men ("The Gender Wage Gap: 2009," 2010). With typical explanations such as differences in experience or education failing to fully explain the wage gap (Blau & Kahn, 2006, 2007), researchers have pointed to negotiation differences between the sexes as a likely contributor to this disparity (Bowles & McGinn, 2008).

While substantial efforts have been made over recent decades to close the gap between men and women in the workplace, persistent differences in pay and advancement exist in the 21st century that cannot be ignored.

We contend that negotiating effectiveness is central to business leadership (Kray & Haselhuhn, 2009); thus, identifying differences in how men and women experience negotiations may shed light on gender gaps in compensation and business participation (cf. Bowles & McGinn, 2008). This leads to the key questions that we address in this chapter: Why do gender differences in negotiation persist in the 21st century workplace? What workplace characteristics impede the resolution of these differences?

To shed light on these questions, we organize this chapter in four sections. First, we describe the multifaceted ways in which gender differences emerge at the bargaining table in the 21st century workplace. Whereas it may be empirically true that men typically demonstrate small but significant economic advantages relative to women in negotiations (Stuhlmacher & Walters, 1999; Walters, Stuhlmacher, & Meyer, 1998), the reasons behind this difference are complex and depend more on the situation than on innate biological factors (Kray & Thompson, 2005). By reviewing the growing literature on gender issues in negotiation, we hope to better understand why gender differences persist. Second, we outline several actions that have been theorized to help close the negotiation gender gap. Third, we discuss unique aspects of the 21st century workplace that present obstacles hindering the degree to which these actions may succeed in leveling the playing field. Fourth, based on the challenges presented by today's workplace, we identify opportunities for the next wave of gender and negotiation research.

SECTION 1: WHY DO GENDER DIFFERENCES IN NEGOTIATION PERSIST IN THE 21ST CENTURY WORKPLACE?

One likely reason why gender differences in negotiation persist is that, until recently, they have been poorly understood both empirically and theoretically. Although gender differences are a perennially popular topic for armchair philosophers, scholarly interest in this question in the negotiation domain has waxed and waned over time. However, substantial strides have been made recently on both fronts, which we review below.

While gender was part of the early investigation of individual differences in negotiation processes and outcomes (e.g., Rubin & Brown, 1975), it quickly fell to the wayside as an uninteresting question that accounted for little variance and lacked theoretical depth. As the negotiation literature became intensely focused on social-cognitive heuristics and biases (Neale & Bazerman, 1991), gender had little to contribute to this conversation.

Another factor inhibiting the study of the negotiation gender gap is the methodological difficulty in doing so. Negotiations are highly interdependent interactions involving multiple parties, thus creating complexity for researchers interested in understanding an individual difference such as gender. As each party in an interaction contributes to the final outcome, even the simplest dyadic negotiation requires a consideration of both negotiators' gender. Negotiation studies are more labor intensive than studies of individual decision making, and the additional complexities introduced by considering each negotiator's gender may have deterred researchers from tackling this topic. Indeed, Kray and Thompson's (2005) review of the literature revealed a deficit of studies examining the full range of possible dyadic compositions (i.e., male–male dyads, female–female dyads, male–female dyads). With few exceptions, studies that do fully explore possible dyad compositions rely on judgments in hypothetical scenarios rather than behavior in negotiation tasks. Finally, perhaps as a result of differences in how gender composition was handled by researchers, contradictions emerged regarding gender's impact in negotiations, rendering unclear conclusions about its explanatory power. In combination, research on gender in negotiations stagnated for decades.

Despite the challenges in studying gender differences at the bargaining table, rising concern over persistent disparities between men and women in career attainment led scholars to continue their efforts. Recent development and application of powerful social psychological theory to explain these differences has provided a boon to this research domain. Rather than asking whether real biological differences exist between men and women negotiators (i.e., *sex* differences), the question became one of differences deriving from societal expectations due to differential social roles (i.e., *gender* differences; Deaux & LaFrance, 1998; Eagly, 1987). Arguably, the modern-day turning point in this nature-versus-nurture debate was the introduction of the highly influential *stereotype threat theory* (Steele, 1997; Steele & Aronson, 1995). In exploring racial and gender gaps in academic achievement, Steele contended that negative stereotypes of social groups created a "threat in the air" that undermined group members' performance. Regardless of whether the stereotype is believed to be true, the mere knowledge that a negative stereotype exists about a social group can create a self-fulfilling prophecy for its members. With this conceptualization of social category-based performance differences deriving from negative stereotypes, the gender conversation in negotiations fundamentally shifted.

Almost immediately after Steele introduced his theory, its potential contribution to the negotiation literature was appreciated. Researchers began measuring and manipulating the activation of gender stereotypes and examining their impact on how men and women negotiated (Kray, Galinsky, & Thompson, 2002; Kray, Thompson, & Galinsky, 2001). By holding constant the mixed-sex composition of dyads and simply manipulating the content of activated stereotypes, performance differences between men and women were shown to flip-flop and even disappear. Rather than being a product of innate differences, the situation emerged as the primary driver of how men and women divide the proverbial pie. On top of this support for nurture-based gender differences, negotiators' beliefs about the role of nature versus nurture in determining negotiating success were also shown to be critical determinants of performance at the bargaining table (Kray & Haselhuhn, 2007). In other words, the belief itself that good negotiators are born that way inhibits negotiators' effectiveness by lowering their goals, reducing their perseverance in pursuit of those goals, and limiting their willingness to risk failure in attempts to learn and develop as negotiators. This belief is also likely to correspond to the endorsement of masculine stereotypes of successful negotiators (cf. Dweck, Chiu, & Hong, 1995). As a result, this dysfunctional belief increases women's vulnerability to the pernicious effects of negative stereotypes and lowers their negotiation performance (Kray, Locke, & Haselhuhn, 2010). In combination, this research provided strong evidence to suggest that gender differences are more a function of negotiators' awareness of and belief in stereotypes than any innate sex differences. To the extent that these stereotypes persist in the 21st century workplace, an in-depth exploration of the effects of gender stereotypes may aid our understanding of the negotiation gender gap in today's organizations.

The Power of Gender Stereotypes

It has long been assumed that men and women differ in the way that they approach negotiation and conflict resolution (e.g., Rubin & Brown, 1975). Underlying these assumptions are gender stereotypes, or lay perceptions about which traits and behaviors characterize an effective or ineffective negotiator. Successful negotiators are typically thought to be assertive, aggressive, and rational. In contrast, unsuccessful negotiators are assumed to be submissive, weak, and emotional (Kray et al., 2001). These perceptions link directly with traditional gender stereotypes: Men are perceived to be independent, assertive, and rational, while women are perceived to be emotional and passive and to demonstrate a concern for others (Bem, 1974; Deaux & Lewis, 1984; Williams & Best, 1982). The congruency between the masculine stereotype and the lay theory of the successful negotiator leads to positive negotiation stereotypes for men. Likewise, the congruency between the feminine stereotype and lay beliefs about unsuccessful negotiators leads to negative negotiation stereotypes for women (Kray & Thompson, 2005).

Given the centrality of stereotype threat theory to understanding gender differences in negotiations, we begin with a brief review of its key tenets. Stereotype threat is characterized by concerns about confirming a negative stereotype about one's social group in a relevant performance domain (Steele & Aronson, 1995). Psychologically, stereotype threat involves both physiological and cognitive stress derived from increased performance monitoring and attempts to suppress negative thoughts and emotions (Schmader, Johns, & Forbes, 2008). Important for understanding the perniciousness of stereotypes are two observations: First, a threatened party need not believe the stereotype to be affected by it; second, greater identification with a domain increases vulnerability to stereotype threat. In other words, the more individuals care about a domain, the more they are likely to be mindful of negative expectations. For example, women majoring in mathematics at an elite university performed worse on a standardized math test when stereotype threat was triggered via a simple request that they check off their gender on an exam prior to commencing the exam relative to when this question was not asked (Spencer, Steele, & Quinn, 1999).

Women Negotiators Face Negative Stereotypes

Building on Steele's work in academic settings, Kray et al. (2001) proposed that negative female stereotypes could be a catalyst for gender differences in the negotiation domain. Challenging the notion that low expectations of women negotiators are *caused by* their historically poor negotiation performance, Kray and colleagues explored whether these stereotypes were in fact *causing* the observed differences in performance. When negative female stereotypes are "in the air," women are expected to experience stereotype threat and confirm the negative stereotype by demonstrating relatively low performance. Because the belief that core abilities are being measured can trigger stereotype threat (Steele, 1997), the perceived diagnosticity of a negotiation was manipulated for mixed-sex negotiating dyads. Claiming performance would be used to diagnose ability was expected to cause negotiators to question what it takes to succeed, thereby activating stereotypically masculine traits (e.g., rationality, assertiveness) and triggering performance deficits for women. Indeed, this claim was sufficient to reduce women's negotiation performance relative to men; under baseline conditions, both genders performed comparably.

Prejudice and Discrimination

The preceding section addressed how stereotypes affect women negotiators' thoughts and behaviors; here, we consider whether gender stereotypes also influence how women negotiators are perceived and treated by others. We distinguish between prejudice, involving negative attitudes toward social groups, and discrimination, involving behavior aimed at denying social groups positive outcomes (Allport, 1954).

To explain why women negotiators may experience these negative hurdles, we consider both the descriptive and prescriptive components of stereotypes: The *descriptive* aspect of gender stereotypes describes how men and women are generally anticipated to behave in negotiation (i.e., men may be aggressive, women may focus on the relationship). The *prescriptive* aspect of gender stereotypes describes how men and women *ought* to behave. Violating prescriptive stereotypes and their concomitant normative expectations, particularly for low-status groups like women, often produces social sanctions (e.g., Rudman, 1998; see also Eagly, Makhijani, & Klonsky, 1992). In negotiations, behavior such as initiating a negotiation or holding firm in the face of requests for concessions may violate prescriptions for women to be agreeable and relatively unconcerned about their own outcomes.

Social Sanctions for Women Negotiators

Women are uniquely faced with a trade-off between increased perceptions of competence (or in negotiations, economic outcomes) at the risk of social censure, termed the *backlash effect* (Rudman, 1998). For example, using a vignette involving an attempt to negotiate a job offer in which the protagonist's gender was manipulated, Bowles, Babcock, and Lai (2007) demonstrated that women who initiated negotiations were perceived to be less nice and more demanding than were men who made the same requests. Importantly, female negotiators anticipated these negative evaluations—in a follow-up study, women were less likely than men to initiate a negotiation, reporting greater apprehension about anticipated backlash (see also Amanatullah & Morris, 2010). Violating the prescriptive gender stereotypes may lead to severe social consequences, particularly when negotiating with men: Women who show concern for their own interests without demonstrating equal care for others are seen as threatening by men and are met with more hostile forms of sexism, such as derogation and active harassment (Berdahl, 2007).

Beyond negotiations, women who violate feminine stereotypes and act in a self-promoting manner (i.e., act according to masculine stereotypes) are seen as less likeable, more dominant, and more arrogant than men who demonstrate similar behavior (Rudman, 1998; Rudman & Glick, 1999. In sum, female negotiators are faced with a trade-off between the material outcomes they could gain from a negotiation and the social consequences of acting in a self-promoting manner. Apparently, women can either succeed economically at the expense of social perceptions (and possibly in terms of future opportunities; Bowles et al., 2007), or they can accept fewer rewards at the bargaining table and maintain positive social standing.

Gender Stereotypes: Beyond Warmth and Competence

To understand why backlash occurs, we first consider two fundamental dimensions of social perception: warmth and competence (Fiske, Cuddy, Glick, & Xu, 2002). Whereas warmth conveys an actor's intention to behave in a cooperative versus competitive manner, competence conveys his or her ability to carry out this intent. Individuals are initially judged in terms of warmth and then in terms of competence (see Cuddy, Fiske, & Glick, 2008, for a review). The traditional female stereotype is derived from these dimensions: Women are typically seen to be warm but not necessarily competent (e.g., Cuddy, Fiske, & Glick, 2007). This is congruent with typical stereotypes of female negotiators—that they have positive intentions (e.g., concerned about the feelings of the other party) but do not possess the skills necessary to achieve their goals (e.g., are passive and emotional). When women are not perceived as warm, not only are they violating gender prescriptions but it may also imply an "uppity" desire to move up the social hierarchy. Backlash functions to bring the violator of social order back down.

Although the bulk of research examining how stereotypes affect perceptions of negotiators has focused on the mandate that women be agreeable and warm, Kray (2012) examined whether subtler aspects of female stereotypes suggesting that women are more gullible, impressionable, and naïve than men (Prentice & Carranza, 2002) may produce negative outcomes for women negotiators. Expectations about women's naïveté were hypothesized to work in concert with women's own admission of their lack of knowledge about negotiating (Babcock, Gelfand, Small, & Stayn, 2006; Kray & Gelfand, 2009) to render women more vulnerable to deception in strategic interactions than men. Building on Ayres and Siegelman's (1995) initial demonstration that women experience gender discrimination at car dealerships (i.e., higher asking prices than their male peers), Kray asked whether women negotiators are especially likely to be deceived in strategic interactions. In an archival study of deception in a real estate transaction simulation in the MBA classroom, female negotiators were significantly more likely to be blatantly deceived compared to male negotiators. Buyers were charged with purchasing a property that would be put to a use inconsistent with sellers' interests. To make this deal, buyers were three times more likely to negotiate in bad faith by blatantly lying to female sellers compared to male sellers. Because both males and females lied more to women than they did to men, it suggests this pattern is driven by a strategic consideration of the likely consequences of engaging in deception (Gneezy, 2005).

Beyond Gender Stereotypes: Emphasizing Economic Outcomes Favors Men

In the previous section, we reviewed the multifaceted effects of gender stereotypes in negotiation. In the next two sections, we discuss other factors that bring about gender differences at the bargaining table. We first consider whether perceptions of gender differences may be exaggerated by an overly narrow focus on economic negotiation outcomes.

The prototypical negotiation may involve a buyer and a seller haggling over the price of a good or service; in reality, however, negotiations often involve multiple dimensions that vary in their quantifiability. Negotiators may be concerned not only with material or financial outcomes (e.g., price of a car), but also with a wide array of nonquantifiable outcomes (e.g., color of the car) and social outcomes (e.g., establishing a solid relationship with the car dealership for ongoing service of the vehicle) (Thompson, 1990). Broadening the spectrum of outcomes to be considered raises the question of whether men and women adopt similar or distinct goals at the bargaining table. A long-standing hypothesis is that men are more concerned with the financial aspects of negotiation, while women place a relative premium on the relationships they form and develop through the negotiation experience (Rubin & Brown, 1975). Because empirical negotiation research has typically relied on quantifiable measures of negotiation performance, for instance, "points" earned in laboratory research or monetary outcomes in salary negotiations, researchers may be "stacking the deck" in favor of male negotiators (Kolb & Coolidge, 1991). While this argument is not new, it is only since 2000 that researchers have begun systematically measuring subjective and relational concerns. In the following, we consider the complementary frameworks in the literature and then consider the ramifications of this research for understanding gender differences.

Negotiators' concerns extend beyond the tangible outcomes of the negotiation (e.g., Thompson, 1990). Recent theoretical and methodological advances shed light on the multifaceted nature of negotiations. For example, Curhan, Elfenbein, and Xu (2006) proposed and tested a four-factor model of subjective value in negotiation. According to this framework, negotiators care about the process, their instrumental outcome, the relationship with their counterpart, and how the negotiation made them feel about themselves (see Chapter 5, this volume). Do men and women differ in the subjective value they gain for themselves and create for their counterpart? Curhan, Elfenbein, and Kilduff (2009) proposed that women may derive less subjective value from negotiations than do men, possibly stemming from lower overall performance expectations by women. Despite these proposed links, most empirical work to date controls for gender rather than examining how it relates to subjective value (e.g., Curhan et al., 2009; Curhan, Elfenbein, & Eisenkraft, 2010).

In contrast to this approach by which gender is statistically eliminated, a growing body of work has specifically examined gender differences in relational concerns that may combine with or supersede economic goals. Considering that negotiation is inherently a relational process (Gelfand, Major, Raver, Nishii, & O'Brien, 2006; McGinn, 2006), negotiation research has arguably focused too much on the negotiators as individuals. Instead, a complete understanding of negotiation requires an account of both individual and relational concerns (Barley, 1991; Gray, 1994).

A number of constructs have been introduced to capture the degree to which individuals demonstrate a concern for their counterpart's interests or for the relationship between the two parties. For instance, Rubin and Brown (1975) discussed the *interpersonal orientation*, whereby negotiators with this orientation are particularly sensitive to the actions of their counterparts. Similarly, Van Lange (1999) discussed the *prosocial orientation*, which describes the degree to which negotiators focus on enhancing social gains rather than personal gains. More recently, Gelfand et al. (2006) proposed that relational self-construals are particularly important in the negotiation context. Relational self-construals are perceptions of the self in terms of the interconnections and relationships one shares with others. This construal provides a relational lens through which affect, cognition, and behavior are interpreted and evaluated based on how they influence these connections.

Relational Concerns Are Stronger for Women

The distinction between economic and relational concerns in negotiation may be helpful for understanding gender differences at the bargaining table. Relational concerns in negotiation are congruent with the traditional feminine stereotype of the caring and nurturing woman (Gelfand et al., 2006). Thus, it may be the case that women are more concerned than men in building and maintaining relationships through negotiation and may be more concerned with relationship outcomes than with material gains (Kolb & Coolidge, 1991).

Empirical research appears to support this position. For instance, Cross, Bacon, and Morris (2000) found that general relationship self-construals are more accessible for women than for men, suggesting that women are more likely to interpret their interactions with others in terms of the relationship. In a negotiation context, Kray and Gelfand (2009) provided some of the first empirical evidence that women actively pursue different goals in negotiation than do men. Specifically, when considering a hypothetical employment negotiation, women reported greater concern over developing a relationship with a potential employer than did men and were in fact more concerned with the relational outcome than with their distributive success. In contrast, men showed equal concern for relational and distributive outcomes. Interestingly, these differences were eliminated when the ambiguity about the appropriateness of negotiating economic terms was reduced: In this case, both men and women reported caring equally about relational and economic terms. If women place greater value on relational outcomes compared to economic outcomes, this may help to explain why they trail men in quantifiable measures of negotiation success—perhaps women are simply prioritizing different objectives altogether.

Negotiators Value Emotional Outcomes

Emotions play a key role in negotiation and can have substantial influence over the negotiation processes and outcomes (e.g., Carnevale & Isen, 1986; Forgas, 1998). Moreover, affect is an important negotiation outcome in and of itself, irrespective of objective gains from the negotiation (e.g., Barry, Fulmer, & Goates, 2006; Barry, Fulmer, & Van Kleef, 2004). Affect, generally, serves a motivational function (Schwarz & Clore, 1983)—individuals are motivated to have positive emotions and to avoid negative emotions. This is particularly true in interactive, competitive domains, such as negotiation, in which individuals act to maximize their overall happiness (Haselhuhn & Mellers, 2005; Mellers, Haselhuhn, Tetlock, Silva, & Isen, 2010).

One important emotional outcome is regret. People are strongly motivated to avoid regret and feel relief when they are able to avoid a potentially regretful outcome (e.g., Richard, van der Pligt, & de Vries, 1996). Both actual and anticipated regret affect negotiator behavior. Galinsky, Seiden, Kim, and Medvec (2002) argued that certain negotiation outcomes, such as having one's first offer accepted, trigger feelings of regret as negotiators consider the counterfactual reality that they should have asked for more. Experiencing this regret can lead to behavioral change—for instance, negotiators who have their first offer accepted in one negotiation may spend more time preparing for future encounters to ensure that it does not happen again (Galinsky et al., 2002).

Building on this work, Kray and Gelfand (2009) argued that feelings of regret in such situations may be primarily a male phenomenon. Given the rampant potential for social backlash, women may feel more anxiety and anticipated regret over the negotiation process than men. In contrast, men's experience of regret may be limited to the quality of the deal they achieve. Consistent with this hypothesis, Kray and Gelfand demonstrated that women were more likely to feel relieved if their first offer was accepted compared to when they achieved the same outcome following several offers and counteroffers. In contrast, men felt more relieved when the negotiation included a series of offers and counteroffers compared to when their first offer was accepted. If men and women have different affective reactions to negotiation outcomes, as this research suggested, the universal motivation to achieve positive emotions and avoid negative emotions may manifest in different goals and behaviors for men and women.

Beyond Gender Stereotypes: Sex Versus the Situation

The preceding section calls into question the dependent variables in the gender and negotiation framework. In other words, can we be sure that men really are better negotiators than women, or has research focused too narrowly on only one dimension of performance? Others have taken a different approach, calling into question whether scholars are looking at the correct *independent* variable. This line of research asks whether gender (or sex) is truly the driver of the performance differences reported in the literature to date, or if there are situational factors or confounding variables that have been overlooked in previous work.

Gender Triggers

Providing more evidence for the "nurture" perspective on gender differences in negotiation, researchers have identified numerous situational factors that elicit gender differences that may not otherwise emerge. In effect, aspects of the situation "trigger" gender-specific concerns or actions that, in turn, lead men and women to negotiate differently. Traditional gender stereotypes, as discussed above, are one example of social or situational factors that elicit gender differences. Other factors, such as the semantics of negotiation or the role negotiators play, have been shown to trigger gender differences as well.

The language of negotiation is one source of gender differences: The term *negotiation* in and of itself can serve as a gender trigger. Whereas terms such as *negotiation* or *bargaining* connote gendered associations and stereotypes, functionally equivalent terms, such as *asking* or *debating* may not have the same implicit connections. To test this proposition, Small, Gelfand, Babcock, and Gettman (2007) examined gender differences in the initiation of negotiation. Following a task with ambiguous performance criteria, participants were given the chance to negotiate their compensation with the experimenter. Some participants were told that people often "negotiated" for a higher payment than they were originally offered, while other participants were told that people often "asked" for additional money. Women were significantly more likely to request a higher payment when it was framed as asking for additional money, compared to when it was framed as a negotiation. In fact, women "asked" for a higher payment just as often as did men. Thus, simply by referring to social interactions as negotiations, researchers and managers may be inadvertently triggering performance differences between men and women.

Another situational cue that can trigger gender differences is a negotiator's role. Bowles, Babcock, and McGinn (2005) demonstrated that whether individuals are negotiating for themselves or on behalf of another party determines whether gender differences emerge in negotiation. Bowles et al. argued that women who negotiate on behalf of someone else are freed from the fear of social backlash effects that accompany self-promotion by women. Results from a simulated salary negotiation supported this assertion (see also Amanatullah & Morris, 2010): While men demonstrated the same level of performance regardless of whether they negotiated for themselves or on behalf of another party, women negotiated a significantly higher salary when negotiating for someone else.

Intriguingly, ambiguity appears to moderate gender differences. Negotiators who have a clear sense of the negotiation parameters (e.g., knowing the range of acceptable or possible outcomes, understanding market values or social norms of fairness, etc.) are less affected by factors that would otherwise trigger gender differences (Bowles et al., 2005). Likewise, Kray and Gelfand (2009) found that gender differences in emotional reactions to having a first offer accepted disappeared when ambiguity about the appropriateness of negotiating was reduced. When it was clearly understood that negotiation attempts are valued, men and women had similar reactions to the negotiation process.

Gender as a Proxy for Status

In addition to raising the question of whether situational factors trigger gender effects, researchers have asked whether the observed differences between male and female negotiators have to do with gender at all. According to this perspective, gender is merely a proxy for other key factors that affect negotiation outcomes, with status being a primary correlate.

The perspective that social status underlies gender differences is not new. For instance, Eagly and Steffen (1984) proposed that traditional gender stereotypes (e.g., women are communal, men are agentic) arise as a result of men and women occupying different positions in society, both today and in the past. Even as contemporary society moves toward greater gender equality, the parameters and constraints of organizational life have been defined in times when men enjoyed far greater opportunities and general success (Kolb & McGinn, 2009). As a result, men are more likely to be in positions of status and power in the workplace, which gives rise to the stereotype of the assertive, agentic man. Women, in contrast, are more likely to be in low-status positions in the workplace (or to be absent from the workplace altogether), leading to the stereotype of the community-focused woman who sacrifices herself for the greater good. In this way, stereotypes that we typically associate with gender are actually reflecting historical differences in social status.

In the negotiation domain, differences in status or power may explain why men and women differ in how they negotiate (Kray & Thompson, 2005; Watson, 1994). According to status-based models of gender and negotiation (Miles & Clenney, 2010), men are perceived as more competent than women, and their actions are seen as more legitimate due to their relatively high social status (Eagly & Wood, 1982). These perceptions then give male negotiators the latitude to employ a wide range of competitive and cooperative negotiation tactics. Due to men's high status, others perceive their agentic behavior as legitimate attempts to achieve negotiation success; thus, these tactics are considered acceptable. In contrast, because women are relatively low status, using the same tactics may be perceived as an attempt to climb up the social ladder; women may then incur backlash as a result of these perceptions. In sum, the status ascribed to men allows them flexibility in the negotiation that women lack. Importantly, it is the relative social status of men and women that is argued to drive these effects rather than gender itself.

Complementing this approach, Galinsky, Shirako, and Kray (2012) examined the necessary and sufficient conditions for stereotype threat in negotiation. Galinsky et al. proposed that negotiator status interacts with performance concerns, such that low-status negotiators feel anxiety in situations in which they feel pressure to perform that high-status negotiators do not feel. These differences in anxiety, then, are expected to lead low-status negotiators to perform worse when their ability is in question—a stereotype threat-like change in performance. Consistent with this prediction, negotiators in low-status roles (e.g., a job candidate as opposed to a recruiter) demonstrated patterns of behavior consistent with those of stereotype threat, achieving less success in situations for which their ability was called into question. Extrapolating these results to the question of gender, it may be that women do not fall prey to stereotype threat due to their gender per se; instead, it may be women's relatively low social status that creates this vulnerability.

Analogous to this line of work, Bowles and Gelfand (2010) examined how status influences the evaluation of deviant workplace behavior. Bowles and Gelfand proposed a model in which high-status individuals were simultaneously more critical of the deviant behavior of low-status individuals and less likely to follow the rules themselves (see Lammers, Stapel, & Galinsky, 2010, for analogous effects of power). Intriguingly, when gender was substituted for status in empirical tests of this model, precisely the same effects emerged—men were more critical of the behavior of women than of other men, while women evaluated the behavior the same regardless of the transgressor's gender. This suggests that in workplace interactions (such as negotiations), gender and status may be inextricably intertwined.

SECTION 2: HOW TO LEVEL THE PLAYING FIELD

As the previous section has detailed, women's negotiation performance suffers mainly as a result of the presence of various situational threats. The very nature of situational factors, however, means that these factors can change. In this section, we describe a variety of possible actions that can be taken by individuals or organizations to help close the gender gap at the bargaining table. Given the prominent function of stereotypes in driving gender differences, we begin with an in-depth discussion of how the pernicious effects of negative female stereotypes can be counteracted. We then turn our attention to actions that can be taken by organizations to level the playing field between men and women.

Countering Negative Stereotypes

Stereotype Reactance: A Motivated Disproval of Negative Stereotypes

Importantly, the existence of negative gender stereotypes need not always harm negotiation performance. When the stereotype is blatantly activated, it can actually motivate women to disprove it. In the work of Kray et al. (2001), while subtle suggestions that stereotypically masculine traits were important to negotiation success led to stereotype threat, the explicit endorsement of gender stereotypes (i.e., stating that men typically do better in negotiation because they possess desirable traits) led to *stereotype reactance*, by which women outperformed their male counterparts. This finding is important for understanding gender differences for two reasons. First, it demonstrates that the same stereotype can trigger different kinds of gender effects depending on how consciously the stereotype is considered by its target. Second, it provides decisive evidence against an innate difference perspective. If varying the level of explicitness of a gender stereotype determines whether men versus women outperform each other, then it cannot be the case that men are innately superior to women in this domain.

Emphasizing Positive Stereotypes Eliminates Threat and Reverses Gender Gap

Beyond considerations of how stereotypes are activated, the content of the stereotype also affects negotiation performance. Building on their previous work, Kray et al. (2002) examined whether negotiators would change their behavior when stereotypically *positive* female traits (e.g., good listening skills, patience) were associated with negotiation success. When these traits were emphasized, the typical gender effect was reversed, with women negotiators outperforming their male counterparts. This once again demonstrates that it is not the case that stereotypes are drawing out inherent differences between men and women negotiators, but rather that the content of the stereotype *causes* these differences in performance. While activating negative stereotypes can reduce negotiation performance, they can also be neutralized by considering that stereotypically feminine traits predict negotiation success. When being female psychologically shifts from being a liability to an asset, performance shifts accordingly.

Does Enhanced Likeability Mitigate Women Negotiators' Social Backlash?

If women face economic sanctions for acting in accordance with female stereotypes (i.e., warm but not competent) and social censure for acting counterstereotypically (i.e., competent but not warm), is there any way for women to capture value at the bargaining table while avoiding social sanctions? One idea for handling this predicament is for women to combine warmth and competence to achieve their goals without bearing social costs (e.g., Babcock & Laschever, 2003). By adopting a "feminine" manner, women are "allowed" to pursue their goals. In support of this assertion, Carli, LaFleur, and Loeber (1995) demonstrated that women who delivered persuasive messages to men using a social style (i.e., leaning toward their counterpart, making eye contact, having a friendly expression) were perceived as more likeable and, as a consequence, were more influential compared to women who delivered the same message using a task-focused style (i.e., firm tone of voice, upright body posture). Similarly, Heilman and Okimoto (2007) found that the backlash effect for (fictional) female managers was reduced when the managers were described as being communal and generally supportive of their employees' needs. A social style appears to signal good intentions, thus enhancing receptivity to women's messages.

Organizational-Level Actions

Kray and Shirako (in press) proposed several steps that organizations can take to reduce the destructive effects of negative stereotypes. For instance, organizations can counteract the effects of gender stereotypes by changing their content—focusing on the positive female characteristics that can lead to negotiation success and deemphasizing the negative aspects of the female stereotype. Individuals' beliefs about the link between gender and negotiation have been shown to be relatively malleable and subject to change, either through regenerating the content of stereotypes (e.g., by associating feminine traits with negotiation success; Kray et al., 2002) or through education (Rudman, Ashmore, & Gary, 2001). Organizations should take advantage of both approaches by highlighting the positive qualities of their female members and by educating all organizational members in reducing prejudice and bias.

Finally, organizations have a responsibility to provide both women and men the tools they need to be successful in negotiations. Negotiation training and education are key in teaching men and women alike the strategies and tactics they need to achieve success at the bargaining table, but this training may be particularly important for women. As noted by Bowles and McGinn (2008), recent legislation in the United States has allocated resources for training women and girls in negotiation, ostensibly because this education is expected to help reduce the wage gap.

While education can help mitigate gender differences by giving both men and women confidence that they can attain positive outcomes, it may help in directly reducing gender stereotypes as well. Novice negotiators are unsure about the traits and characteristics that lead to negotiation success and may therefore be relatively reliant on stereotypes to inform how they approach negotiations. Exposure to a wide range of negotiation situations, and a wide range of negotiators, should help individuals to recognize that both stereotypically masculine and stereotypically feminine traits are necessary for optimal negotiation performance (cf. Lax & Sebenius, 1986).

Indeed, the most powerful impact of training programs for women may be simply to instill the belief that it is possible to improve as negotiators. Individuals hold implicit beliefs about the fixedness or malleability of negotiation skill, and these beliefs have important implications for the goals negotiators set and the outcomes they are able to attain (Kray & Haselhuhn, 2007). Individuals who believe that negotiation is an innate ability focus on their immediate performance, reduce effort in the face of challenges, and ultimately fail to achieve their goals when the going gets tough. Individuals who believe that negotiation is a skill that can be developed are primarily concerned with improving and growing as negotiators over time and exert effort at the bargaining table regardless of their perceived chances for immediate success. This perseverance serves them well and allows them to both create and claim greater value at the bargaining table.

While implicit negotiation beliefs have not been shown to differ by gender, our research has shown that women's implicit beliefs are critical in determining their response to negative stereotypes. Whereas previous research has shown a general pattern of reactance, by which women react against negative stereotypes by improving their performance (Kray et al., 2001; Kray, Reb, Galinsky, & Thompson, 2004), we demonstrated that only women with malleable implicit negotiation beliefs are able to dedicate the effort and wherewithal necessary to achieve success. Thus, teaching women that they can become better negotiators through negotiation education may aid women not only by minimizing gender stereotyping or bias but also by giving women the beliefs necessary to overcome the challenges that they may face.

SECTION 3: CHALLENGES IN CLOSING THE GENDER GAP IN THE 21st CENTURY WORKPLACE

The preceding section outlined several strategies for individuals and organizations to close the negotiation gender gap. However, the ability of negotiators to make use of this information to reduce the gender gap may be constrained by the organizational context. In this section, we describe two attributes of the 21st century workplace that present significant challenges to the application of the actions described. In particular, we focus on the tendency of the contemporary workplace to minimize the discussion of gender, as well as the increased reliance on competition and narrowly defined performance metrics in the workplace.

Unintended Consequences of the Gender-Neutral Workplace

The 21st century workplace is often characterized by a commitment to gender neutrality. In short, many companies endeavor to treat all organizational members equally, regardless of gender. While the intention behind a gender-blind workplace may be noble, such policies have unintended consequences that may ironically impede organizations' efforts to achieve equality at the bargaining table.

At a basic level, organizational commitment to a gender-blind workplace inhibits companies' ability to learn about and capitalize on inherent (and unavoidable) differences between men and women. This is a potential concern for several reasons. First, by eliminating gender from the conversation, companies may not address gender-specific issues (e.g., pregnancy).

Failure to address such issues directly can inadvertently cause greater bias against women as they must negotiate issues that are not shared by men (e.g., Greenberg, Ladge & Clair, 2009). By attempting to take gender out of the equation altogether, organizations may be unable to account adequately for genuine biological differences between men and women.

Biological differences aside, a commitment to a gender-neutral workplace may also hinder companies' ability to understand how men and women react to their environment at a sociocognitive level. While academic research has furthered our understanding of how female stereotypes affect women's experience at the bargaining table, we know relatively little about how gender stereotypes, either positive or negative, affect men. Organizational attempts to move the focus away from gender exacerbate this knowledge gap. Thus, attempts to educate organizational members may be challenged by an organization's incomplete understanding of the comprehensive effects of gender stereotypes.

Finally, companies that endorse a gender-blind approach may inadvertently promote, rather than mitigate, gender differences in negotiation (cf. Kray & Shirako, in press). Research on racial stereotypes suggests that stereotype threat may be heightened in organizations that adopt color-blind policies and procedures rather than explicitly valuing racial diversity in the workplace (Purdie-Vaughns, Steele, Davies, Ditlmann, & Crosby, 2008). Organizations may observe similar effects with regard to gender stereotypes. In contrast to a gender-neutral workplace, acknowledging gender stereotypes gives women the chance to react against the negative perceptions instead of allowing the dangerous beliefs to remain "in the air" (Kray et al., 2001).

Stacking the Deck: Male-Centered Policies in the 21st Century Workplace

More than ever before, the 21st century workplace is characterized by a competitive, performance-driven mind-set. Recent high levels of unemployment highlight the competition inherent in securing and maintaining positions at all levels of the organization. Companies that evaluate employees along a standard measure may do so in the name of fairness—after all, men and women alike are held to the same set of standards. At the same time, however, companies that narrowly define performance along metrics of material gains and losses may inadvertently tilt the playing field in favor of male employees. Organizations that focus exclusively on observable, short-term outcomes (e.g., immediate financial performance) rather than longer-term performance measures (e.g., building client relationships) may stack the deck in favor of men in three ways: First, as outlined in detail above, women and men may prioritize different goals at the bargaining table, and an overly narrow focus on short-term performance outcomes may overlook valuable contributions women make to the organization.

Second, holding men and women to the same rigid set of standards ignores historical imbalances that lead men and women to face different challenges at the bargaining table. For example, individuals—both men and women— generally benefit from being part of an extensive social network (see Chapter 9, this volume). Having a broader set of social connections leads to greater access to unique resources, provides possible alternatives to a current negotiation, and can generally provide information needed to help to reduce the ambiguity of a negotiation (Kolb & McGinn, 2009; Seidel, Polzer, & Stewart, 2000). However, because men have been in the workplace longer than women, and networks tend to be homophilous (Brass, 1985), men, on average, have access to a more extensive network of possible negotiation partners and counterparts than do women. This discrepancy in social networking adds yet another barrier for women to overcome at the bargaining table.

Finally, the competitive atmosphere promoted by many 21st century organizations may set expectations for how negotiations should be conducted in the workplace. These expectations may feed into stereotypes of how negotiators should behave, which may in turn hinder efforts of female negotiators to overcome negative stereotypes. Specifically, we previously described research in which women were able to avoid social backlash by cloaking agentic behavior with a warm, personal approach. However, this research primarily investigated perceptions in a general workplace context. How does this advice translate at the 21st century bargaining table, which fundamentally involves competition? Kray and Locke (2012) proposed that women's demonstration of warmth signals a lack of competitive intent that may lead them to be perceived as "softies" at the bargaining table. If women negotiators are perceived to be more cooperative, they may indeed reap social rewards by being well liked, but at the economic cost of counterparts acting more competitively to take advantage of their cooperation (cf. Lax & Sebenius, 1986). Essentially, acting warmly may signal that a negotiator has relatively modest demands, which allows their counterparts to demand more (Van Kleef & De Dreu, 2010).

Consistent with this theorizing, women who negotiated with a social style in a distributive negotiation were perceived as more likeable by their counterparts but suffered economically as their counterparts (both men and women) negotiated more aggressively (Kray & Locke, 2012). Importantly, though, men who adopted a social style suffered no economic penalty for doing so. Kray and Locke also found that women who adopt a social style are indeed able to leverage their perceived cooperative intent to expand the pie in an integrative context, but once again, their counterparts claimed the entirety of the created value. Finally, relying too heavily on likeability may increase women's vulnerability to benevolent sexism (Good & Rudman, 2010; cf. Glick & Fiske, 1996). Taken together, this suggests that it may be premature to conclude that this Catch-22 is solved by having women cloak their competitive negotiation goals with communal styles.

SECTION 4: UNANSWERED QUESTIONS IN GENDER AND NEGOTIATION RESEARCH

In Section 3, we outlined two aspects of the 21st century workplace that may hinder efforts to level the playing field between male and female negotiators. Of particular import, we argued that attempts to promote a gender-blind work environment provide a unique challenge to reducing the negotiation gender gap as such policies mask important biological and social psychological differences between men and women. In the final section of the chapter, we describe two areas of future research that are guided by these challenges: taking the male perspective to understand better how men experience negotiation in the face of positive or negative stereotypes and reexamining fundamental, biological factors in the negotiation process.

Taking the Male Perspective

Much of the research on gender in negotiation has focused on the barriers and challenges women face at the bargaining table. It is important, however, also to understand the pressures that men may face and how these pressures may affect the negotiation process. To the extent that the male perspective has been considered, men are often assumed to enjoy an advantage in terms of positive performance expectations and outcomes (e.g., Kray et al., 2001; Kray & Thompson, 2005; cf. Walton & Cohen, 2003). Intriguing contradictions, however, have emerged in empirical work. For example, Kray et al. (2001) demonstrated that when negative female stereotypes (and thus positive male stereotypes) were explicitly activated, men paradoxically did worse in a negotiation compared to when these positive masculine stereotypes were implicit. This finding suggests that the weight of positive expectations directed at men created a pressure that ultimately undermined their performance.

Recent research has begun to investigate the effects of positive masculine stereotypes from the male's perspective. Vandello, Bosson, Cohen, Burnaford, and Weaver (2008) introduced the concept of *precarious masculinity*, which posits that men feel pressure to uphold societal perceptions of "manliness." They proposed that manhood, but not womanhood, is perceived to be a malleable characteristic that requires constant validation. Thus, in the face of explicit positive stereotypes, men may feel pressure to live up to these descriptions of the "typical" man to maintain their masculinity. More recently, Moss-Racusin, Phelan, and Rudman (2010) suggested that this concern has merit. In videos of simulated job interviews, men who violated typical gender stereotypes by demonstrating modesty were judged as less likeable and of lower status. Thus, it appears as though the backlash effect is germane to men as well as to women—men who fail to act in accordance with prescriptive masculine gender stereotypes are subject to social sanctions as well.

Future research should carefully examine the implications for precarious masculinity in a negotiation context. If men feel pressure to perform, or to act in ways that are consistent with traditional male stereotypes (e.g., agentic, competitive), this may predict how men will behave in negotiation. In initial research to this end, we have examined how social pressure may underlie gender differences in ethical behavior (Kray & Haselhuhn, 2012; cf. Gilligan, 1982). We argued that the pressure felt by male negotiators to live up to positive gender stereotypes would lead them to process ethical dilemmas pragmatically and to view ethically questionable negotiation tactics as legitimate means of achieving negotiation success. As individuals often engage in unethical behavior as a way to reach goals that they might not otherwise achieve (Schweitzer, Ordóñez, & Douma, 2004), men may be more likely to engage in strategic justification of questionable tactics as a way to fulfill the social stereotype of the successful male negotiator. Consistent with this prediction, we found that men were more pragmatic in their ethical reasoning, demonstrating egocentrism in their ethical judgments and endorsing unethical negotiation tactics as a means of attaining their goals.

Reexamining Sex Differences

For several reasons, research examining inherent differences between men and women in negotiations has fallen out of favor. This is partially attributable to the current political climate, in which the mere suggestion of possible intrinsic sex differences is met with an outcry, as evidenced by the firestorm that erupted after Larry Summers remarked that women may lack "intrinsic aptitude" to succeed at the upper echelons of science and engineering (Kray, 2007). Another primary reason for the lack of recent research is that little evidence exists that inherent sex differences matter, at least not to the same degree as socially constructed and construed differences. However, recent advances in technology have made it possible to understand better the precise factors that may mediate or moderate differences in how men and women negotiate.

For instance, as previously discussed, emotions are key factors in determining negotiation processes and outcomes (Barry et al., 2004, 2006). Recent application of functional magnetic resonance imaging (fMRI) technology to simplified negotiation situations has not only confirmed the critical role of emotion in making decisions in these contexts but also has isolated the specific neuroactivation that occurs when the decisions are made. For instance, the bilateral anterior insula cortex, an area associated with negative emotion, is activated when individuals are faced with what they perceive to be an unfair offer (Sanfey, Rilling, Aronson, Nystrom, & Cohen, 2003). In fact, rejecting perceived unfair offers can be its own reward: de Quervain et al. (2004) demonstrated that punishing unsporting behavior in abstracted bargaining games activated the same brain circuits involved in reward processing. The fMRI technology could be used to answer conclusively questions about how men and women negotiate. For example, both men and women believe that women are more emotional than men in negotiation, and men are more rational than women (Kray & Thompson, 2005). Observing patterns of brain activation during simplified negotiation exercises could conclusively answer the question of whether there is a biological basis for these common lay beliefs.

Other recent developments have identified biological moderators of behavioral sex differences. For instance, anthropological research has established the facial width-to-height ratio as a sexually dimorphic trait that is independent of body size (Weston, Friday, & Liò, 2007). Intrasex differences in facial structure have been linked to aggression and dominance in men only, with wider facial width-to-height ratios associated with more aggressive behavior (Carré & McCormick, 2008; Carré, McCormick, & Mondloch, 2009). For instance, men with wider facial ratios are more likely to retaliate to perceived slights by others (Carré & McCormick, 2008) and are more likely to act in their own self-interest, even if it means violating another's trust (Stirrat & Perrett, 2010). Researchers have theorized that intrasex selection has allowed physically (facially) imposing men more leniency in their behavior toward others as their stature minimizes the chance of retribution for their actions (Stirrat & Perrett, 2010).

Building on this work, Haselhuhn and Wong (in press) examined whether facial characteristics moderated gender differences in the propensity to engage in unethical behavior during a negotiation. Ethically questionable tactics, such as deception, are common in negotiation (O'Connor & Carnevale, 1997; Schweitzer, 2001), and research has demonstrated that men are more likely to engage in these tactics than are women (e.g., Dreber & Johannesson, 2008; Lewicki & Robinson, 1998). As hypothesized, facial width-to-height ratios moderated this gender effect, with this ratio correlating positively with deception by male negotiators and unrelated to female negotiators' use of deception.

CONCLUSION

In this chapter, we have highlighted advances over the past decade in understanding gender differences in negotiation in order to understand why these differences persist in the 21st century workplace. We examined the pernicious stereotypes that threaten female negotiators' ability to achieve success at the bargaining table, both from the perspective of the focal negotiator (i.e., stereotype threat) and from the perception of their counterparts (i.e., prejudice and discrimination). To reduce many stereotype threat effects, it is important to consider the content of the activated stereotype and how consciously it is considered, along with implicit beliefs about what drives success in negotiations. For gender effects derived from social perception, more research is needed to understand how these negative consequences can be avoided. At this point, one practical contribution of this research is to show a reflection of the predicament women face at the bargaining table, without necessarily offering definitive solutions. We are optimistic that seeing the role of prejudice and discrimination more clearly is the first step toward moving beyond the difficulties they create for women negotiators.

Our perspective on the literature to date is that we have made considerable progress in understanding the power of gender stereotypes, yet we continue to have an incomplete understanding of gender differences in negotiation more broadly. To this end, our chapter includes an examination of additional negotiation outcomes, typically harder to quantify than dollar figures, differing in likely importance to men and women. Given the host of situational factors that trigger gender differences, issues of status and power may be at the heart of the gender gap. And, though our perspective is deeply rooted in the nurture-based view of gender differences, we acknowledge that very real nature-based differences between the sexes must also be considered for a comprehensive picture of gender to emerge. Given that a full consideration of these differences is difficult in today's gender-blind workplace, it is imperative for future academic research to address such issues. Our goal for this chapter was to highlight the many subtleties and complexities that characterize the relationship between gender and the task of negotiating. Only by understanding all aspects of the negotiation—the negotiators, the situation, and the organizational context—can 21st century organizations begin to level the playing field between the sexes.

REFERENCES

Allport, G. W. (1954). *The nature of prejudice*. Cambridge, MA: Addison-Wesley.

Amanatullah, E. T., & Morris, M. W. (2010). Negotiating gender roles: Gender differences in assertive negotiating are mediated by women's fear of backlash and attenuated when negotiating on behalf of others. *Journal of Personality and Social Psychology, 98*, 256–267.

Ayres, I., & Siegelman, P. (1995). Race and gender discrimination in bargaining for a new car. *American Economic Review, 85*, 304–321.

Babcock, L., Gelfand, M., Small, D., & Stayn, H. (2006). Gender differences in the propensity to initiate negotiations. In D. De Cremer, M. Zeelenberg, & K. Murnighan (Eds.), *Social psychology and economics* (pp. 239–259). Mahwah, NJ: Erlbaum.

Babcock, L., & S. Laschever. 2003. *Women don't ask.* Princeton, NJ: Princeton University Press.

Barley, S. R. (1991). Contextualizing conflict: Notes on the anthropology of disputes and negotiation. In M. Bazerman, R. Lewicki, & B. Sheppard (Eds.), *Research on negotiation in organizations* (pp. 165–199). Greenwich, CT: JAI Press.

Barry, B., Fulmer, I. S., & Goates, N. (2006). Bargaining with feeling: Emotionality in and around negotiation. In L. Thompson (Ed.), *Negotiation theory and research* (pp. 99–127). Hove, NY: Psychology Press.

Barry, B., Fulmer, I. S., & Van Kleef, G. A. (2004). I laughed, I cried, I settled: The role of emotion in negotiation. In Gelfand, M. and Brett, J. (Eds.), *The handbook of negotiation and culture: Theoretical advances and cross-cultural perspectives* (pp. 71–94). Palo Alto, CA: Stanford University Press.

Bem, S. L. (1974). The measurement of psychological androgyny. *Journal of Consulting and Clinical Psychology, 42,* 155–162.

Berdahl, J. L. (2007). Harassment based on sex: Protecting social status in the context of gender hierarchy. *Academy of Management Review, 32,* 641–658.

Blau, F. D., & Kahn, L. M. (2006). The U.S. gender pay gap in the 1990s: Slowing convergence. *Industrial and Labor Relations Review, 60*(1), 45–66.

Blau, F. D., & Kahn, L. M. (2007). The gender pay gap: Have women gone as far as they can? *Academy of Management Perspectives, 21,* 7–23.

Bowles, H. R., Babcock, L. C., & Lai, L. (2007). Social incentives for gender differences in the propensity to initiate negotiations: Sometimes it does hurt to ask. *Organizational Behavior and Human Decision Processes, 103*(1), 84–103.

Bowles, H. R., Babcock, L., & McGinn, K. L. 2005. Constraints and triggers: Situational mechanics of gender in negotiation. *Journal of Personality and Social Psychology, 89,* 951–965.

Bowles, H. R., & Gelfand, M. (2010). Status and the evaluation of workplace deviance. *Psychological Science, 21,* 49–54.

Bowles, H. R., & McGinn, K. L. (2008). Untapped potential in the study of negotiation and gender inequality in organizations. In J. P. Walsh & A. Brief (Eds.), *Academy of management annals* (pp. 99–132). New York: Routledge.

Brass, D. J. (1985). Men's and women's networks: A study of interaction patterns and influence in an organization. *Academy of Management Journal, 28,* 327–343.

Carli, L. L., LaFleur, S. J., & Loeber, C. C. (1995). Nonverbal behavior, gender, and influence. *Journal of Personality and Social Psychology, 68,* 1030–1041.

Carnevale, P. J. D., & Isen, A. M. (1986). The influence of positive affect and visual access on the discovery of integrative solutions in bilateral negotiation. *Organizational Behavior and Human Decision Processes, 37,* 1–13.

Carré, J. M., & McCormick, C. M. (2008). In your face: Facial metrics predict aggressive behavior in the laboratory and in varsity and professional hockey players. *Proceedings of the Royal Society B: Biological Sciences, 275,* 2651–2656.

Carré, J. M., McCormick, C. M., & Mondloch, C. J. (2009). Facial structure is a reliable cue of aggressive behavior. *Psychological Science, 20,* 1194–1198.

Cross, S. E., Bacon, P. L., & Morris, M. L. (2000). The relational-interdependent self-construal and relationships. *Journal of Personality and Social Psychology, 78,* 191–208.

Cuddy, A. J. C., Fiske, S. T., & Glick, P. (2007). The BIAS map: Behaviors from intergroup affect and stereotypes. *Journal of Personality and Social Psychology, 92*, 631–648.

Cuddy, A. J. C., Fiske, S. T., & Glick, P. (2008). Warmth and competence as universal dimensions of social perception: The stereotype content model and the BIAS map. *Advances in Experimental Social Psychology, 40*, 61–149.

Curhan, J. R., Elfenbein, H. A., & Eisenkraft, N. (2010). The objective value of subjective value: A multi-round negotiation study. *Journal of Applied Social Psychology, 40*, 690–709.

Curhan, J. R., Elfenbein, H. A., & Kilduff, G. J. (2009). Getting off on the right foot: Subjective value versus economic value in predicting longitudinal job outcomes from job offer negotiation. *Journal of Applied Psychology, 94*, 524–534.

Curhan, J. R., Elfenbein, H. A., & Xu, H. (2006). What do people value when they negotiate? Mapping the domain of subjective value in negotiation. *Journal of Personality and Social Psychology, 91*, 493–512.

Deaux, K., & LaFrance, M. (1998). Gender. In D. Gilbert, S. T. Fiske, & G. Lindzey (Eds.), *Handbook of social psychology* (4th ed., pp. 788–827). New York: Random House.

Deaux, K., & Lewis, L. L. (1984). The structure of gender stereotypes: Interrelationships among components and gender label. *Journal of Personality and Social Psychology, 46*, 991–1004.

De Quervain, D. J.-F., Fischbacher, U., Treyer, V., Schellhammer, M., Schnyder, U., Buck, A., et al. (2004). The neural basis of altruistic punishment. *Science, 305*, 1254–1258.

Dreber, A., & Johannesson, M. (2008). Gender differences in deception. *Economics Letters, 99*, 197–199.

Dweck, C. S., Chiu, C., & Hong, Y. (1995). Implicit theories and their role in judgments and reactions: A world from two perspectives. *Psychological Inquiry, 6*, 267–285.

Eagly, A. H. (1987). *Sex differences in social behavior: A social-role interpretation*. Hillsdale, NJ: Erlbaum.

Eagly, A. H., Makhijani, M. G., & Klonsky, B. G. (1992). Gender and the evaluation of leaders: A meta-analysis. *Psychological Bulletin, 111*, 3–22.

Eagly, A. H., & Steffen, V. J. (1984). Gender stereotypes stem from the distribution of women and men into social roles. *Journal of Personality and Social Psychology, 46*, 735–754.

Eagly, A. H., & Wood, W. (1982). Inferred sex differences in status as a determinant of gender stereotypes about social influence. *Journal of Personality and Social Psychology, 43*, 915–928.

Fiske, S. T., Cuddy, A. J. C., Glick, P., & Xu, J. (2002). A model of (often mixed) stereotype content: Competence and warmth respectively follow from perceived status and competition. *Journal of Personality and Social Psychology, 82*, 878–902.

Forgas, J. P. (1998). On feeling good and getting your way: Mood effects on negotiation cognition and bargaining strategies. *Journal of Personality and Social Psychology, 74*, 565–577.

Galinsky, A. D., Seiden, V. L., Kim, P. H., & Medvec, V. H. (2002). The dissatisfaction of having your first offer accepted: The role of counterfactual thinking in negotiations. *Personality and Social Psychology Bulletin, 28*, 271–283.

Galinsky, A. D., Shirako, A., & Kray, L. J. (2012). The minimal stereotype threat effect. Unpublished manuscript. Northwestern University.

Gelfand, M. J., Major, V. S., Raver, J. L., Nishii, L. H., & O'Brien, K. (2006). Negotiating relationally: The dynamics of the relational self in negotiations. *Academy of Management Review, 31*, 427–451.

The gender wage gap: 2009. (2010). Retrieved November 1, 2010, from http://www.iwpr.org/pdf/C350.pdf

Gilligan, C. (1982). *In a different voice: Psychological theory and women's development.* Cambridge, MA: Harvard University Press.

Glick, P., & Fiske, S. T. (1996). The ambivalent sexism inventory: Differentiating hostile and benevolent sexism. *Journal of Personality and Social Psychology, 70,* 491–512.

Good, J. J., & Rudman, L. A. (2010). When female applicants meet sexist interviewers: The costs of being a target of benevolent sexism. *Sex Roles, 62,* 481–493.

Gneezy, U. (2005). Deception: The role of consequences. *American Economic Review, 95,* 384–394.

Gray, B. (1994). The gender-based foundations of negotiation theory. In R. J. Lewicki, B. H. Sheppard, & R. Bies (Eds.), *Research on negotiation in organizations* (Vol. 4, pp. 3–36). Greenwich, CT: JAI Press.

Greenberg, D., Ladge, J., & Clair, J. (2009). Negotiating pregnancy at work: Public and private conflicts. *Negotiation and Conflict Management Research, 2,* 42–56.

Haselhuhn, M. P., & Mellers, B. A. (2005). Emotions and cooperation in economic games. *Cognitive Brain Research, 23*(1), 24–33.

Haselhuhn, M. P., & Wong, E. M. (in press). Bad to the bone: Facial structure predicts unethical behaviour. *Proceedings of the Royal Society B: Biological Sciences.*

Heilman, M. E., & Okimoto, T. G. (2007). Why are women penalized success at male tasks? The implied communality deficit. *Journal of Applied Psychology, 92,* 81–92.

Kolb. D. M., & Coolidge, G. C. (1991). Her place at the table: A consideration of gender issues in negotiation. In J. W. Breslin & J. Z. Rubin (Eds.), *Negotiation theory and practice* (pp. 261–277). Cambridge, MA: PON Books.

Kolb, D. M., & McGinn, K. (2009). Beyond gender and negotiation to gendered negotiations. *Negotiation and Conflict Management Research, 2*(1), 1–16.

Kray, L. J. (2007). Leading through negotiation: Harnessing the power of gender stereotypes. *California Management Review, 50,* 159–173.

Kray, L. J. (2012). *Gender discrimination in negotiators' ethical decision making.* Unpublished manuscript. University of California, Berkeley.

Kray, L. J., Galinsky, A. D., & Thompson, L. (2002). Reversing the gender gap in negotiations: An exploration of stereotype regeneration. *Organizational Behavior and Human Decision Processes, 87,* 386–410.

Kray, L. J., & Gelfand, M. (2009). Relief versus regret: The impact of gender and negotiating norm ambiguity on reactions to having one's first offer accepted. *Social Cognition, 27,* 414–432.

Kray, L. J., & Haselhuhn, M. P. (2007). Implicit negotiation beliefs and performance: Longitudinal and experimental evidence. *Journal of Personality and Social Psychology, 93,* 49–64.

Kray, L. J., & Haselhuhn, M. P. (2009). What it takes to succeed: An examination of the relationship between negotiators' implicit beliefs and performance. In C. L. Hoyt, G. R. Goethals, & D. R. Forsyth (Eds.), *Leadership at the crossroads: Leadership and psychology* (pp. 213–229). Westport, CT: Praeger.

Kray, L. J., Haselhuhn, M. P., & Schweitzer, M. E. (2012). *Male pragmatism in negotitators' ethical reasoning.* Unpublished manuscript. University of California, Berkeley.

Kray, L. J., & Locke, C. (2012). *Women negotiators' interpersonal styles: Economic versus social outcomes at the bargaining table.* Unpublished manuscript. University of California, Berkeley.

Kray, L. J., Locke, C., & Haselhuhn, M. P. (2010). In the words of Larry Summers: Gender stereotypes and implicit beliefs in negotiations. In A. A. Stanton, M. Day, & I. Welpe (Eds.), *Neuroeconomics and the firm* (pp. 101–115). Northampton, MA: Edward Elgar Publishing.

Kray, L. J., Reb, J., Galinsky, A., & Thompson, L. (2004). Stereotype reactance at the bargaining table: The effect of stereotype activation and power on claiming and creating value. *Personality and Social Psychology Bulletin, 30,* 399–411.

Kray, L. J., & Shirako, A. (in press). Stereotype threat in organizations: Its scope, triggers, and possible interventions. In M. Inzlicht & T. Schmader (Eds.), *Stereotype threat: Theory, process, and application.* New York: Oxford University Press.

Kray, L. J., & Thompson, L. (2005). Gender stereotypes and negotiation performance: A review of theory and research. *Research in Organizational Behavior Series, 26,* 103–182.

Kray, L. J., Thompson, L, & Galinsky, A. (2001). Battle of the sexes: Gender stereotype confirmation and reactance in negotiations. *Journal of Personality and Social Psychology, 80,* 942–958.

Lammers, J., Stepel, D. A., & Galinsky, A. D. (2010). Power increases hypocrisy: Moralizing in reasoning, immorality in behavior. *Psychological Science, 21,* 737–744.

Lax, D. A., & J. K. Sebenius. 1986. *The manager as negotiator: Bargaining for cooperation and competitive gain.* New York: Free Press.

Lewicki, R. J., & Robinson, R. (1998). Ethical and unethical bargaining tactics: An empirical study. *Journal of Business Ethics, 17,* 665–682.

McGinn, K. L. (2006), Relationships and negotiations in context. In L. Thompson's (Ed.) *Negotiation theory and research* (pp. 129–144). New York: Psychology Press.

Mellers, B. A., Haselhuhn, M. P., Tetlock, P. E., Silva, J., & Isen, A. M. (2010). Predicting behavior in economic games by looking through the eyes of the players. *Journal of Experimental Psychology: General, 139,* 743–755.

Miles, E. W., & Clenney, E. F. (2010). Gender differences in negotiation: A status characteristics theory view. *Negotiation and Conflict Management Research, 3,* 130–144.

Moss-Racusin, C. A., Phelan, J. E., & Rudman, L. A. (2010). When men break the gender rules: Status incongruity and backlash against modest men. *Psychology of Men and Masculinity, 11,* 140–151.

Neale, M. A., & Bazerman, M. H. (1991). *Cognition and rationality in negotiation.* New York: Free Press.

O'Connor, K. M., & Carnevale, P. J. (1997). A nasty but effective negotiation strategy: Misrepresentation of a common-value issue. *Personality and Social Psychology Bulletin, 23,* 504–575.

Prentice, D. A., & Carranza, E. (2002). What women and men should be, shouldn't be, are allowed to be, and don't have to be: The contents of prescriptive gender stereotypes. *Psychology of Women Quarterly, 26,* 269–281.

Purdie-Vaughns, V., Steele, C. M., Davies, P. G., Ditlmann, R., & Crosby, J. R. (2008). Social identity contingencies: How diversity cues signal threat or safety for African Americans in mainstream institutions. *Journal of Personality and Social Psychology, 94,* 615–630.

Richard, R., van der Pligt, J., & de Vries, N. (1996). Anticipated regret and time perspective: Changing sexual risk-taking behavior. *Journal of Behavioral Decision Making, 9,* 185–199.

Rubin, J. Z., & Brown, B. R. (1975). *The social psychology of bargaining and negotiation.* New York: Academic Press.

Rudman, L. A. (1998). Self-promotion as a risk factor for women: The costs and benefits of counterstereotypical impression management. *Journal of Personality and Social Psychology, 74*, 629–645.

Rudman, L. A., Ashmore, R. D., & Gary, M. L. (2001). Unlearning automatic biases: The malleability of implicit prejudice and stereotypes. *Journal of Personality and Social Psychology, 81*, 856–868.

Rudman, L. A., & Glick, P. (1999). Feminized management and backlash toward agentic women: The hidden costs to women of a kinder, gentler image of middle-managers. *Journal of Personality and Social Psychology, 77*, 1004–1010.

Sanfey, A. G., Rilling, J. K., Aronson, J. A., Nystrom, L. E., & Cohen, J. D. (2003). The neural basis of economic decision-making in the ultimatum game. *Science, 300*, 1755–1758.

Schmader, T., Johns, M., & Forbes, C. (2008). An integrated process model of stereotype threat effects on performance. *Psychological Review, 115*, 336–356.

Schwarz, N., & Clore, G. L. (1983). Mood, misattribution, and judgments of well-being: Informative and directive functions of affective states. *Journal of Personality and Social Psychology, 45*, 513–523.

Schweitzer, M. (2001). Deception in negotiations. In S. Hoch & H. Kunreuther (Eds.), *Wharton on making decisions* (pp. 187–200). New York: Wiley.

Schweitzer, M. E., Ordóñez, L., & Douma, B. (2004). Goal setting as a motivator of unethical behavior. *Academy of Management Journal, 47*, 422–432.

Seidel, M. L., Polzer, J. T., & Stewart, K. J. (2000). Friends in high places: The effects of social networks on discrimination in salary negotiations. *Administrative Science Quarterly, 45*(1), 1–24.

Small, D. A., Gelfand, M. Babcock, L., & Gettman, H. 2007. Who goes to the bargaining table? The influence of gender and framing on the initiation of negotiation. *Journal of Personality and Social Psychology, 93*, 600–613.

Spencer, S. J., Steele, C. M., & Quinn, D. M. (1999). Stereotype threat and women's math performance. *Journal of Experimental Social Psychology, 35*, 4–28.

Steele, C. M. (1997). A threat in the air: How stereotypes shape intellectual ability and performance. *American Psychologist, 52*, 613–629.

Steele, C. M., & Aronson, J. (1995). Stereotype threat and the intellectual test performance of African-Americans. *Journal of Personality and Social Psychology, 69*, 797–811.

Stirrat, M., & Perrett, D. I. (2010). Valid facial cues to cooperation and trust: Male facial width and trustworthiness. *Psychological Science, 21*, 349–354.

Stulmacher, A. F., & Walters, A. E. (1999). Gender differences in negotiation outcomes: A meta-analysis. *Personnel Psychology, 52*, 653–677.

Thompson, L. (1990). Negotiation behavior and outcomes: Empirical evidence and theoretical issues. *Psychological Bulletin, 108*, 515–532.

U.S. women in business. (2009). Retrieved August 15, 2009, from http://www.catalyst.org/publication/132/us-women-in-business

Vandello, J. A., Bosson, J. K., Cohen, D., Burnaford, R. M., & Weaver, J. R. (2008). Precarious manhood. *Journal of Personality and Social Psychology, 95*, 1325–1339.

Van Kleef, G. A., & De Dreu, C. K. W. (2010). Longer-term consequences of anger expression in negotiation: Retaliation or spillover? *Journal of Experimental Social Psychology, 46*, 753–760.

Van Lange, P. (1999). The pursuit of joint outcomes and equality in outcomes: An integrative model of social value orientation. *Journal of Personality and Social Psychology, 77*, 337–349.

Walters, A. E., Stuhlmacher, A. F., & Meyer, L. L. (1998). Gender and negotiator competitiveness: A meta-analysis. *Organizational Behavior and Human Decision Processes, 76,* 1–29.

Walton, G. M., & Cohen, G. L. (2003). Stereotype lift. *Journal of Experimental Social Psychology, 39,* 456–467.

Watson, C. (1994). Gender versus power as a predictor of negotiation behavior and outcomes. *Negotiation Journal, 10,* 117–127.

Weston, E. M., Friday, A. E., & Liò, P. (2007). Biometric evidence that sexual selection has shaped the hominin face. *PLoS ONE, 2,* e710.

Williams, J. E., & Best, D. L. (1982). *Measuring sex stereotypes: A thirty nation study.* Berkeley, CA: Sage.

Section 5

Negotiators as Organizational Managers in the 21st Century

12

From Individual Competence to Organizational Capability: Leveraging Insights From Organizational Learning to Improve Negotiated Results in the 21st Century Enterprise

Jonathan Hughes, Sara Parker Enlow,
Jessica Siegel, and Jeff Weiss

INTRODUCTION

Twenty-first century organizations are increasingly virtual and networked. The average Fortune 500 firm derives approximately one third of its revenue and market capitalization from alliances with other companies (deMan, Duysters, & Neyens, 2009; Margulis & Pekar, 2001). Firms also continue to outsource more and more of their operations—from research and development (R&D), to product design, to manufacturing, as well as internal management infrastructure (e.g., information technology [IT], human resource [HR], finance). In fact, the average company currently spends one half of every dollar in revenue with external suppliers (Minahan & Vigoroso, 2002).

Organizations today are tied to one another by a series of contracts that they must negotiate and renegotiate as they strive to innovate and adapt to rapid change. Not only have negotiations between and among organizations become more pervasive, but also they have become more complex. While research on negotiations has generated useful insights about how to get better results in a *particular* negotiation, little guidance exists for today's managers about how best to maximize negotiated outcomes across the thousands of negotiations they conduct and oversee. The purpose of this chapter is to do just that. As we argue, we believe that organizational learning[1] is key to addressing this challenge. Put simply, to achieve better results across many negotiations, managers need to put in place a means to capture knowledge from negotiations, translate that knowledge into an organized set of useful lessons, and disseminate those lessons in a way that enables the organization to learn from one negotiation to the next.

We begin with a brief discussion of organizational learning and explain why investment in organizational learning is particularly important in the context of 21st century negotiations. Leveraging insights from theories of organizational learning, we then offer a framework to guide managers in understanding which organizational learning methods are best suited for different types of negotiations. Borrowing a common managerial practice—segmentation—we extend our framework to provide guidance regarding which types of negotiations warrant more or less investment in organizational learning. We also describe a number of challenges to enabling organizational learning regarding negotiation in 21st century organizations and offer some suggestions for future research to help organizations address those challenges.

WHY ORGANIZATIONAL LEARNING IS IMPORTANT WITH RESPECT TO NEGOTIATION

Negotiations are pervasive in today's organizations. Companies outsource a wide variety of business functions (Barthelemy & Adsit, 2003; Zhu, Hsu, & Lillie, 2001) and rely on an ever-broader network of external suppliers not only for raw materials, but also for inputs that require a high degree of intellectual property, including complex engineered components and R&D and design services. Companies also increasingly rely on alliance and channel partners to develop, market, sell, and distribute goods and services jointly (Dittrich, Duysters, & deMan, 2007; Gomez-Casseres, 1996; Hughes & Weiss, 2007). These complex external relationships require negotiations both at their inception and on an ongoing basis as agreements are implemented after a contract is signed. Changing market conditions often require firm negotiators to revisit contract pricing, volume, and terms (as underscored by the recent financial crisis), and different interpretations of contractual terms (which often become apparent only as agreements are implemented) likewise require business partners to negotiate resolution of multiple issues after initial contract execution.

While any single negotiation may not involve significant value for an organization, the cumulative effect of these negotiations can be tremendous. Moreover, many agreements are implemented by individuals who did not participate in initial contract negotiations. Given an increasingly mobile workforce (e.g., Broschak, 2004; Parker, Wall, & Cordery, 2001), different individuals will be involved in the negotiation of a firm's agreements with its customers, suppliers, and alliance partners from year to year. This context of changing negotiation agents, along with an increasing volume of negotiations with enormous value at stake, have converged to make the need to leverage organizational learning in the service of negotiations an imperative for 21st century organizations.

By *organizational learning*, we refer to Kim's (1993) definition: "increasing an organization's capacity to take effective action" (p. 43). Kim argued that organizational learning is dependent on, but distinct from, individual learning. He wrote, "The heart of organizational learning [is] the process through which individual learning becomes embedded in an organization's memory and structure" (p. 37). Organizational learning refers to the systems organizations put into place to capture individual learning and make that learning a part of the organization's memory so that others may take more effective action based on that learning. Although learning does originate at the individual level, it becomes organizational learning when the organization itself acquires knowledge beyond that of its individual members (Hedberg, 1981; Huber, 1991). Researchers have recognized that an organization that can learn and adapt has a competitive advantage compared to organizations that cannot use learned knowledge to meet new environmental demands (Argote & Ingram, 2000; Spender & Grant, 1996).

While negotiation success is, in part, a function of individual negotiator skill, it is also a function of the systems in place within an organization, such as the ways negotiators are managed (including by means of the instructions they receive and the incentives to which they are subject), the processes by which contracts are reviewed and approved, and so on (Ertel, 1999; Movius & Susskind, 2009). Consider the example of pharmaceutical and lab assay testing company Aventis. Because licensing arrangements and alliance partnerships were becoming increasingly important to the organization's success, the company put in place a systematic negotiation process and set of tools for negotiators of these arrangements. Part of the program was a negotiation review process that required facilitated debriefs at the end of each high-value negotiation. Negotiation teams extracted lessons from their experiences so that their learning could be leveraged by others at Aventis in future negotiations. The teams not only noted helpful strategies and tactics for negotiating with counterparts but also captured important advice for management about ways they could enable teams to be more effective and efficient in the future (for example, by providing expedited approval processes, access to certain expertise, etc.).

There are several specific characteristics of modern negotiations that necessitate an *organizational* (vs. individual) approach to negotiations. First, many negotiations today have a strong "ripple effect"—one negotiated outcome creates expectations and sets precedent for future negotiations, both with the same party and with others.[2] Negotiation precedent or ripple effects have become increasingly significant due to the continued evolution of information technology, which facilitates efficient spread of information, reduces information search costs, and thus significantly increases market, price, and cost transparency (Granados, Gupta, & Kauffman, 2005; Sinha, 2000). Today, the Internet provides access to vast amounts of data about prices, costs, and negotiated terms and conditions. Firms have built businesses around proprietary databases of information about various cost structures and about negotiated transactions (Kimball, 2010). Buyers of various goods and services can communicate with one another quickly and efficiently. As a result, negotiated outcomes can quickly become known in the marketplace; these outcomes tend to have significant anchoring effects and thus set a precedent for other negotiations. For example, the price and terms a salesperson agrees with a customer have an impact on the expectations of the same customer in future negotiations with that salesperson. Moreover, they are also likely to influence the expectations of other individuals from the same customer company when they negotiate with other salespeople from that company. In many cases, that single negotiated outcome, if and as knowledge about it becomes known, will also affect the expectations of other customers in the same market.

When negotiations are "precedent intense" (that is, the negotiated outcome creates significant expectations and precedents for future negotiations), organizational learning enables organizations to benefit from these effects rather than be harmed by them. For example, with effective capture and leverage of knowledge, a purchasing manager will know when a supplier has agreed to better terms or a more favorable price with another division in his or her company and can demand similar pricing and terms from that supplier.

A second characteristic of modern negotiations that makes organizational learning important is that only a relatively small percentage of today's interfirm negotiations conclude in any meaningful sense at contract signing—in many of today's negotiations, the value of the negotiation is not realized until implementation of the agreement (Ertel, 2004; Ertel & Gordon, 2007). In particular, outsourcing contracts and strategic alliance contracts are two types of increasingly common business arrangements for which contract implementation typically happens over the course of multiple years (Gartner Group, 2003; IBM, 2007; Schaffhauser, 2006). During multiyear contract implementations, employees turn over, taking with them important knowledge about the deal and their counterparties. In addition, issues often arise (such as new government regulations, changes in market and competitive conditions, unforeseen design or manufacturing issues, or evolution or revolution in technology) that may result in problems or opportunities that were impossible to anticipate or preemptively address during the initial negotiations, even with contingent agreements. Therefore, more negotiations (both formal and informal) are required to adapt the agreement to changing circumstances over time.

Moreover, the individuals and teams responsible for implementing these long-term agreements are rarely those who contracted for them in the first place (see Chapter 13, this volume). For example, while two companies' business development teams may have negotiated an alliance between their firms, individuals from sales and marketing teams or product development groups on each side might be the ones who actually need to work together to implement the arrangement. Similarly, a chief procurement officer or senior commodity manager might negotiate a strategic supply arrangement, but project managers and engineers might be the ones who need to work on a day-to-day basis with staff from the supplier to implement the contract. Frequently, the various individuals charged with implementation of negotiated agreements are not formal negotiators, and they are rarely trained in effective negotiation practices and skills (Corporate Leadership Council, 2004; Huber, 2004; Willcocks & Griffiths, 2010). They often have had little knowledge of, or involvement in, the negotiation of the contractual arrangement under which they must operate. Without effective organizational learning—which enables the transfer of knowledge about the contract and lessons from negotiations with the other side—those responsible for implementation waste precious time renegotiating (often ineffectively) issues that may have already been resolved during the contracting stage.

A third and final characteristic of today's negotiations that makes organizational learning important is that they are conducted by an increasingly mobile workforce.[3] Organizations that put in place mechanisms to capture knowledge from past negotiations and apply them to future negotiations with the same or different counterparties (even as the individuals conducting those negotiations change) enable their employee negotiators to be more productive and efficient, thus conserving scarce organizational time and staff resources, and achieve consistently better results (Kesting & Smolinski, 2007).

In all of these circumstances—precedent-intense negotiations, long-term implementations, and changing negotiation agents—the efficiency or inefficiency of the negotiation process, as well as the value of negotiated outcomes, are likely to be significantly affected by the process and outcomes of *prior* negotiations. Organizations that are able to capture and apply relevant knowledge and learning from one negotiation to others are thus able to negotiate transactions more efficiently and achieve more favorable outcomes.

Although there has been a great deal of progress in the study of negotiations over the past few decades, many of these emerging issues and challenges have not been adequately addressed by the extant literature. For example, although 21st century interfirm negotiations often involve repeat transactions between the same parties, much of the research examining negotiations has focused on one-time transactions between negotiators (Mannix, Tinsley, & Bazerman, 1995; Neale & Northcraft, 1991). This research has provided useful insights about the dynamics involved in dyadic negotiations, such as individual differences in negotiating behavior (e.g., Elfenbein, Curhan, Eisenkraft, Shirako, & Baccaro, 2008; Stuhlmacher & Walters, 1999), anchoring and first offers (e.g., Galinsky & Mussweiler, 2001), and the role of emotions (e.g., Van Kleef, De Dreu, & Manstead, 2004). However, the bulk of this literature examines experimental dyads engaging in a one-time negotiation (see Mannix et al., 1995) with little background, context, or relationship history. There is almost never a simulation of future interactions (actual or potential) between the parties. Some research in the negotiations literature has begun to address the issue of repeat transactions or recurring negotiation relationships (Greenhalgh & Chapman, 1998; Sheppard, 1995; Sheppard & Tuchinsky, 1996). However, we are unaware of research to date that effectively simulates or explores the challenges inherent in the kinds of interfirm negotiations that are increasingly common and with which today's managers must contend.

Maximizing the overall value of the myriad negotiations undertaken within organizations today requires managers to make decisions about how to allocate limited firm resources optimally, such as negotiator time, specific negotiation expertise, and management oversight time. The role of management in ensuring optimal allocation of limited firm resources has been examined (e.g., Bourgeois, 1980), but there is no formal treatment in the negotiation literature regarding how a firm's managers should best allocate limited resources across many negotiations to achieve globally optimal outcomes for the firm. Nor is there any research on how to make efficient trade-offs between achieving an optimal negotiated outcome on *a specific transaction* and achieving optimal results across *multiple negotiated transactions*.

Fortunately, theories of organizational learning offer a multitude of insights that can be directly applied to the challenge of maximizing negotiation effectiveness at an organizational level. In fact, the field of organizational learning grew from a need to address some of the very challenges we have articulated. These theories describe how organizations can draw lessons from their experiences and information from their environment to take more efficient and effective action in a complex, dynamic world where resources are limited, and useful knowledge tends to leave the organization through staff turnover. As Peter Senge (2006) wrote:

> As the world becomes more interconnected and business becomes more complex and dynamic, work must become more "learningful." It is no longer sufficient to have one person learning for the organization, … It's just not possible any longer to "figure it out" from the top, … The organizations that will truly excel in the future will be [those] that discover how to tap people's commitment and capacity to learn at *all* levels of the organization. (p. 4)

This certainly rings true with respect to negotiation today. Given the vast number of negotiations that take place at all levels of today's organizations and the characteristics of many modern negotiations discussed, an organizational approach to negotiation learning (vs. relying on a few smart negotiators) is critical.

There are many ways organizations can learn; centers of excellence, after-action reviews, repositories of documented lessons, and changes to standard operating procedures are but a few means of learning and sharing knowledge that have been explored extensively in the organizational learning literature (e.g., Carley, 1992; Frost, Birkinshaw, & Ensign, 2002; Garvin, Edmondson, & Gino, 2008; Levitt & March, 1988; Moore & Birkinshaw, 1998; Zack, 1999). For the manager trying to choose among these various methods and others, theories of organizational learning provide some insights concerning which types of learning methods will be most efficacious in different situations based on (a) the type of knowledge being transferred (tacit or explicit) and (b) the frequency of the task (how routine or variable it is) (e.g., Dixon, 2000; Hansen, Nohria, & Tierney, 1999; Nonaka & Takeuchi, 1995).

In the following, we explore these organizational learning insights and derive a framework that provides guidance to managers regarding how best to enable organizational learning regarding different types of negotiations. We then discuss how to prioritize organizational learning investments across different types of negotiations based on the concept of segmentation, as used in the marketing (e.g., Claycamp & Massey, 1968; Reich, Gordon, & Edwards, 1973) and supply chain management literatures (e.g., Dyer, Cho, & Chu, 1998), and describe a number of specific organizational learning methods that are suited to different types of negotiations.

STRATEGIES FOR ENABLING ORGANIZATIONAL LEARNING REGARDING NEGOTIATION

Type of Knowledge and Negotiation Complexity

Organizational Learning Insight 1: Distinguish Between Tacit and Explicit Knowledge

Two types of knowledge—tacit and explicit—have been explored extensively in the literature on organizational learning (e.g., Grant, 1996; Kogut

& Zander, 1992; Nonaka & Takeuchi, 1995; Ryle, 1984; Polanyi, 1966), and a fundamental insight from theories of organizational learning is to distinguish between these two types of knowledge. Tacit knowledge is a "feeling in the fingertips" (Stewart, 2001). Nonaka (1991) wrote that tacit knowledge refers to knowledge that cannot be easily expressed; it is

> ... rooted in action and in an individual's commitment to a specific context—a craft or profession, a particular technology or product market, or the activities of a work group or team ... [it] consists partly of technical skills—the kind of informal, hard-to-pin-down skills captured in the term "know-how." (p. 98)

At the other end of the spectrum is explicit knowledge—knowledge that is relatively easy to document, explain, and transfer. In other words, explicit knowledge "can be laid out in procedures, steps and standards ... [or] translated into checklists and specifications" (Dixon, 2000).

Application to Negotiations

To some degree, all negotiations involve both tacit and explicit knowledge. For example, sales teams need to understand the specifications of their products, delivery timelines, and pricing models (explicit knowledge); they also need to know when is just the right moment to call on a customer, what combination of features to highlight to which customers, when to compromise (and when not to), and when to move to closing (tacit knowledge). That said, depending on the situation, negotiation success is sometimes more reliant on explicit knowledge and other times more reliant on tacit knowledge. We argue that this is a function of the negotiation's complexity—the more complex the negotiation, the greater the need to leverage and rely on tacit knowledge; the more straightforward the negotiation, the greater the need to rely on explicit knowledge. This notion was supported by Watkins and Rosen (2000), who argued that, in less-complex negotiations, more complete information is available and therefore "most of what you need to know can be learned in advance" (that is, prior to "at-the-table" negotiations) (p. 11). In contrast, they argued that the more a negotiation is complex, uncertain, or ambiguous, the more negotiators must learn as they negotiate, in incremental steps through interactions with their counterparts (as less information is available prior to at-the-table negotiations).

While the notion of negotiation complexity has received little formal definition in the literature, there is ample treatment, and a fair degree of consensus, on a number of key variables that could reasonably be deployed, collectively, to define negotiation complexity. These include the number of parties (firms) involved; the number of *agents* representing those firms (each with their own agendas, styles, etc.) who are involved; the degree to which each party (firm) has heterogeneous and perhaps conflicting interests; the degree of mutual trust and understanding between or among parties or specific negotiators (a function in part of their reputations); the number of issues to be negotiated and the degree of interconnectedness among them; the availability of precedents or marketplace standards to guide negotiators in resolving issues to be negotiated; ZOPA (zone of possible agreement) size;[4] and balance of power (Bazerman & Neale, 1992; Fisher, Ury, & Patton, 1991; Raiffa, 1982).

We contend that more complex negotiations call for greater reliance on tacit knowledge. The intricacies of these negotiations are difficult to articulate in writing and rarely will organizations encounter exactly the same combination of complexities in different negotiations. Complex negotiations require significant creativity and individualized strategies and thus rely heavily on tacit knowledge of negotiators. Conversely, more straightforward negotiations involve fewer variables; strategies should be easier to define, document, and repeat. The less complex the negotiation, the less there is a need for creativity, and the more it makes sense to repeat what worked well previously. Hence, if the negotiation is more straightforward (less complex), the more useful is explicit knowledge.

Organizational Learning Insight 2: Employ Different Means for Sharing Tacit and Explicit Knowledge

Tacit and explicit knowledge call for different means of knowledge sharing. As Stewart wrote (2001, p. 124): "Almost all explicit knowledge belongs in the domain of structural capital ... documents, databases ... procedures, etc." Explicit knowledge is thus highly scalable—it can be used hundreds or thousands of times by many people in different locations, across different contexts. Hansen and colleagues (1999) called this a "codification" approach—one of storing knowledge and connecting people to relevant documents. They observed management consulting firms Ernst & Young and Andersen Consulting using such an approach—investing in documenting knowledge, with the intention of reusing it many times on similar projects. Because it is so amenable to documentation, explicit knowledge can be efficiently shared in writing (e.g., in databases, templates, or formal procedures).

The codification approach stands in contrast to the "personalization" approach that Hansen and colleagues argued makes more sense when tacit knowledge is the focus. The best way to share tacit knowledge is to connect individuals with relevant experience (as tacit knowledge is so difficult to articulate in written form). They noted that consulting firms McKinsey & Company and Bain & Company have pursued a business strategy focused on providing creative, analytical, highly individualized advice, which called for a knowledge management strategy primarily designed to "develop networks for linking people so that tacit knowledge can be shared" (Hansen et al., 1999, p. 109). While tacit knowledge may not be easy to explain in words, it is often demonstrable (Stewart, 2001). When tacit knowledge is to be shared, the most effective approach involves connecting people who can demonstrate what they know, provide the context necessary to explain complex situations, and discuss the interplay of many variables.

These organizational learning insights and the previous discussion lead to two strategies for leveraging organizational learning about negotiations to increase negotiator effectiveness (and thereby improve negotiated outcomes):

1. For *complex* negotiations, managers should institute a *personalization* approach to organizational negotiation learning, focused on *connecting individuals* who have relevant experience and knowledge.
2. For more *straightforward* (less-complex) negotiations, managers should institute a *codification* approach to organizational negotiation learning, capturing knowledge in written form and making that (written) knowledge available to those who will later need it.

Frequency of the Task and Negotiation "Precedent Intensity"

Organizational Learning Insight 3: Employ Push Strategies for Routine Tasks and Pull Strategies for Novel Tasks

Organizational learning theory distinguishes between "push" and "pull" strategies of knowledge sharing. When an organization executes a push strategy, it deems certain knowledge useful and centrally distributes that knowledge to appropriate users, without their explicit request; knowledge is "pushed out" (via standard operating procedures, training, templates, and other job aids, etc.). To a user of the knowledge, it "appears automatically" without them needing to search for it (Dixon, 2000, p. 69). A pull strategy, however, requires individuals to seek the knowledge they need at the time they need it. Thus, this is a more decentralized approach. The individual user of the knowledge (rather than the organization) is the initiator—he or she actively looks for or requests the knowledge (e.g., by searching a database or other electronic repository or by consulting others within the organization).

A third insight from theories of organizational learning thus involves determining whether a push or a pull strategy of knowledge sharing is most appropriate based on the frequency of the need for that knowledge (Boh, 2007; Dixon, 2000). When tasks are more routine (in the sense that they are more frequently occurring), a push strategy for sharing knowledge is sensible (Brown & Hagel, 2005; Dixon, 2000; Hagel & Brown, 2008; Hidding & Catterall, 1998). Efficiency is the driver behind this strategy. Seeking knowledge requires effort (e.g., to formulate a question, determine where to look, to search and cull through information). The more organizations can make appropriate knowledge readily available (i.e., push it out) to those who need it for activities they conduct regularly, the more efficiently individuals can perform these tasks.

Conversely, tasks that are nonroutine (occurring less frequently) are more amenable to a pull strategy of knowledge sharing. A pull strategy is sensible for nonroutine tasks because humans' capability to process information is limited (Grise & Gallupe, 2000; Miller, 1978; Simon, 1960). Pushing knowledge out to people who need that knowledge infrequently (and may, in fact, not be sure when they will need it) can cause "information overload" (Edmunds & Morris, 2000). When too much unsolicited information is communicated, receivers cannot process it efficiently without higher levels of distraction, stress, and errors (Klapp, 1986). However, when knowledge is easily retrievable at the time it is needed, users can efficiently seek out important knowledge for tasks they undertake less frequently without becoming overloaded. Thus, a pull strategy is sensible when the task is infrequent or nonroutine.

Application to Negotiations

Many negotiations are "routine" in the sense that they are similar to previous negotiations and likely to be similar to future negotiations as well.

They might involve the same parties or similar issues. Most often, these negotiations have significant "precedent intensity" (they are likely to be affected by, and to affect, the outcomes of other negotiations). For example, one such negotiation might be the annual renewal of a supply contract. The price and terms agreed to this year are likely to have a significant impact on next year's contract negotiations, and while market or business changes might introduce some differences, the key issues are likely to be the same, and prior terms will almost certainly exert a strong anchoring effect (Richardson, 2007). Hence, this is a negotiation with a notable degree of precedent intensity. Pushing knowledge out for use in preparing for and conducting precedent-intense negotiations (e.g., through standard operating procedures and standard contract forms and term sheets) allows negotiators to apply previously generated solutions to current problems, thereby enabling them to achieve high-quality negotiated outcomes efficiently, with less investment required to plan and prepare (Kesting & Smolinski, 2007).

Such negotiations stand in contrast to negotiations for which precedential impacts are likely to be negligible. An example might include negotiation of the acquisition of a small company with unique technology or the negotiation of a licensing agreement with that company. While the value of the specific negotiation in question may be significant, such negotiations are likely to be relatively infrequent and outcomes determined more by situation-specific factors or ingrained marketplace standards (e.g., common ratios used to determine purchase price for company acquisitions, such as N times firm revenue). For these types of nonroutine, infrequent negotiations, appropriate knowledge and information should be accessible on an as-needed basis (e.g., in searchable databases, through access to experts).

The organizational learning insight mentioned and this discussion leads us to the following strategies:

1. For negotiations with *strong precedent intensity*, managers should use a *push* organizational learning strategy, distributing relevant knowledge to negotiators without their having to request it.
2. For negotiations with *weak precedent intensity*, managers should use a *pull* organizational learning strategy, making relevant knowledge available on demand, when negotiators seek it.

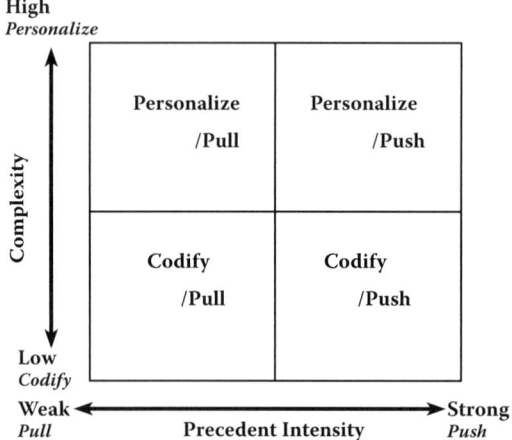

FIGURE 12.1
Enabling organizational learning in different types of negotiations.

These two variables—complexity (or type of knowledge) and precedent intensity (or frequency of the task)—combine to form a model that provides guidance regarding which organizational learning methods are most appropriate for different types of negotiations (see Figure 12.1).

While assessing a negotiation's complexity and precedent intensity tells us something about *how* best to enable organizational learning regarding that type of negotiation (through codification or personalization, push or pull), it does not help us identify which negotiations warrant more or less *investment* in organizational learning effort. Organizational learning regarding negotiation—including capturing negotiation experiences, interpreting them, and then translating resultant insights into new (more effective) actions—requires effort and investment (e.g., financial investments in knowledge management tools, negotiator time to review negotiations and draw lessons from them, negotiator time to locate others and draw on their experiences as they prepare for and conduct negotiations). While insights from organizational learning provide useful guidance about which means of sharing knowledge are more and less effective for different types of negotiations, they offer little help to managers who need to decide where and how to focus limited time and resources to maximize the returns their firm realizes across hundreds or thousands of negotiations. To address this increasingly pressing question, we must consider an additional important variable—negotiation value.

Negotiation Value

Logically, negotiations that involve more value warrant greater investment in learning. However, it is a nontrivial issue to assess the value at stake in any individual negotiation. A simple proxy might be the NPV (net present value) of the total financial value defined in the contract. This, however, is known only after the contract is negotiated and is therefore of limited utility in determining what degree of investment to make in accessing organizational learning regarding negotiation (e.g., as one prepares or conducts the negotiation). Nonetheless, in many cases, a first-order task of negotiation planning can be to estimate the likely total financial value of the agreement that may result. In many firms, this is regularly done in both sales and purchasing negotiations by reviewing the financial value of the last contract with a given counterparty or reviewing agreements with other counterparties that are deemed similar. While imperfect, such initial preparation is very low cost (assuming some system exists to store and retrieve prior contracts) and is likely to provide pragmatically useful guidance about the approximate value of the contract to be negotiated and thus the approximate degree of (further) effort warranted in accessing and using organizational learning in that negotiation.

However, the *financial* value of an *agreement* may not be an accurate reflection of the actual value of that negotiation. For example, consider a sourcing negotiation with a supplier of highly technical components for incorporation into a company's flagship product. It may be that the total cost of these components is relatively small, relative to the company's other purchases. However, these components may be crucial to product performance and provide marketplace differentiation for the company's most important products, which generate a majority of the firm's revenue. As this example illustrates, the concept of "revenue or financial value *at risk*" may be a better way to conceptualize the value of certain negotiations, although significant work would need to be done to enable rigorous definition and calculation of this concept.

In addition, because of the precedent intensity of many 21st century negotiations, the value of any given agreement may not reflect the incremental value that may be added or lost in *other* negotiations as a result of precedent effects. For example, consider the salesperson who grants a discount to a customer. While that particular negotiation may involve relatively little value (revenue), in a transparent marketplace, other customers are likely to learn of the discount and demand similar price concessions (both from the same salesperson and from the salesperson's colleagues). Multiplied over many other customers, the value impacted by the precedent this negotiation set may be significantly larger than the value of the initial discount. We refer to the value (positive or negative) of precedential impacts such as these as the "valence value" of a negotiation.

This discussion leads to our next strategy:

> To *prioritize* organizational learning efforts, focus most on negotiations that are of *high value* or those that have *high valence value*.

A MODEL FOR SEGMENTING NEGOTIATIONS

Although these three criteria—value, complexity, and precedential effect—may sometimes be positively correlated with one another (e.g., high-value negotiations may often be complex as well), they are nonetheless causally independent. Together, they form a model that can be used to categorize, or segment, different types of negotiations (see Figure 12.2).

The concept of segmenting interfirm business relationships is a well-established managerial practice (particularly with respect to customer relationships and increasingly with respect to supplier and alliance relationships)

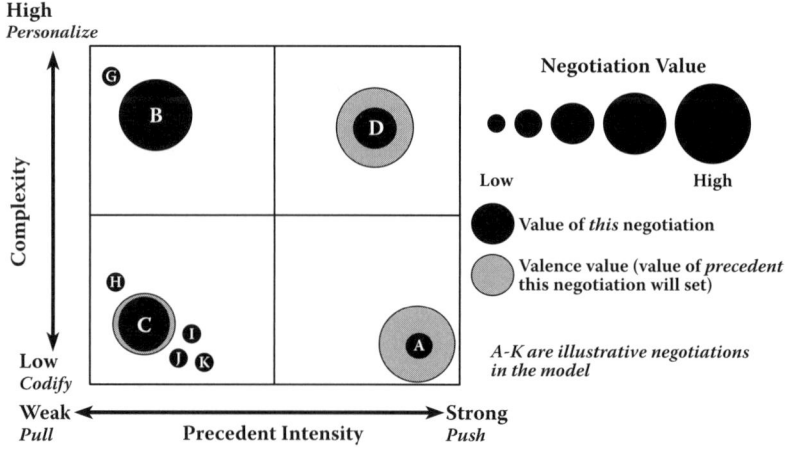

FIGURE 12.2
A model for segmenting negotiations.

and a topic that has been extensively explored in the popular business literature and to some extent in the academic management literature (Bensaou, 1999; Dyer et al., 1998; Svensson, 2004). The purpose of segmentation is to use a set of standard variables to group different members of a population (e.g., customers, suppliers) into subsets such that limited resources can be optimally allocated to manage relationships and so appropriate relationship management strategies can be employed. For example, according to accepted sales and marketing theory and practice, customers can be grouped into segments that respond in the same way to a particular mix of marketing messages and vehicles (Claycamp & Massey, 1968; Reich et al., 1973). In the supply chain management world, suppliers can be grouped into segments that are best suited to different relationship management approaches, such as "arm's-length" or "partner" models (Dyer et al., 1998).

Segmentation helps managers determine the optimal allocation of scarce resources and enables them to define appropriate strategies and operating procedures to enable effective and efficient execution of important business activities. While we believe segmentation of negotiations would help meet the same goals,[5] we are not aware of any treatment of this topic in the academic literature.

By way of illustration, Circles A through K denote different examples of negotiations in Figure 12.2. Figure 12.2 shows two separate dimensions—complexity on the *y*-axis and precedent intensity on the *x*-axis—creating four different quadrants into which negotiations may be classified. Each circle within the diagram represents a specific (illustrative) negotiation, and the size of the circle indicates the value of the negotiation (in two ways: the fully shaded circle represents the value of the current negotiation, and the patterned circle represents the value of the precedent set by the negotiation). As an example of how to interpret the figure, consider Negotiation A. Negotiation A is placed low on the complexity continuum (therefore, it is a relatively straightforward negotiation). The value of Negotiation A itself is relatively small (as evidenced by the small, fully shaded circle), but it is located high on the precedential intensity continuum and has high valence value (as indicated by the relatively large patterned circle), meaning that the precedent this negotiation sets will have a strong impact on later negotiations. In the following, we discuss key attributes of these illustrative negotiations and one or two specific, practical learning mechanisms appropriate for each of the four types of negotiations (represented by the four quadrants) in the model.

Negotiation Context: Low Complexity/Strong Precedent Intensity—Organizational Negotiation Learning Strategy: Codify, Push

As described, Negotiation A in the model is a relatively low-value negotiation that is not particularly complex but has very strong precedential intensity. This negotiation might be one between a health insurance company and a physician's practice, for which the reimbursement terms agreed to in this negotiation are likely to be discovered by many other network health care providers. Alternatively, this could be a negotiation between a supplier and customer with a relationship that spans multiple goods and services, across multiple business units. While the value at stake in a particular negotiation may be small, the terms agreed to in that negotiation might set a powerful precedent for future negotiations (of much greater value) between the same two organizations over issues such as ownership of intellectual property, service-level guarantees, and indemnification. Given its high valence value, this negotiation warrants some attention from an organizational learning perspective (as argued previously, negotiations involving greater value merit more investment in learning).

In addition, this negotiation's low complexity indicates the appropriateness of a codification (vs. personalization) approach to sharing knowledge (Strategy 2). Its precedent intensity suggests that a push (vs. pull) strategy is likely to be most efficient and effective (Strategy 3). One useful means for capturing and pushing out explicit negotiation knowledge is through contract templates with standard terms and conditions that cover large numbers of similar negotiations. While we are not aware of any discussion in the negotiation literature about the use of standard contracts as a means for learning, the concept is consistent with ideas about the role of documented procedures as a vehicle for organizational learning (e.g., Miner & Mezias, 1996).

Many organizations use standard contract templates, and a few—including one major software company—have worked to make such templates even more helpful by adding annotated language that negotiators can use to (a) explain legal contract terms in a way that is easy to understand and clearly connected to important business objectives, (b) allay counterparty concerns, and (c) and persuade external counterparts of the reasonableness of the firm's negotiating positions.[6] This annotated language is a codified form of knowledge that negotiators can leverage during fairly routine negotiations they undertake regularly. As an added benefit, this software company has found that, as negotiators use such language with different counterparts, they are able to hone the arguments in different ways to suit the communication needs of different counterparties (e.g., negotiators might need to shape the argument differently for attorney counterparts than for line-of-business counterparts). These different "spins" on the annotated language can be captured and shared with the company's other negotiators, furthering the organization's learning.

A primary risk of codifying standard contract terms and conditions is inflexibility and an inability to adapt to change effectively (Kesting & Smolinski, 2007). The more effort organizations put into perfecting their standard contracts, the more risk there is of dysfunctional rigidity and hence the less effective such terms are likely to be over time as the market continues to evolve. To allow for a limited number of exchanges during negotiations, defined trade-off matrices can be created—within controlled parameters (to limit precedential risks)—to help negotiators arrive efficiently at better outcomes. Common examples of such trade-offs that we have observed in practice include longer contract duration tied to defined reductions in price; higher or lower prices tied to specific, committed purchase volumes; and higher or lower pricing defined against different indemnification terms and assumption of risk. Such defined trade-off options take advantage of likely differences (e.g., risk tolerance, discount rate/time value of money, business strategies) across multiple negotiation counterparties within a defined negotiation segment.

To ensure that standard terms and conditions and allowed trade-offs are appropriately updated in response to changing market conditions, an organizational feedback mechanism can be incorporated as well. Such a feedback mechanism allows for the efficient capture of the experiences of multiple individual negotiators, including insights into which terms and conditions create the greatest conflict (e.g., risk of impasse). Standard terms and conditions can then be modified over time based on such feedback (again, furthering the organization's learning).

Negotiation Context: High Complexity/Weak Precedent Intensity—Organizational Negotiation Learning Strategy: Personalize, Pull

Illustrative Negotiation B in the model is one of high value and high complexity but with limited precedential intensity. It could be a negotiation over the licensing of novel intellectual property that could significantly affect a company's future market competitiveness. Such a negotiation might involve individuals from engineering, R&D, legal, strategy, and other departments, as well as a number of issues, and significant uncertainty (e.g., about future market conditions, how easily or not the technology can be commercialized) and thus be quite complex. Precedential intensity may be relatively low, however, as the outcome is likely to be determined more by situation-specific factors than by prior deals with the same party or negotiations with other parties over similar issues. Moreover, the organization may not contemplate engaging in any similar licensing negotiations in the foreseeable future.

Given its value, this type of negotiation merits some attention from an organizational learning perspective. (Illustrative Negotiation G stands in contrast to Negotiation B; while Negotiation G is also complex and has weak precedential effect, its low value makes it less likely that the effort to search for and transfer knowledge will yield enough benefit to warrant much learning investment.) Because it is complex, Negotiation B is likely to require greater reliance on tacit knowledge than explicit knowledge; hence, a "personalization" approach to learning likely makes sense (Strategy 1). Also, the weaker precedential effect suggests making use of a pull strategy for knowledge sharing (Strategy 4). For this type of negotiation, it might make sense to implement a social networking mechanism to connect individuals who have dealt with similar complex issues or to set up a simple "yellow pages" of negotiators who can be called on (directly, in a personalized way) for input or consultation on an as-needed basis.

When there is a need to share complex (tacit) knowledge, organizational learning methods are most successful when they facilitate connections between individuals who have at least some shared context and regularly occurring informal contact (Hansen et al., 1999; Stewart, 2001). Consider the experience of one global IT company: The company's account executives frequently negotiate and renegotiate deals for IT services with customers around the world. "In response to requests, we have tried in numerous ways to connect account executives—directories, social networking sites—to facilitate sharing of knowledge and experiences among the group," said the company's head of account executive enablement. "Unfortunately, it never seems to work in practice. Everyone wants to receive assistance, but no one really wants to take the time to provide it" (personal communication, Nov. 2010). While the account executives have some shared context (they perform similar roles in different geographies), the ties among them are rather weak; there is little incentive or social pressure, therefore, to spend time helping someone they do not know. The company has experienced greater success, however, in facilitating connections among account executives who serve the same industry and geography and have a shared reporting structure. These individuals connect more frequently and therefore are more likely to (a) know when someone in the group has had a similar negotiation experience and (b) reach out for and receive help as there is some existing tie to draw on and a greater likelihood of reciprocation.

Negotiation Context: Low Complexity/Weak Precedent Intensity—Organizational Negotiation Learning Strategy: Codify, Pull

Negotiation C involves fairly significant value but is not especially complex and involves little precedential intensity. Consider, for example, a pharmaceutical company negotiating an in-licensing deal with a biotechnology firm. The pharma company may do a few such deals, and each will be a bit different; however, each could involve fairly significant value. Negotiations H, I, J, and K are also of low complexity and weak precedent intensity, but by contract they involve relatively low value. These might be negotiations between suppliers and customers over details of a particular shipment or alliance partners about project deadlines, for example.

Negotiation C's value suggests that it warrants attention from a learning perspective. Its relatively low complexity suggests a codification approach to sharing knowledge (Strategy 2), and its relatively low precedential effect suggests a pull strategy (Strategy 4). For this type of negotiation, a searchable database of negotiation lessons (codified knowledge, available on demand) might be useful.

Use of such a database, however, naturally means that one must be created and populated with relevant lessons. As the example of the global IT company showed, getting busy negotiators to contribute to such efforts can be difficult, but it is not impossible. Consider the example of a company in the insurance business, with teams of negotiators who adjust various types of claims (from maritime, to aviation, to health, to pollution, etc.) (Ertel & Gordon, 2007). This organization created a multilayer approach to negotiation reviews. At the conclusion of all negotiations, managers require negotiators to answer a few simple questions (such as, "Did you try anything new?" and "Did you learn anything in this negotiation?"). In many negotiations, "no" is an acceptable answer. However, anyone who indicates that they have not learned anything new in 10 or 12 negotiations can expect to be tapped by their manager and encouraged to contribute. When negotiators indicate that they learned something new or witnessed something interesting, they are prompted to have a brief conversation with their manager about whether it warrants a short write up in the negotiation knowledge base or a debriefing session with the team. After some initial contests to encourage population of the negotiation knowledge base, the program took off—teams now regularly submit lessons and are able to find other useful lessons as well. The key to getting negotiators to contribute, they found, was making the process simple and efficient, ensuring a degree of management oversight and accountability, and letting negotiators themselves determine when greater effort to extract and share lessons was warranted.

Negotiation Context: Strong Precedent Intensity/High Complexity—Organizational Negotiation Learning Strategy: Personalize, Push

Negotiation D is a complex negotiation involving relatively modest value. However, with fairly strong precedential intensity, this negotiation may have an impact on the value achieved in other negotiations to a significant degree. This might be the negotiation of a small acquisition, for example. There may be only modest value involved in the direct negotiation, but if the purchase is motivated by a goal of acquiring a capability or technology that will place the company in competition with one of its alliance partners, it could have significant financial impact on other negotiations with the alliance partner or with customers to which the company cosells with its partner.

Because of its high complexity, this type of negotiation lends itself to a personalization method of knowledge sharing (Strategy 1), and its strong precedent intensity suggests that a push learning strategy is warranted (Strategy 4). While codified negotiation preparation templates might be a means for capturing and sharing explicit knowledge on an as-needed basis (codify/push), KLA-Tencor, a leading manufacturer of process control and yield management solutions for the semiconductor and related microelectronics industries, uses them in a different way. In both sales and procurement, select employees are trained in negotiation strategies and the use of negotiation preparation templates. It is not the specific form of the templates themselves that is of concern to management, but the thinking and preparation that they inculcate. Consequently, many employees leverage the content of the templates but put it in a different form. Negotiator colleagues then often use the preparation templates as the basis for dialogue, asking probing questions and sharing their experiences from similar negotiations.

There are several benefits of using templates within such a framework (where they are tightly coupled with structured dialogue among negotiators). The templates provide, and reinforce use of, a common language regarding negotiation among different negotiators in the organization, making sharing of knowledge and experiences easier. They also shape the thinking of negotiators (particularly those who are less experienced)—in effect, making some amount of tacit knowledge about effective preparation for negotiation more explicit and aiding the transfer and absorption of tacit knowledge. The questions instantiated in these templates prompt negotiators to gather and analyze information (some of which is tacit, and some explicit) that is likely to be important to achieving successful negotiated outcomes. As negotiators use the forms regularly, they absorb that tacit knowledge, thereby improving their negotiation skill.

Negotiation centers of excellence and role rotation of individuals in negotiation-intensive roles are other mechanisms that show promise as vehicles for personalized negotiation knowledge sharing coupled with a push strategy. Centers of excellence are formal organizational structures that are recognized for their knowledge and "mandated to make that knowledge available throughout the firm" (Kubr, 2002, p. 429). A formal, cross-functional negotiation center of excellence in which individuals from various functions who negotiate (e.g., sales, procurement, contracts, licensing) convene to discuss negotiation experiences and lessons learned enables the sharing of knowledge and insight, both within and across functional units. For example, sales and procurement representatives can share their experiences negotiating with different parts of the same counterpart organization. They can also role-play one another's counterparts, given their respective experiences (e.g., someone from sales can role-play a salesperson from another organization to assist a colleague from procurement in his or her negotiation preparation).

Regular rotation of individuals in negotiation-intensive roles (e.g., of procurement staff into sales roles, salespeople into procurement roles, and individuals in both sales and procurement back and forth with line-of-business roles) shows promise as well. Many companies use job or role rotation—"lateral transfers of employees between jobs in an organization" (Campion, Cheraskin, & Stevens, 1994, p. 1518)—to develop leaders by giving them a broad perspective on the company's operations and helping them develop a diverse network of relationships within the company. Job rotation has the added benefit of maintaining and increasing employee knowledge and motivation. Job rotations have been positively related to promotion rate, salary growth, knowledge and skill acquisition, and various career benefits, such as organizational integration and personal development (Campion et al., 1994). Further, job rotation has been directly linked to learning within the organizational context (Ortega, 2001). As such, rotating employees among negotiation-intensive roles can be expected to result not only in multiple personal and professional benefits, but also in greater organizational learning with regard to negotiation.

Job rotations and negotiation centers of excellence also facilitate the development of internal networks of productive relationships between individuals in negotiation roles and with their internal constituencies. Greater understanding and trust reduces the likelihood of conflict arising from agent-principal misalignment (Deutsch, 1958; Rousseau, Sitkin, Burt, & Camerer, 1998) and can be expected to facilitate greater organizational negotiation effectiveness. Moreover, as these organizational learning practices facilitate connections among individuals, they are useful for the transmission of tacit knowledge and therefore are especially applicable in the context of complex negotiations.

THE CHALLENGE OF A DIVERSE, DISTRIBUTED WORKFORCE

We have described several strategies for achieving better overall negotiated results through effective organizational learning. While the nature of 21st century negotiations makes organizational learning critical, today's complex, global, distributed working environment creates considerable challenges for implementing these strategies. Negotiations often involve the input and participation of individuals in very different roles, from different functions. Salespeople must work with their counterparts in finance, who prepare analyses to support different deal structures; lawyers contribute their expertise on terms and conditions; technical product managers, engineers, and delivery managers help define purchasing requirements for negotiations with suppliers and assist in the design of solutions to be proposed to customers during sales negotiations; business managers and functional representatives provide input on priorities and trade-offs. These myriad individuals represent different functional areas and have different backgrounds, perspectives, goals, priorities, and incentives (Atkin & Rinehart, 2006; Brett, Friedman, & Behfar, 2009; Brodt & Thompson, 2001). For example, salespeople might be most concerned with meeting customer needs and requirements and closing the deal, while staff in the finance department focus on profitability, cash flow, return on investment, and other financial metrics. Attorneys look most carefully at legal risks, while project managers are most concerned with whether solutions can be implemented.

Further, the global nature of today's organizations means that negotiators (and those with whom they must collaborate internally) are often geographically dispersed (some working from offices, others working from their homes, still others working from client sites or other remote locations) around the world. They may speak different languages and have very different cultural norms for communicating and sharing knowledge. Complicating matters further, they may have very different views about what constitutes acceptable (and effective) negotiation behavior, given their different cultures and backgrounds (see Chapter 13, this volume).

This creates considerable challenges for organizations attempting to implement the strategies described in this chapter. For example, regarding Strategy 1 (for complex negotiations, use a personalization approach to organizational learning focused on connecting individuals with relevant experience and knowledge)—in 21st century organizations, individuals who have relevant experience and knowledge may come from very different functions or geographic locations compared to those who are seeking to leverage that experience and knowledge. A business development manager may have knowledge relevant to an alliance manager who is negotiating a new alliance contract, for example. A procurement lead in Houston, Texas, may have lessons or experience in dealing with a raw materials supplier that could be leveraged by another procurement lead in Brisbane, Australia. Even if these individuals are *aware* of who has relevant knowledge (a difficult task in and of itself), research has shown that weak ties between disparate organizational functions can make it difficult to share complex knowledge, and (as noted previously) there is often less motivation for individuals who are weakly tied to make the effort required to share knowledge (Hansen et al., 1999). In addition, because individuals from different functions have different backgrounds, goals, priorities, and incentives, they might advise very different trade-offs, leading to different negotiated strategies and outcomes. A salesperson might advocate taking on more risk to close a deal, while an account manager may be more risk averse due to concerns about the availability of delivery staff to complete work on time and at high quality, for example. These varied viewpoints need to be taken into account in a "personalized" approach to organizational learning (e.g., by including multiple roles in a negotiation center of excellence or including several functions in a job rotation program) if negotiated outcomes for the firm *overall* are to be maximized.

Regarding Strategy 2 (for less-complex negotiations, use a codification approach to organizational learning, capturing knowledge in written form and making that knowledge available to those who will later need it)—defining what knowledge should be captured and codified can be difficult when negotiators are dispersed in different functions throughout the organization and across geographic boundaries. First, what constitutes important "learning" might be different to different groups (lessons that matter to salespeople might be different from those that matter to attorneys; negotiation advice for supply chain managers who *implement* agreements might be different from advice useful for commodity sourcing managers who *negotiate* agreements). Organizations therefore face the task of determining what knowledge to capture and how to organize such knowledge effectively so that individuals from different functions with different needs can readily find what is relevant to them. Second, as noted, what constitutes an effective negotiation strategy or lesson in one part of the world may not be appropriate in another. As a result, lessons or advice must be captured together with contextual information describing when they are appropriate for use (which is easy to take for granted), or negotiators must be experienced enough to ascertain when certain strategies or approaches do not translate well in their context (and they must be willing to sift through those that do not to find those that do).

Aventis, the pharmaceutical company referenced previously, implemented an effective solution to address this challenge. Following negotiations of high-value deals, a facilitated review was required. The output of each review was a set of key lessons in the form of one or two prescriptive sentences. Along with each lesson, a short story about the experience was written to provide context for why the team advised as it did. For example:

Advice: *Consult with Legal well before beginning negotiations over contract terms and conditions, but do not bring them to meetings with the other side until a high degree of trust and rapport has been established.*

Here is what happened that led us to formulate this advice...

By reading the story of one negotiation team, other negotiators were able to better assess the applicability of the team's advice to their own negotiations.

SUGGESTED DIRECTIONS FOR FUTURE RESEARCH

In this chapter, we have derived several strategies from theories of organizational learning and described a number of useful organizational learning methods to guide managers as they strive to improve overall negotiated outcomes for their organizations. Next, we present some possible directions for future study, arguing that more research is needed to understand the efficacy and costs and benefits of different organizational learning methods with respect to negotiation.

Organizational Learning in the Negotiation Context

As noted, a challenge to organizations in the 21st century is how to compete successfully when a complex, global, distributed working environment creates considerable challenges for implementing these strategies. Previously, we discussed some strategies for overcoming these hurdles. Moreover, a primary contention of this chapter is that companies that enable organizational learning (that is, put in place the means to capture individual learning and make that learning a part of the organization's memory so that others may take more effective action based on that learning) will achieve improved negotiated outcomes overall. In this chapter, we have linked insights from existing organizational learning research to the context of negotiations and relied primarily on anecdotal evidence to support the use of certain organizational learning practices (e.g., directories of experts, standard contracts with annotated language, centers of excellence) to facilitate enhanced negotiation learning and effectiveness by firms. While we believe this analysis yields useful ideas for managers who are responsible for maximizing the value of negotiated outcomes and optimizing the allocation of resources across many negotiations, we are unaware of any research to date that examined the efficacy of these organizational learning practices specifically in the negotiation context. We therefore believe that more empirical research into the costs and benefits of various approaches to organizational learning with respect to negotiation should be undertaken.

To examine the impact of these proposed methods and strategies, a set of measurable characteristics should be defined to assess an organization's overall negotiation effectiveness or results. These outcome characteristics can be correlated with the use of the specific negotiation learning methods described here. Such research will help managers begin to understand which negotiation learning methods contribute most to a firm's overall negotiation effectiveness.

For example, we have argued (based on insights drawn from organizational learning theory) that personalized means of knowledge sharing (such as centers of excellence and role rotation) are most effective for complex negotiations, which rely heavily on the tacit knowledge of negotiators. We have also argued that codified forms of knowledge (such as standard contract templates with annotated supporting language) are the most efficient means for knowledge sharing in less-complex negotiations. Longitudinal empirical research could be useful in assessing and refining these assertions.

The Complexities of a Team-Based or Distributed Workforce

In addition, although progress has been made in understanding some of the issues that occur in teams of negotiators (e.g., decision rules, interpersonal processes) (Bazerman, Mannix, & Thompson, 1988; Buttery & Leung, 1998; Mannix, Thompson, & Bazerman, 1989; Thompson, Peterson, & Brodt, 1996), further research is needed that addresses how to enable better negotiated outcomes when negotiations involve the participation of a diverse, distributed group of people. We know little about how teams develop shared negotiation goals or how managers can guide development of shared goals in cross-functional negotiating teams. Building on the work of Keenan and Carnevale (1989) concerning ingroup cooperation, some recent research has begun to address this issue, recognizing that collectives such as teams often consist of subgroups with conflicting interests (Brodt & Thompson, 2001; Halevy, 2008). Several questions remain, however. How can managers balance the unique interests and priorities of different internal constituencies participating in negotiations to achieve the best negotiated outcomes for the organization as a whole? Can organizational learning mechanisms guide negotiation teams in making trade-offs that provide the greatest benefit to the organization overall?

Interconnectedness of Modern Negotiations

Finally, negotiations today are often not independent, one-time transactions; rather, they are an interconnected series of events, impacted by an organization's reputation and previous negotiations (through precedential effects). For example, the terms a company agrees to with one alliance partner may become known to another and have an impact on the terms that the organization expects to be offered in a similar deal. A company's sales team may develop a reputation for agreeing to lower prices at the end of a fiscal year to meet revenue targets; therefore, customers may hold off on ordering until year end, sparking a flurry of negotiations in the final days of the year. Customers of a particular service company may know that they can always get a better deal by escalating to management, so managers become ever more involved in negotiations. In all of these situations, previous negotiations and organizational reputation affect the negotiation process and negotiated outcomes. Although we can describe these processes anecdotally, we know little about exactly how and under what circumstances they come about since much of the negotiations research focused on one-time transactions (e.g., Mannix et al., 1995; Neale & Northcraft, 1991). Some negotiation scholars have argued that organizations must take a coordinated, systematic approach to managing negotiations (Ertel, 1999; Movius & Susskind, 2009), and further research in this area is warranted.

For example, a significant body of literature has examined the development of organizational reputation (Rindova et al., 2005; Rindova, Petkova, & Kotha, 2007; Yang, 2007), but we know less about how more specific organizational reputations—such as reputations for negotiating—are developed and how they may influence business transactions. How does an organization's reputation with respect to negotiation influence the way its potential customers, suppliers, and alliance partners approach negotiations with that organization? How do organizations build and leverage organizational reputation in an increasingly transparent marketplace to achieve more favorable negotiated outcomes? These questions have yet to be addressed.

CONCLUSION

A significant body of literature emphasizes the importance of organizational learning for 21st century firms (e.g., Hitt, Dacin, Levitas, Arregle, & Borza, 2000; Miner & Mezias, 1996), which need to be increasingly adaptable and innovative (Wang & Lim, 2008). Similarly, an emerging body of literature is beginning to address the scope and complexity of interfirm negotiations. We have described several characteristics of 21st century negotiations that necessitate an organizational approach to negotiation learning and have provided preliminary practical guidance for managers based on organizational learning insights. We also have outlined future research that we feel warrants attention given the complexity of the 21st century organizational landscape.

Negotiation scholars are beginning to view negotiation as an organizational competence, not simply an individual skill—and this is a welcome development. We argue that the next phase in the evolution of negotiation theory and practice requires a move beyond analysis and management of a firm's negotiations as independent transactions. The interconnected nature of organizational negotiations, in part a function of reputational and precedent effects, coupled with an increasingly dynamic and transparent business environment, means that negotiations need to be understood (by academics) and managed (by executives or by practitioners) in a more integrated fashion. We believe that insights from the organizational learning literature are a valuable resource to guide further research and the development of improved management techniques.

NOTES

1. By *organizational learning*, we refer to Kim's definition (1993): "increasing an organization's capacity to take effective action" (p. 43). Organizational learning, as we use the term in this chapter, refers to the systems organizations put into place to capture individual learning and make that learning a part of the organization's memory so that others may take more effective action based on that learning.
2. See the work of Hudson and McArthur, 1994; McGinn and Keros, 2002, on the dynamics associated with "repeat transactions" with the same counterparties.
3. For more information on increased worker mobility, see, for example, the work of Parker et al. (2001); Broschak (2004); Nicholson (1996); and Liljegren and Ekberg (2009).

4. We suggest that negotiations with either a very small ZOPA or a very large ZOPA are apt to be more complex. Negotiations with a small ZOPA have fewer opportunities for negotiators to reach agreement and therefore are, naturally, more difficult; those with a large ZOPA have a wide range of possible outcomes that could be acceptable to both parties. The more knowledgeable and effective at negotiating a given party is, the more likely the party is to capture a larger share of the value at stake in the negotiation.

5. See the work of Ertel, 1999, for a discussion of the benefits of Grupo Financiero Serfin's negotiation categorization scheme.

6. See the work of Fisher et al. 1991, for explication of the power of (perceived) legitimacy in negotiations.

REFERENCES

Argote, L., & Ingram, P. (2000). Knowledge transfer: A basis for competitive advantage in firms. *Organizational Behavior and Human Decision Processes, 82,* 150–169.

Atkin, T. S., & Rinehart, L. M. (2006). The effect of negotiation practices on the relationship between suppliers and customers. *Negotiation Journal, 22,* 47–65.

Barthelemy, J., & Adsit, D. (2003). The seven deadly sins of outsourcing. *Academy of Management Executive, 17,* 87–100.

Bazerman, M. H., Mannix, E. A., & Thompson, L. L. (1988). Groups as mixed-motive negotiations. In E. J. Lawler & B. Markovksy (Eds.), *Advances in group processes* (pp. 195–216). Greenwich, CT: JAI.

Bazerman, M. H., & Neale, M. A. (1992). *Negotiating rationally.* New York: Free Press.

Bensaou, M., (1999). *Portfolios of buyer-supplier relationships. MIT Sloan Management Review, 40,* 35–44.

Boh, W. F. (2007). Mechanisms for sharing knowledge in project-based organizations. *Information and Organization, 17,* 27–58.

Bourgeois, L. J. (1980). Performance and consensus. *Strategic Management Journal, 1,* 227–248.

Brett, J. M., Friedman, R., & Behfar, K. (2009). How to manage your negotiating team. *Harvard Business Review, 87,* 105–109.

Brodt, S., & Thompson, L. (2001). Negotiating teams: A levels of analysis approach. *Group Dynamics: Theory, Research, and Practice, 5,* 208–219.

Brown, J. S., & Hagel, J. J. (2005). The next frontier of innovation. *McKinsey Quarterly, 3,* 83–91.

Broschak, J. P. (2004). Managers' mobility and market interface: The effect of managers' career mobility on the dissolution of market ties. *Administrative Science Quarterly, 49,* 608–640.

Buttery, E. A., & Leung, T. K. P. (1998). The difference between Chinese and Western negotiations. *European Journal of Marketing, 32,* 374–389.

Campion, M. A., Cheraskin, L., & Stevens, M. J. (1994). Career-related antecedents and outcomes of job rotation. *Academy of Management Journal, 37,* 1518–1542.

Carley, K. (1992). Organizational learning and personnel turnover. *Organization Science, 3,* 20–46.

Claycamp, H. J., & Massey, W. F. (1968). A theory of market segmentation. *Journal of Marketing Research, 5,* 388–394.

Corporate Leadership Council. (2004). *Maximizing returns on HR outsourcing investment.* Washington, DC: Author.

deMan, A. P., Duysters, G., & Neyens, I. (2009). *Third state of alliances—2009.* Canton, MA: Association of Strategic Alliance Professionals.

Deutsch, M. (1958). Trust and suspicion. *Journal of Conflict Resolution, 2,* 265–279.

Dittrich, K., Duysters, G., & deMan, A. (2007). Strategic repositioning by means of alliance networks: The case of IBM. *Research Policy, 36,* 1496–1511.

Dixon, N. (2000). *Common knowledge: How companies thrive by sharing what they know.* Boston: Harvard Business School Press.

Dyer, J. H., Cho, D. S., & Chu, W. (1998). Strategic supplier segmentation: The next "best practice" in supply chain management. *California Management Review, 40,* 57–77.

Edmunds, A., & Morris, A. (2000). The problem of information overload in business organizations: A review of the literature. *International Journal of Information Management, 20,* 17–28.

Elfenbein, H. A., Curhan, J. R., Eisenkraft, N., Shirako, A., & Baccaro, L. (2008). Are some negotiators better than others? Individual differences in bargaining outcomes. *Journal of Research in Personality, 42,* 1463–1475.

Ertel, D. (1999). Turning negotiation into a corporate capability. *Harvard Business Review, 77,* 55–70.

Ertel, D. (2004). Getting past yes: Negotiating as if implementation mattered. *Harvard Business Review, 82,* 60–68.

Ertel, D., & Gordon, M. (2007). *The point of the deal: How to negotiate when yes is not enough.* Boston: Harvard Business School Press.

Fisher, R., Ury, W., & Patton, B. (1991). *Getting to yes.* New York: Penguin Books.

Frost, T. S., Birkinshaw, J. M., & Ensign, P. C. (2002). Centers of excellence in multinational corporations. *Strategic Management Journal, 23,* 997–1018.

Galinsky, A. D., & Mussweiler, T. (2001). First offers as anchors: The role of perspective-taking and negotiator focus. *Journal of Personality and Social Psychology, 81,* 657–669.

Gartner Group. (2003). *IT outsourcing contracts reach $47M average.* Retrieved September 29, 2010, from http://www.gartner.com/press_releases/pr5may2003a.html

Garvin, D. A., Edmondson, A. C., & Gino, F. (2008). Is yours a learning organization? *Harvard Business Review, 86,* 109–116.

Gomez-Casseres, B. (1996). *The alliance revolution.* Cambridge, MA: Harvard University Press.

Granados, N., Gupta, A., & Kauffman, R. (2005). Transparency strategy in internet-based selling. In K. Tomak (Ed.), *Advances in the economics of information systems* (pp. 80–112). Hershey, PA: Idea Group.

Grant, R. (1996). Prospering in dynamically-competitive environments: Organizational capability as knowledge integration. *Organization Science, 7,* 375–387.

Greenhalgh, L., & Chapman, D. I. (1998). Negotiator relationships: Construct measurement, and demonstration of their impact on the process and outcomes of negotiation. *Group Decision and Negotiation, 7,* 465–489.

Grise, M., & Gallupe, B. R. (2000). Information overload: Addressing the productivity paradox in face-to-face electronic meetings. *Journal of Management Information Systems, 16,* 157–185.

Hagel, J. J., & Brown, S. (2008). From push to pull: Emerging models for mobilizing resources. *Journal of Service Science, 1,* 93–110.

Halevy, N. (2008). Team negotiation: Social, epistemic, economic, and psychological consequences of subgroup conflict. *Personality and Social Psychology Bulletin, 34,* 1687–1702.

Hansen, M. T., Nohria, N., & Tierney, T. (1999). What's your strategy for managing knowledge? *Harvard Business Review, 77,* 106–116.

Hedberg, B. (1981). How organizations learn and unlearn. In P. C. Nystrom & W. H. Starbuck (Eds.), *Handbook of organization design* (Vol. 1, pp. 3–27). Oxford, UK: Oxford University Press.

Hidding, G. J., & Catterall, S. M. (1998). Anatomy of a learning organization: Turning knowledge into capital at Andersen Consulting. *Knowledge and Process Management, 5,* 3–13.

Hitt, M. A., Dacin, M. T., Levitas, E., Arregle, J., & Borza, A. (2000). Partner selection in emerging and developed market contexts: Resource-based and organizational learning perspectives. *Academy of Management Journal, 43,* 449–467.

Huber, G. P. (1991). Organizational learning: The contributing processes and the literatures. *Organization Science, 2,* 88–115.

Huber, N. (2004). *Don't let IT staff manage outsourcing deals, warns Gartner.* Computer weekly.com. Retrieved November 14, 2010 from http://www.computerweekly.com/Articles/2004/04/30/202119/Don39t-let-IT-staff-manage-outsourcing-deals-warns.htm

Hudson, R. L., & McArthur, A. W. (1994). Contracting strategies in entrepreneurial and established firms. *Entrepreneurship Theory and Practice, 18,* 43–59.

Hughes, J., & Weiss, J. (2007). Simple rules for making alliances work. *Harvard Business Review, 85,* 122–131.

IBM. (2007). *Extend the business value of outsourcing: Turning provider relationships into innovation partnerships.* Retrieved September 29, 2010, from http://www-935.ibm.com/services/au/gts/pdf/extend_the_business_value_of_outsourcing-white_paper.pdf

Keenan, P. A., & Carnevale, P. J. D. (1989). Positive effects of within-group cooperation on between-group negotiation. *Journal of Applied Social Psychology, 19,* 977–992.

Kesting, P., & Smolinski, R. (2007). When negotiations become routine: Not reinventing the wheel while thinking outside the box. *Negotiation Journal, 23,* 419–438.

Kim, D. H. (1993). The link between individual and organizational learning. *Sloan Management Review, 34,* 37–50.

Kimball, G. (2010). *Outsourcing agreements—A practical guide.* New York: Oxford University Press.

Klapp, O. E. (1986). *Overload and boredom: Essays on the quality of life in the information society.* Westport, CT: Greenwood Press.

Kogut, B., & Zander, U. (1992). Knowledge of the firm, combinative capabilities, and the replication of technology. *Organization Science, 3,* 383–397.

Kubr, M. (Ed.). (2002). *Management consulting, a guide to the profession* (4th ed.). Geneva, Switzerland: International Labour Office.

Levitt, B., & March, J. G. (1988). Organizational learning. *Annual Review of Sociology, 14,* 319–340.

Liljegren, M., & Ekberg, K. (2009). Job mobility as predictor of health and burnout. *Journal of Occupational and Organizational Psychology, 82,* 317–329.

Mannix, E. A., Thompson, L. L., & Bazerman, M. H. (1989). Negotiation in small groups. *Journal of Applied Psychology, 74,* 508–517.

Mannix, E. A., Tinsley, C. H., & Bazerman, M. (1995). Negotiating over time: Impediments to integrative solutions. *Organizational Behavior and Human Decision Processes, 62,* 241–251.

Margulis, M., & Pekar, P. (2001). *The next wave of alliance formations: Forging successful partnerships with emerging and middle-market companies.* Los Angeles: Houlihan Lokey Howard & Zukin.

McGinn, K. L., & Keros, A T. (2002). Improvisation and the logic of exchange in socially embedded transactions. *Administrative Science Quarterly, 47,* 442–473.

Miller, J. (1978). *Living systems.* New York: Wiley.

Minahan, T., & Vigoroso, M. (2002). *The spending analysis benchmark report: Dissecting a corporate epidemic.* Boston: Aberdeen Group.

Miner, A. S., & Mezias, S. J. (1996). Ugly duckling no more: Pasts and futures of organizational learning research. *Organization Science, 7,* 88–99.

Moore, K., & Birkinshaw, J. (1998). Managing knowledge in global service firms: Centers of excellence. *Academy of Management Executive, 12,* 81–92.

Movius, H., & Susskind, L. (2009). *Built to win: Creating a world-class negotiating organization.* Boston: Harvard Business Press.

Neale, M. A., & Northcraft, G. B. (1991). Behavioral negotiation theory. In L. L. Cummings & B. M. Staw (Eds.), *Research in organizational behavior* (pp. 147–190). Greenwich, CT: JAI Press.

Nicholson, N. (1966). Careers in new context. In P. Warr (Ed.) *Psychology at work* (4th ed.). London: Penguin Books.

Nonaka, I. (1991). The knowledge-creating company. *Harvard Business Review, 69,* 96–104.

Nonaka, I., & Takeuchi, H. (1995). *The knowledge-creating company: How Japanese companies create the dynamics of innovation.* New York: Oxford University Press.

Ortega, J. (2001). Job rotation as a learning mechanism. *Management Science, 47,* 1361–1370.

Parker, S. K., Wall, T. D., & Cordery, J. L. (2001). Future work design research and practice: Towards an elaborated model of work design. *Journal of Occupational and Organizational Psychology, 74,* 413–440.

Polanyi, M. (1966). *The tacit dimension.* London: Routledge & Kegan Paul.

Raiffa, H. (1982). *The art and science of negotiation.* Cambridge, MA: Harvard University Press.

Reich, M., Gordon, D. M., & Edwards, R. C. (1973). A theory of labor market segmentation. *The American Economic Review, 63,* 359–365.

Richardson, J. (2007). How negotiators choose standards of fairness: A look at the empirical evidence and some steps toward a process model. *Harvard Negotiation Law Review, 12,* 415–444.

Rindova, V. P., Petkova, A. P., & Kotha, S. (2007). Standing out: How new firms in emerging markets build reputation. *Strategic Organization, 5,* 31–70.

Rindova, V. P., Williamson, I. O., Petkova, A. P., & Sever, J. M. (2005). Being good or being known: An empirical examination of the dimensions, antecedents, and consequences of organizational reputation. *Academy of Management Journal, 48,* 1033–1049.

Rousseau, D. M., Sitkin, S. B., Burt, R. S., & Camerer, C. (1998). Not so different after all: A cross-discipline view of trust. *Academy of Management Review, 23,* 393–404.

Ryle, G. (1984). *The concept of mind.* Chicago: University of Chicago Press.

Schaffhauser, D. (2006). *Research: Trends in data center outsourcing.* Retrieved September 29, 2010, from http://www.sourcingmag.com/content/c060424a.asp

Senge, P. M. (2006). *The fifth discipline: The art and practice of the learning organization* (Rev. ed.) New York: Currency Doubleday.

Sheppard, B. H. (1995). Negotiating in long-term mutually interdependent relationships among relative equals. In R. J. Bies, R. J. Lewicki, & B. H. Sheppard (Eds.), *Research on negotiation in organizations* (Vol. 5, pp. 3–44). Greenwich, CT: JAI Press.

Sheppard, B. H., & Tuchinsky, M. (1996). Micro-OB and the network organization. In R. M. Kramer & T. R. Tyler (Eds.), *Trust in organizations* (pp. 140–165). Thousand Oaks, CA: Sage.

Simon, H. (1960). *The new science of management decision.* New York: Harper and Row.

Sinha, I. (2000). Cost transparency: The net's real threat to prices and brands. *Harvard Business Review, 78,* 43–54.

Spender, J. C., & Grant, R. M. (1996). Knowledge and the firm: Overview. *Strategic Management Journal, 17,* 5–9.

Stewart, T. A. (2001). *The wealth of knowledge: Intellectual capital and the twenty-first century organization.* New York: Currency.

Stuhlmacher, A. F., & Walters, A. E. (1999). Gender differences in negotiation outcome: A meta-analysis. *Personnel Psychology, 52,* 653–677.

Svensson, G. (2004). Supplier segmentation in the automotive industry: A dyadic approach of a managerial model. *International Journal of Physical Distribution and Logistics Management, 34,* 12–38.

Thompson, L. L., Peterson, E., & Brodt, S. E. (1996). Team negotiation: An examination of integrative and distributive bargaining. *Journal of Personality and Social Psychology, 70,* 66–78.

Van Kleef, G. A., De Dreu, C. K. W., & Manstead, A. S. R. (2004). The interpersonal effects of emotions in negotiations: A motivated information processing approach. *Journal of Personality and Social Psychology, 87,* 510–528.

Wang, H., & Lim, S. S. (2008). Real options and real value: The role of employee incentives to make specific knowledge investments. *Strategic Management Journal, 29,* 701–721.

Watkins, M., & Rosen, S. (2000). *Rethinking preparation in negotiation.* Boston: Harvard Business.

Willcocks, L., & Griffiths, C. (2010). The crucial role of middle management in outsourcing. *MIS Quarterly Executive, 9,* 177–193.

Yang, S. U. (2007). An integrated model for organization—public relational outcomes, organizational reputation, and their antecedents. *Journal of Public Relations Research, 19,* 91–121.

Zack, M. H. (1999). Managing codified knowledge. *Sloan Management Review, 40,* 45–58.

Zhu, Z., Hsu, K., & Lillie, J. (2001). Outsourcing—A strategic move: The process and the ingredients for success. *Management Decision, 39,* 373–378.

13

Great Deal, Terrible Contract:
The Case for Negotiator Involvement
in the Contracting Phase

Deepak Malhotra

INTRODUCTION

Managers and executives negotiate constantly—big deals and small—but after reaching agreement and reaching across the table for a handshake, negotiators will often disengage, leaving some key decisions in the contracting phase to lawyers. In contexts as varied as labor-management bargaining, private equity deal making, joint venture structuring, and trade agreements between nation-states, there is an observable transition between what we might call the *negotiation phase*, in which concessions are made, diverging interests are reconciled, and agreement is reached, and the *contracting phase*, in which the agreement is translated into a legal document that codifies the deal. Notably, across all of these negotiation contexts—and many others—the parties that are at the table before versus after this transition may differ: Managers and executives drive the negotiation process; lawyers drive the contracting process.

There is no shortage of reasons for this passing of the baton. First, the increasing technical complexity of contracts makes it difficult for most managers and executives to play a heavy hand in the drafting of contracts. Second, the fast and increasing pace of business puts pressure on negotiators to move on to the next order of business as soon as they can disengage from the current deal. Third, most managers and executives will admit that, compared to high-stakes negotiation, the process of translating the deal into legalese is boring and uneventful. Any of these factors, and perhaps many others, can drive a wedge between the negotiating and contracting phases of deal making, with managers and executives responsible for decision making during the former and lawyers taking greater control in the latter, even when all parties understand that coordination between legal and managerial perspectives is to be a continued concern.

The objective of this chapter is to help negotiators recognize the dangers, or pitfalls, associated with disengaging too much from the contracting phase of deal making. While many managers and executives see contracting as nothing more than a legal formality for transliterating what they have already negotiated, in fact the contracting process can have powerful effects on the kind of deal—and relationship—that negotiators attain at the end. An understanding of these consequences should (a) encourage managers and executives to stay at the bargaining table during the contracting phase and (b) equip them to manage the contracting phase such that it yields contract structures that can help build trust and reduce conflict in the relationship. This chapter also analyzes why these issues take on a special importance in the domain of 21st century deal making, in which an increasing number of negotiations will take place across borders and cultures.

As I argue, the reason many managers and executives overlook the importance of their involvement during the contracting phase is that they see contracts merely from an economic and legal perspective—both of which emphasize formal means of risk mitigation. In contrast, those who understand the psychological dimension of contracts (i.e., how contracts and the contracting process influence perceptions of the deal, interpersonal attributions, and norms surrounding conflict resolution) are in a much stronger position to negotiate *better* outcomes and relationships, not just safer ones.[1] As it turns out, managers and executives are often best suited to the task of identifying and pursuing such opportunities. In contrast, the training, incentives, and job descriptions of the legal team tend to motivate action aimed primarily at achieving compliance with the law, minimizing risk, and ensuring the legal enforceability of promises and agreements (Bagley, 2005). The problem then is not with lawyers, who contribute tremendous expertise in the process of negotiation, but with the crowding out of managerial and relational perspectives when it comes to embodying the deal in written language.

This chapter leverages existing research on the interplay between contracts and trust; insights from the psychology of judgment, decision making, and negotiation; as well as a series of real-world case analyses to (a) offer prescriptive advice to managers and executives who negotiate in domains characterized by high stakes, uncertainty, and long-term relationships, (b) identify interesting and important questions that remain unanswered, which future research might tackle, and (c) emphasize through illustration how the need for negotiators to participate more actively in the contracting process (than they may be inclined to) is becoming all the more critical due to the increasingly international and cross-cultural nature of exchange in the 21st century, in which the risks of misunderstandings, the need for trust building, and the degree of uncertainty regarding the structure and prospect of long-term collaboration are all high. The core of this chapter discusses five key contracting pitfalls that can derail an otherwise soundly negotiated agreement and then draws implications for negotiation practitioners and scholars who are interested in creating more resilient outcomes and relationships.

CONTRACTS: THE DOMINANCE OF LEGAL AND ECONOMIC PERSPECTIVES

To understand why the scholarship and practice of negotiation has failed to spill over into the domain of contracting, it is useful to consider the dominant perspectives that have shaped how academics and practitioners view the role of contracts. As I suggest in the following, the dominance of legal and economic perspectives on contracting have (de facto) crowded out psychological and strategic perspectives. Furthermore, whereas the psychological lens would seek to yield prescriptive advice to negotiators, the legal and economic perspectives have emphasized normative and descriptive approaches to the role of contracting. This has created a deep divide, in the minds of negotiators and negotiation scholars, between negotiating and contracting; the former is seen as relevant to *decision makers,* and the latter is seen as involving little (if any) strategic choice (Bagley, 2005). In her book, *Winning Legally*, Constance Bagley (2005, p. 5), argued that this is a problematic perception: "To paraphrase Clemenceau, legal matters are too important to leave to the lawyers. As we'll see, managers can and should seek legal counsel to understand their legal and strategic alternatives, but ultimately they must make the hard decisions." While both Bagley (2005) and I are concerned with the extent to which legal issues are ignored by managers, our focus differs. Bagley (2005) focused on the need for managers to be "legally astute"—that is, to increase their understanding of the law so that they can make wiser and more ethical business decisions. Here, I focus on the need for managers to participate in what are typically considered *legal decisions*—that is, managers as negotiators should partner with their legal team on whether, when, and how to translate the deal into a contract. In this formulation, lawyers are not to be substituted, but complemented, by managers and executives.

The traditional legal perspective on contracts and the contracting process ignores negotiation altogether. One of the earliest—and certainly the most primitive—of principles in the legal theory of contracts is *pacta sunt servanda*, a Latin phrase that translates into "agreements must be kept" (Wehberg, 1959). Based on this principle, the breach of a legal contract allows victims of the breach to pursue remedy through the force of law.[2] Notably, the legal perspective on contract law does not pay much attention to the process by which an agreement is reached in the first place—what we would call the negotiation process. Fundamentally, from a legal perspective, the role of contracts (and contract law) is to facilitate exchange and social relations by enforcing (presumably negotiated) agreements.

In his seminal book, *Economic Analysis of Law*, Richard Posner (1972) elaborated this perspective in suggesting that contract law has three functions. First, it furnishes incentives (e.g., through awarding damages) that aim "to minimize breakdowns in the process of exchange" (p. 42). Second, it helps to reduce transaction costs by creating a set of "normal terms" that negotiators would otherwise have to craft idiosyncratically. Third, it provides guidance to would-be transaction partners, through a vast and accumulating body of case law, on potential pitfalls and contingencies to consider prior to initiating an exchange relationship. Posner's (1972) work is representative of the vast literature in the field of "law and economics" in that it is more descriptive and normative with regard to the law and legal institutions than prescriptive with regard to the behavior of individual parties in a transaction.

The dominance of legal and economic perspectives on the role of contracts spills over into other domains of scholarship as well. Organizational theory research on contracts, for example, is largely consistent with the legal and economic perspectives. This work, much of it stemming from the literature on transaction-cost economics (TCE), argues that when the stakes are sufficiently high, contracts help facilitate exchange by reducing uncertainty (Williamson, 1979) and mitigating the risk of opportunism (Walker & Weber, 1984; Williamson, 1985). Thus, contracts are seen, foremost, as instruments for mitigating or managing the risks inherent in exchange relationships. Unlike the legal and economic perspectives, however, TCE research *does* speak to the role of negotiation—but this role is an entirely passive one (Crocker & Reynolds, 1993; Williamson, 1991, 1996). Instead of providing would-be negotiators with prescriptive advice, the TCE perspective offers a descriptive lens on interfirm governance, with a focus on predicting the conditions (e.g., the degree of asset specificity) under which contractual structures will emerge. In this formulation, the structure of the exchange relationship and the environment determine the negotiated outcome. This approach is interesting because it does not ignore the negotiation phase as much as diminish its significance.

THE NEGOTIATION LENS

Now consider the background and perspective of negotiation scholars (see Malhotra & Bazerman, 2008). Negotiation research has its roots in economics, with early work on the topic rooted in game theoretic paradigms that rose to prominence after the publication of von Neumann and Morgenstern's (1947) seminal work, *Theory of Games and Economic Behavior.* Whereas the legal, law and economics, and organizational theory perspectives we considered focused on contracting more so than negotiation, the game theoretic approach to bargaining emphasized negotiation over contracting: In this literature, the "negotiated outcome" and the "contract" were essentially synonymous (see Rubinstein, 1982).[3,4] Notably, however, for the two decades that followed, most research in negotiation—much of it involving formal modeling—clung to variations of the assumption that negotiators had fixed, known preferences and behaved in ways that would maximize their expected utility. This had important consequences. By focusing excessively on presumptions of rationality, most models of bargaining assumed away something quite important: the negotiator's role in decision making. Instead, this research focused primarily on descriptive and normative accounts of the bargaining process and negotiated outcomes—not so different from the disciplinary perspectives we considered. This is quite remarkable with hindsight: The mainstay of negotiation research in the current day is to understand the mistakes negotiators may make and to offer advice and insights to mitigate such behaviors.

Published in 1982, Raiffa's *Art and Science of Negotiation* seemed to mark the official transition toward an emphasis on describing negotiators as they are (warts and all), not how they should be, and then offering prescriptions on the basis of descriptive (vs. normative) analyses of bargaining situations. While research on negotiation continues in multiple disciplines—including law, economics and, increasingly so, computer science—scholarship aimed at prescriptive advice is largely conducted by researchers who have a background in psychology or "micro"-organizational behavior (Bazerman, Curhan, Moore, & Valley, 2000; Bazerman & Neale, 1992; Lewicki, Saunders, & Barry, 2006; Malhotra & Bazerman, 2007; Thompson, 2005). The result is that research on negotiation strategy is most often conducted by those who have little interest or expertise in contracts and the contracting process. Indeed, with few exceptions (e.g., Lax & Sebenius, 2006; Subramanian, 2010), there is little overlap between those who work on negotiation strategy and those who study the structure (and structuring) of contracts.

WHY BUILD THIS BRIDGE?

The central premise of this chapter is that the tendency of negotiation scholars and practitioners to focus on *deal making*, but not *deal drafting*, is problematic. Real-world negotiators who disengage from the contracting phase of the deal underestimate the potential (negative) consequences of entirely outsourcing this important task. Similarly, scholars who ignore the potentially significant effects of contract structure and the contracting process do a disservice to those who wish to understand how best to manage their long-term relationships and maximize value in the deals they structure.

This is not to say that managers and executives need to be involved in every contracting meeting and decision or that lawyers can be sidelined in important negotiations. Rather, the key is for lawyers and managers to understand the different skills and perspectives they bring to the table: Lawyers understand the law, and their primary reason for being at the table is to identify and mitigate potential risks; managers and executives undergird the business relationships and understand the commercial interests at stake, and their primary objective is to structure a relationship that maximizes value. A contracting strategy that focuses blindly on maximizing expected value from the deal might fail to target manageable risks or to protect against nefarious tactics from an unscrupulous counterpart; meanwhile, a contracting strategy that focuses entirely on eliminating every potential risk will probably create little, if any, value.

The primary task of managers, when negotiating, is to make wise, informed decisions regarding risk-reward trade-offs, for which a legal perspective is necessary, but not sufficient. Ultimately, it is the manager's job to ensure that the deal that is drafted is consistent with the deal that was negotiated—in substance and in spirit. In the sections that follow, I identify five common contracting pitfalls that are more likely when the manager-as-negotiator (cf. Lax & Sebenius, 1986) exits the stage before a contract is in place.

PITFALL 1: CONTRACTS THAT SIGNAL DISTRUST

After 12 years as manager of the New York Yankees—a period in which the Yankees made the playoffs each year and won the World Series four times—Joe Torre was offered a 1-year contract renewal that could give him up to $1.6 million more than his previous average compensation. But, there was a problem: The offer lowered Torre's base pay but included a very large incentive component for reaching the playoffs and winning the World Series. While this is a standard structure in many types of compensation contracts, Torre saw it differently: "I'd been there 12 years and did not feel motivation was needed. … I explained that and the fact that the incentives, which to me I took as, you know, an insult" (*New York Times* online, Oct. 19, 2007). The structure of the contract apparently signaled to Torre that Yankees' management did not trust him to put forth sufficient effort in the absence of financial incentives. Torre rejected the offer and instead went to the Los Angeles Dodgers, where he was paid *less* in total compensation than the Yankees had offered as a base salary. The following year, the Dodgers made it to the playoffs. The Yankees did not.

Hall and Bennett (2010) tell the story of a similar incident: A large, privately held firm in the Middle East offered an experienced British executive the opportunity to join the company and take over as head of the retail business. The two sides reached an agreement, but the executive made clear that he had commitments to his current employer that would delay his ability to make the transition for 6 months. Recognizing how desperate the retail division was for new leadership, and betting that there might be at least some degree of flexibility with regard to the executive's departure from his current employer, the head of human resources (HR) offered an incentive to the British executive: a "join-soon bonus" that would give an *extra* $200,000 to the executive if he joined the firm immediately and a reduction to the bonus of $40,000 for each month's delay. This bonus would improve the executive's compensation if he joined any earlier than in 6 months and make him no worse off if he could not. The result? In a phone conversation a few days later, the executive told the head of HR that the provision seemed to suggest that he was not trusted to put forth a good faith effort to join as soon as possible: "I found it slightly insulting. It seems to imply that it takes a lot of money to motivate me—I would work hard to join quickly in any case. It's not the money that is keeping me at my current job longer; it's just that I feel like I have a duty to do a good job" (Hall & Bennett, 2010; Case C, p. 1).

Many contracts include provisions (e.g., performance pay, earn-outs, and vesting schedules) that are designed to create incentives for desired behavior. The problem is that in some contexts such provisions do not clearly signal a desire to coordinate expectations and reward performance. They signal distrust: *You won't work hard unless money is on the line.* Certainly, financial incentives can provide motivation (Jensen & Meckling, 1976), and may even enhance perceptions of fairness (Newman & Milkovich, 1990). The problem arises when the extent to which incentives (vs. other rewards) are being leveraged is seen as excessive—or counternormative—from the perspective of the target. The result is a soured relationship at best. Joe Torre found himself having to clarify this point when Hank Steinbrenner, the son of the Yankees' principal team owner, George Steinbrenner, voiced his frustration with Joe's perceived disrespectful behavior:

> (He) thought I was disrespectful because I said I was insulted. But the insult came from the incentive-based situation. And unless you understand what sport is all about and how important winning is to you, I don't think you understand the insult part of this thing. (*New York Times* online, Oct. 24, 2007)

Incentives are not the only types of provisions that may signal distrust in certain contexts. Other such provisions may include penalty clauses and harsh deadlines (e.g., exploding offers). The problem for negotiators is that such provisions are typically part of the boilerplate contracts that firms use across multiple negotiations. These "standard provisions" are often not even negotiated explicitly; they emerge during the contracting phase.

In other instances, such language is explicitly added into the deal *after* the negotiated agreement has been reached. A few years ago, a Harvard Business School student negotiated a deal with an angel investor in which they agreed on everything (valuation, equity stake, possibility and process of additional investment in future rounds, etc.). The following week, the student asked his lawyer to move the process forward. The lawyer, in turn, drafted a contract that was entirely consistent with what had been negotiated and sent it to the angel investor. The investor read the contract and almost pulled out of the deal. The reason? Each provision had been crafted in a way that favored the student and limited the rights of the investor—it represented an entirely one-sided interpretation of every element of the terms that were negotiated. Indeed, no matter how carefully a deal is reached, there remain many ways of crafting language that can tilt the contract to either side's advantage. In the lawyer's defense, he was merely safeguarding his client's interests. But, by not staying involved in the contracting phase of the deal, the student had given his lawyer free reign to draft language that might offend the other side.

Implications for Negotiators

How might negotiators avoid such consequences? One option would be to reconsider the use or scope of contractual incentives, or other potentially insulting provisions, when the target is someone with a reputation for being conscientious and intrinsically motivated (Deci & Ryan, 1985; Lepper, Greene, & Nisbett, 1973) or in cultures where there are norms that support a strong work ethic. Alternatively, those who draft such contracts should seek to reframe their motivation for doing so: The same provision can be presented as an incentive for performance or as a means by which the organization plans to share the value created when positive outcomes are achieved. Because the other party's response to such provisions— whether to reciprocate positively or to be offended—will depend in large part on the attributions the other party makes regarding the negotiator's intentions for including them (Pillutla, Malhotra, & Murnighan, 2003), it is important for contracting parties to manage the attribution process actively so distrust is not signaled.

Another potential solution was suggested by a book publisher with whom my coauthor and I were negotiating a contract. The negotiations, on behalf of the publisher, were conducted by the editor—but the scope of these negotiations was limited to the major issues: advance on royalties, royalty rate, deadlines, and so on. The negotiation process was smooth, and a lot of goodwill was created between the parties. Once the two sides had agreed to the key elements of the deal, the negotiation was handed off by the editor to the "contracting department" of the publishing house. In the days that followed, negotiations became much more frustrating as the contracting department asked to include a number of heavy-handed provisions (e.g., regarding restrictions on competitive works) that favored the publisher. While we were able to reach mutually acceptable language on every provision, the process soured us on the publisher. But, something quite interesting had happened: Our positive perceptions of the editor were unchanged. By "outsourcing" the negotiation of small (but thorny) issues to the contracting department, the publishing house had created a process in which negative attributions and mistrust, if any, would not soil the important long-term relationship that is needed between authors and editors. More generally, if negative attributions are likely, and if proposing potentially insulting provisions cannot be avoided, a solution may be to outsource aspects of the negotiation to parties that can take the blame without sacrificing the key relationships. Here is another useful role that attorneys can, and often do, play to facilitate the deal-making process.

This discussion yields the following strategies for negotiators:

Strategy 1: Reconsider the use of contractual incentives for motivating performance when (a) the target individual has a reputation for conscientiousness and intrinsic motivation or (b) there are cultural norms promoting a strong work ethic.

Strategy 2: If contractual incentives for motivating performance are to be included, reframe the motivation for their inclusion in a way that deemphasizes the risks you perceive from the other party and emphasizes the benefits that you can share with the other party.

Strategy 3: If contractual incentives for motivating performance are to be negotiated, seek to outsource these negotiations to agents or entities that can absorb negative perceptions without hurting the relationship between principals.

PITFALL 2: CONTRACTS THAT CODIFY TOO MUCH

There is a subsidiary of a large firm in the financial industry whose primary product is an electronic platform that banks, broker-dealers, and other financial institutions use to execute trades (e.g., stocks) for their customers. This subsidiary has two divisions that are relevant to this story: the sales division and the relationship management division. The sales division is responsible for bringing in new customers and signing the initial contract, which is usually for 3–5 years. Once the contract is signed, the customer is handed over to a relationship manager (RM), who is responsible for "managing the relationship" and for all future renewals when the current contract expires.

Every so often, in this firm, a RM would be heard complaining to colleagues of receiving "one of those calls." The RM would be referring to a situation that arose every few weeks: A client would call the RM and report that a trade had failed to initiate due to the client firm's error and ask that the RM help expedite the processing of this trade so that it cleared when it was supposed to do so. The RM would inform the client that, as explained in their contract, the problem would take 2–3 business days to fix. Inevitably, the client would respond that it was critical that it be solved the same day lest the client face customer wrath and regulatory sanctions. The RM would then have to spend an entire day fixing the problem—almost literally walking the trade (i.e., the paperwork) through various aspects of the organization (tech support, compliance, processing, etc.). At one meeting, at which I was present, a vice president (VP) of the firm proposed a solution:

> This problem has been going on for years. *They* make a mistake, *we* end up having to fix it. Why don't we simply do what FedEx does? We know that we *can* process things quicker when it is really necessary. Let's charge the client for expedited processing. That will discourage mistakes, all the while

increasing our revenue if and when problems do arise. Let's stop complaining and just put this service in the contract.

This seemingly ideal solution was opposed by every one of the RMs—the same group that had complained for years about the problem. Why? As one RM explained to the VP:

> Do you know how little "relationship managing" we actually do? Everything we do for our clients is mandated by contract. … But when the contract term expires, and the client is considering whether to stay with us, or go to a competitor, they do not remember a single day when we did what we were supposed to by contract. They remember the *one* day on which they were desperate, and the contract couldn't help them; only *we* could help them— and we did. That's why they stick with us.

As the RM went on to point out, charging for such a service may generate $100–$200,000 in additional annual revenue, but if going "beyond the contract" helped to retain even one of the 300+ customers of the firm, that would be worth millions of dollars.

Trust requires that parties see each other as well intentioned (Mayer, Davis, & Schoorman, 1995). Overly detailed contracts crowd out trust because they make it impossible to learn about the intentions of the other party (Malhotra & Murnighan, 2002). As the RM's response suggests, not every potential contingency that can be articulated should be included in the contract. Parties build trust when contracts are incomplete. Unfortunately, when the contracting phase is controlled by lawyers, the tendency is to try to make contracts as complete as possible and to stipulate every conceivable right, responsibility, and eventuality in the document. Wise negotiators (e.g., the RM) can facilitate the contracting process by articulating the business case for when a reliance on the contract is suboptimal. Lumineau and Malhotra (2010) provided evidence for the proposition that too much detail can be costly. They showed that the level of contractual detail in an interfirm contract makes it more likely that parties will engage in rights-based (Ury, Brett, & Goldberg, 1988), rather than interest-based, negotiations when a dispute arises, and that such behavior increases the costs of dispute resolution. In related work, Malhotra and Lumineau (2010) showed that too many control provisions in a contract make it less likely that firms will continue to work together after experiencing conflict.

Implications for Negotiators

Notably, if the decision whether to include a fee for expedited process had been left to the lawyers or the finance department of the firm, it would almost certainly have been implemented—it made perfect sense from a traditional, economic perspective. However, negotiators need to be wary of contracts that seek to codify too much. The RM example underscores the value of *strategic incompleteness*: Contracts that are overly detailed, and which seek to identify every right and responsibility for each party, will minimize risks but will crowd out a necessary condition for the building of trust—volition. For trust attributions to take hold, the trusted party's behavior needs to be seen as discretionary (cf. Gambetta, 1988). Economists have long posited that contracts are necessarily incomplete (Hart & Moore, 1988), which is usually regarded as a lamentable sign of imperfection. The negotiation lens suggests that in certain contexts, contracts should be *incomplete by design*.

> Strategy 4: Avoid putting into the contract every right and responsibility that was (or could have been) negotiated and instead seek to create space for parties to behave volitionally after the contract has been signed. Behaviors that produce relatively little revenue when priced but relatively high levels of goodwill when given away for free are ideal candidates for exclusion from the contract.

PITFALL 3: CONTRACTS THAT CLARIFY TOO MUCH

Consider the negotiations (2005–2008) between the United States and India regarding the "civilian nuclear agreement," according to which India agreed to separate its military and civilian nuclear facilities and place the latter under International Atomic Energy Agency safeguards in exchange for full nuclear cooperation by the United States (in contravention to the commitment of the United States to the Non-Proliferation Treaty).[5] One of the (many) problems that arose during these multiyear negotiations pertained to the consequences if India tested another nuclear weapon. Support for the agreement, in the United States, was contingent on assurances that India would not test another weapon; support in India was contingent on the Indian government not being perceived as having ceded its sovereign right to test weapons if desired.

Here was a stalemate, but with a strange twist. The real problem with these incompatible positions was not that the two sides could not *agree* on how to structure the deal—it was that there was no easy way to write down the agreement on paper. Each side knew that any agreement, no matter what language was used to write it down, would involve both sides knowing that if India tested another weapon, which of course it *could* do, the United States would be forced to terminate the agreement due to domestic and international pressure. It really did not matter what was—or was not—in the signed agreement. The practical reality was that there was no way to stop India from testing a nuclear weapon if it wished, and there was no way to stop the United States from pulling out of the agreement if India tested—and the latter reality was the best reason for India not to test a weapon in the first place. In other words, everyone agreed on everything—there was no misunderstanding. But, try writing this down in actual words, and you had a problem. For months, negotiators labored over how to write a few sentences that would be acceptable to each side. Any language akin to "if India tests a nuclear weapon …" was a nonstarter in India; taking out such language was unacceptable in the United States.

The eventual solution was an approach that runs contrary to the instincts of most lawyers: The agreement had to be written in language that was as *ambiguous* as possible, thereby allowing each side to interpret the agreement (to its constituency) in the most favorable way.

Implications for Negotiators

As this case reveals, negotiators sometimes need to be wary of contracts that seek to clarify too much. The nuclear negotiations underscore the need for *strategic ambiguity*: Contracts that are overly precise may rob negotiators of the psychological and political flexibility they need at the outset of a complex relationship, for example, when the negotiators represent hard-lined constituencies. Some arrangements are easy to understand and agree to in principle but are very difficult to write down with precision—especially at the outset of what is expected to be a long-term, evolving relationship. Strategic ambiguity may also play an important role in business relationships, especially in early-stage cross-cultural relationships, for which both parties fear that an explicit commitment to collaborate is risky, but being explicitly noncommittal is likely to send a very negative signal. Introducing some degree of ambiguity regarding the nature of the relationship and the strength and length of commitment may provide both parties with the flexibility and freedom needed to overcome initial hesitations and pursue early-stage collaboration with "no strings attached."

The nuclear negotiations provide an additional insight regarding the role of contracts in managing conflict. If the purpose of a contract is to *resolve* conflicts that will emerge in the future, then contract language should be as unambiguous as possible. If, however, the purpose of the contract is to *prevent* conflicts from derailing negotiator efforts at the outset of a relationship, then sometimes the solution is to create and leverage strategic ambiguities in contractual language. As an example, consider the role of control provisions in contracts, which are designed to prevent conflicts from arising in a relationship (Williamson, 1985). However, in their analysis of 102 interfirm disputes, Malhotra and Lumineau (2010) found that too many control provisions in the contract diminish trust and make it less likely that interfirm disputes, if they arise, will be resolved in such a way that the parties will continue to work together. In other words, the types of provisions (e.g., control provisions) that are best able to prevent the onset of conflict may not be the best suited for conflict resolution if a dispute nonetheless arises.

Similarly, an appreciation for strategic ambiguity may help negotiators handle complex agreements that are to be translated into different languages. On the one hand, it is important to reduce the risk of miscommunication, so translations should be as close to perfect as possible. On the other hand, allowing parties on each side to draft language that is better suited to—and acceptable in—its culture, even if the language deviates slightly from what a literal translation would require, may help create a more harmonious and resilient relationship.

> Strategy 5: When the negotiated agreement is inherently self-enforcing, but neither party wishes to acknowledge (or publicize) the factors and conditions that sustain it as such, consider using strategically ambiguous language that allows each party to enter the relationship without losing face or feel that it has promised or committed too much.

PITFALL 4: CONTRACTS THAT FAIL TO INCLUDE APPROPRIATE CONTINGENCIES

In late 2006, three Harvard students founded a business that blended social networking technology with the growing interest in amateur stock market investing (Wasserman & Malhotra, 2008). In November of that year, when the company was only weeks old, the three cofounders drafted a contract that would serve as the basis for their partnership. Among other things, they agreed that the three cofounders would receive a roughly equal share of equity in the company, with a slight premium (approximately 5%) for one of the founders, Michael, who had come up with the idea for the business.

Problems surfaced approximately 2 months later, when Michael began to feel that he was doing a disproportionate amount of the work: He had cancelled other plans for the holiday season to focus on raising money for the startup while one of his cofounders was vacationing with family and the other was still working on his consulting business. By February, Michael was close to securing funding from an angel investor and had been working hard on revising the business plan. His cofounders, he felt, were not working nearly as hard. In light of this, Michael felt that a redistribution of the equity was warranted. The problem was that their original agreement was supposed to have put the equity split issue to rest.

The problem was compounded by the fact that Michael's cofounders, who were willing to give up some equity to keep Michael happy, did not agree that they had been shirking their duties. More important, they were concerned about how easy it seemed for Michael to dismiss their existing agreement as irrelevant. On the one hand, this appears to be a classic example of self-serving biases that lead to overclaiming of credit in teams (Caruso, Epley, & Bazerman, 2006; Epley, Caruso, & Bazerman, 2006). On the other hand, this is a context in which such biases can lead to truly vexing problems: Michael's ability to trust his partners in the future was predicated on their willingness to renegotiate the equity splits in a way that he deemed fair; meanwhile, his cofounders' trust in him would plummet if he were seen as someone who would renege on existing agreements whenever it suited his needs.

The problem for these cofounders, in part, can be traced to the drafting of their initial agreement: The contract failed to include contingency provisions that would address foreseeable conflicts and preempt future mistrust. Consider that many of the justifications that Michael presented when arguing for an increase in his equity stake (e.g., having secured an angel investor and working over the holiday season) could have been anticipated and addressed at the time the contract was initially signed.

For example, the cofounders could have discussed the importance of angel funding at the outset and included an equity bonus (e.g., 2%) for whoever secured an acceptable angel investor. Had such a provision been included in the initial contract, there would be less conflict in the future. Notably, negotiating such a bonus would have been relatively easy at the outset, before anyone had actually secured angel funding, because there would be no reason for the founders to have sharp disagreements on the issue. The conflict was sure to be much greater after one of them had identified an investor; after the fact, Michael unsurprisingly placed a much higher value on his accomplishment than did the other cofounders.

Implications for Negotiators

Even though negotiators understand that certain conflicts will emerge over time, contracts often fail to reflect these concerns. Wisely structured contracts carefully and appropriately accommodate such concerns through the use of contingency provisions (e.g., an equity bonus for securing angel funds). Michael and his cofounders could—and should—have included contingency provisions for a host of issues that they had the capacity to identify and address at the outset. For example, partners to an entrepreneurial venture should be aware of the possibility that one or more of the founders will exit the firm, or reduce involvement, sooner than initially anticipated. If this happens too early in the venture, the remaining cofounders are likely to be frustrated—especially if the exiting founder is walking away with his large equity stake intact. Anticipating this, wise cofounders will create a "vesting schedule" for the stock options given to each founder; the vesting schedule (which should be discussed with Pitfall 1 in mind) is essentially a contingency provision that delineates what portion of the equity stake a founder must relinquish for failing to stay for a specified period of time (usually 3 to 5 years). (Notably, Michael and his cofounders did not have a vesting schedule in place, which created another conflict the following year when factors beyond his control forced one of the cofounders to work only part-time on the venture.) Notably, this is an area in which the experience and expertise of lawyers can be useful; lawyers who have structured similar deals previously are a great resource for information on the types of contingencies that may be appropriate in the current contract.

Strategy 6: Seek to include contractual contingencies that resolve a conflict before it arises when both of these conditions are met: (a) The conflict that will likely emerge in the future can be identified with some degree of provision, and (b) the parties are likely to have more biased perceptions regarding the conflict after versus before it arises.

PITFALL 5: CONTRACTS THAT IGNORE THE LEVEL OF UNCERTAINTY

Let us revisit the cofounders' example from the previous section. I mentioned that one of the mistakes the cofounders made was their failure to include contingency provisions that would have preempted future conflict. There was also a second, and perhaps more critical, mistake: The contract ignored the high degree of uncertainty in the business context and therefore contained provisions whose scope far exceeded what the negotiators could have reasonably contracted at the time of signing.

The negotiators, all experienced entrepreneurs, were well aware that their relationship would evolve over time, and that their evaluations of each founder's level of commitment and ability to add value would be updated as the business model was vetted by investors and evolved over the coming weeks. If these estimates were to be significantly revised in the weeks ahead—as was probable, given how early in the venture they were negotiating—the partners should have waited to apportion at least some of the firm's equity until after some uncertainty was resolved. And yet, the contract included language regarding equity distribution that brazenly ignored the high level of uncertainty that each negotiator knew existed.

Rigid, overreaching contracts that fail to accommodate uncertainty seem to reflect a strategic myopia among negotiators (cf. Streich & Levy, 2007) or perhaps a forecasting failure regarding how things will change in the future (cf., Gilbert, Gill, & Wilson, 2002). Notably, however, even when negotiators understand that the relationship will evolve over time and that it would be wiser to tackle certain issues at a later date, contracts often fail to reflect these concerns, suggesting that the mistake is often an overemphasis during the contracting phase on making sure that nothing is left unaddressed. This again implicates the need for negotiator vigilance in the contracting phase.

Implications for Negotiators

Pitfalls 4 and 5 seem to push in opposite directions. Pitfall 4 warns against *excluding* contingency provisions that might help preempt conflict, whereas Pitfall 5 argues against *including* provisions that create too much rigidity in areas of the relationship that are subject to great uncertainty. To help reconcile this seeming conflict, and to illustrate the issue that confronts managers and executives as negotiators, let us consider the following quotation by a man who (for good reason) is not typically associated with negotiation: Donald Rumsfeld, the former secretary of defense under President George W. Bush. Known for inane, circuitous, and contemptuous answers to media inquiries, Secretary Rumsfeld did, at least on one occasion, state something profound in response to a journalist's question. Here is what he said:

> As we know, there are known knowns; there are things we know we know. We also know there are known unknowns; that is to say we know there are some things we do not know. But there are also unknown unknowns—the ones we don't know we don't know. (February 2002)

This provides a useful framework for thinking about Pitfalls 4 and 5. In most deals, the issues that confront negotiators can be meaningfully categorized as things that are *known,* things that are *known unknowns*, and things that are *unknown unknowns.* For example, a book deal negotiation between an author and a publisher includes consideration of things that are known (e.g., how many copies the author's previous books have sold, where the author is employed, etc.); things that are known to be unknown (e.g., how many copies the current book will sell, when exactly the author will finish writing the book, etc.); and things that the negotiators do not even know that they do not know (the unknown unknowns). We would have a hard time listing the unknown unknowns with any precision (because if we could list them, even as general classes of events such as "negligence," they would be known) but can imagine a host of issues that the parties are unlikely to have even considered at the time of the negotiation, no matter how well prepared they were. For example, imagine publishing contracts that were signed prior to the emergence of the Internet; these may contain language that fails to address whether the publication rights to online books are granted to the publisher or reside with the author.

Wisely structured contracts carefully and appropriately accommodate each of these categories of issues. The knowns are easy to accommodate in the contract: You do so with a *standard provision*. For example, the contract may include a higher advance on royalties in recognition of the fact that the author has a previous best seller. The known unknowns are a bit more difficult to accommodate, but they can be addressed using *contingency provisions*. These are precisely what we considered in Pitfall 4. For example, it is unknown how many books will eventually be sold, but both sides understand that book sales are a key element of the deal (making it a known unknown). Publishing contracts use contingency provisions—in this case, royalty rates—that tie author compensation to eventual book sales.

The last category is the trickiest because contract language cannot be used to address unknown unknowns.[6] The unknown unknowns are the stuff of Pitfall 5. Indeed, contracts, by creating too much rigidity across too many domains of the relationship, are more likely to create or exacerbate unknown-unknown problems than to solve them. This was the case in the example with the three cofounders: Michael felt that he was working harder than the others; this unanticipated problem was made much harder to resolve because the founders had already apportioned all 100% of the firm's equity. The founders would have been wiser to distribute only a portion of the equity (say, 50%, with vesting schedules) at the outset and then agreed in principle to a similar distribution of the remaining equity at a later date, provided there were no material changes in each founder's ability or willingness to contribute. On the other hand, there are at least two reasons for not setting aside too much equity for a later distribution. First, the less equity that is distributed at the outset, the less commitment parties will have to the venture. Second, deferring equity distribution raises the concern that the next negotiation will take place after the company valuation has increased, thereby raising the stakes (and possibly, aggressiveness) of the future negotiation. This suggests that the right answer will require balancing these concerns: not setting aside so much equity that commitment today is too low and stakes tomorrow are too high, but setting aside enough to create slack in an environment where too much is currently unknown.

More generally, partners in a new business venture would be naïve to try to create strict provisions regarding each party's responsibilities and contributions at the outset of the relationship; if the language is overreaching, it will be rejected for fear of creating too many constraints in a domain in which there is great uncertainty. Entrepreneurs in their role as negotiators often seem to understand this; in the contracting phase—often due to pressure from legal advisers—this understanding is often not reflected in the contract that is drafted. While lawyers can help identify and craft appropriate contingencies, trying to resolve all future conflicts this way can lead to reliance on provisions that are not sensitive to the fact that relationships will evolve; when the future state of the world is realized, the basis of the contingency may seem inappropriate.

> Strategy 7: The higher the degree of uncertainty at the time of the contract, the more that negotiators should (a) consider postponing the drafting of contract provisions that are relevant to the uncertainty, (b) create norms and guidelines surrounding renegotiation of provisions in the event that the relationship materially changes, and (c) increase efforts to build trust and social capital between the parties.

NEGOTIATORS AS TRUST BUILDERS IN THE 21st CENTURY

In the previous sections, I have discussed five potential pitfalls regarding contracts that can undermine even well-negotiated and well-intentioned deals. Each of these pitfalls—signaling distrust, having too much codification and clarification, and failing to include contingencies or accommodate uncertainty—are more likely today than they were only a few decades ago. The reason is the tremendous increase in cross-cultural and international negotiations, in which parties to the table are facing not only a greater deficit of initial trust but also very different norms regarding contracts and the contracting process. Managing these differences, again, is a task for deal makers; it cannot be easily outsourced. Consider the following example:

A Chinese executive recently shared with me his beliefs regarding how a difference in perspective regarding the role of contracts often creates an interesting—albeit frustrating—impediment in negotiations between U.S. and Chinese firms:

When negotiations are concluded, the American lawyers we deal with want to gather everything that was said or implied in the negotiation, and write it down in the contract. When the Chinese resist this effort, trust breaks down—for both sides. The Americans say, "How can we trust someone who is unwilling to write down their commitments on paper?" Meanwhile, their Chinese counterpart is saying, "How can we trust someone who will not do anything unless it is written down on paper?" We both end up not trusting each other. We see the role of contracts very differently.

This executive's tale suggests that too much codification (Pitfall 2), or contracting over too broad a domain of issues (Pitfall 5), is not the only problem when deal making takes a cross-cultural turn; what *qualifies* as "too much" codification and what the scope of the contract should be are issues that also need to be negotiated. The example also sheds new light on the age-old observation that cultures differ in whether a particular tactic is seen as ethically acceptable in the context of negotiation (Lewicki & Robinson, 1998). Usually, the debate is whether a mutually acknowledged "bad behavior" (e.g., lying or deceiving in negotiation) is considered too far out of bounds in a particular context. No one really debates whether lying is ethically better or worse than telling the truth; everyone agrees that truth tellers are more ethical than liars, and truth telling remains the gold standard of behavior, regardless of whether someone expects it in an actual negotiation. The executive's observation suggests that a qualitatively different problem can also emerge in cross-cultural negotiations: *You may disagree about which behavior is the gold standard.* In the example, the two cultures fundamentally disagreed about whether putting as much as possible in the contract was really preferable to keeping some (or many) items out. Strategy 1 (avoid provisions that signal distrust in certain cultures) and Strategy 4 (avoid delineating every right and responsibility in the contract) become especially important to consider and follow in light of this discussion.

If writing a more comprehensive contract increases trust in one culture but can diminish trust in another, it provides further evidence that the contracting phase should not be divorced from the negotiation phase: Managers and executives should coordinate with their lawyers (and the parties across the table) when making decisions regarding what should go into the contract. Negotiators would also be wise to coordinate on *when* they should discuss the contract. In some cultures, merely bringing up the contract, or specific provisions, too early in the negotiation can signal distrust (Pitfall 1). Here, again, we see that negotiators will need to be more sensitive about which behaviors and contract structures signal distrust across different cultures.

As a final example, consider a problem that deal makers in India have often faced: the reluctance of Indian negotiators to discuss "exit" clauses or breakup provisions in the event the partnership is unsuccessful. As reported by both Indian and U.S. negotiators, there is a tendency for the Indian counterpart to avoid discussing the possibility of failure or dissolution, making it difficult to include contingency provisions that could ameliorate matters in the event that the parties decide to go their separate ways. This reluctance seems rooted, foremost, in a culture that prides itself on "getting things done," even if finding a solution requires creative or unorthodox means of tackling the problem. While such confidence may be reassuring, it also creates a barrier to structuring the most effective contract. For negotiators, the key insight is that while it may be economically rational and legally advisable to include certain types of provisions (e.g., clauses aimed at unwinding failed collaborations), it is dangerous to ignore the culture-specific psychology surrounding the discussion and inclusion of such provisions. Here, Strategies 2 and 3 (regarding how best to introduce provisions that might signal distrust) and Strategy 5 (regarding the use of strategic ambiguity) may be especially useful.

A GUIDE TO FUTURE RESEARCH

An analysis of the five pitfalls identified in this chapter not only provides practitioners with some useful insights regarding how to manage negotiations and the deal process, but also raises a number of questions for future research. Here are some potential avenues of future research related to each pitfall.

Contracts That Signal Distrust

Researchers have long debated whether and how contracts may sour relationships and, in particular, whether incentives may signal distrust

(Bohnet, Frey, & Huck, 2001; Fehr & Fischbacher, 2002; Frey, 1997; Rigdon, 2009). Dating to the work of Macaulay (1963), and as reiterated more recently by Ghoshal and Moran (1996), the mere suggestion or introduction of contracts may signal distrust of the other party's intentions, thereby disrupting what may otherwise be a cycle of trust and reciprocity leading to mutual trust development (Pillutla et al., 2003). A slightly different mechanism was proposed by Tenbrunsel and Messick (1999), who argued that the existence of a control mechanism (e.g., a penalty clause) can change the "decision frame" that guides the information processing and behavior of exchange partners. As a result, contractual provisions designed to protect against opportunism may, ironically, promote such behavior by inducing a "business" rather than "ethical" framing of the interaction.

While the possibility that contracts will signal (or invoke) mistrust has long been established (but see Rigdon, 2009), little attention has been given to examining the *conditions* under which contracts (or certain types of provisions) will signal mistrust. For example, distrust-signaling provisions will likely have different consequences depending on *when* they are proposed. Prior research on trust development provided competing predictions. Bottom, Gibson, Daniels, and Murnighan (2002) found that trust breaches are easier overcome when they occur early in the relationship because such breaches are evaluated coolly and calmly by victims. This suggests that including a penalty clause for nonperformance (or an incentive for enhanced performance) may be less damaging at the start of a relationship between erstwhile strangers than when it is (suddenly) interjected into an existing relationship between parties that are supposed to trust each other already. On the other hand, Lount, Zhong, Sivanathan, and Murnighan (2008) argued that a breach of trust early in relationships is more devastating because of a primacy effect: In the absence of other information regarding the counterpart's trustworthiness, the breach takes on special importance. Future research that tests these competing predictions regarding the appropriate timing of sensitive contract provisions would be of tremendous value. Notably, the answer may well differ across cultural contexts: Cultures in which negotiators are less inclined to discuss detailed proposals too early in the relationship may also be especially sensitive early on to provisions that signal distrust. Testing the effects of timing, and the moderating effect of cultural context, seems especially important for 21st century researchers. Finally, while attributions-based models of trust are widely accepted (Ferrin & Dirks, 2003; Kramer, 1999;

Mayer, Davis, & Schoorman, 1995; McKnight, Cummings, & Chervany, 1998; Weber, Malhotra, & Murnighan, 2005), there is relatively little work that examined how trust attributions can be effectively managed (Kim, Dirks, Cooper, & Ferrin, 2006). For example, if negotiators have little choice but to propose contracts that can signal distrust, how might they do so most safely? Future research in this domain could examine, for example, the kinds of justifications and frames that a negotiator can leverage to minimize negative attributions related to the proposal. Here again, which justifications and frames will be most effective will depend on the cultural context. For example, it may be easier for negotiators to mitigate negative attributions by blaming the need for a contract on corporate policy in large (or public) versus small (or family-run) businesses; in the case of small or family-run businesses, which are relatively more common in some cultures than in others, negotiators may need to justify their demands for sensitive provisions by arguing that these are designed to protect the relationship (i.e., they protect "us," and not just "me"). Thus, additional research could help provide greater understanding of whether and when contracts will signal mistrust, when the consequences will be most severe, and how the damage can be managed or mitigated. For example, we may discover that the risk of signaling distrust is amplified in cross-cultural exchanges and when contracts (or certain types of provisions) are not institutionalized aspects of business practice. Meanwhile, I expect that culture moderates (a) whether contracts are most likely to signal distrust when proposed early versus late and (b) how negotiators may best shape the attributions of the other party to minimize distrust attributions.

Contracts That Codify Too Much

More systematic and extensive research is warranted when we consider how negotiators could implement strategic incompleteness in the contracts they structure. The very notion of strategic incompleteness begs the question: How do we decide what to include versus exclude from the contract? For example, in how much detail should rights and responsibilities of each party be specified in the contract? Prior research suggested that too little specification may lead to coordination problems even among well-intentioned parties, while too much specification can make the relationship too rigid for strategic adaptation to changing environments. As Vlaar (2008, p. 18) has noted:

> The relationship between contracting and interorganizational performance is likely to follow a curve-linear path, where too little contracting gives rise to chaos and destructive or opportunistic behaviour and where too much contracting causes rigidity and curbs creativeness and entrepreneurial activities.

More recently, Malhotra and Lumineau (2010) have demonstrated that the degree of contract completeness may be less important than the types of provisions that are included. More specifically, coordination-oriented provisions lead to enhanced perceptions of competence and a greater desire to continue collaborating even after a dispute, whereas control-oriented provisions have mixed results: They enhance perceptions of competence but reduce perceptions of goodwill, potentially diminishing the willingness to continue collaboration in the shadow of conflict. This line of research suggested that the types of provisions that should be included or excluded may be a function of the context: Environments in which competence-based trust is critical may favor the inclusion of both coordination and control provisions, whereas environments in which it is critical for parties to create goodwill may demand a reduced emphasis on control provisions. These issues become especially important in the domain of cross-cultural negotiations, for which both competence and goodwill are harder to gauge.

Another avenue of study on these issues would be to examine further which subset of a firm's products and services should be priced into the contract and which should be given away for free. These questions have been studied only cursorily in the past, but prior research serves as a useful point of departure. Cialdini (1993) has written extensively about the power of reciprocity and the tendency of recipients to reciprocate even unsolicited and unwanted gifts, suggesting a role for exchange-related activities that are not tied to formal agreements. The power of token, unilateral concessions was emphatically demonstrated by James and Bolstein (1992), who found that respondents were almost twice as likely to complete a questionnaire when they received a $1 bill as a gift "in the envelope," as opposed to an incentive that credibly guaranteed $50 if and when the questionnaire was returned. Additional research is clearly warranted and should focus on providing more rigorous answers to the question that is at the heart of strategic incompleteness: When is the goodwill and trust created by excluding a contract provision more valuable than the revenue created (or risk reduced) by including it in the contract? As one example, research on loss aversion and the endowment effect (Kahneman, Knetsch, & Thaler, 1991) would suggest that parties would be more receptive to paying "high" prices on services that have previously not been offered than paying "moderate" prices on those that have previously been given away for free. To the extent that the increase in cross-cultural negotiations makes it more likely that negotiators are engaging with a party for the first time or are early in the relationship, this also raises questions about how to set the appropriate precedent. Might token concessions made at the start of a relationship limit negotiation options later in the relationship? And if so, which types of concessions are more likely to be precedent setting in different cultures. For example, it may be easier to make token, unilateral concessions in cultures (e.g., in some East Asian countries) that have norms surrounding gift giving in early-stage relationships but much more difficult in cultures in which concessions are likely to be interpreted as weakness.

Contracts That Clarify Too Much

Strategic ambiguity has received little attention in research on negotiation, although it has recently surfaced in the study of protracted conflicts. Atran and Axelrod (2008) referred to the possibility of leveraging "creative ambiguity" as a solution to reconciling seemingly incompatible positions that are tied to sacred values:

> During World War II the U.S. government promised the American people and its allies that it would accept nothing less than "unconditional surrender." But the government and people of Japan were adamant that the Emperor must be preserved. Realizing this, the United States reframed the meaning of "unconditional surrender" by making clear that it would graciously allow the Emperor of Japan to retain his title and liberty. People often apply the "same" sacred values in different ways, which facilitates creative use of ambiguity. ... For both Israelis and Palestinians, "The Land" is sacred, with Jerusalem at its center. ... Israeli political leaders creatively reinterpreted the historical scope of "The Land," first to justify claims on Gaza and then to justify leaving it. If Palestinians, who simply refer to Jerusalem as "The Holy" (*Al Quds*), can reframe their idea of the city to include only its Arab suburbs and part of the Temple Mount (*Haram Al-Sharif*), then Israel might be willing to accept the Palestinian capital there. (pp. 235–236)

In contrast, Pressman (2007), in his evaluation of the history of Israeli–Syrian negotiations, cautioned against reliance on strategic ambiguity, especially in contexts for which an eventual, final agreement will require disambiguation:

> Ambiguity, an artifice so essential to diplomacy and conflict resolution, can end up as a destructive factor rather than a constructive one. It may help bridge gaps, but it can create problems when the parties turn (inevitably, if the process is to succeed) to concrete implementation. ... (p. 351)
>
> The absence of clarity helps draw the parties closer and agree to hold talks. Yet it becomes problematic when the talks shift toward implementation and diplomatic formulations must be translated into, for example, lines on a map. (p. 379)

Future research that extends beyond case studies to more rigorously evaluate the implementation of strategic ambiguity, as well as the boundary conditions for its successful use, would fill an important gap in the research. As an example of how such research might be structured, consider the work by Ginges, Atran, Medin, and Shikaki (2007), who surveyed "moral absolutist" Israeli settlers and Palestinian refugees regarding their willingness to consider compromise on sacred values. They found, not surprisingly, that an offer that contains a taboo trade-off (e.g., Palestinians will recognize Israel as a Jewish state in exchange for a two-state solution) can trigger anger as well as support for violent opposition. More interestingly, if an incentive (e.g., billions of dollars of support will be provided to Palestinians) is included to sweeten the offer, the level of anger and support for violence *increases* among those who would be receiving the sweetened offer. Similar survey research could be structured with respect to offers that make taboo trade-offs more or less ambiguous; one way to make difficult trade-offs palatable may be to make the details more ambiguous. Likewise, research on early-stage cross-cultural business relationships may be an ideal context in which to study the effects of strategic ambiguity on outcomes because the level of commitment to the proposed relationship can vary dramatically in such contexts. In early-stage ventures for which the value proposition is unclear, and when both parties are unsure whether they are committed to the relationship, some level of ambiguity regarding the nature of the relationship may provide each party the flexibility and freedom it needs to overcome initial hesitations and pursue early-stage collaboration; meanwhile, if one party is committed and the other is not, strategic ambiguity may not help as it sends a bad signal to the committed party.

Also important, especially in cross-cultural research, is the need to evaluate the potentially harmful effects of strategic ambiguity on future contracts. While strategic ambiguity may be useful for navigating sensitive issues that arise today, it may also exacerbate discrepancies in perspective over time, creating greater difficulty when the parties negotiate (or renegotiate) contracts in the future. This seeming dilemma—of balancing current and future contracting needs—provides fertile ground for future researchers.

Contracts That Fail to Include Appropriate Contingencies

Prior research on contingency provisions has enumerated their benefits primarily from two perspectives. Raiffa (1982) and Bazerman and Gillespie (1999) have pointed out that contingency provisions help parties to overcome *current conflicts* regarding future events. For example, if a potential employee is arguing that he or she will be a spectacular salesperson and deserves a high salary, but the employer is less confident, then the two parties can resolve the conflict about how well the salesperson will perform by including a contingency in the employee's compensation (e.g., a commission on sales). Malhotra and Bazerman (2007) added that merely proposing a contingency contract can also help detect deception in negotiation. If the salesperson is unwilling to take a slightly lower salary in exchange for a high commission, the employer may deduce that the salesperson is not as confident in his or her abilities as he or she claims.

The founders' example described in the chapter points to another area in which contingencies can be useful: Contingency provisions can mitigate *future conflicts*. For example, including a bonus for securing angel funding would not serve to resolve any current disagreements between cofounders regarding future performance but would help resolve conflicts that may arise at a later date. Bazerman and Gillespie (1999) argued that contingency provisions are not used often enough to resolve current disagreements. I would propose that they are even less often used when the conflict they address will not erupt until some date in the future. Research that explores when such contingency provisions are appropriate and the conditions that facilitate their adoption would serve as a useful extension of existing research on contingency contracts. For example, laboratory experiments that have previously examined whether parties are wise enough to craft contingency agreements to solve current conflicts (Thompson, Gentner, & Loewenstein, 2000) could be adapted to include conditions in which the conflict would only arise later in the relationship. This would allow us to test whether the proposition (i.e., contingency clauses are even less likely to be adopted when conflict will arise in the future) is correct.

Contracts That Ignore the Level of Uncertainty

Prior research on psychological contracts has acknowledged that contracts of the written document variety cannot and should not attempt to represent the entirety of the rights and obligations of each party (Robinson & Rousseau, 1994; Rousseau & Parks, 1993). Rather, there is a presumption of good faith in most business relationships and an acknowledgment that when certain types of unforeseen problems arise, contracts will not contain the answer; the solutions will need to be negotiated, and these negotiations will fare much better if the parties have a reservoir of trust on which to rely (Lumineau & Malhotra, 2010).

Furthermore, while prior research has studied negotiations that take place in existing *relationships* (Valley, Neale, & Mannix, 1995), there is considerably less focus on the topic of "renegotiating" existing *agreements*. This is somewhat surprising, given how pervasive renegotiation is in practice. For example, most employee compensation negotiations are, in fact, renegotiations of an existing agreement, but negotiation researchers typically only consider the "initial" employer–employee negotiation. Other examples for which the current negotiation is strongly affected by previous agreements include renegotiations of labor–management contracts (Malhotra & Hout, 2007), renewals in most vertical relationships (e.g., distribution and supplier contracts) and "postsettlement settlements" in virtually any domain of business (Raiffa, 1985). Future research might usefully focus on issues that become important in such contexts, such as (a) how negotiators should change their strategy when postsettlement settlements or future renewals of the contract are expected; (b) how contracts should be structured so that they balance the need for security today with flexibility tomorrow; and (c) how the tendency to overly discount the future affects the contracts that negotiators favor—and what effect this has on future negotiations?

CONTRACTS AS INSTRUMENTS OF TRUST

Considerable attention has been devoted in recent years to examining the interplay between contracts and trust (see Vlaar, 2008, for a review). This research has developed along three distinct lines of inquiry (Puranam & Vanneste, 2009). The first examines how (preexisting) trust influences the form and degree of contract that emerges (e.g., Argyres, Bercovitz, & Mayer, 2007; Corts & Singh, 2004; Gulati, 1995; Kalnins & Mayer, 2004). The second focuses on how contracts and trust interact, for example, the role that trust plays as a moderator of the relationship between contractual governance and performance (Poppo & Zenger, 2002). The third domain of research has sought to examine the effects of contractual governance on the development of trust (Macaulay, 1963; Malhotra & Murnighan, 2002).

The current chapter relates to the third domain but differs in multiple ways from the perspective that organizational behavior researchers have typically adopted. First, I have focused not only on contract structure but also on the contracting process. Second, I have adopted a negotiation, or deal-making, lens—heavily influenced by research in psychology—to identify the key problems that can emerge when the contracting phase is ignored by managers and executives. Third, I have avoided taking a stance on whether contracts "help or hurt" trust or whether they are "complements or substitutes"; rather, I have acknowledged that the modal state of the world is one in which business relationships require both contracts and trust and have explored some of the problems that this coexistence creates. Finally, in identifying key insights for practitioners and scholars, I have placed a heavy emphasis on understanding and solving the problems that arise as negotiators try to balance risk mitigation and value creation.

The key insight for negotiation practitioners is, at a general level, quite clear: It is important to stay at the table even after an agreement is reached and hands have been shaken. In important deals, characterized by long-term relationships, changing economic conditions, the possibility of repeat business, and the need for continued coordination and cooperation, the contracting process and contract structure are critical factors that require *negotiator* attention, not simply legal review. More specifically, this chapter has identified five potential pitfalls that can plague negotiated agreements in which the contracting process has been ignored—and has provided strategies for avoiding them.

The implication for negotiation scholars is that our focus should not be limited to deal-making strategies, tactics, and attitudes that lead to (or impede) agreement. In important deals, what happens after the deal is done—that is, the contracting phase—is also important to explore.

In the previous sections, I have identified a number of specific questions that future research might fruitfully tackle. Because of the well-established tradition of emphasizing prescriptive advice (rooted in descriptive analysis), negotiation scholars are perhaps better suited to answering these questions than are legal or economic scholars. But, to do so most effectively, negotiation scholars will likely have to collaborate with—or at least learn from—those who have already spent decades examining contracts and the contracting process from a descriptive and normative lens.

NOTES

1. As we shall also see in the numerous examples that follow, reaching better outcomes tends also to make the relationship more resilient and safer in the long run.
2. Under common law, requirements for a legal contract include, for example, offer and acceptance, consideration, and an intention to enter into a legal relationship.
3. In his seminal paper, "Perfect Equilibrium in a Bargaining Model," Rubinstein (1982) stated: "When I refer in this paper to the *Bargaining Problem*, I mean the following situation and question: Two individuals have before them several contractual agreements. Both have interests in reaching agreement, but their interests are not entirely identical. What 'will be' the agreed contract, assuming that both parties behave rationally?" (p. 97)
4. There are other domains of game theory research that focus on contracts and deemphasize or ignore negotiation.
5. The following example is based on the author's personal conversations with former U.S. Under Secretary of State Nicholas Burns, who helped negotiate the deal on behalf of the United States.
6. Even *force majeure* clauses are aimed at known unknowns.

REFERENCES

Argyres, N. S., Bercovitz, J., & Mayer, K. J. 2007. Complementarity and evolution of contractual provisions: An empirical study of IT service contracts. *Organization Science, 18*, 3–19.

Atran, S., & Axelrod, R. 2008. Reframing sacred values. *Negotiation Journal, 24*, 221–246,

Bagley, C. E. 2005. *Winning legally: How to use the law to create value, marshal resources, and manage risk.* Boston: Harvard Business School Press.

Bazerman, M. H., Curhan, J. R., Moore, D. A., & Valley, K. L. 2000. Negotiation. *Annual Review of Psychology, 51*, 279–314.

Bazerman, M. H., & Gillespie, J. J. 1999. Betting on the future: The virtues of contingent contracts. *Harvard Business Review, 77*, 155–160.

Bazerman, M. H., & Neale, M. A. 1992. *Negotiating rationally.* New York: Free Press.

Bohnet, I., Frey, B. S., & Huck, S. 2001. More order with less law: On contract enforcement, trust, and crowding. *American Political Science Review, 95*, 131–144.

Bottom, W. P., Gibson, K., Daniels, S., & Murnighan, J. K. 2002. When talk is not cheap: Substantive penance and expressions of intent in the reestablishment of cooperation. *Organization Science, 13*, 497–513.

Caruso, E., Epley, N., & Bazerman M. H. 2006. The costs and benefits of undoing egocentric responsibility assessments in groups. *Journal of Personality and Social Psychology, 91*, 857–871.

Cialdini, R. B. 1993. *Influence: Science and practice* (3rd ed.). New York: HarperCollins College.

Corts, K. S., & Singh, J. 2004. The effect of repeated interaction on contract choice: Evidence from offshore drilling. *Journal of Law, Economics, and Organization, 20*, 230–260.

Crocker K. J., & Reynolds K. J. 1993. The efficiency of incomplete contracts: An empirical analysis of Air Force engine procurement. *RAND Journal of Economics, 24*, 126–146.

Deci, E. L., & Ryan, R. M. 1985. *Intrinsic motivation and self-determination in human behavior.* New York: Plenum.

Epley, N., Caruso, E., & Bazerman, M. H. 2006. When perspective taking increases taking: Reactive egoism in social interaction. *Journal of Personality and Social Psychology, 91*, 872–889.

Fehr, E., & Fischbacher, U. 2002. Why social preferences matter: The impact of non-selfish preferences on competition, cooperation, and incentives. *The Economic Journal, 112*, 133.

Ferrin, D. L., & Dirks, K. T. 2003. The use of rewards to increase and decrease trust: Mediating processes and differential effects. *Organization Science, 14*, 18–31.

Frey, B. 1997. A constitution for knaves crowds out civic virtues. *The Economic Journal, 107*, 1043–1053.

Gambetta, D. 1988. Can we trust trust? In D. Gambetta (Ed.), *Trust: Making and breaking cooperative relationships.* Cambridge, MA: Blackwell.

Ghoshal, S., & Moran, P. 1996. Bad for practice: A critic of the transaction cost theory. *Academy of Management Review, 21*, 13–47.

Gilbert, D. T., Gill, M. J., & Wilson, T. D. 2002. The future is now: Temporal correction in affective forecasting. *Organizational Behavior and Human Decision Processes, 88*, 430–444.

Ginges, J., Atran, S., Medin, D., & Shikaki, K. 2007. Sacred bounds on rational resolution of violent political conflict. *Proceedings of the National Academy of Sciences of the United States of America, 104*, 7357–7360.

Gulati, R. 1995. Does familiarity breed trust? The implications of repeated ties for contractual choice in alliances. *Academy of Management Journal, 38*, 85–112.

Hall, B. J., & Bennett, N. S. 2010. *Recruiting Andrew Yard* (Harvard Business School Cases, 911-028, 911-029 and 911-030). Boston, MA: Harvard Business School Publishing.

Hart, O., & Moore, J. 1988. Incomplete contracts and renegotiation. *Econometrica, 56*, 755–785.

James, J. M., & Bolstein, R. 1992. Large monetary incentives and their effect on mail survey response rates. *Public Opinion Quarterly, 56*, 442–453.

Jensen, M. C., & Meckling, W. H. 1976. Theory of the firm: Managerial behavior, agency costs and ownership structure. *Journal of Financial Economics, 3*, 305–360.

Kahneman, D., Knetsch, J. L., & Thaler, R. H. 1991. Anomalies: The endowment effect, loss aversion, and status-quo bias. *Journal of Economic Perspectives, 5*, 193–206.

Kalnins, A., & Mayer, K. J. 2004. Relationships and hybrid contracts: An analysis of contract choice in information technology. *Journal of Law, Economics, and Organization, 20*, 207–229.

Kim, P. H., Dirks, K. T., Cooper, C. D., & Ferrin, D. L. 2006. When more blame is better than less: The implications of internal vs. external attributions for the repair of trust after a competence- vs. integrity-based trust violation. *Organizational Behavior and Human Decision Processes, 99*, 49–65.

Kramer, R. M. 1999. Trust and distrust in organizations: Emerging perspectives, enduring questions. *Annual Review of Psychology, 50*, 569–598.

Lax, D. A., & Sebenius, J. K. 1986. *The manager as negotiator: Bargaining for cooperation and competitive gain.* New York: Free Press.

Lax, D. A., & Sebenius, J. K. 2006. *3-D negotiation, Powerful tools to change the game in your most important deals.* Boston: Harvard Business School Press.

Lepper, M. R., Greene, D., & Nisbett, R. E. 1973. Undermining children's intrinsic interest with extrinsic rewards: A test of the overjustification hypothesis. *Journal of Personality and Social Psychology, 28*, 129–137.

Lewicki, R. J., & Robinson, R. J. 1998. Ethical and unethical bargaining tactics: An empirical study. *Journal of Business Ethics, 17*, 665–682.

Lewicki, R. J., Saunders, D. M., & Barry, B. 2006. *Negotiation.* Boston, MA: McGraw-Hill Irwin.

Lount, R. B., Zhong, C. B., Sivanathan, N., & Murnighan, J. K. 2008. Getting off on the wrong foot: The timing of a breach and the restoration of trust. *Personality and Social Psychology Bulletin, 34*, 1601–1612.

Lumineau, F., & Malhotra, D. 2010. Shadow of the contract: How contract structure shapes inter-firm dispute resolution. *Strategic Management Journal, 32*, 532–555.

Macaulay, S. 1963. Non-contractual relations in business. *American Sociological Review, 28*, 55–70.

Malhotra, D., & Bazerman, M. H. 2007. *Negotiation genius.* New York: Bantam Books.

Malhotra, D., & Bazerman, M. H. 2008. Psychological influence in negotiation: An introduction long overdue. *Journal of Management, 34*, 509–531.

Malhotra, D., & Hout, M. 2007. *Negotiating on thin ice: The 2004–2005 NHL dispute (A) and (B)* (Harvard Business School Cases 906-038 and 906-039). Boston, MA: Harvard Business School Publishing.

Malhotra, D., & Lumineau, F. 2010. Trust and collaboration in the aftermath of conflict: The effects of contract structure. *Academy of Management Journal, 54*(5), 532–555.

Malhotra, D., & Murnighan, J. K. 2002. The effects of contracts on interpersonal trust. *Administrative Science Quarterly, 47*, 534–559.

Mayer, R. C., Davis, J. H., & Schoorman, F. D. 1995. An integrative model of organizational trust. *Academy of Management Review, 20*, 709–734.

McKnight, D. H., Cummings, L. L., & Chervany, N. L. 1998. Initial trust formation in new organizational relationships. *Academy of Management Review, 23*, 473–490.

Newman, J. M., & Milkovich, G. T. 1990. Procedural justice challenges in compensation: Eliminating the fairness gap. *Labor Law Journal, 41*, 575–580.

New York Times online (2007, Oct. 19) Torre calls Yankees bonus offer an insult. Available at http://www.nytimes.com/2007/10/19/sports/baseball/19cnd-torre.html

New York Times online (2007, Oct. 24) In interview, Torre details meeting with the Yankees. Available at http://www.nytimes.com/2007/10/24/sports/baseball/24torre.html?pagewanted=print

Pillutla, M., Malhotra, D., & Murnighan, J. K. 2003. Attributions of trust and the calculus of reciprocity. *Journal of Experimental Social Psychology, 39*, 448–455.

Poppo, L., & Zenger, T. 2002. Do formal contracts and relational governance function as substitutes or complements? *Strategic Management Journal, 23*, 707–726.

Posner, R. 1972. *Economic analysis of law*. Boston: Little, Brown.

Pressman, J. 2007. Mediation, domestic politics, and the Israeli-Syrian negotiations, 1991–2000. *Security Studies, 16*, 350–381.

Puranam, P., & Vanneste, B. S. 2009. Trust and governance: Untangling a tangled web. *Academy of Management Review, 34*, 11–31.

Raiffa, H. 1982. *The art and science of negotiation*. Cambridge, MA: Harvard University Press/Belknap.

Raiffa, H. 1985. Post-settlement settlements. *Negotiation Journal, 1*, 9–12.

Rigdon, M. 2009. Trust and reciprocity in incentive contracting. *Journal of Economic Behavior and Organization, 70*(1–2), 93–105.

Robinson, S. L., & Rousseau, D. M. 1994. Violating the psychological contract: Not the exception but the norm. *Journal of Organizational Behavior, 15*, 245–259.

Rousseau, D. M., & Parks, J. M. 1993. The contracts of individuals and organizations. *Research in Organizational Behavior, 15*, 1–43.

Rubinstein, A. 1982. Perfect equilibrium in a bargaining model. *Econometrica, 50*, 97–109.

Rumsfeld, D. Press briefing (2002, February).

Streich, P., & Levy, J. S. 2007. Time horizons, discounting, and intertemporal choice. *Journal of Conflict Resolution, 51*, 199–226.

Subramanian, G. 2010. *Negotiauctions: New dealmaking strategies for a competitive marketplace*. New York: Norton.

Tenbrunsel, A. E., & Messick, D. M. 1999. Sanctioning systems, decision frames, and cooperation. *Administrative Science Quarterly, 44*, 684–707.

Thompson, L. 2005. *Heart and mind of the negotiator* (3rd ed.). Upper Saddle River, NJ: Prentice Hall.

Thompson, L., Gentner, D., & Loewenstein, J. 2000. Avoiding missed opportunities in managerial life: Analogical training more powerful than individual case training. *Organizational Behavior and Human Decision Processes, 82*, 60–75.

Ury, W. L., Brett, J. M., & Goldberg, S. B. 1988. *Getting disputes resolved*. San Francisco: Jossey-Bass.

Valley, K. L., Neale, M, A., & Mannix, E. A. 1995. Friends, lovers, colleagues, strangers: The effects of relationships on the process and outcome of dyadic negotiations. In R. J. Bies, R. J. Lewicki, & B. H. Sheppard (Eds.), *Research on negotiation in organizations* (Vol. 5, pp. 65–93). Greenwich, CT: JAI.

Vlaar, P. W. L. 2008. *Contracts and trust in alliances: Discovering, creating, and appropriating value*. Cheltenham, UK: Elgar.

Von Neumann, J., & Morgenstern, O. 1947. *Theory of games and economic behavior* (2nd rev. ed.). Princeton, NJ: Princeton University Press.

Walker, G., & D. Weber. 1984. A transaction cost approach to make-or-buy decisions. *Administrative Science Quarterly, 29*, 373–391.

Wasserman, N. T., & Malhotra, D. 2008. *Negotiating equity splits at UpDown* (Harvard Business School Case 809-020). Boston, MA: Harvard Business School Publishing.

Weber, J. M., Malhotra, D., & Murnighan, J. K. 2005. Normal acts of irrational trust: Motivated attributions and the trust development process. In R. M. Kramer (Ed.), *Research in organizational behavior* (Vol. 27, pp. 75–101). New York: Elsevier/JAI.

Wehberg, H. 1959. Pacta sunt servanda. *The American Journal of International Law, 53*, 775–786.

Williamson, O. E. 1979. Transaction cost economics: The governance of contractual relations. *Journal of Law and Economics, 22*, 3–61.

Williamson, O. E. 1985. *The economic institutions of capitalism*. New York: Free Press.

Williamson, O. E. 1991. Comparative economic organization: The analysis of discrete struc-tural alternatives. *Administrative Science Quarterly, 36*, 269–296.

Williamson, O. E. 1996. *The mechanisms of governance*. New York: Oxford University Press.

14

The "New" World of Negotiating: Interactions Mediated by Information Technology

Ritu Agarwal, Siva Viswanathan, and Animesh Animesh

INTRODUCTION

Negotiations are widely used by entities such as individuals, teams, firms, countries, and others to conduct a variety of transactions. Fundamentally, negotiation is a market mechanism to allocate the gains from a trade, which may be to share or divide limited resources, create something new that neither party can create on its own, or resolve a dispute and conflict between the transacting parties. Bargaining, auctions, and bartering or exchanges can all be considered different forms of negotiation. New information technologies (ITs) spawned by the Internet have enabled negotiations to occur between entities that may be geographically dispersed and even virtual "strangers." The effects of IT on negotiations include the birth of online auctions (e.g., ebay.com), "spot" markets for selling consulting services (e.g., eLance.com), and companies that enable the monitoring of remote workers (e.g., oDesk.com), among numerous other examples too abundant to list.

The goal of this chapter is to explore how the ubiquity of IT and its mediation in the interaction among parties in a transaction has altered the landscape of negotiations. We develop a framework that describes (a) the influence of IT on the *prenegotiation (or "contact"-related) stage*, the initial stage of negotiation between parties considering making a contractual agreement with each other; (b) the influence of IT on the *negotiation (or "contract"-related) stage,* in which the negotiating parties seek to reach a contractual agreement; and (c) the influence of IT on the *postnegotiation (or "control"-related) stage,* during which the parties are engaged in communications with each other and various activities to ensure that the terms of the contract are faithfully executed (Carmel & Nicholson, 2005; Nooteboom, 1993). We explore the nature of activities in each of these negotiation stages and describe how the Internet and other recent developments in ITs have influenced the transaction costs associated with these activities. As such, we approach the effects of IT on negotiations through a "transactions cost" lens and discuss how technology has altered these costs in the three crucial negotiation stages of contact, contract, and control. We conclude by noting how the new IT-related mechanisms for negotiation yield important implications for managers as well as raise critical questions for future research. Before describing the three stages of negotiation comprising our framework, we begin by briefly reviewing literature associated with transaction costs so that there is an understanding about what we mean by taking a transaction cost approach to the subject of negotiation.

A TRANSACTION COST APPROACH TO NEGOTIATING

The outcome of a successful negotiation is typically an agreement that is referred to as a contract. The parties in negotiation use the contract (which may be communicated formally/informally, explicitly/implicitly, orally, or in writing) to commit to certain actions in return for specified benefits, to clarify terms of agreement, to delineate punishments for noncompliance and rewards for compliance, and to reduce risk (Lupia & Strøm, 2008). The costs of reaching such agreements are known as *transaction costs,* which Kreps (1990, p. 743) defines as follows:

> When undertaking a transaction, parties to the transaction must incur several sorts of costs. ... [Some] costs are incurred before the transaction takes place. If the transaction is to be governed by a written contract, the contract must be drafted. Whether governed by a contract or simply by verbal commitments, the terms of the transaction must be negotiated. [Other] costs are incurred in consummating and safeguarding the deal that was originally struck.

Negotiation participants spend time and effort to obtain an agreement that is acceptable to all stakeholders. These expenditures, which depend on the complexity of the agreement being sought, make transaction costs an important factor in determining the nature of negotiations as well as the likelihood of successful negotiations (Lupia & Strøm, 2008). Transaction costs arise for a variety of reasons and are manifested in many different forms (Hobbs, 1996). For example, the parties in the negotiation may need to expend effort to find each other, such as a buyer seeking the lowest-cost seller for a specific product. Because of the effort involved in performing a thorough and extensive search for the best partner, boundedly rational behavior may occur, leading the information seeker to settle for a less-than-optimal solution. Each party may possess different types, quantity, and quality of information, thereby creating information asymmetry and shifting the bargaining power toward the party that is more well endowed. When transactions occur between parties that have not contracted before, transaction costs created by opportunistic behavior by one of the parties may exist.

The three stages of negotiation that each involve several activities are fraught with transaction costs. Figure 14.1 identifies the activities in each stage and is designed to help negotiators understand and manage transaction costs for each activity via the help of IT. Next, we discuss the negotiation stages and the activities within each, together with the related IT interventions that affect the transaction costs of these activities, each stage in turn.

THE CONTACT STAGE

The *contact stage* is a "prenegotiation stage" since it occurs *prior* to the actual commencement of the negotiation, or contract, stage. In technology-mediated settings such as the Internet, the nature of the contact stage is one that typically *lacks* interpersonal or face-to-face exchange between the negotiating parties. In general, the key task confronting a negotiator here is a search for information. Core activities by individual negotiation parties include (a) search for a (buyer/supplier) partner; (b) search for product information, including price and product attributes, (c) search for

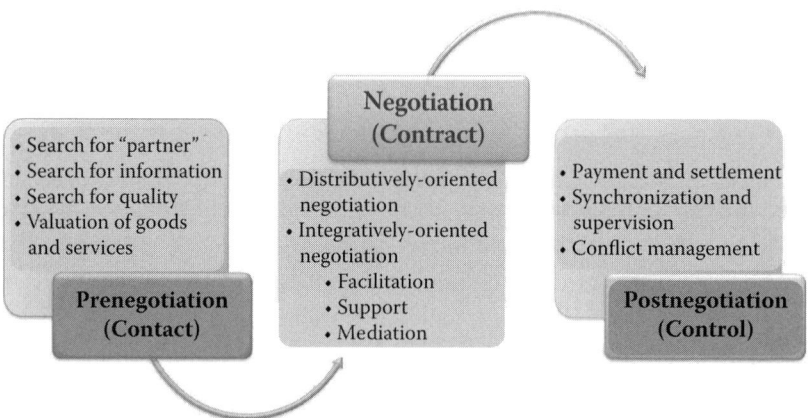

FIGURE 14.1
The stages of negotiation and associated activities.

information about the quality of the goods and services that will potentially be exchanged and the quality or reputation of potential partners, and (d) determination of the true value of the good to be exchanged. Next, we describe the transaction costs typically associated with each activity and illustrate how recent developments in IT have changed the nature of these costs.

The Impact of IT on the Search for a Partner

Risks and uncertainties are an integral part of all negotiations and transactions, and a significant amount of information gathering and processing is required to reduce these uncertainties. Of these, the foremost is the search for the right transaction partner offering the right products or services at the right price. Parties can incur significant search costs, and search costs are often considered one of the primary costs of transacting in a marketplace. Search costs can include the cost of acquiring information about products and sellers, as well as the time and effort incurred in searching for the right transaction partner.

Prior to discussing specific search costs, we note that technology also allows efficient matching of actors for a negotiation transaction and thus enables new markets. For example, Internet technology has revived bartering, a primarily cashless trade negotiation. A traditional bartering process is often impractical or inefficient due to the difficulty in finding a match between parties who have precisely what the opposite wants and possesses. However, using the Internet, it is efficient to swap both physical products and services. Tools provided by companies such as swap.com allow a party to list the product/service it wants or can offer. The automated matching tool then uses proprietary algorithms to show all the items that one can receive in lieu of the items offered, as well as information about the other party offering that item. Once the parties accept the offers, the trade is completed. These online services eliminate geographical barriers, simplify the timing problem with bartering, and speed up the process. Further, some systems also offer trade credits when one party cannot find something immediately. Such bartering facilitation services enabled by the Internet lower the cost of negotiation by providing access to an extensive database of barter offers. The automated matching tool simplifies the negotiation process and increases the contracting efficiency.

Buyer's Search Cost

Search costs play a significant role in consumer buying decisions. High search costs can lead to inefficient outcomes for parties in a transaction. For instance, in traditional markets for professional services, including physicians, car mechanics, lawyers, and the like, consumers are often forced to stick to a service provider as it is costly to search for cheaper or better alternatives. Search costs can thus create high switching costs for consumers, leading to inefficient outcomes. In the extreme case, very high search costs can even lead to market breakdown. For instance, buyers as well as sellers of antiques or rare collectibles often find it too costly to search for the right transacting partners, delaying trades, sometimes for years.

Recent advances in IT, including the Internet and Web 2.0 technologies, have had a dramatic impact on search costs incurred by buyers as well as sellers. Electronic marketplaces such as eBay and Amazon and search technologies such as Google and Yahoo!, have made it easy to search for and obtain information on a number of facets of sellers and their offerings. In addition to general search services such as Google and Yahoo!, online shopbots, also known as shopping agents or product comparison agents, have grown in popularity. The last few years have witnessed the growth of a number of online shopbots that serve to provide information about sellers and products to help consumers make purchase decisions. The earlier shopbots were price comparison engines such as PriceScan, mySimon, among others, that helped consumers compare prices for the same product offered by competing retailers. BargainFinder, one of the earliest price comparison engines developed by Andersen Consulting, enabled consumers to compare prices of compact disks at different online retailers.

One of the primary outcomes of reduced search costs for buyers has been an increase in competition among sellers, leading to lower prices and more efficient markets. Ease of comparing prices among competing sellers increases price competition, leading to average lower market prices. Theoretical models (e.g., Bakos, 1997; Stahl, 1989) have shown how lowering buyer search costs for price information can reduce the bargaining power of sellers and their ability to extract monopolistic profits and improve consumer welfare. Commensurate with the exponential growth of online shopping and commerce, there has been a growth of empirical studies examining the role of emerging ITs and electronic marketplaces on a variety of market outcomes.

Seller's Search Cost

While the role of the online marketplace in lowering the search costs for buyers and the resulting impact on market prices and outcomes have been well studied by a number of researchers (see, for instance, Alba et al., 1997; Bakos, 1997, 1998; Bapna, Goes, Gupta, & Yiwei, 2004; Ratchford, Lee, & Talukdar, 2003; Smith, Bailey, & Brynjolfsson, 1999), much less is known about their impact on the search costs incurred by sellers. As Kuruzovich, Viswanathan, and Agarwal (2010) noted, "Both buyers and sellers incur search costs in market transactions; while buyers search for products that fit their needs, sellers search for customers whose product preferences and valuations match the sellers' offerings" (p. 1702). In one of the few studies examining the impact of online marketplaces on seller search costs, Kuruzovich et al. (2010) found that online marketplaces offer the potential to reduce search costs for sellers in much the same way as they do for buyers, and the impact of ITs on seller search costs and the resulting outcomes are equally as important. Using data from over 80,000 auctions of used cars online, they found that the lower search costs in online markets enable sellers to relist their vehicles in sequential auctions to search for the best buyer. More important, they found that increased searching by sellers leads to a higher sale price, and the benefits from increased searching are higher in markets with greater dispersion of prices. These findings suggest that the increased access to different types of information as well as the reduction in search costs for both buyers and sellers stemming from the growth of online markets can have significant implications for market participants. However, the impact of these technological developments for any individual participants depends on a number of factors and would require a careful consideration of the context.

Search Costs and the Long Tail of Commerce

Reduction in buyer search costs combined with the reduction in costs for sellers of reaching consumers have given rise to another interesting phenomenon: the long tail of commerce. According to Brynjolfsson, Hu, and Smith (2006):

> While consumers certainly do benefit from lower prices online, our research finds that they derive far more value from another important characteristic of Internet markets—the ability of online merchants to help consumers locate, evaluate, and purchase a far wider variety of products than they can via traditional brick and mortar channels. (p. 67)

For instance, compared to traditional book retailers that carry between 40,000 and 100,000 unique titles, Internet retailers like Amazon.com carry over 3 million titles. More interestingly, Brynjolfsson et al. (2006) found that 30–40% of Amazon's sales come from this "long tail" (Anderson, 2004) of books—products that are not normally found in traditional brick-and-mortar stores. Along similar lines, the Internet also facilitates the growth of the long tail of sellers by enabling small sellers (e.g., microbrewers and specialty retailers such as Extend-ITs.com that sell seat belt extenders for airline passengers) to reach customers globally at a low cost. The long tail of products and sellers is largely attributable to the ability of sellers to increase their reach at relatively low costs of production and distribution compared to traditional channels, as well as to the ability of sellers to aggregate demand for niche products that could be distributed across a wide geographic region. In addition, the availability of a variety of search technologies and recommendation systems (e.g., Amazon's recommendation system that recommends rare or niche products based on an analysis of customer preferences and purchase histories—products that would otherwise not have been in their consideration set) have dramatically increased the ability of consumers to discover niche as well as emerging products and services. The Internet has helped the long tail of sellers in several product categories, including news, music, stock photography, and beer, among others.

In a more recent study, Brynjolfsson, Yu, and Smith (2010) compared the change in the sales distribution of books on Amazon.com between 2000 and 2008 and found that the long tail has grown longer, with niche books accounting for 36.7% of Amazon's sales. In addition to benefiting small and niche sellers, the growth of the long tail also increases consumer welfare. Brynjolfsson, Hu, and Smith (2003) showed that the ability to purchase previously hard-to-find products increases consumer welfare by almost $1 billion, which is almost five time larger than the consumer welfare resulting from increased competition or lower prices.

The Impact of IT on the Search for Information

Although the Internet still accounts for only a small fraction of overall retail sales, a vast majority of consumers use the Internet to search for products and services and to gather the requisite information for decision making. Several research studies have examined the role of such increased information availability for buyers as well as sellers.

Search for Price Information

In one of the early studies of the impact of the Internet for consumers, Brynjolfsson and Smith (2000) found that Internet retailers charge lower prices than conventional retailers, and that price dispersion was lower online than in the traditional channel, suggesting the impact of lower search costs for buyers in online environments. A study by Baye and Morgan (2001) found that establishing a market for price information leads to more competitive pricing by firms. Another study by Baye, Morgan, and Scholten (2003) showed that consumers using price comparison engines such as Shopper.com to shop for the lowest prices online saved an average of 16% compared to purchasing at the average listed price. Even when just two firms listed their prices for a product, consumers were found to save 11% over the average price. Interestingly, these savings increased to 20% when there were more than 30 firms listing their prices on these shopbots.

Similar impacts of the Internet and online channels on prices have been documented in a number of sectors and industries. In a study of the impact of e-commerce on the retail brokerage sector, Bakos et al. (2005) found that online brokerages charged much lower prices than their off-line counterparts, even after accounting for any quality differences. In another study of the impact of online referral services in the auto-retailing sector, Scott-Morton, Zettelmeyer, and Silva-Risso (2001) found that consumers who used online referral services while shopping for new cars paid on average 2% less than off-line customers. They also found that dealer margins for vehicles sold to customers referred by online referral services were significantly lower than for vehicles sold to other customers.

Arnold and Pénard (2007) examined the role of online referral services in the auto-retailing sector and found that when the difference in buyer bargaining abilities is not too large, buyers who use the referral service will pay a lower price, on average, than buyers who do not use the referral service. In such a case, weak bargainers are shown to benefit the most from the availability of an online referral system. Their findings are consistent with the empirical results of Scott-Morton et al. (2001; Scott-Morton & Zettelmeyer, 2004; Scott-Morton, Zettelmeyer, & Silva-Risso, 2003). Thus, the impact of increased availability of price-related information on consumer purchase decisions and outcomes was not restricted to online transactions but also carried over to purchases made in traditional channels, thereby affecting the balance of power of the transacting parties.

Search for (Nonprice) Product Information

Books, CDs, stocks, and other search goods for which quality and product characteristics can be easily ascertained have traditionally been the products most suited for online purchases. For less-expensive products such as books and CDs, the convenience and ease of access offered by the online channel may outweigh any potential risks associated with their purchase. Convenience and ease of shopping may again favor search products such as airline tickets and tickets for entertainment and sports events. The ability to compare prices for standardized products made a substantial difference to the bargaining power of consumers relative to sellers. Over time, with the growth of sales in other categories, including services, and the need to compare not only prices but also a plethora of characteristics and features of these offerings have led to a growth of shopbots and agents specializing in product comparison. Product comparison sites such as BizRate.com enable consumers to compare products and sellers on multiple attributes. These price comparison engines specialize in collecting and aggregating information about product features and attributes from a number of retailers, enabling consumers to make easy comparisons. Such product comparison sites are most useful for product categories with quantifiable attributes such as physical dimensions, warranty period, or other objective characteristics.

Experience goods and credence goods—goods and services for which quality cannot be easily conveyed and for which prior experience is valuable to judge quality—have been typically slower to take off online. However, all this has changed with the growth of online sites that not only enable users to compare objective attributes such as weight, shipping costs, and other features but also enable other users to share their experiences and subjective information. Sites such as Epinions.com enable consumers to learn not only about the features of different products and services but also about the evaluation of other users of these services. More important, in addition to helping consumers compare and evaluate differentiated product and service offerings, these sites enable consumers to find the right match for their own preferences and needs. There has been a dramatic growth of specialized online information intermediaries, such as autobytel.com and Edmunds.com for automobile purchases; Travelocity.com, Expedia.com, and Orbitz.com for air travel; Hotel.com and TripAdvisor.com for hotels and vacations; and other aggregators such as Kayak.com and Bookingbuddy. Such infomediaries provide detailed objective information as well as subjective reviews and user experiences and aid consumers in identifying the offerings that best meet their needs. Rather than focus purely on providing price-related information, these services seek to provide detailed product information to aid consumers' decision making.

While the availability of increased price information and the ease of comparing prices have clearly led to increased price competition among sellers, shifting the balance of power in favor of consumers, the impact of increased availability of product-related information and the ease of product-related searches is less obvious. On the one hand, the ability for consumers to identify the offering that provides the best fit is likely to decrease their price sensitivity and enable multiple sellers with differentiated offerings to charge higher prices to their target audience. On the other hand, the ability of consumers now to differentiate low-quality sellers from high-quality sellers decreases the power of low-quality sellers, shifting the balance in favor of sellers with higher-quality offerings.

A number of empirical studies have analyzed the impact of online product information availability on market outcomes. In a study of consumers shopping for wines, Lynch and Ariely (2000) found that increasing access to information about the quality of different wines had a marked impact on the price sensitivity of consumers. Consumers with access to quality information on the wines were willing to pay a higher price, suggesting that the impact of availability of quality information may outweigh the impact of increased price information in certain markets. Lynch and Ariely (2000) also found that increasing the ease of comparing prices across different retailers increased the price sensitivity for common wines sold by the competing merchants but not for wines unique to one merchant. Their findings suggest that sellers with unique merchandise would still have greater bargaining power and maintain higher prices, while low-cost retailers would be able to undercut rivals for generic products. While the results indicated that merchants stand to benefit from the increased availability to product and quality information available to consumers, it is interesting to note that such transparency also benefits consumers. Lynch and Ariely (2000) found that consumers were able to choose wines that better fit their tastes when they used the experimental electronic interfaces to obtain quality information.

Although the popular press as well as early research studies focused on the potential of online channels and the Internet to lower prices, researchers and practitioners are increasingly becoming aware of the important role of nonprice information available online. In a study of the impact of online infomediaries in the auto-retailing sector, Viswanathan, Kuruzovich, Gosain, and Agarwal (2007) examined an extensive dataset of over 16,000 consumers who obtained price and product-related information from online infomediaries as part of their new vehicle purchase process. They found that consumers who obtained price-related information paid a lower price on average, while consumers who visited "product specialist" infomediaries and obtained product-related information paid higher prices on average for the same vehicle. In addition to highlighting the differential impact of price and product-related outcomes for consumers, their study also identified a novel mechanism for sellers to differentiate price-sensitive customers from "product enthusiasts" who are less sensitive to price.

Going beyond the impact of online price and product information on market prices, researchers have also examined the impacts of lower search costs on other outcomes. In addition to lower final prices, the use of search tools and online information sources has led to a dramatic reduction in the amount of time spent by consumers searching for products and services. In another study of the impact of online infomediaries in the auto-retailing sector, Kuruzovich, Viswanathan, Agarwal, and Gosain (2008) found that the ease of obtaining different types of information online—price versus product information—has important implications for whether consumers consummate their online search through referred purchase or extend their search into the physical marketplace. Kuruzovich et al. (2008) found that consumers who seek and find price-related information are more likely to purchase based on the referral provided by the online infomediary. On the other hand, consumers who seek and find product-related information are less likely to purchase based on online referrals and are more likely to extend their search to the traditional channel. These findings further highlight the nuanced role of different types of information and their ability to alter the bargaining power of different parties in a transaction across multiple channels.

In summary, while the lower search costs for price information are likely to increase consumer price sensitivity, the lower search costs for product and quality-related information could decrease consumer price sensitivity. The net effect would depend on the magnitude of reduction of these search costs as well as other context-specific factors. As acknowledged by Viswanathan et al. (2007), even in the case of product-related search costs "depending on the specifics of the context, and more importantly, on whether information accentuates or attenuates the differences, the availability of product information could lead to higher or lower prices for consumers" (p. 91). Interestingly, as sellers face pricing pressures due to lower search costs for consumers, they tend to adopt alternate strategies, such as differentiating their products and services from their rivals, to overcome the adverse effects of price competition. For instance, Smith and Brynjolfsson (2001), in their analysis of consumer choice data from an online price infomediary, Dealtime.com, found that although consumers benefit from lower prices on average, there exists significant price dispersion in online markets, suggesting that retailers use a number of strategic options to mitigate price pressures.

The Impact of IT on the Search for Quality

With the growth in the number of options available to consumers, there is also an increased need for credible signals of quality. IT has led to the emergence of a number of mechanisms for signaling quality for individuals and firms alike. Reputation mechanisms, ratings and reviews, trust and certification seals, online word of mouth, among others, serve to reduce information asymmetry between negotiating parties, thereby alleviating transaction costs.

Most markets suffer from significant information asymmetries between parties in a transaction. A number of quality-signaling mechanisms have evolved to help reduce the frictions and the likelihood of market collapse. As noted by Akerlof (1970), when there is significant quality uncertainty and buyers are unable to differentiate between high-quality and low-quality sellers, the average quality of sellers in the market drops as bad sellers tend to drive out good ones. Mechanisms such as certifications, warranties for products and services, buy-back guarantees, costly branding, among others, have been used by sellers to build trust and convey the quality of their offerings.

As compared to offline settings, online markets are characterized by a greater presence of information asymmetry and trust deficits. The ability to verify the identity of brick-and-mortar merchants and factors such as investment in premier locations, investment in store assortments, and personal communication with customers often serve to mitigate information asymmetry and trust deficits in traditional settings. In addition to the lack of such tangible features, online transactions are typically anonymous, and the ability to trade anonymously remains a primary source of uncertainty in online environments (Resnick, Kuwabara, Zeckhauser, & Friedman, 2000). Further, concerns about quality of the products, delivery and shipping, and issues such as fraudulent or unauthorized access, attacks on computers by hackers, privacy, and security concerns, among others, create frictions that reduce the efficiency of transactions. While a few large firms such as Amazon.com, Google, and Yahoo! have managed to establish their identities through significant investments in their brands, a vast majority of transactions occur among less-well-known parties.

Online markets have developed a number of mechanisms to help buyers and sellers overcome issues stemming from information asymmetry prevalent in these markets. As noted by Özpolat, Gao, Jank, and Viswanathan (2010), online shoppers can typically get information regarding the reliability of merchants and the quality of their offerings from three broad categories of sources before entering into a transaction.

Online sellers provide a significant amount of *first-party information.* Researchers have found that the quality of the Web site design (Schlosser, White, & Lloyd, 2005), the presence of contact information, availability of privacy policy (Tsai, Egelman, Cranor, & Acquisti, 2011), and performance reports and testimonials (Kim & Benbasat, 2006) may all be useful in inducing trust. However, first-party information is clearly less credible and, in most cases, is not sufficient to overcome issues of trust and security fully.

In addition to first-party information, online sellers and markets can facilitate transactions by the provision of *second-party information.* A number of successful online markets and sellers such as Amazon.com and eBay have developed sophisticated reputation and feedback mechanisms. Consumers on Amazon.com, for instance, can provide numerical ratings and detailed textual reviews of products and services offered. Although noisy, these online ratings and reviews provide valuable information based on personal experiences—information that can help reduce quality uncertainty for new customers. Such "online word of mouth" has been shown to have a significant impact on purchase behaviors of consumers. While it has been well recognized for decades that word of mouth was a valuable source of information for shoppers (Katz & Lazarsfeld, 1955), with the ability to collect detailed data and measure online word of mouth, there has been a growing interest in understanding how it has an impact on shoppers.

Researchers have begun to examine the impact of online word of mouth in a variety of online markets and have found that such online recommendations and reviews have a rather strong effect on sales and the success of transactions. Chevalier and Mayzlin (2006) examined the effect of online reviews provided by customers at Amazon.com and Barnesandnoble.com and found that positive reviews for a book led to an increase in sales and market share, findings that are consistent with those of Chevalier and Goolsbee (2003).

Interestingly, they also found that the marginal (negative) impact of 1-star reviews was greater than the (positive) impact of 5-star reviews. In a study of the impact of online reviews of craft brewers on sales, Clemons, Gao, and Hitt (2006) found that the mean of consumer ratings is a useful predictor of sales. Further, they found that the mean of the top quartile of user ratings was the strongest predictor of sales. In a study of online word of mouth relating to TV shows, Godes and Mayzlin (2004) examined which aspects of online word of mouth were important and found that higher dispersion (rather than volume) of online word of mouth was related to higher future sales. Their findings also suggested that online word of mouth is more important early in a product's life. Chintagunta, Shyam, and Sriram (2010) measured the impact of online user reviews of movies from Yahoo! Movies on their box office performance and found that the valence of the reviews (rather than the volume of reviews) had a significant and positive impact on box office revenues.

A number of studies have also examined the effectiveness of eBay's online feedback mechanism, which enables users to rate one another after a transaction. Ratings are either positive (1), neutral (0), or negative and can be accompanied by brief feedback. According to Resnick and Zeckhauser (2002), more than 52% of buyers and 60% of sellers posted a feedback after a transaction. Several studies (e.g., Dewan & Hsu, 2004; Eaton, 2002; Ederington & Dewally, 2003; Houser & Wooders, 2006; Kalyanam & McIntyre, 2001; Livingston, 2005; Melnik & Alm, 2002) have attempted to estimate the value of such reputation/feedback for sellers, and most found that there is a causal relationship between seller reputation and sale price. Further, negative feedback tended to have a stronger effect on sales compared to positive feedback. According to Cabral and Hortacsu (2004), a 1% increase in the fraction of negative feedback on eBay correlated with a 9% decrease in price and a 1%–2% increase in the probability of the seller exiting the market. These findings highlight the increasingly important role of online word of mouth and reputation mechanisms in not only facilitating transactions but also empowering both customers and high-quality sellers.

Second-party information such as user reviews and ratings, despite being low cost and powerful mechanisms in stimulating cooperation among traders, still suffer from being noisy and unreliable predictors of quality due to the anonymity of the sources. Such unreliable information has the potential to bias reputation and trading decision of agents (Dini & Spagnolo, 2005). Naturally, researchers (e.g., Ye, Gao, & Viswanathan, 2009) as well as practitioners continue to assess the performance of different reputation mechanisms and seek to improve their efficacy.

An alternative to second-party information is *third-party mechanisms*. Third parties such as certification intermediaries can provide independent verification of a seller's trustworthiness. In the online setting, such independent verification is usually provided by specialized trust certification companies such as buySAFE, TRUSTe, and VeriSign. Online merchants who meet their standards of privacy, security, and service quality are allowed to display a trust seal on their Web sites.

Other agencies such as Better Business Bureaus (BBB) also publish directories of trusted online retailers. In a study of the value of such third-party trust seals, Özpolat et al. (2010) examined over a quarter million online transactions and found that online trust seals provided by third parties not only increased the probability of completion of purchase but also served as substitutes for shopper experience as well as seller size. Thus, these third-party mechanisms helped smaller retailers most of all to increase their trustworthiness and negotiating power relative to those in markets lacking effective quality-signaling mechanisms.

The Impact of IT on the Valuation of Goods and Services

Negotiations among transacting parties typically break down due to a lack of agreement on the value of the goods/services being traded. Developments in information and communication technologies now enable parties to gain a better understanding of the value of the products being traded. One of the fastest growing market mechanisms, online auctions, allows buyers and sellers to discover the value of the good or service under consideration.[1] Online auctions have become popular not only because of the ease of conducting such auctions but also because they are often considered the perfect market mechanism. In theory, auctions enable the efficient allocation of goods and services as the items auctioned are often sold to the highest bidder, that is, the individual or firm valuing it the most.

There are four standard auction types (Klemperer, 1999): the English auction, the Dutch auction, the first-price sealed-bid auction, and the second-price sealed-bid auction. Of these, the English auction, or the ascending price auction, in which the bidding starts low and increases until the highest bid is reached, has been the most popular auction type in traditional settings. The English auction is considered equivalent to a second-price sealed-bid auction, which is often used as the benchmark. One of the attractive properties of auctions for a seller is that a well-designed auction is a "truth-telling" mechanism. In other words, the best strategy for a bidder is to bid his or her true valuation for the item. Bidding lower increases the probability of the bidder losing the item, while bidding higher increases the probability of winning but at a valuation above one's true value for the item. A well-designed auction can thus help the seller elicit the true valuation of the item from each bidder.

In an auction in which the product has a common value, a bidder can use other bidder's bid information provided by the auction platform to form and revise his or her willingness to pay (Roth & Ockenfels, 2002). The online auction provides detailed history information, which allows bidders to incorporate information gathered from the earlier bids of others in the same auction or other related auctions into their own valuation (Kauffman & Wood, 2006; Roth & Ockenfels, 2002). Usually, negotiators are expected to know the valuation of the product or service in question. However, in many real-life situations, negotiators may not be aware of exactly how much they value the product, which may lead to inefficient trades (Hossain, 2008). In such cases, an online auction employing a second-price format, in which the highest bidder wins the auction but pays the price based on the bid of the second-highest bidder, and allowing bidders to submit as many bids as they want can enable bidders to learn more precisely about their own private valuations for the good in a boundedly rational learning process (Hossain, 2008).

An online auction platform provides the bid history information and constant updates to the latest winning bids efficiently. It also allows bidders to change the bids many times to experiment strategically and learn more about their preferences. Bidders get more information any time the price changes as a result of either their own bid or some other bidder's bid, as contemplating the relation between their valuation and the posted price is cognitively easier, whereas gathering such information by comparing with any other hypothetical price is infinitely costly (Hossain, 2008).

Kauffman and Wood (2006) observed that bidders also learn from their past experiences in online auctions. They suggested that after losing a previous auction bidders will likely update their valuation of the item upward or bid a higher amount closer to their actual valuation if they were shading their bids (i.e., bidding below their actual valuation).

Online auctions also aid sellers in the negotiation process. In traditional markets, content providers set a price for advertising real estate, but as stated, most valuations are suboptimal as the real valuation of their advertising spot is unknown, which makes the negotiation process inefficient. A technology-enabled solution to alleviate such inefficiency arising due to content providers' inability to assess the value of its product is keyword auctions, also known as sponsored search auctions. Sponsored search auctions, in which advertisers bid for better placement in the listing of search results on services such as Google and Yahoo!, have emerged as the dominant form of online advertising as well as the primary revenue model for online search engines. As with other auctions, sponsored search auctions allow search engines to sell their online "real estate" to the advertisers (bidders) with the highest valuations. As described, the ability of online auctions to enable both sellers and buyers discover the market value of their goods and services have made them a staple market mechanism for individuals and businesses alike.

THE CONTRACT STAGE

The contract or negotiation stage is about *how* to determine the terms of the transactions. In this stage, negotiators engage in the process of interacting with the other party to jointly identify possible solutions with the goal of reaching a consensus. All the activities involved in arriving at the terms of a contract and finalizing a contract involve transaction costs. Technology-enabled tools allow negotiators to improve the effectiveness and efficiency of the contracting process and reduce the transaction costs associated with the contracting stage. There are two approaches to determining the terms of the contract: a distributively oriented approach (which is "zero sum" or "win-lose" in nature) and an integratively oriented approach (which is *not* zero-sum, hence potentially win-win in nature). Next, we describe what these two contract-related approaches entail, the IT interventions that may assist negotiators in engaging in each of these contract-related approaches, and the impact of IT on the associated transaction costs of contracting.

The Impact of IT on Distributively Oriented Negotiating

Parties engaging in distributive negotiation attempt to reach agreements about how to allocate shares of scarce resources. Given the zero-sum nature of distributive negotiations, each party focuses on maximizing its own pay-offs while conceding only enough to its opponent to obtain a basic agreement. Each party views the other as an adversary, shares information that increases its chances of winning, and attempts to learn as much as possible about the other party's positions, needs, and minimum acceptable demands.

Technology supports a distributive negotiation approach in the form of electronic auctions (e-auctions), which are a special case of automated negotiations (Klein, 1997). Auctions are market mechanisms that employ an explicit set of rules to allocate resources and determine the prices based on the bids from market participants (McAfee & McMillan, 1987). A variety of transactions that employ face-to-face negotiations among multiple participants can be conducted using auctions (Kaufmann & Carter, 2004). Emergence of the Internet and consequent lowering of overhead cost in conducting an auction, which traditionally has been used for negotiating trades of large monetary value, has allowed use of auctions for negotiating the price in low monetary value transactions. Online auctions make it easier and more efficient to negotiate the price of a product or service. Computational power and flexibility provided by technology allows automation of the auction rules and processes. Modifying the rules and processes embedded in the technology-enabled auction platform can create a wide variety of auction formats to suit diverse negotiation needs.

Forward Auctions

An auction can be initiated by either a buyer or a seller. An auction started and controlled by a seller is referred to as a forward auction. In a forward auction, generally, one seller sells a product or service to a group of potential buyers. Sellers such as Dell employ forward e-auctions conducted through their Web site (http://dellauction.com) to sell old or excess inventory. Small firms or individuals can also conduct forward auctions by using a technology platform created by intermediaries like eBay. Sellers' use of forward e-auction increases their negotiation speed and efficiency because instead of negotiating individually with each of the potential buyers (contacted through channels such as classifieds) they let the marketplace determine the price—one of the critical terms of the negotiation (Guttman & Maes, 1999). Relative to the seller, the buyers in the forward e-auction incur higher effort because instead of interacting directly with the buyer they compete with multiple (often unknown) participants on the same side of the table by placing multiple bids in the auction.

Reverse Auctions

A reverse auction (or procurement auction) involves a buyer setting up the auction to invite bids from a group of sellers. As opposed to forward auctions, which are ascending price auctions, prices in reverse auctions typically start high and descend when the auctions progress. Traditionally, firms negotiate with a relatively small number of suppliers for procurement transactions to develop long-term cooperative relationships with their suppliers. However, the advent of electronic auctions, which radically reduce transaction costs and increase seller competition, has enabled firms to engage in technology-enabled negotiation with a large number of sellers. Dynamically negotiating a price for a product or service through an e-auction shifts the burden of determining the price to the marketplace, thereby reducing the complexity of the negotiation process for the buyer. Moreover, e-auctions lower the supply cost and benefit the buyer by locating efficient suppliers or lowering the administration cost. However, the majority of the cost savings to the buyer comes from squeezing the profit margins of the supplier (Rothkopf & Whinston, 2007). Therefore, the low supply costs negotiated through an e-auction may not be sustainable. A firm deciding to use electronic auctions as the mode of negotiation faces uncertainty about the effect of such auctions on the long-term strategic buyer–supplier relationships (Kaufmann & Carter, 2004).

Price negotiation is one of the most time-intensive activities in the purchasing process compared to negotiation over quality and delivery performance terms (Emiliani, 2000). E-auctions have replaced negotiations for supplier selection and price setting (Rothkopf & Whinston, 2007); however, primary focus on the price dimension of the procurement negotiation at the expense of other supplier attributes such as quality, reliability, and terms of delivery leads to alienation of the suppliers, especially the incumbent suppliers, who may refuse to participate in such procurement auctions (Elmaghraby, 2007). To minimize the negative impact of negotiations through auctions, practitioners recommend that an auction should be used to enable the price discovery process during negotiations rather than using it as a substitute for the negotiation process (Elmaghraby, 2007). Buyers are advised to invest in learning about supplier capabilities and prequalify suppliers, clearly communicate the product specifications, and actively engage in postauction negotiations on nonprice attributes to make the final award decision (Elmaghraby, 2007). Although the auctions adopt explicit sets of rules to conduct the transaction, in reality rules are unclear and constantly changing (Subramanian, 2010) as the buyer or sellers (depending on type of auction) can negotiate about the auction rules when the auction is being set up and can negotiate postauction with a few top bidders to finalize the transaction. Given these challenges in negotiating using e-auctions, it has been suggested that a new set of concepts, skills, strategies, systems, and structures is needed to adopt electronic auctions successfully (Kaufmann & Carter, 2004).

E-auctions primarily focusing on price are lacking since allocation based only on price does not take into account the ability of the providers and the potential quality of work, especially in the case of procurement (B2B) auctions. Advances in the technology allow parties in an auction to move beyond the price-centric negotiation to include multiple attributes that are essential for complex transactions (i.e., dealing with nonstandardized products whose quality is difficult to assess). As a result, in addition to determining prices dynamically, auctions can be used to determine nonpricing terms, such as payment method and credit. For example, the Web-based procurement platform developed by elance.com allows parties to deal with the complexities inherent in IT procurement, such as price discovery, resolution of vendor quality, and identification of vendor fit with the buyer or project (Snir & Hitt, 2003). Multiattribute e-reverse auctions automate the procurement process with multiple negotiable attributes, such as price, quality, delivery, and other factors (Bichler & Kalagnanam, 2003, 2005; Talluri, Narasimhan, & Viswanathan, 2007). Combinatorial procurement auctions have been developed that allow bidders to bid on combinations of items. Complex combinatorial computations enabled by technology to allow bidders to exploit their economies of scale or cost synergies between items in various combinations may transform the distributive negotiation process into an integrative one (Rothkopf & Whinston, 2007).

The e-auction platforms have also incorporated online social networking tools to facilitate negotiation of transactions. For example, Propser. com, which provides a system to support lending negotiations, uses online social networks to mitigate adverse selection problems in lending (Lin, Prabhala, & Viswanathan, 2009). Parties in the negotiation create and maintain relationships in online social networks. The social network of each party can facilitate transactions by providing information that may reduce the risk of *opportunism* and alleviate the perception of the other party as an adversary. Overlaying the social network structure on the negotiation platform enables relationship-oriented rather than task-oriented interactions among negotiators, which leads to more concessions being granted (Greenhalgh & Gilkey, 1993; Kurtzberg & Medvec, 2003), more information sharing, and a more cooperative attitude (McGinn & Keros, 2002) among socially embedded negotiators. Thus, the inclusion of social networks in the negotiation platform may lower the adverse impact of distributive negotiation and increase the likelihood of successful negotiation (Pesendorfer & Koeszegi, 2007).

Interestingly, in some contexts, such as advertising, the e-auction mechanism (such as the one used by Google to allot advertisement slots) has replaced the traditional price-based negotiations with a process that takes into account both the price and the quality of the advertisement (as the ad slots are allotted based on the advertisers' bids as well as their advertisement's historical click-through rate, which is an indicator of the ad's quality). On the other hand, some modifications in the format of e-auctions, such as the all-pay auction variant (referred to as pay-to-bid or penny auction) developed by companies like Swoopo, have led to a more extreme distributive process. In Swoopo auctions, bidding starts at a penny and goes up in 1-cent increments. Each bid costs the bidder (e.g., x cents per bid). Although each auction has a scheduled closing time, the time is extended by t seconds whenever someone submits a bid (Thaler, 2009). Even though the bidder who wins in a penny auction may make significant profits, collectively, bidders lose money in these transactions.

The Impact of IT on Integratively Oriented Negotiating

Integrative negotiations involve a joint effort directed at finding a solution that will be perceived as beneficial to both parties. Integrative negotiations are referred to as non-zero-sum games in which parties collaborate to search for ways to increase the total payoff and share norms that value reasoned, analytic, and objective problem solving. In short, the distributive process consists primarily of concession making, whereas the integrative process involves both concession making and a search for mutually profitable alternatives.

The integrative negotiation approach has been built into a variety of IT tools that are employed by negotiators to facilitate negotiations, support negotiations, as well as to mediate negotiations (Kersten & Lai, 2008).

These tools allow the parties to a negotiation transaction to be better prepared and to conduct negotiations better, thus improving the efficiency of the negotiation process.

IT tools *facilitate* negotiations by enabling communication, storage, and exchange of information. Lowering of the barriers of geography, time, and distance due to globalization has increased the reliance of negotiators on computer-mediated communication (CMC) tools such as e-mail, instant messaging, document sharing, videoconferencing, and so on to conduct negotiations. It is well accepted that the communication medium has an impact on behavior and outcomes, however, the empirical results examining the relative advantages of CMC versus face-to-face interactions are mixed. Researchers suggested that reduced interpersonal and social context cues in CMC may adversely affect behavior in negotiation processes. The difficulty in establishing rapport and relationships when primarily using CMC tools may not allow participants to effectively manage conflict resolution in a negotiation process (Drolet & Morris, 2000; Morris, Nadler, Kurtzberg, & Leigh, 2002), thus leading to a more distributive negotiation process. On the other hand, it has been shown that negotiators using a CMC medium such as e-mail are more likely to divide the surplus equally and arrive at integrative (i.e., win-win) agreements as compared to negotiators in a face-to-face context (Croson, 1999). The lack of social cues in a CMC medium, which may be detrimental for establishing rapport, may facilitate integrative agreement by leveling the playing field between strong and weak negotiators and reducing the opportunities to engage in confrontation negotiation tactics (Croson, 1999). Characteristics of the CMC medium (in particular, text-based CMC tools) such as reviewability, revisability, and asynchrony can facilitate an integrative negotiation outcome by making negotiators task focused and encouraging rational decision-making approaches (Delaney, Foroughi, & Perkins, 1997; Pesendorfer & Koeszegi, 2007; Rangaswamy & Shell, 1997; Wilkenfeld, Kraus, Holley, & Harris, 1995).

Further, the CMC medium is more effective in the generation of diverse and creative options (Daly, 1993; Gallupe, Cooper, Grise, & Bastianutti, 1994; Nunamaker, Dennis, Valacich, & Vogel, 1991). This increased consideration set of alternative solutions to the negotiation problem available to negotiators facilitates the formation of integrative agreements (Croson, 1999). Although the negotiators using CMC may generate more options, the CMC tools cannot help the negotiators decide among solutions (Daly, 1993). To assist negotiators in decision making during negotiations, a special category of IT, referred to as a negotiation support system (NSS) can be used.

IT tools in the form of an NSS can *support* the negotiation process by expanding the abilities of the negotiators to assess the negotiation problem and the possible implications of alternative solutions (Kersten & Lai, 2008). The NSS increases the processing capability of negotiators by providing simulation and optimization models, visualization tools, and access to expert knowledge (Hordijk, 1991; Kersten & Lai, 2008). In addition to allowing negotiators to exchange messages and transaction offers, computer-supported negotiation tools can help negotiators understand priorities and constraints of their counterparts, predict the opponents' moves, and suggest countermoves (Kersten & Lai, 2008). The NSS also allow negotiators to understand their own preferences better by incorporating several utility assessment techniques, such as conjoint analysis, that can be used by negotiators to disaggregate their priorities (Rangaswamy & Shell, 1997). The systems also provide real-time, subjective evaluations of the value of offers and counteroffers to the negotiators (Rangaswamy & Shell, 1997).

A wide variety of NSSs has been developed that differ in the level of analytical support provided for the negotiators (Vetschera, 2007). Tools such as NEGO (Kersten, 1985) and PERSUADER (Sycara, 1990) support prenegotiation strategy formulation, whereas tools such as MEDIATOR (Jarke, Jelassi, & Shakun, 1987) and ONDINE (Nyhart & Samarasan, 1989) also allow for some form of actual interactive negotiations (Eliashberg, Gauvin, Lilien, & Rangaswamy, 1992). Tools such as Negotiator Assistant (NA; Rangaswamy & Shell, 1997) employ a multistage process that enables negotiators to prepare for, execute, and evaluate negotiated solutions.

For example, NA allows negotiators to specify all the issues and options for each issue within the negotiation domain and then rate the issues and the options within each issue. Based on these ratings, the NA system conducts conjoint analysis, constructs a set of sample settlement packages, and allows negotiators to explore their options in the context of an overall agreement covering all issues simultaneously. The system visually presents the trade-offs between the settlement packages and allows negotiators to refine their preferences. In the negotiation stage, the system allows negotiators to send offers, counteroffers, and other messages over the computer network. Following an agreement, the system takes the role of a third-party mediator. It examines the final agreement by comparing the accepted package with all other possible packages in the negotiation set and suggests a list of packages that are, based on the inputs of both parties, more advantageous than the current settlement package for one or both sides without making either side worse off (Rangaswamy & Shell, 1997).

It has been shown that an NSS reduces a negative climate (Delaney et al., 1997), allows the negotiators to achieve higher joint outcomes and more balanced agreements as compared to face-to-face negotiations (Foroughi, Perkins, & Jelassi, 1995), and increases negotiator's satisfaction (Delaney et al., 1997). However, it is important to note that a majority of NSSs have not been applied to real-life negotiations (Al-Sakran & Serguievskaia, 2006).

Technology can be used to *mediate* negotiations by influencing the process and proactively shaping it such that parties reach an agreement. This set of tools completely automates the negotiation process using software agents that mediate the negotiations on behalf of the negotiators. These agents act (either reactively or proactively) with varying degrees of autonomy on behalf of the negotiators and have the capability to learn, cooperate, and collaborate (Kersten & Lai, 2008). The agents interact with other agents in an agent-based marketplace based on the common negotiation protocol and individual strategies (Boutilier, Shoham, & Wellman, 1997). A variety of methods, such as Bayesian learning (Zeng & Sycara, 1998) and fuzzy similarity rules (Sierra, Faratin, & Jennings, 1999), is used by agents to determine which negotiation strategy is more successful, and approaches such as the notion of expected value of information (Howard, 1966) and utility (von Neumann & Morgenstern, 1944) are used by agents to deal with uncertain, partial, tentative, or generic information within a negotiation (Klusch, 2000). The negotiators provide their agents in an agent-based marketplace, like Kasbah (Maes, Guttman, & Moukas, 1999) and Tête-à-Tête (Guttman, Moukas, & Maes, 1998), with information about their preferences and their negotiation strategy (Kersten & Lai, 2007). The agents then search for other agents who are likely to engage in a negotiation and enter into negotiations. Another class of technology tools partially automates the negotiation process by which software takes over the role of the traditional human mediator. These tools, such as CyberSettle and SmartSettle, have generally been used for negotiations involved in resolving postnegotiation disputes and are discussed in greater depth in the section on the postnegotiation stage.

THE CONTROL STAGE

The control stage or postnegotiation stage of exchange between parties can be temporally viewed as commencing once the contract has been signed. As with the other stages of negotiation, mediation by technology has affected the manner in which a range of postnegotiation activities can be conducted. The negotiating parties often need to exchange value in monetary form, requiring mechanisms for payment and settlement. Depending on the nature and content of the contract, it may be necessary for the exchange parties potentially to engage with each other postsettlement, such as synchronizing work activities and exchanging information when tasks are interdependent. For example, in a contract in which one party engages another for specific design work, an exchange of requirements may be necessary. Likewise, when the contractor delivers a design, the buyer may provide feedback for further iterations. Often, the parties may need to supervise the work of the other, such as in contracts that are priced based on time and materials, the buyer needs a mechanism for ensuring that the effort expended by the seller is consistent with the charge that is levied. Overall, in this final stage of negotiation the overarching concern is with ensuring that the "terms" of the contract are adequately met. Finally, when conflicts arise, the negotiating parties need mechanisms to assist in their resolution. We note that while actions related to synchronization and monitoring involve the negotiating parties who have entered into a contract, payments and conflict management are typically reliant on the existence of a supporting policy and regulatory structure.

Each of these control activities involves transaction costs that are affected when the transaction is conducted on an electronic platform. In the case of payment, to the degree that electronic payment systems are faster and able to mitigate risks of opportunistic behavior through mechanisms such as automated credit checks and privacy and security assurances, they increase efficiency and reduce the transaction costs incurred by the negotiating parties. The real-time and asynchronous ability to track work and exchange intermediate work products (through technologies ranging from e-mail to shared workspaces and documents enabled by google. docs) reduces the transaction costs associated with the synchronization and coordination of work, as well as supervision. Indeed, Overby (2008) argued that monitoring capability offered by IT in terms of authenticating process participants and tracking activity moderates the effects of the synchronicity needs of a process and its "virtualizability." Finally, a number of online tools for managing and resolving conflicts in trade have emerged. Variously referred to as online dispute resolution (ODR), Internet dispute resolution (iDR), and electronic automated dispute resolution (eADR), the focus of this class of technologies is on facilitating the resolution of disputes in an online medium, from beginning to end (Katsh & Rifkin, 2001).

The Impact of IT on Payment and Settlement

Postcontract, negotiating parties engage in an exchange of value, typically in the form of a monetary payment. The Internet has proved to be a transformational technology in reducing the inefficiencies associated with paper-based and physical payment processes. In general, electronic payment systems fall into two broad categories: electronic cash, which includes smart card systems and online cash systems, and account-based systems such as credit and debit systems (Abrazhevich, 2001). Examples of the former include the Chipknip electronic cash system used extensively in the Netherlands, which allows value to be loaded onto smart cards and utilized for payments at parking meters and in shops, and the Octopus card used in Hong Kong with similar capabilities.

Since approximately 2000, perhaps the most striking effect of technology on postnegotiation payments is the ability for individuals and organizations to exchange small amounts of value in the form of "micropayments" in a cost-efficient manner. Referred to as online cash systems, the popular payment mechanism offered by PayPal, founded in 1999, exemplifies this capability. Used extensively in consumer-to-consumer auctions and increasingly in online purchases, PayPal has grown virally, and in 2010, supported payments were in 23 currencies, with a total payment volume of $71 billion, of which 25% was accounted for by cross-border transactions (Bielski, 2010). Making payments through PayPal is simple, safe, and inexpensive for users, contributing to its phenomenal growth (Schwartz, 2001).

The second category of electronic payment systems is fundamentally account based. In its simplest and most ubiquitous form, an account-based electronic payment may be in the form of a credit card number that a buyer provides online to settle a trade. The online credit card-processing providers (such as that supported by Visa and numerous small providers, including authorize.net, merchantone.com, and gotmerchant.com) perform the necessary authentication, approval, and confirmation of the transaction, considerably simplifying the task of payment. Similarly, electronic debit systems offered by most banks allow for the electronic transfer of cash from a user's bank account to a merchant or trading partner. The benefits of e-payments can be substantial, ranging from reduced costs for payer and payee, lower risk of fraud and theft, and improvements in transparency (Jolly, 2008). The Gartner Group, a consulting and advisory organization, provides estimates of the cost savings from electronic invoicing: An electronic bill costs 50% less than a paper bill ($5 for the latter versus $2.50 for the former), while the cost of processing incoming payments is reduced from $10 to $3.

Today, mobile payments represent the new frontier in electronic cash. With the growing use of smart mobile devices in both personal and organizational domains, consumers are availing themselves of the convenience, speed, and simplicity of using these devices to pay for purchases. As with the tethered scenario in which payments are made using a computer connected to the Internet, a variety of payment alternatives are now available for mobile platforms. To illustrate, PayPal now offers a complete mobile application with the same functionality as the online mechanism. In late 2010, traditional competitors in the mobile business (AT&T, Verizon, and T-Mobile) launched a joint venture named ISIS to build a national payments network (Hsu, 2010). To overcome the traditional limitations of electronic payments such as a lack of trust between trading parties, new technology services such as Venmo (http://www.venmo.com) allow a credit card or a bank account to be linked to a mobile phone and used to exchange cash between "friends." In short, the number and sophistication of IT tools that facilitate and simplify the payment process have increased substantially and are expected to exhibit robust growth, consistent with the growth of mobile and wireless applications.

Choosing the appropriate digital payment mechanism for a specific contract can be a complex task, and no one solution dominates in all circumstances. The user may face constraints imposed by the intermediary facilitating the contract (such as an auction completed on eBay supports a specific set of payment types) or may be resource constrained (such as not owning a credit card). MacKie-Mason and White (1997) described a methodology for evaluating alternative schemes that included an extensive list of 30 evaluation criteria, such as ease of exchange, transactions delay, financial risk, portability, and unobtrusiveness. They noted that the final choice of type of electronic payment was largely a function of the needs of the decision maker (who could be a buyer, a seller, or an intermediary), and as such, proposed that a decision maker-centric approach to selection that accounts for these needs is optimal.

The Impact of IT on Synchronization and Supervision of Work

As noted, in many instances transacting parties need to coordinate and synchronize work activities after the contract has been executed. Furthermore, buyers may have a need to monitor the effort expended by the seller on a specific engagement. The capabilities of IT to alleviate coordination costs are well documented (e.g., Malone, Yates, & Benjamin, 1987). More than two decades ago, Malone et al. argued that IT innovations, as a result of their power to reduce the costs of processing and communicating information, would lead to greater use of markets as opposed to hierarchies for coordinating work. This prediction has been handsomely affirmed by the phenomenal growth of electronic markets.

Synchronizing work requires that all parties have easy access to each other's intermediate work products and are able to share and resolve issues that may arise during the execution of a task efficiently. For example, an IT contractor developing a complex software application in an offshore location from the client may have a question about a specific user requirement. If such a query can be addressed in a rapid manner, it naturally reduces the time delay in project completion. The same capabilities of IT that facilitate integrative negotiation (viz., communication, storage, and exchange of information) also play a crucial role in supporting work synchronization and monitoring. Widely available tools for this include e-mail, instant messaging, document storage and sharing, collaborative project management tools, shared calendaring, and videoconferencing. Such collaboration software helps overcome spatial and temporal constraints, enabling the coordination of work across time and space.

Numerous empirical studies, both field-based and experimental, have examined the effects of collaboration software on outcomes. Although a complete review of this literature is beyond the scope of this chapter, summaries of findings are available in the work of Treude, Storey, and Weber (2009) and Wainer, Novoa Barsottini, Lacerda, and Magalhães de Marco (2009). We note that an overwhelming conclusion from these studies was that despite the lack of social cues and other limitations of the electronic medium, the tools help to improve the time and effort involved in coordinating work significantly, especially when the parties involved are not colocated. IT for synchronizing work is particularly useful in the coordination of complex supply chains (e.g., Dedrick, Xu, & Zhu, 2008). The benefits of IT in such settings can be complex and nuanced; for example, Sanders (2008) found that specific patterns of IT use were associated with operational coordination, and these were distinct from the patterns that facilitated strategic coordination.

Argyres (1999) presented a compelling example of how IT helps reduce transaction costs in the context of the design of the B2 stealth bomber. This highly complex engineered product was constructed by four companies that coordinated their work almost entirely on digital platforms. Argyres noted that in this instance IT "aided coordination by making information processing less costly" (p. 162.). Additional benefits obtained from the IT included more efficient project governance (by establishing a shared "technical grammar" for communication among the stakeholders) and improved measurement of work output.

A number of specific IT tools for the monitoring of work have emerged. Such tools may be utilized within an organizational setting, where supervisors are able to "observe" virtually what employees are doing, or in contracts across organizations and individuals. Examples of tools in the former category include Refog, EmployeeMonitoring, and software sold by Spytech. We note that while such tools provide detailed accounts of what employees are doing when using the technology platform of their employers and, purportedly, improve productivity and morale, they are controversial in regard to potential privacy invasion. A study conducted by the U.S. General Accounting Office (GAO) examined the electronic monitoring policies of 14 private-sector companies and found that all of them routinely stored employees' electronic transactions, including e-mail messages, Internet sites visited, and computer file activity (GAO, 2002). A survey conducted by the American Management Association (AMA) and ePolicy Institute in 2007 reported that two thirds of employers monitored employees' Web site visits, and 28% of employers had fired workers for e-mail misuse. Consumer privacy advocates (e.g., privacyrights.org) argue that there is a need to balance the employer's right to information with the employee's rights to privacy.

Web-based IT tools that facilitate the supervision of work between contracting parties are also now available. For example, a company called oDesk (http://www.oDesk.com) provides the foundation for contracting on technology development projects. Buyers with a need for technology services can find qualified contractors on the site and enter into an agreement for specific work. The site provides a "work diary" for the parties in the contract; the buyer can view the seller's effort in real time, review intermediate work products and provide feedback, and supervise the execution of work. For contracts that are based on time and materials pricing, through the automated monitoring facility the buyer is able to verify that the contractor has expended the effort that the client is billed for. In other words, oDesk supports both the synchronization and the supervision of work between the contracting parties.

The Impact of IT on Conflict Management

Postcontract conflicts and disputes are inevitable in any negotiation setting. A buyer may renege on payment, or a seller may provide goods that are not of the agreed-on quality. Acknowledging the growing significance of electronic transactions, governments of many nations have begun to evolve policy and legislation to safeguard the rights of the transacting parties (Hörnle, 2009). An evolving field of cyberspace law is beginning to articulate formally the principles and methods for the resolution of such disputes (Lim, 2007). ODR uses the concept of a third-party intermediary supported by information and communication technology to offer a more efficient mechanism for resolving disputes that arise in electronic transactions (Katsh & Rifkin, 2001).

Thiessen and Zeleznikow (2004) identified a number of benefits associated with ODR, including an elimination of the need to meet face to face, easy availability of synchronous and asynchronous communication, elimination of geographical and spatial constraints among the parties engaged in conflict resolution, a greater chance of cooperation, and a more comprehensive approach that can assist in a speedier and fairer resolution of the conflict. Thus, it is easy to see that managing postnegotiation conflicts electronically can be efficacious in significantly reducing transaction costs.

A number of distinct approaches to online conflict management are in existence today, and several of them are supported by IT tools and systems (Conley, 2007; Thiessen & Zeleznikow, 2004). We provide several illustrative examples. Cybersettle is an online conflict resolution system that utilizes univariate blind bidding to resolve monetary disputes. Parties that decide to adopt Cybersettle's technology use a double-blind bid system to negotiate. A party that initiates the process provides confidential offers for a prespecified number of rounds. The opposing party provides the same number of counteroffers corresponding to each round. The system compares parties' offers and counteroffers on a round-by-round basis. When the offer is greater than or equal to the opposition's counteroffer, the claim instantly settles. The tool is designed to motivate the parties to reach a settlement quickly since the values that would cause them to exit the negotiation can be submitted online. The double-blind process, facilitated by online technology, reduces the likelihood of opportunistic behavior by one of the parties. Also, the confidentiality of offers and counteroffers ensures that information asymmetry with respect to each party's reservation prices is minimized. Many companies have used Cybersettle to expedite various types of insurance claim settlement (such as bodily injury claim resulting from an auto, general liability or uninsured/underinsured motorist claim, worker compensation claims, etc.), ranging from $500 to $13 million. This asynchronous tool allows parties to settle disputes faster, 24 hours a day, 7 days a week. It has been shown that such a tool can shorten the claim cycle by reducing the time from offer to settlement; thus, it makes the negotiation process more efficient.

Other examples of electronic conflict management tools include Smartsettle; its Web site provides Web-based negotiation technology that allows parties to reveal their willingness to accept without the concern about revealing their hand. However, Smartsettle rewards an early move into the zone of agreement by providing a better final settlement to those parties who negotiate in a professional manner (i.e., quickly accepting what is fair and equitable). A third instance of IT-based tools in support of conflict resolution is ECODIR (http://www.ecodir.org), an ODR process that provides a robust platform for orchestrating negotiations, mediation, and ultimately recommendations. The parties in conflict are first provided the opportunity to negotiate with each other on the ECODIR electronic platform for 18 days. If no resolution is reached within 18 days, ECODIR appoints a human mediator, who interacts with the conflicting parties on the same platform and brings the process to closure, through either consensual resolution or a recommendation based on principles of fairness. As noted on the Web site, "ECODIR helps consumers find a solution through a flexible, inexpensive, and quick process."

In summary, although all economic transactions are associated with a variety of risks, transactions conducted electronically between parties who may be geographically dispersed and contracting for the first time are arguably inherently riskier. When conflicts arise because one party fails to deliver on its contractual obligations, there is a need for interventions that can effectively settle the dispute. In nonvirtual settings, conflict resolution can be a long and arduous process, fraught with inefficiencies. When conflict resolution is orchestrated electronically, it eliminates some of these inefficiencies, saving the disputing parties both time and money.

This chapter has treated the process of negotiation as consisting of three major stages: contacting, contracting, and controlling. Each of these stages involves multiple activities that have transaction costs associated with them. IT has played a significant role in reducing these transaction costs, and negotiators today have access to a broad array of IT tools to assist them in the three stages. Yet, while the promise of IT to mitigate the transaction costs of negotiating is substantial and supported by a growing body of evidence, it is not clear if these benefits can be equally exploited by all organizations and individuals. When transactions cross national boundaries, they often involve parties that operate in distinct political, social, and economic climates. The IT interventions described in this chapter need to be equally accessible to all parties engaged in a negotiation for value to be created. We consider the possibility that the global nature of the 21st century workplace may involve locations where there are disparities in access to IT interventions.

ARE IT-ENABLED TRANSACTIONS EQUALLY ACCESSIBLE IN THE GLOBAL WORKPLACE OF THE 21ST CENTURY?

Although the Internet is a global resource and is, in principle, available to managers everywhere, in practice there are three factors that constrain accessibility in the 21st century global workplace. First, the existence of a digital divide, which fundamentally denotes unequal access to the Internet and other computing technologies, has been widely acknowledged (Servon, 2002). The divide has been documented between nations (Robison & Crenshaw, 2010) and within nations (Agarwal, Animesh, & Prasad, 2009), among the rich and poor (Jansen, 2010), and between rural and urban populations (Stern, Adams, & Elsasser, 2009). Unequal access to technologies implies that all individuals and organizations in the digitally "poor" sections of society cannot participate in the new world of negotiation enabled by IT. For example, broadband access that enables transacting parties to avail themselves of the resources of the Internet exhibits considerable variation in availability, price, and quality (Agarwal et al., 2009).

A second constraint that organizations and individuals face with respect to the accessibility of IT interventions that support negotiations is global variations in government policy in regard to freedom of information and expression. Governments of certain nations have instituted policies that restrict access to certain Web sites for their residents for a variety of political and social reasons. The Chinese have frequently been implicated for blocking access to specific Web sites (Joint Hearing, 2006), and recently Iran has as well (Iran Human Rights Documentation Center, 2009). As a consequence, depending on their geographic location, negotiation partners may have unequal and, in some instances, no access to some IT interventions.

A final impediment constraining the use of IT tools for negotiation is simply the technological sophistication of the trading partners. Many of these IT interventions require their users to be reasonably competent and comfortable with using computing technologies, and some, particularly those related to searching for information, require sophisticated navigational skills. As such, the value created by these tools for managers is predicated on transacting parties knowing about the existence and their ability to utilize the tool in an effective manner such that they are availed of all of its functionality. The expected benefits in terms of reducing transactions cost may not be appropriated in the absence of a basic foundation of technological literacy.

QUESTIONS IN NEED OF FUTURE RESEARCH

As illustrated in the numerous examples provided in this chapter, by mitigating the transaction costs incurred at various stages of the negotiation process, IT has considerably transformed and expanded the opportunities available to managers. These transformations span the gamut from the ability to locate potential partners unconstrained by geography, to ascertain partner and product quality, to negotiate prices and other outcomes that are preferred and value generating, and as necessary, to manage the relationship once the negotiation has been concluded and an agreement reached. This "new" world of negotiating will increasingly become a defining characteristic of the 21st century workplace, and we envision an accelerating mediation by technology in negotiations of all varieties. For scholars, these trends pose some intriguing research questions that warrant further work. We identify a few next.

The first question relates to amplifying the "digital literacy" of managers. As noted, knowledge about the availability of various IT interventions that can aid with negotiation as well as the ability to use technology effectively are crucial prerequisites for availing themselves of the new opportunities afforded by IT. This has implications for organizational processes related to recruitment, socialization, and training, as well as the culture of the organization. What managerial actions would be efficacious in creating the type of organizational culture that would encourage experimentation with new technologies and motivate managers to learn about innovations? What is the most effective way to identify during a selection process, a priori, the willingness of potential hires to be innovative with their use of technology? And, what training and development opportunities need to be made available to managers for them to become productive users of the IT-based negotiation tools?

A second significant research question emerges from the unequal access to technology to which we alluded. As organizations expand operations globally, and as they seek to exploit location-specific cost advantages and leverage diverse talent that may not be available domestically, there is a likelihood that their ability to locate appropriate partners and engage in negotiation and trading may be limited by the availability of the right set of tools and technology. While this expectation is plausible and supported by anecdotal evidence, there is limited empirical data to substantiate it. Future research could focus on measuring and documenting the disadvantages that accrue to organizations as they attempt to initiate negotiation transactions in different parts of the world. For example, would it be more value creating to select partners purposively from certain geographies as opposed to a broad-based global search? Are all parties within a geographic region equally able to "offer" their products and services on a digital platform? Findings from such studies could inform organizations and their managers about the "best" places in the world to negotiate with through technology.

A final set of questions that merits further research arises from the widely documented cognitive constraints and biases inherent in managerial decision making (e.g., Tversky & Kahneman, 1981, 1986). Tversky and Kahneman proposed prospect theory as an explanation for circumstances in which individual behavior deviates from theories of rational choice. Individuals evaluate alternatives based on whether they perceive the alternative to be a loss or a gain: A response to losses is typically more extreme (referred to as loss aversion) than a response to perceived gains from the alternative. Such biases will inevitably influence the manner in which managers conduct various activities in the negotiation stages and may cause, for example, a suboptimal partner to be selected, a price negotiation to be prematurely terminated, or inadequate coordination and follow-up once the agreement is reached. There are two issues here that are in need of rigorous research. First, what is the magnitude and nature of these biases, and what is their effect on the negotiation outcome? Field and laboratory experiments that place managers in negotiating situations, both face to face and mediated by technology, could be used to investigate this question. Second, can negotiation technologies be designed such that they help managers in the 21st century workplace overcome their cognitive constraints and biases? We are already seeing examples of such systems in the technologies described in this chapter, and systems designers could seek to craft better and more sophisticated tools that would allow each stage of negotiation to be conducted optimally.

NOTE

1. Online auctions are discussed in detail in the next section, in which we examine the role of this electronic market mechanism in facilitating the contract stage activities and its impact of the costs of the contracting stage of negotiation.

REFERENCES

Abrazhevich, D. 2001. Classification and characteristics of electronic payment systems. In K. Bauknecht, S. K. Madria, & G. Pernul (Eds.), *Electronic commerce and Web Technologies: Second international conference, EC-Web 2001, lecture notes in computer science* (pp. 81–90). Berlin: Springer-Verlag.

Agarwal, R., Animesh, A., & Prasad, K. 2009. Social interactions and the "digital divide": Explaining variations in Internet use. *Information Systems Research, 20,* 277–294.

Akerlof, G. A. 1970. The market for "lemons": Quality uncertainty and the market mechanism. *The Quarterly Journal of Economics, 84,* 488–500.

Alba, J., Lynch, J., Weitz, B., Janiszewski, C., Lutz, R., Sawyer, A., & Wood, S. 1997. Interactive home shopping: Consumer, retailer, and manufacturer incentives to participate in electronic marketplaces. *Journal of Marketing, 61*(3), 38–53.

Al-Sakran, H. and I. Serguievskaia, 2006. A framework for developing experience based e-negotiation system. *Journal of Computer Science, 2*(2), 180–184.

Anderson, C. 2004. The long tail. *Wired Magazine, 12*(10), 170–177.

Argyres, N. S. 1999. The impact of information technology on coordination: Evidence from the B-2 "stealth" bomber. *Organization Science, 10*(2), 162–180.

Arnold, M. A., & Pénard, T. 2007. Bargaining and fixed price offers: How online intermediaries are changing new car transactions. *Review of Network Economics, 6,* 134–160.

Bailey, J., Brynjolfsson, E., & Smith, M. D. 1999. Understanding digital markets: Review and assessment. In E. Brynjolfsson & B. Kahin (Eds.), *Understanding the digital economy*. Boston: MIT Press.

Bakos, J. Y. 1998. The emerging role of electronic marketplaces on the Internet. *Communications of the ACM, 41*(8), 35–42.

Bakos, Y. 1997. Reducing buyer search costs: Implications for electronic marketplaces. *Management Science, 43*, 1676–1692.

Bakos, Y., Lucas, H. C., Oh, W., Simon, G., Viswanathan, S., & Weber, B. 2005. The impact of e-commerce on competition in the retail brokerage industry. *Information Systems Research, 16*, 352–371.

Bapna, R., Goes, P., Gupta, A., & Yiwei, J. 2004. User heterogeneity and its impact on electronic auction market design: An empirical exploration. *MIS Quarterly, 28*(1), 21–43.

Baye, M. R., & Morgan, J. 2001. Information gatekeepers on the Internet and the competitiveness of homogeneous product markets. *American Economic Review, 91*, 454–474.

Baye, M. R., Morgan, J., & Scholten, P. A. 2003. The value of information in an online consumer electronics market. *Journal of Public Policy and Marketing, 22*, 17–25.

Bichler, M., & Kalagnanam, J. 2005. Configurable offers and winner determination in multi-attribute auctions. *European Journal of Operational Research, 160*, 380–394.

Bielski, L. 2010. What's PayPal up to? *ABA Banking Journal, 102*(7), 26–29.

Boutilier, C., Shoham, Y., & Wellman, M. P. 1997. Economic principles of multi-agent systems. *Artificial Intelligence, 94*(1–2), 1–6.

Brynjolfsson, E., Hu, J. Y., & Smith, M. D. 2006. From niches to riches: Anatomy of the long tail. *Sloan Management Review, 47*, 67–71.

Brynjolfsson, E., & Smith, M. 2000. Frictionless commerce? A comparison of Internet and conventional retailers. *Management Science, 46*, 563–585.

Brynjolfsson, E., Yu, J. H., & Smith, M. D. 2010. *The longer tail: The changing shape of Amazon's sales distribution curve*. Working paper. Retrieved from http://ssrn.com/abstract=1679991

Brynjolfsson, E., Hu, Y., & Smith, M. 2003. Consumer surplus in the digital economy: Estimating the value of increased product variety at online booksellers. *Management Science, 49*, 1580–1596.

Cabral, L., & Hortacsu, A. 2004. The dynamics of seller reputation: Theory and evidence from eBay. *The Journal of Industrial Economics, 58*(1), 54–78.

Carmel, E., & Nicholson, B. 2005. Small firms and offshore software outsourcing: High transaction costs and their mitigation. *Journal of Global Information Management, 13*, 33–54.

Chevalier, J., & Goolsbee, A. 2003. Measuring prices and price competition online: Amazon and Barnes and Noble. *Quantitative Marketing and Economics, 1*, 203–222.

Chevalier, J. A., & Mayzlin, D. 2006. The effect of word of mouth on sales: Online book reviews. *Journal of Marketing Research, 43*, 345–354.

Chintagunta, P. K., Shyam, G., & Sriram, V. 2010. The effects of online user reviews on movie box office performance: Accounting for sequential rollout and aggregation across local markets. *Marketing Science, 29*, 944–957.

Clemons, E., Gao, G., & Hitt, L. 2006. When online reviews meet hyperdifferentiation: A study of the craft beer industry. *Journal of Management Information Systems, 23*, 149–171.

Conley, T. M. 2007. Online dispute resolution. In M. Malkia & A.-V. Anttiroiko (Eds.), *Encyclopaedia of digital government* (pp. 1268–1274). Hershey, PA: Idea Group Reference.

Croson, R. T. A. 1999. Look at me when you say that: An electronic negotiation simulation. *Simulation and Gaming, 30*, 23–37.

Daly, B. A. 1993. The influence of face-to-face versus computer-mediated communication channels on collective induction. *Accounting Management Information Technology, 3,* 1–22.

Dedrick, J., Xu, S., & Zhu, K. 2008. How does information technology shape supply-chain structure? Evidence on the number of suppliers. *Journal of Management Information Systems, 25,* 41–72.

Delaney, M. M., Foroughi, A., & Perkins, W. C. 1997. An empirical study of the efficacy of a computerized negotiation support system (NSS). *Decision Support Systems, 20,* 185–197.

Dewan, S., & Hsu, V. 2004. Adverse selection in electronic markets: Evidence from online stamp auctions. *The Journal of Industrial Economics, 52,* 497–516.

Dini, F., & Spagnolo, G. 2005. Reputation mechanisms and electronic markets: Economic issues and proposals for public procurement. In K. V. Thai, A. Araujo, R. Y. Carter, G. Callender, D. Drabkin, R. Grimm, et al. (Eds.), *Challenges in public procurement: An international perspective* (pp. 227–247). New York: Academic Press.

Drolet, A. L., & Morris, M. W. 2000. Rapport in conflict resolution: Accounting for how face-to-face contact fosters mutual cooperation in mixed-motive conflicts. *Journal of Experimental Social Psychology, 36,* 26–50.

Eaton, D. H. 2002. Valuing information: Evidence from guitar auctions on eBay. *Journal of Applied Economics and Policy, 24,* 1–19.

Ederington, L. H., & Dewally, M. (2003). A comparison of reputation, certification, warranties, and information disclosure as remedies for information asymmetries: Lessons from the on-line comic book market. Working paper, Price College of Business, University of Oklahoma, Norman, OK.

Eliashberg, J., Gauvin, S., Lilien, G. L., & Rangaswamy, A. 1992. An experimental study of alternative preparation aids for international negotiations. *Group Decision and Negotiations, 1,* 243–267.

Elmaghraby, W. 2007. Auctions within e-sourcing events. *Production and Operations Management, 16,* 409–422.

Emiliani, M. L. 2000. Business-to-business online auctions: Key issues for purchasing process improvement. *Supply Chain Management: An International Journal, 5,* 176–186.

Foroughi, A., Perkins, W. C., & Jelassi, M. T. 1995. An empirical-study of an interactive, session-oriented computerized negotiation support system (NSS). *Group Decision and Negotiation, 4,* 485–512.

Gallupe, R. B., Cooper, W. H., Grise, M.-L., & Bastianutti, L. M. 1994. Blocking electronic brainstorms. *Journal of Applied Psychology, 79,* 77–86.

General Accounting Office (GAO). 2002. *Employee privacy: Computer-use monitoring practices and policies of select companies.* United States General Accounting Office, Report to the Ranking Minority Member, Subcommittee on 21st Century Competitiveness, Committee on Education and the Workforce, U.S. House of Representatives.

Godes, D., & Mayzlin, D. 2004. Using online conversations to study word of mouth communication. *Marketing Science, 23,* 545–560.

Greenhalgh, L., & Gilkey, R. W. 1993. The effect of relationship orientation on negotiators cognitions and tactics. *Group Decision and Negotiation, 2,* 167–186.

Guttman, R. H., Moukas, A. G., & Maes, P. 1998. Agent-mediated electronic commerce: A survey. *Knowledge Engineering Review, 13,* 147–159.

Guttman, R., & Maes, P. 1999. Agent-mediated integrative negotiation for retail electronic commerce. *Lecture Notes in Artificial Intelligence, 1571,* 70–90.

Hobbs, J. E. 1996. A transaction cost approach to supply chain management. *Supply Chain Management, 1,* 15–27.

Hordijk, L. 1991. Use of the RAINS model in acid rain negotiation in Europe. *Environmental Science Technology, 25*, 596–603.

Hörnle, J. 2009. *Cross-border Internet dispute resolution*. London: Cambridge University Press.

Hossain, T. 2008. Learning by bidding. *Rand Journal of Economics, 39*, 509–529.

Houser, D., & Wooders, J. 2006. Reputation in auctions: Theory, and evidence from eBay. *Journal of Economics and Management Strategy, 15*, 353–369.

Howard, R. 1966. Information value theory. *IEEE Transactions on Systems Science and Cybernetics, 2*, 22–26.

Hsu, T. 2010, November 16. AT&T, T-Mobile and Verizon partner on Isis mobile payment project. *Los Angeles Times*. Available at http://latimesblogs.latimes.com/technology/2010/11/att-t-mobile-and-verizon-partner-on-isis-mobile-payment-project.html

Iran Human Rights Documentation Center. 2009. *Ctrl+Alt+Delete: Iran's Response to the Internet*. Retrieved January 8, 2011 from http://www.iranhrdc.org/httpdocs/English/pdfs/Reports/Ctr+Alt+Delete%20--%20Iran%27s%20Response%20to%20the%20Internet.pdf

Jansen, J. 2010, Nov 24. Use of the Internet in higher-income households. Pew Internet & American Life Project Project. Accessed Dec. 14, 2011 from http://pewinternet.org/~/media//Files/Reports/2010/PIP-Better-off-households-final.pdf

Jarke, M. M., Jelassi, T., & Shakun, M. F. 1987. MEDIATOR: Towards a negotiation support system. *European Journal of Operational Research, 31*, 314–334.

Joint Hearing. 2006. *The Internet in China: A tool for freedom or suppression?* (Committee on International Relations, Serial Number 109-157). Washington, DC: U.S. Government Printing Office.

Jolly, H. 2008. Winning vendors over to e-payments. *Journal of Payments Strategy and Systems, 2*, 175–181.

Kalyanam, K., & McIntyre, S. 2001. Returns to reputation in online auction markets, Retail Workbench Working Paper, Leavey School Business, Santa Clara University, CA.

Katsh, E., & Rifkin, J. 2001. *Online dispute resolution: Resolving conflicts in cyberspace*. San Francisco: Jossey-Bass.

Katz, E., & Lazarsfeld, P. F. 1955. *Personal influence: The part played by people in the flow of mass communications*. New York: Free Press.

Kauffman, R. J., & Wood, C. A. 2006. Doing their bidding: An empirical examination of factors that affect a buyer's utility in internet auctions. *Information Technology Management, 7*, 171–190.

Kaufmann, L., & Carter, C. R. 2004. Deciding on the mode of negotiation: To auction or not to auction electronically. *Journal of Supply Chain Management, 40*, 15–26.

Kersten, G. E. 1985. NEGO-Group Decision Support System. *Information and Management, 8*, 237–246.

Kersten, G. E., & Lai, H. 2007. Negotiation support and e-negotiation systems: An overview. *Group Decision and Negotiation, 16*, 553–586.

Kersten, G. E., & Lai, H. 2008. Negotiation support and e-negotiation systems. In F. Burstein & C. W. Holsapple (Eds.), *Handbook on decision support systems 1: Basic Themes* (pp. 469–508). Berlin: Springer-Verlag.

Kim, D. J., & Benbasat, I. 2006. The effects of trust-assuring arguments on consumer trust in Internet Stores: Application of Toulmin's model of argumentation. *Information Systems Research, 17*, 286–300.

Klein, S. 1997. Introduction to electronic auctions. *International Journal of Electronic Markets, 7*, 3–6.

Klemperer, P. 1999. Auction theory: A guide to the literature. *Journal of Economic Surveys, 13*, 227–286.

Klusch, M. 2000. Agent-mediated trading: intelligent agents and e-business. In A. L. G. Hayzelden & R. Bourne (Eds.), *Agent technology applied to networked systems*. Chichester, UK: Wiley.

Kreps, D. M. 1990. *A course in microeconomic theory*. Princeton, NJ: Princeton University Press.

Kurtzberg, T., & Medvec, V. H. 2003. Can we negotiate and still be friends? In R. J. Lewicki, B. Barry, & D. Saunders (Eds.), *Negotiation. readings, exercises, and cases* (pp. 281–286). Boston: McGraw-Hill.

Kuruzovich, J., Viswanathan, S., Agarwal, R., & Gosain, S. 2008. Marketspace or marketplace? Online information search and channel outcomes in auto retailing. *Information Systems Research, 19*, 182–201.

Kuruzovich, J., Viswanathan, S., & Agarwal, R. 2010. Seller search and market outcomes in online auctions. *Management Science, 56*, 1702–1717.

Lim, F. Y. 2007. *Cyberspace law: Commentaries and materials*. London: Oxford University Press.

Lin, M., Prabhala, N. R., & Viswanathan, S. 2009. Can social networks mitigate information asymmetry in online markets? In *Proceedings of the 30th International Conference on Information Systems*, December. Phoenix, AZ.

Livingston, J. A. 2005. How valuable is a good reputation? A sample selection model of internet auctions. *The Review of Economics and Statistics, 87*, 453–465.

Lupia, A., & Strøm. K. 2008. Bargaining, Transaction costs, and coalition governance. In T. Bergman, W. C. Müller, & Kaare Strøm (Eds.), *Cabinets and coalition bargaining: The democratic life cycle in western Europe* (pp. 51–84). Oxford, UK: Oxford University Press.

Lynch, J. G., & Ariely, D. 2000. Wine online: Search cost affect competition on price, quality, and distribution. *Marketing Science, 19*, 83–103.

MacKie-Mason, J. K., & White, K. 1997. Evaluating and selecting digital payment mechanisms. In G. Rosston & D. Waterman (Eds.), *Interconnection and the Internet* (pp. 113–134). Mahwah, NJ: Erlbaum.

Maes, P., Guttman, R. H., & Moukas, A. G. 1999. Agents that buy and sell. *Communications of the ACM, 42*, 81–91.

Malone, T. W., Yates, J., & Benjamin, R. I. 1987. Electronic markets and electronic hierarchies. *Communications of the ACM, 30*, 484–497.

McAfee, R. P., & McMillan, J. 1987. Auctions and bidding. *Journal of Economic Literature, 25*, 699–738.

McGinn, K. L., & Keros, A. T. 2002. Improvisation and the logic of exchange in socially embedded transactions. *Administrative Science Quarterly, 47*, 442–473.

Melnik, M. I., & Alm, J. 2002. Does a seller's ecommerce reputation matter? Evidence from eBay auctions. *Journal of Industrial Economics, 50*, 337–350.

Morris, M., Nadler, J., Kurtzberg, N., & Leigh, T. 2002. Schmooze or lose: Social friction and lubrication in e-mail negotiations. *Group Dynamics: Theory, Research, and Practice, 6*, 89–100.

Nooteboom, B. 1993. Firm size effects on transaction costs. *Small Business Economics, 5*, 283–295.

Nunamaker, J. F., Dennis, A. R., Valacich, J. S., & Vogel, D. R. 1991. Information technology for negotiating groups: Generating options for mutual gain. *Management Science, 37*, 1325–1346.

Nyhart, J. D., & Samarasan, D. K. 1989. The elements for negotiation management: Using computers to help resolve conflict. *Negotiation Journal, 11*, 43–62.

Overby, E. 2008. Process virtualization theory and the impact of information technology. *Organization Science, 19*, 277–291.

Özpolat, K., Gao, G., Jank, W., & Viswanathan, S. 2010. *The value of online trust seals: Evidence from online retailing*. Working Paper. Retrieved from http://ssrn.com/abstract=1592480

Pesendorfer, E., & Koeszegi, S. T. 2007. Social embeddedness in electronic negotiations. *Group Decision and Negotiation, 16*, 399–415.

Rangaswamy, A., & Shell, G. R. 1997. Using computers to realize joint gains in negotiations: Towards an "electronic bargaining table." *Management Science, 8*, 1147–1163.

Ratchford, B. T., Lee, M. S., & Talukdar, D. 2003. The impact of the Internet on information search automobiles. *Journal of Marketing Research, 40*, 193–209.

Resnick, P., Kuwabara, K., Zeckhauser, R., & Friedman, E. 2000. Reputation systems. *Communications of the ACM, 43*, 45–48.

Resnick, P., & Zeckhauser, R. 2002. Trust among strangers in Internet transactions: Empirical analysis of eBay's reputation system. *Advances in Applied Microeconomics, 11*, 127–157.

Robison, K. K., & Crenshaw, E. M. 2010. Reevaluating the global digital divide: Sociodemographic and conflict barriers to the Internet revolution. *Sociological Inquiry, 80*, 34–62.

Roth, A. E., & Ockenfels, A. 2002. Last-minute bidding and the rules for ending second-price auctions: Evidence from eBay and Amazon auctions on the Internet. *American Economic Review, 92*, 1093–1103.

Rothkopf, M. H., & Whinston, A. B. 2007. On e-auctions for procurement operations. *Production and Operations Management, 16*, 404–408.

Sanders, N. R. 2008. Pattern of information technology use: The impact on buyer–suppler coordination and performance. *Journal of Operations Management, 26*, 349–367.

Schlosser, A. E., White, T. B., & Lloyd, S. M. 2005. Converting Web site visitors into buyers: How Web site investment increases consumer trusting beliefs and online purchase intentions. *Journal of Marketing, 70*, 133–148.

Schwartz, E. I. 2001. Digital cash payoff. *Technology Review, 104*, 62.

Scott-Morton, F., & Zettelmeyer, F. 2004. The strategic positioning of store brands in retailer-manufacturer negotiations. *Review of Industrial Organization, 24*, 161–194.

Scott-Morton, F., Zettelmeyer, F., & Silva-Risso, J. 2001. Internet car retailing. *The Journal of Industrial Economics, 49*, 501–519.

Scott-Morton, F., Zettelmeyer, F., & Silva-Risso, J. 2003. Consumer information and discrimination: Does the Internet affect the pricing of new cars to woman and minorities? *Quantitative Marketing and Economics, 1*, 65–92.

Servon, L. 2002. *Bridging the digital divide: Technology, community, and public policy*, Malden, MA: Blackwell.

Sierra, C., Faratin, P., & Jennings, N. 1999. Deliberative automated reasoning using fuzzy similarities. In *Proceedings of the EUSFLAT-ESTYLF, Joint Conference on Fuzzy Logic, Palma de Mallorca, Spain* (pp. 155–158). September.

Smith, M. D., Bailey, J., & Brynjolfsson, E. 1999. Understanding digital markets: Review and assessment. In E. Brynjolfsson & B. Kahin (Eds.), *Understanding the digital economy* (pp. 99–136). Cambridge, MA: MIT Press.

Smith, M. D., & Brynjolfsson, E. 2001. Customer decision making at an Internet shopbot: Brand still matters. *The Journal of Industrial Economics, 49*, 541–558.

Snir, E. M., & Hitt, L. M. 2003. Costly bidding in online markets for IT services. *Management Science, 49*, 1504–1520.

Stahl, D. O. 1989. Oligopolistic pricing with sequential consumer search. *American Economic Review*, *79*, 700–712.

Stern, M. J., Adams, A. E., & Elsasser, S. 2009. Digital inequality and place: The effects of technological diffusion on Internet proficiency and usage across rural, suburban, and urban counties. *Sociological Inquiry, 79*, 391–417.

Subramanian, G. 2010. *Negotiauctions: New dealmaking strategies for a competitive marketplace*. New York: Norton.

Sycara, K. P. 1990. Negotiation planning: An A.I. approach. *European Journal of Operational Research, 46*, 216–234.

Talluri, S., Narasimhan, R., & Viswanathan, S. 2007. Information technologies for procurement decisions: A decision support system for multi-attribute e-reverse auctions. *International Journal of Production Research, 45*, 2615–2628.

Thaler, R. H. 2009. Paying a price for the thrill of the hunt. *The New York Times*. Retrieved January 8, 2011, from http://www.nytimes.com/ 2009/11/15/business/economy/15view.html

Thiessen, E., & Zeleznikow, J. 2004. Technical aspects of online dispute resolution challenges and opportunities. In M. Conley Tyler, E. Katsh, & D. Choi (Eds.), *Proceedings of the Third Annual Forum on Online Dispute Resolution*. July. Melbourne, Victoria, Australia.

Treude, C., Storey, M.-A., & Weber, J. 2009. *Empirical studies on collaboration in software development: A systematic literature review* (Technical Report DCS-331-IR). Victoria, BC: Department of Computer Science, University of Victoria.

Tsai, J. Y., Egelman, S., Cranor, L., & Acquisti, A. 2011. The effect of online privacy information on purchasing behavior: An experimental study. *Information Systems Research, 22*, 254–268.

Tversky, A., & Kahneman, D. 1981. The framing of decisions and the psychology of choice. *Science, 211*, 453–458.

Tversky, A., & Kahneman, D. 1986. Rational choice and the framing of decisions. *Journal of Business, 59*, S251–S278.

Vetschera, R. 2007. Preference structures and negotiator behavior in electronic negotiations. *Decision Support Systems, 44*, 135–146.

Viswanathan, S., Kuruzovich, J., Gosain, S., & Agarwal, R. 2007. Online infomediaries and price discrimination: Evidence from the automotive retailing sector. *Journal of Marketing, 71*, 89–107.

von Neumann, J., & Morgenstern, O. 1944. *The theory of games and economic behavior*. Princeton, NJ: Princeton University Press.

Wainer, J., Novoa Barsottini, C. G., Lacerda, D., & Magalhães de Marco, L. 2009. Empirical evaluation in computer science research published by ACM. *Information and Software Technology, 51*, 1081–1085.

Wilkenfeld, J., Kraus, S., Holley, K. M., & Harris, M. A. 1995. Genie: A decision support system for crisis negotiations. *Decision Support Systems, 14*, 369–391.

Ye, S., Gao, G., & Viswanathan, S. 2009. The good, the bad, or the ugly? An empirical investigation of revoking behavior on eBay. In *Proceedings of the 30th International Conference on Information Systems*, December. Phoenix, AZ.

Zeng, D., & Sycara, K. 1998. Bayesian learning in negotiation. *International Journal of Human-Computer Studies—Evolution and Learning in Multiagent Systems, 48*, 125–141.

Section 6

Commentaries

15

Negotiating in a Brave New World: Challenges and Opportunities for the Field of Negotiation Science

Michele J. Gelfand and Ya'akov (Kobi) Gal

INTRODUCTION

Contributors to this volume have collectively paved the way for a new revolution in the field of negotiation science. *The Psychology of Negotiations in the 21st Century Workplace* is a tour de force. The territory covered in the book is simply astounding, including such basic processes as fairness, trust, competition, and cooperation, to social structure and networks, to organizational learning and national culture—all of which capture part of the complex "elephant" that is negotiation. Each chapter draws on new and exciting theoretical and empirical developments from a wide variety of disciplines to inform key learning that can be distilled for managers, practitioners, and anyone who needs to manage interdependence with others in their daily lives. And, the authors have each grounded their theoretical, empirical, and practical discussions of negotiation in situ—in the particular features of the 21st century organizational landscape that invariably affect the process and outcomes of negotiations in this brave new negotiating world. Put simply, this volume exemplifies the science-practitioner model at its very best.

Unlike other volumes in the field, this collection is particularly unique in that it not only takes a look *back* on the seminal theories, the empirical discoveries, and the practical wisdom of decades of negotiation research but also provides a thoughtful window into the *future* of the science and practice of negotiation and the contextual realities that negotiators will face. Negotiations in the 21st century, as many of the chapters illustrate, are much more complex; they are "wired," they are global, they are networked, and they occur in increasingly flattened and fluid organizational structures (Goldman & Shapiro, Chapter 1, this volume). In this new 21st century workplace, negotiations are *connected*; they take place across a much broader array of actors—with peers, supervisors, customers, suppliers, alliance partners, and even computer agents—who are embedded in wider social networks, and they take place across many new forms of social media. By providing us with an analysis of the critical features of the 21st century organization in which negotiations are embedded, the chapters in this book provide an infinite number of research ideas for decades to come.

In this commentary, we take the opportunity to take a bird's-eye view of the volume to make *explicit* some of the *implicit* scientific mandates that the authors address. We highlight the need for new conceptualizations of negotiation that are better matched to the organizational realities in the 21st century workplace; we discuss neglected scholarly territory and critical research gaps that desperately await investigation; above all, we champion a *negotiation science* that transcends disciplines and recommend new intellectual mergers that are required to address the complex organizational realities of negotiation that this volume identifies.

RECONCEPTUALIZING NEGOTIATION

While the book is diverse in its content, all the authors make clear that the way that we have fundamentally conceptualized negotiations in the past needs to be much broader, and the questions we ask need to change accordingly. Negotiation research, inherited from economics with a heavy game theoretic and prescriptive emphasis, has examined many cognitive, motivational, and emotional psychological processes that are inherent to the "game" negotiators are playing (Bazerman, Curhan, Moore, & Valley, 2000; Thompson, Wang, & Gunia, 2010), as well as the social and communication processes that occur as negotiators interact, exchange passes or volleys, to gain points (Weingart & Olekalns, 2004). Negotiations, using this game metaphor, were often seen as one-shot, delimited interactions between actors—largely divorced from the social context—in the service of completing the game (Kramer & Messick, 1995).

The chapters in this book challenge us to reconceptualize negotiations from largely one-shot, delimited interactions to a view of negotiations as involving many actors over networks, over time, and over space. They make clear that negotiations often extend within and across organizational boundaries, and that what happens at the table *does not end at the table.* Above all, they collectively highlight the sports metaphor that has dominated negotiation research (Gelfand & McCusker, 2002), which assumes that what happens on the field ends when the game is over and does not affect the next game. However, this metaphor does not fit these new organizational realities.

Accordingly, this volume invites new metaphors, new theoretical perspectives, and novel research questions to match the realities of the 21st century workplace. For example, the fact that negotiations often involve repeated transactions between parties in ongoing relationships embedded in networks that exist virtually invites a "network metaphor of negotiation" in contrast to a sports metaphor. The network metaphor suggests that dynamics that occur at the negotiation table can have downstream numerous "ripple effects" for negotiators' relationships, their social networks, and organizations more broadly. In this view, negotiation failures (for example, feeling unfairly treated) can have important downstream costs for future willingness to negotiate and the ability to reap high economic outcomes over the long run (see Elfenbein & Curhan, Chapter 5, this volume). For example, as discussed in this volume, while injustices (Conlon & Ross, Chapter 2; Roloff, Brockner, & Wiesenfeld, Chapter 3); negative emotions (Cropanzano, Becker, & Feldman, Chapter 6); and unethical behavior (Lewicki & Hanke, Chapter 8) might be tolerated in a one-shot deal, they could present large future costs for negotiators in repeated, networked transactions. On the flip side, this conceptualization also suggests that *successes* that occur at the negotiation table (for example, feeling fairly treated) can have many positive ripple effects in repeated transactions in the future—engendering more trust, cooperative behavior, and more "idiosyncratic credits" for future behavior (Hollander, 1958). Importantly, positive or negative carryover effects at the negotiation table need not be confined to the parties' relationships: They can extend to individuals' trust or mistrust in the organization, their proclivity to engage in prosocial behavior or revenge and sabotage, and ultimately their organizational commitment or lack thereof (see Pinkley, Chapter 4, this volume, and Elfenbein & Curhan, Chapter 5, this volume, for related discussions).

This new conceptualization further suggests that given that negotiators are invariably embedded in networks of interpersonal relationships (Brass & Labianca, Chapter 9, this volume), dynamics that occur at the negotiation can also have widespread ripple effects *across networks*. As Roloff et al. (Chapter 3, this volume) note, negotiations can be "overheard" by others, with the failures or successes at the negotiation table ultimately spreading throughout networks. Indeed, in the new 21st century workplace, negotiations do not end at the organizational door: Negotiated outcomes can become quickly known in the marketplace, where technology allows information about negotiation to be posted through various social media (Agarwal, Viswanathan, & Animesh, Chapter 14, this volume). Take, for example, the disgruntled employee or customer who "vents" through Twitter or Facebook about his or her negative negotiation experiences with an organization online.

In all, this view of negotiation implies that previous research findings that fit with a "one-shot deal" will need to be revisited and expanded to address the *dynamics of negotiation* and how they become dispersed across people, networks, social media, and time. It begs new questions such as, How do the basic psychological and social processes in one negotiation affect negotiation dynamics over a much longer timeframe? To what extent are negotiation processes contagious to others—how are observers of negotiations and their networks affected by the negotiations they witness? To what extent does a negotiator's reputation spread across networks and with what implication for future negotiations? How do changes in negotiation networks, as is often the case given the increasingly mobile workplace, affect negotiations over time? For example, how do negotiators who "inherit" mistrust and mistreatment by others negotiate their relationships with this lingering psychological past? How is trust repaired in negotiations when it involves negotiators who were not part of the original process? Implicit in this discussion is that we need to move beyond standard criteria of economic capital achieved in a one-shot negotiation to include new criteria that matter in the networked view of negotiation. Criteria such as subjective value at the individual level (Elfenbein & Curhan, Chapter 5, this volume); relational capital at the dyadic level (Gelfand, Smith, Raver, Nishii, & O'Brien, 2006); and reputation and social capital at the network level (Brass & Labianca, Chapter 9, this volume) are currencies that loom large in the 21st century workplace. Fundamentally, this networked view of negotiation implies that previous research findings and gold standard criteria that fit with a one-shot deal will need to be revisited.

In addition to inviting new ways to conceptualize negotiation and new criteria for evaluating negotiation success, the chapters in this book highlight important research gaps in the literature. They suggest that the brave new negotiation science needs to be multilevel in its focus, global in its reach, and interdisciplinary its structure, each of which are discussed in the following material.

THE OPEN SYSTEMS VIEW OF NEGOTIATION: IMPLICATIONS FOR CROSS-LEVEL MODELING IN NEGOTIATION

Chapters in this book hint at the fact that negotiations in the 21st century workplace function within the larger organizational contexts in which they are embedded. They foreshadow an *open systems view* of negotiation that includes inputs from various aspects of organizational systems that can constrain or afford dynamics at the table. To date, the negotiation literature has been primarily micro in its orientation and has largely been separated from its organizational roots. Rarely is negotiation discussed in connection to other central topics in organizational behavior, such as leadership, organizational culture, structure, human resource management, or organizational change. For example, chapters on organizational behavior in the *Annual Review of Psychology* have rarely discussed conflict management; likewise, reviews of the negotiation literature have rarely discussed conflict as it relates to organizational processes and performance (De Dreu & Gelfand, 2008). As we have previously argued (Gelfand, Leslie, & Keller, 2008), the time is ripe to connect negotiation to its organizational roots and to examine how features of organizations constrain or enable microlevel negotiation dynamics. This requires cross-level theories that link organizational culture, leadership, human resource (HR) systems, the structure of networks, among other features of the organizational landscape to psychological and social dynamics in negotiations. Next, we highlight some exciting opportunities that illustrate this intellectual spirit with some concrete examples.

Organizational Culture as an Affordance and Constraint of Negotiation Dynamics

An open systems view of negotiation suggests that *organizational culture*—basic assumptions, shared values, common understandings, and patterns of beliefs and expectations that are typically taken for granted (Schein, 1992)—can have important cross-level influences on negotiation dynamics in organizations. For example, although there are idiosyncratic ways of managing conflict at the individual level, organizations often provide strong situations—or develop distinct conflict cultures—that guide organizational members' attitudes and conflict behaviors at the microlevel (Gelfand et al., 2008; Gelfand, Leslie, Keller, & De Dreu, 2010). Organizations or units therein vary on the degree to which they cultivate what we have referred to as *dominating* conflict cultures (characterized by conflict management norms that encourage active confrontation to win conflicts publicly); *collaborative* conflict cultures (characterized by management norms for active, cooperative discussion of conflict); *avoidant* conflict cultures (characterized by conflict management norms of passive withdrawal in response to conflicts to maintain harmonious relationships); or *passive-aggressive* conflict cultures (characterized by norms for conflict management that are both disagreeable and passive and for which it is normative to handle it in the form of passive resistance). Recent research indeed has shown empirical support for the existence of conflict cultures at the organizational level and has shown that leaders' conflict management styles are a strong predictor of organizational conflict cultures, with important consequences at the macrolevel, such regarding as creativity, turnover, and customer service (Gelfand, Leslie, et al., 2010).

The cross-level impact of organizational conflict cultures on dynamics at the negotiation table remains wide open territory. For example, how people make meaning about their counterparts' negotiation behavior may be determined in part by macroconflict cultures. Collaborative conflict cultures may afford more positive sensemaking of others' fairness behavior (what Roloff et al. call "perceived fairness authenticity" in Chapter 3, this volume). Put differently, the same behaviors (asking others for voice, providing advance notice) might be interpreted much differently in a passive-aggressive or dominating conflict culture in which individuals would be more inclined to question others' motives. Conflict cultures might affect negotiator trust development and trust repair (Lewicki & Hanke,

Chapter 8, this volume); degree of revenge or forgiveness after mistreatment (Bies & Trip, Chapter 7, this volume); or more generally the ability to develop high subjective value (Elfenbein & Curhan, Chapter 5, this volume). Conflict cultures have implications for leveling the gender negotiation playing field. As Haselhuhn and Kray (Chapter 11, this volume) so aptly note: "The competitive atmosphere promoted by many 21st century organizations may set expectations for how negotiations should be conducted in the workplace. These expectations may feed into stereotypes of how negotiators should behave, which may in turn hinder efforts of female negotiators to overcome negative stereotypes" (page 314). Stereotype threat at the individual level could likely be affected by organizational conflict cultures, being exacerbated in dominating conflict cultures and reduced in collaborative conflict cultures. Put differently, the macro-organizational context plays a major role in the affordance or constraint of stereotype threat and women's ability to negotiate on a level playing field. These brief examples aside, more generally, future research needs to look at how organizational culture affects microdynamics in negotiations.

The Role of Leaders in Affording and Constraining Negotiation Dynamics

Relatedly, the impact that organizational leaders have on negotiations is an important area for future research. To date, research on negotiation has largely remained separate from studies of organizational leadership and vice versa. Leaders have long been argued to have a large impact on behavior in organizations, in part through their influence on organizational culture, as discussed, but also in their direct influence through their own moral values, ideals, and behavioral role modeling (Schein, 1992). Indeed, early studies showed a direct link between leadership and conflict dynamics. Lewin, Lippitt, and White (1939) found that boys in clubs with democratic leaders were friendlier, more spontaneous, and more cooperative as compared to boys in clubs with laissez-faire or autocratic leaders who were more competitive. Lewin et al. (1939) attributed these differences in conflict behavior to the pattern of interactions or "social climate" created by the different leadership styles. So it is in the domain of negotiations, in which leaders have the ability to profoundly influence negotiation dynamics in organizations.

For example, leaders can play a central role in creating a workplace environment that promotes transparency ultimately to build trust—a foundation of negotiations—by modeling their own trustworthiness so that individuals can trust the organization and thus trust each other more (see Bies & Tripp, Chapter 7, this volume). Leaders can also play a major role in modeling compassion, temperance, and justice, which are key drivers of forgiveness—another foundational aspect of conflict and negotiations in which trust has been violated (Fehr & Gelfand, 2011). Leaders can help to structure social networks to enhance trust and reduce unethical behavior (see Bies & Tripp, Chapter 7, this volume, and Lewicki & Hanke, Chapter 8, this volume) and can leverage social networks in helping to identify which representatives are in the best position to manage intergroup conflict in organizations (Brass & Labianca, Chapter 9, this volume). At a more macrolevel, leaders have the ability to facilitate organizational learning over negotiations with customers, suppliers, and alliances and other constituencies by encouraging, rewarding, and supporting people to share tacit knowledge about negotiations and by developing linking mechanisms for them to do so (for example, by creating negotiation centers of excellence and role rotation; see Chapter 12, this volume, by Hughes, Enlow, Siegel, & Weiss) and by ensuring that there is continued coordination between the contracting process and the contracting phase (see Malhotra, Chapter 13, this volume). Leaders can also have an impact on negotiation dynamics by directly creating HR management systems that emphasize the importance of negotiation skills throughout the organization, for example, through extensive training and seminars and by including evaluations of such competencies in performance appraisals. More generally, the impact of leaders on negotiation dynamics should be an intellectual priority in future research.

National Culture as an Affordance and Constraint of Negotiation Dynamics

Chapters in this book have all touched on the global context of negotiation in the 21st century. They highlight the fact that negotiators in many walks of life need to manage their interdependence with people who are from very different cultures than their own. A negotiation science in the 21st century sorely needs to take on this global challenge and incorporate it into the questions we ask, the samples we gather, and the conclusions we make about *human* behavior in negotiation. Psychological research has been shown to rely heavily on researchers and participants from Western societies (Arnett, 2008), a group of people who have been described as "the WEIRDest people in the world" (Henrich, Heine, & Norenzayan, 2010) to indicate the fact that they are largely "*W*estern, *E*ducated, *I*ndustrialized, *R*ich, and *D*emocratic" (p. 61). Indeed, in an analysis of six major psychological journals published between 2003 and 2007, Arnett (2008) found that 73% of the authors were from U.S. institutions. Combining the United States with European and English-speaking countries, 98% of the authors were based in Western societies. Moreover, 68% of the samples in these studies were drawn from the United States, and 27% were in European and English-speaking countries. In other words, 95% of all the samples in the six major psychological journals were from Western societies.

Negotiation research is no exception. We recently conducted a similar analysis of research on negotiation to examine whether this field also exhibits the tendency toward cultural centrism (Gelfand, Severance, Fulmer, & Al Dabbagh, in press). We analyzed two recent comprehensive reviews of the literature (an *Annual Review of Psychology* chapter by Thompson et al., 2010, and an APA handbook chapter on negotiation by Gelfand, Fulmer, & Severance, 2010) and did a content analysis on the geographic distribution of the author affiliations and sample locations on all of the studies cited. Consistent with prior studies (Arnett, 2008; see also Adair, Coelho, & Luna, 2002; Bauserman, 1997), we found that the United States, together with European and English-speaking countries, represented 95% of all of the authors on papers cited in these reviews (with 77% of them from the United States and the rest from Western Europe, the United Kingdom, Canada, Australia, and New Zealand), with the remaining authors coming from Asia (3%) or Israel (2%). A full 90% of the samples on which these studies were based were from the United States and European and English-speaking countries (with 74% of these from the United States), and over 85% of the studies used student samples. The rest of the samples were mainly from Asia (6%) or Israel (2%). Participants in other nations in the Middle East, Latin America, or Africa made up roughly a total of 2% of all samples. By way of comparison, the proportions of the authors and samples in the United States and Western countries in the field of negotiation are somewhat higher than those in the field of psychology as a whole reported by Arnett (2008). There is no doubt that research on negotiation has been heavily dominated by Western authors and Western samples.

The limited focus in negotiation research on Western nations, particularly on American samples, is concerning this new 21st century workplace.

Arnett (2008) pointed out that Americans make up merely 5% of the total world population, a percentage that is expected to diminish continually over coming years. Henrich et al. (2010) further proposed that the WEIRD samples (i.e., Western, educated, industrialized, rich, and democratic) are in fact outliers among the general human population. Given the very different environments to which they are accustomed, Henrich and colleagues suggested that WEIRD people are unlikely to be representative of the rest of the world's population and may even be the *worst* samples from which to generalize scientific research. Indeed, even basic perceptual phenomena—such as visual illusions (Segall, Campbell, & Herskovits, 1966), color perception (Roberson, in press), and neural structure and function (Chiao, 2009) are subject to cultural variation.

Negotiation science needs to step up to this global challenge and continually question whether the assumptions, theories, questions, methods, and conclusions are universal or are in fact applicable to only WEIRD samples. Cross-cultural research can also identify new explanations for age-old findings in the West. For example, we have recently argued that cultural differences in negotiation can be understood as default strategies (Yamagishi, 2010) that are ecologically rational (Gelfand et al., in press). That is, many of the negotiators' biases, motivations, and strategies that have been documented as universal "facts" may reflect Western individuals' adaptations to a particular (and unique) ecological niche. In particular, American samples tend to operate in everyday structural contexts in which there are uniplex and weak social ties (Morris, Poldony, & Ariel, 2000); high relational, job, and residential mobility in that people change relationship partners, jobs, and residences with great frequency (Oishi, 2010; Schug, Yuki, Horikawa, & Yakemura, 2009; Schug, Yuki, & Maddux, 2010); and weak everyday situations (Gelfand et al., 2011), all of which reinforce and sustain high descriptive norms for individualism, competition, looseness, and egalitarianism. Gelfand et al. (in press) noted that the ecological niche of American samples affords and constrains a default strategy in negotiations that could be referred to as the *individual's asserting and maximizing self-interest strategy* (IAMS; Hashimoto & Yamagishi, 2009). The IAMS strategy in negotiation assumes that individuals believe that they are supposed to "be all they can be"—to stand out, be unique, express oneself, and promote self-interest, often through competition. It assumes that people are able to enter and exit social relationships with relative ease and to have swift trust. And, it assumes economic capital takes precedence over relational capital in contexts in which relationship partners change frequently. Importantly, these assumptions are perfectly "rational" in the context of the ecological niche in which these samples navigate.

By contrast, Gelfand et al. (in press) argued that East Asian samples tend to operate in everyday structural contexts in which they are embedded in strong, multiplex networks (Morris et al., 2000); have low relational, job, and residential mobility (wherein people *do not* change relationship partners, job, and residences with great frequency; Oishi, 2010; Schug et al., 2009, 2010); and navigate contexts in which there is high situational constraint (Gelfand et al., 2011). The highly constrained ecological niche of East Asian samples affords a default strategy that could be referred to as the *not to offend others strategy* (NOOS; Hashimoto & Yamagishi, 2009). The NOOS departs in numerous ways from the IAMS strategy in its assumptions about what is "socially wise." It assumes as its basis that individuals' behavior should be calibrated with the duties and expectations of the group; that one should be modest and avoid behaviors that threaten one's reputation (particularly in low-mobility contexts in which one cannot enter and exit relationships easily), which could result in ostracism, the ultimate "psychological death"; that developing trust, particularly with strangers, is "dangerous" and takes much more time given strong ingroup–out-group distinctions. Within this strategy, relational capital looms larger than economic capital for securing the loyalty and commitment of negotiation partners in contexts for which there is low mobility, closed networks, and high constraint. This perspective also suggests that cultural effects can be dynamic—that is, when ecological environments change, strategies change in *all* cultures (Chiu, Gelfand, Yamagishi, Shteynberg, & Wan, 2010; Yamagishi, 2010), which helps us to avoid assuming within-culture strategies are used in between-culture negotiations, as cautioned by Tinsley, Turan, Weingart, & Dillon-Merrill (Chapter 10, this volume). More generally, it suggests that strategies that are perceived as the most ecologically rational will guide negotiation behavior (cf. Gigerenzer, 2005; Kruglanski & Gigerenzer, 2011), thus producing different (but equally valid) "cultural rationalities" in negotiation (Gelfand et al., in press).

As with organizational culture, the cross-level impact of national cultures on dynamics at the negotiation table remains wide open territory. There are many exciting empirical possibilities on culture and negotiation that await future investigation, and there are scores of ideas that can be gleaned from the chapters in this book. Pinkley (Chapter 4, this volume) aptly asks how applicable conventionally prescribed negotiation strategies apply in negotiations when one's negotiation counterparts are diversified across cultures. Roloff et al. (Chapter 3, this volume) identify challenges in managing fairness concerns across the negotiation table with great psychological distance between diverse parties. Results from Western samples that are discussed throughout the book need to be revisited in future research. For example, are the markers of deceptive messages culturally universal (Lewicki & Hanke, Chapter 8, this volume)? How does culture affect the dynamics of trust development and decline? Are the dimensions of subjective value universal or culture specific (Elfenbein & Curhan, Chapter 5, this volume)? Are there differences in standards used to evaluate fairness in negotiation (Conlon & Ross, Chapter 2, this volume)? What are universal and culture-specific triggers of revenge (Bies & Tripp, Chapter 7, this volume)? How does culture influence the nature of contracting (Malhotra, Chapter 13, this volume)? How does the structure of social networks in different cultures affect negotiation behavior (Brass & Labianca, Chapter 9, this volume; Gelfand, Severance, Fulmer, & Al Dabbagh, in press; Morris et al., 2000)? In all, the global context of negotiation mandates that the science of negotiation becomes global in its scope.

THE INTERDISCIPLINARY MANDATE: TOWARD A NEGOTIATION SCIENCE

Finally, this book makes clear that to understand negotiations in the 21st century workplace, we will need to go outside our familiar psychological territory to partner with disciplines that have different conceptualizations, methods, and scientific worldviews. A perusal of the chapters in this book and the research cited reveals that psychological research on negotiation, with some exceptions, generally exists in its own "scientific silo." While each chapter offers important insights into the complex elephant of negotiation, there needs to be much more bridging within and across disciplines to connect these theoretical and empirical dots. As Karl Popper (1963) noted, "We are not students of some subject matter, but students of problems. And problems may cut right across the borders of any subject matter or discipline" (p. 88). The value—if not the necessity—of interdisciplinary perspectives is indisputable. Many of the greatest scientific breakthroughs have been made possible through interdisciplinary research. From the mapping of the genome to understanding the global map of terrorism, it is clear that science benefits from multiple perspectives that require expertise from different disciplines. The study of negotiation is perfectly suited to interdisciplinary perspectives. It invariably involves insights from economics, psychology, political science, sociology, organizational behavior, and computer science, among many other disciplines. Together, they all contribute to what could be called a *negotiation science* for the 21st century.

There are many exciting "disciplinary mergers" between psychology and other disciplines to exploit fully. Collaborations between psychologists and computer scientists are positioned to bear much scientific fruit. For example, individuals in the 21st century are increasingly negotiating with computer agents, requiring teams of artificial intelligence researchers and psychologists to understand how they adapt to each other. The literature on psychological and social processes has been driven by human–human interactions; thus, there is a critical need to compare human–agent dynamics with human-human dynamics. Does the literature on negotiation biases, justice, trust, emotions, among other topics, apply to how humans respond when they know they are interacting with a computer agent? Pioneering studies conducted by Nass and colleagues have highlighted the conditions under which humans respond to computers the same as they do toward other humans (Nass, Fogg, & Moon, 1996; Reeves & Nass, 2003). According to the "media equation" principle, social dynamics surrounding human–computer interactions mirror those that solely comprise groups of humans. However, studies about the effects of computers on human behavior in negotiation settings have not produced conclusive results. For example, research has shown that people accept lower offers from computer proposers than from human proposers in simple take-it-or-leave-it ultimatum games (Blount, 1995). Yet people also exhibit reciprocal behavior toward agents in a manner that is similar to their interaction with other humans (van Wissen, van Diggelen & Dignum, 2009), and research has also shown that when people negotiate to form groups, they behave similarly to the predictions of cooperative game theory (Bachrach, Kohli, & Graepel, 2011). The similarities and differences between human-agent and human–human negotiations warrant much more empirical attention.

Likewise, artificial intelligence scientists have a keen interest in developing agents that effectively negotiate, requiring a deep knowledge of human psychology. Recent models of agent design have used opponent modeling approaches and use learning to adapt to people's negotiation strategies. Representative works include Byde, Yearworth, Chen, Bartolini, and Vulkan (2003), who constructed agents that bargain with people in a market setting by modeling the likelihood of acceptance of a deal, and Oshrat, Lin, and Kraus (2009), who used density estimation techniques to estimate people's acceptance of offers in a repeated multiattribute negotiation scenario and showed that agents outperformed people.

Learning techniques have also been applied to model the belief hierarchies that people use when they make decisions in one-shot interaction scenarios (Ficici & Pfeffer, 2008; Gal & Pfeffer, 2007). Zuckerman, Kraus, and Rosenschein (2007) used machine learning to allow agents to predict which strategy would be chosen by people in settings that demand coordination among several possible strategies. Research in artificial intelligence is also increasingly integrating *emotional* cues into agents' decision-making strategies, illustrating that exhibiting emotions can improve agents' performance as compared to agents that negotiate strategically only using decision theory (Antos & Pfeffer, 2011).

And, negotiation research on agents has also been increasingly applied to gender and culture. Katz, Amichai-Hamburger, Manisterski, and Kraus (2008) showed that agents who take gender differences into account outperform those who do not, and Gal, Kraus, Gelfand, Khashan, and Salmon (2011) showed that an adaptive agent can negotiate with people across different cultures in strategic settings in which agreements are not binding. More generally, there is a growing consensus among researchers on the applicability and relevance of psychological theories regarding agent design for human–computer interaction. This work highlights the interdisciplinary nature of human–computer negotiation, which requires the combination of different theories and methods to develop effective agents for human–computer negotiation applications.

Computational models of negotiation are also critical for examining complex negotiation dynamics. Over the past several years, scholars have been studying conflict through the lens of dynamical systems theory (e.g., Coleman, Vallacher, Nowak, & Bui-Wrzosinska, 2007; Nowak et al., 2010; Nowak, Vallacher, Bui-Wrzosinska, & Coleman, 2006), an increasingly influential paradigm in many areas of science (Johnson, 2001; Schuster,

1984; Strogatz, 2003; Vallacher, Read, & Nowak, 2002). A *dynamical system* is a set of interconnected elements (e.g., beliefs, feelings, and behaviors) that change and evolve over time. The system as a whole evolves and changes as a result of interactions among the individual elements in the system. Applying dynamical modeling to conflict situations can provide a number of insights. For example, dynamical modeling suggests that successfully changing any element of a relationship in a conflict (e.g., level of trust) is a function of the status of the other elements (e.g., each party's motives, attitudes, actions) of this relationship. Dynamical research can also identify basic parameters that account for sudden and dramatic changes in the nature of a conflict relationship (Nowak, 2004). The dynamical systems approach has been suggested as a way to conceptualize and investigate such conflict-related phenomena as emotion (Thagard & Nerb, 2002), attitude change (Nowak, Szamrej, & Latane, 1990), cooperation and competition (Liebovitch et al., 2008), and conflict intractability (e.g., Coleman et al., 2007), among others.

Dynamical systems theory offers a rich array of new metaphors, constructs, and principles that might be fruitfully applied to the negotiation literature. Dynamic system constructs such as attractors, emergence, and self-organization can serve as useful metaphors to help the researcher understand the dynamic nature of negotiations (e.g., Vallacher & Nowak, 1994). Second, the dynamical systems approach provides social scientists with tools that facilitate the mathematical description of the hypothesized mechanisms underlying specific negotiation dynamics. Thus, although social science theory is typically expressed verbally, the dynamical systems tools translate these theories into computer simulations. Dynamical models allow researchers to identify the assumptions inherent in our theories that are difficult to identify when theories are maintained in their verbal form. Finally, the dynamical systems approach has implications for the types of empirical methodologies developed and employed in research. Typically, traditional social sciences focus on the central tendency of variables and ignore important dynamics reflected in variables' variances. Further, dynamical systems models and methods push the social sciences to focus on events as they unfold over time (Bui-Wrzosinska, 2005).

Partnerships between negotiation scholars and neuroscientists are another natural scientific merger. For example, the emerging areas of social neuroscience (Heatherton, Macrae, & Kelley, 2004) and neuroeconomics (Zak, 2004), which focus on the use of neuroscience methods to understand human behavior, are ripe for integration with negotiation theory and research. Biological factors have been shown to play an important role in a wide range of organizational phenomena, such as entrepreneurship (White, Thornhill, & Thompson, 2006), occupational choice (Dabbs, De la Rue, & Williams, 1990), and job satisfaction (Arvey, 1989). Indeed, the growing momentum on this topic can be seen in a recent special issue of *Organizational Behavior and Human Decision Processes* devoted to biological processes in organizations (Shane, 2009). Existing models of negotiation rarely examine the role of biological factors, but recent research showed the promise of neuroscience for the study of decision making (Rilling & Sanfey, 2011; Sanfey, Rilling, Aronson, Nystrom, & Cohen, 2003); punishment (de Quervain et al., 2004); ingroup trust and cooperation (De Dreu et al., 2010); procedural and distributive justice (Dulebohn, Conlon, Sarinopoulos, Davison, & McNamara, 2009); social influence (Mason, Dyer, & Norton, 2009); and gender differences (Severance & Gelfand, 2011), among other topics. The emerging field of cultural neuroscience (Chiao, 2009) also has the potential to shed new light on cultural variation in basic processes in negotiation such as trust, reciprocity, cooperation and competition, fairness, revenge, and forgiveness. For example, Zak and colleagues (Zak & Fakhar, 2006; Zak, Kurzban, & Matzner, 2005) found that cultural differences in interpersonal trust and cooperation can be explained in part by differences in consumption of estrogen-like molecules that are linked to oxytocin. Using functional magnetic resonance imaging (fMRI) techniques, Zhu, Zhang, Fan, and Han (2007) measured brain activity of Western and Chinese participants and provided neuroimaging evidence that culture shapes the way the self is represented in the human brain. More generally, integrating theories and models of biological sciences into negotiation research will extend current research by helping to identify the precise mechanisms that account for negotiation dynamics and has the potential to help us understand the evolutionary bases of this universal process.

Related to the integration of biological sciences and negotiation science is the need to link negotiation research focused on humans to that of other species. There is an abundance of research on conflict processes among chimpanzees (de Waal, 2000); spotted hyenas (Wahaj, Guse, & Holekamp, 2001); dolphins (Weaver, 2003); crayfish (Huber, Panksepp, Yue, Delago, & Moore, 2001); bees, ants, and other insect communities (Trivers & Hare, 1976), as well as many other species. This research provides examples of important concepts, metaphors, and questions that are relevant for human negotiation behavior. For example, Flack, de Waal, and Krakauer, (2005) demonstrated that *third-party policing,* the physical intervention by a third party into a conflict between two primates, is common among the pig-tailed macaques, and that eliminating the high-power interveners caused the social system to destabilize, leading to more conflict, less sociopositive interaction, and less reconciliation among other pigtail macaques (see the discussion of ripple effects in this commentary). As another example, research has shown that *crowding* among capuchin monkeys decreased aggression, play, and social grooming (van Wolkenten, Davis, Gong, & de Waal, 2006), suggesting that primates may avoid social encounters and adopt a conflict avoidance strategy in contexts of high density (cf. our discussion of the NOOS strategy as practiced by humans in highly constrained environments). More generally, by reaching out and partnering with primatologists, we will be better able to address the fundamental question of how human negotiation behavior varies from other species.

These examples aside, there are many other possible disciplinary mergers that await negotiation science in the 21st century. Psychological perspectives on negotiation can be fruitfully integrated with theories and research on social structure found in sociology and legal anthropology, with frames detected with methods found in computational linguistics, with research on cultural consensus and associated methods found in cognitive anthropology, among others. To be sure, while there is limitless potential for interdisciplinary partnerships, much needs to be done to capitalize fully on the differences that invariably bring the most creative research products. As noted in an editorial in *Science*, "In the years to come, innovators will need to jettison the security of familiar tools, ideas and specialties as they forge new partnerships" (Kafatos & Eisner, 2004, p. 1257). Scientific disciplines have their own cultures, and interdisciplinary teams will invariably find that they are managing cultural conflict even as they pursue common intellectual questions. Differences in worldviews, scientific language, and priorities that are entrenched in different disciplinary paradigms will make the research process both more rewarding and more difficult (and more time consuming). New structures and scientific outlets will need to be created to counter the discipline-focused tradition that characterizes academe. The benefits, in our view, far outweigh the costs. Interdisciplinary research can inspire creative breakthroughs; provide outside perspectives on models, applications, and methods; and identify crucial deficiencies and oversights in projects or previous research (Nissani, 1997).

CONCLUSION

In this commentary, we have discussed the need for new conceptualizations of negotiation, the need for connecting microdynamics to its multilevel context, and the need for a negotiation science that has many scientific players across disciplines and cultures working together at the same table to study similar questions. In highlighting the complex realities of negotiating in the 21st century, this book has moved the field into new and exciting scientific territory.

ACKNOWLEDGMENT

We thank Rebecca Mohr for her assistance with this chapter and U. S. Army Research Laboratory and the U. S. Army Research Office grant number W911NF-08-1-0144 for their support of this work.

REFERENCES

Adair, J. G., Coelho, A. E. L., & Luna, J. R. (2002). How international is psychology? *International Journal of Psychology, 37*, 160–170.

Antos, D., & Pfeffer, A. (2011). Using emotions to enhance decision-making. In *International Joint Conference on Artificial Intelligence*. Barcelona, Catalonia, Spain. July 2011.

Arnett, J. J. (2008). The neglected 95%: Why American psychology needs to become less American. *American Psychologist, 63*, 602–614.

Arvey, R. D. (1989). Job satisfaction: Environmental and genetic components. *Journal of Applied Psychology, 74*, 187–192.

Bachrach, Y., Kohli, P., & Graepel, T. (2011). Rip-off: Playing the cooperative negotiation game. In *Proceedings of the International Conference on Autonomous Agents and Multi-Agent Systems*. Taipai, Taiwan. May.

Bazerman, M. H., Curhan, J. R., Moore, D. A., & Valley, K. L. (2000). Negotiation. *Annual Review of Psychology, 51*, 279–314.

Bauserman, R. (1997). International representation in the psychological literature. *International Journal of Psychology, 32*, 107–112.

Blount, S. (1995). When social outcomes aren't fair. *Organizational Behavior and Human Decision Processes, 63*, 131–144.

Bui-Wrzosinska, L. (2005). *The dynamics of conflict in a school setting*. Unpublished master's thesis, Warsaw School for Social Psychology, Warsaw, Poland.

Byde, A., Yearworth, M., Chen, K. Y., Bartolini, C., & Vulkan, N. (2003). Autona: A system for automated multiple 1–1 negotiation. In B. Yearmore et al. (Eds.). *Proceedings of the 4th ACM conference on electronic commerce* (pp. 198–199). San Diego, CA. June 2003.

Chiao, J. (Ed.). (2009). *Cultural neuroscience: Cultural influences on brain function. Progress in Brain Research.* New York: Elsevier.

Chiu, C.-Y., Gelfand, M. J., Yamagishi, T., Shteynberg, G., & Wan, C. (2010). Intersubjective culture: The role of intersubjective perceptions in cross-cultural research. *Perspectives in Psychological Science, 5,* 482–493.

Coleman, P. T., Vallacher, R. R., Nowak, A., & Bui-Wrzosinska, L. (2007). Intractable conflict as an attractor: A dynamical systems approach to conflict escalation and intractability. *American Behavioral Scientist, 50,* 1454–1475.

Dabbs, J. M., De la Rue, D., & Williams, P. M. (1990). Testosterone and occupational choice: Actors, ministers, and other men. *Journal of Personality and Social Psychology, 59,* 1261–1265.

De Dreu, C. K. W., & Gelfand, M. J. (2008). Conflict in the workplace: Sources, functions, and dynamics across multiple levels of analysis. In C. K. W. De Dreu & M. J. Gelfand (Eds.), *The psychology of conflict and conflict management in organizations* (SIOP Frontiers series; pp. 3–54). New York: Erlbaum.

De Dreu, C. K. W., Greer, L. L., Handgraaf. M. J. J., Shalvi, S., Van Kleef, G. A., Baas, M., et al. (2010). The neuropeptide oxytocin regulates parochial altruism in intergroup conflict among humans. *Science, 328,* 1408–1411.

de Quervain, D. J.-F., Fischbacher U., Treyer, V., Schellhammer M., Schnyder, U., Buck, A., et al. (2004). The neural basis of altruistic punishment. *Science, 305,* 1254–1258.

De Waal, F. B. M. 2000. Primates: A natural heritage of conflict resolution. *Science, 289,* 586.

Dulebohn, J. H., Conlon, D. E., Sarinopoulos, I., Davison, R. B., & McNamara, G. (2009). The biological bases of unfairness: Neuroimaging evidence for the distinctiveness of procedural and distributive justice. *Organizational Behavior and Human Decision Processes, 110,* 140–151.

Fehr, R., & Gelfand, M. J., (forthcoming). The forgiving organization: A multilevel model of forgiveness at work. *Academy of Management Review.*

Ficici, S. G., & Pfeffer, A. (2008). Simultaneously modeling humans' preferences and their beliefs about others' preferences. In *Proceedings of the international joint conference on autonomous agents and multi-agent systems (AAMAS).* Estoril, Lisbona, Portugal. May.

Flack, J. C., de Waal, F. B. M., & Krakauer, D. C. 2005. Social structure, robustness, and policing cost in a cognitively sophisticated species. *American Naturalist, 165,* E126–E139.

Gal, Y., Kraus, S., Gelfand, M. J., Khashan, H., & Salmon, E. (2011). An adaptive agent for negotiating with people in different cultures. *ACM Transactions on Intelligent Systems and Technology, 3,* 1–27.

Gal, Y., & Pfeffer, A. (2007). Modeling reciprocity in human bilateral negotiation. In *Proceedings of Association for the Advancement of Artificial Intelligence.* Vancouver, BC, Canada. July.

Gelfand, M. J., Fulmer, A., & Severance, L. (2010). The psychology of negotiation and mediation. In S. Zedeck (Ed.), *Handbook of industrial and organizational psychology.* (pp. 495–554) Washington, DC: American Psychological Association.

Gelfand, M. J., Leslie, L., & Keller, K. (2008). On the etiology of conflict cultures in organizations. *Research in Organizational Behavior, 28,* 137–166.

Gelfand, M. J., Leslie, L., Keller, K., & De Dreu, C. (2010). *Cultures of conflict: How leaders and members shape conflict cultures in organizations.* Paper presented at the annual conference of the Academy of Management, Montreal, Canada. August.

Gelfand, M. J., Raver, J. L., Nishii, L. Leslie, L. M., Lun, J., Lim, B. C., et al. (2011). Differences between tight and loose cultures: A 33-nation study. *Science, 332*, 1100–1104.

Gelfand, M. J., & McCusker, C. (2002). Metaphor and the cultural construction of negotiation: A paradigm for theory and practice. In M. Gannon & K. L. Newman (Eds.), *Handbook of cross-cultural management* (pp. 282–314). New York: Blackwell.

Gelfand, M., J., Severance, L., Fulmer, C. A., & Al Dabbagh, M. (in press). Explaining and predicting cultural differences in negotiations. In G. E. Bolton & R. Croson (Eds.), *The Oxford handbook of economic conflict resolution.* New York: Oxford University Press.

Gelfand, M. J., Smith, V. Raver, J., Nishii, L., & O'Brien, K. (2006). Negotiating relationally: The dynamics of the relational self in negotiations. *Academy of Management Review, 31*, 427–451.

Gigerenzer, G. (2005). Is the mind irrational or ecologically rational? In F. Parisi & V. L. Smith (Eds.), *The law and economics of irrational behavior* (pp. 37-67). Stanford, CA: Stanford University Press.

Hashimoto, H., & Yamagishi, T. (2009, September). *Self-sustaining mechanism behind Japanese interdependence.* Paper presented at the GCOE 3rd international symposium: Socio-ecological approaches to cultural and social psychological processes, Hokkaido University, Sapporo, Japan.

Heatherton, T. F., Macrae, C. N., & Kelley, W. M. (2004). A social brain sciences approach to studying the self. *Current Directions in Psychological Science, 13*, 190–193.

Henrich, J., Heine, S. J., & Norenzayan, A. (2010). The weirdest people in the world? *Behavioral and Brain Sciences, 33*, 61–135.

Hollander, E. P. (1958). Conformity, status, and idiosyncrasy credit. *Psychological Review, 65*, 117–127.

Huber, R., Panksepp, J. B., Yue, Z., Delago, A., & Moore, P. (2001). Dynamic interactions of behavior and amine neurochemistry in acquisition and maintenance of social rank in crayfish. *Brain, Behavior, and Evolution, 57*, 271–282.

Johnson, S. (2001). *Emergence: The connected lives of ants, brains, cities, and software.* New York: Scribner.

Kafatos, F., & T. Eisner. 2004. Unification in the century of biology. *Science, 303*, 1257.

Katz, R., Amichai-Hamburger, Y., Manisterski, E., & Kraus, S. (2008). Different orientations of males and females in computer-mediated negotiations. *Computers in Human Behavior, 24*, 516–534.

Kramer R.M. & Messick, D.M. (1995) *Negotiation as a social process,* Thousand Oaks, CA: Sage Publications.

Kruglanski, A. W., & Gigerenzer, G. (2011). Intuitive and deliberate judgments are based on common principles. *Psychological Review, 118*, 97–109.

Lewin, K., Lippitt, R., & White, R. (1939). Patterns of aggressive behavior in experimentally created "social climates." *Journal of Social Psychology, 10*, 271–299.

Liebovitch, L. S., Naudot, V., Vallacher, R., Nowak, A., Bui-Wrzosinska, L., & Coleman, P. (2008). Dynamics of two-actor cooperation competition conflict models. *Physica A, 387*, 6360–6378.

Liebovitch, L. S., Vallacher, R., Nowak, A., Bui-Wrzosinska, & Coleman, Peter, T. (2007). Dynamics of two-actor cooperation-competition models. Under review with *Negotiation and Conflict Management Research.*

Mason, M. F., Dyer, R., & Norton, M. I. (2009). Neural mechanisms of social influence. *Organizational Behavior and Human Decision Processes, 110*, 152–159.

Morris, M. W., Poldony, J. M., & Ariel, S. (2000). Missing relations: Incorporating relational constructs into models of culture. In P. C. Earley & H. Singh (Eds.). *Innovations in international and cross-cultural management* (pp. 669–678). Thousand Oaks, CA: Sage.

Nass, C., Fogg, B., & Moon, Y. (1996). Can computers be teammates? *International Journal of Human-Computer Studies, 45,* 65.

Nissani, M. (1997). Ten cheers for interdisciplinarity: The case for interdisciplinary knowledge and research. *The Social Science Journal, 34,* 201–216.

Nowak, A. (2004). Dynamical minimalism: Why less is more in psychology. *Personality and Social Psychology Review, 8,* 183–192.

Nowak, A., Bui-Wrzosinska, L., Coleman, P., Vallacher, R., Jochemczyk, L., & Bartkowski, W. (2010). Seeking sustainable solutions: Using an attractor simulation platform for teaching multistaker holder negotiation in complex cases. *Negotiation Journal, 26,* 49–68.

Nowak, A., Szamrej, J., & Latane, B. (1990). From private attitude to public opinion: A dynamic theory of social impact. *Psychological Review, 97,* 362–376.

Nowak, A., Vallacher, R., Bui-Wrzosinska, L., & Coleman, P. (2006). Attracted to conflict: A dynamical perspective on malignant social relations. In A. Golec & K. Skarzynska (Eds.), *Understanding social change: Political psychology in Poland* (pp. 33–50). Hauppauge, NY: Nova Science.

Oishi, S. (2010). The psychology of residential mobility: Implications for the self, social relationships, and well-being. *Perspectives on Psychological Science, 5,* 5–21.

Oshrat, Y., Lin, R., & Kraus, S. (2009). Facing the challenge of human-agent negotiations via effective general opponent modeling. In *Proceedings of international conference on autonomous agents and multi-agent systems* (pp. 377–384). Budapest, Hungary. May.

Popper, K. R. 1963. *Conjectures and refutations: The growth of scientific knowledge.* New York: Routledge and Kegan Paul.

Reeves, B., & Nass, C. (2003). *The media equation: How people treat computers, television, and new media like real people and places* (CSLI Lecture Notes S.). Palo Alto, CA: Center for the Study of Language and Informatics.

Rilling, J. K., & Sanfey, A. G. (2011). The neuroscience of social decision-making. *Annual Reviews of Psychology, 62,* 23–48.

Roberson, D. (in press). Culture, categories, and color: Do we see the world through t(a) inted lenses? In Gelfand, M. J., Chiu, C. Y., & Hong, Y. Y. (Eds.), *Advances in culture and psychology* (Vol. 2). New York: Oxford University Press.

Sanfey, A. G., Rilling, J. K., Aronson, J. A., Nystrom, L. E., & Cohen, J. D. (2003). The neural basis of economic decision-making in the ultimatum game. *Science, 300,* 1755–1758.

Schuster, H. G. (1984). *Deterministic chaos.* Vienna, Switzerland: Physik Verlag.

Schein, E. H. (1992). *Organizational culture and leadership: A dynamic view.* San Francisco: Jossey-Bass.

Schug, J. R., Yuki, M., Horikawa, H., & Takemura, K. (2009). Similarity attraction and actually selecting similar others: How cross-societal differences in relational mobility affect interpersonal similarity in Japan and the United States. *Asian Journal of Social Psychology, 2,* 95–103.

Schug, J., Yuki, M., & Maddux, W. W. (2010). Relational mobility explains between- and within-culture differences in self-disclosure toward close friends. *Psychological Science, 21,* 1471–1478.

Segall, M. H., Campbell, D. T., & Herskovits, M. J. (1966). *The influence of culture on visual perceptions.* Indianapolis, IN: Bobbs-Merrill.

Severance, L., & Gelfand, M. J. (2011). The impact of estradiol on negotiation outcomes: Toward a bio-social model of negotiation. Unpublished manuscript.

Shane, S. (2009). Introduction to the focused issue on the biological basis of business. *Organizational Behavior and Human Decision Processes, 110*(2), 67–69.

Strogatz, S. (2003). *Sync: The emerging science of spontaneous order.* New York: Hyperion Books.

Thagard, P., & Nerb, J. (2002). Emotional gestalts: Appraisal, change, and the dynamics of affect. *Personality and Social Psychology Review, 6,* 274–282.

Thompson, L., Wang, J., & Gunia, B. (2010). Negotiation. *Annual Review of Psychology, 61,* 491–515.

Trivers, R. L., & Hare, J. (1976). Haplodiplody and the evolution of the social insects. *Science, 191,* 250–263.

Vallacher, R. R., & Nowak, A. (1994). *Dynamical systems in social psychology.* San Diego: Academic Press.

Vallacher, R. R., Read, S. J., & Nowak, A. (2002). The dynamical perspective in personality and social psychology. *Personality and Social Psychology Review, 6,* 264–273.

Van Wolkenten, M. L., Davis, J. M., Gong, M. L., & de Waal, F. B. M. (2006). Coping with acute crowding by capuchin monkeys (*Cebus paella*). *International Journal of Primatology, 27,* 1241–1256.

Wahaj, S. A., Guse, K., & Holekamp, K. E. (2001). Reconciliation in the spotted hyena (*Crocuta crocuta*). *Ethology, 107,* 1057–1074.

Weaver, A. (2003). Conflict and reconciliation in captive Bottlenose dolphins, *Tursiops truncatus. Marine Mammal Science, 19,* 836–846.

Weingart, L. R., & Olekalns, M. (2004). Communication processes in negotiation. In M. J. Gelfand & J. Brett (Eds.), *Handbook of culture and negotiation* (pp. 143–157). Palo Alto, CA: Stanford University Press.

White, R. E., Thornhill, S., & Thompson, E. (2006). Entrepreneurs and evolutionary biology: The relationship between testosterone and new venture creation. *Organizational Behavior and Human Decision Processes, 1000,* 21–34.

van Wissen, A., van Diggelen, J., & Dignum, V. (2009). The effects of cooperative agent behavior on human cooperativeness. *Proceedings of the International Conference on Autonomous Agents and Multi-Agent Systems.* Budapest, Hungary. May.

Yamagishi, T. (2010). A niche construction approach to culture. In M. J. Gelfand, C. Y. Chiu, & Y. Y. Hong (Eds.), *Advances in culture and psychology* (Vol. 1, pp. 251–308). New York: Oxford University Press.

Zak, P. J. (2004). Neuroeconomics. *Philosophy Transactions Royal Society, 359,* 1737–1748.

Zak, P. J., & Fakhar, A. (2006). Neuroactive hormones and interpersonal trust: International evidence. *Economics and Human Biology, 4,* 412–429.

Zak, P. J., Kurzban, R., & Matzner, W. T. (2005). Oxytocin is associated with human trustworthiness. *Hormones and Behavior, 48,* 522–527.

Zhu, Y., Zhang, L., Fan, J., & Han, S. (2007). Neural basis of cultural influence on self-representation. *NeuroImaging, 34,* 1310–1316.

Zuckerman, I., Kraus, S., & Rosenschein, S. (2007). Using focal points learning to improve human-machine tactic coordination. *Journal of Autonomous Agents and Multi-Agent System, 22,* 289–316.

16

Integrating Negotiation Research
With Team Dynamics

Leigh Thompson, Erika Richardson, and Brian Lucas

INTRODUCTION

This volume has explicitly positioned negotiation in the complex and challenging world of the workforce. Instead of using the well-worn terms *negotiation* and *negotiators*, Goldman and Shapiro use the more provocative and rarer *employees* and instead of using the vacuous terms *situation and context*, they use the much more meaningful terms *workplace* and *industry*. Similarly, instead of referring to negotiated outcomes, the contributors have referred to contracts (e.g., Malhotra, Chapter 13, this volume). In so doing, this important volume has reminded scholars that the study of negotiation outside the context of organizations, whether it be firms or a home business, is quite frankly not that meaningful to managers.

In this commentary chapter, we reflect on how negotiation research has been an excellent student, comrade, and proponent of team and group research. We explore the synergistic relationship between negotiation research and team research and suggest ways it may continue to grow and prosper; we attempt to remain true to the grounding theme of the volume in the workplace. We use the chapters in this volume to highlight how team and group research has informed negotiation as well as speculate on new vistas for research.

In truth, many or most of the researchers in this volume are aligned with both the field of negotiation and group research. Not surprisingly, the theorizing of negotiation scholars has been deeply influenced by group research in social psychology. Our commentary examines how group research has influenced negotiation research and where some opportunities may lie. We use the organizing structure of the volume to guide our selective review of team and group dynamics. Specifically, we first explore fairness and justice in the context of groups and teams and then examine emotional and affective processing, social influence, and organizational influence.

FAIRNESS IN TEAMS AND NEGOTIATION

The contributors to this volume have provocatively highlighted how fairness considerations may thwart negotiator effectiveness or at the very least give rise to conflict or inconsistent decision making. Fairness considerations are an essential aspect of the twin tasks of negotiation: expanding the pie and dividing the pie. Negotiation researchers often admonish managers that even after the pie has been expanded, it must be divided. From a mixed-motivational perspective, the act of dividing or allocating resources has been considered the "competitive" aspect of negotiation, whereas the process of expanding the pie has been considered the "cooperative" aspect (Lax & Sebenius, 1986; Walton & McKersie, 1965).

Behavioral researchers have identified a disturbingly long list of biases in terms of how individuals make "faulty" fairness judgments. Some of these biases include egocentrism (e.g., allocating more for oneself than others, cf. Messick & Rutte, 1992; evaluating one's own contributions as more important than others, Ross & Sicoly, 1979); self-serving bias (Allison, Messick, & Goethals, 1989; van Avermaet, 1974); inconsistent use of fairness rules (e.g., equality with friends, equity with strangers, Austin, 1980; equality for benefits but equity for burdens, Sondak, Neale, & Pinkley, 1995); framing effects (Bazerman, Loewenstein, & White, 1992); selective recall of one's own contributions to the exclusion of other's contributions (Messick & Sentis, 1979); and excessive preoccupation with the payoffs or outcomes of others (van Avermaet, 1974).

Teams and groups are faced with decisions about how to allocate scarce resources and reward members. Not surprisingly, several "fairness" biases have been identified in the groups literature, including the ingroup bias effect, procedural justice and group value theory, and social utility. We discuss these next.

Ingroup Bias

The ingroup bias effect is probably the most well-known group-level bias. It simply states that members of groups regard their own group to be more superior and more worthy than members of out-groups (Kramer, 1991; Wills, 1981). This effect is true even when groups are randomly assigned and formed on the basis of chance (Tajfel, 1970). The ingroup bias effect influences not only subjective ratings of one's own and other groups (e.g., my group is superior to the out-group) but also allocation decisions. For example, people allocate more rewards to ingroup members than to out-group members, even in the absence of any justifying criteria (Diekmann, Samuels, Ross, & Bazerman, 1997).

In a similar vein, research on equity theory in groups and negotiations has revealed that people expect outputs to be commensurate with inputs (i.e., equity theory; Adams, 1963). However, pervasive biases cloud people's perceptions of the relative inputs and outputs of themselves and others. In this volume, we discuss the implications of experiences of "injustice" in negotiations. The authors explain how perceptions of a negotiation counterparty's "fairness" may lead to more cooperation among parties and, presumably, more integrative agreements (or in some cases, more negotiator compliance). Tying the literature from both the negotiation and organizational justice streams of research, in Chapter 2 of this volume Conlon and Ross present eight justice-enhancing techniques that promote fairness in mixed-motive disputes. In addition, Conlon and Ross account for a real-world context, in which social networking Web sites (SNWSs) influence perceptions of negotiator fairness. In this vein, the authors address how contemporary avenues for gaining information (i.e., Facebook pages) affect early perceptions of one's negotiation counterpart.

Similarly, Pinkley (Chapter 4, this volume) enumerates negotiation strategies that help both employers and employees achieve fair negotiated outcomes. Pinkley concentrates on compensation, suggesting that current compensation negotiation research should be updated to suit a burgeoning diverse and technologically savvy workforce. The author argues that prior research has concentrated on same-gender negotiating parties, suggesting that beneficial negotiation strategies may differ for women as opposed to men (i.e., in *anchoring the negotiation*). Furthermore, Pinkley examines differences between online and face-to-face communication, suggesting that virtual communication may affect the utility of classic compensation negotiation strategies. For example, instead of the traditional post-job interview salary negotiation, many companies using online recruitment methods ask candidates to report their salary expectations when they apply. Pinkley explains that a job candidate can avoid the pressure to report a low salary expectation (in an effort to remain competitive with the other applicants) through a sequential anchoring process. That is, an applicant can initially state that his or her expectations are consistent with the market but anchor the negotiation with a numerical salary value only after securing the job.

Procedural Justice and Group Value Theory

In their seminal book, Thibaut and Walker (1975) widened the lens of equity theory not only to focus on outputs per se but also to consider the manner in which justice is enacted. Thus, Thibaut and Walker distinguished distributive justice from procedural justice. Tyler and Lind and their colleagues provocatively demonstrated that, in many cases, disputants and negotiators are much more concerned about how justice is enacted rather than their actual monetary outcomes (Lind & Tyler, 1988; Tyler & Degoey, 1995). For example, Tyler (1987) found that disputants' satisfaction in court adjudications was more influenced by whether they believed that the judge had "heard" their case than by the actual judgment handed to them. Similarly, employees who believe they have been mistreated are more likely to exit and exhibit work withdrawal (Boswell & Olson-Buchanan, 2004). The term *voice* became a key construct measure of whether disputants experienced procedural justice.

Lind and Tyler's (1988) group value model of justice argues that individuals who are strongly identified with their groups and organizations may put aside their self-interest and act in a way that helps the group. Key to the model is the idea that people in groups evaluate leaders in terms of their ability to be fair and impartial. Thus, the authenticity of the group leader is key.

In Chapter 3 of this volume, Roloff, Brockner, and Wiesenfeld suggest that negotiators should appear "authentically fair" rather than just "fair." The authors assert that fair outcomes may only seem valuable if they are delivered with intent or are intrinsically, rather than strategically, motivated. Negotiators may evaluate authenticity by attributing their counterpart's actions to personal or contextual factors, reasoning that a negotiator who is personally motivated has greater congruence between their intentions and actions than a negotiator who is motivated by environmental factors. Finally, the authors note moderating factors in today's workplace, mentioning how both physical distance, for which the counterparts are spatially separated, and psychological distance, for which the counterparts are culturally separated, may negatively influence perceptions of authenticity in negotiation counterparts.

Social Utility

Social utility was introduced as the idea that people are excessively preoccupied with how well others do relative to themselves when a perfectly rational person should only be concerned about his or her own outcomes. This leads to a variety of paradoxical behaviors, such as attaching more value to less money, depending on how much the other party is receiving.

Loewenstein, Thompson, and Bazerman (1989) compared how much satisfaction people associated with different allocations of money between themselves and others; they found that satisfaction is highest in cases of equal outcomes, but if inequity must exist, they strongly prefer that they benefit relative to others rather than vice versa. Bazerman et al. (1992) pitted pure self-interest against social utility by asking managers (negotiators) to indicate which of several salary payoffs they preferred. Manager-negotiators were often willing to accept a lower absolute salary if that meant that they were not underpaid relative to others. Messick and Sentis (1979) found that people unconsciously select fairness rules in a self-serving fashion; for example, when people have worked more hours, they believe they are entitled to more than someone who has worked fewer hours, holding constant the amount of work actually done. Yet, when they have worked fewer hours and accomplished more, they expect to be paid more.

Recently, social utility in negotiation research has moved beyond strictly economic measures of utility (such as money and resources) and has focused on other considerations, such as satisfaction. In Chapter 5 of this volume, Elfenbein and Curhan emphasize the necessity for subjective value measures, above and beyond objective value measures, in negotiations. The authors illustrate the relative importance of subjective value—that is, the overall feelings and sentiments that follow a mixed-motive interaction—to common people and negotiation professionals alike. Furthermore, Elfenbein and Curhan assert that positive subjective value can lead to future objective outcomes due to the positive relationship between the negotiators. Finally, the authors discuss several factors (i.e., extraverted personality, identifying subjective value outcomes, etc.) that can beneficially affect a negotiator's postnegotiation subjective value. For example, Elfbein and Curhan argue that a negotiator can enhance his or her counterpart's subjective value by treating the counterpart with respect. A negotiator can signal this respect by asking questions, listening, showing trustworthiness, and making the entire negotiation process efficient.

In sum, research in the area of groups and fairness has revealed that individuals most certainly depart from the prescriptions of economic models. Their judgments tend to be highly self-serving and egocentric. Further, there is a strong link between fairness judgments and behavior.

EMOTIONAL AND AFFECTIVE PROCESSING IN TEAMS AND NEGOTIATION

Once negotiation broke free of the "don't feel, don't tell policy" inherited from the superrational cognitive information-processing paradigm, emotions have become a legitimate area of study in negotiation. Several burgeoning research findings conspired to create a new look at how people make decisions and behave in the face of emotion. A key influence in this area of research was the distinction between two routes to persuasion: the cognitive, rational information-processing route and the mercurial, affective route (Chaiken, Wood, & Eagley, 1996). Another influence was the research findings on how temporary mood states affect the nature and quality of decision making. From the groups and teams literature, we briefly highlight four affect-based group phenomena and discuss their impact on negotiation research: positive mood effects, negative mood effects, affective contagion, and relational and task conflict. We then highlight how these four themes emerge in the chapters in this volume.

Positive Mood

Carnevale and Isen (1986) were the first to study the impact of positive mood on negotiation behavior. In their investigation, positive affect was temporarily induced by having research participants read funny comic strips; positive mood led to more integrative agreement than did neutral moods. Kurtzberg, Naquin, and Belkin (2009) found that beginning an e-mail transaction with humor resulted in increased trust and satisfaction, higher joint gains, as well as higher individual gains, as compared to those who did not use humor. In sum, for quite some time, positive mood was considered to be nearly uniformly conducive for negotiation in terms of improving outcomes and inducing cooperation from the counterparty.

More recent research focusing on nuances of mood and affect, however, suggest a more complex picture. Sinaceur and Tiedens (2006) suggested that anger expressions help negotiators claim more of the proverbial pie when their counterparts have poor alternatives. Individuals who were subject to angry versus nonangry negotiation counterparts were more concessionary when they felt they had few options rather than many (Sinaceur & Tiedens, 2006). Although positive moods contribute to joint outcomes, negative moods are just as influential to negotiated agreements, especially in a distributive sense.

In Chapter 6 of this volume, Cropanzano, Becker, and Feldman review the literature on mood and emotion in negotiation and reason that both constructs weigh heavily on negotiation processes and outcomes. For example, envy may increase the probability that a negotiator will use deception in a negotiation, whereas guilt or shame may lead to more concessionary behaviors. Furthermore, the authors assess the effect of affect on relationships in negotiations, reasoning that stronger relationship commitments may have an impact on negotiation outcomes. Finally, the authors provide directions for future research, arguing that "negative mood states" should be explored in terms of the beneficial effects they may have on mixed-motive interactions.

Negative Mood

Researchers quickly realized that negative or bad moods might have nonobvious effects on negotiation. Negotiators who are really angry and feel little compassion for the counterparty are less effective in terms of expanding the pie than are happy negotiators (Allred, Mallozzi, Matsui, & Raia, 1997). In contrast, negotiators who display "strategic anger" are more likely to gain concessions from their opponent because the counterparty will assume the angry person is close to their reservation point (Van Kleef, DeDreu, & Manstead, 2004). Angry negotiators induce fear in their opponents; thus, their opponents are more likely to succumb when they are motivated (Van Kleef et al., 2004).

In Chapter 7 of this volume, Bies and Tripp also examine a particular type of negative mood, revenge. The authors discuss the ways in which employees seek revenge, while also exploring how organizational managers can implore their workforce to respond more cooperatively. For example, Bies and Tripp explain that when a victim has lower status than his or her harm-doing counterpart and the level of procedural justice in the organization is high, the victim will be less likely to retaliate with vengeful actions. The authors explain that "intentions matter" and show how revenge partially stems from the assumption that the harm doer intended to do harm. On a practical note, Bies and Tripp argue that employees should always be explicit about their intentions when communicating sensitive or emotionally charged information over the contemporary media of e-mail or text.

Researchers have moved beyond the simple question of how a particular mood affects the outcome of a negotiation and raised the interesting question of how moods might affect the behaviors of negotiators. Arguably, negotiators who are deceived feel particularly emotional. In Chapter 8 of this volume, Lewicki and Hanke explore the interesting question of how deception affects a negotiator's self-view (i.e., as a victim of deception) and his or her view of others (i.e., as a perpetrator of deception). They argue that trust is a vital factor in the negotiation process, and that deception diminishes negotiator trust. In this vein, Lewicki and Hanke present strategies that negotiators use to deceive their counterparts. Some strategies are considered marginally ethical but are generally accepted, such as competitive bargaining (i.e., making an inflated opening offer) and emotional manipulation (i.e., faking anger). Other strategies are generally agreed to be inappropriate, such as maliciously defacing an opponent's reputation or using bribery to gather information. The authors also present tactics that counterparts can use to avoid being the victim of deception, including trust and relationship building and asking probing questions to reveal inconsistencies in a counterpart's arguments. Finally, Lewicki and Hanke show how modern-day media of communication may add or detract from negotiator trust.

Affective Contagion

Contagion models of affect argue that one person's moods can infect those of others. Certain social conditions may augment the impact of moods as well, such as the fact that powerful people are more contagious than are others. For example, Anderson and Thompson (2004) found that positive affect of powerful negotiators shaped the quality of negotiation processes and outcomes more than the positive affect of less-powerful negotiators. Powerful individuals' trait positive affect was the best predictor of negotiators' trust for each other and of whether they reached integrative outcomes and predicted joint gains above and beyond negotiators' trait cooperativeness and communicativeness.

Relational and Task Conflict

Jehn (1995) drew a distinction between two types of group-level conflict: affective conflict and task conflict. Behfar, Peterson, Mannix, and Trochin (2008) expanded Jehn's distinction to introduce a third type of conflict: process conflict. Several studies suggested that affective conflict (characterized by negative emotions) was detrimental for negotiation, in contrast to fact-based conflict or task conflict, which was effective (Jehn & Mannix, 2001). However, a groundbreaking meta-analysis of relational and task conflict suggested that both types of conflict hurt group performance (DeDreu & Weingart, 2003). They found that relationship conflict was also highly negatively correlated with team performance; surprisingly, task conflict was negatively correlated with team performance and team satisfaction.

SOCIAL INFLUENCE IN GROUPS AND NEGOTIATION

Social influence is a timeless topic in team and group research dating back to the famous Asch (1956) and Milgram (1963) studies of conformity and obedience, respectively. Cialdini's (1993) provocative book on influence clearly captured the attention of negotiation researchers. The research on social influence has provided an extremely wide-ranging set of studies from which negotiation research has benefited. When we look at the field of negotiation, there are several compelling theoretical and empirical examples of social influence. We discuss the following: power, gender (in terms of status and pseudostatus), and culture.

Power and Negotiation

Research on power in groups has yielded a provocative set of findings. Powerful people are less inhibited (Keltner, Gruenfeld, & Anderson, 2003), take more risks (Galinsky, Gruenfeld, & Magee, 2003), and are more expressive (Keltner, Gruenfeld, Galinsky, & Kraus, 2010) than are less-powerful individuals. People with higher status make less-accurate judgments about the personality and emotions of others than do low-status people (Keltner et al., 2003). In negotiation, power promotes an action orientation. High-power individuals are more likely to initiate a negotiation than low-power individuals, and once in the negotiation, high-power negotiators are more likely to make the first move (Magee, Galinsky, & Gruenfeld, 2007), which can influence economic outcomes (Galinsky & Mussweiler, 2001). Power can also have indirect advantages for negotiators. In high-power negotiators, anger produces cognitive focus, which allows them to claim more value, whereas low-power negotiators lose cognitive focus when angry and claim less value (Overbeck, Neale, & Govan, 2010).

Gender and Negotiation

Eagley and her colleagues soberly demonstrated that women are not only accorded less value in groups and teams but also are devalued (Eagly & Johnson, 1990; Eagly & Karau, 1991). Similarly, Rudman (1998) suggested that there is a backlash against women. Women are penalized for embodying masculine traits, such as agency and dominance. Unfortunately, both of these skills may be necessary for effective negotiation. Kray, Thompson, and Galinsky (2001) borrowed Steele's (1997) implicit stereotyping theory to argue that when gender stereotypes are primed, this negatively affects women at the bargaining table. In a similar fashion, Bowles, Babcock, and McGinn (2005) examined "strong" versus "weak" situations in negotiation and found that the greatest gender differences in salaries and economic negotiation outcomes occurred in industries in which the compensation standards were ambiguous. Similarly, women perform better when negotiating on behalf of someone besides themselves.

In this volume's Chapter 11, Haselhuhn and Kray provide a thorough review of gender issues in negotiation and discuss why gender differences persist in today's workplace. For example, relative to men, women are stereotyped as warm but incompetent. When female negotiators perform actions inconsistent with this stereotype, they are socially sanctioned (backlash effects) more than their male counterparts. Furthermore, the incentive structure and focus on economic outcomes in negotiations favor male stereotypes. They argue that the language commonly used in negotiations (i.e., *negotiating for* vs. *asking for* a higher salary) may serve as "gender triggers" that make gender differences salient. The authors also describe actions that have been proposed to help close the negotiation gender gap. For example, organizational initiatives that emphasize positive female stereotypes (i.e., good listening skills) and actively attempt to reduce prejudice and bias can help minimize gender differences. However, the authors admonish that workplace norms of competition and a lack of discussion of gender issues may minimize the effectiveness of these initiatives.

Culture

Research on culture in groups and teams has also stimulated negotiation research. Culture is treated in terms of a fixed trait as well as temporarily activated. For example, Brett and Okumura (1998) examined culture as a fixed trait when they compared Japanese with U.S. negotiators and found that joint gains were significantly lower in intercultural negotiations, as opposed to intracultural negotiations. Gardner and her colleagues used a priming methodology to temporarily induce an independent versus interdependent orientation in negotiators to activate cultural differences that influence behavior. For example, Seeley, Gardner, and Thompson (2007) induced different relationship construals (independent vs. interdependent) by having negotiators read a short paragraph. They then examined how negotiators allocated resources in a dispute situation with a narrow (almost nonexistent) bargaining zone. They found that in team negotiations, independently oriented negotiators were more generous and constructive than were interdependently oriented negotiators.

In Chapter 10 of this volume, Tinsley, Turan, Weingart, and Dillon-Merrill investigate how cultural membership-cued stereotypes affect cross-cultural negotiations. They describe three factors that shape how cultural stereotypes affect negotiations and offer strategies for managing them. First, the effects of cultural stereotypes depend on the accuracy of the negotiators' stereotypes. Another factor is the level of ethnocentrism triggered by the cultural stereotype as ethnocentrism is positively correlated with the negativity of the cultural stereotype. A third factor is the extent to which negotiators behave in a consistent manner with their cultural group stereotype. Negotiators should realize that often cultural factors interact with the environment to produce inconsistent behavior. To help navigate cross-cultural negotiations, the authors suggest that negotiators learn about other cultures to increase stereotype accuracy to recognize that a cultural variable can interact with the situational context to produce stereotype-inconsistent behavior, to take a "culture-blind" approach and view the counterpart as an individual, and finally, to adopt a "multicultural" approach to enhance the positivity of cross-cultural stereotypes.

ORGANIZATIONAL PERSPECTIVES IN GROUPS AND NEGOTIATION

The organizational perspective in many ways holds the greatest promise for negotiation research. Negotiation research has profited in many ways from its strong roots in social psychology's small group and team paradigm. However, because social psychology stops short of social groups larger than a small team, it is the field of sociology and macro-organizational behavior that may very well represent the next frontier of research. We briefly discuss social networks, reputation, technology, and learning.

Social Networks

Social networks of organizational actors, embedded in work teams and groups in an organization, regularly negotiate. In this volume, Brass and Labianca discuss in Chapter 9 how social networks research may increase negotiators' power and influence at the bargaining table. For example, negotiators' network centrality, occupation of structural holes, and number of weak ties can all enhance their power and influence. Thus, it is important to recognize social network building as a strategic/motivational factor for negotiators and as an outcome variable in negotiations research. The authors recognize that organizations are becoming flatter, and negotiations are increasingly involving cross-functional and interorganizational participants. Consequently, it is becoming increasingly important for negotiators to consider their bargaining networks.

One of the implications of social network theory for the study of negotiation is that it is often the case that the parties who appear at the negotiation table are not actually those who will take on the ultimate responsibility for honoring the terms of the deal. For example, a negotiated deal may occur between a procurement division of a large company and a key supplier. Ultimately, the managers who use the procured resources may act in ways that are contrary to the terms of the contract. In this volume, Chapter 13, Malhotra draws the distinction between the *negotiation* phase, during which a negotiated agreement is reached, and the *contracting* phase, during which the agreement is codified in a legal document. He observes that many managers leave the deal-making process after the negotiated agreement but before the contracting phase. He argues that lack of managerial participation in the contracting phase is ultimately detrimental because it can result in a final deal that reflects the economic stipulations of the agreement but not the relational aspects. Inattention to relational considerations may result in contracts that signal distrust through excessive monetary incentives, mask honest intentions with fine print, and create rigid, binding terms that strain the relationship, especially during times of uncertainty.

Reputation

Arguably, it is only in the context of organizations and social networks that reputation is meaningful. Croson and her colleagues examine reputations and find that reputations are built fairly quickly in negotiation communities (Glick & Croson, 2001). They found four distinct reputations in negotiation communities: liar-manipulators, tough-but-honest, nice-and-reasonable, and finally, cream puffs. People use tough or manipulative tactics in a defensive fashion with liars and tough negotiators but in an opportunistic fashion with cream puffs. Anderson and Shirako (2008) tracked the development of reputations among individuals who engaged in multiple negotiation tasks across several weeks. The authors found that, on average, individuals' reputations were only mildly related to their history of behavior. However, the link between reputation and behavior was stronger for some individuals than others—specifically for individuals who were more well known and received more social attention in the community. In contrast, for less-well-known individuals, their behavior had little impact on their reputation. The findings have implications for negotiation behavior among groups and teams in organizations.

Technology

Whereas the common advice is to negotiate face to face, that is often an impossibility in the virtual workplace. Whereas conducting multimillion-dollar deals over the Internet would have seemed implausible as little as 10 years ago, it is commonplace today. The study of the impact of technology on group behavior spread like wildfire during the past 15 years. Because many of the empirical observations were nonobvious or different from what we know of face-to-face interaction, this captured the attention of the negotiation community. One of the first studies of technology's impact on negotiation behavior was conducted strictly via the Internet among full-time management students (Moore, Kurtzberg, Thompson, & Morris, 1999). In this study, some students negotiated with another student from their university (ingroup member) and some negotiated with a student from a different university (out-group member). In addition, some negotiators exchanged personal information with the other party, and some did not. The authors found that both membership in a social group and mutual self-disclosure improved the quality of agreements negotiated with information technology (IT). When neither common ingroup status nor a personalized relationship existed between negotiators, negotiations were more likely to end in impasse. Other studies have found that gender may be a key mediating variable in terms of the quality of negotiated agreements. For example, when females negotiate, their agreements are of higher quality when they have visual contact; however, the opposite is true for males, who reach better agreements in absence of visual contact (Swaab & Swaab, 2009).

In Chapter 14 of this volume, Agarwal, Viswanathan, and Animesh provide an overview of how IT has had an impact on the landscape of negotiations. Specifically, the authors explore how IT has altered the *transaction costs*, or the costs required to reach a contracted agreement, of three stages of negotiation. In the prenegotiation, or contact, stage of negotiation, IT has substantially lowered costs associated with searching for an optimal transaction partner. This has transformed both the way consumers purchase and the way sellers make markets. For example, online merchants have given rise to the long tail phenomenon, by which small-scale sales accumulate into substantial revenue. The impact of IT is also seen at the negotiation, or contract, stage. Online auctions support distributive bargaining approaches, and a vast amount of IT is designed to increase effectiveness of integrative bargaining situations by facilitating organization, communication, and efficiency. In the postnegotiation, or control-related, stage, IT facilitates synchronization to allow each party to fulfill the contract and provides oversight to ensure the terms of the deal are followed. Also, electronically mediated conflicts are often more efficiently reducing, saving both parties time and money.

Learning

The investigation of learning and performance over time has made great strides in the last decade of research. For example, Moreland's studies of transactive memory in teams suggest that people develop a shared cognitive system for completing tasks (Moreland, Argote, & Krishnan, 1998). Their now-famous transistor radio study revealed that holding constant the amount of training that people received, it was the group context that best predicted whether the team would be successful in assembling the radio once the instructions were removed (Liang, Moreland, & Argote, 1995).

Loewenstein, Thompson, and Gentner (1999) used theory from cognitive psychology to formulate a theory of analogical learning and transfer. They found that the ability to transfer concepts learned in one domain or context is quite limited, leading to the "inert knowledge problem." By actively comparing two or more examples or cases that illustrate the same concept, the ability to transfer knowledge to a new situation greatly increases. Bazerman and others extended this research finding by showing that diverse analogical training (training with multiple concepts) is superior to specific analogical training (training with a single concept) in facilitating joint value creation (Moran, Bereby-Meyer, & Bazerman, 2008). Negotiators trained with a contingent contract and a logrolling analogy created more value in a later negotiation than those trained with two contingent contract analogies. Surprisingly, diverse analogical training enhanced performance on the other integrative issues in the negotiation.

In this volume, Hughes, Enlow, Siegel, and Weiss in Chapter 12 emphasize that negotiation is an organizational competence, and hence concepts of organizational learning are crucial for enhancing workplace negotiation ability. First, the authors emphasize the importance of capturing knowledge from previous negotiations. Beyond the skills of individual negotiators, this knowledge can include organizationally embedded knowledge such as how negotiators are managed or how contracts are reviewed. The authors then provide a framework for translating organizational knowledge into practical lessons that can be disseminated across the organization. To determine which aspects of negotiation warrant investments in organizational learning, the authors propose using the concept of segmentation, or grouping a population into subsets to allocate resources and manage relationships optimally.

CONCLUSION

Negotiation research has blossomed from social psychology's great body of research in group behavior. The team perspective offers several intriguing vantage points for the negotiation scholar, who may be interested in the question of how a team, ostensibly on the same side of the negotiation table, allocates scarce resources, or how members of a larger organization negotiate with one another. By examining the negotiator in the workplace, new theoretical questions can be raised, and provocative empirical designs may be crafted. To be successful in offering prescriptive advice for the manager in the 21st century workplace, negotiation scholars must continue to conduct theory-grounded research. We have suggested in this review that group research based in social psychology as well as sociology is paramount for the continued success of the field. Collaborations that combine microfocus on groups with macrofocus on how those groups are networked will capture the attention of managers as well as help to integrate research within the field.

REFERENCES

Adams, J. S. (1963). Toward an understanding of inequity. *Journal of Abnormal and Social Psychology, 67,* 422–436.

Allison, S. T., Messick, D. M., & Goethals, G. R. (1989). On being better but not smarter than others: The Muhammad Ali effect. *Social Cognition, 7,* 275–296.

Allred, K. G., Mallozzi, J. S., Matsui, F., & Raia, C. P. (1997). The influence of anger and compassion on negotiation performance. *Organizational and Human Decision Processes, 70*, 175–187.

Anderson, C., & Shirako, A. (2008). Are individuals' reputations related to their history of behavior? *Journal of Personality and Social Psychology, 94*, 320–333.

Anderson, C., & Thompson, L. (2004). Affect from the top down: How powerful individuals' positive affect shapes negotiations. *Organizational Behavior and Human Decision Processes, 95*, 125–139.

Asch, S. (1956). Studies of independence and conformity: A minority of one against a unanimous majority. *Psychological Monographs, 70*, 1–70.

Austin, W. (1980). Friendship and fairness: Effects of type of relationship and task performance on choice of distribution rules. *Personality and Social Psychology Bulletin, 6*, 402–408.

Bazerman, M. H., Lowenstein, G. F., and White, S. B. (1992). Reversals of preference in allocation decisions: Judging an alternative versus choosing among alternatives. *Administrative Science Quarterly, 37*, 220–240.

Behfar, K. J., Peterson, R. S., Mannix, E. A., & Trochin, W. M. K. (2008). The critical role of conflict resolution in teams: A close look at the links between conflict type, conflict management strategies, and team outcomes. *Journal of Applied Psychology, 93*, 170–188.

Boswell, W. R., & Olson-Buchanan, J. B. (2004). Experiencing mistreatment at work: The role of grievance filing, nature of mistreatment, and employee withdrawal. *Academy of Management Journal, 47*, 129–139.

Bowles, H. R., Babcock, L., & McGinn, K. (2005). Constraints and triggers: Situational mechanics of gender in negotiations. *Journal of Personality and Social Psychology, 89*, 951–965.

Brett, J., & Okumura, T. (1998). Inter- and intracultural negotiation: U. S. and Japanese negotiators. *Academy of Management Journal, 41*, 495–510.

Carnevale, P. J., & Isen, A. M. (1986). The influence of positive affect and visual access on the discovery of integrative solutions in bilateral negotiation. *Organizational Behavior and Human Decision Processes, 37*, 1–13.

Chaiken, S., Wood, W., & Eagly, A. H. (1996). Principles of persuasion. In E. T. Higgins & A. Kruglanski (Eds.), *Social psychology: Handbook of basic mechanisms and processes* (pp. 211-238). New York: Guilford Press.

Cialdini, R. B. (1993*). Influence: The psychology of persuasion* (Rev. ed.). New York: Quill.

DeDreu, C. K. W., & Weingart, L. R. (2003). Task versus relationship conflict, team performance, and team member satisfaction: A meta-analysis. *Journal of Applied Psychology, 88*, 741–749.

Diekmann, K. A., Samuels, S. M., Ross, L., & Bazerman, M. H. (1997). Self-interest and fairness in problems of resource allocation: Allocators versus recipients. *Journal of Personality and Social Psychology, 72*, 1061–1074.

Eagly, A. H., & Johnson, B. T. (1990). Gender and leadership style: A meta-analysis. *Psychological Bulletin, 108*, 233–256.

Eagly, A. H., & Karau, S. J. (1991). Gender and the emergence of leaders: A meta-analysis. *Journal of Personality and Social Psychology, 60*, 685–710.

Galinsky, A. D, Gruenfeld, D. H., & Magee, J. C. (2003). From power to action. *Journal of Personality and Social Psychology, 85*, 453–466.

Galinsky, A. D., & Mussweiler, T. (2001). First offers as anchors: The role of perspective-taking and negotiator focus. *Journal of Personality and Social Psychology, 81*, 657–669.

Glick, S., & Croson, R. (2001). Reputations in negotiation. In S. J. Hoch, H. C. Kunreuther, & R. E. Gunther (Eds.), *Wharton on making decisions.* (pp. 177–186). New York: Wiley.

Jehn, K. A. (1995). A multimethod examination of the benefits and determinants of intragroup conflict. *Administrative Science Quarterly, 40,* 256–282.

Jehn, K. A., & Mannix, E. A. (2001). The dynamic nature of conflict: A longitudinal study of intragroup conflict and group performance. *Academy of Management Journal, 44,* 238–251.

Keltner, D., Gruenfeld, D. H., & Anderson, C. (2003). Power, approach, and inhibition. *Psychological Review, 110,* 265–284.

Keltner, D., Gruenfeld, D. H., Galinsky, A., & Kraus, M. W. (2010). Paradoxes of power: Dynamics of the acquisition, experience, and social regulation of social power. In A. Guinote & T. K. Vescio (Eds.), *The social psychology of power* (pp. 177–208). New York: Guilford Press.

Kramer, R. M. (1991). Intergroup relations and organizational dilemmas: The role of categorization processes. *Research in Organizational Behavior, 13,* 191–228.

Kray, L. J., Thompson, L., & Galinsky, A. D. (2001). Battle of the sexes: Gender stereotype confirmation and reactance in negotiations. *Journal of Personality and Social Psychology, 80,* 942–958.

Kurtzberg, T. R., Naquin, C. E., & Belkin, L. Y. (2009). Humor as a relationship-building tool in online negotiations. *International Journal of Conflict Management, 20,* 1044–1068.

Lax, D., & Sebenius, J. (1986). *The manager as negotiator: Bargaining for cooperation and competitive gain.* New York: Free Press.

Liang, D. W., Moreland, R., & Argote, L. (1995). Group versus individual training and group performance: The mediating role of transactive memory. *Personality and Social Psychology Bulletin, 21,* 384–393.

Lind, E. A., & Tyler, T. R. (1988). *The social psychology of procedural justice.* New York: Plenum Press.

Loewenstein, G. F., Thompson, L., & Bazerman, M. H. (1989). Social utility and decision making in interpersonal context. *Journal of Personality and Social Psychology, 57,* 426–441.

Loewenstein, J., Thompson, L., & Gentner, D. (1999). Analogical encoding facilitates knowledge transfer in negotiation. *Psychonomic Bulletin and Review, 6,* 586–597.

Magee, J. C., Galinsky, A., & Gruenfeld, D. H. (2007). Power, propensity to negotiate, and moving first in competitive interactions. *Personality and Social Psychology Bulletin, 33,* 200–212.

Messick, D. M., & Rutte, C. G. (1992). The provision of public goods by experts: The Groningen study. In W. B. G. Liebrand, D. M. Messick, & H. A. M. Wilke (Eds.), *Social dilemmas: Theoretical issues and research findings* (pp. 101–109). Oxford, UK: Pergamon.

Messick, D., & Sentis, K. P. (1979). Fairness and preference. *Journal of Experimental Social Psychology, 15,* 418–434.

Milgram, S. (1963). Behavioral study of obedience. *Journal of Abnormal and Social Psychology, 67,* 371–378.

Moore, D., Kurtzberg, T., Thompson, L., & Morris, M. W. (1999). Long and short routes to success in electronically-mediated negotiations: Group affiliations and group vibrations. *Organizational Behavior and Human Decision Processes, 77,* 22–43.

Moran, S., Bereby-Meyer, Y., & Bazerman, M. (2008). Stretching the effectiveness of analogical training in negotiations: Teaching diverse principles for creating value. *Negotiation and Conflict Management Research, 1,* 99–134.

Moreland, R. L., Argote, L., & Krishnan, R. (1998). Training people to work in groups. In R. S. Tindale, L. Heath, J. Edwards, E. Posavac, F. B. Bryant, Y. Suarez-Balcazar, et al. (Eds.), *Theory and research on small groups* (pp. 37–60). New York: Plenum.

Overbeck, J. R., Neale, M. A., & Govan, C. L. (2010). I feel, therefore you act: Intrapersonal and interpersonal effects of emotion on negotiation as a function of social power. *Organizational Behavior and Human Decision Processes, 112,* 126–139.

Ross, M., & Sicoly, F. (1979). Egocentric biases in availability and attribution. *Journal of Personality and Social Psychology, 37,* 322–336.

Rudman, L. A. (1998). Self-promotion as a risk factor for women: The costs and benefits of counterstereotypical impression management. *Journal of Personality and Social Psychology, 74,* 629–645.

Seeley, E., Gardner, W., & Thompson, L. (2007). The role of the self-concept and social context in determining the behavior of power-holders: Self-construal in intergroup vs. dyadic dispute resolution negotiations. *Journal of Personality and Social Psychology, 93,* 614–631.

Sinaceur, M., & Tiedens, L. Z. (2006). Get mad and get more than even: When and why anger expression is effective in negotiations. *Journal of Experimental Social Psychology, 42,* 314–322.

Sondak, H., Neale, M. A., & Pinkley, R. (1995). The negotiated allocation of benefits and burdens: The impact of outcome valence, contribution, and relationship. *Organizational Behavior and Human Decision Processes, 64,* 249–260.

Steele, C. M. (1997). A threat in the air: How stereotypes shape intellectual identity and performance. *American Psychologist, 52,* 613–629.

Swaab, R. I., & Swaab, D. F. (2009). Sex differences in the effects of visual contact and eye contact in negotiations. *Journal of Experimental Social Psychology, 45,* 129–136.

Tajfel, H. (1970). Aspects of national and ethnic loyalty. *Social Science Information, 9,* 119–144.

Thibaut, J., & Walker, L. (1975). *Procedural justice: A psychological analysis.* Hillsdale, NJ: Erlbaum.

Tyler, T. R. (1987). Conditions leading to value-expressive effects in judgments of procedural justice: A test of four models. *Journal of Personality and Social Psychology, 52,* 333–344.

Tyler, T. R., & Degoey, P. (1995). Collective restraint in social dilemmas: Procedural justice and social identification effects on support for authorities. *Journal of Personality and Social Psychology, 69,* 482–497.

Van Avermaet, E. (1974). *Equity: A theoretical and empirical analysis.* Unpublished doctoral dissertation, University of California, Santa Barbara.

Van Kleef, G. A., DeDreu, C. K. W., & Manstead, A. S. R. (2004). The interpersonal effects of emotions in negotiations: A motivated information processing approach. *Journal of Personality and Social Psychology, 87,* 510–528.

Walton, R. E., & McKersie (1965). *A behavioral theory of labor negotiations.* New York: McGraw-Hill.

Wills, T. A. (1981). Downward comparison principles in social psychology. *Psychological Bulletin, 90,* 245–271.

17

Commentary and Future Directions for Negotiations

Chia-Jung Tsay and Max H. Bazerman

INTRODUCTION

We are fortunate to have the role of commentators on an interesting collection of papers. There are many nuggets that are fascinating and useful. We have made multiple copies of Pinkley's (Chapter 4) list of compensation issues that will be useful in advising students in the future. Even experienced negotiators would be wise to heed the intriguing and counterintuitive findings that Malhotra (Chapter 13) offers regarding the risks in leaving contracts to the lawyers, even when that is simply what is believed to be appropriate. Practitioners are likely to gain new perspectives from Agarwal, Viswanathan, and Animesh (Chapter 14), who discuss the impact of information technologies on the search costs incurred in negotiators' attempts to reduce risks and uncertainties, offering more systematic categorizations of technology-facilitated interactions that will become more relevant with our increasing dependence on web-based forums.

On top of the many valuable tools and ideas that this volume presents to negotiators, several chapters explore important literatures relatively untapped by negotiation scholars. They offer constructive syntheses, translating theories from those literatures and discussing their meaning within negotiations. For example, Brass and Labianca (Chapter 9) consider the relational aspects of negotiations by delving into the extensive social networks literature, underlining the value of a better understanding of the dynamic nature of relationships.

In another promising direction, Hughes, Enlow, Siegel, and Weiss (Chapter 12) draw upon the literature in organizational learning to pose ways in which negotiators may better capture knowledge, complementing the prescriptive approach that has the potential to have greater impact for practitioners. Such views, along with the substantial institutional investment in and benefits of training (Bazerman & Neale, 1982; Coleman & Lim, 2001; Thompson, Gentner, & Loewenstein, 2000), may inform our intuitive notion of the naturally gifted negotiator (Kray & Haselhuhn, 2007; Thompson, 2005, 2007) and our automatic privileging of natural talent (Tsay & Banaji, 2011). By more fully appreciating negotiations as a function not only of individual skill but also of relationships and organizational competence, negotiators stand to gain much in joint processes and outcomes.

Beyond the lessons that negotiators may learn from the chapters mentioned above, we focus our commentary on the three core topics that are central to the current volume on negotiation—fairness, emotions, and diversity. We are delighted that these issues are so central to this volume, and use our limited space to expand on the future of each of these three topics.

FAIRNESS AND ETHICALITY

Being fair in negotiation matters. People like to deal with fair opponent negotiators, and reputations are important. The deliberate use of deception or strategic tactics can be costly, with consequences to all parties. Yet, as several of the pieces in this volume note (Conlon & Ross, Chapter 2; Roloff, Brockner, & Weisenfeld, Chapter 3), this connection between fairness, procedural justice, and behavioral ethics is underrepresented in the literature. This volume moves towards fixing this discrepancy.

Conlon and Ross (Chapter 2) do a fine job of connecting the vast literature on procedural justice to the area of negotiation, specifically to the issue of cooperativeness. But, Roloff, Brockner, and Weisenfeld (Chapter 3) highlight a fascinating challenge and implicit criticism of the recommendations from the prior procedural justice literature: negotiators can follow all of the rules from the procedural fairness literature, and still not get the benefits if they are perceived as inauthentic in their desire for procedural fairness. This may sound obvious, but it goes against much of the prior literature on procedural justice. In fact, Roloff, Brockner, and Weisenfeld suggest an interesting dilemma: if negotiators use the procedural justice literature strategically to improve performance, they are likely to lose authenticity. When they lose authenticity, they may not get the value suggested by the vast procedural justice literature as it has been studied to date.

We see this argument as paralleling the recent work on the downside of goal setting. Ordonez, Schweitzer, Galinsky, and Bazerman (2009) argue that when clear goals are imposed, people are often motivated to ignore performance dimensions that are not part of the goal, to cheat to get to the goal, and to act in a variety of other dysfunctional ways. For example, in this volume, Malhotra (Chapter 13) suggests that while contractual provisions for incentives may increase perceptions of fairness, they may actually lead to a negative impact on the relationship. Similarly, we see Roloff, Brockner, and Weisenfeld (Chapter 3) bringing to light that when procedural justice criteria are used as a checklist, lack of authenticity is a likely result, effectively eliminating the benefits of being procedurally just.

One striking aspect of this research harkens to observations by Conlon and Ross about the lack of connectivity between the literatures on procedural fairness and negotiation. This seems true despite the procedural justice literature having early roots in the topic of negotiation. In 1986, Lewicki, Sheppard, and Bazerman edited the first volume of *Research on Negotiation in Organizations*, and roughly a third of the volume focuses on procedural justice, with papers by Tyler, Greenberg, Folger, Brett, and Bies and Moag. Twenty-five years later, the outlined connection between these fields is still lacking.

Perhaps even more disturbing is the lack of connectivity between procedural justice and the rapidly emerging areas of behavioral ethics (Lewicki & Hanke, Chapter 8) and trust (Bies & Tripp, Chapter 7). As Enron and other ethically-challenged organizations pushed the scholarly community to develop research insights about how to change ethical behavior, the procedural justice literature has been noticeably absent. Similarly, as the trust game and the trust literature have emerged in behavioral decision research and behavioral economics, the role of procedures has not been at the forefront of the intellectual dialogue. If we want to understand ethical failings in negotiation (Lewicki & Hanke, Chapter 8), there is an obvious need to know how the processes that govern a negotiation affect perceptions of trust, the ethicality of the process setter, and the negotiation processes and outcomes that ensue.

From our perspective, the other critical gap that we see in much of the existing justice and ethics work is a focus limited to intentional, conscious decisions. One of the most important intellectual trends in the field of behavioral ethics is increased attention to the role of unintentional ethics actions. Bazerman (one of the authors of this commentary) observes that a common classroom experience is that during the debriefing of a negotiation simulation, one party is angry at the other for his unethical action, but the target of the hostility is quite confident that he did absolutely nothing wrong. How does this occur?

Our view is that this common experience is quite consistent with the emerging literature on bounded ethicality in negotiations (Bazerman & Tenbrunsel, 2011; Chugh & Bazerman, 2007). That is, it is common for negotiators to engage in unethical acts without knowing that they are doing anything wrong. Pinkley (Chapter 4) highlights the common example of negotiators overstating what they will bring to the partnership and their control over future events; there is ample evidence that this can occur without the negotiator knowing that he or she is doing so (Caruso, Epley, & Bazerman, 2006).

Psychologists similarly document ways in which humans discriminate without knowing that they are doing so (Banaji & Bhaskar, 2000; Greenwald & Banaji, 1995; Greenwald et al., 2002; Greenwald, McGhee, & Schwartz, 1998). For example, in negotiations, we can act toward opponent negotiators differently based on gender and ethnic background (Chugh & Bazerman, 2007; Banaji, Bazerman, & Chugh, 2003). The specification of the multitude of ways in which negotiators can act unethically, and yet without their own awareness, is a topic of active research and is worth the attention of the negotiation literature.

In recent years, work related to bounded ethicality has been fast growing, and holds much relevance for negotiators. For example, negotiators might heed the empirical work that points to the ease with which unethical acts that occur through incremental changes (Gino & Bazerman, 2009) or intermediaries (Paharia, Kassam, Greene, & Bazerman, 2009) can go unnoticed, contributing to potential misunderstandings that erode both the relational and economic value of negotiations. Such effects are likely to be exacerbated by competitive contexts (Ku, Malhotra, & Murnighan, 2005; Malhotra, 2010), cognitive strain (Carnevale & Lawler, 1986; Gilbert

& Hixon, 1991; Gilbert, Pelham, & Krull, 1988), and cynical tendencies to attribute negative intentions to others (Kruger & Gilovich, 1999; Tsay, Shu, & Bazerman, 2011).

EMOTIONS

Just as we may not consciously recognize when we make unfair decisions, recent research has also illuminated the many ways in which we may not know how moods and emotions influence our judgments. Not only do we each bring our own respective emotional "baggage" to the negotiating table (Barsade & Gibson, 2007), the interpersonal aspects of dyadic and group negotiations also demand that we pay much more attention to this fast-growing area of research.

Recent work has highlighted the dynamic nature of emotions (Filipowicz, Barsade, & Melwani, forthcoming) and the automatic ways in which our emotions can affect others' emotions (Barsade, 2002). In this volume, Cropanzano, Becker, and Feldman (Chapter 6) suggest that the growing dependence on cross-cultural communication and teams confronts negotiators with the need to better understand the wide range of expressions of and reactions to affect (Adam, Shirako, & Maddux, 2010). Furthermore, our increasing reliance on technology-based media also brings to the forefront the more universal aspects of affective cues that emerge consistently through a widening and diversifying set of negotiators. The impact that affect has on negotiators, relationships, and negotiation processes and outcomes cannot be taken lightly.

From Cropanzano, Becker, and Feldman's (Chapter 6) comprehensive overview of the emergence of work on moods and emotions in negotiations, we see the importance of both types of affect: the more intensely-felt emotions that have more specific causes and targets, and the moods that may be more diffuse but are still powerful as they linger and are less easily recognized. While there has been much evolution in how scholars have thought about the impact of moods in organizations, the complexities and at times contradictory findings about how they affect negotiations can be daunting. This may be the case especially for practitioners who prefer more cleanly delineated strategies that have tighter relationships between cause and effect.

With more specifically targeted emotions, there appear to be findings that may be more amenable to practitioners' use (Kopelman, Rosette, & Thompson, 2006; Thompson, Medvec, Seiden, & Kopelman, 2001). The literature has thus far focused more on the role that negative emotions, such as anger, have for behaviors, performance, value-claiming, and joint outcomes. A body of work has also shed light on how such effects may be moderated by the level of motivation to consider the others' emotions (Van Kleef, De Dreu, & Manstead, 2004a, 2004b), the target of experienced emotions (Steinel, Van Kleef, & Harinck, 2008), as well as others' power and status (Overbeck, Neale, & Govan, 2010; Sinaceur & Tiedens, 2006).

Despite some of the individual and even joint gains that may be attributed to the expression of an emotion such as anger, it would be prudent to take caution in such expression. This is not only because of the complex ways in which emotions can serve as information and affect the other party, but also because of the potential downsides that can result from emotional outbursts. When we take a more long-term and relational view, there may be consequences for future interactions (Van Kleef & Dreu, 2010), such as exclusion from future coalitions in multiparty negotiations (Beest, Van Kleef, & Dijk, 2008). In the case of dyadic negotiations, our desire to avoid impasse may contribute to conceding to the angry negotiator. However, when given other alternatives in multiparty negotiations, that same preference can lead us to leave the angry negotiator in favor of a different party who has not communicated anger.

There have been significant contributions in recent years as scholars further refine the area of emotions. There is a fast-growing literature on the more nuanced ways to understand positive and negative emotions (Han, Lerner, & Keltner, 2007; Lerner & Keltner, 2000, 2001; Lerner & Tiedens, 2006), as well as the influence of the incidental emotions (Forgas, 1995, 1998) that are not directly related to the targets or interactions but which still can have a powerful impact on negotiations.

While emotions scholars have gained much ground in recent years, practitioners' focus on tangible outcomes and quantifiable value may pose some obstacles for negotiators to reap the full benefits of such work. One growing area of research, outlined by Elfenbein and Curhan (Chapter 5) in this volume, is perhaps more likely to appeal to and influence negotiators in practice. This work may more effectively bridge the gap between emotions scholars and the field of negotiations: the concept of *subjective value*

(SV)— defined by Curhan, Elfenbein, and Xu (2006) as "social, perceptual, and emotional consequences of a negotiation."

Not only do negotiators care about their perceived fairness of the process and outcome, feelings of competence, and rapport and trust established with other parties, they often use these perceptions to understand their own performance and guide future behavior. Furthermore, as this group of scholars has established (Curhan, Elfenbein, & Eisenkraft, 2010; Curhan, Elfenbein, & Kilduff, 2009), subjective value is likely to positively influence future interactions by contributing to greater transparency and reciprocity. This allows negotiators to draw upon "relational capital" (Gelfand, Major, Raver, Nishii, & O'Brien, 2006) and ultimately come to more integrative outcomes.

In other important work on emotions, Bies and Tripp (Chapter 7) tackle the damaging impact of emotions, such as revenge, on negotiations and organizations. The authors systematically explore the antecedents, moderators, and expressions of revenge, such as how individuals engage in aggressive responses when their goals have been frustrated or when they perceive that they have lost face. Bies and Tripp discuss how revenge and avoidance can endure over months or longer, and become more likely— and reconciliation less likely—when individuals construe conflict in self-serving ways (Bies & Tripp, 1995, 1996) or hold greater relative power (Aquino, Tripp, & Bies, 2001, 2006; Kim, Smith, & Brigham 1998).

The consequences of revenge can be severe, escalating conflict instead of "righting" the scorecard in negotiations. These "revenge scholars" note the ways in which certain twenty-first century changes can heighten the likelihood that negotiators follow through with these intensely negative emotions. These challenges include the proliferation of media-lean technologies that efficiently allow us access to wider networks than ever, while also stripping away the nonverbal opportunities to develop confidence and trust in relationships.

As such, Lewicki and Hanke (Chapter 8) highlight another promising area for negotiations scholars in the continued examination of the role of nonverbal, affective, and visual information. While there has been some work investigating the rich set of nonverbal behaviors, both displayed and leaked, discussions about nonverbal information in the context of negotiations have often focused on deception detection. For example, practitioners may want to understand and use microexpressions (Ekman, 1999) to prevent exploitation by "trained liars."

We propose additional future research investigating not just the use of nonverbal information to guard against bad behavior, but also the nature of our automatic and nonconscious use of this type of information. In preliminary new work, Tsay and colleagues find that even in domains in which sound is explicitly and consistently valued for the evaluation of performance, professionals and novices alike actually rely on visual over audio information in rapid social judgment of individuals and groups. It would be valuable to further explore the dissociation between the information we report valuing versus that which we actually use. These initial findings also suggest several potential implications for negotiations, such as the persistence of automatic impressions, the risks in overweighting expert opinion, and the conditions under which more information actually contributes to a reduced quality of negotiation performance and outcomes.

There has also been some interesting research suggesting that individual differences in abilities to recognize and understand emotions correlate with important negotiation outcomes (Elfenbein, Foo, White, Tan, & Aik, 2007; Mayer, Roberts, & Barsade, 2008; Mueller & Curhan, 2006). To extend such research further, how well might naïve perceivers be able to predict which dyads give up prematurely and only arrive at impasse? How quickly, through nonverbal information alone, can perceivers predict which dyads are particularly able to establish rapport and come to more optimal individual and joint outcomes? If perceivers are indeed good at such social judgment, what affective or visual cues might they be using as heuristics in assessing the quality of the actual interactions?

Thompson et al. (2001) suggest that at least for distributive bargaining, the "poker face" may be most conducive to reaching optimal outcomes. Do experienced negotiators also go forward with the assumption that hiding emotions is the best strategy? What kinds of consequences might there be from this deliberate masking of emotions, when it comes to integrative bargaining? There is some exciting work that points to the value of emotional expression for revising others' assumptions of negotiations as a fixed-pie interaction, in turn promoting integrative behavior (Pietroni, Van Kleef, De Dreu, & Pagliaro, 2008). It is our hope that such research and future work might help train negotiators to become more effective without sacrificing authenticity, and foster the conditions that allow negotiators to become better equipped to create value together and arrive at more integrative outcomes.

DIVERSITY

The previous section hinted at the need to better understand the different meanings and construals of affective expressions (Adam et al., 2010), given the frequency with which we are encountering dissimilar others. In an age where the workplace is increasingly diverse, with a greater presence of women in a broad swath of work arenas and with the flattening of the international economy, it becomes incumbent on scholars to help practitioners become more attuned to differences between groups and the dangers of implicit discrimination, as well as new approaches to facilitate communication and interactions with those unlike oneself. In this section, we expand upon our earlier brief mention about the impact of our nonconscious beliefs and how they contribute to discriminatory practices and suboptimal outcomes in the face of different others.

Until recently, scholars and practitioners have questioned the value of some diversity research. For practitioners, while the increasing diversity was becoming quite visible, there may have been a question of whether investment is worthwhile, considering that female representation in the upper ranks of management remained disproportionately low considering the significant advances that women have made in many domains (Haselhuhn & Kray, Chapter 11; Helfat, Harris, & Wolfson, 2006).

As for the research on the impact of gender diversity on negotiations, two decades ago, Neale and Bazerman (1991) argued that despite hundreds of studies examining gender, there was little evidence to support a main effect for gender differences in negotiator performance (Lewicki & Litterer, 1985). Thompson (1990) argued that even the evidence that does exist must be viewed skeptically, as researchers have not been consistent in reporting gender differences and many studies report them as secondary analyses. The implication is that there may be an even larger number of studies that have tested gender differences, but which have never been reported due to a lack of a statistically demonstrable effect.

This view was pretty common, and other scholars reached similar conclusions. Lewicki and Litterer (1985) believed that "...there are few significant relationships between personality and negotiation outcomes." Similarly, Hermann and Kogan (1977) posited that "from what is known now, it does not appear that there is any single personality type or characteristic that is directly and clearly linked to success in negotiation." There was some consensus that individual traits and characteristics, such as gender, were overrated as variables in negotiation.

However, the problem was actually due to the way that gender was being studied in the context of negotiation. Linda Babcock and her colleagues (Babcock, Gelfand, & Small, 2006; Babcock & Laschever, 2003; Bowles, Babcock, & McGinn, 2005; Kray & Babcock, 2005) have done a phenomenal job of demonstrating that the problem was in how researchers specified the problem. In short form, when negotiators are forced to negotiate in a defined structure, such as a lab experiment, the differences between men and women were small and inconsistent. But, there were big differences that researchers were missing, such as how gender affects propensities to initiate negotiations (Babcock & Laschever, 2003), how gender largely determines economic payoffs in outcomes (Kray & Thompson, 2005), and how the gender of initiators affects the likelihood of social risks and sanctions incurred (Bowles, Babcock, & Lai, 2007).

These effects, such as decrements in performance even in high-performing women, may be attributed in part to the threat of being judged or treated stereotypically (Steele, 1997; Steele & Aronson, 1995). Women may also be reminded of their female identity and shift negatively in their implicit attitudes towards certain domains (Steele & Ambady, 2006). A traditionally male-dominated domain, such as negotiation, poses an environment ripe for the self-fulfilling prophecy that the female negotiator would be less effective. Haselhuhn and Kray (Chapter 11) present the aptly named concept of "gender triggers," the social or situational cues that lead to gender differences in negotiations. These can include the language or framing of the interaction, the type of role that the negotiator holds, and the level of ambiguity involved. Other recent work has also shown the impact of gender and sex stereotypes on negotiation performance, through expectations of male superiority in negotiating ability, gendered social norms, and pay expectations (Bowles & McGinn, 2008).

In this volume, Haselhuhn and Kray (Chapter 11) offer particularly insightful glimpses of the impact of gender diversity, which will become increasingly important in the 21st century. Given the recent research covering the significant effects of gender on negotiation processes and outcomes, the prescriptive advice in this volume holds promise for facilitating more transparent and open communication, as well as capturing better outcomes for all parties. Haselhuhn and Kray's chapter (Chapter 11) also presents some thorough and excellent discussion that clarifies some of the psychological underpinnings of gender differences in negotiation performance and outcomes, tying in consideration of gender-based affective responses to negotiation outcomes. In addition, they call to attention the literature's relative neglect of the relational aspects of negotiations, which contribute to our understanding of how gender affects negotiations.

Whether diversity and dissimilar others come in the form of gender, ethnicity, or culture, the vast literature from social psychology does much to inform us. Turning to the impact of ethnic and cultural diversity on negotiations, Tinsley, Turan, Weingart, and Dillon-Merrill (Chapter 10) examine how differences may be magnified. Information about visible social categories (Brewer & Feinstein, 1999; Fiske, 1998) can become the basis of automatic assumptions and expectations (Fiske & Taylor, 1991) about other parties, resulting in shifts in behavior and negotiation processes and outcomes. Furthermore, not only can we be nudged through subtle contextual or physical cues towards assumptions about how others might behave in accordance with various associated stereotypes, our behaviors can also be quite malleable. Our awareness of the stereotypes that may be associated with ourselves can push us towards behaviors that may or may not be consistent with those stereotypes.

The authors also offer some interesting discussion regarding the power of valenced stereotypes, drawing from previous work that shows how positive, neutral, and negative stereotypes influence negotiation processes and outcomes (Kray, Thompson, & Galinsky, 2001). Above and beyond the competitive nature of negotiations in general, negotiators would do well to better understand how intercultural negotiations can increase the likelihood that negative emotions are elicited by the automatic association of dissimilar others with negative stereotypes.

Another valuable perspective is the differentiation between intracultural versus intercultural stereotypes. Tinsley, Turan, Weingart, and Dillon-Merrill (Chapter 10) offer an intriguing discussion about our failure to account for how dissimilar others adjust during intercultural interactions. This calls to attention our assumption that others will behave towards us just as they would towards those from their own cultures, in a fascinating extrapolation of our tendencies to ignore the cognitions and perspectives of others (Bazerman & Neale, 1982). A myopic focus on potential cross-cultural differences may again result in inaccurate assumptions and sub-optimal outcomes if we neglect the influence of the norms or rules of the specific negotiation (Adam et al., 2010; Moore, 2004).

In addition to considering others' perspectives and the specific rules of the negotiation, there are other ways to reduce the potentially harmful effects of the ways in which we quickly use social categories as part of our information set, which may be magnified in cross-cultural negotiations. Rather than the assumption of negotiations as a zero-sum interaction in which parties necessarily win or lose parts of the mythical fixed pie (Bazerman, Magliozzi, & Neale, 1985), it would be worthwhile to focus on the shared goal of creating value together and reaching more integrative outcomes by making wise trade-offs with negotiation partners (Baron & Bazerman, 2002).

IS THE 21ST CENTURY REMARKABLY DIFFERENT? A CAUTIONARY NOTE

The editors and the authors have done a fantastic job of highlighting how society is changing and how this will affect the nature of negotiations in upcoming decades. By reconciling and balancing our naïve assumptions about negotiations with a better understanding of the importance of a myriad of other factors contributing to negotiation processes, negotiators can potentially use more finely-tuned levers through which they can enact powerful transformations during negotiations, and ultimately, create greater joint value.

It is useful to note that the core conceptual frameworks still remain in place throughout this volume, which does not speculate far into completely new topics or frameworks. The changing world provides insight into the structural characteristics that affect how we use the core tools in existing conceptual frameworks of negotiation. We still want to provide good advice to negotiators. We still need to think about the decisions of the other side. And, we still need to think about how the situation affects the decisions of both parties—we simply have some new situations in which to respond. Thus, for us, this volume is a testimony to the strengths of the negotiation field as it has developed over the last three decades, and we look forward to seeing a productive role for knowledge from the field of negotiations over the upcoming decades.

REFERENCES

Adam, H., Shirako, A., & Maddux, W. W. (2010). Cultural variance in the interpersonal effects of anger in negotiations. *Psychological Science, 21*(6), 882–889.

Aquino, K., Tripp, T.M., & Bies, R.J. (2001). How employees respond to personal offense: The effects of blame attribution, victim status, and offender stat us on revenge and reconciliation in the workplace. *Journal of Applied Psychology, 86,* 52–59.

Aquino, K., Tripp, T.M., & Bies, R.J. (2006). Getting even or moving on? Power, procedural justice, and types of offense as predictors of revenge, forgiveness, reconciliation, and avoidance in organizations. *Journal of Applied Psychology, 91,* 653–658.

Babcock, L., Gelfand, M., & Small, D. (2006). Propensity to initiate negotiations: A new look at gender variation in negotiation behavior. In D. De Cremer, M. Zeelenberg, and J. K. Murnighan (Eds.) *Social psychology and economics.* Mahwah, NJ: Lawrence Erlbaum Associates.

Babcock, L. & Laschever, S. (2003). *Women don't ask: Negotiation and the gender divide.* Princeton: Princeton University Press.

Banaji, M., Bazerman, M., & Chugh, D. (2003). How (un)ethical are you? *Harvard Business Review, 81*(12), 56–64.

Banaji, M. R. & Bhaskar, R. (2000). Implicit stereotypes and memory: The bounded rationality of social beliefs. In D. L. Schacter & E. Scarry (Eds.), *Memory, brain, and belief* (pp. 139–175). Cambridge, MA: Harvard University Press.

Baron, J., & Bazerman, M. H. (2002). Enlarging the pie by accepting small losses for large gains. In R. Gowda, J. C. Fox, R. Gowda, J. C. Fox (Eds.), *Judgments, decisions, and public policy* (pp. 322–352). New York: Cambridge University Press.

Barsade, S. (2002). The ripple effect: Emotional contagion and its influence on group behavior. *Administrative Science Quarterly, 47,* 644–675.

Barsade, S. & Gibson, D. (2007). Why does affect matter in organizations? *Academy of Management Perspectives, 21,* 36–59.

Bazerman, M. H., Magliozzi, T., & Neale, M. A. (1985). The acquisition of an integrative response in a competitive market. *Organizational Behavior and Human Decision Processes, 35*(3), 294–313.

Bazerman, M. & Neale, M. (1982). Improving negotiation effectiveness under final offer arbitration: The role of selection and training. *Journal of Applied Psychology, 67*(5), 543–548.

Bazerman, M. & Tenbrunsel, A. (2011). *Blind Spots: Why we fail to do what's right and what to do about it.* Princeton: Princeton University Press.

Beest, I., Van Kleef, G. A., & Dijk, E. (2008). Get angry, get out: The interpersonal effects of anger communication in multiparty negotiation. *Journal of Experimental Social Psychology, 44*(4), 993–1002.

Bies, R.J. & Tripp, T.M. (1995). The use and abuse of power: Justice as social control. In R. Cropanzano and M. Kacmar (Eds.), *Organizational politics, justice, and support: Managing social climate at work* (pp. 131–145). New York: Quorum Press.

Bies, R.J. & Tripp, T.M. (1996). Beyond distrust: "Getting even" and the need for revenge. In R.M. Kramer & T. Tyler (Eds.), *Trust and organizations* (pp. 246–260). Thousand Oaks, CA: Sage.

Bowles, H., Babcock, L., & Lai, L. (2007). Social incentives for gender differences in the propensity to initiate negotiations: Sometimes it does hurt to ask. *Organizational Behavior and Human Decision Processes, 103*(1), 84–103.

Bowles, H.R., Babcock, L., & McGinn, K. L. (2005). Constraints and triggers: Situational mechanics of gender in negotiation. *Journal of Personality and Social Psychology, 89,* 951–965.

Bowles, H. & McGinn, K. (2008). Gender in job negotiations: A two-level game. *Negotiation Journal, 24*(4), 393–410.

Brewer, M. & Feinstein, A. (1999). Dual processes in the cognitive representation of persons and social categories. In S. Chaiken, & Y. Trope, *Dual processes in social pyschology* (pp. 255–270). New York: Guilford Press.

Carnevale, P.J. & Lawler, E.J. (1986). Time pressure and the development of integrative agreements in bilateral negotiation. *Journal of Conflict Resolution, 30,* 636–659.

Caruso, E., Epley, N., & Bazerman, M. (2006). The costs and benefits of undoing egocentric responsibility assessments in groups. *Journal of Personality and Social Psychology, 91*(5), 857–871.

Chugh, D. & Bazerman, M.H. (2007). Bounded awareness: What you fail to see can hurt you. *Mind and Society, 6*(1), 1–18.

Coleman, P. T. & Lim, Y. (2001). A systematic approach to evaluating the effects of collaborative negotiation training on individuals and groups. *Negotiation Journal, 17,* 363–392.

Curhan, J. R., Elfenbein, H. A., & Eisenkraft, N. (2010). The objective value of subjective value: A multi-round negotiation study. *Journal of Applied Social Psychology, 40,* 690–709.

Curhan, J. R., Elfenbein, H. A., & Kilduff, G. J. (2009). Getting off on the right foot: Subjective value versus economic value in predicting longitudinal job outcomes from job offer negotiations. *Journal of Applied Psychology, 94,* 524–534.

Curhan, J. R., Elfenbein, H. A., & Xu, H. (2006). What do people value when they negotiate? Mapping the domain of subjective value in negotiation. *Journal of Personality and Social Psychology, 91,* 493–512.

Ekman, P. (1999). Basic emotions. In T. Dalgleish and M. Power (Eds.). *Handbook of cognition and emotion.* Sussex, UK: John Wiley & Sons, Ltd.

Elfenbein, H., Foo, M., White, J., Tan, H., & Aik, V. (2007). Reading your counterpart: The benefit of emotion recognition accuracy for effectiveness in negotiation. *Journal of Nonverbal Behavior, 31*(4), 205–223.

Filipowicz, A., Barsade, S. & Melwani, S. (forthcoming). Emotional transitions in social interactions: Beyond steady state emotion. *Journal of Personality and Social Psychology.*

Fiske, S. (1998). Stereotyping, prejudice and discrimination. In D. Gilbert, S. Fiske, & G. Lindzey, *The Handbook of Social Pyschology* (pp. 357–411). New York: McGraw-Hill.

Fiske, S., & Taylor, S. (1991). *Social cognition.* New York: McGraw-Hill.

Forgas, J. P. (1995). Mood and judgment: The affect infusion model (AIM). *Psychological Bulletin, 117,* 39–66.

Forgas, J. P. (1998). On feeling good and getting your way: Mood effects on negotiator cognition and bargaining strategies. *Journal of Personality and Social Psychology, 74,* 565–577.

Gelfand, M. J., Major, V. S., Raver, J. L., Nishii, L. H., & O'Brien, K. (2006). Negotiating relationally: The dynamics of the relational self in negotiations. *Academy of Management Review, 31,* 427–451.

Gilbert, D. T. & Hixon, J. G. (1991). The trouble of thinking: Activation and application of stereotypic beliefs. *Journal of Personality and Social Psychology, 60,* 509–517.

Gilbert, D. T., Pelham, B. W., & Krull, D. S. (1988). On cognitive busyness: When person perceivers meet persons perceived. *Journal of Personality and Social Psychology, 54,* 733–740.

Gino, F. & Bazerman, M.H. (2009). When misconduct goes unnoticed: The acceptability of gradual erosion in others' unethical behavior. *Journal of Experimental Social Psychology*, 45(4), 708–719.

Greenwald, A. G. & Banaji, M. R. (1995). Implicit social cognition: Attitudes, self-esteem, and stereotypes. *Psychological Review*, 102, 4–27.

Greenwald, A. G., Banaji, M. R., Rudman, L. A., Farnham, S. D., Nosek, B. A., & Mellott, D. S. (2002). A unified theory of implicit attitudes, stereotypes, self-esteem, and self-concept. *Psychological Review*, 109, 3–25.

Greenwald, A. G., McGhee, D. E., & Schwartz, L. K. (1998). Measuring individual differences in implicit cognition: The implicit association task. *Journal of Personality and Social Psychology*, 74, 1464–1480.

Han, S., Lerner, J.S., & Keltner, D. (2007). Feelings and consumer decision making: The appraisal-tendency framework. *Journal of Consumer Psychology*, 17, 158–168.

Helfat, C. E., Harris, D. & Wolfson, P. J. (2006). The pipeline to the top: Women and men in the top executive ranks of U.S. corporations. *The Academy of Management Perspectives*, 20(4), 42–64.

Hermann, M. G. & Kogan, N. (1977). Effects of negotiators' personalities on negotiating behavior. In D. Druckman (Ed.), *Negotiation: Social psychological perspectives*. Beverly Hills, CA: Sage.

Kim, S.H., Smith, R.H., & Brigham, N.L. (1998). Effects of power imbalance and the presence of third parties on reactions to harm: Upward and downward revenge. *Personality and Social Psychology Bulletin*, 24, 353–361.

Kopelman, S., Rosette, A., & Thompson, L. (2006). The three faces of Eve: Strategic displays of positive neutral and negative emotions in negotiations. *Organization Behavior and Human Decision Processes*, 99 (1), 81–101.

Kray, L. J. & Babcock, L. (2005). Gender in negotiations: A motivated social cognitive analysis. In A. Kruglanski & J. Forgas (Eds.), *Frontiers in social psychology*. NY: Psychology Press.

Kray, L. J. & Haselhuhn, M.P. (2007). Implicit negotiation beliefs and performance: Longitudinal and experimental evidence. *Journal of Personality and Social Psychology*, 93, 49–64.

Kray, L. J. & Thompson, L. (2005). Gender stereotypes and negotiation performance: A review of theory and research. In B. M. Staw & R. Kramer (Eds.), *Research in organizational behavior series* (Vol. 26, pp. 103–182). Greenwich, CT: JAI Press.

Kray, L. J., Thompson, L., & Galinsky, A. (2001). Battle of the sexes: Gender stereotype confirmation and reactance in negotiations. *Journal of Personality and Social Psychology*, 80, 942–958.

Kruger, J. & Gilovich, T. (1999). "Naive cynicism" in everyday theories of responsibility assessment: On biased perceptions of bias. *Journal of Personality and Social Psychology*, 76, 743–753.

Ku, G., Malhotra, D., & Murnighan, K. (2005). Towards a competitive arousal model of decision making: A study of auction fever in live and internet auctions. *Organizational Behavior and Human Decision Processes*, 96(2), 89–103.

Lerner, J.S. & Keltner, D. (2000). Beyond valence: Toward a model of emotion-specific influences on judgment and choice. *Cognition and Emotion*, 14, 473–493.

Lerner, J. S. & Keltner, D. (2001). Fear, anger, and risk. *Journal of Personality & Social Psychology*, 81, 146–159.

Lerner, J.S. & Tiedens, L.Z. (2006). Portrait of the angry decision maker: How appraisal tendencies shape anger's influence on cognition. *Journal of Behavioral Decision Making* (Special Issue on Emotion and Decision Making), *19*, 115–137.

Lewicki, R. J. & Litterer, J. A. (1985). *Negotiation.* Homewood, IL: R. D. Irwin.

Lewicki, R. J., Sheppard, B. H., & Bazerman, M. H. (1986). *Research on negotiation in organizations.* New York: JAI Press.

Malhotra, D. (2010). The desire to win: The effects of competitive arousal on motivation and behavior. *Organizational Behavior and Human Decision Processes, 111*, 139–146.

Mayer, J., Roberts R., & Barsade, S.G. (2008). Human abilities: Emotional intelligence. *Annual Review of Psychology, 59*, 507–536.

Moore, D. A. (2004). The unexpected benefits of final deadlines in negotiation. *Journal of Experimental Social Psychology, 40*(1), 121–127.

Mueller, J. & Curhan, J. (2006). Emotional intelligence and counterpart mood induction in a negotiation. *International Journal of Conflict Management, 17*, 110–128.

Neale, M. A., & Bazerman, M. H. (1991). *Cognition and rationality in negotiation.* New York: Free Press.

Ordonez, L.D., Schweitzer, M.E., Galinsky, A.D. & Bazerman, M.H. (2009). Goals gone wild: The systematic side effects of over-prescribing goal setting. *Academy of Management Perspectives, 23*(1), 6–16.

Overbeck, J. R., Neale, M. A., & Govan, C. (2010). I feel, therefore you act: Intrapersonal and interpersonal effects of emotion on negotiation as a function of social power. *Organizational Behavior and Human Decision Processes, 112*, 126–139.

Paharia, N., Kassam, K.S., Greene, J.D. & Bazerman, M.H. (2009). Dirty work, clean hands: The moral psychology of indirect agency. *Organizational Behavior and Human Decision Processes, 109*(2), 134–141.

Pietroni, D., Van Kleef, G. A., De Dreu, C. W., & Pagliaro, S. (2008). Emotions as strategic information: Effects of other's emotional expressions on fixed-pie perception, demands, and integrative behavior in negotiation. *Journal of Experimental Social Psychology, 44*(6), 1444–1454.

Sinaceur, M. & Tiedens, L. Z. (2006). Get mad and get more than even: When and why anger expression is effective in negotiations. *Journal of Experimental Social Psychology, 42*(3), 314–322.

Steele, C. (1997). A threat in the air: How stereotypes shape intellectual identity and performance. *American Psychologist, 52*(6), 613–629.

Steele, C. M. & Aronson, J. (1995). Stereotype threat and the intellectual test performance of African-Americans. *Journal of Personality and Social Psychology, 69*, 797–811.

Steele, J. & Ambady, N. (2006). "Math is hard!" The effect of gender priming on women's attitudes. *Journal of Experimental Social Psychology, 42*(4), 428–436.

Steinel, W., Van Kleef, G., & Harinck, F. (2008). Are you talking to me?! Separating the people from the problem when expressing emotions in negotiation. *Journal of Experimental Social Psychology, 44*(2), 362–369.

Thompson, L. (1990). Negotiation behavior and outcomes: Empirical evidence and theoretical issues. *Psychological Bulletin, 108*(3), 515–532.

Thompson, L. L. (2005). *The mind and heart of the negotiator* (3rd ed.).Upper Saddle River, NJ: Pearson/Prentice Hall.

Thompson, L. L. (2007). *The truth about negotiations.* New York: The Financial Times Press.

Thompson, L., Gentner, D., & Loewenstein, J. (2000). Avoiding missed opportunities in managerial life: Analogical training more powerful than individual case training. *Organizational Behavior and Human Decision Processes, 82*(1), 60–75.

Thompson, L. L., Medvec, V. H., Seiden, V., & Kopelman, S. (2001). Poker face, smiley face, and rant 'n' rave: Myths and realities about emotion in negotiation. In M. A. Hogg & R. S. Tindale (Eds.), *Blackwell handbook of social psychology: Group processes* (pp. 139–163). Malden, MA: Blackwell.

Tsay, C. & Banaji, M. (2011). Naturals and strivers: Preferences and beliefs about sources of achievement. *Journal of Experimental Social Psychology, 47*, 460–465.

Tsay, C. Shu, L., & Bazerman, M. (2011). Naiveté and cynicism in negotiations and other competitive contexts. *Academy of Management Annals, 5*, 495–518.

Van Kleef, G. A. & Dreu, C. (2010). Longer-term consequences of anger expression in negotiation: Retaliation or spillover? *Journal of Experimental Social Psychology, 46*(5), 753–760.

Van Kleef, G. A., De Dreu, C. K. W., & Manstead, A. S. R. (2004a). The interpersonal effects of anger and happiness on negotiation behavior and outcomes. *Journal of Personality and Social Psychology, 86*, 57–76.

Van Kleef, G. A., De Dreu, C. W., & Manstead, A. R. (2004b). The interpersonal effects of emotions in negotiations: A motivated information processing approach. *Journal of Personality & Social Psychology, 87*(4), 510–528.

Author Index

Subject Index